Building Green

Building
Green

A COMPLETE HOW-TO GUIDE
TO ALTERNATIVE BUILDING METHODS

EARTH PLASTER • STRAW BALE
CORDWOOD • COB • LIVING ROOFS

Clarke Snell & Tim Callahan

LARK BOOKS
A Division of Sterling Publishing Co., Inc.
New York

Library of Congress Cataloging-in-Publication Data

Snell, Clarke.
  Building green : a complete how-to guide to alternative building methods :
earth, plaster, straw bale, cordwood, cob, living roofs / Clarke Snell & Tim
Callahan.
        p. cm.
  Includes bibliographical references and index.
  ISBN 1-57990-532-3 (pbk.)
  1. Ecological houses. 2. Sustainable buildings—Design and construction.
I. Callahan, Tim, 1954- II. Title.
TH4860.S6397 2005
690'.837—dc22
                                      2004022417

10 9 8 7 6 5 4 3

Published by Lark Books, A Division of
Sterling Publishing Co., Inc.
387 Park Avenue South, New York, N.Y. 10016

Distributed in Canada by Sterling Publishing,
c/o Canadian Manda Group, 165 Dufferin Street
Toronto, Ontario, Canada M6K 3H6

Distributed in the United Kingdom by GMC Distribution Services,
Castle Place, 166 High Street, Lewes, East Sussex, England BN7 1XU

Distributed in Australia by Capricorn Link (Australia) Pty Ltd.,
P.O. Box 704, Windsor, NSW 2756 Australia

If you have questions or comments about this book, please contact:
Lark Books
67 Broadway
Asheville, NC 28801
(828) 253-0467

Manufactured in China

ISBN 13: 978-1-57990-532-3
ISBN 10: 1-57990-532-3

For information about custom editions, special sales, premium and
corporate purchases, please contact Sterling Special Sales Department at
800-805-5489 or specialsales@sterlingpub.com.

EDITORS:
Terry Krautwurst and Kathy Sheldon

ART DIRECTOR: Kristi Pfeffer

COVER DESIGNER: Barbara Zaretsky

COVER PHOTOGRAPHY:
Stewart O'Shields and Clarke Snell

ILLUSTRATOR: Olivier Rollin

PRODUCTION: Jackie Kerr

ASSISTANT EDITORS:
Rebecca Guthrie and Nathalie Mornu

ASSOCIATE ART DIRECTOR: Shannon Yokeley

EDITORIAL ASSISTANCE: Delores Gosnell

ART PRODUCTION ASSISTANCE: Jeff Hamilton

ART INTERNS:
Biljana Bosevska, Brad Armstrong,
Christopher Dollar, Bradley Norris, and
Sara House

The authors and publisher wish to
specially thank photographer
Don Gurewitz for contributing his
photographs of traditional buildings
from around the world. All photos
by Don Gurewitz are copyright
Don Gurewitz.

Dedicated To

In loving memory of Hazel Clarke, who
taught me how to gut a fish and that you
should always leave a place cleaner than
you found it.

—Clarke Snell

Hic labor, hoc opus est...

—Tim Callahan

Contents

Introduction

You and everyone else who decides to read this book

share a common interest: green, or alternative, building. But what is that? What do those words mean?

The term "green building" carries a variety of connotations, ranging from a focus strictly on the healthfulness or environmental impact of building materials and practices to much broader definitions. (For more on this, see the sidebar What is Green Building? in chapter 1.) Fundamentally, it's an acknowledgment that modern construction is out of sync with the ecosystem of the planet. Green building, then, is the search for better building choices from an environmental perspective.

"Alternative building" is a somewhat less specific and more encompassing term, a reference to the entire spectrum of efforts, motives, methods, and approaches people are exploring today towards better ways to build housing. As an adjective, "alternative" is defined as "affording a choice of two or more things or courses of action." "Alternative building," then, embodies the simple fact that in every act of building, there is a choice, and that choice is up to you.

In this book, we use the two terms almost interchangeably, or at least in the same context, the same spirit. At their core they both refer to the search for choices outside the current modern norms of building. Certainly, regardless of whether you prefer the term "green" or "alternative," the one thing that we all share is the desire for a choice. We've looked around at available new housing options, everything from mobile homes to spec houses to architect-designed and contractor-built custom homes, and, for one reason or another, we haven't found what we're searching for. Our collective response has been, "Okay, what else is there?" There must be an alternative.

Fortunately, there is—in fact, there are many. And in this book, we don't just talk about them—we show them to you. In these pages, right before your eyes, we design and build a little building that demonstrates a variety of materials, techniques, and concepts that are all practical alternatives to what passes for housing in our modern industrial world.

IN PURSUIT OF A DREAM

But this book is about far more than just the mechanics of building green. It's fundamentally about creating a house that is uniquely yours. Just as the language you grew up with rolls easily off your tongue, just as the clothes you wear reflect your sense of style and comfort, there is a house—a beautiful, healthful, nurturing house—that corresponds to who you are. This real place is often relegated to being a dream, the elusive "dream house" for which so many are forever searching. But why?

At some point on our long journey from the cave to the cubicle, we abandoned the art of creating our own shelter. Somewhere back on your family tree, your ancestors built their homes using local materials harvested from or near the site. Everyone knew how to build because building was a basic part of life; you grew up doing it. The housing system used had evolved slowly in response to a particular physical environment and the needs of the culture that was developing it. In other words, it was specific to a time, a place, and a people. You already knew what to build and how to build it because that knowledge and those skills were part of your upbringing. Put simply, your house was a part of you.

In contrast, most of us today couldn't possibly find and gather together all our own building materials; we wouldn't know how best to build with them if we could find them; and we really aren't sure exactly what we'd build anyway.

The good news is that all is not lost. You can overcome these problems. Because the fact is that, despite all the cell phoning, shrink-wrapping, and computer dating of our advanced civilization, the basic relationship of human to house hasn't changed in all of these years. To create a house that is uniquely and specifically yours, you still need only to be in sync with your exact site and your particular, unique, idiosyncratic human needs. And the know-how and skills and self-awareness to do just that are entirely within your—anyone's—reach.

FROM HERE TO THERE

In this book we give you a solid introduction to both the theory and the praxis—the hands-on how-to—of green building.

In Part One, we start with a primer on the basics. First, we take a look at what goes into making a house, any house. We discuss concepts such as structure, building loads, thermal mass, insulation, and more. From there we move on to outline some strategies for manifesting these basics in sensible ways. It's here that we start to take issue with how modern houses are being constructed, and learn the advantages gained by simply taking responsibility for the specifics of your own housing. For example, though your local contractor and city planner seem to overlook it, you can harness the largest power source known to humanity for free and in perpetuity to help heat, cool, and power your house. It's called the sun, and in this section you'll begin to see how easily you can incorporate the sun's power into any home design.

Part One, then, is the fundamentals-and-theory section of the book. But what about Part Two? How can we show you how to actually *apply* the fundamentals and theory? How can we give you the down-in-the-dirt practical experience of construction itself?

It would be hard enough if we knew you personally and could tailor instruction to your situation, but of course that's not the case. What's more, there are all sorts of alternative materials and techniques out there that you really need to experience before you can intelligently decide which approaches and choices are right for creating your particular house.

In an ideal world, you might gain that experience by getting involved in a series of projects that together expose you to a wide variety of materials and techniques—or better yet, you might actually construct a series of buildings, each with a different focus. But who among us has the time or money to do all of that as a learning experience?

MEET OUR LITTLE BUILDING

Our solution, we think, is the next-best approach to actual hands-on experience: In Part Two, we create a small, efficient, carefully thought out green building for you, one that incorporates and compares a wide spectrum of alternative materials and construction techniques, and we document the process in photos and text every step of the way, from site selection to finishing touches.

Our intent, in effect, is to reach up out of this book, grab you by the shoulders, and pull you onto the building site with us to show and teach you how to use a whole host of popular alternatives to conventional building practices, all incorporated into a single, small structure. In a sense, the building is an alternative-techniques-and-materials sampler, in the tradition of needlework samplers from centuries past. Among its many alternative features and innovations are a practical living roof system, a gravel trench foundation, lightweight insulated concrete stem walls (the waterproof walls that lift a building away from the ground), a simple and versatile post-and-beam framework, passive solar design, and both earth and lime plasters covering four different popular alternative wall systems: straw bale, cob, cordwood, and modified stick-frame.

Green building concentrate. Our little building, though diminutive in size, has all the comforts of a whole house and features a wide spectrum of alternative materials and construction techniques, ranging from site-conscious, passive solar design to a living roof and four different wall systems.

However, our little building is far more than a conglomeration of materials thrown together merely as a demonstration for the purposes of producing a book on the subject. We wanted to give you a true feel for what goes into a real house. We placed each material consciously as part of a careful, thoughtful design that integrated our exact site, our specific needs, and a combination of site-harvested, locally available, and store-bought building materials to create a beautiful, functional, energy-efficient, and long-lasting building with a clear purpose. As you'll see when you read chapter 1, that makes our little building a perfect introduction to the entire process of creating a green building. Don't let its diminutive size fool you, either. Though it's certainly small, our little building has all the comforts of home: heat, running water, kitchen, bed, couch, desk, storage, kids' space, privacy, outdoor space, and a place to entertain guests.

In essence, our little building gives you a step-by-step tutorial to the complete creation of a simple, thoughtfully created house—*and* to the use, advantages of, and challenges presented by different alternative materials and techniques. What's more, virtually every detail of the construction process is explained through text, more than 1,000 how-to photographs, and some 70-plus illustrations.

MEET US

Both this book and our little building are the result of a pleasant creative collaboration between myself (Clarke Snell) and my coauthor, Tim Callahan. Tim is a master craftsman, having built everything from fine guitars and expensive yachts to custom timber-frame homes. He's also a conventional building contractor who has extensive experience with the ins and outs of modern building techniques.

I, on the other hand, got into building from the alternative end of the spectrum. I have experience with a wide variety of alternative and conventional building materials and techniques; have researched alternatives to conventional construction for many years; have built my own passive solar, partially earth-sheltered home; and am the author of *The Good House Book: A Common-Sense Guide to Alternative Homebuilding.*

Tim and I designed our little building together. Tim was the structural engineer and was involved in much of the building process, including much of the more subtle woodworking. I was the main, day-in-and-day-out builder and technician on most of the "alternative" stuff. As for the book itself, I wrote the main text while Tim added a number of special sidebars contributing his perspective and passing on some valuable tricks of the trade.

Tim's encyclopedic knowledge, inquisitive nature, and road-weary skepticism about some "natural," "green," and "alternative" building claims were a great complement to my stubborn focus on innovation and my tarnished though still-kicking idealism. Together, our two perspectives combined to create a special building, and, we hope, a genuinely useful, helpful book.

What a team. That's me, the ever-inquiring true believer, on the left. Tim, the seasoned skeptic, is (of course) on the right. We're both experienced builders. Our little building and this book are the results of our combined perspectives and our shared interest in exploring possibilities.

HOW TO USE THIS BOOK

In a sense, this work can be seen as two closely interrelated books: a basic green building primer (Part One) and a how-to manual on specific techniques and detailing (Part Two). Our intent is that both the beginner and the hardened veteran can be served by these same pages.

Though our approach to the basics of construction and alternative strategies is novel enough to be interesting even to experienced builders, the how-to sections are written so that they can stand alone. If you're an experienced builder, you might choose to skip the primer and use the how-to chapters as a construction reference for specific building details of the different approaches we document. For example, if you want only to check out our innovative approach to living-roof detailing, go right to that section. The combination of explanatory text, how-to photos, and construction drawings should serve you well.

If you're a beginner, please take your time and read the whole book from beginning to end long before you plan on starting a building project. The chapters in Part One are critical for helping you understand the basics of construction and for helping you define a clear vision of what you want your house to be. In a sense, those chapters serve as an extended glossary that will greatly increase what you learn from the actual construction.

When you move on to read the step-by-step how-to discussions in Part Two, keep in mind that as we created our building we made decisions based on our particular situation. Naturally, your site, your needs, and your project will be different. The specifics of how we designed and built our building would be worthless to you if you couldn't translate them to the specifics of your own situation. However, thanks to all the work we've done together in the beginning of the book, you'll have the conceptual background to watch what we do and try to imagine if and how it might apply to your potentially very different situation.

To help you in that process, each how-to chapter starts with a discussion of materials and techniques within the context of the general concepts discussed in Part One. Then we go on to describe and show you, by way of text and photos and illustrations, how we applied those concepts—our thought processes, materials choices, and installation techniques. Finally, because each site and every builder is different, we end each chapter with an overview of some of the possible variations to our approach, contrasting solutions that different climates, environments, builders, and building uses might engender.

Of course, regardless of the thoroughness of this book's instructions, there's still no substitute for actual doing. If you have little to no construction experience, this book can be only a start; we hope you'll use it as a launching point for the real thing. And finally, we hope you'll pay particular attention to our Epilogue, Your Green Building, and the Tim's Take sidebars, in which we've done our best to pass along to you a reality-based perspective on what to expect when you do get involved in building. We've made lots of mistakes and would love to spare you the trouble of making the same ones. (Don't worry, you'll discover plenty of your own.)

All right; the stage is set. Let's get this journey under way.

•

Basics

Unlike birds or wasps, people don't build houses purely by instinct. To create a building that matches our climate, our site, and our needs, we have to think and plan. For the modern human without access to an indigenous, culturally specific building system, the thinking process and the building process must be even more intimately intertwined. In these first four chapters, we introduce the concepts and the thought process that you'll need, both to understand our little building and to start on the road to creating your own.

Chapter 1 - **Why Green Building?**

Chapter 2 - **Building Fundamentals**

Chapter 3 - **Alternative Building Strategies**

Chapter 4 - **Design**

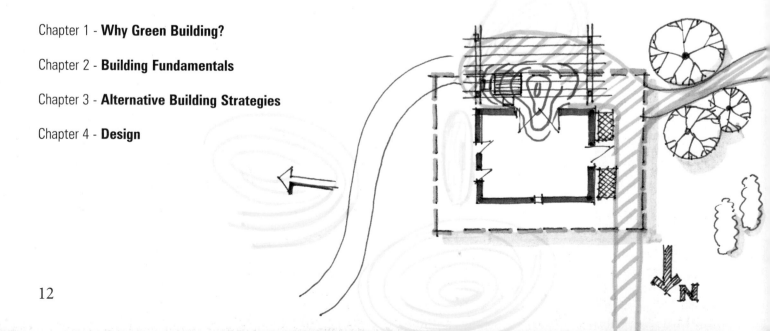

Chapter 1
Why Green Building?

As I'll point out throughout this book, modern building isn't going to be a lot of help on your journey to a green home, a house that is beautifully, specifically, and uniquely yours. Today, housing is usually just one more cog in the economy. The result is an array of modular materials that can be efficiently transported over long distances and sold by the square foot to create housing systems that can be built anywhere, in any climate. This makes buying and selling easy, but abandons the concept of creating structures that mesh with a specific site and a specific person, i.e., you.

Alternative building to the rescue! In my definition, alternative or green building (see the sidebar, What Is Green Building?, on page 17) are catchall terms for both a broad philosophy and a host of specific building practices and techniques that, taken as a whole, can help anyone find the way to their own special, here-in-the-flesh, no-more-dreaming home.

But wait: Although it's tempting to jump right into the hands-on how-to of green building, it'd be a mistake. Trust me, patience is important here. Because the most crucial alternative presented in this book isn't about materials or techniques. It's about perspective, about looking at and understanding housing and the construction process in new, alternative ways. Once you understand that perspective, the design, materials, and techniques will fall right into place.

In order to pave the way for this new perspective, let's explore three questions: (1) what does a house do, (2) why doesn't modern housing do it, and (3) what are the alternatives?

WHAT DOES A HOUSE DO?

There are many kinds of buildings. They range from a metal cage with a little wheel for housing a gerbil to a huge underground concrete bunker for housing a nuclear warhead. The operative word here is "house." Every building is designed to house something. Though you can use the information in this book to build a shed to house tools, our primary goal is to learn about buildings meant to house humans. Cleverly, we call these buildings "houses."

A house, then, is a building designed to sustain human life. This is an important concept, because it points out that houses do the same job as some other familiar structures designed to sustain human life: our bodies.

The human body, the original house, sustains human life by providing four basic functions. First, it's a *self-supporting structure* that defines an inside (you) and an outside (the world). This structure is an interconnected network of bones—our skeleton—that creates a space for our heart to beat, lungs to breathe, and stomach to digest.

Second, the body *maintains a stable temperature* inside in the face of fluctuating temperatures outside. Our bodies accomplish this in two ways: (1) by creating temperature—heat through metabolizing foods, and cool through sweating, breathing, and other heat-dissipating maneuvers—and (2) by storing heat, especially in the wonderfully efficient heat sink that is the water that makes up some 70 percent of our mass.

Whole house. With elegant simplicity, this humble abode nurtures human life by providing the same four basic functions that sustain our bodies: a supporting structure, temperature control, separation from the elements, and connection to those same elements.

Third, the human body creates a *separation from outside elements* that could damage us. For example, our skin keeps out unfiltered water and air, and our immune systems fight off invading pathogens.

Finally, the body *maintains a constant connection,* or exchange, with the outside. Oxygen, food, and water come in while carbon dioxide, urine, and feces go out in a constant cycle that must be perpetuated almost completely uninterrupted from the day we're born to the day we die. We see then that the body is a miraculous house delicately and exquisitely crafted to create space, regulate temperature, and maintain a constant separation from and exchange with the outside.

Initially, the body was all the house we needed. But as we started moving about the planet, humans encountered climates that pushed our bodies beyond their job descriptions. Not a species to be denied, we used our bulging brains to come up with ways of augmenting our bodies. Clothing was an innovation, a second skin, that allowed our bodies to maintain a stable interior temperature while exposed to lower outside temperatures. Housing was another, more ambitious innovation developed to help our bodies sustain human life in the difficult climates and environments we encountered as we fanned out across the planet.

So we're ready to answer our first question: What does a house do? From a functional point of view, the answer is simple. A house sustains human life by mirroring and augmenting the four basic functions the body provides: (1) A house is a self-supporting structure that defines an inside and an outside. (2) A house maintains an interior temperature that sustains human life in the face of exterior temperatures that wouldn't. (3) A house creates a separation from the outside that protects both the house and its inhabitants from destructive forces. (4) A house allows the constant exchange with the outside that its inhabitants need to survive.

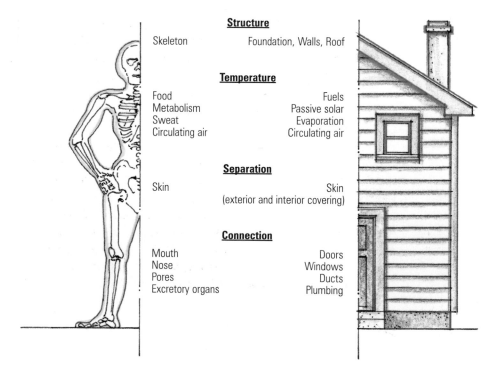

Figure 1
THE AUGMENTED BODY:
THE FOUR FUNCTIONS OF A HOUSE

Structure

Skeleton	Foundation, Walls, Roof

Temperature

Food	Fuels
Metabolism	Passive solar
Sweat	Evaporation
Circulating air	Circulating air

Separation

Skin	Skin
	(exterior and interior covering)

Connection

Mouth	Doors
Nose	Windows
Pores	Ducts
Excretory organs	Plumbing

What Is Green Building?

Let's face it: "green building" is a nebulous term. Broadly, it refers to an attempt to consciously create buildings with an eye to how they interact with our planet's ecosystem. But this means different things to different people. For some, it means focusing on creating a healthy indoor environment inside buildings. For others, it makes sense to focus on improving the mass-produced materials that predominate in modern construction. For still others, it's about eschewing mass-produced components and centralized systems altogether in favor of site-harvested resources, including building materials, electricity, water, and food.

My own approach to "green building" centers on the concept of "sustainability": the simple notion that the way of life we choose must not lead to circumstances that prevent that way of life from continuing. In order to create a building to serve that end, I believe, five basic traits need to be considered:

1) Low Construction Impact. Building, almost by definition, is initially a destructive act. Land usually has to be at least minimally cleared and reshaped, holes need to be dug, and material resources refashioned to serve the building. A "green" building minimizes its impact on the building site and the environment at large through careful, conscious design and by utilizing replenishable materials that create a minimum of ecological destruction through their use.

2) Resource Efficiency through the Life of the Building. The impact of a building's construction is only part of the story. Once a building is built, people move in and use it. This human use requires environmental resources for such things as heating, cooling, water, and electricity. A "green" building provides these human needs efficiently, conserving resources.

3) Long Lasting. Natural resources in the form of building materials, tools, and fuels, as well as human energy and ingenuity, come together to create a building. The longer that building lasts, the longer the time before the environment is asked to give up those resources again to replace the building. Therefore, the longer a building lasts, the "greener" it is.

4) Nontoxic. To sustain healthy lives, we need to sustain a healthy indoor and outdoor environment. A "green" building, then, needs to provide a healthy indoor environment while doing nothing to harm the outdoor environment.

5) Beautiful. One of the biggest sources of our environmental woes is the constant and polluting movement of humans about the planet. To create a sustainable lifestyle, we need to stay put more of the time and derive more of our social, physical, and spiritual sustenance from our own backyards. For example, it takes a long time to build healthy soil to grow good food; to build a network of friends and compatriots that will be the basis for community; to nurture the trees and other plants that will be part of a house's cooling strategy. These things simply won't happen if you aren't sufficiently seduced by your home to stay there for the many years it will take to turn it into a real place that nurtures both its inhabitants and the environment. A "green" house, then, needs to be beautiful, a place that is as hard to leave as a lover and as unthinkable to neglect as your own child.

Grappling with these issues in their full depth is complex. It often requires compromise, and always demands a combination of idealism and realism. For instance, imagine two neighbors building houses of exactly the same size. One person is determined to build using only site-harvested "natural materials" that require little energy to produce and that create almost no pollution in the process. The other is using some site-harvested materials in combination with some mass-produced materials that are more energy-intensive in order to create a building that will use less energy through its lifetime to provide warmth and other services to its inhabitants.

Which builder is "greener"? To even try to answer that question you'd need to know the *embodied energy* (the energy required for production, transportation, and installation) of all the materials involved, the relative energy efficiency of the two buildings, how long each will last, how much maintenance each will require, and many other factors, both technical and personal to the owners involved.

In the end, "building green" is a deeply personal process in which you make judgments as to how a building will best merge with your own personal mode of survival, be it computer programming or subsistence farming, to create the most beneficial impact on your environment, both local and global. An ideally "green" building, then, must be a very specific thing, matching your idiosyncratic personal needs with the fabric of your exact local environment. As you read further, you'll discover that striving for this ideal is what this book is all about.

Specific building connected to a culture.
These intricate screen walls are part of an ancient technology for utilizing desert winds to cool interior spaces.

Nonspecific building connected to life-support systems. This is a typical modern house in the United States. It's basically a box hooked up to life-support systems that supply warm and cool air, water, light, and power. Its materials have been transported from many miles away. Its features allow this same building to be constructed in a variety of climates without concern for site-specific variables such as the path of the sun. But they also strap this building to expensive, wasteful, and polluting solutions to problems that often could be better solved with attention to the details of local climate, terrain, and building materials.

WHY DOESN'T MODERN HOUSING DO IT?

Who could deny that the human body is a mind-boggling miracle? Imagine: each of us is safely housed within a bundle of blood, bone, and guts nurturing a little glow of life while suspended in a sea of constant change and danger. The miracle becomes even more astounding when you consider the long, slow, evolutionary process of give and take that produced the human body. Our bodies don't struggle with the sea of nature around us because we developed with it, within it, as part of it, over time.

Housing, likewise, originally developed slowly within particular human cultures and in response to specific climates and environments. Using materials from the site and techniques developed out of long experience with an exact location and climate, each culture around the world crafted a unique style of housing from the fabric of their surroundings. In other words, traditional housing approaches were specific to the culture, climate, and environment from which they sprung. The results were astounding. Consider the igloo, a building using the thermal mass of ice to enclose heat and repel snow, or the ancient Egyptians' intricate system of screens, wind scoops, and ventilation domes that produced interior cooling amid burning desert heat. These solutions are masterpieces in their context, but would fail miserably if they switched places.

We live in a different world today. People are moving around; cultures are intermingling. An urban lifestyle predominates that doesn't change with the seasons and isn't connected to a specific climate or locale. The glue that holds us together is a world economy of frantic buying and selling to each other. The housing of this world is general. It isn't connected to a climate, set of available local resources, or specific group of people. Instead, it's designed to be flexible, to be used in any of a variety of environments and climates and by any of a variety of people. The modern concept of housing is to build a strong box and hook it to adjustable life-support systems that provide temperature, light, and air circulation as well as bring water in and flush waste out. Such a box can be mass-produced as a unit, as with a mobile home, or assembled from standardized, mass-manufactured, easily transportable parts. This house can be plopped down almost anywhere in the world and be ready to go. Differences in climate are accommodated by a simple twist of the control knobs.

The strength of this approach, its apparent flexibility, is also its fatal flaw. Housing solutions that don't arise out of a slow, intricate interaction between a place and a people cannot possibly hope to nurture the delicate interaction between that place and those people that's required for the survival of both. The result: modern housing is often simply dangerous. Off-gassing from synthetic materials, the poison chlorine in "sanitized" drinking water, even the effects of living under a fake sun (artificial light), are only a few of the dangers facing the people. Erosion and loss of wildlife habitat from forest clear-cutting, pollution from burning coal to produce electricity, and wasteful resource depletion represented by the mountains of cut-off pieces of modular units constantly headed for the dump, are just a few of the perils for the place. But we don't even need this analysis to know that modern housing isn't working. As you learn in a trip to any mobile home sales lot, modern housing somehow falls flat. It just doesn't feel right.

Housing is supposed to be a sublime temple of union between two ancient partners, the human and nature. That's just not something you can hook up to a truck and pull off a parking lot. It's also not something you can write a check for and plant haphazardly based on the locations of roads and shopping malls.

WHAT ARE THE ALTERNATIVES?

The problem isn't with the modern house; it's with our concept of what a house is supposed to be. A modern house is designed to be mass-producible and serviceable with standardized parts so that it can be easily constructed, sold, altered, and resold. Those are great properties for a commodity, but have nothing to do with the mission of a house. Once we remember that a house's job is to be a conduit and filter between an exact environment and an exact group of people, our course is clear: each act of building needs to grow out of the site it inhabits; it needs to work with the environment and climate that surround it; and it needs to fit its inhabitants like a glove—quite literally, because both a glove (clothing) and a house are augmentations of the human body. Put simply, the creation of a house is something that each of us has to be involved in on an intricate and personal level.

Is this a house? The core component of green or alternative building isn't a technique or material; it's a perspective, a change in concept of what a house should be. This manufactured home, specific neither to a place nor to the people who will live in it, is starkly contrary to that concept.

This, then, is the real "alternative" in green building. It isn't a specific technique or material, but simply a change in perspective. It means getting personally involved, so that your house is the symbiosis of where you live and who you are.

How do you accomplish this? First, the negatives: most of us don't have extended experience with a specific environment and climate, or a clear cultural context, or, to be blunt, a clear personal identity. We don't know enough about where we live or who we are, so we don't know what to build or how to build it. The positives: we still have the big brains and creative drives that our ancestors used to find their elegant solutions in specific situations. Once we regain the respect for the magical confluence that is a truly specific house, we'll amaze ourselves with our own sublime solutions.

Tim's Take
On "Alternative" and "Green" Building

Over the past 30-plus years, I've either witnessed or participated in numerous building projects that involved "alternative" or "green" materials and approaches. Too many of those buildings failed the tests of time and everyday use, either spatially, structurally, practically, or all of the above. I admit that, as a result, I felt a certain cynicism whenever I ran into someone who was on fire about the latest "alternative" building trend.

Then, several years ago, I met Clarke Snell while we were working on a construction project together and he was completing his first book, *The Good House Book*. We had many conversations regarding the dearth of articles and books that tell the real truth about building and building materials. In the course of those discussions, I realized that one reason why some of my early forays into green building—and those of others, too—had stumbled had to do with two major issues: attachment to a particular ideology or material, and lack of experience or common sense.

As we talked, we began to see an opportunity. With our combined knowledge and experience, we might be able to produce a work that could be a truthful guide to both the pleasures and pitfalls of green building. From that notion sprung yet another: instead of just talking about materials and techniques in our book, we'd *show* our readers. We'd design and construct a little green building, and document every step with how-to photos. The result is the book you hold in your hands. I think it turned out to be just as we'd pictured it: full of information, helpful, and honest. I hope you think so, too.

In the spirit of that honesty, though, I have to make a confession: That "little green building" we built took us *much* longer to finish and presented way more challenges than we'd anticipated, despite the fact that we're both highly experienced at construction, design, and creative problem-solving.

The moral of this story: Never mind whether it's "alternative," "green," or some other descriptive catch phrase. Building of *any* kind is hard work. It always takes more time and more money than people generally plan on. It requires patience and stick-to-it-iveness. It requires the ability to make decisions with an open and critical eye that can objectively research and judge the strength and adequacy of materials in a given application. It requires basic and not-so-basic skills, or at least the willingness to learn them well. It takes imagination and energy, perseverance and perspiration.

So please: Resist the temptation to jump into green building just because you like a certain concept or ideology or the look of a particular material or technique. Before you declare, "I can do that!", STOP! Read this book. Think about it. Then, if you're still sure you've got what it takes, good. Go for it.

Many shades of green. "Green" buildings run the spectrum from very simple structures to much more elaborate homes. Though their features vary, all reflect their owners' awareness of environmental concerns when making design and/or materials decisions. *Top:* This little adobe cottage in New Zealand features a living roof and a solar panel for running a small water pump. *Bottom:* This more conventional looking home features mass-produced energy and resource efficient composite block walls as well as both passive and active solar design elements. (See page 210 for more on composite block construction.)

THE PROCESS

At about this point I can expect to hear a frustrated how-to voice from the peanut gallery, "Hey, less yammerin', more hammerin'! We've identified the challenge and defined our goal. Let's build something!"

Sorry, but you're still going to have to be patient. There are four distinct steps to creating your unique house, and no skipping is allowed.

Step 1: Get in touch with the physical evidence and feelings that sent you searching for alternatives to the modern house/commodity unit. This step is what led you to pick up this book and it's what you're working on now. This is where you come to understand that a house needs to be an exact intersection between a specific place and specific people. In reality, that translates into a mandate to take personal responsibility for the thing you call a home. Once you accept that as your mantra, you're ready to move on to the next step.

Step 2: Okay, perhaps a slight panic attack is in order: you're in charge of something, but all you know is what you don't want. You don't really know what it is or how to make it. Believe me, this is no problem; you're already way ahead of the game. You just need to slow down and take some time to understand the basics of what makes a house, any house, function. Conceptually, this is pretty straightforward stuff, covered in the next chapter. By the time you're done, you'll have put a face on the beast. Buildings will no longer be mysterious hulks. You'll be able to go into any building and ask yourself some basic questions: what's holding it up, how is it creating and maintaining temperature, how does the structure provide both protection from and connection to the outside world. You can start putting words to things that you like and don't like about the buildings around you.

Step 3: Your next step is to create general strategies for achieving the basic elements of housing in a sensible, "green" way. It's here that you start defining alternatives to modern approaches. Having already defined a house as something that exists to sustain human life, and examined how a house mimics the functions of the human body, you'll have the perspective necessary to explore some elegant general solutions that modern housing simply ignores. We cover this in chapter 3, Alternative Building Strategies.

Step 4: Now you're ready to start thinking about creating a specific building that manifests what you've learned in conjunction with an exact physical site and a set of exact personal needs. This is the design and (at last!) construction phase—and in the case of this book, it's where we show you the design and construction of our specific little building. This is the bulk of the book, Part Two, starting with chapter 5.

All right. Now let's get down to business and explore the fundamentals of how a house is put together.

Time to get to work. "Green," "alternative," whatever; no matter what you call it, at some point in the process it's time to start hammering that dream of yours into reality. Understanding the concepts behind green building is important, but so is developing the basic skills necessary to make it happen.

Chapter 2
Building Fundamentals

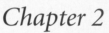

For most of us, home is primarily an emotional concept. If our

parents were divorced, we're said to be the product of a "broken home." If our parents got along, we lived in a "loving home." Home is a feeling. There's no place like home. However, as pointed out in the last chapter, home at its core is functional. It's a (1) structure that helps our bodies (2) maintain a stable temperature and create a delicate (3) separation from and constant (4) connection with the world around us.

By looking at the physical data, as well as by connecting with our gut feelings, many of us have come to the conclusion that modern housing isn't cutting that mustard. Though our desire for alternatives may come primarily from our reactions to—our feelings about—the housing around us, our ticket out of the modern-housing rut is thinking. We have to think about every aspect of what we're doing as we plan and build. We'll be using a lot of feeling, too, but we simply have to cultivate the discipline of thinking and problem-solving in the building context. Fortunately, the fundamentals of housing really aren't that complicated. In this chapter, we'll cover the basics of how buildings provide the four essential functions that define a house.

Conceptually, these basics are simple applied science, so be forewarned: this chapter is essentially a review from your high school science classes. But please, don't stare out the window or throw spitballs this time around. I'll try to make it brief and painless. This stuff is critical. Keeping it all in mind through the process of design and construction can make the fundamental difference between a good and bad building.

The real trick will come in trying to apply these basics to your specific place and to you as a specific person, in making them sprout from you and your site. Remember, it doesn't matter how ecological, beautiful, inexpensive, or whimsical your building is. If it doesn't supply the four basic functions, it isn't a house. We'll keep these functions in the forefront of our discussions throughout this book. So should you as you plan, design, and build your home.

Finally, a disclaimer: My apologies to any engineers, meteorologists, and various scientists who might take umbrage at the simplifications that follow. My goal here is simply to get you thinking about the ways that the natural world comes together to create a building, so that you can do just that.

FUNCTION ONE: STRUCTURE

Everything in this world has to stand on its own two metaphorical feet. Be it an amoeba, raindrop, or skyscraper, everything physical has some kind of self-supporting structure. This is because in order to exist on this planet, you have to withstand forces: the force of gravity pulling you down; the force of air moving against you; the force of Aunt Emma pinching your cute little cheek.

In fact, to a large degree it's structure that allows us to group things, to define them as being related. For example, humans come in all shapes and sizes and can have any of an almost unlimited number of other variations. Yet we all withstand the physical forces of the world with the same basic skeletal structure which causes us to stand, move, and look fundamentally similar. Our skeletons define us as related. It's the same with buildings. All buildings, whether a shack or a palace, share the same basic structural elements, because they all must withstand certain physical forces.

Ancient strength. Long-standing pyramids such as this ancient Mayan temple owe their strength to weather-resistant material arrayed in a strong structural configuration.

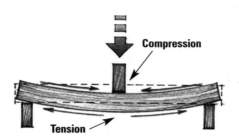

Figure 1
BENDING

A heavy load pushing down on this beam causes one side to be squeezed in compression while the other is stretched in tension. Bending is the result.

Compression

Tension

Bending to breaking. Squeezing one side while stretching the other puts a lot of stress on a material. When the strain gets to be too much, something has to give. The weight of everything on the floor above this beam, or floor joist, eventually caused it to break.

Figure 2
SHEAR

Cracks in concrete block walls are often caused by the ground beneath settling. The part of the wall on the settling area moves, while the section on solid ground stays put. The wall splits in two, with one half sliding vertically past the other, creating a vertical crack between the sections.

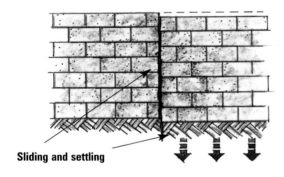

Sliding and settling

Shear damage. *Left:* Notice how the crack in this basement concrete block wall doesn't follow the mortar joints but creates a straight vertical line, breaking both blocks and joints. The foundation beneath has settled unevenly, creating a vertical shear force that caused this wall to split into two pieces. Even this tiny crack is enough to allow water to flow into the basement from the earth behind it. *Right:* The weight of water pushing against a wall, called hydrostatic pressure, is a horizontal shear force that can break a wall in two.

Figure 3
TORSION

Four walls connected together and attached to a foundation at the bottom and to a roof at the top can be twisted when wind forces hit the system at an oblique angle.

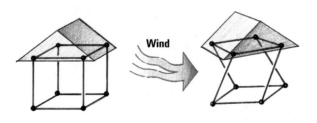

Wind

Tree torsion. Wind isn't the only source of torsion that a building might encounter. Here, a tree has grown too close and is pushing on this barn, creating a slowly increasing torsion force that's twisting the building.

LOADS

The forces that buildings withstand are called "loads." *Dead loads* are static, permanent, downward forces such as the weight of the building itself. *Live loads* are transient forces such as wind, snow, and your kid's punk band practicing in the basement. *Lateral loads* are live loads that push on a building from the side, such as wind and driving rain on a wall. *Uplift* is the force of wind pushing up on a roof.

There are a number of ways that loads can put stress on the structure of a building. *Compression* is a force that squeezes something together. *Tension* is a force pulling something apart. A material *bends* when it is squeezed on one side while being stretched on the other. *Shear* is a force that causes two parts of a body to slide past each other in a parallel direction. *Torsion* or *twisting* can occur when a force approaches something from an angle. (See figures 1, 2, and 3.)

The structural materials of most buildings act as *compression members;* the building's loads are transferred primarily by compressing these materials. Compression members must be rigid and have a certain thickness or they will bend and potentially fail. Some examples are bricks and wooden studs. It's also possible to create structure with *tension members,* which transfer loads by being stretched in tension. You can apply more force to a material in tension because the stress is evenly distributed throughout the volume of the material. Think of a thin stick, for example. You can snap it easily by bending it, a combination of compression and tension, but there's no way you are going to pull it apart, the application of tension alone. For this reason, tension members can be light and thin.

The shape of a structure, and of its structural elements, also affects its ability to carry loads. The same pile of materials configured into different shapes can result in structures of vastly differing strengths. Take a bunch of bricks and stack them without mortar into a vertical wall. It won't take much effort to push the thing over. Now, take the same bricks and stack them in a series of circles, each overlapping the one below slightly toward the center, and you'll end up with a three-dimensional arch, called a dome, of vastly superior structural strength. The same would be true if you stacked your bricks in a configuration of leaning triangles called a pyramid. Ancient buildings such as the Roman Pantheon—a 2,000-year-old freestanding concrete dome—and the 5,000-year-old Great Pyramids in Egypt, built of stacked stone, attest to the incredible strength of these archetypal shapes.

The strength of shape. *Top two:* This little unmortared rectangular wall of bricks…is a pushover…to push over. *Bottom two:* If you restack the bricks…creating a pattern that twists each course into a slightly smaller circle than the one before it…you end up with a three-dimensional arch, called a dome, that is structurally strong and difficult to topple.

Tension topper. The roof of this combination yurt and dome, called a Yome, is a tensile structure. The entire fabric membrane, which is stretched over a fixed set of support points, serves as a tension member that carries the load applied to any part of it.

The most common shapes used in buildings are the rectangle, arch, and triangle (see figure 4). Used alone, the rectangle is intrinsically weak. In buildings, diagonal and cross braces are used to divide rectangles into multiples of much stronger triangles. Post-and-beam framing would be impossible without utilizing this geometric trick. Rectangular and triangular panels, such as plywood sheathing, can also be incredibly strong braces because they disperse loads throughout their entire surface area (see figure 5).

Another type of brace is the buttress, defined as "a projecting support built into or against the outside of a wall." This simple concept can be used elegantly to create strength from weakness. For example, the single relatively flimsy rectangle of a conventionally stick-framed wall becomes quite strong when combined with other flimsy rectangles—the other three walls of a four-wall building, which together form an open-topped cube. A more graphic example is the concrete buttresses you'll often see bracing modern concrete construction.

Big buttresses. *Top:* These concrete buttresses help this parking garage's open concrete walls withstand the considerable forces of daily traffic while allowing the interior space to remain open and unobstructed by structural wall supports. *Bottom:* Another approach is to bring the buttress inside and use it to create an interior wall. Here, an interior stick-framed partition wall buttresses the long exterior wall.

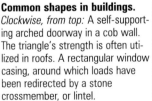

Common shapes in buildings. *Clockwise, from top:* A self-supporting arched doorway in a cob wall. The triangle's strength is often utilized in roofs. A rectangular window casing, around which loads have been redirected by a stone crossmember, or lintel.

Figure 4
THE INTRINSIC STRENGTH OF SHAPES

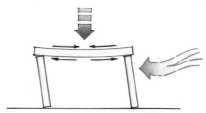

Rectangle
Alone, rectangles are intrinsically weak in response to either downward or lateral forces.

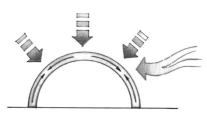

Arch/Dome
Downward forces on this arch cause both its inside and outside surfaces to compress, squeezing the structure into a tighter, more stable state. Imagine this arch in three dimensions, a dome, and you can see that lateral and downward forces are the same and therefore both are met with a strengthening compression of the structure.

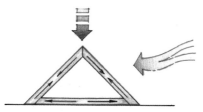

Triangle
Downward forces on this triangle create a balancing opposition of forces: the compression on the top two sides is balanced by the tension on the bottom side.

Figure 5
BRACING WITH PANELS

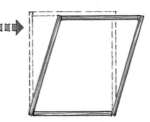

These four pieces of wood nailed together create a rectangular frame that's structurally weak.

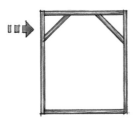

Adding two diagonal braces creates two strong triangles that add considerable structural strength.

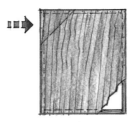

The same effect is achieved when a panel, such as a sheet of plywood, is added to the unbraced wall. Instead of single triangles that redistribute some of the loads, this piece of plywood disperses those loads over its entire surface area. It's as if a strengthening triangle has been stretched out in both directions.

Diagonal bracing. *Left:* This hefty permanent diagonal brace creates a strong triangle to help support a beam in this timber-frame building. *Right:* Temporary diagonal braces turn an empty rectangle into a series of triangles, providing structural support until this wall's permanent structure can be built.

Tim's Take
On Shapes and Sharing the Load

Consider two common objects: a cardboard box and a bicycle wheel.

A box with both ends taped closed is a surprisingly strong structure. If you cut through the tape on one end, though, it's not nearly as strong. Cut the other end, and the box collapses with just a small amount of pressure.

The end panels strengthen the box by serving as joined triangles—each rigid flap, whether square or rectangular, can be divided into triangles that connect opposite points. When the flaps are connected, those triangles form a reinforcing diaphragm, a kind of connective tissue, that distributes loads exerted on one point or area through the structure.

A bicycle wheel, though an entirely different shape, works similarly. The wheel's small spokes form a series of triangles that can hold an amazing amount of weight. In a rapidly spinning and changing dynamic, each spoke picks up a fraction of the forces being put on the wheel and shares that load with every other spoke around the rim.

In both the box and the wheel, the principle is the same: Opposing forces find a dynamic balance by being distributed throughout the entire structure. A weak shape is made strong by thoughtfully combining it with stronger shapes. This is the secret to building strong structures. When faced with a situation that pits the structure you want to build against the realities of load limitations, think about adding shapes as strengtheners. (For one example of such a situation, see my sidebar The Wall Truss, on page 413.)

As you consider the shapes you might incorporate into your building, imagine all of the forces that would come into play as they move throughout the structure. Take the time to look at as many other buildings as you can and see if you can figure out the ways other builders have used shapes to solve the structural challenges unique to their situations.

Figure 6
SHAPES

Box
Taped together, the flaps form a diaphragm that distributes forces equally.

Bicycle Wheel
Downward force from the weight of the bicycle and rider is distributed around the wheel's rim by the triangular configuration of spokes.

Adding flaps adds triangles, which create rigidity.

Without ends

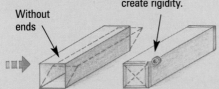

THE BASIC STRUCTURE OF BUILDINGS

Regardless of the shapes or material configurations used, all buildings deal with loads in the same basic way: by transferring them to the ground. Every building uses some variant of the same three components to accomplish this task: *foundation, walls,* and *roof.* In turn, each of these elements is manifested in one of two basic configurations: *skeletal* or *monolithic.* Skeletal structures are made up of a series of members separated by space yet connected together to form a supporting framework. One example is the legs on a table. Monolithic structures consist of a single mass acting as a unit. A boulder is a monolithic unit. So is the water in a bathtub.

FOUNDATIONS

The true foundation of every building is the earth itself. The constructed foundation of a building has two jobs: (1) to firmly connect the building to the earth and (2) to disperse loads exerted on the building over a wide enough area of that earth to allow the building to be supported. To accomplish these tasks, a foundation must first access solid, dry ground. The firm connection to the earth is usually accomplished by the foundation's own weight. Distribution of loads is achieved by passing them through a wide, monolithic unit.

Foundations come in two basic flavors: *pier* (skeletal) and *continuous* (monolithic). Pier foundations are basically an array of smaller monolithic foundations working together to distribute the building's loads. Continuous foundations are made up of a single

Figure 7
PIER FOUNDATION

Pier foundations are made up of several small monolithic foundations, the wide pads connecting the columns and the rest of the building's framework to the ground. Each pier handles the loads from a particular part of the building.

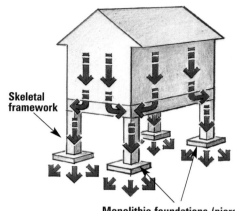

Skeletal framework

Monolithic foundations (piers)

Figure 8
FOUNDATION EXAMPLES

Concrete pier

The wide base is the actual pier foundation. The rest of the concrete is the beginning of a column that continues as a post above ground.

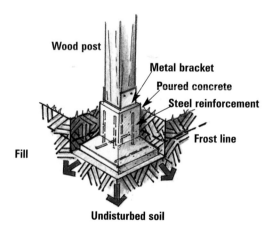

Wood post

Metal bracket

Poured concrete

Steel reinforcement

Frost line

Fill

Undisturbed soil

Pier start. These are the four structural piers that make up part of the foundation of the little building featured in this book.

Continuous Poured Concrete

This foundation type is the most common in modern building. The base is called the footer. The wall built or poured on top and extending above the surface is called the stem wall.

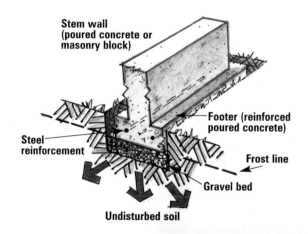

Stem wall (poured concrete or masonry block)

Footer (reinforced poured concrete)

Frost line

Steel reinforcement

Gravel bed

Undisturbed soil

Continuous concrete. This is a conventional poured-concrete continuous foundation for a basement. Concrete block walls will be built on top of it.

Figure 9
SKELETAL STRUCTURES

A wood-frame building's structural members work much like the bones in a skeleton, distributing the weight to the foundation.

Timber framing. Fewer, larger members are used, creating a dense, heavy structure. Notice the numerous triangles that strengthen this structure.

Stick-framing. More, smaller members create a lightweight structure.

monolithic mass, such as concrete, or a series of interlocking units that form a single mass, such as stone. This mass is poured or laid around the entire perimeter of the building.

A well-conceived foundation is designed to deal with the particular loads of the building it serves. For example, a modern fabric tent is very light, so its dead load is minimal. But it must be able to withstand substantial lateral loads in the form of wind and rain. That's why a basic tent foundation consists of the thin tips of very light poles (piers) that distribute the small dead load, and strong stakes driven into the ground to firmly hold the building in response to wind.

WALLS

In terms of structure, walls exist to distribute loads to the foundation. They must be strong enough to bear the dead weight of the roof, and rigid enough to resist lateral loads. Again, there are two basic conceptual flavors: skeletal and monolithic.

Skeletal walls are made up of individual vertical members called *columns* attached to horizontal members called *beams*. A timber frame building has skeletal walls made of a few large, strong columns connected to thick, heavy beams. Conventional stick-framed buildings have skeletal walls constructed of many smaller, light columns, also called *studs,* connected by thin beams on the top and bottom, also called *top and bottom plates.* Described simply, the loads from specific parts of a skeletal building are transferred by specific individual members to the foundation. The picture becomes more complicated in real life, where diagonal braces, sheet materials such as plywood, other elements such as plank siding, and monolithic infills such as cob and straw bales also take part in evening out the distribution of building loads in a skeletal structure.

Monolithic walls can be conceived of as a single column stretched sideways to fill the space of the entire wall (see figure 10). These walls act as a unit whose entire volume distributes loads to the foundation. Monolithic walls can consist of a single integrated mass—such as poured concrete, molded cob (a mix of clay, sand, straw, and water), or rammed earth—or they can be made up of interlocking units that function together as a single mass, as is the case with walls made of concrete blocks, adobe, and stone.

Figure 10
MONOLITHIC WALL STRUCTURES

A downward force on a monolithic wall spreads out through the wall's volume. A column is a tall, compact monolithic wall. When elongated, the column becomes what we think of as a wall. Building blocks stacked in an interlocking pattern also form a monolithic wall.

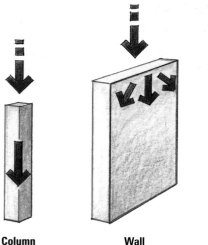

Column   **Wall**   **Stacked block wall**

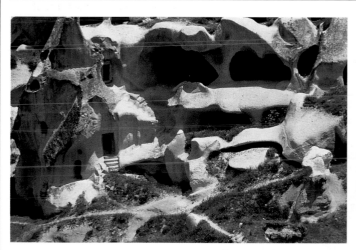

Integrated mass monolithic walls. *Left:* This building was carved by hand from sandstone hills in Turkey. *Right:* This hospital in the U.S. is constructed of poured concrete.

Interlocking block monolithic walls.
Left: These buildings are made of sun-dried mud bricks (adobe) such as those stacked in the right foreground, waiting to be used. *Right:* Fired clay bricks placed and mortared in an interlocking pattern can yield an extraordinarily strong structure, as evidenced by this tall brick chimney.

Skeletal roof structures. Though their materials and layouts vary, all these roofs are skeletal in nature. (Top left) log rafters creating a round roof; (top right) rafters with plywood decking; (middle) trusses; (bottom) poured concrete with integrated beams

Monolithic roof structures. *Top to bottom:* mud roof on a granary in Mali; dome roofs, St. Mark's Cathedral in Venice, Italy; superadobe dome under construction

ROOFS

The roof archetypally defines a building. Your foundation and walls can be just a few thin poles on the dirt, but put a roof on top and instantly the structure feels like something. Structurally speaking, the roof simply has to carry its own weight and any direct environmental forces exerted by snow, wind, rain, and the occasional tree limb or football. These loads are considerably reduced if the roof is sloped to allow physical materials such as rain and snow to slide off rather than build up. (Even flat roofs are sloped slightly to prevent water from collecting.) All loads on the roof are transferred to the walls below.

Roofs can be skeletal or monolithic, but by far most of the buildings you probably come in contact with have *skeletal roofs*. Wood is a wonderful roofing material because it's light but very strong in response to compression and tension forces. Other materials such as steel and bamboo also are used. The sloping forms of skeletal roofs can take on a variety of configurations, including shed, gable, and hip. Most of these forms incorporate the strength of the triangle to allow using relatively small-dimensioned members over wide spans. Flat concrete roofs like those found in parking lots and on commercial buildings either are poured over a skeletal structure of steel beams or are strengthened by thickened areas that essentially create integrated concrete beams.

Figure 11
ROOF FRAMING: GRAVITY, PITCH, AND TRIANGLES

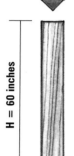
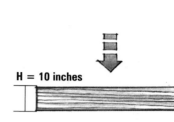
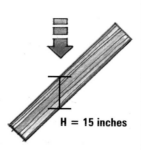

These three drawings show the same piece of wood, 1½ inches thick x 10 inches wide x 60 inches (5 feet) long, in different relationships with gravity.

H = 60 inches

H = 10 inches

H = 15 inches

a) Here, the downward thrust of gravity is carried by the full 60-inch length of the board.

b) When the board is laid flat, say as a beam in a flat roof, the amount of material resisting gravity is reduced to 10 inches.

c) If the same piece of wood is oriented diagonally so that H = 15 inches, say as a rafter in a pitched roof, its ability to resist the bending force of gravity is more than doubled. That's because as H increases, its resistance to bending increases by the square of the increase.

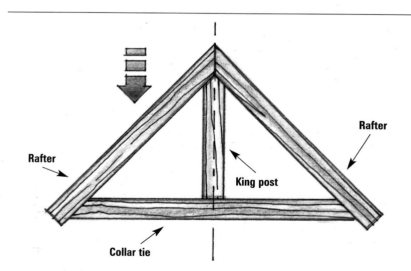

Rafter

Rafter

King post

Collar tie

d) This principle explains why, in building, the higher the pitch of a roof, the smaller the roof-framing members can be dimensioned. Adding the strength of the triangle to a roof design allows the dimensions to be reduced even further. For example, by creating two strong, mutually bracing triangles in the configuration shown here, a simple truss, the width of the rafters can be reduced with no sacrifice in strength.

Monolithic roofs come in the form of domes and vaults. Many ancient buildings have domed roofs—the Taj Mahal, for example—but you just don't see them that much in modern cities or housing. However, ferrocement water cisterns and the ceramic and superadobe houses pioneered by architect Nader Khalili are examples of monolithic domes in a modern context.

HYBRIDS

As with most conceptual simplifications, our foundation, wall, and roof divisions can become blurred. The division between foundation and wall, for example, is fuzzy in some buildings.

Monolithic walls gain strength from being wide and massive, so sometimes the walls of monolithic structures are all the foundation that's needed. Stone retaining walls and Earthships, buildings with walls made of stacked automobile tires rammed tightly with earth, are both examples of this.

Domes and pyramids often utilize one element to serve all three structural functions. A skeletal example is the tepee, basically a many-sided pyramidlike shape made of long sticks that function as the structural foundation, walls, and roof. A monolithic example is the igloo, a dome made of snow. In this mind-boggling building, snow blocks are cut and stacked so that the walls lean in on each other, simultaneously forming the roof. The wide, heavy blocks are massive enough to function also as the building's foundation. Inside, the heat from a lamp melts the underside of the blocks, which then refreeze as ice, sealing the blocks together like mortar.

CONNECTIONS

It's easier to twist your ankle than to break your leg. That's because the weak point in a structure is often the place where two units meet. In building, you need not only a strong foundation, walls, and roof; you need strong connections between those elements. Most buildings use a variety of materials connected in a myriad of ways. Often, connecting two materials takes creative problem-solving, acrobatic physical prowess, a lot of muscle, and/or special tools.

Good connections also require an understanding of the specific kinds of forces they're designed to resist. An earthquake puts different stresses on a building than does a hurricane. A building in a valley will experience different forces than a building on top of a nearby mountain. The better a building's connections are tailored to its site's exact, worst-case scenario conditions, the longer that building will last.

FLOORS

To be thorough, we need to quickly mention floors in a structural context. In the building we create in this book, and in most small, single-story buildings without framed floors, the floor has no true structural function. Its structural job is to support the people and stuff that inhabit the space, but it doesn't contribute to the overall structure of the building. However, in some buildings floors *can* be integral to the structural integrity. In multistory buildings, for example, floors act as a structural diaphragm by distributing some of the lateral loads taken by a given wall to the rest of the structure. This is why, for example, you can stomp on an upstairs floor and rattle a plate on a wall downstairs.

Two for the price of one. These dirt-packed tires stacked like bricks in a U-shaped configuration are wide and heavy enough to serve as both the foundation and walls of the building, called an *Earthship* by its inventors. See page 55 for a photo of a finished Earthship.

Tim's Take
On Making Connections

Building involves creatively assembling different parts and materials so that they work together as a whole. If you want a building to last, you must choose the appropriate connectors to join the varied pieces. Each situation poses its own challenges, depending on the materials and joining task involved, so you have to make your choices wisely.

There are several classes of connections, and corresponding fasteners, in construction:

1) Mechanical fasteners. These are the most commonly used, and include nails, screws, and bolts.

2) Chemical fasteners. These include glue and other compounds that create a bond between two or more components.

3) Welded connections. This is literally the physical union of two separate parts. They melt together and become one.

Mechanical fasteners are by far the most widely used, especially when joining dissimilar materials. There are literally hundreds of different fastener types; nails, screws, and bolts are only the beginning. Your local industrial bolt and fastener supply store can be a great resource for finding the right fasteners for a given situation, and for finding answers to any questions you may have. A web search for "specialty fasteners" will turn up an eye-opening array of possibilities, too.

Typically, the most attractive connections can be accomplished when using similar materials. Using only water, clay can be joined to clay to become one with itself. When properly joined with the appropriate glue, the chemical bond between two pieces of wood is stronger than the wood itself, and nearly invisible.

A welded connection, properly sized and executed, is incredibly strong and truly a thing of beauty. (If you're considering using welded connections in your structure, however, be sure they're performed by an expert welder; this is not the place for you to be learning this skill.)

Joining materials of different composition—wood to metal, cob to wood, glass to wood, etc.—takes a bit more ingenuity.

With all of the materials possibilities, and ways of putting them together, the methods of achieving solid connections are nearly infinite. Look under tables and chairs, look in your basement, look all around you. Unless something is monolithic, one solid piece, it is made up of pieces held together with *something*. See what you can discover.

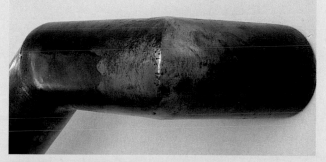

Connections. *Top:* This bracket was mechanically fastened with bolts to the wooden post and the concrete below, creating a solid connection. *Middle:* This bracket was chemically fastened to the metal below it by soldering. The material to which it's mechanically fastened with screws is a composite lumber, itself a chemical fastening of wood chips and recycled plastic. *Bottom:* The pieces of this stair rail have been melted together by welding, creating, in essence, a single piece of metal.

FUNCTION TWO: TEMPERATURE

With the exception of volcanoes, geysers, and other heat originating from geothermal sources, the sun creates and maintains our planet's temperature. In a very real sense, sunlight also creates the heat within the human body. Through photosynthesis, plants turn sunlight into edible energy that's consumed by animals and metabolized into tissue. Humans, in turn, burn plant and animal tissue in their metabolic furnaces, creating a temperature that stays consistently in the area of 37° C (98.6° F). How close the earth's air temperature is to this human temperature at any given place on the planet is the main determining factor in human comfort and, in many situations, survival.

One of housing's primary functions is to maintain indoor air that has a temperature closer to that of the human body than the air hanging around outside at any given moment. To do that, a house has to be capable of first creating and then maintaining a comfortable temperature.

CREATING HEAT

There are two basic strategies for creating warmth inside a building: (1) increasing the temperature of the air around the building and (2) increasing the temperature of the air inside the building. Both of these strategies almost always depend on the sun's energy. The air temperature around a building is higher (duh) when the sun is shining on it than when it isn't. Higher outside temperatures mean (duh again) that inside temperatures don't have to be raised as much. The air temperature inside buildings is usually raised by (1) solar energy, in other words sunlight, passing through glass-covered openings, and/or (2) solar energy released by burning fuels. The wood in stoves, petroleum (oil, propane, natural gas) for furnaces, and coal for electricity for baseboard heaters are all solar energy stored in the form of plant tissue and later burned to create heat. The only exceptions to the above are electricity generated in nuclear power plants and some forms of geothermal heat.

Direct sun. Without the Sun, our planet would be cold, dark, and dead. Direct sunlight lights up and heats up our world. By putting glass-covered openings in the right places, our buildings can reap those same life-giving benefits.

Ancient sunshine. The energy in the propane fueling this fire is solar energy that reached the earth millions of years ago and was used to create plant and animal tissue that, over many more millions of years, was slowly transformed from dead organisms into petroleum. Fossil fuels such as these are increasingly rare souvenirs of a younger sun.

CREATING COOL

Logically enough, the two basic strategies for creating cooler air inside a building are: (1) decreasing the air temperature around the building and (2) decreasing the temperature of air inside the building. Again, both strategies are usually directly related to the sun's energy and are accomplished by way of three possible mechanisms: shading, evaporative cooling, and wind.

Shading, of course, is the blocking of the sun's rays. Shading is accomplished on the outside by trees and other plants, as well as by building features such as awnings, arbors, and roof overhangs. Inside, shading is provided by the building's roof as well as by window and door coverings such as awnings and curtains.

Evaporative cooling is the lowering of air temperature through evaporation, a process also driven by the sun. (See the sidebar, Evaporative Cooling.) It's accomplished outdoors by the same plants that provide shade, as well as by ponds, dew, the earth itself, and anything else that can give water up to the hot air. Indoors, evaporative cooling can be accomplished directly by breezes passing over plants, human bodies, fountains, or even bowls of water, and mechanically by burning fuels to run air conditioning units or swamp coolers.

Wind is produced by the rotation of the earth and the sun's energy which, put simply, heats air, causing it to rise and displace cooler air, which falls. The result is air movement, or wind. This wind feels cool both because of its role in evaporative cooling and because in most cases it's air moving from cooler, higher regions of the atmosphere. (Please forgive my simplifications, meteorologists.) Wind also can be mechanically produced by burning fuels to run fans or air-conditioning units.

Two evaporative cooling systems. The three machines on the top and the three plants on the bottom cool air using the same physical mechanism, evaporation.

Evaporative Cooling

There are two basic principles behind evaporative cooling: (1) heat is required to make water evaporate, or change from a liquid to a vapor, and (2) when air heats up, its ability to hold water vapor increases.

As a result of those two factors, when warm, dry air comes in contact with a source of water—a lake, dew, a transpiring plant, or your sweating body—the thirsty air gives up some of its heat, causing evaporation, in order to take on some of the moisture. Heat is pulled from the air, and thus the temperature drops. This is evaporative cooling.

The sun is the motor behind all of this cooling, because its heat is both the source of the warming air and the differences in air pressure (the wind) that move that air. HVAC and other mechanical air-conditioning units mimic natural evaporative cooling. Most of these systems mechanically force a liquid to evaporate, causing the temperature inside to drop. "Inside" could mean the interior of a refrigerator, or of a building. The evaporated liquid, i.e. gas, is compressed back into a liquid, built-up heat is dissipated to the outside air, and the whole process starts over again. Again, the sun, in the form of coal-fired electricity, propane, or natural gas, is usually the motor behind this cooling.

MAINTAINING TEMPERATURE

However you create temperature, all that effort is moot if you can't maintain it. There are two basic techniques for maintaining temperature: (1) storing it and (2) slowing its movement.

Storing: Thermal Mass

Everything stores temperature; thus, everything to some extent is a *thermal mass:* something with weight that has a temperature. Some things can store more temperature, heat or cold, per unit volume than others. For example, water is an effective thermal mass. A frozen lake stays frozen long after outside air temperatures rise above 32°F, largely because of its thermal mass. Likewise, that same body of water in summer stays warmer than the surrounding air on a cool night because it has stored the sun's heat during the day.

Similarly, your body, which is 70 percent water, is able to maintain its stable temperature largely due to that water's thermal mass. Building materials that are good thermal masses, such as concrete, rock, clay (fired brick, cob and adobe), and water, are used to store temperature that is produced inside the building.

Slowing: Insulation

Changes in temperature are due to the movement of heat. Stored cold is diminished by the movement of heat into its turf. Stored heat is lost because heat is always looking for something cold to warm up.

Heat moves in three ways: radiation, convection, and conduction. *Conduction* is the transfer of heat from molecule to molecule through a material, such as a pot on a stove. *Convection* is the transfer of heat by physically moving molecules from one place to another, such as the steam rising off a pot on the stove. *Radiation* is the transfer of heat through space by means of electromagnetic energy. The sun heats the earth through vast empty space with radiant energy.

These three concepts often work together. Let's imagine, for example, a metal wood-burning stove. Heat moves through the metal by conduction; it moves away from the stove in all directions through radiation; and that radiant energy heats up air causing it to rise through convection, thus making the air at the ceiling warmer than that at the floor.

You can't stop heat from moving, from trying to find equilibrium, but you can slow it down by sticking something in its way. Any material that prevents the movement of heat is called *insulation.* The type of insulation chosen depends on the kind of heat movement you're trying to thwart. In building, the relative resistance to heat transfer that a material exhibits is often expressed in a measurement called *R-value.* For our purposes, all we need to know is that the higher the R-value, the more resistant a given volume of a material is to the flow of heat.

Conduction is best slowed by any thick, airy stuff that forms a complicated web of circuitous routes that the heat must traverse on its trip through the material. This is the principle behind most things we normally label as insulation, including fiberglass, polystyrene foam, and forms of organic cellulose such as recycled newspapers, cotton, and straw bales.

Thermal mass. *Top:* Although the air temperature is obviously below freezing, the water in this pond isn't frozen because its mass is still holding heat collected when outside temperatures were higher. *Bottom:* The mass of this tile floor, ceramic tile over an insulated concrete slab, and the interior brick wall are collecting the sun's heat and will give it back slowly to the air after the sun has gone down.

Radiation is best slowed by reflection. Purely reflective materials have (1) a low thermal mass so as not to store heat that would then radiate and (2) a surface that reflects heat energy, such as that provided by a white or metallic coloration. An unpainted metal roof, for example, does a good job of reflecting the pounding heat of the sun away from a building.

Convection is slowed by preventing air movement. Many, many materials won't let air move through them. Seamless materials such as plaster, concrete, and cob allow basically no convective heat loss through their volume. In most buildings, convective heat loss is noticeable only around punctures or gaps in the walls and roofs, which are often made to accommodate windows, doors, vents, plumbing, and electricity. One strategy is to carefully seal those punctures; another is to create a sacrificial air mass that isolates the living space from the outside. This is the idea behind an air lock or mudroom.

FUNCTION THREE: SEPARATION

Have you ever watched a bunch of ants devour a piece of food left lying on the sidewalk? The same thing would probably happen to us if our bodies couldn't move. You think that you're driving to work or taking a walk, but in a very real sense you're just running away from ants. Movement is perhaps the most basic way that our bodies separate us from danger. Internally, our bodies have an immune system that protects us from pathogens. Externally, our bodies have skin that protects us from the outside by keeping the outside out and the inside in.

In the same way, buildings need protection. Unfortunately, most of them are stationary, so movement's out, and we don't have the sophistication to create biological immune systems for buildings. So it's a building's skin that must do the major work of protection, or separation, from the outside.

THE FORCES OF DECAY

The job of a building's skin is to separate the building from the omnipresent natural forces of decay. Interestingly, we can conceive of these forces as the four classical elements: fire (which, of course, in this sense is the sun), water, air, and earth.

Sun

Our fiery sun intermittently and endlessly pours down on a building with incredible intensity, disappears, and then returns with a fury. This constant cycle of heating and cooling puts terrific stress on a building's skin. Ultraviolet (UV) wavelengths of sunlight react chemically with many materials causing them to break down. The sun also has an intense drying effect.

Water

Water can be a building's worst enemy. First, it's a changeling. Water is the only substance that exists as a solid, liquid, and gas at temperatures found normally on the surface of the earth. So what? So water can enter a crack in concrete as a liquid, for example, and then expand as it freezes into ice causing more cracking or even struc-

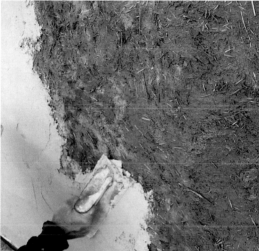

Resisting temperature flow. *Top:* The straw bales in this wall are excellent insulation against conduction, and the mud plaster will stop air flow, acting as insulation against convection. *Bottom:* The finish coat of white lime plaster will do a good job of reflecting the sun's heat, providing insulation against radiation.

Water and Air: The Issue of Condensation

Water vapor in air is called *humidity*. Air at any given temperature can hold a certain amount of water vapor. The hotter the air, the more water it can hold. The *relative humidity* of air at a given temperature is a measure of how much water vapor it's holding compared to how much it could potentially hold. For example, air with a relative humidity of 80 percent is holding 80 percent of the water it potentially could hold at that temperature. When warm humid air cools down, it will eventually reach a temperature where it must give up some of the water it's holding. This is called *condensation,* and the temperature at which condensation will occur for air with a given relative humidity is called the *dew point*.

Because a major goal of most buildings is to create an interior temperature different than that of the outside air, buildings often have cool surfaces on which warmer, humid air will cool down enough to create condensation. For example, warm humid outside air entering a crawlspace through a foundation vent will eventually find a cool surface, perhaps concrete foundation walls or the decking of the floor, that will lower its temperature to the dew point and release moisture. So, now we have a situation where water has condensed in a cool, dark place—exactly the kind of hangout favored by molds, fungus, and termites.

It's important to remember, when considering protecting a building from water's destructive potential, that it's not just liquid moisture that you have to keep in mind. Don't ignore condensation. It's an issue that'll come up throughout this book, and for good reason.

Quadruple whammy. Here we can see all four forces of decay working together to break down this building. Sun and water have conspired to rust the metal roofing while the wind has been tugging away at it. A nail has come loose as a result, allowing the wind to begin to bend and even tear the metal. Meanwhile, sunlight has dried the visible roof rafter enough to cause cracking, which let water in. Freeze/thaw cycles widened the cracks. The wood eventually became soft and wet enough to invite carpenter ants and bees to burrow in and create nests. This in turn attracted woodpeckers, who've pecked at the wood to get at the insects.

tural failure. Second, liquid water is basically formless, so it can fit into the tiniest hole or crevice in a building's skin. Third, it's virtually alive. Water's high surface tension allows it to crawl upward against the force of gravity. This is called capillary action and is part of the mechanism behind water's movement through plants and blood's movement through your body. But it also allows water to crawl around your building in an almost sentient search for openings. Fourth, it's everywhere. Water falls from the sky, travels through the ground, and hides in the air. It makes up most of the surface of the planet and most of the mass of your body.

Air

Moving air, or wind, tears at a building's skin looking for weaknesses. As we've already learned, the weakest parts of a building are its connections. Wind preys on these connections, pulling roofs away from walls or one shingle off another. Wind combined with rain or snow also acts as a conduit for water, propelling and driving it into areas of the building where gravity alone could never take it.

Earth

Earth in this sense means life forms—all the plants, insects, and animals that spring from the earth. This life sustains itself by digesting organic material, stuff that is living or has lived. Rot is the process by which living things break down organic material. All the organic material in a building will eventually rot; the only question is how long it will take.

Various bacteria, fungi, insects, and even animals such as mice and woodpeckers all are driven to find yummy things somewhere on or in your house.

The Quadruple Whammy

Sorry, but the story gets worse, because these four formidable forces seldom work alone. Instead, they work together, creating a destructive power greater than the sum of the parts. For example, the freezing, thawing, and drying actions caused by the sun make many materials split and crack. This alone wouldn't be so serious, except that those splits and cracks provide avenues for water to enter—perhaps with the help of wind. Even so, things aren't so bad, because plain water doesn't rot things. It does, however, attract life forms, such as fungi and molds, which in turn do eat. Rot is the result.

BUILDING SKINS

Buildings have an exterior and interior skin. The exterior skin is basically all those surfaces that separate the building from the outside. This includes the surfaces of the roof, walls, windows, doors, chimneys, and anything else on the outside of the building. Not surprisingly, the interior skin is all the analogous surfaces that comprise the interior surfaces of the building. In this fundamentals chapter, we concern ourselves only with the exterior skin.

There are two basic categories of exterior building skins: *integrated* and *applied*. Materials with an outer surface that's resistant to the forces of decay have integrated skins. Stone and concrete are examples. Materials that need to have a protective coating applied to their surface, such as straw bales and rigid insulation, have applied skins. Many materials are durable in some situations and not in others, so they may or may not need an applied skin. Cob and adobe, for instance, are very durable in sun and wind, but much less so when exposed to lots of water. For that reason, they're often left unplastered in hot, dry climates, but commonly plastered in wetter climates. Wood is often given an applied skin of paint or sealer, but can also be treated as an integrated-skin material. The difference arises from the specific application and type of wood.

Wall skins feast. This building is a smorgasbord of wall skins. First, there's the stone stem wall's integrated skin. Moving up, there's the integrated skin of the log wall. Above that and on the second floor is a lapped board-and-batten siding skin, made of wide wooden boards whose intersecting seams are covered with narrow battens. The small entrance room's wall skin consists of lapped cedar shingles, also called shakes.

All-purpose seamless skin. Both the walls and roof of this adobe building in Mali are covered with the same seamless coat of plaster. Notice the wooden water spouts that project far past the walls to carry rainwater off the flat roof.

Lapped roof skins. *Left:* These slate shingles have protected this incredibly steep roof for many years and are still going strong. *Right:* These asphalt shingles are trying to mimic the far superior, much more expensive slate.

As with structure, the weakest points in a building's skin are the breaks in and transitions between materials. For this reason, applied skins are usually either *lapped* or *seamless.* Shiplap siding and shingles are examples of lapped skins, while plaster is an example of a seamless skin. Breaks or punctures, such as windows, doors, chimneys, and water pipes, are perhaps the most crucial places in a building's skin. These spots require careful detailing to seal out air, insects, and, most of all, water. A combination of trim and durable sheet metals called *flashing*, sometimes in complex configurations or soldered together, are usually used to seal, or weatherize, these difficult areas.

Tim's Take
On Flashing: "Be the Water"

Flashing, in its barest form, is fabricated from galvanized steel, aluminum, or copper, and is intended to move water away from a spot where it might intrude and cause damage. Since buildings are made up of many pieces, with many joints, it behooves us to think carefully about how water moves around and about them. While water means life for us mammals, it can be the kiss of death to our houses if it finds its way inside.

My brother engineers roofs for residences and large commercial structures. His advice when considering flashing details is, "Be the water." In other words, look for every conceivable way water might enter your house or get past that flashing you're installing.

Obviously, gravity and wind are the primary movers of water and should be the first concern. In the absence of wind, gravity is a reasonably predictable force. Water flows downhill...though my brother claims water *can* flow uphill, and I believe him. Wind, capillary action, surface tension, and Murphy's Law occasionally constellate to move water into places that defy all reasoning.

Learning to execute good flashing details is an art. You can get only a general idea from drawings and descriptions, and it's difficult to see good flashing on completed buildings because the crucial aspects are by definition covered. As you try to "be the water" and create good flashing details, you'll definitely need to use your common sense. And when in doubt, don't hesitate to ask for experienced advice.

Chimney flashing. This brick chimney is carefully flashed with two overlapping series of copper pieces. The first series, which isn't visible, is composed of L-shaped pieces called step flashing that extend under the last slate shingle in each course and bend up onto the chimney. The second series of pieces, called counter flashing, has one side set into the mortar and the other side (the triangular shapes you see here) bent down over the step flashing. This complex system allows little chance for water to sneak along the chimney and into the house.

FUNCTION FOUR: CONNECTION

Housing is a paradox, because the same potentially destructive natural elements that we try to keep away from our homes are the ones we seek out when looking for a place to build a house. The main trick of housing, then, is figuring how to keep natural elements out on one front while inviting those same elements in somewhere else.

THE FORCES OF LIFE

Let's take a yin-yang perspective and look at the elements of decay from the flip side.

Sun

Yes, the sun can cause problems for a building's skin. But we've already learned that it's also the fundamental source of all heat for buildings, so we just can't stay mad at it. Besides, our bodies need sunlight in order to manufacture vitamin D and to reset our biological clocks. We also need sunlight to see. We can either use stored sunlight in the form of electricity to run lights or we can use it directly for illumination, a practice called *daylighting* in the architecture trade.

Water

We drink water, bathe in water, cook with water, and are basically made of water. We need water in or near our homes. There are a number of ways that humans can access water: (1) directly from the groundwater reservoir, or aquifer, by drilling wells; (2) from the groundwater reservoir as it comes to the surface in the form of springs; (3) from rivers, ponds, and lakes; or (4) by intercepting water as it falls from the sky, a technique called *rain catchment.*

Air

The phenomenon of air is simply amazing. We're engulfed by an ocean of air called the atmosphere. Every little animal and insect is constantly sucking up oxygen and wheezing out carbon dioxide. Every tiny plant is doing the opposite, gasping for carbon dioxide and coughing up oxygen. In the face of this constant change, the makeup of air stays remarkably constant everywhere near the surface of the earth, allowing all of those plants, animals, and insects a guarantee of just what they need with every breath. This is made possible by air circulation, or wind.

A building must maintain this natural circulation—it must breathe, or the inhabitants will eventually use up all the oxygen, necessary for life, and would breathe in too much carbon dioxide, a poison to humans.

There are several basic strategies for maintaining healthy air exchange with the outside. The most obvious is placing holes in the building to allow outside air to move freely through the interior space. This is called *natural ventilation* and can be maximized by being conscious of prevailing winds and careful window and door placement. Another approach is to seal the building against air infiltration and to mechanically create circulation by using air pumps and fans, as is the case with modern HVAC (heating, ventilation, and air conditioning) systems. A third option is to

Sun. Our bodies need sunlight for such functions as producing Vitamin D and resetting our biological clocks. The more time we spend indoors, the more we need to invite sunlight into our buildings. Here, sunlight creates beautiful patterns on a cob building's earthen walls.

Water. A reliable, clean source of water must be a centerpiece of any building project designed for human habitation. A healthy human body can go many days without food, but water is a much more urgent necessity.

create a situation where air can circulate through the walls of a building, sometimes called "breathable walls," without gaining or losing much heat in the process. The idea here is that differences in pressure between the inside and outside will be equalized by air squeezing through microscopic holes in a thick wall of an appropriate material. (A disclaimer: I have no proof that this technique works. Some people scoff at it, and others swear by it.)

Earth

A building that doesn't give us easy access to the earth—in other words, the world outside—isn't a house, it's a prison. Houses need a connection to food, water, and a whole host of other things that reside in the world outside our homes. Houses need to create an easy flow between inside and outside, an easy conduit for movement to maintain this connection to the earth. Doors are the archetypal solution to this problem, and of course all buildings have doors. The careful placement of doors as well as the conscious design of interior and exterior rooms is a large part of what defines the flow between inside and out.

Many things in modern life don't come in through the front door, but also are important elements in many people's home lives. Phone service, water, and electricity are examples of connections to the outside that are made through conduits, pipes, and wires instead of direct human movement into the outside world. To a large extent, your concept of connection to the earth is defined on a personal level based on the laundry list of interactions and resources that correspond to your life.

Air. Breathing no air will kill you in minutes. Breathing bad air can kill you in minutes, hours, days, or years. As modern life grinds on, our need for truly fresh air becomes ever more of a challenge, one we have to meet by carefully planning how a building accesses and maintains quality indoor air.

Earth. Every building is physically supported by the earth, yet many buildings functionally separate us from the outside. A successful house simply has to encourage a comfortable connection to our true home: the earth.

WHERE ARE WE NOW?

Okay, so we've covered some of the basics of what makes up a house. We've put a face on the four functions a house has to provide. Now it's up to you to do some research of your own: Start looking at the buildings you come across each day and try to analyze them based on what we've discussed in this chapter. What is the building's basic structure? Are the foundation and walls skeletal or monolithic? How are the various elements connected? How does the building create and maintain a comfortable temperature? Is it doing an adequate job of separation from the forces of decay, or do you see signs of water leaks, rot, or insect damage? Does the building feel connected to the outside, with such features as natural ventilation and daylighting, or is it closed off and reliant on mechanical systems?

Looking at buildings in this way is actually a lot of fun. You'll be surprised at how quickly you'll start to get a feel for how buildings work. But it's also vitally important preparation—without this basic knowledge, without thinking about and observing and learning from the buildings around you, you'll really be in the dark when it comes to thinking about what you want to build and how you want to build it.

Most of the material covered here really is just applied grade-school science. But we've organized that science within the context of a powerful realization: that a house exists to nurture human life by augmenting the human body, by providing the same kinds of functions. This perspective defines clearly the things our buildings need to provide. What's more, it allows us to uncover some real blind spots in modern housing construction, and to explore alternatives—the subject of the next chapter.

A good house. This little building uses a combination of locally harvested (wood and bamboo) and mass-produced (corrugated roofing and plywood) materials to provide a strong skeletal structure that's lifted away from water and protected from the sun. (Notice the triangle braces on the front two corner posts.) Shading and natural ventilation provide cooling in a hot climate. Connection to the outside is ample and direct. The whole package is very simple yet elegant because it so clearly connects the needs of its specific inhabitants with the exact spot on which it's set. You need to find a combination of design, materials, and techniques that fits your situation just as nicely.

Chapter 3

Alternative Building Strategies

Imagine you're an Inuk living in northern Canada sometime in the 19th century.

It's getting colder, the kids are wanting their privacy, and you need a place to cook your blubber when there's a blizzard. It's time to build a house.

Do you have to design it? No, you know exactly what you're going to build and how you're going to build it. It's going to be a nice little dome with a small entrance tunnel. You'll make the whole thing from the snow on which you're standing. You'll only have to decide where to put it and perhaps adjust the dimensions to suit the size of your family. Maybe you'll add some personal touches, and perhaps even develop an innovation that others will copy, bringing it into the local building vernacular. But you'll move forward comfortably without a design consultation. The planning for your house has already taken place over many hundreds of years by generations of your forebears. You watched people build, and helped build, any number of these shelters as you were growing up. You're confident and calm as you break ground, cutting and laying the first snow block of your new pad.

For most of us, the process of building a house is going to be harder. The dominant building vernacular of our culture, the mobile home and contractor-built spec house Model Number Two, isn't working for us, so we basically have to start from scratch. We took the first step in the last chapter by studying the fundamental concepts behind a building and its interaction with nature. The next step is to form that information into some general strategies, alternative approaches that will apply to all of our specific situations.

ALTERNATIVE STRATEGIES: STRUCTURE

Modern techniques create incredibly strong structures. Just look at the Hoover Dam or your local skyscraper. The materials used are often sensible and practical. For example, it's hard to beat the roof trusses used in modern residential construction. As we learned in the last chapter, they use the strength of the triangle to create a powerful structure from small-dimensioned wood members. Wood is renewable, and the small dimension allows the members to be made out of small, young trees.

There's a weakness here, though, and it stems from the modern, generalized, mass-production mindset: The materials and structural approach for most modern buildings are determined before the place it will occupy or the occupants themselves are identified. This produces waste, inefficiency, and missed opportunities for creating lasting structures that truly suit and sustain their occupants and sites.

THROW AWAY THE COOKIE CUTTER

The solution is simple: the structure of each building needs to be designed specifically for that building. This may sound obvious, but it often isn't the way things are done. Building codes create general guidelines, and builders, being careful not to be held liable for problems, tend to meet or exceed these guidelines regardless of the specific situation. The result, as we'll discuss in more detail in chapters 7 and 11, is that modern buildings often overuse concrete in their foundations and overuse structural wood members in their walls. These materials create pollution in their manufacture

Enough's enough. The simple foundation on this little building does its job of lifting the walls away from water and creating support for a floor of small log beams and stick decking.

and transport. If the construction of a house causes undue pollution, then that construction is causing danger for the very things the house is supposed to nurture: human life and nature.

MINIMIZE YOUR IMPACT

The obvious answer to the above quandary might seem to be to completely swear off the use of these modern materials. But the truth is, every material that's transported causes pollution. In the short run, building is a destructive act. It's our job to be conscious of this fact and minimize the destructive aspects as much as possible. If using some concrete, for example, will allow a building to last a lot longer than not using it, we may actually be saving energy and preventing pollution by using it. That's a complicated equation, one with no general answers.

As green builders our general structural strategy has to be to use just enough of the right materials to create a structure that will be as strong as we need it in the worst case scenario, i.e. those times when loads are the most extreme in our specific situation.

For example, in the little building featured in this book, our design includes some wide, often heavy walls and an extremely heavy living roof. For that reason, we chose to use concrete in our foundation—but we made a little go a long way. By looking around our land instead of the aisles of a builder's supply, we were able to find some locust posts to serve as the walls' structural supports. We felt the heavy load of the roof was best carried by store-bought kiln-dried lumber, so we didn't hesitate to choose that modern material for that purpose. In some cases we created our own fasteners, and in others we happily used off-the-shelf hardware, depending on the particulars of the task at hand. In this way, we created a beautiful, powerful, long-lasting structure using a reasonable amount of materials.

THINK SKELETAL VS. MONOLITHIC

The majority of modern buildings use skeletal structures to create their walls and roofs. Many of those concrete-and-glass buildings clawing at the sky in cities have a skeletal structure made of steel. The conventional house, even if faced with brick, tends to have a structure of small wooden members holding up the walls and roof.

In contrast, many popular materials in the alternative/natural/green building worlds are capable of forming monolithic walls that will support the roof of the building. Cob, straw bale, and cordwood are examples. We utilize all three materials in the walls of the little building in this book—but not as vital structural elements. We strongly recommend NOT starting your building career or your first foray into these materials by using them to hold up your roof. Here's why:

First, building a skeletal structure makes the construction process easier. The materials you use to create the building's skeleton will be sufficiently weather-resistant to remain uncovered during initial construction. Once installed, kiln-dried wood can stand in the rain for months without damage, for example. (Don't leave it stacked in a mud puddle, though.) Once you cover your roof, the skeleton will, for all practical purposes, be protected, and you'll have a dry place to build your walls. Materials like cob and cordwood are difficult if not impossible to build with in the rain. In addition, walls made of these materials can be damaged if rained on excessively before being covered by a roof. The same goes double or quadruple for straw bales. Sure, you can become the wind's plaything and try to create a temporary fabric roof, or you can run around like a maniac covering everything with tarps. But why create stress unnecessarily? Why let life-giving rain be a source of tension, anxiety, and regret?

If you're a beginner, there's an even more urgent reason to start with a skeletal structure. Remember that stuff in the last chapter about bracing and buttressing? Skeletal structures are wonderful because they can be stiffened after the fact. This makes them great for beginners to build. If it looks a bit rickety as you're putting it up, just add some more bracing here or there. Also, skeletal structures go up pretty quickly, so it's more economical to hire someone to help, or easier to coax an experienced friend over to lend a hand, for that particular phase of construction. In contrast, load-bearing walls built of cob or cordwood take longer to build up, experienced help can be hard to find, and if the walls aren't strong enough, there's not much you can do about it.

In future chapters we'll point out other specific differences between skeletal and monolithic applications of these materials as we install them in our little building. For now, we'll keep our point simple: We wouldn't feel comfortable letting a friend truly inexperienced in building try to create monolithic walls that will carry a roof load, whether out of cordwood, cob, or straw. Some proponents of these materials will disagree with us strongly. Nonetheless, new inexperienced friends, that's our advice. Use it as you will. We say, first build a little building with a skeletal structure and the infill that interests you. If you have the confidence after that, do all the monolithic wall-building your heart desires.

Roof rewards. *Top:* A roof not only protects your cob from rain while it's still curing on the wall, it also gives you a shady, dry place to mix and lay the cob. *Bottom:* Adding a tarp to an already sheltering structure protects these straw bales from rain until plaster can be applied.

ALTERNATIVE STRATEGIES: TEMPERATURE

If you travel down the streets of a typical planned suburban subdivision, you'll see near-identical houses, chosen from three available models, facing each other on each side of the street. As you turn a corner or take a curve, all the houses you encounter continue to face the street as if they need to keep an eye on you. This simple phenomenon belies a devastating blunder, one that alone provides conclusive evidence of how oblivious we've become to the natural forces that make our lives possible. These houses, with their manicured lawns and treeless streets, are truly lost in the wilderness. Why? Because they're placed haphazardly in relation to the sun. They've forgotten where the sun is. Any navigator can tell you that you don't know where you are if you don't know where the sun is.

Of course, the inhabitants of these houses aren't lost on the planet. They have cars poised to comfortably transport them to exact locations to purchase any convenience they desire. However, they are lost in their own backyards, because they use a fake sun to replace the real one. High electricity bills, air pollution, and a house that can't function in a winter storm "power outage" are a few of the consequences.

USE THE SUN

The sun is the single most predictable climatic element of any building site. For any place on the planet, you can calculate the exact spot the sun will occupy in the sky at any given moment on any given day from now until our nearest star eventually burns out. Except for hiding behind clouds, the sun bears no surprises.

We've already learned that a building's interior temperature is maintained basically by a combination of accessing and creating separation from solar energy, either directly as sunlight or indirectly through stored-solar fuels such as wood, petroleum, and coal.

So let's review: the sun beats down on us, we know exactly when and where in the sky it will be beating down on us, and its energy is the source of all the heat and cool in our building. These facts scream out at us to utilize the direct sun and its predictable behavior, its reliable beating down. *Passive solar design* is the conscious placement of a building and associated materials so that the sun's direct energy is manipulated to affect the temperature inside the building. Once you look at the fundamentals, it's simply and obviously the only way to go.

Besides, as the human population of our planet continues to rise, it's paramount to understand that all sources of heating fuel are finite. Heat requires combustion and combustion requires fuel. Many of our fuel sources, such as coal and petroleum, take literally millions of years to produce. Wood, on the other hand, is quickly replenishable, but we could never replace it fast enough to supply the entire world with heat. Ultimately it doesn't matter how efficient our usage, the human population of earth will eventually drive the demand beyond the supply.

Furthermore, the combustion of all of these fuels puts massive amounts of pollution into the air. Can anyone truly stand in the horrible air engulfing Los Angeles, Mexico City, or Rome and say that our fuel combustion practices aren't a disaster? Of course, the combustion of the sun is also finite, but when the sun's fuel runs out, life won't be possible on this planet anymore anyway. In addition, that combustion is occurring far outside of our atmosphere's protective envelope, so we don't have to breathe the product of its smokestack. Ironically, our combustion of fuels is damaging our atmosphere by creating holes that allow dangerous ultraviolet radiation from the sun's combustion to reach us.

I'm a big fan of debate and the relativity of truth, but this is an issue, like life and death itself, over which we have no control. The decision to base our heating and energy technology on the power of the sun is not open to sensible debate. There simply is no other long-term solution, and any naysaying comes either from ignorance or in service to some special interest. We have to finally and permanently admit the simple beauty of our situation: It's all about the sun.

Three Kinds of Solar Power

Passive solar refers to dealing directly with the sun's energy, both by inviting it into and blocking it out of a building. *Active solar* refers to collecting sunlight's direct heat and moving it to a different place for use in the building. An example is hydronic floor heating, which uses a liquid that's heated on the roof of a building by the sun and pumped to a storage tank, then circulated through pipes in the floor to create room heating. Another example of active solar is *photovoltaics,* which is the conversion of direct sunlight collected outside a building into electricity used inside the building. A third kind of solar power, one that uses solar energy stored in the form of plant and animal tissue, such as wood and fossil fuels, doesn't really have a name. Let's call it *reactivated solar.*

Active solar. Glycol, a liquid with a low freezing point, is passed through pipes in these panels, where it's heated by the sun and then pumped into coils in a tank in the house. The coils, called a heat exchanger, give up the collected heat to water that surrounds them and send the liquid back to the roof to be heated again. The heated water is then used for domestic hot water or is run through pipes in the floor to heat the house, a process called hydronic heating.

Passive solar. Passive solar design encompasses both inviting in and keeping out the sun's intense energy. This large north-facing porch overhang creates a cool, shaded outdoor room in summer and protects the building's walls from solar radiation, which helps keep the interior cooler also. Uncovered windows on the building's south side are open to the sun's lower winter path, and the building's interior has mass to store the solar heat pouring in during those months.

Reactivated solar. Wood contains solar energy stored as plant tissue.

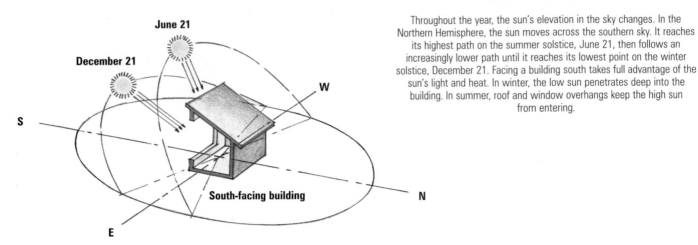

Figure 1
THE SUN'S CHANGING PATH

Throughout the year, the sun's elevation in the sky changes. In the Northern Hemisphere, the sun moves across the southern sky. It reaches its highest path on the summer solstice, June 21, then follows an increasingly lower path until it reaches its lowest point on the winter solstice, December 21. Facing a building south takes full advantage of the sun's light and heat. In winter, the low sun penetrates deep into the building. In summer, roof and window overhangs keep the high sun from entering.

CREATING PASSIVE SOLAR TEMPERATURE

Passive solar design is based on a useful property of the sun's path through the sky: In winter the sun is low in the sky and in summer it's high. This simple fact makes it possible to place a building so that its interior will get lots of warming sunlight in the winter, when it's cold, and very little of that same sunlight in the summer, when it's hot. This basic idea is so sublime because it allows the use of the same building elements to create both heat and cool. For example, a good thermal mass set inside the building in front of glass-covered openings can store winter solar heat during the day and then release it back to the building at night. Such a mass is most often placed in the floor because that's where most of the sunlight hits. Concrete slabs and adobe floors are examples. In the summer, this same mass is protected from the sun by the building's roof and other elements, so it becomes cool and can accept extra heat from the air to help keep the interior cooler.

Similarly, the building's windows can serve a double purpose. If you place most of a building's glass toward the winter sun, which in the Northern Hemisphere would be the south side of the building, that glass will allow solar heat to enter the building in winter, but will be shaded by the roof in summer. Thus, the same windows create both heat and cool. The limited amount of sunlight through east and west windows in the winter, combined with the fact that a window alone has very little insulation value, adds up to these windows being a net heat loss in winter. In summer, the rising sun to the east and very hot setting sun to the west cannot be stopped by roof or window overhangs; therefore east and west windows can cause overheating in the summer. In this case, the same windows cause heat loss in winter and overheating in summer, so they should be minimized, at least from the point of view of dealing with direct sunlight.

Another elegant dual-purpose passive solar material is deciduous plants. Thoughtfully placed deciduous trees and plants create cooling shade and evaporative cooling around a building in summer and, after losing their leaves, allow solar heat to access and heat up thermal mass inside a building in winter.

Roof overhangs. The overhangs over these south-facing doors are sized to allow the welcome heat of the low winter sun's rays in, while keeping the unwelcome heat of the higher summer sun out.

Double-duty deciduous plants. The birch trees growing close to the south and west of this little house provide shade and evaporative cooling throughout late spring and summer. After losing their leaves, the trees let ample, warming sunlight flow into the interior of the house in fall and winter.

Heating and cooling with the same materials. In the winter, the glass in these south-facing doors admits solar energy to be stored in the thermal mass floor. In summer, it provides a shaded visual connection to the outside, or the doors can be opened to let in cooling fresh air from the shaded exterior. The tile on the floor, which is installed on top of an insulated concrete slab, also provides both heating and cooling. In the winter, the mass collects and stores solar energy to heat the building. In the summer, the shaded mass is cool and accepts heat from the air, helping to keep interior temperatures lower.

MAINTAINING PASSIVE SOLAR TEMPERATURE

The same mass that helps a passive solar building create temperature through storage will help maintain that temperature. Conventional forced-air furnaces heat air and move it around, but they don't store heat. Thermal mass floors and thick thermal mass walls, such as those made of adobe or cob, store heat and give it back slowly to the air as the mass cools. This process takes time. The more mass a building has, the longer it will take to cool down or heat up, and the more stable its temperature will be in response to outside fluctuations. This trait can be embellished by partially burying a building in the side of a hill, also called *berming*, which allows the building to access the huge, stable thermal mass of the earth.

Thermal mass *can* be too much of a good thing, though. If you have too much mass in your floor, for example, it will be able to store a substantial amount of heat, but it will also take a lot of heat to warm the floor once it has cooled down. In other words, too much mass causes a building's solar thermostat to respond very slowly. On the other hand, a building with too little mass will fill its solar "storage tanks" early on a sunny day. The solar heat shining in for the rest of the day will be heating only the air, which will cause overheating. In addition, after the sun goes down, the small mass won't have stored enough heat to keep the building warm through the night.

Keep in mind, too, that thermal mass alone won't maintain temperature. As with any modern building approach, careful placement of insulation is important in passive solar design. Since we're being conscious of the sun's role, however, new opportunities are immediately obvious. For example, why use the same materials on all walls? Some materials are both good thermal masses and decent insulation. One such material is cob, a combination of mass (clay and sand) and insulation against conduction (straw). Another example is composite blocks made of wood chips bonded with concrete. Why not use one of these materials on the south side (in the Northern Hemisphere) where its mass can add some heat to the building in winter? On the sunless north side, it's definitely a better idea to use as much insulation as possible, so straw bales might be a good choice. Perhaps the east and west sides are going to hold most of the weight of the roof, so we might choose strong wood framing here with an infill of recycled newspaper insulation.

Berming. This house is set into a south-facing hill. The entire first story is snug out of the cold winter wind while being open to the winter sun's warming rays. Insulation between the north wall and the earth behind it allows the building to be partially blanketed by 55°F earth, making it easier to raise indoor temperatures above this mark when needed in winter. It's as though the insulated north wall is in a temperate climate where the outdoor temperature always hovers between 50° and 60°F, even while the rest of the house is dealing with a snowy winter or sweltering summer. (See chapter 14 for more on this.)

Insulation. As part of the passive solar strategy of the little building we built for this book, we chose to match the unique insulative properties of straw bale, cordwood, and cob to deal with specific temperature storage problems on each of three walls, shown here in various stages of construction. We'll discuss each situation in detail in upcoming chapters.

DESIGNING WITH PASSIVE SOLAR

We've just touched on some of the basics of the elegant simplicity that is passive solar design. Though we'll go into more detail in the descriptions of decisions we made for our little building, this book can't provide you with all the information you need to do a thorough study of passive solar. Before you build anything designed for human habitation, even a playhouse or workshop, read more about passive solar design and get a firm grip on how it applies to your specific situation. Though we've focused our examples on climates that require winter heating and summer cooling, the same basic strategies can be adjusted for any climate.

In fact, before moving on, let's look at some of the basics as they might be applied in three different climate types. Of course, climate is actually a continuum, which means that each act of building has to look closely at the specifics of the exact climate at the site. We are making blunt abstractions as a learning tool to get across basic concepts. It's also important to remember that a house is an organic whole and temperature is only one aspect. For these examples, we're talking about a house that's designed only with temperature in mind. The tug and pull of other needs will adjust these archetypes. Also, these examples assume that the building is in the Northern Hemisphere.

Cold Climate

In cold climates, houses should be long and thin along the east-west axis to maximize solar exposure to winter sun. A longer southern wall displays more surface area to the sun and shorter east and west walls allow for deep penetration of that sun into the building. The shorter east and west walls also minimize exposure to the overheating western sun in the summer. The amount of southern window and door glass, or glazing, should be carefully designed to match the amount of thermal mass in the building. Don't use too much glass! Much of this mass should be placed where the winter sun will reach it. The floor is a good spot. Eastern and western glazing should be chosen based on other needs, such as lighting, natural ventilation, or views; it's a net loss in terms of solar heating. North glass should be minimized.

Cold winter design. Angled south-facing windows allow the low winter sun to penetrate deeply into this Earthship, while berming on its north side takes advantage of the earth's stable, moderating temperature.

Roof overhangs, as well as door and window awnings and arbors, should be shorter, allowing maximum sun penetration in early and late winter. Use curtains to avoid overheating in late summer.

Insulation should be maximized where possible, for example in the attic or roof. Consider berming the north side into a south-facing hill, or superinsulating the north side with straw bales or the like. Insulate under the mass floor and behind a bermed wall to create a buffer from the stable, yet colder-than-human-comfort earth. (We'll discuss this concept in more detail in chapter 14.) Dense evergreen trees to the north or in the direction of the prevailing winter wind are helpful. Keep the south face clear of obstruction, with the exception of deciduous trees placed strategically to provide leafy shade in summer but allow solar exposure in winter. Carefully choose your backup heat source to augment your design. For example, the huge thermal mass of a masonry wood-burning stove can act as a solar mass when the sun is out, in addition to being an energy-efficient and comparatively clean-burning source of reactivated solar heat.

Fairly Cold/ Fairly Hot Climate

The siting and shape of a building in this climate should follow essentially the same principles as in the cold climate. The same southern window-to-mass ratio applies. Here, though, you need to be more concerned with cooling. Adding more east, west, and north windows will encourage natural ventilation. Creating longer overhangs and awnings will block more of the early and late summer sun. This will also cause a decrease in solar heating in the early and late winter, but it's a tradeoff that makes sense in this situation. Another option is to plant arbors placed in front of windows and doors with deciduous vines; the foliage in summer provides shading while its absence in winter allows solar entry.

Milder climate design. This building has a south-facing exposure and a similar layout to the building shown on page 55, but is tweaked to a wetter, milder climate. The addition of roof overhangs protects walls against frequent rains and provides some shading. East and west (left wall shown) windows allow for cooling summer ventilation.

Insulation is important here, though radiant barriers (reflective materials applied to a surface of the roof somewhere under the final covering) may outweigh extra roof insulation in importance. The north side of the house can be a wonderful cool patio in the summer, so northern doors and windows are much more appealing in this climate. Extending the east and west roof overhangs to create porches blocks the hot rising and setting sun and creates cool places to relax or comfortable outdoor work areas. Plant trees for shade, but be careful not to block prevailing summer breezes. Using dense evergreens to hold back winter winds is still a good idea. Backup heat is almost always needed even in the best passive solar designs, but make sure what you choose isn't too much or too little for your situation.

Hot Climate

In many hot climates, there's still a need for some winter heating. In these situations, southern glass and mass can be used, but the focus of living should be shifted to the north side, with outdoor courtyards and patios serving as full-fledged living spaces for much of the year. The long, thin shapes of our buildings above can give way to designs that create shaded inner courtyards, perhaps facing north. Glass should be shaded and placed to encourage natural ventilation. Roof overhangs should be extended to create sun-sheltered living spaces all around the building, with the possible exception of the south side. A thermal mass shaded from the sun and connected to the earth, as with a bermed wall or slab-on-grade floor, can tap into the earth's massive stable temperature, often between 50° and 60° F. If the mass is used only for cooling, no insulation is needed between it and the earth, though a gravel bed, plastic vapor barrier, or similar measure should be included to prevent condensation.

In certain situations, an open floor plan along with a cooling tower—a large, roof-mounted vent—can encourage cooling. Hot air rises through the roof vent, causing cooler air to be pulled inside through low northern windows. This air can be further cooled by north plantings near the windows and by interior water fountains or other water sources, all of which will encourage evaporative cooling. In conventional designs, the attic can be used as the cooling tower and an attic fan can increase the ventilation.

If a thermal mass is used as part of a cooling strategy, as described above, then insulating the interior is as important here as in other climates. However, in tropical regions where little or no heating is required and cooling breezes and shading are amply available, insulation is of negligible importance. Instead, lots of openings in the form of doors and windows or walls made of woven bamboo or similar materials allow cooling air circulation, and tall trees on all sides shade the building's roof.

Extreme heat design. This building is all about protection from solar heat. Its compact shape exposes only a small surface area to the sun's rays. Thick cob walls slow the penetration of heat. The interior courtyard creates a shaded, ventilated outdoor room.

ALTERNATIVE STRATEGIES: SEPARATION

As we've said before, our approach to housing alternatives is all about perspective. That premise certainly applies to the topic of separation. The general modern approach to the forces of decay is to treat them as enemies: if it wants to come in, keep it out; if it's alive, kill it.

One problem with this approach is that it makes an enemy of the very things that define our survival. In a real sense, it makes enemies of ourselves. Take, for instance, the idea that you dissuade insects from eating your house by poisoning them. The trouble is that insects are carbon-based life forms that take in oxygen and give off carbon dioxide; in other words they're similar to us. By poisoning them, especially in and around our houses, we poison ourselves.

Another problem with this perspective is that you just can't win. You can't fight the sun, water, wind, and life, because they're everywhere, omnipresent, the whole ball of wax. On top of that, poor little modern housing is often expected to fight off these superpowers using the same strategies in a variety of different climates. As a result, there's a constant flow of new and improved supermaterials crowding the shelves of your local builder's supply. Ironically, this means that modern building is often experimental and untested. Until recently in many parts of the U.S., for instance, arsenic-laced pressure-treated wood was required by law for applications that touched the ground or masonry. You can still see little kids crawling around on whole playgrounds made of the stuff. Today, this process has been outlawed because it has finally been proven that poisoning wood with arsenic is dangerous to people. One day it was against the law *not* to use it, and the next it was against the law *to* use it.

Rejecting water. Notice the lack of roof overhangs and gutters on these small storage buildings. They're built with the notion that water can be sealed out by wrapping the entire space with water-resistant painted metal. But even if water doesn't find its way inside (I'm betting it will, by seeping behind those windows with the flanges installed on top of the siding, a mistake), water will still pour off the roof onto the ground all around the building. It'll splash up onto the siding, get under the building, and generally make a nuisance of itself.

Redirecting water. In our little building, the living roof absorbs water, limiting roof run-off, and the huge overhang and well-sloped grading direct water away so efficiently that we don't even need a gutter on this eave wall. In addition, the overhang creates a useful outdoor space, in this case a potting area complete with shelving and a sink.

Drip edge. The groove cut into this granite windowsill is a drip edge. When water runs over and beneath the sill, the drip edge interrupts the flow long enough for gravity to take over, causing the water to fall away from the wall.

REDIRECT INSTEAD OF REJECT

Personally, I didn't need to wait around for science to prove that arsenic-treated wood was dangerous. I knew it already; not because I'm a genius, but because I had a different perspective, the same one we've established in this book: a house needs to create and sustain a delicate balance of simultaneous separation from and connection to the same elements of nature. That pretty much precludes poison as a strategy. Now, don't get the wrong impression. I'm not demonizing modern materials. Science has given us some great stuff and you'll find some of it in almost every building in the industrialized world. Metal roofing, for example, is a useful, durable material and you'll often see it on even the purest eco-hut. What I'm saying is that we need to choose materials wisely and not expect them to do the impossible.

In general, we can phrase our alternative strategy to separation very simply: redirect, rather than exclude or reject, the forces of decay.

Redirecting Water

What does it mean to redirect rather than reject? In the case of water, it means creating a comfortable route for water to flow over and away from the building. *Flashing* blocks the flow of water at crucial breaks in materials long enough for gravity to carry it away. A *drip edge* directs water away from rather than toward vulnerable building components. Large roof *overhangs* direct water away from walls into gutters or directly onto properly graded and landscaped ground. Short water-resistant walls, called *stem walls*, lift vulnerable wall materials off the ground away from rain splash and accumulated snow. In walls, redirecting water means either creating multiple layers of surfaces for water to flow down, called *drainage planes*, or using materials that are capable of taking on and giving off water vapor, as in breathable plaster systems with some form of cellulose insulation.

Drainage Planes

A drainage plane is a surface that's impervious enough to water to allow gravity to carry it away. A conventional stick-framed wall uses multiple drainage planes to redirect water. To start with, the plywood sheathing placed over studs is a good drainage plane in itself. However, the first "official" drainage plane is created by covering the plywood sheathing with a layer of overlapping, tar-impregnated, water-resistant paper. The tarpaper, in turn, is covered with an exterior skin—either siding or metal lath and cement stucco—that doesn't bond with the

paper. When it rains, most of the
water flows down this second
drainage plane, the exterior skin.
Any water that makes it behind the
skin flows down the tarpaper.
This system very effectively redirects
water, and can create a situation
where liquid water may never come
in contact with the wood.

In the real world, however, that
doesn't always happen. Water can get
behind the paper, especially around
poorly flashed doors and windows,
for example. Water that makes it to
the sheathing or framing and
insulation can get trapped behind
all of those drainage planes. If
chronic, this trapped water can
cause major problems.

Hygroscopic Walls

A different approach is to create
what's called a *hygroscopic wall*, a
wall that uses materials that can
take on and give off water vapor in
response to humidity changes without sustaining damage. All forms of organic
cellulose, including wood, straw, and recycled newspapers, have this ability within
certain moisture ranges. The idea here is to allow the wall to become a part of the
humidity cycle of the air around it, which greatly reduces the chance of trapping
water and can, as we'll explain later, lead to improved indoor air quality. To envision
how this works, consider the example of a straw bale wall. A single drainage plane of
relatively vapor-permeable plaster is bonded to the bales themselves. In the best-case
scenario, any liquid water falling on the plaster will be directed away, leaving the
system to adjust to humidity changes in the air. However, even if the plaster absorbs
some liquid water that then wicks into the bales, they won't be harmed if they have
ample time and the right conditions to dry out between wettings.

Obviously, this system is more vulnerable to liquid water than a well-installed
conventional drainage-plane system like the one described earlier. In warm, arid
climates, this isn't a problem because potential soakings are separated by plenty of
drying time and are driven out by dry air that wants the moisture the walls contain.
In wetter climates, the possible advantages of hygroscopic walls need to be carefully
protected by keeping as much liquid water off the walls as possible through diligent
use of stem walls, overhangs, and drainage systems. All four of the walls of the little
building featured in this book employ the hygroscopic strategy, so we'll discuss the
topic more in future chapters.

Figure 2
REDIRECTING WATER

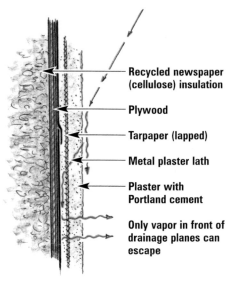

- **Recycled newspaper (cellulose) insulation**
- **Plywood**
- **Tarpaper (lapped)**
- **Metal plaster lath**
- **Plaster with Portland cement**
- **Only vapor in front of drainage planes can escape**

Drainage Planes

Conventional stick-framing uses multiple drainage
planes to effectively keep liquid water away from
cellulose materials, leaving open the possibility
that liquid water making it past the drainage
planes might get trapped there.

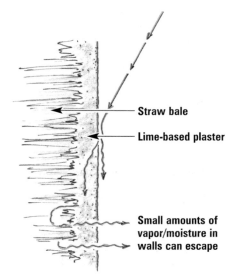

- **Straw bale**
- **Lime-based plaster**
- **Small amounts of vapor/moisture in walls can escape**

Hygroscopic Walls

Another approach is to allow cellulose materials,
such as wood, straw, and recycled newspapers,
to take on and give off water vapor and small
amounts of liquid water absorbed through their
exterior skins. The gamble here is that the wall
could become overloaded with more water
than it can give off before the onset of mold,
fungus, and rot.

Living proof. Plants don't just redirect the sun's energy; they use it to grow more shading, evaporative-cooling foliage. Plants, then, can be a self-maintaining, even self-improving, skin for a building's roof.

Redirecting Sun

Mass-produced modern and site-produced traditional materials can make excellent skins when it comes to redirecting the sun. Both a lime-washed earth plaster and a light-colored metal roofing, for example, stand up to UV very well and double as radiant insulation by reflecting the sun's heat. Still, these materials are no match for constant solar attack. The common modern practice of clear-cutting land before building would put a lot of strain on either material by maximizing possible exposure to harsh sunlight. On the other hand, the simple strategy of selective cutting to leave shade trees would help both materials do their job.

Of course, big trees often aren't an option and falling limbs and leaves can cause problems of their own. Another approach to achieve the same goals would be to shade the roof by covering it with plants, called a living or green roof, and to shade the walls by extending the roof over them with large overhangs. Living roofs use a waterproof membrane, insulation, drainage, growing medium, and plants to create an incredibly durable roof skin that's very resistant to both UV damage and damage due to freeze-thaw cycles—the two banes of any roof skin. These roofs have a lot of other advantages. Happily, our little building has a living roof, so we'll cover the topic in detail later in the book.

Redirecting Wind

Wind is the most site-specific of all the forces of decay. You can look up estimated rainfall and solar insolation (a measure of the sun's energy hitting an area) for a general region and assume it's accurate for your specific site. Wind is a different matter. You really need to spend time *on* an exact spot to get a feel for the seasonal wind patterns there. Although modern materials perform wonderfully against wind, it's rare for a contractor or architect to have this kind of extended experience with a site. In addition, modern house siting is often view-driven, which results in plunking a building on top of a hill to expand the view, and never mind that this also tends to expose the building to the most wind.

Weather to build? This open meadow on top of a hill offers panoramic views and lots of sun. It seems a great house site. On the other hand, hilltops without tree cover can be very windy. Cold winter winds would make a house up here hard to keep warm, and wind-driven rain would put a lot of stress on the building's protective skin. A better idea might be to nestle the house somewhere down on the hill's south face, where it will be open to the winter sun but protected from the winter wind.

By spending enough observation time on a site, you can decide the best place to put a building to protect it from cold winter winds, open it up to cooling summer breezes, and hide it from powerful, destructive wind patterns. Trees, land contour, or rock outcroppings, may already exist on the site to serve as natural wind breaks. Using such elements may be as simple as pulling the building a bit off the top of that hill with the awesome view. Put a fire pit up there instead, and go look at the view when you have a chance to really enjoy it.

Redirecting Life ("Pests")

As we've seen, in many respects the modern approach to separation is just a tweak away from a slightly more sensible alternative. When it comes to dealing with life as a destructive force, the modern, often building-code-required, approach is simply scary: poison. Fortunately for us, it's actually easier and safer to redirect life than to kill it.

For example, termites can be redirected by creating physical barriers to their movement into the house. Traditional metal termite barriers don't keep termites out entirely, but do force the insects to create a tell-tale tunnel across the barrier to an entry point, allowing you to easily locate and close up that entry—a better method than poisoning the entire perimeter of your home. Also, special materials have become available in some areas recently that do benignly prevent entry. One is sand of a particular grain size; the other is wire screen of a particular mesh size. The sand is too large to be carried away by the termites, but too small to support tunnel construction. Similarly, the gaps in the metal mesh are too small for the termites to crawl through.

Remember too, as we learned in the previous chapter, that most life is attracted to water. Mold, fungi, and termites can't thrive in dry places, so if you keep your edible building materials dry, these forces of decay usually won't be a problem. We'll cover different strategies for creating self-drying walls in upcoming chapters as we build the walls of our little building. Please just follow this simple, seemingly obvious rule: Don't poison your house.

Dry, high, and bug-free. All the edible components of this building are lifted off the ground by a small concrete wall, called a stem wall. In combination with roof overhangs and sloped drainage, this strategy keeps the building's materials dry and therefore much less interesting to molds and insects. For termites, the height off the ground makes it harder to find the cellulose they're seeking. As a final measure, a metal barrier was placed over the stem wall to force any termites that might be crawling through cracks in the concrete to come out into the open, where their tunnels will be visible.

ALTERNATIVE STRATEGIES: CONNECTION

Everything that keeps us alive comes from the outside: outside our bodies and outside our houses. Everyone would agree that we need to keep a constant connection to the light-, water-, oxygen-, and food-filled outside. Modern building, however, takes the worried-mother approach to connection. It just doesn't quite trust the outside and wants to keep your connections on a tight leash. Instead of opening up to the sun, let's just close the drapes and turn on the light. Just to be safe, we'd better kill everything in that water. Rather than letting scary fresh air in, let's use an air freshener. In some houses, the main connection to the outside is through the TV. Collecting food can consist of quick transitions between air-conditioned house to garage to air-conditioned car to air-conditioned shopping center. This all may sound like an exaggeration, but, sadly, it often really isn't. Let's face it: modern housing is basically paranoid about the outside. The less neurotic alternative is to consciously and carefully invite the outside directly in.

Tale of two windows. *Top:* The sun is never low in the sky to the north (in the Northern Hemisphere), so north-facing windows provide even, indirect, glare-free light year-round. Someone reclining on this sofa with his or her back against the far wall can read a book by the light of this north-facing window on any day of the year, regardless if the day is sunny or cloudy. *Bottom:* It's hard to imagine why the windows in this building were installed at all. They're high, in the shadow of the roof, and the shades are always drawn, necessitating the use of electric lights on even sunny days.

DESIGN FOR SUNSHINE

We've already consciously placed our building in relation to the sun to create and maintain temperature. Now we just need to tweak things to gain the added benefit of having the sun be our daylight illumination. This may sound obvious, but good daylighting is a real art. Direct sun can cause headaches and eye strain, so you need to find ways to use reflected and ambient sunlight in work and reading areas. This is made more difficult because you're often already inviting the sun to come streaming in to create winter heat.

One answer is to create a *Trombe wall,* which is basically a masonry wall set inside a big window. The wall has vents in the top and bottom that passively circulate the heat absorbed by the wall in a process called *thermosiphoning.* At the same time, the masonry wall is shading the interior, so you get solar heat without solar glare.

On the other hand, sunlight streaming in on a cold winter day can be a beautiful, uplifting sight, so another option is to create a sort of boiler room. This space can be an attached sunroom or greenhouse, or simply a section of the living space that you don't need to sit in on a sunny winter day. This boiler room then stores solar energy that will supply other, shaded parts of the house's open floor plan with heat. Every task or activity asks for a specific kind of illumination, so if your daylighting is going to be effective, you'll need to design carefully. Remember, your house and the sun can combine to form a lamp, but it's a lamp that can't be moved, so place it carefully.

WATER IN: CONSIDER THE SOURCE

"Innocent until proven guilty" is a wonderful foundation for a justice system, but it's a stupid tenet when talking about maintaining a connection between our delicate thread of life and the equally delicate ecosystem outside. Everyone admits that chlorine is a poison. It has been used extensively as a chemical weapon. And municipalities widely use it to kill (there's that word again) microbes in water.

Call me a worrywart, but I'm not waiting around for some study to tell me that chlorine is rotting my liver or causing cancer of the spleen. I'm not putting it in my drinking water! In my opinion the chlorination of water is an act of desperation taken by people asked to do the impossible: safely collect, store, and disseminate clean drinking water for millions (or hundreds of thousands, or thousands) of people from a single source.

Wisely, you've decided to take charge of your own situation, so you only have to supply clean water to a single household. Regardless of your water source—spring, well, rain catchment, or the mystery of municipal service—filtering is a relatively easy, safe method for removing anything in the water that you don't want. You can test your water and adjust your filtering based on what you find.

After an initial test, many people with wells don't do any filtering because they assume that the combination of natural, biological land treatment the water receives as it filters through the ground and the dark cold environment of the aquifer insures a biologically benign brew. Of course, it's always possible that human-made contaminants have crashed the party, so other people decide to filter anyway. The issues are basically the same for springs.

To the best of my knowledge, those who collect rain catchment water for drinking always use filtering. The sky has become polluted, so rainwater, once considered clean, isn't necessarily clean anymore. Also, there's a pretty good possibility that bird droppings and other impurities on the roof could contaminate the water.

Municipal water should be tested, too. Often, all that's left that needs to be filtered is the poison the city put in: chlorine.

Pure simplicity. This simple, inexpensive, point-of-use water filter screws onto a faucet and is certified to reduce many known carcinogens, lead, mercury, bacteria, and even some of the poisonous chlorine that contaminates most municipal water. A wide variety of other filters and filtering systems are available. After testing a water source, you can choose the approach that best suits your situation.

WATER OUT: CONSIDER THE IMPACT

What happens to that sanitized (chlorinated) drinking water after it's poured down the drain? In cities, it's combined with feces from toilets, motor oil and auto chemicals from repair shops, a variety of toxins from local factories, and everything and anything else that goes down any drain. This huge mess descends on the municipal sewage treatment plant where a complex process of cleanup takes place. In other words, we take water that we've gone to great lengths to sanitize, mix it with a horrible array of toxins, and then go to great efforts to clean it up again. It's basically treated as toxic waste. I'm sorry to be such a pain in the neck, Modern World, but that just doesn't make sense.

Fortunately, once you take responsibility for one little building as opposed to thousands, the problem is made much simpler. We just need to keep the potentially dangerous stuff out of the water. In a domestic household, that dangerous stuff consists mainly of human feces and any chemical cleansers, pesticides, and other toxins we may use.

As a first step, use biodegradable soaps and citrus-based cleansers, and forget the pesticides altogether. As for human feces, what's it doing in the water in the first place? Let's just keep it out. And if we have any meat grease or other things that just intuitively seem like they're going to be nasty in water, let's keep them out, too. Okay, now what we have going down the drain is basically clean water with some dirt, vegetable pieces, and other basically harmless solids. This water, commonly called *greywater* to distinguish it from *blackwater* that contains human urine and feces, can be utilized directly by outdoor plants.

But what about the feces? Well, what's really so scary about that anyway? Once separated from the water, you're left with a small amount of solids that are made up of food waste and microorganisms from your body. It's easy to compost the stuff into a nutrient-rich, useable soil. That's what happens in any barn, and we can accomplish

It happens, but what to do with it? It's not a question of whether we'll produce feces daily; it's a question of what to do with it. One option is to encase it in a concrete coffin, also called a septic tank (left), and let the fetid liquid slowly ooze out into trenches in your yard, officially called a "leach field," like this one filled with corrugated pipes wrapped with Styrofoam peanuts (right).

Another bad option. You can flush your waste into the public water supply, where it combines with every other chemical or compound washed down any person's or business' drain. The water will end up at a sewage treatment plant, where steps will be taken to "clean" it, probably including adding more chlorine, before it's released back into the environment.

Dirt simple solution. Another choice is to separate out the small amount of fecal solids and combine them with kitchen scraps, yard clippings, sawdust, and straw in a simple composting system that creates odor-free, nutrient-rich soil that plants love. This is our composted humanure soil.

the same thing without the smell by using some form of composting toilet. People buy composted cow manure in bags at the local nursery to use as a soil amendment. Why not just make some for free at home?

If you think that sounds weird, it may be helpful to realize that the same thing is being done on a massive scale down at your local sewage treatment plant. Composting of solids is a basic step in the procedure. It's also the same process that's going on in any septic tank. The difference in our situation is that since we're not dealing with water, we can use aerobic (oxygen-consuming) microorganisms to break down our solids. This allows us to obtain higher temperatures, which more efficiently kill parasites. The end result is beautiful black dirt, not some sludge in the bottom of a septic tank that's pumped out and taken to the landfill.

We don't have the space to go into this issue in detail. There's a lot to learn about creating greywater systems and safely composting human feces. Obviously, if you aren't going to do them right, you shouldn't do them at all. For now, we're trying to get across a general design concept: By dealing conscientiously with the water coming in and leaving your house, you can create useful materials out of what is generally considered dangerous waste.

PAY ATTENTION TO AIR QUALITY

As we've said, the atmosphere is one big mass of air that remains amazingly constant in the face of constant change. We can't be separated from that air for more than a couple of minutes and survive. Our goal in housing, then, is exceedingly simple: make sure that indoor air and outdoor air are one and the same. Unfortunately, we can't just leave the windows and doors open all the time and move on to the next problem. The catch, obviously, is that in most places most of the time we need indoor air that has a different temperature than outdoor air. This is a problem with no truly elegant, straightforward solution. However, we can come up with some basic guidelines.

First, to have good indoor air, you need good outdoor air. Incredibly, in this day and age, finding clean outdoor air is a problem in many parts of the world. If you can't access good outdoor air, then you have no choice but to seal up your house and use air exchangers, filters, and humidity control to emulate the outdoor air of the good old days.

Moving air. Healthful air is constantly moving and mixing. If it wasn't, you'd keep breathing in the carbon dioxide that you just exhaled. There are different strategies for keeping air moving through a building. *Top:* Here, building openings are kept closed and a machine blows air, cooled through forced evaporation, into the interior while pumping byproduct heat to the air outside. *Bottom:* A more direct solution is to open a window.

However you initially access good air, next you have to make sure that whatever makes up the indoors doesn't mess up the air that you're bringing in from outdoors. There are basically two categories of stuff that'll do that: human-made and biological. The human-made stuff can be avoided by choosing the right materials. The concept is pretty simple, really: Don't use anything made of noxious toxins that will leach poisons into the air. In practice, this is harder than it sounds because everything from sofa cushions to common paints to carpeting to kitchen cabinets can contain such pollutants. I go into buildings all the time that reek from a chemical soup of off-gassing materials.

The biological pollutants are things such as molds and fungi. They can be avoided by designing an indoor environment that's sufficiently dry and promotes constant air exchange with the outside. This is definitely the hardest part of the clean-air puzzle. How do you create winter air exchange in a cold climate without losing heat? How do you encourage cooling, natural ventilation in a humid climate without creating indoor mold and fungus problems? There are many answers from a variety of perspectives offered to these and other, related questions.

As mentioned in the last chapter, some people suggest that you create walls that allow air exchange through their volume, so called "breathable walls." The advantage here is that the exchange is slow and therefore the air is warmed or cooled as it moves through the wall and reaches the inside at much the same temperature as the existing interior air. I simply don't know if this approach works.

Others counsel the use of hygroscopic walls, which use materials that can take on and let off water vapor in response to changes in ambient humidity (see page 59). Confusingly, such walls also are referred to as "breathable." The concept is that the interior air will be kept at a constant acceptable humidity level that won't encourage the growth of molds or fungi. This doesn't help with air exchange, but does help keep indoor air clean. The strategy definitely works, but can be difficult to accomplish in wet climates. It also requires careful detailing in construction. If liquid water is allowed entry, you can quickly create mold in the materials that were designed to prevent it. All the walls in our little building are conceived with variants of this concept, so we'll discuss it in more detail later.

In some ways, the modern approach makes a lot of sense. You create a basically airtight building and then allow machinery to breathe for it. If you monitor the indoor air quality and adjust it with filters, humidity control, and the like, you can create some really nice air. You have the added advantage of being able to regulate that air's temperature. Personally, I just don't like this solution. Like the name implies, modern *heating, venting, and air conditioning (HVAC)* "forced air" systems seem to be forcing things. They require a lot of power, which creates air pollution, and they don't work when the power is out. I want a freer connection to life-giving air.

An interesting variant on this concept is *heat-recovery ventilation (HRV)*, in which a constant supply of fresh air is provided by two moving columns of air, one coming in, the other going out. These columns are separated only by a thin piece of metal, which allows heat from the warmer column being exhausted to be given up to the cooler air coming in. This simple heat exchanger is powered with energy-efficient, low-wattage fans. Perhaps HRV in combination with warm weather natural ventilation (in other words, open windows) would create a good system.

Of course, this is really an issue that needs close scrutiny in the context of your specific climate. I can pretty much guarantee one thing: you'll create good indoor air quality only through careful design and skillful execution in construction. Take this seriously!

LIVE OUTSIDE, TOO

We're trying to cover a lot of ground in a single book. As a result, we're having to be a bit antiseptic about our approach. Problem: blah. Solution: blah-blah. Of course, life is much richer and more complicated than that. So much feeling, intuition, and alchemy go into making a space where humans can really relax and feel at home. That realm is very subjective, a personal magic that we all have to seek out for ourselves. Again, however, there are some basic guidelines, and a prominent one is physical connection to the outside. I hate to keep harping on modern buildings, but this is another place where they so often fail. The unused front yard of meticulously mown grass. The back yard with its haphazard swing set and splotchy patches of dirt scratched bare by the marauding family pooch. These places are dead, but why?

Most often it's because outdoor spaces aren't seen for what they really are: outdoor rooms. In this book, we've been describing an alternative, a perspective that sees a house more as a concept than a building. A house is the intersection between you and nature; so why stop it at the door? Cooking, relaxing, and many other daily routines can be turned into joyous events just by moving them outdoors. Often, we don't do things outside simply because we haven't created the appropriate spaces. A simple solar camping shower—a black plastic sack hung on a pole—along with a wooden pallet for a floor and a few plantings for privacy can make an outdoor bathroom fit for royalty. With a few more amenities, such as a sink and a mirror, you might find yourself bathing under the sky most of the time. Similarly, a patio with an awning, outdoor stove, table, and chairs makes a comfortable place to cook in the heat of summer. If you also plant an adjacent vegetable garden, you may find yourself happily spending more time outside than inside during parts of the year.

The key to making these spaces work is to treat them literally as outdoor rooms. There have to be smooth transitions from inside to out. There need to be walls of some kind, whether plantings, fences, fabric decorations, or some other kind of dividers. They can't be places you have to set up; they should be full-fledged rooms ready to be used.

While outside, many of the challenges of connection, such as daylighting and air exchange, are solved. Moreover, outdoor rooms are inexpensive to create and can allow you to build a smaller indoor space. Once you decide that connection to the outside is an important function of a house, moving at least some of the house outside quickly becomes an obvious way to accomplish this goal.

Outdoor rooms. A building is automatically connected to the space around it by proximity. What you do with that space is up to you. *Top:* The space around this building is of no use to humans. In fact, most people would go out of their way to avoid it. *Bottom:* Some tables and chairs, an open, welcoming entry, and simple decorations create a space that invites human use and connects the outside to the inside.

LESS POWER TO YOU, MORE FROM YOU

All of the above connection strategies are simple, sensible, yet some would say radical approaches in the modern context of housing, because they tend to favor working with natural processes rather than relying on technological means. But let's face it: Modern life has altered the way we connect to many things. We don't physically visit; we talk on the phone. We don't walk to a well; we turn on a faucet. We don't carry heat indoors in the form of wood; we turn a power knob that accesses electricity, which sets mechanisms in motion to create temperature. For most people, a lot of these "modern conveniences" have become basic necessities. I'm typing away on a computer right now. How many people do you know who could make their living without access to a phone? For us, the choice isn't really *if* we'll use technology, but *how* and *how much*.

The "how much" is a personal matter that I don't need to get into. A lot of people are looking for a lifestyle change, a way to simplify. Creating a building can be a good way of materializing that desire. However, only you know what modern doodads you need to make your way in the world.

I *can* say a few words about the "how," and that discussion ties into our talk about connections. The thing that drives all the modern conveniences, of course, is some sort of power. The search for ways to plug into that power, as with everything else we've discussed in this chapter, becomes much more interesting when you take control over your building. First off, we've done a lot of good already by using passive solar and daylighting. These choices considerably lower our power demand and expand our options. Next, we need to start looking at each demand for power and decide what's the appropriate form for the need.

It's All Solar Power

The first thing to point out about energy is that—surprise!—it's all about the sun. With the exception of our modern-day Frankenstein monster, nuclear power, all of our energy sources originate with the sun. For example, all electricity, whether generated directly from the sun or by burning coal or some other fossil fuel, is reformed solar energy. Our only real choice is how we utilize the sun.

Reduce Your Use

The modern approach is to use electricity for almost everything. Electricity is a highly refined form of power. Its advantage is that it can be moved quickly in exact amounts. Delicate electronics and motors need exact amounts of power infused at exact rates. Electricity is perfect for such needs.

Hot water, on the other hand, is created by dumping a bunch of heat into a container of water. Electricity is way too fancy for this application. The big, blunt sun blasting away bombastically is the perfect vehicle for heating water. There are lots of ways of using sun to heat water; some are simple and inefficient, others are fancy and very efficient. There's an approach to creating at least some hot water for almost any budget in almost any climate.

Now, chances are that you'll need to supplement that solar hot water. You still don't want elegant electricity keeping some tank of water constantly hot just waiting for that one hour a day you'll want to use it. A much better approach is to use a

It's all solar power. The choice is how we use it. For example, much of the electricity that powers the modern world is created by burning some form of stored solar energy, very often coal. This creates huge amounts of air pollution. As if that isn't bad enough, much of what's produced is lost as resistance, basically friction, in the long journey through power lines from where it's made to where it will be used. Worse yet, in order to force it through all of that resistance, electricity has to be sent over these lines at extremely high, dangerous voltages.

tankless, also called *on-demand,* hot-water heater. These efficient little units usually use some kind of gas to heat water as you need it. In other words, when you turn on the tap, it starts heating the water—a better idea, don't you think?

Next, open your fridge. There's a lot of room in there and lots of that stuff, such as condiments, can be stored at room temperature. Why not get a smaller, energy-efficient fridge?

Now, let's look at those light bulbs. Don't tell me that they're incandescents! Those dinosaurs create mostly heat. No kidding, somewhere around 90 percent of the energy from those bulbs is emitted as heat, and you get a little 10 percent bonus of some byproduct illumination. Compact fluorescent bulbs use one-fifth the energy to create the same light. They also continue to get less expensive all the time. Use compact fluorescents.

Make Your Own

Okay, now we've reduced our demand for electricity down to a fraction of the modern norm. We still need a little for those light bulbs and delicate electronic things that we can't do without, but our lower usage has put within reach the direct use of the sun's energy to produce electricity. There are three ways to do this: photovoltaics, wind energy, and hydropower.

Photovoltaics (PV) is the conversion of light, in our context sunlight, into electricity. PV has a long history of development and has been tested and improved through its use over many years of human space exploration, as well as several decades now of earthbound applications.

Domestic photovoltaic systems, commonly called *solar power systems,* are almost perpetually becoming more efficient and less expensive. The equipment is durable and modular, so problems tend to be easy to identify and fix. If you were trying to supply electricity to a typical modern energy-hog building, a photovoltaic system would be very expensive. But because we've just hugely reduced our electricity needs, a simple system that can accommodate most modest needs is probably within reach. The advantages are huge: producing your own electricity that isn't affected by storms or other causes of municipal power outages. In many locales, you can even sell your excess electricity back to the power company.

As mentioned in the last chapter, the sun powers the winds, so *wind energy* is a form of solar power too. Wind power can be harnessed by mounting a small, swiveling, specially designed turbine or turbines to a pole on or near your home. The turbine spins, turning an alternator that generates electricity. Because wind is the most site-specific

Right power for the right job. Here are two devices sitting in the sun trying to get some work done. The one on the left is helpless. It needs an infusion of exact units of power coming at a particular speed and volume. The one on the right, a bowl of water, is already hard at work heating water. Direct sunlight is the perfect power source for this job. This simple device is the concept at the core of all solar hot water heaters.

Sunlight solar power. When the sun hits these PV panels, an electric current is created that can be used directly or stored.

natural element, a lot of data should be collected before determining whether there's enough wind around to be useful. There is equipment that can be purchased to make this assessment automatically and accurately.

Falling water also is a form of solar power, called *hydropower* or *hydroelectricity*, because the sun is the engine that drives the precipitation that creates all naturally falling water. Hydropower works essentially the same as wind power. A turbine is set in the path of falling water, which spins the turbine, which turns an alternator that creates electricity. It's really incredibly simple. The only real challenge is creating a safe spot to install the turbine so that changes in the amount of falling water, a huge rain for example, won't affect its performance. If you're blessed with a source of falling water with enough *head* (the amount of vertical fall) and *flow* (the volume of water falling in a given time, as in gallons per minute) near a building that's going to use electricity, there's almost no excuse for not installing a hydroelectric system. (Being completely broke, of course, is always a good excuse.)

All of these solar power sources create direct current, which allows them to be combined easily into a single system.

Wind solar power. Simply put, the sun heats up air, causing it to rise and displace colder air, which falls. The result is wind. Making electricity using the wind is conceptually simple. The blades on this small turbine spin in the wind and rotate a shaft that in turn spins a rotor in a generator, very similar to if not the same as the alternator in your car, which produces electricity.

Water solar power. The sun is the engine behind the constant cycle of evaporation and precipitation that keeps water falling from high places to low all over the planet. The only real difference between this hydroelectric setup and the wind power system is that falling water, instead of wind, spins the turbine.

WHERE ARE WE NOW?

This chapter has been organized pretty much along the lines of us (all the cool people reading this book and learning about better ways to do things) against them (all those dips involved in business-as-usual conventional building). In fact, I hope it's clear that we've created this imaginary whipping boy called "modern building" only by artificially congealing a bunch of systemic, boneheaded traits that are prevalent in commercial building into one horrendous entity. It's a convenient technique—create good and evil to show contrast—but of course it's not entirely fair or accurate.

The reality is that the modern world has made some invaluable contributions to the history of building: insulated glass and the cordless screw gun are two examples that come to mind. In fact, in many ways modern building isn't that far removed from the past. Many apparently modern, often maligned building materials, such as concrete, wood, metal, and glass, actually have ancient origins. Many wonderful houses are built with modern materials and techniques.

In addition, I've spent years as a conventional construction worker and can tell you that people in the building trades work hard, generally aren't paid that well, and often have to deal with obnoxious jerks for clients. The real difficulty isn't people, ignorance, laws, or even materials. Modern building's real problem is trying to house billions of people in crowded cities without access to abundant local resources. I'd like to see any group build a cob ecovillage to house the 20 million people who live in the New York City metropolitan area. Of course, the argument would be that we need to create a network of smaller villages, which would necessitate a complete restructuring of our economy and social structure, which would….

At about this point you may be saying, "Look, I just want to get my hands dirty and maybe eventually try to build something for me and my family." I agree. I may be a lot of things, but I'm not dumb enough to claim that I have a solution to the world's problems. But I am trying to create a context to help explain the reasons and thinking behind the decisions made while creating the little alternative building demonstrated in this book, in hopes that with that perspective you can go out and build a version that's just right for you.

So far, we've decided to take charge (chapter 1); we've looked at the fundamentals of building (chapter 2); and we've molded those fundamentals into basic strategies (this chapter). Now we have the background to confidently move forward on a real building project. Let's do it.

Chapter 4
Design

What, exactly, do you want to build?

At first, that question may seem silly; you want to build a house, of course, or maybe some other kind of structure. But if you think about it for a minute, the fact that you can't answer more precisely, in much more detail, might be the reason why you picked up this book in the first place.

The process of deciding exactly what you want to build is called design, and it is by nature a highly personal progression. Obviously, if your building is going to be a reflection of your exact needs connecting with your exact site, the design has to come from you. This is not to say that you shouldn't get help from architects or other professionals, but the core of the project simply has to be a direct product of your thoughts and feelings.

Because design is so personal, it's difficult to give general advice on how to go about it. I've chosen an approach that works for me, and it's the process we used to design the little building featured in this book. The best I can do in this chapter, then, is to explain the design approach I've personally chosen to use and describe how that approach was applied to create a design for our little building. Hopefully, that will at least give you an idea of where to start in your own design process.

DEVELOP A VISION

I can say one thing with confidence about your situation: you need to consciously and confidently create a design for any building you want to construct. I'm not talking about professionally rendered blueprints, necessarily, or even drawings of any kind. It simply means that you need to be clear in your own mind about what you're trying to accomplish. The main difference between buildings that work and those that don't is simply clarity of vision in design linked with careful, even loving, follow-through in construction.

How can you develop that clarity of vision? Let's explore some concepts.

IMAGINATION AND DREAMS

In some ways, this can be the most difficult part of a building project, one that at times is ignored almost completely. That's because design is a process of imagining, and imagining is a skill with which we can sometimes lose touch. It can be dismissed as daydreaming, or ignored as the sole property of the artist or visionary. But in fact, imagining is a tool as real as a hammer. The better you wield it, the more focus you give it, the better will be your building.

Of course, you probably know the main thing, the core thing, about the building you want to build. For example, you want a house, a workshop, a guest room, a study, a doghouse—whatever. But again, these are general answers. What is it that sets one house or workshop apart from another? The answer is, a dream. Your dream is what is

What do dreams look like? These two houses are fundamentally similar. They're about the same size and shape, face south, have two-foot overhangs and steep gable roofs covered in metal, and were built within a few miles of each other. Yet each has a different, specific, and unique feel. That's because the dream behind each house is different, and personal. It's obvious that they were built for specific people, not as spec houses to be sold on the open market. It's not the materials used or the money spent, but the consciousness of a need to nurture a certain feeling, a personal and specific way of life, that gives these houses their unique character.

specific to your building; it's the source of your desire for that building. On the surface, your thoughts may express themselves as the need for more room or a place that you own rather than rent, but underneath there's something deeper, more fundamental. It's a certain way you expect to feel there, a certain way your life is going to be easier, more relaxed, or in some way more fulfilled. That feeling is the essence of your building, and it needs to be brought out into the open. You need to be able to express it clearly.

Okay, so yes, I am talking about feelings and your need to get in touch with them. But make no mistake. All this dreaming and imagining business is practical, nuts-and-bolts stuff. This building doesn't exist. Right now it's a dream, a rumbling in your gut, a gnawing feeling of need. The measure of your success is going to be how clearly you understand the underlying dream and how fully you bring it to the light of day.

PLACES AREN'T THINGS

Materializing your dreams and feelings into a design, a place, isn't an esoteric process. We're just not used to talking this way. But the fact is, feelings are already the way we identify places. Places aren't essentially physical; they're defined by what happens there.

Let's imagine, for example, a pond. What is it? Well, it started as some running water. Then an obstruction appeared, perhaps a dam built by beavers or humans, or perhaps some collected debris, and the water started pooling up. Like a magnet, the still water attracted all sorts of life: frogs, dragonflies, aquatic plants. Trees took root in the wet soil and larger animals came to drink the water and eat the assembled smaller plants and animals. As the trees grew, birds and

The same, but different. Both of these buildings are made of mud, millet straw, and sticks. Yet the feeling created by each is vastly different. The one on the left invites you inside with open doors while commanding awe and respect in your approach. In other words, it demands a change in your frame of mind, a perfect effect for a mosque. The building on the right is small, cozy, and easy to approach, but access is limited to a tiny door at the top of a ladder. The building is convenient and functional for users, but strangers and animals are clearly not invited in: exactly the feeling that a grain storage shed should encourage.

squirrels made them their home. Eventually, a tire swing was hung from the old oak, and the yelps of children playing were added to the rest of the cacophony of this busy place.

What, then, is this pond? There is no single thing you can point to that describes it. Instead, the pond is really just the sum of the things that happen there. It is a system. A healthy system is something that encourages the same kinds of things to happen over and over again in a self-sustaining cycle. The pond we've described is such a system. A good building is, too.

Think of the building of which you have the fondest memories. How would you describe it? Would you talk about the structural configuration, the roof surface, or the way the doors are attached to their frames? No, you'd probably describe things such as

Tale of two cities. Both of these buildings are places of business opening out onto a street. The glass-and-steel concoction on the top was designed by modern professionals and is an impressive technical feat, but it has no relationship to its local climate or environment. It's so dead that it needs an electric machine to breath for it. The building on the bottom was created by local craftspeople without drawings or permits. Thick mass walls, shutters, overhangs, and natural ventilation replace the inoperable windows and air conditioning of its modern cousin. Doors opening directly onto the street are inviting and approachable.

The Curse of Design

How do we create places that nurture life-enriching feelings and events? I hate to break it to you, but it's not easy in this day and age. Think about that pond described on the previous page: it just happened. There was an initial impetus, the pooling of water, and then a virtual infinitude of elements and moments created the ever-changing system. The only constants were the physical coordinates on the planet earth and the general repeating seasons of the climate.

The same was originally true of housing. No one sat down and thought up the tepee or adobe pueblo. These weren't designs, but organic systems that developed slowly over time along with a particular human culture in response to a particular climate and environment. Thus, just like the pond, these buildings slowly became something specific, inseparable from a time, people, and place.

Modern buildings are often just the opposite. We are a people from different cultural contexts all mixed together, and this mix is constantly changing as we move from job to job and city to city. No specific people combined with no specific place creates buildings that aren't connected to the people or place. Make no mistake: this is a disaster.

A real place, like a pond or a good building, works because it's part of a time and place. It isn't static, but a set of interactions that has been set in motion. In short, it was born, will grow, change, and eventually die. In a sense, it is alive. By destroying the connection between a specific building, time, people, and place, we've rendered our buildings lifeless. The examples most of us share are large grocery stores, department stores, and shopping malls.

This is not merely a matter of aesthetics; it's a matter of connecting to life. Beneath the environmental and health issues that plague many modern buildings lies this simple, sad fact. They have no feeling, and when you stop feeling, you die. A building without feeling is dead, and you can't truly live inside something dead. Remember, the purpose of a house is to sustain human life. Your goal is to create a building that nurtures life.

That's daunting, because let's face it, we're modern people with jobs, families, busy lives, dreams, and no clear idea of what building will bring them all together. Our tepee and adobe pueblo are the mobile home and spec house. These buildings did not really come from us. They're the result of a specific economy, not a partner to our deep, tangible personal needs. And that is the essence of the "alternative building" movement: to create buildings that are a marriage of each of our individual needs and the spot we've chosen to call home.

It's important not to underestimate the scope of that task. Just replacing wood with straw, for example, doesn't get at the heart of the problem. We have no choice but to start from scratch and slowly, clearly, and deliberately define the different elements that need to come together to make that exact place, that feeling, that we're seeking. It's only because we're basically clueless, because we've been stripped of the cultural heritage of an indigenous building system, that we have to resort to this clunky process. We have to design.

a morning spent talking with someone you love at a kitchen table, with soft sunlight and a gentle breeze streaming through open windows. You might not specifically remember that the window glass was old and wavy, that each window opened out and had six panes, and that outside there was a little arbor holding vines, all of which together created a calming, dappled light. You might not have been conscious of the beautiful little arch that created the alcove you were sitting in, or of how the ceiling height was lower over the table, which made the spot feel secluded and comfortable while still connected to the kitchen.

You might not have specifically identified these and a myriad of other elements, but they all came together to create a feeling that you remember. What's more, just like the frogs in the pond, you were drawn back again and again to that same spot at that same time of day. This kitchen is really defined for you by the things that happened there. It's a place that's difficult to describe but easy to feel. A good building, then, is a place that engenders specific, desired things to happen again and again. It is a space that creates a certain, desired feeling.

DESIGN WITH PATTERNS

Okay, so we're going to base our approach to design on our insight that buildings are places that nurture repeating events and create desired feelings. (Remember that wonderful sunlit kitchen where we had relaxing talks with loved ones?) But what, exactly, encourages those events to happen? Let's look again at the two examples we've already touched on: the pond and the kitchen. With a bit of scrutiny, we can identify physical elements that make the events and therefore the feelings possible.

Every place we call a "pond," for instance, has a source of flowing water and some kind of dam or physical obstruction and concave shape that causes that water to pool up. The exact form these elements may take and the way they interact is complicated and variable, but within every pond is that relationship. If the water isn't flowing, it's not a pond, but a puddle. If there's no obstruction or concave shape to hold the water, it's a stream or marsh.

As we look more closely at a number of ponds, we'll start to notice the variety of forms that these same elements can take, and the way these differences affect the kinds of repeated events that occur there. For example, a suburban backyard pool could be called a pond. The "concave area" and "dam" are a poured concrete bowl, and the flowing water is constantly circulated in a closed loop by a pump through filters. The impervious bowl and surrounding concrete patio prevent any plant life from gaining a foothold. Chlorine in the water and aerosol bug sprays or citronella candles discourage wildlife and insects from using the water. As a result, the specific form the physical elements take in this situation to create the pond-defining pooling water encourage a specific, limited set of other kinds of events to occur: the splashing of children, the reclining of barbeque chefs, the churning of the pump, the turning of the electric meter, the regularly scheduled chlorine treatments.

Without the plants and animals and the complex interactions and constant change that they bring, this suburban pond is an entirely different place than the naturally occurring one described earlier. If the goal of the human-made pond is to create a place to swim that's unencumbered by the complexity of other living species, then the form of the dam and the water source chosen are perfect. But if the goal is to

mimic the flourishing, sustainable system of a natural pond, then the space created is a failure. In a very real sense, it's a dead space, and the form that the fundamental physical elements have taken is what killed it.

The contrast between this dead concrete pond and its healthy tree-, plant-, and animal-filled cousin teaches us something profound. Though at their core they each share the same fundamental relationship between physical elements and repeating action—a source of flowing water, a concavity, and a dam coming together to create a pool—the form these elements takes drastically changes the kinds of events that will happen there. And that, in turn, completely alters the entire identity, the inherent feel of the place.

The same thing can be said about buildings. The wonderful kitchen that we described earlier keeps us coming back not because it has a door, some windows, and a table. Most kitchens have these features. It's the exact form that these elements take that affects the kind and quality of experiences that people will have there.

Consider that kitchen's windows, for example. Our description mentioned a wonderful, sunlit morning, so some of those windows have to be to the east to let in the morning sun. However, direct sunlight is harsh and creates glare. The kind of glass, number of panes, height of the sill, thickness of the wall, and other elements of the window come together to create a calming, dappled light. The windows, in turn, work together with myriad elements to create the feeling that makes us want to return.

What we've learned is that choosing the forms various building elements will take isn't simply a matter of aesthetics, but drastically affects the events that occur there.

In order to design a space, then, you need to decide what kinds of things you want to have happen in a place, and then decide what elements you require and the specific forms they need to take in order to encourage those things to happen repeatedly. In other words, you have to identify a combination of both a specific form of an element and the action that it will encourage. I don't know an accurate word to define this relationship, but the term chosen by Christopher Alexander, et al, in their milestone design books that are the guiding templates for this approach (see the sidebar on the next page, Whose Idea Is This, Anyway?) is "pattern," so that's the word I use here.

All of this may sound like you're going to need to do a lot of esoteric, intellectual conceptualizing in order to design your house. But that's not our approach. Most of

What's in a pond? Both of these bodies of water share the same relationship between basic physical elements and a repeating series of events. But the specific physical forms of the elements in each case encourage drastically different events to occur, creating places that feel worlds apart. *Left:* The dam and shape of this pool are made of earth. The pooling water creates a magical combination of water and earth that enriches the soil, attracting a variety of plants that in turn bring forth a menagerie of insects and animals. The complex interactions of life create an ecosystem that is self-sustaining. *Right:* This pool's dam and shape are made of concrete intended to prevent plant growth around the pond. The pooling water isn't replenished but recirculated, and chemicals are added to stifle the natural attraction of life forms to water. As a result, the series of events encouraged here is strictly regulated, preventing the complexity of interaction that creates a self-sustaining system.

Whose Idea Is This Anyway?

About 25 years ago an architect named Christopher Alexander published a book called *The Timeless Way of Building* (New York: Oxford University Press, 1979) that laid out the philosophy behind an approach to architecture that he and a number of colleagues had been working on. Together, two years earlier, they had published a book called *A Pattern Language* (New York: Oxford University Press, 1977) that was a practical method for putting the philosophy into practice. Ever since, their ideas have strongly influenced the world of building design and, perhaps surprisingly, also the fields of artificial intelligence and computer programming.

I, too, have found their ideas extraordinarily helpful. This chapter is my personal expression and adaptation of that design approach, based on the concept of "patterns." As I say elsewhere, I don't think this is the only way to think about building design. And I certainly have no idea whether it's "the best way," whatever that might mean. However, this book's core concept is to take you through the entire process of creating a small house, from basic building fundamentals to a finished building. Part of that process is design, and in order to take you on that part of the journey, I needed to introduce you to the concepts behind our particular design approach. I can only give you enough conceptual background here to enable you to follow the simplified pattern language that I present as the design for the little building we constructed for this book. I hope I've accomplished that goal. In any case, please consider this only a beginning. I highly recommend studying *The Timeless Way of Building* and *A Pattern Language*. If I could recommend only two sources to anyone interested in building, these would be the books.

the work can be done by simple observation. All you really need to do is start being conscious of all the places, especially buildings, that you encounter, and try to identify specific elements that engender a specific kind of action.

Again, this may sound daunting, but it's actually easy to do. In fact, the closer you look at any building, the more of these elements you'll find.

For example, what is a door? A physical description does nothing to capture it. Just like our pond, a door isn't a thing, but a place where specific events happen over and over. A door is a place that invites people to move from one space to another. So what? Well, once we define a door in this way, as a relationship between place and action, we can look at every door we come across and decide whether the place does a good job of encouraging the action.

This is the key to the design process. By looking at the buildings around you, you can quickly identify relationships between elements and actions, relationships that we are calling patterns, that a building needs. And for each kind of place, you can find examples that work, that draw their intended action to them like a magnet. Just as helpful will be all the examples that *don't* work. By comparing and analyzing the two types, you'll discover the elements that each kind of place seems to need in order to really do its job.

How can you tell what works and what doesn't? In some cases, it'll be obvious. A leaking roof isn't working. Most often, however, you'll need to use the barometer by which, whether we're aware of it or not, we all measure a place: how it feels.

I hope that much has become clear. Because we're dealing with relationships rather than just things, feelings are much more accurate descriptors than words. Take one last look at the place "pond," for example. We've spent some time getting acquainted with the relationship between some of the elements and actions that define "pond." So, what's the difference between a "pond" and a "lake?" Well, we could say that a lake is big and a pond is similar but smaller, but clearly that doesn't capture the difference. We could spend a lot of time trying to quantify the distinctions, but what would that get us?

If our goal is to create a certain kind of place, the most direct route is to find a place that has a feeling we like, get in touch with what happens there to create that feeling, and then try and identify the fundamental elements that are enabling the actions that create the feeling. It's actually a simple and fun game to play.

IDENTIFYING PATTERNS

The basic concept behind this particular design approach, then, is to pull your attention away from things and toward relationships. Instead of thinking of a building as an assemblage of windows, doors, wood studs, or straw bales, think of it as a series of relationships between spaces made up of physical elements and the activities that are generated there. There's a simple three-step process to this game. For each kind of place (1) identify its general context, (2) define the problem or goal that generally presents itself there, and (3) express a solution to the problem. That solution will be the pattern that we can apply to our situation, our design.

For example, take the place we've already identified: a door. There are lots of kinds of doors that serve different purposes, so first we'll need to be more specific. Let's say it's an exterior door, a door that serves as an entryway. Okay, so entryway is our context.

Now, let's go out and look at some entrances to buildings. One thing we'll soon notice is that there are two basic types of entrances: those that create some kind of transition and those that are abrupt. We'll also find that, almost without exception, an entrance with a transition feels better than one without.

Alright then, that's our problem or goal: *an entrance to a house needs to supply a smooth transition between the vastly different worlds of outside and inside.*

Now we can work on solving the problem of how to provide a smooth transition by observing and thinking in more detail about the entryways around us. What, exactly, makes a good transition? The first thing we might notice is that uncovered entrance doors are physically uncomfortable to use. For example, imagine yourself standing outside an uncovered doorway waiting to be let in on a rainy day. Your shoulders are hunched; perhaps you're holding a newspaper over your head to catch that drip coming off the roof. Basically, you're miserable and not feeling very welcome.

There's that word "feeling" again. This uncovered doorway simply doesn't feel right. In fact, even if it wasn't raining this place still wouldn't have a good feeling, because an entrance is

Less than welcome. To get into this house you have to walk up the steps, grab the screen door, move down a step as you open it, move back up to the tiny landing while you hold the screen open with your body, fumble with your keys and finally open the door. If it's raining, you'll get wet, too.

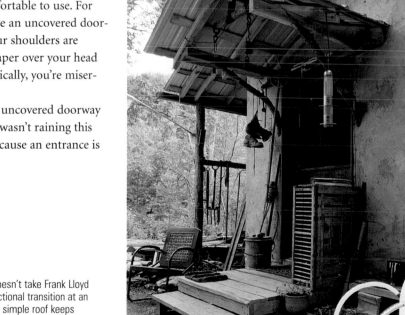

More than welcome. It doesn't take Frank Lloyd Wright to create a nice, functional transition at an entryway. In this example, a simple roof keeps people entering and exiting out of the rain. Chairs invite lingering as people come and go. The feeling is "Hey, thanks for coming by! If I'm not here, hang out a minute, maybe I'll show up."

Figure 1

A TRANSITIONAL ENTRYWAY PATTERN

This illustration fleshes out a full-fledged entrance transition. As you come up the gravel drive and stop your car at the short stone wall or bamboo hedge, the first change you notice is the stone path, which takes you through a clear gate that separates the outside world from home. The first destination on the short path is an arbor-covered seat where you can pause before going indoors, or perhaps sit with a child who has come out to greet you. Next, you move toward the entrance where an arbor and a covered porch create complex changes in light, and wind chimes repeat sounds that over time come to be identified with this place. The entrance itself is covered with a porch that will shelter people waiting at the door from rain or snow. There's a bench and table next to the door for lingering as people come and go.

more than just a place to get in and out. It's the place where you pause for final conversation as you say goodbye to good friends. It's the place where you excitedly greet loved ones coming home. It's the place where you linger to prepare yourself for the transition between busy-outside-world person to relaxed-indoor-world person. Most importantly, perhaps, it's the final place that defines the level of privacy and sets the tone of difference between the outside world and your inner sanctum. This place, then, is critical and deserves careful consideration.

What would an entrance that fulfilled all of these needs look like? In other words, what's our solution to the problem? After closely comparing and contrasting more entrances and trying to distill the essence of a good one, we might state our solution like this:

Create an entrance that provides a clear separation between the inside and outside worlds. Set the entrance back from the street or parking area and make the pathway to the entrance experience a series of changes. For example, if there is an asphalt street or concrete sidewalk, make the path of stone, broken brick or mulch. Cover the doorway with a roof that will keep people who linger there dry. Add an arbor or porch with vines that create a change of light and change of view. Create a change of direction in the path or a change of sound, for example with a fountain or wind chimes. Add a physical barrier that retains a connection to the street, such as a simple gate or knee-high stone wall. The objective is to maintain a connection to the outside while creating a real and dramatically different feeling in the person preparing to enter or leave the house.

We still haven't described a particular entryway. But we've identified the elements we think need to come together to make a working entryway, an entryway that creates the feeling that we're looking for. In other words, we've identified the relationship between action and physical elements that we'll call the pattern "entryway." A sketch of the pattern might take the form of the illustration shown on the left.

As you look more closely at the buildings around you, you'll be able to identify a myriad of such patterns. Look, too, at the patterns others have noted or created, such as those in *A Pattern Language* and the ones you'll find in this chapter. The next step will be to decide which of these patterns you need or want in your building and how they should combine, or come together, to create the feelings you imagine.

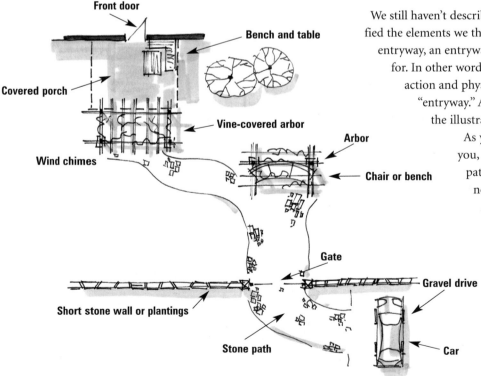

Front door

Bench and table

Covered porch

Vine-covered arbor

Arbor

Wind chimes

Chair or bench

Gate

Gravel drive

Short stone wall or plantings

Stone path

Car

CREATE YOUR BUILDING'S PATTERN LANGUAGE

Every building is a story told by the feelings the building engenders. The patterns we've been discovering are the words that make up those stories. In order to create your own story, then, you need to build a progression of patterns, linking related patterns much as you would words when forming sentences, to create the pattern language of your building.

The first step is to choose a central dream, the core feeling from which the entire story will germinate. Once you've identified the single pattern that best expresses the essence of your building, you can then add to this pattern a second that flows from the first. This second pattern should be less broad in scope. It should identify a problem or goal created by the first pattern and solve it. The third pattern will identify another context created by the first or second pattern and solve a problem related to it, and so on. This list of patterns will grow outward, like ripples from a pebble tossed into a pond, until the building seems whole. It will become the pattern language for your building. It's a tool you can use to clearly imagine your building before you start to build it.

I know that all of this might sound abstract to you right now. I can only encourage you to take the time to try creating some pattern languages. You'll discover that what might seem like a mystifying process is actually concrete and basic. You'll find yourself simplifying and solving a dauntingly nebulous problem—creating a building out of thin air—by identifying things you like in the existing world of buildings and then applying them, one by one, to your situation.

The best way to learn how to create a pattern language is to make one, so let's create a language for our little building.

OUR BUILDING: APPLYING PATTERN LANGUAGE

As I've said, the pattern language for a specific building is a highly personal thing. Yours will be based on your situation, your own tastes, your own likes and dislikes, and a variety of other factors entirely unique to you.

To really understand the language created to imagine and design the little building we construct in this book, you'd have to know a lot about how my wife and I live, the land we live on, our outlooks, and our dreams. Of course, getting to know us is not the reason you're reading this book. So I've simplified the actual language I present here. My goal is just to give you some idea of how the process works, and to give you a better idea of the purposes behind our actual construction decisions.

THE CORE PATTERN

We live on three acres of old tobacco field that are connected to about 50 acres of pasture and woods that we own with neighbors. Our home is about 25 miles away from a small city of about 60,000 people. We work at home and try to spend as much time tending our little homestead as we can, so we don't travel much. However, we have lots of good friends spread out in cities all over the country. Our broad dream is to bring the city and country incarnations of our lives together. Because we don't travel much, we have to bring the city to us. So we want to create a wonderful place that will coax friends from the city to come visit. Our task then is to imagine the physical place that will keep bringing our city friends back to it. We'll call this relationship the pattern "guest cottage in the country." Here's how we describe the pattern:

Context: Guest Cottage in the Country

Problem: Guests feel comfortable when they have their own space, a home away from home, but it can be difficult to create such a place inside an already busy household.

Discussion: When you live outside a city, in a rural area that requires a substantial drive to reach, guests often need to be able to stay a while to be coaxed to come for a visit. Extended visits can be wonderful; they give the rural dweller some contact to city culture and give city folks a chance to enjoy some fresh air and quiet. However, if guests staying several days don't have their own space, they can feel like they're intruding, and in fact visits can sometimes be disruptive because the guests are on vacation and consequently have different needs than the hosts, who are still going about their daily business.

Solution: Give guests their own little building with a nice view and plenty of privacy. Keep it close enough to the main house so that guests will feel connected, yet far away enough so that they can really unwind and feel they have their own little place in the country. Make sure that that the cottage connects well to the outdoors and has a nice patio and plenty of plants and wildlife around.

A PROGRESSION OF OTHER PATTERNS: SITING

Of course, once we'd defined the core pattern for our building, we needed to determine where to put that building and how to orient it with other elements on our property, both those existing now—natural elements such as the sun and terrain, and human-made elements such as our house—and those we planned to add "someday." A building needs to be conceived in connection with a definite place.

To that end, we developed a hierarchical list of patterns that flowed from and further defined the core pattern. We looked at each pattern in order and tried to fully imagine it before adding the next pattern and imagining it in the same way. Making simple sketches of each pattern as we went, we slowly combined the sketches to create a playful, expressive graphic version of the patterns—the elements and feelings we wanted in and around the little building. Here is a sampling of seven patterns we used. In the first several, which are various contexts related to siting, you'll find both an overview of our specific situation and the basic problem-discussion-solution structures of the patterns that were behind our decisions and that hopefully may apply to others' situations. The accompanying drawings are composites of the sketches that went along with each pattern.

Context: Site Repair

The area where we park our cars has a long, sordid history. It began as the construction parking and delivery area during the building of our house. We have since tried to improve that blunt space by creating a parking circle which, though we measured and planned turned out to be too small. At present, it's an awkward space altered by grading that has become the ad hoc repository for firewood, some tools, building materials, and miscellaneous junk that I swear crawled there on its own. This spot

Figure 2
GUEST COTTAGE IN THE COUNTRY

Our core pattern is best described as the feeling we had while drawing our dream house as kids. You know: the little cottage in the woods with friendly squirrels and rabbits and a happy sun that smiles sweet rays on a little garden in the yard. We're all older now and have found the real world different from that image. However, maybe we can capture some of its magic in a little place we build not for real life, but for our friends' well-earned vacations from real life.

clearly needs some act of repair. Since we want our guests to feel free to come and go, it seems that their place should be convenient to the cars, so it makes sense to somehow connect the guest cottage to this damaged site. This project, then, will be a conscious act of repair to this spot.

Problem: People tend to build on the most beautiful sections of a lot or piece of land, but this flies in the face of the basic nature of the act of construction.

Discussion: Common to the construction of any habitable building are two unavoidable facts: First, the act of construction is always initially destructive. Second, an inhabited building focuses human attention where it is built. The beauty of a place comes from the fact that it is complete. Imagine, for example, a meadow with trees, a babbling stream, and a view of distant mountains. Placing a building here will require clearing, at the minimum, and probably dirt-moving, too. These actions will disrupt something that developed over a long period into a whole place, a spot that lives. On the other hand, a house encourages the inhabitants to care for the area around it. Trees are planted for shade here, the soil is developed for a vegetable garden there, a small stone wall is built to separate the garden from a patio. If a site is chosen that needs attention, perhaps to fix some previous human folly, then the initially destructive act of building can actually lead to continued acts of repair.

Solution: Leave the most beautiful areas of a site alone to thrive and be enjoyed as they are. Build new structures in places that for some reason need help or will be neglected if left alone. Plan your building so that it is a positive act of repair to its site.

Site Repair. Building is often destructive to a site, but our project was an act of repair to a spot that had previously been damaged. *Top:* Before we started building, our chosen site was neglected and a mess from a previous construction folly. *Bottom:* We used our project to focus some loving attention on the site, repairing and beautifying it.

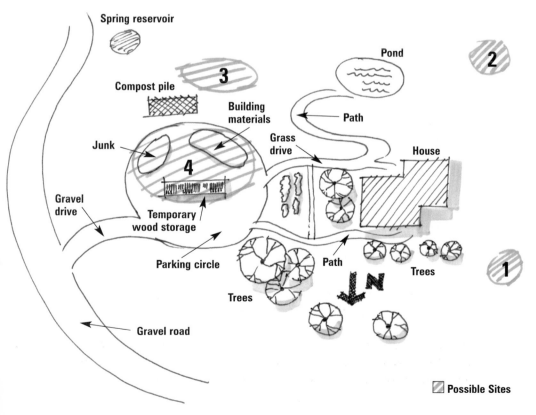

Spring reservoir

Compost pile

3

Building materials

Junk

4

Pond

Path

2

Grass drive

House

Gravel drive

Temporary wood storage

Parking circle

Path

Trees

N

Trees

1

Gravel road

Trees

◨ **Possible Sites**

Figure 3
SITE REPAIR

Our first task was to choose an approximate site for the building. We knew from our core pattern that the guest cottage needed to be close to our house, but also private and connected to plants and wildlife. Looking around, we identified four possible sites. Number 1 is a nice meadow that looks out on the surrounding mountains. In fact, it's so nice that it'd be a shame to mess it up with a building. Number 2 is nestled lower on the same hill, more at the level of our house. It seemed too far from the cars to be practical for the comings and goings of guests. Number 3 overlooks our pond, but it's on a steep bank. Number 4 is reasonably flat, has good sun, and is convenient to the parking area. It was also a mess from a previous and unsuccessful attempt we'd made to create a parking circle. Rather than disrupt existing beautiful places with the initially destructive act of building, we decided to use the opportunity to build our cottage on this site, to repair this troubled spot.

South-facing pattern realized. Our plan to site the building so that it would open onto a sunny patio and provide solar warmth in winter worked out nicely.

Context: South-Facing Building

We live in a climate with four real seasons, including about six months that require an indoor temperature higher than that outside. For that reason, we need our building to be sited in a generally southerly direction with few obstructions to block the sun. There needs to be open land to the south that is easily accessed and private, so that guests will be encouraged to see the building as both a useable indoor and outdoor space, therefore vastly increasing its apparent size. This works out great with our decision to repair the old car circle. If we keep the cars behind the building, they'll be to the north and the building will open to the south. It may take a bit of earth moving, but we'll be able to access plenty of sunlight and have a nice open space in front of the building to the south.

Problem: Buildings that are sited without regard to the sun's position and movement are both inefficient and unappealing. Buildings that are placed consciously relative to the sun in their climate are strongly connected to their surroundings and draw people to them.

Discussion: This is basically the "passive solar" pattern, something that we've discussed in some detail elsewhere, but we're approaching it here from the point of view of feeling. I used to live in the oppressive heat of Texas. Approaching any house without ample tree cover elicited a tangible feeling of dread, whereas houses with shaded roofs instantly felt welcoming. There is an analogous feeling linked to buildings and their relationship with the sun for every climate and site.

Solution: Orient your building so that its interaction with the sun brings pleasure and comfort to the people around it.

Figure 4
SOUTH-FACING BUILDING

We'll position our building forward on the site and face it south to give it open access to the sun and a sunny front patio in the winter. Because our house is to the east and slightly north, this siting will both accomplish our goal of privacy for the cottage and give us the opportunity to use passive solar strategies. Now that it's clearer exactly where we'll put the building, we can fine-tune our act of repair to the site: (1) we'll fix drainage problems with a stone retaining wall to the east of the building, (2) we'll move the compost pile away from the cottage and closer to our house, and (3) we'll formally abandon our failed car circle and create room for parking spaces behind the cottage.

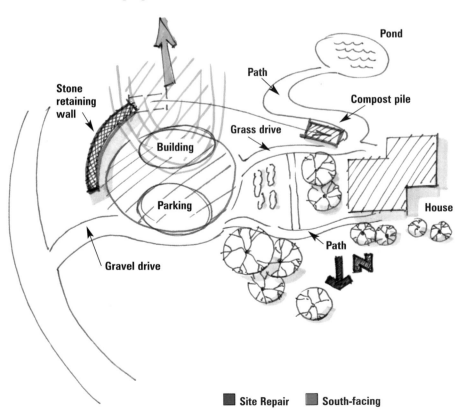

Context: Outdoor Rooms

A guest cottage alone near car parking isn't a very romantic country vacation image. We need to plan other buildings and plantings that will help define the outdoor space into useable rooms. We intend to build a workshop to the north eventually that will act as a buffer from the cars and comings and goings to and from the main house. The placement of the two buildings will create a courtyard that will be a public space for working, socializing, and outdoor cooking.

We also need to be conscious of how this small complex connects to our house. Our goal, really, is to create two connected homes. Of course, we live here and our house has a strong presence, but we want our guests to feel that, while they're here, they live here, too. So we need to create both a strong separation and connection between the two spheres. We'll place the cottage so that you can see our house from it, but we'll keep our distance by creating gardens and other plantings between the two buildings connecting them with walking paths. The workshop and courtyard will be the focal point of the two spheres, a place that we all share equally.

Problem: We build houses because we need indoor space, but we often neglect the fact that we also use outdoor space. The area around a building and especially between buildings can either invite activity, attention, and life or be unused, ignored, and basically dead.

Discussion: Most of us see the importance of planning and organizing interior space. We need different kinds of spaces for different activities, and each space has its own feel that goes with what happens there. Bedrooms are more secluded and sub-

Connecting buildings to create outdoor rooms. *Left:* In this neighborhood, buildings are close to one another, but the spaces in between are undefined. There's simultaneously a lack of privacy and no invitation to gather. There's no shade for relaxing or working outside. The result: all the space is basically wasted and unused. *Right:* Buildings in this neighborhood create useful outdoor spaces. Buildings and walls are clustered together, creating private, shaded courtyards that can also function as fences to keep some animals in and others out. Buildings are set together in narrow rows that, along with the occasional tree, create shaded paths between. Even the roofs are utilized as outdoor rooms. Notice the two mats for sleeping under the open sky on hot, dry nights.

Figure 5
OUTDOOR ROOMS

Our building's main goal is to provide a small but complete home, so that guests can have a complete life while visiting us. But a single building is often like an indoor island floating in a sea of outdoors. To feel like a whole place, the space around our cottage has to be useful and multifaceted. We've been needing a workshop and more outdoor work space around our place, so we decided to combine the workshop with the guest cottage. This creates a lot of nice outdoor spaces and gives our cottage a range of public and private realms. Multiple plantings between the house and the site create a nice separation, while several paths and a view from each building to the other maintain a connection.

■ **Outdoor rooms**

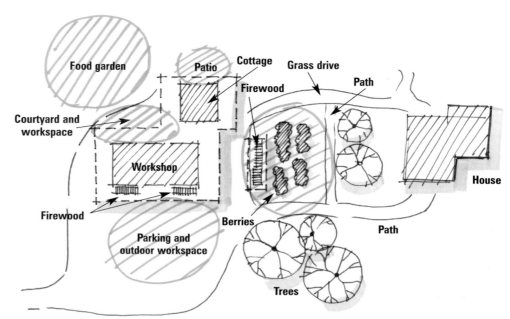

dued. They have doors for privacy. Kitchens are active, public spaces that need to encourage free movement and easy interaction. The same is true of outdoor spaces, and it's useful to conceive of them as outdoor rooms with clear identities analogous to their inside cousins. For example, an outdoor room designed for relaxation needs first to have a feeling of enclosure including a back (in other words, a direction from which no one will approach), some kind of shade, and comfortable places to sit or recline. A play area needs sunlight, at least some level ground, and freedom from major dangers such as cars and other machines.

Solution: Conceive of all the spaces around and between your buildings as outdoor rooms. Give them a clear shape, defined by other buildings, trees, hedges, gardens, etc.

Context: Car Connection

The main possession most guests will bring with them is their car, and it will likely serve as storage for things needed only on occasion. So, we need to keep some kind of connection between the cottage and parking area. We'll make the path to the car covered and pleasant, so that someone can stroll there while thinking absentmindedly of something else. However, this is a secluded country vacation, so we want to create a visual separation from the cars. The shop needs to completely shield the cottage from the sights and, to whatever extent possible, sounds of vehicles coming and going.

Problem: More often than not, people arrive at and leave from their houses in cars. Yet, cars are often an awkward presence around homes and the area of connection between car and building is neglected, ugly, and ill-considered.

Discussion: Most of us accept cars as a part of modern life, but only in an ambivalent sort of way. We need them, but somehow don't want to acknowledge them. This leads to a kind of housing-design schizophrenia. A house will have a clear front entrance with a curved walkway passing flower beds on the way to a covered porch and strong door. But the covered area for the car will be situated next to a side entrance that goes through the laundry room into the kitchen. The result is that the attractive main entrance is seldom used, though it's still maintained, and the always used "secondary" entrance is neglected and drab.

Solution: Create a room for cars that is beautiful and functional, perhaps including a vine-covered arbor or other living features. Place this room near the main entrance to the house, so that the most direct route from the car is through the front door.

Figure 6
CAR CONNECTION

Are you starting to see how a lineage of patterns can build on one another? Our planned shop building not only will create a useable sheltered courtyard between the two buildings, but it will also hide the cars from guests who've come to leave the city behind. In addition, our south-facing exposure will further focus attention away from the cars and towards the sun. To complete this pattern, we'll create a nice vine-covered shelter for the vehicles off the north of the shop. Also, we'll use the roofs of the shop and cottage to shelter a path to the cars that will turn that mad dash through the rain to get a book or luggage into a nice stroll with a glimpse of stars or the setting sun.

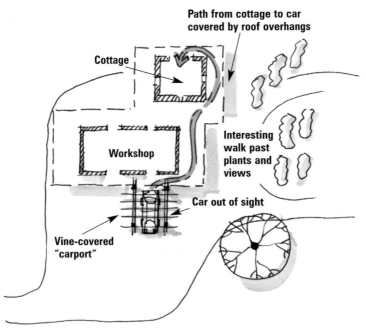

Path from cottage to car covered by roof overhangs

Cottage

Interesting walk past plants and views

Workshop

Car out of sight

Vine-covered "carport"

Context: Progression from Private to Public Spheres

Our goal is to give our guests their own place, a home away from home. In order to do that we need to create spaces for them that will allow the full range of possible human interactions. That's going to be a challenge in such a small building. Our present layout helps. The most public sphere is the car parking to the north. This gives way to a slightly less public workshop, which in turn gives way to the more intimate but still public courtyard. The interior of the building itself and the southern patio need to complete the transition to privacy. The only problem is that the most private area, the inside of the building, is close to the public courtyard. We'll need to carefully place any windows in this north wall to be conscious of privacy. We'll also have to put a lot of focus on creating a very private patio to the south. We can do this with a lot of plantings and a nice plant-covered arbor that will shade the area in the summer.

Problem: A house and its surroundings need to accommodate a complex variety of human interactions simultaneously, from the very intimate to the very public.

Discussion: Different relationships and situations require spaces that provide correspondingly different degrees of intimacy and openness. This applies also to outdoor spaces. These relationships and many more form a complex web that a house has to accommodate simultaneously.

Solution: Organize your landscape, as well as your building's interior, in zones of privacy, progressing from the least to the most. Outdoors, the driveway and parking areas will be the most public and become increasingly private as you approach the house. At the house itself, the first zone, nearest the main entrance, will be the most public, and as you move through the house you'll pass through spaces that are designed to be more and more private.

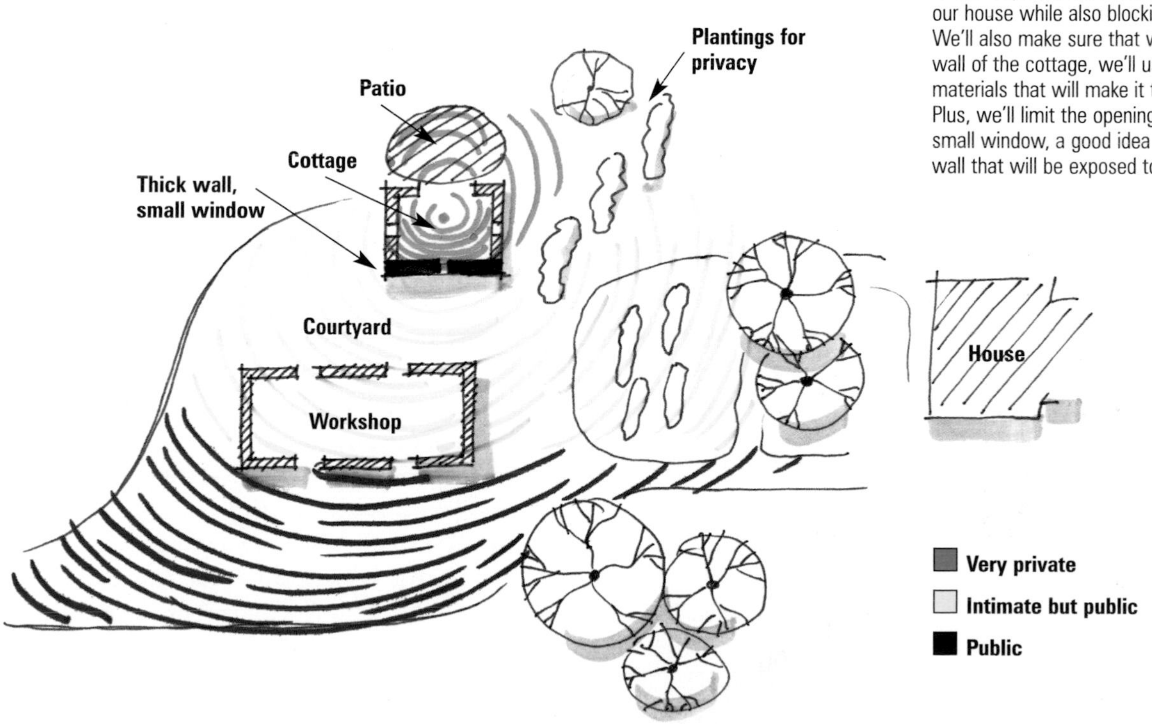

Figure 7
PROGRESSION FROM PRIVATE TO PUBLIC SPHERES

This pattern builds beautifully on what has come before. The main thing we need to do here is to emphasize the privacy of the inner sanctum. To do that we'll put plantings to the southwest that will further separate the southern patio visually from our house while also blocking harsh western sun. We'll also make sure that when we build the north wall of the cottage, we'll use techniques and materials that will make it thick and soundproof. Plus, we'll limit the openings in the wall to one small window, a good idea anyway on a cold north wall that will be exposed to winter winds.

Plantings for privacy

Patio

Cottage

Thick wall, small window

Courtyard

Workshop

House

■ Very private
□ Intimate but public
■ Public

SOME MORE PATTERNS

I hope you get the idea of how we slowly created a language by carefully considering contexts, problems, and solutions, and building each pattern on top of the one before it. The thought may also have occurred to you that such a process could be never-ending; you can just keep getting deeper and deeper into the myriad ways of making a building whole. In fact, the actual language I created to design this building is too long to cover in full detail here. But I do want to mention several other patterns, to give you some additional insight into why and how our building took the shape that it did. Here, without the context/problem/solution discussions, are descriptions of several other patterns and how they relate to our building.

Figure 8
SHELTERING ROOF AND OTHER PATTERNS

Our large sheltering roof plays an integral role in many of our patterns by helping to create transitions and outdoor spaces. It also grounds the little building and creates a feeling of a complete, secure haven. The paths from the house and the car space provide ample opportunities for a pleasant and interesting entrance transition, which comes to a head at the vine-covered arbor over the door. Our simple entrance room expands the space by creating a seamless transition between the inside of the building and the large open patio.

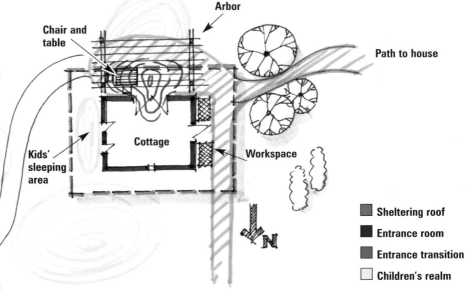

Food garden

Badminton and play space

Arbor

Chair and table

Path to house

Kids' sleeping area

Cottage

Workspace

N

■ Sheltering roof
■ Entrance room
■ Entrance transition
□ Children's realm

Our sheltering roof. Our roof's huge overhangs are our little building's strongest archetypal gesture. The addition of the living roof layer ties the building into its natural surroundings, helping to create a roof that conveys a nurturing, secure feeling of home.

Sheltering Roof

Our building needs to be tiny, both because of a small budget and because we want to create a whimsical, storybook country experience. However, it's important that the building feel like a complete home, a real place to hang your hat. For this reason, we need a very strong archetypal roof that creates a powerful image of secure shelter. We'll create a low-pitched roof with huge overhangs to the east and west that will really set the cottage firmly in the landscape. These overhangs will create nice outdoor rooms on the east and west faces of the building that can be used as work areas, outdoor sleeping porches, or just places to hang out in the shade. They'll also serve as much of the covered walkway to the cars as part of the "car connection" pattern, and they'll be integral to our interaction with the sun by shading much of its brutal afternoon rays. And to really bring the roof into play as a part of the living space, we'll make it a living roof, complete with green, flowering plants.

Roof wars. *Left:* These simple buildings exude an almost idyllic image of "houseness," and to a large degree their roofs are responsible. The low-sloped gables with broad overhangs stretch out over rooms nestled into the volume of the roof itself. The shed porch roofs create useful outdoor space under their canopy. The thick tiles give the rooftops dimension and stature. *Right:* This building's roof line is similar to the other buildings', but the effect is the opposite. The roof seems just stuck on. The strange gable with a picture window over the porch feels like it fell from the sky and landed there. The tiny overhangs offer no feeling of shelter, and the thin shingles don't help either. I could go on, but let's just check the feeling meter: I'm getting a reading of zero.

Entrance Room

One of the fun challenges of our design process is to make a single room feel like a complete house. To do that, we need to try to blend the outside and inside, so that both are used seamlessly and at the same time. This will greatly increase our cottage's size and functionality. We'll try to create a hybrid "room" that encompasses the area just outside, including, and just inside the entrance. We'll install a small area of tile or stone that's the same color just inside and outside the door, to tie the space together visually and create the feeling of a room that straddles both sides. Finally, we'll furnish the room with a small table and a chair next to the door on the outside. The south arbor and roof overhang will help, too. A visitor coming or going can comfortably pause and talk to someone who is standing at the door.

Children's Realm

People staying with children simply won't have enough room inside this tiny building. Children could sleep on the floor, or if it's nice outside everyone could sleep on the patio. It might be possible to create an outdoor children's sleeping area on the exterior side of the east wall. Parents could watch their children through the window. The area could be screened and made whimsical with a colorful fabric bunting, so that kids feel like they're having an adventure. Kids are going to want to be outside around here anyway, so it seems a good idea to have them set up camp near the courtyard to the north and the gardens and play space to the east.

It's important to remember that the same spaces often lend themselves to a diversity of patterns. This space, for example, is also perfect for an entirely different relationship: tool storage and outdoor workspace. The large overhang and east-facing wall would shelter tools, materials, and projects from rain and snow.

Children's realm. Perhaps we'll build a little platform here under the windows to double as a bench and a place for kids to sleep. If we can encourage the kids to see the outside area as their own, the adults can have a more relaxing time inside.

Winter Sunlight/ Summer Shade

Because this is such a tiny space, our problem won't be too little sunlight. The building is facing south, so the orientation should create cool summers and great winter solar gain. In fact, we need to be careful to correctly size the south glass, because if there is too much, there will be no refuge from the sun on bright winter days. Also, we'd get overheating in the day and lose heat too quickly at night.

Figure 9
THE INTERIOR

Only now are we getting to the topic that many people might consider the beginning of design: the interior layout. Because we've worked from the outside in, we can feel secure and relaxed as we start filling in the building. It's time to think about placing windows and doors, being careful to allow only so much sun through our southern glass as our mass will be able to store without overheating. Knowing about our eventual workshop and courtyard, we can plan a special view toward the mountains to the north without sacrificing interior privacy. We can conceive how to creatively supply the basics in such a small space: the bed, desk, kitchen, and bath. We can also carefully add features that will make our space richer, like the partition by the bed and the beveled window reveals, both of which add a change of light.

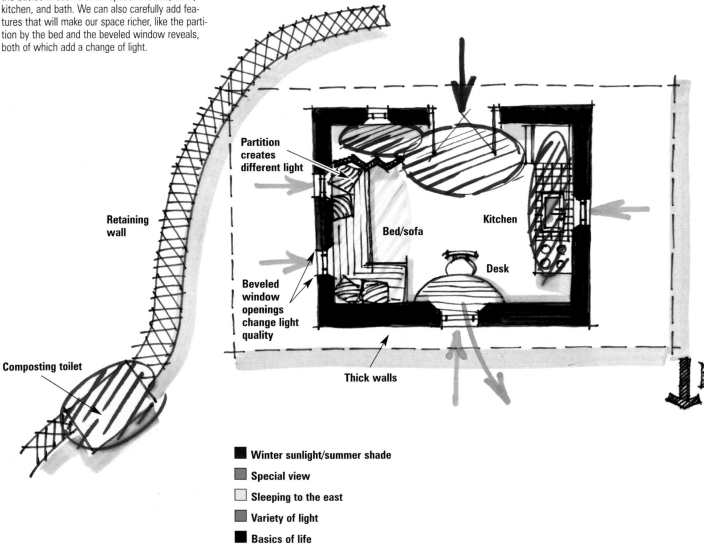

Partition creates different light

Retaining wall

Kitchen

Bed/sofa

Desk

Beveled window openings change light quality

Composting toilet

Thick walls

- ■ **Winter sunlight/summer shade**
- ▨ **Special view**
- ☐ **Sleeping to the east**
- ▨ **Variety of light**
- ■ **Basics of life**

Special View

Our attempts to create privacy in a busy little complex will necessarily cut off wide panoramas of the mountains around us. However, with correct placement of the north or west windows along with thoughtful planting we should be able to create a beautiful focused view of the mountains. We'll be sure to set one of these windows in such a way that this view will be framed best from a single spot in the cottage, perhaps the bed, or a north window above a desk. A similar effect could be created looking west from the south patio. In the end, the effect will be more serene and powerful than the expansive, picture-window mountaintop vistas many area houses have.

Sleeping to the East

I'm totally sold on this concept, one that's practiced in many cultures. I notice how, every morning in our bedroom, I look to the east window to gauge the time of day. It keeps me in touch with how light it is at different times of morning at different times of the year. It's also why I've lived without an alarm clock for many years. In this tiny building, perhaps anywhere the bed is placed would accomplish this pattern. Still, it seems right to place the bed along the east wall next to the east-facing windows. This will also allow parents to keep an eye on children sleeping just outside the windows by their bed.

Variety of Light

Light, more than anything else, defines a place. A range of qualities of light within a building creates a rich variety of places and allows people to choose a mood that matches their own or that's appropriate to the task at hand. We're creating a single room that needs to feel like a complete house, so we need varieties of light to define a mix of places in the small space. Thick walls with beveled window openings would create areas of relative shade next to windows. We can accentuate this by adding trellised plantings outside a window or two that will add dappled, moving light as the sun shines through leaves. We can also create a partial interior partition at the south foot of the combination bed/couch, so that two people could sit and read, with one person's back to the north wall and the other's back against the partition. This would make a closetlike space to the south while creating an area of relative darkness at the bed's foot.

Differing views. *Left:* One strange modern building trend is to wrap office buildings in inoperable glass windows. Workers inside swim in an air-conditioned fishbowl with a panoramic view of an outdoor world from which they're completely separated. A smaller, house-size version of the same phenomenon is the status-symbol picture window overlooking a grand view. But that omnipresent view can quickly become mundane through constant exposure, and the effect can also be that of a fishbowl. *Right:* This is the north window of our little building. Rather than creating an omnipresent picture window shot of the picturesque mountains, we elected to make the view special by framing it so that you'll really only see it when entering the front door or sitting at the desk.

Variety of light. Not all light is created equal. Different kinds of light encourage different moods and activities. Therefore it's important to match the right kind of light to the desired mood and action in a given space. Here, the varying colors and shapes of the bottles, combined with the undulation of the cob into which they're set, create a light experience unique to this place.

Basics of Life

We all need food, water, shelter, and clothing as a bare minimum to survive. So of course our little guest house has to accommodate these basics. We'll include a tiny kitchen on the west side with a sink, small stove, counter, and storage space. The water pipe from our spring reservoir to the house is buried directly in front of the cottage, so we'll be able to tap into that. We'll provide hooks and a small closet area for clothes and luggage. People are used to having an indoor bathroom, but it doesn't make sense to include one in such a tiny building. Guests will be able to brush their teeth and wash up at the kitchen sink. We'll put a nice little composting toilet in a whimsical structure built into the retaining wall between the shop and the building, close enough to the cottage overhangs to allow a guest to get there comfortably when it's raining. We'll also create a beautiful outdoor solar shower, a treat that many people have never experienced, on the private south patio overlooking the pond. If it's too cold outside, guests can always bathe at our house.

Frankie's place. All the elements and variables that come together in this exact box in this exact spot make Frankie a happy cat.

Housing Design: A Success Story

Frankie is a cat we live with. One day we absent-mindedly set a little, well-used apple basket on the floor, and Frankie was drawn to it like a bird to its nest. The basket was on the tile in front of a south-facing, floor-to-ceiling window next to a glass door. Frankie loved to squeeze into that little basket and bask in the sun. Every morning when we sat down to breakfast, he'd crawl in with his head propped on the edge in such a way that he could see both us and the outside.

One morning, for some reason, we'd moved the basket slightly; it had been turned 90 degrees and moved about one foot to the east just slightly out from directly in front of the window. I noticed that Frankie wasn't in the basket that morning. I moved the basket back to its spot, and Frankie immediately came back and got in.

There was something exact about that basket in that spot that worked for him. Lots of variables came together in a way that almost forced him to act. When it was slightly changed, the spell was broken. The basket simply didn't serve his needs anymore.

This is a simple example of the challenge of good housing design. What are all the elements that need to come together, and in what exact way, to create your little basket in the sun?

THE PROCESS OF DESIGN

As I've said, the exact approach appropriate for creating a pattern language and fleshing out a design for a building must be specific to the situation. Certainly, you should have a fairly definite idea of your site before you get too far into the design process. On the other hand, designing for a while can help give you some insights into pinpointing a site. Even a playhouse destined for a small suburban backyard could be placed on a number of possible sites, each of which might offer drastically different access to sun, connection to the house, and so on. You really just have to dive in and see what process your situation dictates. And remember, there's absolutely nothing wrong with starting over when you hit a dead end. The best barometer is how much fun you're having.

If you're not having fun, all I can say is, why not? You're not spending any money; you don't have to do this in the rain or snow; you can stop and start at your whim; and your job is to dream the best building that you can imagine. Believe me, it isn't going to get better than this.

Take your time and languish in the luxury of possibilities. The beauty of creating a hierarchical pattern language is that it truly allows you to imagine each pattern individually. Bask in each pattern. Celebrate it. Imagine its most beautiful expression right there in your building. Only then, move on to the next one. Remember that this process is about creating a clear image of your building in your mind. The clearer this image is, the easier all the subsequent steps will be.

PLAYING AT BUILDING: FLOOR PLANS, MODELS, AND MOCKUPS

All through the design process, you should spend a lot of time outside walking around possible sites, roughly measuring things, and checking out the positions of the sun, trees, and other elements of your chosen spot. Make a lot of rough sketches, like the ones shown in the previous section. Mess with your design as much as you want. It's only a tool and it's yours to push, stretch, and otherwise do with what you will.

Once a general floor plan has begun to take shape, start creating it in two- and three-dimensional space. Make simple cardboard cutouts to scale of the elements you imagine inside and out, and move them around on a cardboard floor plan. This step is important because you don't want to go to all the trouble of building your wonderful little building and then find out you really needed an extra six inches of interior space to fit in that cool salvage sink and stove. Making a soft clay model also is helpful, because it gives you an image in three dimensions and is easy to modify. Or you can try any of the many simple, inexpensive computer programs that allow

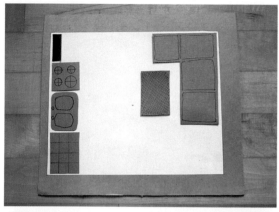

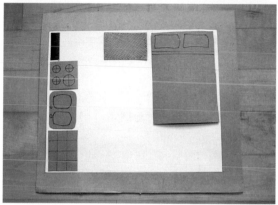

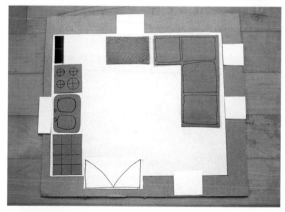

A 2-D floor model. Once you've determined a building's general dimensions and floor outline, you can consider the size and layout of primary interior elements (including windows and doors) and make accurate, to-scale cutouts of them. For example, if you use a ½-inch-per-1-foot scale, a 2 x 3-foot sink will become a 1 x 1½-inch cutout. Once you've made cutouts of all major elements, move things around to your heart's content until you get exactly what you want. In our model, the light brown cardboard background represents our building's thick walls, the white paper is the floor area, and the white cutouts on the walls are windows and doors. On the left (west) side are cutouts symbolizing counter space, stove, sink, and heater. A desk/table is on the north side, and the bed/sofa is on the right (east). In the middle photo, the sofa's trundle bed has been pulled out.

A scale model. This is one of two scale models that my wife, Lisa, made of our house (not the guest cottage) before we built it. All the roofs come off and the two floors can be separated. She also made tiny versions of features such as our bathtub, masonry wood stove, and furniture. Using the model, we were able to simulate how sunlight would move through the windows and onto our thermal mass floor and walls, try different layouts for our stove, and generally get familiar with our plan to see if it seemed just right for our needs. Making the model and "playing" with it was time well spent.

you to create floor plans and 3-D scale models. They take a bit of effort to master, and the graphics seem to make everything look like cheap motels, but many of the programs allow you to easily adjust plans, view the building from any angle, and take walking tours of the inside of your planned space. Once you've gotten far enough, you might even build a 3-D scale model of the building.

It's also very helpful to make an actual-size mockup of the space. You can do this on-site with bamboo poles, rope, some old sheets, or anything else that will mark off the dimensions. This is a great way to start cementing down your exact siting. You can mock up window and door placements, even move in furniture and play house for an afternoon. Another, perhaps easier, approach along the same lines is to tape out a space on the floor of a large room (see photos below). Create life-size versions of all the floor plan elements and move them around. This is a great way to see if your image of space matches reality. Can that bed really fit there? Will the table tennis table and the life-size Elvis statue really work in the loft of your cabin? You're about to find out. This indoor taping method has the advantage of being weatherproof, so it can be left in place throughout the design process.

Mock cottage in the country. This is a life-size mockup of our little building. Notice that we're working with basically the same layout we came up with in the 2-D model. The blue tape line represents the inside walls and the blue tape shapes on the left are the counter, sink, stove, and heater, respectively. The pillows are the sofa that becomes a bed. The cardboard is the desk and the chair is, well, a chair.

CHOOSING MATERIALS

By the time you've thoroughly fleshed out a pattern language, you'll have gradually constructed the feeling of the place you want to create in your mind. By focusing on individual patterns, you'll also have gained fairly detailed mental images of many places both inside and outside your building. Using those images, you can create a clear floor plan and firm up how your building and its site will interface with the sun.

Now it's time to make some decisions about materials to match your design. Note that, although for many readers the materials featured in these pages may have been the main reason they picked up the book, this is our first mention of the subject. This is because choosing materials before you've created a clear design is clearly a case of putting the cart before the horse.

Once you have a design, however, you need to know what materials you're going to use, because your choices will affect the size of your building and many other factors, including siting, site work, and virtually everything else from here on out.

OUR BUILDING: MATERIALS CHOICES

Because materials choices are design-specific, the best I can do for you here is outline the thinking that went into choosing the materials for our little building, with the hope that you'll find lots of information that you can apply later to your own situation. Also, I won't go into extensive detail now regarding the specifics of how we used the materials we chose; I'll save that for the chapters dedicated to the actual construction. For the time being, I'll focus just on the process of deciding which materials we'd incorporate into our design.

Of course, a major influence in our particular approach to materials was that we were purposefully creating, for this book, a building intended to demonstrate a variety of green building techniques using a variety of popular alternative building materials.

Nonetheless, as with any building project, we wanted to be highly conscious of materials selection, making our choices based on the suitability of particular materials for particular purposes and applications. Our project's small size was an advantage, because it allowed us to play and experiment a bit. Also, we intended to use as much material as we could find on the land, and then fan out from there to the local mill, and finally the hardware store. Our overriding goal, naturally, was to make a building that will last a very long time and age gracefully.

Our building is in a climate that has four real seasons. Our pattern language had already defined a south-facing building that's slightly longer on its east-west axis, is only 10 feet deep, and has huge overhangs to the east and west. It has a large door and a window to the south, an open floor plan and windows for cross ventilation to the east and west, and only a small window in the north wall. This is a classic setup for passive solar winter heating and summer cooling. So we needed to choose materials that support that basic design.

The north side of a building is usually the coldest. The building itself shades its north face in the winter, and winter winds often come from the north also. So for our north wall, we needed a material that offers superior insulation against conductive and convective heat loss. Because the sun never hits the wall, which is also exposed to the wind, a material with thermal mass would probably be a bad idea. For this reason, we chose to use straw bales on the north.

The south side of our building would, by far, receive the most sun in the cold months. For that reason, it made sense to use a material that combines thermal mass and insulation. (We'll discuss this reasoning in more detail in chapter 8.) We knew there was plenty of good clay at the site, based on the material we'd found when we excavated our driveway. So a south wall of cob made with clay from the site seemed like a good solution.

Neither cob nor straw bales is the best choice for walls that need a lot of shelving or other elements that might be added or changed after construction (more on this, too, in later chapters). Our design's east wall featured a little closet and a window seat on the inside, and a built-in children's sleeping area and/or workspace/tool-storage zone on the outside. Next to the north face, this wall would get the least winter sun, so we needed something insulative. Cordwood can be nailed into easily, and is therefore great for creating shelving and other add-ons. It's also readily available on-site—we live in a wooded area and heat our house with firewood—so we chose cordwood for our east wall.

Figure 10
DETERMINING OUR BUILDING'S FOOTPRINT

Before we can accurately site our building, we need to know how much ground it covers, also called its footprint. As you can see here, our building is about 14 x 13 feet from the outside of its thick walls, and 22 x 17 feet including the roof overhangs.

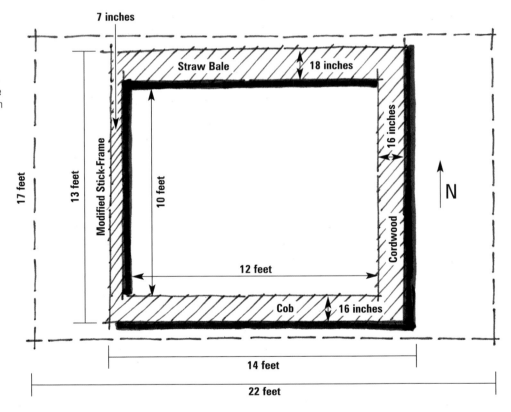

Our west wall will be where all the systems, including an indoor and outdoor sink and a propane stove and space heater, are installed. This wall will also have extensive interior and exterior shelving. Conventional stick-framing accommodates plumbing and other conduit-based systems easily. Its flat surface and easy nailing makes it even better at accepting shelving, sinks, counters, and the like than cordwood. For all of these reasons, we decided to create a modified stick-frame wall on the west.

There are a lot more materials decisions we'll make along the way. We'll talk about each material and its context as we get ready to actually install it in the building. For now, we've got enough information to move on to siting our building, because we now know its full footprint—in other words, its dimensions and the surface area it will cover—and have a clear picture of the building's eventual form and relationships with other site elements.

FOLLOW YOUR FEELINGS

Let's return to the gentle snowdrift where our imaginary Inuit friends have just finished home-sweet-igloo and are sitting down with the kids for a relaxing evening. Their building process hasn't included all of this pattern language and design hubbub, because their design language is expressed as a natural, integral part of the building process. Just as many people aren't conscious of the grammatical structure that they use fluently, these people aren't conscious of the grammar of their buildings. To them patterns are just words they know and use as forms of expression. This allows them to adjust their building as they go, designing on the fly, so to speak. While we have to do all of this clunky preparation, we need to try to keep the spontaneous feeling of their approach alive in our process.

Although you must deeply imagine, draw, plan, and replan your building before starting, you also should maintain an attitude of playfulness and intuition as you actually start to build. Your building will be a real thing, an exact thing, sitting on an exact place, facing an exact direction. A piece of paper with scratches on it won't tell you precisely where the building needs to sit, or exactly where in the wall that window should go to catch the morning winter sun, or just where a built-in shelf will be within easy reach of the door. These decisions have to be felt and realized through the act of construction. On a modern construction site it's usual to see people hunched over plans, pointing at symbols and tapping on calculators. I'm a fan of all of these activities, but you also have to stop and look at the sun, sense all the forces at work at your site, feel from within the home you want to build. You've got to step back and imagine the effect of what you're doing regardless of what that paper says.

Just remember that native Inuk. Be your own culture; plan and build not only with logic and common sense, but with spirit and intuition. Follow your feelings.

PART TWO: BUILDING

Structure

The next three chapters deal with setting our little building consciously, carefully, and solidly on a specific piece of ground. First, we'll decide exactly where our building needs to sit in relation to the sun, water, wind, and earth of our site, a process called siting. Next, we'll alter the land to fit our design. This step is called site work, and it entails creating a seat for our building and making sure that water is flowing away from it. Finally, we'll set the basic framework of our building—its foundation, wall, and roof structure—onto our carefully prepared site.

Chapter 5 - **Siting**

Chapter 6 - **Site Work**

Chapter 7 - **Structure**

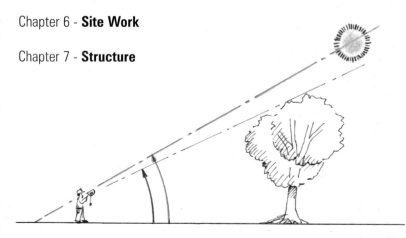

Chapter 5
Siting

Siting is where all of the varied and rich information we've just

covered—from the reasons for and functions of housing to the science and intuition of creating a home that is specifically yours—literally comes "down to earth." It's a focusing of all you know about buildings in general and your desired building in particular onto an exact spot. Though it's a process that precedes any actual construction, it's an act that will profoundly affect every aspect of your building, from the first day of construction to its final day on earth.

To the beginner, siting can seem nebulous, not as directly a part of the building process as, say, digging a foundation trench or installing a window. After all, in essence you're preparing an exact spot for something that doesn't yet exist. In reality, siting is one of the most densely concrete acts of construction because it touches so much of what the building will be: its temperature on a winter day; the quality of light caressing your face on a lazy Sunday morning in bed; your experience of a cool summer breeze; the way your friends feel as they walk from their car to your front door, and on and on.

Certainly, siting requires both great preparation and focus of purpose. On the other hand, the process can be completely relaxed and free from the pressures of time. No work has begun; no decisions have been set in stone. As of yet you have no building problems; only, perhaps, worries that reside in the abstract future. You have to strike a balance between the ominous finality and relaxed playfulness that is inherent in the process of siting.

The moment you set out with hammer and stakes to begin the life of your new building, the wisdom of all of the planning and preparation you've done should be a warm glow of purpose in the pit of your stomach. At this point, you should have a clear image of what you want to create, the building that you want to feel on this spot. Everything about that image and all you know about how to make it needs to come to bear as you decide exactly where your building will spend its life.

Smart siting. *Left:* These buildings carved directly from sandstone formations are sited closely together for shade. *Right:* This little cob home is sited so that it's shaded in summer by deciduous trees and is warmed by the sun in winter, when the trees are leafless and the sun's path is lower.

GENERAL CONTEXT: SITING

Your job is to bring the exact environment of your site into a union with your plans. To do so, you'll need to consider the forces at work on your site; those four elements of nature that are both the forces of decay and the objects of desire for your building. You need to consider exactly how sun, water, air, and earth are expressed on your site.

SUN

At this point, you should have a clear idea of what kind of relationship your building needs to have with the sun. Are they going to be good friends, your building inviting the sun in on cold winter mornings? Or is the sun just a bully in your climate, something better to be avoided? Chances are the answer is some combination of the two, as reflected by the passive solar concepts that by now you've integrated into your design.

There are a lot of things you can change about a building, but its orientation to the sun isn't one of them. So the task at hand is one of the most pivotal aspects of siting: to place your building carefully in alignment with your solar design strategy. To do that, you'll need to have a clear idea of where the sun is going to be in the sky at different times of day throughout the year. You'll also need to determine whether, and how, obstructions such as large trees, nearby ridges, or buildings shade the site at different times.

By far the best way to research this is to visit the site often, or live there, for a year or more and take note of the sun's position in the sky on a daily, weekly, or at least monthly basis. The lessons can be dramatic. For example, in cold climates physical obstructions to the south such as trees or ridges can divide a field that's sunny and open in the summer into two climate zones in the winter. One section can be covered with snow and never see the sun for months, while just feet away the other section is snow-free and basking in sunlight for much of the day. After a full year of these kinds of lessons, the best solar siting will be crystal clear.

If you don't have the option of observing your site over time, you can create a "solar map" that will give you the same information: the changing paths of the sun over your site at different times of the day and year, and any obstructions that may diminish or shade that solar energy. The sidebar starting on page 104, Mapping the Sun, describes the procedure.

In some situations, you won't need detailed solar mapping information. For instance if you have a flat, open site, then clearly you'll be getting lots of sun and you'll just need to use a compass to orient your building based on your passive solar design. If you're concerned only about a ridge to your south that might block the winter sun, then you might just figure out the sun's path on the winter solstice, its lowest path of the year, and then use the simple protractor/sextant described in the sidebar to see if the sun clears the ridge on that day. If it does, you'll know that you'll always get full sun. The more complicated your terrain and the less personal experience you have with your site, the more detailed your solar mapping should be.

My advice is: when in doubt, map. It's fun to do and not much work, and siting your building accurately is just too important to leave to chance. Later you'll need to make other decisions, such as how large to make window and door overhangs and the proper ratio of glass to mass on your building's south face, that aren't part of siting but that require a clear understanding of your building's relation to the sun.

Blinded by the view. Many modern houses are sited based on the view they afford from a deck or picture window. However, distant mountains or a picturesque river have nothing directly to do with your physical building. It's your site's microclimate—the way the sun, water, air, plants, animals, and soil interact right there—that should be the focus of your siting. Figure out first how your building will interact with its exact physical environment, then think about views. This building has a killer view, but also a killer driveway and killer wind exposure.

Good sun, bad sun. Let's assume this building was built in a climate with cold winters and hot summers. Because the sun's path through the sky changes with the seasons (see figure 1, page 52), we know that if this is a south-facing wall in the Northern Hemisphere, then the only time of year the sun could pour in like this would be winter, when sunlight would help heat the building. If, on the other hand, this wall is facing directly west, then this is hot late afternoon sun most likely in the summer, but definitely not the winter. In this orientation, the sunlight would be heating the building when cooling is needed. So whether or not this wall is an intelligent design decision is based solely on how it's oriented to the sun.

Mapping the Sun

To create a solar map, first you'll need to make a graph that plots the sun's paths over your site at different times and months of the year, including its lowest path at winter solstice (December 21) and its highest path at summer solstice (June 21). These two paths are the bottom and top, respectively, of a site's "solar window," the hours throughout the year when strong sunlight is available at a given spot, minus any obstacles. Then, on the same graph, you'll mark the positions and highest points of any buildings, trees, ridges, or other potential obstructions. Objects that fall within the solar window will block the sun during some part of the year.

Making the Graph

First, lay out a graph that on one axis plots the horizontal orientation of south, east, and west (with south at the midpoint) and on the other—vertical—axis indicates altitude, starting at horizon or ground level (see figure 1). Mark off intervals of 20 degrees on both axes, as shown. The horizontal axis represents the *azimuth angle* (see figure 2), the number of degrees that an obstacle, or the sun at a given time, is east or west of south. The vertical axis represents the *altitude angle* (see figure 3), the number of degrees that an obstacle, or the sun at a given time, is above horizontal, or ground level.

Figure 1
GRAPH FOR SOLAR MAPPING

Using graph paper or by drawing your own grid lines, create a graph that plots east to west orientation on the horizontal axis and altitude on the vertical axis. Mark off intervals of 20 degrees along the horizontal axis and 20 degrees along the vertical.

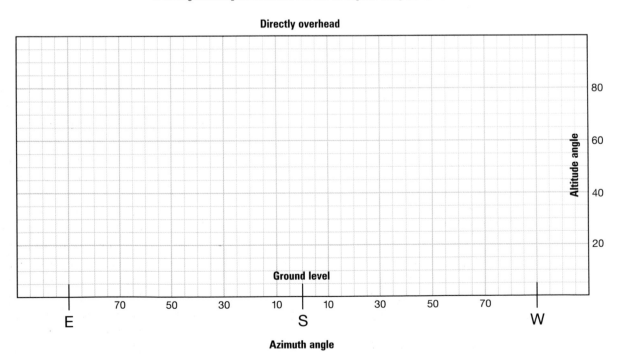

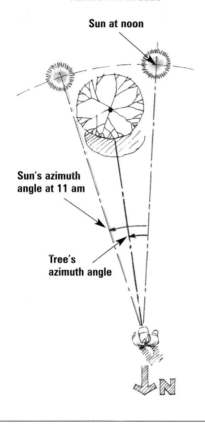

Figure 2
AZIMUTH ANGLES

Sun at noon

Sun's azimuth
angle at 11 am

Tree's
azimuth angle

Figure 3
ALTITUDE ANGLES

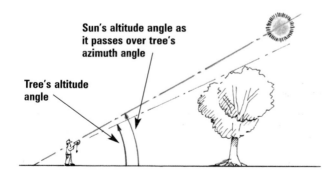

Sun's altitude angle as
it passes over tree's
azimuth angle

Tree's altitude
angle

Now, by marking the azimuth and altitude angles of the sun's position each hour as it moves in an arc across your site on the summer and winter solstices, you can plot the top and bottom of your site's solar window. You can also plot the sun's path during other months of the year, too, if you wish. Don't panic! Fortunately, you don't have to measure any of these angles yourself. The sun's movement through the sky is well-documented, and there are many sources—book and websites on passive solar design—from which you can get this information. All you need to know is your latitude, and you'll find charts listing the solar azimuth and altitude angles at different times of the day for the solstices as well as for the other months of the year. Just mark the angles on your chart and you'll have plotted the sun's varying paths. (Some software programs and websites will create an entire solar window chart for you; all you need to do is enter your latitude, or, in some cases, zip code and print out the resulting chart.) (See page 106, figure 4.)

Mapping

Once you have a graph of your solar window, all that's left is to plot the positions and elevations of landmarks on the horizon as well as those of any potentially sun-blocking obstacles. To do that, you need only a simple compass and a protractor converted to a homemade sextant (see photos, pages 106 and 107).

To measure an object's azimuth angle, stand at your site and point the compass in the direction of the object that you want to plot. Turn the degree dial until the magnetic pointer is aligned on the north/south axis, which will mean it's pointing to 180 degrees at its south end. Count the number of degrees east or west from south to where the compass is pointing, and you'll have the azimuth angle. For example, if the compass pointer reads 210 degrees, then the azimuth angle of the object is 30 degrees west of south. If the compass reads 140 degrees, then the azimuth angle is 40 degrees east of south. (Note: Your compass needle aligns itself to magnetic

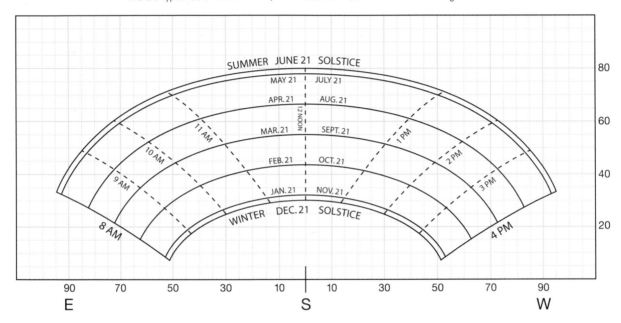

Figure 4
SOLAR WINDOW CHART
This is a typical solar window chart, in this case for a location at latitude 36 degrees north.

Compass. This inexpensive camping compass is perfect for measuring the azimuth angles of landmarks and obstacles. Here, the compass is pointing at an object that has an azimuth angle of exactly 90 degrees, or due east, from south.

north/south. True north/south can deviate by as much as 30 degrees from magnetic north/south, depending on your location. If you live in an area where the variance is more than a few degrees, be sure to adjust your compass readings accordingly, so that they represent orientation to true north/south. You can find this information for your area in many sources, including websites and books on passive solar design.)

To make the sextant for measuring altitude angles, just tie one end of a short piece of string to a weight, such as a plumb bob, and the other to the hole in the center of the protractor. Then, with a black marker, draw a straight line between the 0 and 180 degree marks, as shown in the photo on the next page. In this setup, the plumb bob will hang at 90 degrees when you sight to a theoretical ground level or horizon, zero degrees. To make a measurement, simply sight along the long black line to the top of the object in question and measure how many degrees away from ninety the weight is hanging. (It helps to have a second person read the angle while you hold the sextant.) This reading is the object's altitude angle.

Now you're ready to use these procedures to map your site's significant landmarks and other potential obstacles. Take your compass and protractor/sextant, along with your solar window

graph, and stand at the building site you're considering. Look to the east and, using your compass, find the azimuth angle (degrees away from south) of an object or landmark on the horizon. Now, using your sextant, find the altitude angle of the same landmark's highest point. On your graph, plot the point where these two measurements meet. Move your gaze more to the southeast and pick another object or landmark—a rise or fall in the horizon ridge, a tree, a building, whatever—and measure and mark its position on the graph. Continue this process around the full panorama from east to south to west, plotting all the significant changes or obstacles in the landscape around your future building (see figure 5).

If you live in a cold climate, be on the lookout especially for obstructions that will block the sun when its daily path is lowest in the solar window—in other words, during late fall, winter, and early spring, when solar heat is most needed. Of course, the mapping process is the same if you want to use physical features of your land to shade your site in a hot climate. But instead of avoiding the shade created by obstacles, you'll want to use it.

If you're unhappy with the results revealed by your solar map, try some different sites in the immediate area. In some terrains, even small adjustments can make a big difference.

Homemade sextant. To determine an object's altitude angle, just sight along the long black line to the top of the object and read how many degrees from 90 (horizontal) the weight is hanging. On my sextant shown here, I've added another, short black line that marks the point that the sun reaches at noon on the winter solstice for our latitude. This is a good reference point for someone trying to read the sextant.

Figure 5
SOLAR MAP

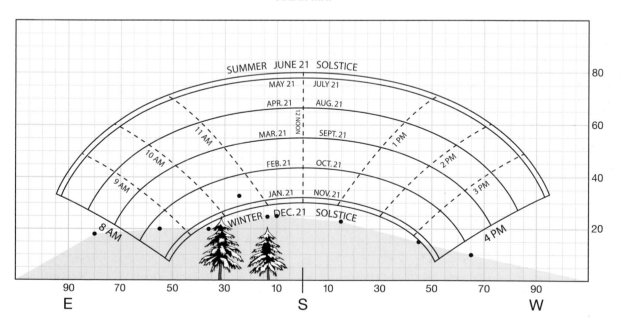

WATER

The water on this planet is a single unit always falling toward itself, seeking unity at the sea. Your job is to determine how to work with the water that's falling through your site.

If you have an orderly flow, such as a small creek, you might want to site your building close enough to it to easily utilize its kinetic energy to create electricity (see page 70). Long electric runs greatly increase the expense of hydropower and other direct-current generating technologies, so close proximity to the source can be important.

If you plan on bringing water into the building for drinking or washing, now's the time to decide where it will come from. If the source is a spring, you'll need to think about how the water will access the house. If you'll be drilling a well for your water, you'll want to do that first to make sure you have the water you'll need. Even in the city, rain catchment is an option, but it needs to be carefully considered at this point. A huge rain catchment cistern—the reservoir in which rainwater is stored—can wreak havoc on a wonderful site plan if it isn't part of the planning from the beginning.

Of course, then there's water's other, potentially destructive, side. Much of the water on your property will fall in an unruly mass from the sky and flow across your site in a complex pattern matching the contours of the land. This water must be coaxed into being absorbed by *swales*—small, human-made valleys—or safely redirected away from your building. It's important to pay close attention to the contours of your site and to place your building away from the natural flow of water or to plan grading, retaining walls, or other

Rising above the situation. This little house is sited in an area where heavy rains often send water flowing over the ground. Instead of redirecting surface water by changing the contour of the land, this house is simply lifted up and out of the way.

physical changes to the site that will redirect falling water. This is important regardless of whether your building is a home or just a shed or playhouse. I continue to be amazed at how often little thought is given to this crucial environmental reality when siting buildings.

AIR

Because it's influenced by so many variables—terrain, vegetation, seasonal fluctuations, and more—wind is the least predictable and most site-specific of all the forces of nature affecting siting. Precipitation charts, solar window data, soil analyses, and similar information sources can help you scope out the other elements on your site, but to really understand the flow of air across the specific place where your building will stand, you generally have to be there—ideally, for a year or more—to observe the wind's behavior first-hand. Wind, then, is a good reason to get at least a general idea of possible sites as soon as you can. Then, as you're thinking and planning, you can be watching the wind. It's fun research: flying a kite on a spring afternoon, observing the breeze under a tree on a hot summer day, or gauging the wind while throwing a snowball on a winter morning.

If you have any thoughts of using the wind to create electricity, you'll probably want to gather more exact data over a period of months using an *anemometer,* a device that measures and records wind speed, to see if you have enough wind for that purpose. If you live somewhere that's known for powerful winds that might damage your building, you can look for physical wind barriers on your site once you've determined the prevailing direction of the winds in question. Hills or dense trees (not too close to the building, though!) in the right place can be amazingly effective windbreaks.

EARTH

Now let's bring this discussion truly down to earth. There are at least three ways that the earth around your building can affect siting: soil, contour, and building materials.

Soil

We've already learned that the soil under a building is its true foundation. In order to finally site a building you need to know something about the loads that building is going to exert on the soil underneath it. Thus, although the design process to this point has evolved primarily within the realm of your imagination, now you must bring that design into the real, physical world and start to define its structural characteristics and the materials you're going to use. If the building is going to be made of massive materials, it will require a more substantial foundation, and, consequently, a more stable soil structure.

Defining a site's soil characteristics might be as easy as digging a hole. Where I live, for example, we have dense clay just under the topsoil. This clay is an adequate foundation for just about any building we could conceive to build on a modest, house-size scale. On the other hand, if you do a little digging and come up with, say, a loose and airy subsoil, you'll need to have a clearer idea about the structure you're going to build before you lock down a site. Though soils in close proximity can vary greatly, it can be helpful to look at the foundations of existing buildings near your site, too. How are they holding up? What are they holding up? If you've made a conscious decision to build a relatively small structure, chances are that your building will be light enough to be accommodated in some way by most site soil conditions. A definite exception is wet soil. If you dig around and find water, just do yourself a favor and find somewhere else to site your building.

Remember, too, that the soil on which your building rests must not only be solid and dry, but also must remain unfrozen throughout the year. This means that you need to determine your site's *frost line:* the depth to which frost penetrates the soil in your area. When water freezes, it expands. If a foundation rests above the frost line, expanding soil moisture can push on the foundation. This phenomenon, called *frost heave,* can lift an entire house, cracking its foundation and twisting its structure. You must place your foundation below the frost line in your area, which varies by local climate. Where I live in western North Carolina, the frost line is 12 inches. In parts of New England, it's more than four feet.

Avoidable mess. This is the crawlspace under a house built at the base of a hill. With every rain, water pours under the house and pools up here. This mess could've been avoided if the ground around the house had been reconfigured slightly to slope gently away from the building. Another solution, of course, would've been to choose another site.

Tim's Take
On Terra Firma (and Not-So-Firma)

When you create a building, you want it to stay in one place. This requires putting the building on a foundation that doesn't move, which in turn means putting the foundation on earth that doesn't move. A simple concept, right? Yes. But actually planting a building's feet on what is truly terra firma is not always so simple.

Of course, one major consideration is the composition of the site's earth, and the load-bearing capacity thereof. As you can see from the table below (which, for our purposes, is best viewed to see relative values), we have a pretty good idea of how much weight the earth in all its many forms will bear. We can see for example, that hard rock can hold 15 times more weight than stiff clay soil can, and that stiff clay can bear twice as much weight as soft clay.

The trouble is, you can't know for sure what lies beneath the surface of your particular site without looking—in other words, without digging. While it can be tricky to estimate the work involved in completing the aboveground construction of a building, it is a real crapshoot to guess what you might find below ground. Depending on what part of the earth you inhabit, scratching the surface of a building site may yield rock, water, clay, sand, shale or any combination of the above.

Be prepared to be surprised. I've found myself using dynamite to remove an unexpected subterranean rock ledge, and have spent days with a jackhammer drilling clay and shale to create footings that I thought would take a morning to dig. Like it or not, you'll have to deal with the mysteries that are revealed when you go subterranean.

Indeed, another major factor to consider is just how deep you'll have to dig before you reach truly solid ground; in other words, the minimum depth at which you can safely put your foundation. Certainly, you need to dig below your site's frost line. But another, equally critical, requirement is less obvious and sometimes overlooked: you must set your foundation on undisturbed soil. Make no mistake: "undisturbed" means soil that has never been excavated before. If the soil on which your site rests was once cultivated for crops, for instance, you'll need to dig down past the deepest point of cultivation. If your site has been leveled with fill dirt, you'll have to dig past the fill. Some disturbed soils can be compacted to be acceptable for building, but I don't recommend it; compacting

soil is very labor-intensive and unless you employ the services of a soils engineer, the outcome can't be assured. Go for the real thing: soil that has not moved in a million years or so.

How do you know when you've reached solid, undisturbed soil that will bear your building's loads? One method for roughly testing the soil's load-bearing capacity is to use a 1/2-inch steel rod with a T-handle at the top and try to force it into the soil. I've done this enough to have gained a pretty good sense of when the earth is giving me adequate resistance. "Adequate" in this case means a lot. I'm a sizeable animal and when I lean my full weight onto that T-handled rod, I don't want to see it penetrate the soil more than about 1/2 inch. If there's ever any question in my mind about a soil's load-bearing capacity, I dig deeper until I find what I'm looking for. This is very important. Some years ago I built a mountainside house that we thought would require an average-cost foundation. By the time we got to undisturbed soil and were comfortable we were on solid ground, the foundation was going to cost the homeowner three times as much, and we'd lost any money we might have made on the job. But it was worth every penny.

Remember: Settle for nothing less than solid, undisturbed ground. If you don't find it, dig until you do, or look for a different site. Everything you're going to do from here on in rests on this, literally. If there's any question in your heart or mind about a site's soil qualities, consult a professional builder or engineer.

LOAD-BEARING CAPACITIES OF SOILS

Class of Soil	Description	Allowable Bearing Weight in Tons Per Sq. Ft.
1	Massive igneous or metamorphic rock in sound condition	100
2	Massive sedimentary rocks	20
3	Hard weathered rock	30
4	Soft weathered rock	15
5	Hard residual silt/dense sand	5
6	Residual silt/sand	3
7	Dense sand	2
8	Stiff clay	2
9	Loose sand	1
10	Soft clay	1
11	Compacted controlled fill	1.5

Contour

We've already discussed the contour of land in relation to solar access and surface water. Now, we're looking at it from two more angles: access and useable space.

Access

How easily will you and others be able to get to your site? This question is often overlooked by novices. Where I live, some realtors drive vehicles resembling tanks so that they can get unsuspecting dreamers to the top of every mountain that might be for sale. The views are great up there, but nobody mentions the costly road that's going to be necessary to access that paradise. You need a level of access that matches the realities of what you're building and how you'll use it. For example, how will you get materials to the site? Is the arrival of a concrete or propane truck somewhere on the horizon? Do you want to walk or drive to access the finished building? These are important questions whether you're building in your backyard or on a remote homestead. Be realistic. The way you approach your building will be a large part of the mood of the entire place. If it's a pain to get there and you're not building a Zen retreat where that pain is part of the allure, you might defeat the project's entire purpose. Don't forget, cars can be given nice, vine-covered "rooms," and roads and paths can be wonderful places—if you plan for them by siting appropriately.

Useable Space

Anthropologists think that the human species first developed in flat terrain, perhaps a tropical savannah. In any case, let's face it: we need flat space to do a lot of what we do. Vegetable gardens need to be reasonably flat or terraced. You need a flat place to work on a car or to play catch. Even to enjoy a beer or game of checkers at a little table, you need some degree of flat land. What I'm saying is, if your site isn't flat, you're going to have to flatten part of it. That could take just a little shovel work, or some heavy machinery and perhaps construction of some retaining walls. Either way, level ground has to be a part of your siting equation. Place your building to make maximum use of this precious flatness. In climates with cool and cold weather, that's probably going to mean placing your building on the north end of the flat area, so that the building doesn't shade it. In very hot climates, you might choose to do the opposite.

Technically, it's possible to drastically change a site's natural contours with machinery, but this dangerous step needs to be taken with care. It took a long time for your land to situate itself the way it is, and indiscriminate tampering can result in all sorts of problems, not the least of which is the loss of precious topsoil due to erosion. On the other hand, every beautiful terraced garden or snugly bermed cottage is the successful result of earthmoving. And if, as is the case with our little building, you'll be repairing an already damaged spot, earthmoving to fix problems and prepare the site can be a positive step. (See chapter 6 for more about earthmoving.)

Tight squeeze. This is a nice, flat road languishing through a picturesque old farm. But the distance between the barn to the left and the steep ridge to the right is too narrow. Trucks of any size carrying building materials or making other deliveries will have trouble getting through here. Maybe you don't need such things, but you'd better be sure before you commit to building somewhere along this road.

If it's not flat, you may have to flatten it. Most humans need some amount of flat area to go about the business of living. These farmers need flat, wet land to grow rice, so they're willing to spend generations drastically altering the landscape to get it.

Building Materials

As part of the design process, you'll have already decided on some of the materials you're going to use in your building. Now you need to think about them in terms of how they affect siting. The presence of useful materials on or around your site can influence your siting choices. For example, perhaps your site is wooded and you're having trouble imagining cutting trees to make room for your building. You could look for a site with desirable lumber to the south of it, for example a couple of large white pines. By cutting them instead of nearby oaks, you'll be losing a couple of fast-growing trees and gaining not only wood that can be milled into lumber for your roof, but also a nice, sunny garden space and better access to the sun for winter heating.

Solar lumber. With a portable sawmill, you can turn the need to clear a bit of room for your building into useable materials and, if the trees are blocking desired sun, better solar access.

Clay and stone are two other valuable materials whose presence might affect your siting choices. For example, you're going to feel a lot better about excavating to create a berm or a flat spot if it produces clay that can be used to make cob to build walls.

Choosing to use off-site materials also affects your siting choices. If you're going to need to have materials delivered, for example, you'll need enough room and convenient access to accommodate them. I'm not talking about just concrete trucks here. Sand for mixing cob, lumber for structural framing, and many other materials also often require large trucks for delivery.

In addition, as you learned in the last chapter, your materials choices influence the size of your building and a variety of other factors that are closely linked to siting: the configuration of your foundation, the thickness of the building's walls, the weight of the roof, and more. The ability of your site's soil to accept loads, in turn, determines if the foundation you're planning will work. If your head is starting to spin, just be patient; all of this will become clearer as we actually go through the process of building. My point for now is that you need to get a clear picture of the material configuration of your building before you can finally determine your exact siting.

SITING APPLIED: OUR LITTLE BUILDING

Because our chosen site is close to our house, we had the advantage of observing the precise local environment for a number of years. We knew the approximate path of the sun at winter solstice, the prevailing winter and summer breezes, and the flow of water over the land. This long personal experience made precise siting much easier.

DEFINING THE FOOTPRINT

This first thing we had to do was clearly define our project's footprint, the ground area that would be covered by the building, outdoor rooms, and anything else in our plan that required space. Here, we were instantly rewarded for all of our pattern language design work. We not only knew the size and shape of the building that we were trying to site, but we had an idea of the sizes of the workshop and courtyard that we planned to create in the future.

Next we needed to decide how much space would be required to park and turn around the cars in the area behind the workshop. We did this by moving our cars around and measuring the amount of space used in pulling in, parking, and turning around to leave. Every car manufacturer publishes the turning radii of their vehicles, so we also researched the turning radius of a typical delivery truck or an ambulance to make sure that we'd be leaving enough space for all eventualities.

It was also time to decide how many cars we wanted to accommodate, like it or not, for daily life and for parties or other events. Personally, I'm ambivalent about cars. I'm highly conscious of the automobile's horrible effects on our ecosystem. But I've also learned that ignoring them won't make them go away. So I try to bring cars into the process of design and siting. Nothing is solved by making everyone inch forward and backward for a half hour trying to get their vehicles in or out of a place.

Using all of this information, we made a to-scale drawing of the entire plan (see figure 6). Then, with our drawing in hand, we walked out to the site to find the right place to nestle everything in. The only tools necessary were a compass, our homemade sextant, a 50- or 100-foot tape measure, a large hammer, some stakes, and another person's help.

Siting tool kit. These are all the tools we need to place our building exactly where we want it.

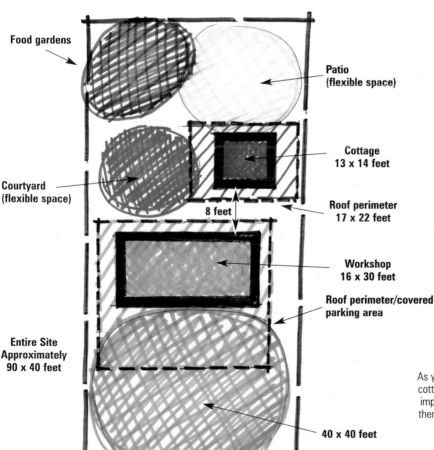

Food gardens

Patio
(flexible space)

Cottage
13 x 14 feet

Courtyard
(flexible space)

8 feet

Roof perimeter
17 x 22 feet

Workshop
16 x 30 feet

Roof perimeter/covered
parking area

Entire Site
Approximately
90 x 40 feet

40 x 40 feet

Figure 6
OUR LONG-TERM SITE PLAN

As you can see, our immediate project, the guest cottage, is a small part of our long-term plan. It's important to site our cottage in such a way that there will be room for all the other elements that will make our little building whole.

Site in the rough. This photo was taken from the northwestern border of our site. From here we need about 90 feet straight ahead and 40 feet to the left to fit everything in our plan onto the site.

At the site, we used our compass to orient ourselves. We knew we wanted our building facing generally south, so we identified that direction and studied the terrain and other elements there for a while, getting a general feel for that portion of the site. Next, we considered the situation overall. The north boundary of our project was already defined by our driveway. In front of this is the flat area that was previously graded out as a parking circle—the area we'd decided to repair by building there. To the south of this, a hill quickly rises to the east.

As our site plan showed, we needed about 90 feet of space from north to south and about 40 feet from east to west. After taking some measurements with the tape measure, it was clear that we'd have to excavate some of the hill to the east to fit everything in. That didn't bother us, because we knew we'd find good clay there that we could use to make our cob wall.

Once we had a good idea of how much room we'd need to accommodate our design and plans for the future, and where we'd need to put everything, we could consider the best ways to utilize our site's natural elements.

ASSESSING THE SUN

Our next task was to map the sun's path. Because the passive solar approach we chose for this building maximizes winter sun for heating and accomplishes summer shading through physical building elements and plantings, we were mainly concerned with obstacles that might block the sun during the heating season.

Again, we used our compass to orient ourselves basically south. In our area, the difference between true and magnetic south is only five degrees west, so a direct compass reading was accurate enough in this situation.

From our vantage point we could see that the southern and eastern horizons are partially blocked by a tree-covered ridge while the western horizon is open and at relatively the same elevation as our site. There are no other possible sun-blocking obstructions to the south of where we were standing.

That meant that we needed only to determine whether the path of the sun through the sky at its lowest point, winter solstice, will be high enough to clear the ridge for a significant portion of that day. We knew that if that was the case, we'd get enough sun on every other day of the winter too.

Not a sun-blocker. This is the view from the front of our site, facing south. Using our homemade protractor sextant, we found that the sun will come up on the east side of this ridge at about 9:30 in the morning and will continue to hit our site uninterrupted until after four in the afternoon on the winter solstice, when the sun takes its lowest and shortest path.

Using the procedures described in Mapping the Sun on page 104, we created a graph of our latitude's "solar window." Then, using our homemade sextant to plot enough points along our horizon ridge to represent its basic contour, we determined that the sun will rise on our site at the winter solstice to the southeast at about 9:30 am and will move unobstructed through the sky before setting to the southwest at around four in the afternoon. Good. We'll be getting plenty of sun even on the shortest day of the year, and we'll continue to get more as the days grow longer.

CONSIDERING WATER AND AIR

Next, we needed to concentrate on water and wind. The hill to the east would bring a fair amount of runoff water to the site, which we'd redirect and slow down for absorption by plants by building the retaining wall that's part of our design. As for wind, I knew that our land's contour seems to funnel most wind into us from the west. This is an advantage of our site in the summer because we'd have an open west wall and large window to invite that breeze inside. In the winter, though, it might drive snow and rain into the west and north walls. The north winds will be blocked by our planned workshop, and if the west winds prove to be too severe we can slow them with some dense plantings.

EARTH ISSUES

Finally, we needed to consider the earth itself. From previous experience, I was confident that the soil a few inches down anywhere in our siting area would produce firm clay and would be adequate for our foundation. Our access is already clearly defined by our existing driveway and the remnant of our failed parking circle. This situation was ideal because we'd be able to drive any needed materials right up to the site, including things that had to be delivered on large trucks. We'd already decided to excavate a portion of the site to the east to create additional flat space. The exact amount would depend on how much flat area we wanted in front of the building and would be best determined after we'd staked out the building and as we were actually doing the excavating.

As for building materials, we knew we'd be getting clay for cob from the excavation. Our site is an old tobacco field, so we wouldn't need to cut any trees to make room for the building. We'd also be able to use some other materials on the property, including some stone piled nearby from a pond excavation, but these wouldn't have any effect on our siting decisions.

With all of this information and observation, we were ready to set stakes to mark the building. As we stood on the site with compass in hand, it seemed right to set the building just a bit west of south to flow better with the hill to the east that falls toward the west. We knew how much room we needed to the south of our already defined northern boundary, and we also knew that we wanted to preserve a grass road that accesses our house to the west of our chosen site. These two parameters along with our desire to be sited slightly west of south pretty much locked down the position of the building. Using our tape measure, compass, and a hammer, we set stakes at the corners of our building and any other points that seemed to need definition.

WHAT WE'VE ACCOMPLISHED

Because we took the time to carefully imagine our building and, perhaps more importantly, other buildings, cars, and outdoor spaces in detail, the sometimes nebulous, nerve-racking act of siting went very smoothly. We could be confident we'd have enough room for everything that would need to happen here for a long time. We also knew that we'd get plenty of sun, that water could be collected and redirected, and that the dirt we needed to excavate would be used as a building material for our project.

Drive-in convenience. This is the existing driveway to our house. It ends in a gravel circle that comprises the northern end of our building site, an ideal situation for deliveries.

Stakeout. These stakes mark the corners of the outside of our building's walls as well as of the roof overhangs. We also put in a few stakes to mark the south end of our future workshop. We also set up a long stick in the center to get a feel for how tall the roof will be.

David and Goliath. In the city, sometimes direct sun just isn't an option. The small building at left, for example, is lost in the shadows of the taller building at right. No amount of creative design can change the path of the sun. That's why the ancient Romans had laws protecting urban landowners' rights to access sunlight.

ONE LAST DEEP BREATH

The last phase before taking the drastic and basically permanent step called site work is to spend some time with your layout. With an outline of your building set exactly where you plan to put it, it's time to go back over your design and pattern language and see if the siting seems right. Your building now feels much more real and defined than it did on paper. As you walk around your staked site imagining the building, you need to ask yourself: Do you feel excited? Do you get an echo of the feeling you hope to create with this building? If not, maybe you need to tweak the design. On the other hand, if you do get an inkling of that feeling you're looking for, revel in it. This is an act of imagination becoming reality that you've worked hard to earn. Enjoy it.

VARIATIONS

Of course, a major theme of this book is that any building you construct should be specific—and thus unique—to you and your site. By showing you in detail how our little building came together, we hope you'll get a good idea about how to create yours. As a contrast, let's consider briefly a couple of other, vastly different, siting situations.

THE CITY

One of the main challenges of siting a building in a city is dealing with solar access. You're almost certain to have all sorts of physical obstructions around you, over which you have no control. If you're building in your backyard, for example, your own house and those of the neighbors, as well as neighborhood trees, public buildings, or what have you will create unique challenges to your plans for utilizing the sun. Even more difficult is the fact that you can't know what might be built nearby in the future—on a vacant lot across the street, for instance. It's a horrible experience to create a nice plan around a bright, sunny space only to have that space permanently shaded by a new building a couple of years later.

Almost every difficult site has within it the seed of some wonderful solutions. For example, a sunny outdoor space, and even a vegetable garden, can be placed on a roof. If you've ever spent time on a roof garden atop a tall building in a crowded city, you know that the experience can be joyous. It feels like you're a king or queen, or at least a court jester with seniority, living on top of your own lofty world.

EXTREMELY HOT CLIMATE

Our site plan works nicely in our situation, but wouldn't be a very good one if we were in an extremely hot climate. We'd be exposed to the hot western sun, with no large shade trees of any kind. I lived in central Texas for many years, and would never consider living in a house there that wasn't surrounded by large, cooling shade trees. Remember, plants don't just lower heat by blocking the sun; they also provide evaporative cooling, which is the mechanism that creates cold air in a refrigerator and air conditioner.

There's a lot you can do with building design if you don't have the perfect site for your climate. For example, if our present site was in a hot region, I'd keep the southern exposure and focus on building design and plantings to provide cooling. First, I'd plant trees long before construction was to begin. This could cause access problems in the building process, so careful planning would be important. Next, I'd move the building's entrance to its north side and turn the courtyard into a private shaded space. The shop could open up onto its north side to create a shaded public outdoor cooking and work space. This simple change in plan would still allow us to heat the interior easily with solar, perhaps without any or only cursory backup heat. I'd also carefully plan overhangs on the south and be vigilant about not putting in too much glass there to avoid overheating.

Hot climate siting. These buildings make the most of a difficult climate by nestling close to one another and a precious tree, thus sharing the tree's shade and creating some of their own. Notice the deep, shaded entrance room in front of the door.

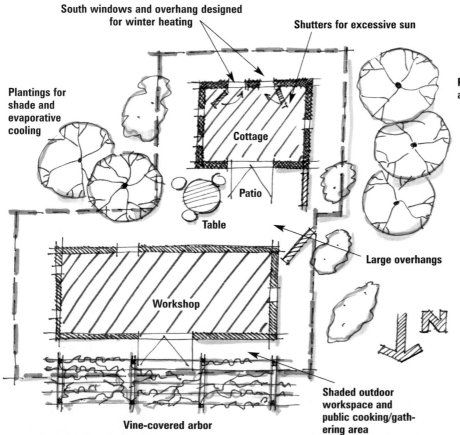

South windows and overhang designed for winter heating

Shutters for excessive sun

Plantings for shade and evaporative cooling

Plantings for shade and evaporative cooling

Cottage

Patio

Table

Large overhangs

Workshop

Vine-covered arbor

Shaded outdoor workspace and public cooking/gathering area

Figure 7
A HOT-CLIMATE SITE PLAN

Here's our project on the same site if it were in a hot climate. Simply by turning our focus from south to north, we'd create a hacienda with lots of shaded exterior and interior space. We'd still want to use the sun for winter heating, so we'd make the south overhang larger to adjust for the shorter heating season. Also, insulated shutters would allow us to close out the sun's heat if there were too much on an early or late winter day.

▨ **Shaded cool mass floors (also provide some winter heat collection)**

Chapter 6
Site Work

All acts of building change the site on which they occur.

The question is: how and how much? Site work is the act of changing a site in preparation for building. It can include clearing land, building roads, flattening contours, redirecting surface water, and digging holes and trenches for foundations. For you as a builder, it's the point of no return. It's the step that brings your building screaming from the womb of imagination into the cruel light of day. From here on out, you've set something in motion that has a life, and you'll be responsible for it.

In the modern context, site work must strike a balance between realism and self-control. On the one hand, I know people who live in a wooded eco-community that's striving to be self-sufficient. The members need to clear trees—lots of them—not only to make room for housing, but also, more drastically, to open up the land to the sun in order to make agriculture possible. Some members, however, are against cutting trees, and this causes conflict within the community. These members aren't being realistic. The community's stated goals of creating housing and practicing sustainable agriculture simply demand cutting trees and clearing land.

On the other hand, I often see site work for constructing apartment complexes and subdivisions that begins with indiscriminate clear-cutting and complete clearing of the entire property. Sure, this makes construction easier for the contracting firm, but it also devastates the microclimate, causes erosion, and almost guarantees that whatever is built there will be lifeless and out of sync with its environment. What's worse, there's often no reason for creating this ground zero other than the fact that it's easy to do with bulldozers and backhoes. These builders are showing no self-control.

You need to walk the path between these extremes by making sure that any site work is in service to the needs of your specific project. If trees need to be cleared to gain solar access to heat your building, clear them. If you need more flat land, flatten it. At the same time, respect your site and be conscious of the potentially permanent nature of your actions. In just a few minutes, a couple of machines can devastate a piece of land. When it comes to site work, the goal is to do just exactly enough and no more.

All buildings alter the place they inhabit. *Top:* This is the site work done for a small house in a self-described "eco-spiritual" intentional community devoted to living with nature. Like it or not, site work often requires nature-destructive acts such as cutting trees, bulldozing land, or spreading gravel. Sometimes, it takes the courage and commitment to do damage that you know you can repair in order to create the best building for a given situation. *Bottom:* This bird's nest sits very lightly on its chosen spot, but it still alters the site significantly.

GENERAL CONTEXT: SITE WORK

By going through the process of siting covered in the last chapter, you'll have evaluated how your building will interact with the sunlight, water, air, and earth on your site. The next step is to actually alter the site physically to match your plans. Unless your site is relatively flat with no unwanted obstructions to your building or the sun; unless the natural flow of surface water works perfectly with your plans; and unless it already offers you the access you need for building materials and other essentials, you're going to have to make physical changes to the land. Though site work encompasses adding things such as retaining walls and trees, initially it's about taking things away or rearranging them.

As I said in chapter 4, it takes a long time and an infinitude of events to create a "place." Your site is already such a place and, unless it's been tampered with recently by humans, it has probably found some sort of balance, a situation of some stability: water flowing without causing erosion; plants growing; insects, birds, and animals finding places to do their thing. Your site work will be successful only if the changes you make don't permanently disrupt this overall stability, this tiny, slowly created ecosystem. If you've chosen a site that needs to be repaired in the wake of some previous human blunder, your site work and act of building can actually help create the stability that your site needs to become a self-sustaining living system, a true place.

CLEARING LAND

The first necessary physical act is to make space for all facets of your project. In some cases that may mean simply moving some things that are in the way, such as a stack of firewood, assorted building materials, whatever. In many situations, however, it involves the often-larger job of moving or removing plants. You may have to clear trees to create solar access, or simply clear brush and weeds. Whatever the scope of the clearing you need to do, be prepared. If you'll be clearing trees and are planning on using the wood for something other than firewood, be ready to process or store the wood right away. For example, as you'll learn in chapter 9, logs destined to be used in cordwood walls need to be debarked immediately after they've been cut.

MARKING CONTOURS

Once your building area is cleaned up and cleared of vegetation, you'll be able to get a really good look at the site's general contours. Unless the terrain is very flat, you're probably going to have to move some dirt around to create a flat spot for your building to sit on. But exactly where and how deep do you need to dig? How much dirt will you need to move, and where will you need to move it?

The clearest way to determine the right dirt-moving strategy is to map your site's contours by measuring, marking, and comparing its elevations at different points. Once that's done, you'll know whether you're going to need a shovel, a tractor, or a backhoe. You'll be able to visually assess how much dirt has to be moved or how high the front of the building needs to be lifted off the ground to be level with the back. Marking and mapping will help you picture how big that planned retaining wall needs to be, or how you might be able to move a little dirt from here and put it over there to make a flat spot. For an explanation of this process, see the sidebar Mapping Site Contours.

Get real. The space this neglected house occupies is quickly being reclaimed by plant and animal life. Some people imagine they can build a house without disturbing plants or animals. They picture an idyllic home surrounded by woods, wildlife, and a vegetable garden. But vegetables and people need sunlight; wildlife eat crops; unwanted plants compete for space. The reality is that you have to stake a claim to an area of sufficient size to accomplish your chosen human tasks.

Some experienced builders might say that you don't really need to map out your entire site thoroughly; that just measuring and marking elevations at the site's four corners will give you all the information necessary for determining where and how much dirt you need to move. That's certainly often true, but I recommend taking an extra half-hour to mark the entire site. It gives you another useful piece of graphic information to consider, in combination with your design sketches, scale model, solar map, and everything else, as you make your final decisions before committing to actually building. You're getting ready to start a lot of work and to spend some hard-earned money, so the more clear information you can gather, the better.

Control yourself. No, this isn't the surface of the moon. It's the site of a mall construction project in a small mountain town. The first thing the builders did was go in and remove every piece of living material, then they completely flattened the place. Replacing plants with asphalt creates run-off problems, raises urban temperatures, and speeds up the deterioration of local air quality. Conscious site work requires restraint.

Mapping Site Contours

To measure and mark your site's contours, you'll need a tool called a *transit* or *builder's level*, a long measuring stick or *transit stick*, and some stakes. A transit is basically a magnifying scope mounted on a tripod. The scope pivots horizontally so that, once the tripod has been leveled, the instrument's crosshairs will always point to the same elevation as it pivots around. You might be able to borrow a transit from a builder friend, or you can rent one. Or, as a substitute, you can use a water level as described on page 123.

To use a transit for marking contours, set up and level the tripod on a spot that offers a clear view of the entire site, and that allows you to position the scope itself above the highest point you plan on measuring. Now, choose a point that's approximately at one corner of where you envision your site and that also seems close to what you want your finished excavation's elevation, also called grade, to be. Put a stake there. This will be the reference point against which you'll compare all other measurements (see the red stake in the illustration on page 122). While someone holds the measuring stick vertical at that spot, look through the tripod and read the measurement where the crosshairs meet the measuring stick's tick marks. Write that measurement down.

Transit and measuring stick.
A transit is a useful tool for comparing a building site's varying elevations, or for ensuring that the depths of trenches or footings are consistent throughout. Simply level the transit and, with the measuring stick held upright at the spot in question, look through the viewer and read the stick where the crosshairs fall, much as you'd read any ruler. Then, keeping the transit set at exactly the same elevation, rotate the transit's scope to other points one at a time, take readings there, and compare those measurements to your initial reading. Higher spots will read lower on the measuring stick, lower spots will read higher.

Next, create a "grid" on the ground. Place stakes spaced equally apart—say, every five feet if the contour changes quickly, or every 10 or even 20 feet if the site is flatter—starting at the reference stake, along one side of your approximate site. Then place corresponding stakes spaced the same distance apart along the opposite side (see illustration, page 122). Now, using the tripod and measuring stick, measure and record the elevation at one of the stakes. Then pull a tape measure from that stake across the site to the corresponding stake on the opposite side. Again using the tripod while someone holds the measuring stick, measure and record the elevation at even intervals—the same spacing you used between stakes—along the tape measure (represented by the green dots in the illustration) and at the opposite stake. Repeat the process, recording the elevations between each pair of stakes, until you've measured the entire grid. (See also photos on pages 127 and 128.)

Because the tripod always points at the same level, the measurement taken at each spot along the grid tells you that point's relative elevation. For example, if the measuring stick at the grade point (A in the illustration) reads 52 inches and the stick up the hill at point B reads 44 inches, you'd know that point B is 8 inches higher than point A. After all the measurements are made, mentally connect the dots between the stakes and other grid points, and—voila!—you'll have a visualization of the shape of the ground now as compared to how you want it to be. To literally create the map, draw a two-dimensional version of your grid on paper. Mark each point with its elevation measurement and write down the elevation measurements at each point.

Figure 1
MAPPING SITE CONTOURS

To mark and map your site's contours, use a transit or water level to compare the elevations of points along a grid defined by two rows of equally spaced stakes placed along opposite sides. Use a measuring tape pulled between each pair of opposing stakes to determine the actual measuring points. In this drawing, measurements are taken every five feet between stakes. The red stake marks the reference point against which all other elevation measurements are compared. The blue dotted line represents grade, the level of the desired finished excavation. The green dots represent the points at which elevation measurements are taken.

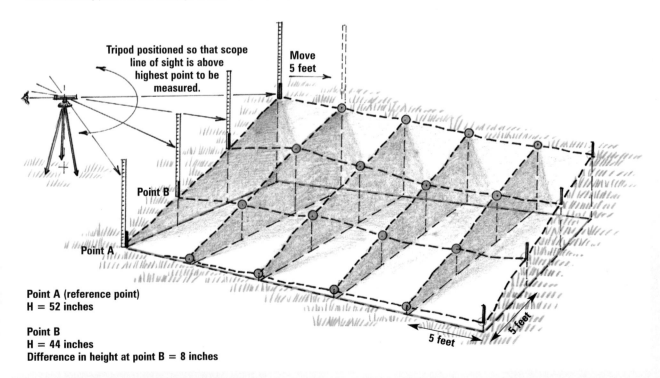

Tripod positioned so that scope line of sight is above highest point to be measured.

Move 5 feet

Point B

Point A

Point A (reference point)
H = 52 inches

Point B
H = 44 inches
Difference in height at point B = 8 inches

5 feet

5 feet

A Homemade Water Level "Transit"

A transit such as the one shown and described on page 121 is the tool of choice among builders for measuring and marking sites. If you can't borrow or rent a transit to measure relative elevations for mapping site contours, though, you can use a simple, inexpensive substitute: a water level.

All you need to make a water level is a container (a five-gallon plastic bucket works nicely), a piece of 3/8-inch clear plastic tubing long enough to reach across the area you want to measure, and a short length of flexible wire.

Poke two small holes side-by-side about 3/4 inch apart near the top of the container. Thread one end of the wire through one of the holes and the other end through the other hole, starting from the inside and pushing the wire through to the outside, to make a small loop on the inside of the bucket. Now slip one end of the plastic tubing through this loop so that the tubing extends deep into the container but doesn't quite touch bottom. Twist or tie the wire ends together to tighten the wire loop around the tubing; it should be just snug enough to keep the tubing from pulling out.

Next, set the container somewhere on or near the site at a spot that's higher than the highest point you want to measure. Fill the container about half full of water; then siphon water into the tube. Be sure there are no air bub-

bles trapped in the water inside the tubing. Your water level is now installed and ready for action.

Water levels work on the simple principle that water seeks its own level. As long as no water spills out of the bucket or the tube, the level of the water in the tube will remain constant, equal to the level of water in the bucket. To use the level, move the tube's long end to a point you want to mark or map, and with a measuring tape measure the distance from the ground to the water level in the tube. Record the measurement, then move the tube to other points, measuring and recording their relative elevations, much as you'd use a transit as described in the sidebar, Mapping Site Contours.

Though accurate and easy to master, water levels take more care to use than a transit. As you move the tube around, cover its open end with your thumb to keep water from spilling. Also, when you take your thumb off to make a measurement, the water will bounce up and down in the tube before it settles. Make sure there's enough empty tube above the water's level to accommodate this sloshing. If any water spills from the tube or bucket, you'll have to start all over again, because all the elevation measurements need to be compared to the same water level.

Figure 2
WATER LEVEL

Used properly, a simple water level makes a good
substitute for a transit. In this example, point B is
15 inches higher than point A.

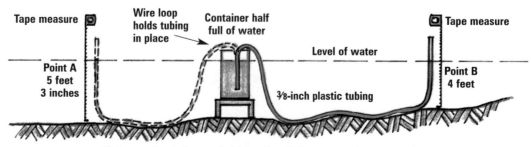

Make sure level of water is higher than highest spot to be measured.

MOVING DIRT

Both clearing land and moving dirt can be done by hand or with machinery such as a bulldozer. What's right for you, of course, depends on your specific situation. If you need to get vehicles to your building and there isn't a road already, you may need to use a bulldozer and perhaps a backhoe to create one. If that's the case, then it makes sense to use that machinery while you've got it to do other site work such as clearing brush and (sometimes) trees. Machines can do things in minutes that would take people days, so let them do their thing. Now's the time to dig that pond you're planning, for example.

On the other hand, take this step *very* seriously. Choose your 'dozer driver as carefully as you would a daycare facility for your kids. Make sure the driver comes well-recommended. If you're having any kind of road built, carefully identify important landmarks, such as streambeds or old trees, that you don't want to disturb, and walk the route with the machine operator. Don't let the operator do anything until you're both in agreement as to what that thing is. *Always* be on site when any big machinery is in action! A good machinery driver can be an artist, so you don't want to get in the way or tell that person how to do the job, but you also don't want to allow any misunderstandings. Big machinery can destroy a site in minutes. Don't let that happen!

Regardless of how you do it, the point of moving dirt is to match your site to your plan. This can include taking a chunk out of a hill into which a bermed building will be inserted, moving dirt from one place to another to create a flat spot, or sculpting land so that surface water flows away from the building. Whether using machines or shovels, always keep in touch with the purpose behind your actions, which is to consciously incorporate and interact with the sun, water, wind, and earth on your site. No more, no less.

Digging tools. The tools in both these photos do basically the same thing: they dig. Each is the right choice for a specific kind of dirt-moving job.

Drastic action. The layers of materials that make up your site—vegetation, topsoil, subsoil, etc.—are the result of millions of years of slow change. Machines can drastically change all of that in minutes. Don't move any soil until you're sure everyone involved knows exactly what needs to be done (and not done), and where.

Working with water. Water doesn't care about your plans. It goes where the laws of physics direct it. You have to place your building where water won't flow, or rearrange dirt to convince water to flow elsewhere. *Left*: This gentle slope was created by grading to redirect water away from the adjacent house. Rows of berry bushes to the right act as swales to help slow surface water runoff. To the left, vegetation flourishes in the soft fill dirt that berms a retaining wall built to help direct water away from the house. *Right*: To build this house, a chunk of the hillside was cut out to create a flat spot. But the ground wasn't built up to slope away from the building, so water flows off the hill directly toward the house. The result is a wet environment that eventually rotted some of the framing, requiring repairs.

Dirt moving is like surgery. It's an initially destructive act that's intended to improve things in the long run. It always leaves a wound, and infectious erosion can set in and spread if care isn't taken. After dirt surgery, immediately apply the appropriate bandage. In some areas of your site that might mean a layer of gravel; in others, planting grass, ground covers, shrubs, or trees will help. With the proper care and attention, the site of the surgery will recover.

Grass-and-straw bandage. If you have to move dirt, make sure you immediately take steps to heal the wound. Here, a huge grass-and-straw bandage has been applied after radical road surgery. Perhaps your holistic building approach will allow you to avoid such invasive Western medicine.

Land heals. Every time I use a table saw, I have an image of cutting off several fingers. That thought has kept me careful and safe over the years. A similar respect is in order for site work. It's scary and requires caution. On the other hand, every farm, garden, and road has required some degree of earthmoving. Given a chance, land heals. The excavation at left became the green expanse at right in a matter of months.

FINAL BUILDING LAYOUT AND FOUNDATION PREP

After you've changed your site to match your plans for construction, the next step is to lay out the building's footprint again, pretty much as you did before, only with even more care. If you needed machinery to move dirt, you'll want to do this layout work while the machines are still around in case you need to tweak anything. Hopefully you checked the grading with a transit or water level as it was going on; recheck it now as you site your building. Consider, too, whether your grading has created areas that may be susceptible to erosion and thus need to be shored up or protected in some way right now. In our project, for example, we decided to build a retaining wall immediately after grading our site, so that a small cut we had made into a hillside wouldn't erode and spill soil into our freshly leveled building area.

Once you've finished laying out your building and shoring up any areas, it'll be time to prepare the site for your foundation. If you've planned ahead, you'll be able to ask that backhoe operator who's getting ready to drive off after grading your site to quickly and inexpensively dig some holes or trenches for your foundation, a task that would take you hours or days to dig yourself.

ORGANIZING SITE WORK

Regardless of your methods, remember that site work really is the point of no return. It might require chainsaws and heavy machinery, or just friends with shovels. But, either way, you need to make sure you're ready. It's a good idea to see site work as a single act.

If you're using rented machinery, obviously you need to be organized so that everything that machine can do gets done quickly. Even if it's just you and a shovel, though, keep in mind that you're preparing your workspace for a process that's going to take a lot of time and probably more money than you think. Once you get into the thick of it, you may become too preoccupied with the construction itself to create sensible organization. Now's a better time.

If you need covered workspace or storage for tools and materials, plan it, make space for it, and create it now. If you're clearing land or grading, don't just assume you'll bandage the wound immediately with grass seed and straw; get that seed and straw now, so that it's on hand when you need it. Consider, too, what you want to do with any soil you remove. If there's good topsoil on the area you'll be excavating, you'll want to scrape it off first and keep it in a separate pile somewhere to spread back over the site before planting your grass, or to use in garden areas. If you intend to use excavated clay or soil to make cob or earth plaster, decide now where the best place to put it is for easy access later.

If you intend to build a retaining wall to hold back a graded area, make sure the necessary materials are onsite, and build it. If you had a driveway or road of any kind put in, complete the job by installing culverts and gravel or surface of your choosing.

All of this can be expensive and time-consuming, but it's absolutely crucial that it be done correctly now, before proceeding with building. The easier the access, the fewer puddles, the less mud, the more organized the materials and work areas, the smoother the construction process will go.

SITE WORK APPLIED: OUR LITTLE BUILDING

Certainly in terms of site work, our site was a piece of cake. We already had an established drive coming directly into a broad circle of gravel adjacent to the site. Truck deliveries and material storage wouldn't be a problem. Part of the reason we chose the site was that it needed repair due to some previous fumbling human shenanigans. Almost anything we did was going to be an improvement, and there were no trees or even topsoil to speak of that needed protecting. Our only issue was the last curve of a gentle hill to the east.

MARKING SITE CONTOURS

Our siting process left us with long sticks marking our building's outline protruding from the various firewood, materials, and junk piles that still littered our site. We replaced the sticks with pieces of brick to mark the building, and cleaned up all the junk lying around. Then, using the procedure described and illustrated starting on page 121, we accurately marked our site's contours (see photos, below). The result was a clear visual representation of the site's contours superimposed over the layout of our building marked with bricks. This allowed us to see where and how much dirt needed to be moved.

From siting to site work. This is how our site looked at the end of the siting process. To prepare the area to be graded, we cleared out the junk and replaced the long sticks marking the building's corners with bricks. The next step was to make a contour map of the site.

Marking Our Site's Contours

▲ **Step 1.** First, we created a grid on the ground where we wanted to measure contours. At left are the stakes set every five feet at the south side of our site, and at right are the stakes on the north side.

▲ **Step 2.** Working with one corresponding pair of stakes at a time, we connected the north and south stakes with a tape measure.

▲ **Step 3.** Next, using a transit, we measured and recorded the elevation at one stake.

▲ **Step 4.** Then we moved along the measuring-tape line connecting the corresponding north and south stakes, and took measurements every 10 feet.

▲ **Step 5.** After taking elevation measurements at and between one pair of stakes, we moved the tape to the next pair, took measurements every 10 feet along that line, moved the tape and recorded elevations between the next pair of stakes, and so on until we'd measured the entire space at 10-foot intervals. Using those measurements, we were able to plot a simple visual grid similar to figure 1 on page 122. We could visualize exactly how much dirt needed to be taken from where.

EXCAVATION

Excavating always makes me uneasy. It's a version of that peculiar human tendency to mess around with nature that, in its unchecked, out-to-lunch expression, has created the hydrogen bomb and the human-rabbit hybrid embryo. Before I start moving dirt for a project, then, I rejuvenate my image of the structure to come, making sure that it's clear enough, that the feeling I'm looking for warrants this kind of surgery. In the case of our little building, I reminded myself that we were actually involved in an act of repair. I pictured an attractive stone retaining wall curving around a comfortable country cottage, and knew that we were doing the right thing.

Luckily, we have a nice neighbor who was willing to loan us his tractor with a backhoe attachment. Even with that powerful tool, and despite the diminutive size of both our building and the gentle slope we were dealing with, it still took a full day to make our small excavation (see photo sequence, next page). To do the same thing by hand probably would've meant a couple of weeks of hard labor for one or two people.

Before we started grading, we set up the transit where it wasn't in the way, so that we could check our elevations often as the excavation proceeded. (If you intend to use a water level instead, make sure to get enough tubing to allow you to set it up out of the way during grading.) Remember, the whole point is to produce a site that's not only flat and solid enough to build on, but that has a contour that will move water away from the building. You don't want to take out more dirt than you intended. If we had removed too much dirt, water would pool up near our retaining wall instead of moving past the south end of the building toward the west.

As we'd hoped, we hit wonderful clay that was perfect for making cob. We staged this clay carefully in a spot out of the way but close to and higher than the site, so that we'd be moving the clay *downhill* when it was time to use it.

When excavating, remember to leave plenty of room for everything in your plan. We had a wide porch and a thick stone retaining wall to accommodate on the east, so we had to excavate well beyond the perimeter of our planned building.

Excavating the Site

▲ **Step 1.** A small tractor with a backhoe attachment is the best of both worlds: small enough to move around easily with minimal impact, but able to move a lot of dirt! Here, Tim scrapes off topsoil before beginning to dig. We stored topsoil in a separate pile from other excavated materials, both so that we could use it again and to keep it out of the subsoil pile that we planned to use for our cob and earth plaster mixes.

▲ **Step 2.** Tim has begun the excavation to make way for the retaining wall on the eastern edge of our building.

◄ **Step 4.** Here the excavation is about half done. Even with the tractor, the job took a long day's work. Notice the pile of clay that we're starting to make above the site to the east. Because we did that, we were able to carry it a short distance to the building in buckets when we needed it to build with. Remember, if you're storing dirt to use as a building material, be sure to separate out as much topsoil as you can.

▲ **Step 3.** Ah, pay dirt! As I'd suspected, we hit wonderful clay that would be perfect for making cob and earth plasters.

PRELIMINARY BUILDING LAYOUT

After we'd moved enough dirt and checked our elevations again with the transit, we got our compass and tape measure and, taking into consideration the desired solar orientation and our site's other physical features, laid out the building's position on the newly graded site (see the photos, below). Then we measured and marked the building's four sides. At this point for this simple building, we just set stakes at the approximate four corner points. Next, we measured outward to see if we'd have enough room for the porches, retaining wall, workshop, parking, and everything else that we'd imagined in our design.

Adjusting solar orientation. With our site excavated and graded, it was time to establish the building's layout and exact orientation. We set our compass against a long, thin piece of wood placed on the ground to denote the south side of the building, and then adjusted the position of the wood piece until we felt it was right. Based on the slope of the excavated hill, the angle of our nearby house, and other subjective factors, we set the building about 15 degrees west of south, still within the range we needed to get excellent winter solar gain.

It's a stakeout. After orienting the building on the finished excavation, we staked the four corners and measured out from these points to make sure we'd have room for everything in our plan. Can you see how the site is sloped slightly to the southeast, in other words toward the camera? This will allow any water that falls close to the building to flow away.

Tim's Take
On Muddy Building Sites

The majority of building sites I've experienced swim in a sea of mud after a hard rain. People often take it for granted that onsite mud during the construction process is okay, to be expected. I think not. Mud at this stage is dangerous, messy, and bad for morale.

Do what you can at the excavation stage to move water away from your building site and create a safe and pleasant working environment. A practical, thoughtful approach to the movement of water around your site can save you from a world of worry and wet—both now, while you're working onsite and need to be able to keep your footing, and in the future, when your building has taken shape and needs to be standing on its own dry feet.

In our project, we ensured that our grading would move water away from our working area. Later, after installing perimeter drains (see the next chapter), we covered the area around the building with pea gravel, in anticipation of its later incarnation as a stone patio. This provided a clean, dry construction site for creating our building, no matter what the weather.

BUILDING THE RETAINING WALL

As soon as we'd oriented our building and confirmed that we'd have enough space for everything, we moved on to build our retaining wall. This was important because the longer we waited to build the wall, the greater the chance that rain would erode our new cut. As I've said, once you start building you take on a certain amount of time pressure and stress, especially at certain junctures, such as this one. Even though you may be anxious to start building, try to finish as much of the final site work as possible before starting to build. Frankly, we compromised and built only as much of the retaining wall as necessary to create our little building. The planned wall actually extends to the northeast end of the building and creates a courtyard behind it. Instead of building that portion of the wall, we dug a temporary trench there to redirect water away from the site. (See page 132, lower right.)

Most of the rocks we used for our wall were fieldstones from a huge pile on our property that farmers had made many years ago, probably when the field was first cleared. I had to scrounge creeks on and around our property for some choice flat stones, especially for those that capped the wall. Between collecting the rock and stacking it, I spent about five days building the wall. Hey, I'm not the most experienced stone mason!

Stacking a Stone Retaining Wall

▲ **Step 1.** A stone mason once told me to "lay stones as if they've already fallen." We laid this wall wide at the bottom and tapered it back into the hill as we went up, which is roughly the shape it would take if you dumped rocks into the cut and they settled on their own.

◄ **Step 2.** If trapped behind something, water can exert enormous pressure. A stone retaining wall works because it allows water to pass through gaps between the rocks. We filled spaces behind the wall and between the rocks with gravel to keep dirt from clogging the wall and preventing water from passing through.

▲ **Step 3.** Laying stone is like putting together a jigsaw puzzle. Sometimes you find rocks that fit incredibly well, as was the case here; other times you search in vain. Don't be afraid to break stone to make it fit.

▲ **Step 4.** The most basic rule of dry-stacking stone is that the rows, or courses, need to overlap in a staggered pattern, much the way bricks are laid. Just think of the rocks as irregular bricks. This pattern creates structural stability.

◀ **Step 5.** We capped the wall with large flat stones, poured gravel into all gaps, and then added a layer of soil from the excavation to complete the grading.

Redirecting water. The functional reason for our wall is to prevent the cut we made from collapsing, and to redirect water away from the building. *Left:* The finished wall slopes back away from the building, creating a shallow valley that carries water flowing down the hill safely away from the building. *Right:* Most projects have time and budget constraints, and this one was no exception. We couldn't afford the time to build the entire retaining wall included in our design, so we dug this temporary trench to redirect water away from our site's north side.

FOUNDATION LAYOUT

With the area graded and the retaining wall built, our site was pretty well prepped and ready to go. The next step was to lay out and dig our foundation. I'll describe the foundation in detail in the next chapter. For now, suffice it to say that we decided to pour four corner pads of concrete and connect them with trenches filled with gravel. We needed to lay these out accurately by defining, first, the four corners and exact rectangle of our little building, and then, second, the rectangle the pads and trenches outside the building would create—both easy jobs, using the techniques described in the sidebar below.

Building Math: Pythagoras, Rectangles, and You

Geometry literally means "to measure the earth," so it's no surprise that various geometric principles have been used to create buildings for thousands of years. One of the most basic and useful formulas is the Pythagorean theorem, which defines the relationship between the sides of a right triangle: $a^2 + b^2 = c^2$.

This simple relationship is incredibly powerful, especially because triangles are used in so many ways in buildings. Thanks to Pythagoras, we can apply the dimensions of their sides to help in innumerable calculations and procedures. Probably the simplest of these is the ability to accurately create a rectangle of a given size, as explained below. Let's say you want to create a rectangle on the ground—such as a building's

Figure 3
MAKING RECTANGLES

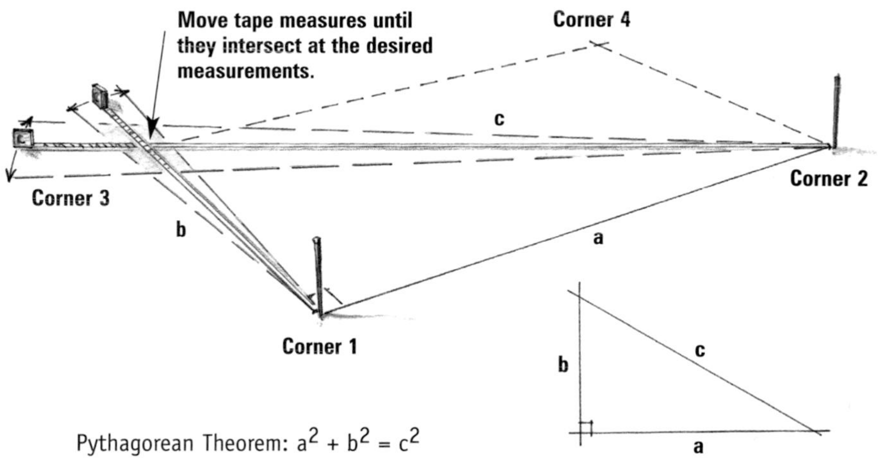

Move tape measures until they intersect at the desired measurements.

Corner 4

Corner 3

Corner 2

b

a

c

Corner 1

b

c

a

Pythagorean Theorem: $a^2 + b^2 = c^2$
Example: Side a = 72 inches; Side b = 36 inches
a^2 (5184) + b^2 (1296) = c^2 (6480)
Square root of 6480 = 80.4984 inches
Diagonal rounded to nearest fraction of an inch:
80½ inches

perimeter—with sides of lengths "a" and "b." First, using the Pythagorean theorem, calculate the diagonal "c" (see figure 3) to the nearest fraction of an inch.

Now, using the three measurements (in inches) and two tape measures, you can lay out the rectangle accurately, with good, square corners.

Measure out and mark a side of length "a" on the ground, and put a stake at each end. Next, starting at one end of "a"

(let's say corner 1), pull a tape measure out to the desired length of "b." From the opposite end of "a" (corner 2), pull a second tape measure out to the calculated length of diagonal "c." The point where the two tape measures cross at their desired lengths—you'll need to adjust them side to side until they do— is the point of corner 3. Place a stake there. To establish corner 4, repeat the process at the other end of "a," running the diagonal tape measure from corner 1 to corner 4.

Laying out the Foundation

▲ **Step 1.** We laid out and staked our building's four corners and perimeter using the Pythagorean theorem, as described in the sidebar on page the previous page. The string tied around the four corners represents the eventual height of our stem wall.

▲ **Step 2.** Next, we had to lay out the spots where we'd dig our footers. Here, Tim is setting a stake to mark the line between the outer corners of the two southern footers.

▲ **Step 3.** We knew the distances between our footers ("a" and "b"), so all we had to do was calculate "c" and round the decimal off to the nearest fraction of an inch

▲ **Step 4.** Using the same technique we employed to lay out the building's rectangle, we pulled two tape measures from their respective southern corners and put a stake where "b" and "c" intersected: the corner of our northwest footer. We repeated the process on the other side to locate the northeast footer.

DIGGING THE FOUNDATION

Finally, we were ready to dig our foundation. The foundation would be the starting point of our building, so of course we needed to make sure that each of its four corners would be at the same height. For that reason, we needed to carefully dig holes for our footers, measuring their depth with the transit. First, we marked the outlines of the four wide corner footers with flour and dug them out with the backhoe; then we marked the outside edges of our foundation trenches with flour and dug the trenches. The process is shown in the photos below.

Construction is a constant logistical calculation. For example, because we'd dug the pier footer holes first, the tractor had to straddle those holes, making digging the trenches difficult. We also had to clean a lot of dirt out of the holes by hand because the trench digging kept filling them up. On the other hand, it was much easier to set the depth of the four corners first and dig the trenches to match. Either approach had its own set of difficulties. The long and short of it is, you will get yourself into tight situations, and there's nothing you can do about it. Do your best to think ahead, but don't beat yourself up if you find yourself painted into a corner. There's always a way out.

Digging the Foundation

▲ **Step 1.** Each foundation stake marked the outer edge of one of the four footers. At each stake, we used flour to mark a 2 x 2-foot square.

▲ **Step 2.** We then dug our footers with the backhoe. Notice the transit set up to the left of the tractor in a spot that's out of the way, but that provides a clear line of sight to the entire area.

◄ **Step 3.** We dug each hole as carefully as possible and checked the depth often with the transit. We cleaned out the last bit of dirt with a pick and shovel. If we went a bit too deep, it wasn't a problem because we could just pour the concrete a bit thicker in that spot.

▲ **Step 4.** Next, we marked the outside of our foundation trenches with flour and dug them with the tractor to the same depth as our footers.

▲ **Step 5.** We checked the depth of our trenches with the transit and carefully rechecked our layout with triangulation as we progressed through the process of digging. Here, we're double-checking the position of the northwest corner (the foreground stake) before starting to dig the final trench, across the north side.

WHAT WE'VE ACCOMPLISHED

By its nature, most site work is violent and initially destructive, and as the builder you're responsible for it. So it can be a stressful process. Were we doing the right thing? Because we'd carefully designed and sited our building, always clearly within the context of how the structure would connect to and be separated from sun, water, wind, and earth, we could go about our site work with clear confidence. We knew that the dirt we moved would be put right back into the walls as cob and earth plaster. We already had the rocks on hand to quickly build a beautiful stone retaining wall that would keep surface water away from our building. We'd carefully planned space for deliveries and material storage that would be convenient to the construction process. And we immediately seeded any open dirt, other than that directly connected to the building, with grass, to start the healing process.

The result of all of this careful work was a nice, flat, dry, well-organized work site that was completely prepared to accept our little building. Most significantly, though, our site work had initiated the act of actually repairing this neglected and once-abused place. We'd started a process that in the end would make our site better able to accept water and nurture life; soon, more plants would be growing around and even on our building. As a result, it will be a more hospitable place for all kinds of animals, including humans. If you can say that about a building project, you know you're on the right track.

VARIATIONS

As we said, excavating and moving large amounts of dirt is not for the faint of heart, and perhaps not for the beginner without the help of someone more experienced. At the same time, picking a site based solely on the ease of site work isn't the answer either. You have to keep an open mind. Let's look at a couple of vastly different examples.

BERMING

In building lingo, a *berm* is a bank of earth placed against exterior portions of a building or retaining wall. There are at least two ideas behind berming a building into the ground. The first is to access the earth's stable temperature as part of a strategy for heating and cooling the building. The second is to nestle the building into the contours of the land, making it blend in. If you completely berm a building, in other words if you put it underground, and add a living roof, you can make it pretty much invisible. There's a kind of paradox at work here, however, because the more you make a building blend into its environment through berming, the more you have to disrupt that environment initially to berm it.

LOW-IMPACT

Some buildings take the opposite approach to blending in. They try to barely touch the ground in a few places and leave the rest of the site alone. In this situation, too, there can be a paradox. If, for example, a house is placed delicately in the woods sitting on only a few small piers, yet it's built of wood cut and trucked from far away, is the purity of intention only an image? Even if the house isn't made of wood, it might quickly consume more wood heating its interior than is represented by the trees creating its tranquil surroundings. A lot more wood could be saved by clearing the land to the south and allowing for solar heating. Of course, as with everything, it all depends on the situation.

Berming dialectics. *Top:* The site work for a bermed building is inherently drastic. *Bottom:* But the result can be a building that truly becomes a part of its site.

Very low impact construction. This little building uses living trees as its corner posts. Its foundation consists of two rocks and a cinder block. An inconspicuous path through woods is the only route of access. Site work, in other words, was virtually nil. The building sits lightly on the land, but it also has no heat, no plumbing, and no electricity. This lack of amenities wouldn't be for everyone, but it didn't prevent its builder from living here through a cold winter; after all, the building is specific to its creator's needs, not to everyone's.

Chapter 7
Structure

Buildings are about differentiating space, defining an inside and an outside. The world doesn't take kindly to being shut out, so you need a strong structure, a fortress able to withstand the relentless burdens of weight, wind, and the myriad other nudges, slaps, and sucker punches that the bullying world throws at innocent little abodes. We covered the basics of structure in chapter 2, but now we're talking about applying those fundamentals in the real world—an entirely different perspective.

The first thing you might notice as we start discussing the hands-on of building is that our neat little intellectual divisions—the four elements that a house must provide—don't line up politely and take their turn being dealt with. You have to think about all of them all of the time, so in this structure chapter we'll be dealing with separation issues such as drainage and termites, temperature issues such as insulating masonry walls, and connection issues such as windows and doors. Even so, remember that the primary focus at this stage is creating a strong structure on which everything else will rely for support.

GENERAL CONTEXT: STRUCTURE

Issues involving structure are sometimes the first hard lessons for the excited alternative builder who's bent on breaking away from the modern-building monster's horrible sweaty grip. When all the polemical dust clears, in many situations modern structural approaches and techniques are hard to beat. The truth is, fortunately, that all approaches to building— whether modern, natural, eco-spiritual, or whatever—share the same structural heritage, which has developed within the stringent confines of the laws of physics.

The modern human is nothing if not an engineer. So it's not surprising that modern life has contributed a solid, analytical approach to structure that has produced a lot of useful goodies such as strong fasteners and strength-adjustable, compression-rated concrete mixes. These developments can actually save resources by allowing the careful molding of materials to the structural loads at hand.

Strong skeleton. All the members of this timber frame are made of basically the same unit—a round log—yet each serves a different function based on where it's installed. The vertical logs set on the concrete foundation are *posts*; the horizontal logs connecting the posts about halfway up are beams, called *ledgers*, which support other beams, called *floor joists*, which are the horizontal logs notched onto the ledgers. Higher up, the horizontal logs capping the posts in the same configuration as the ledgers are simply called *beams*. They support the *rafter* logs, which angle downward from their attachment to the top horizontal log or *ridge beam*. Notice how the rafters have been hewn flat along their exposed faces to ready them for roofing materials.

Modern construction wasteland. Most acts of conventional building are accompanied by a huge pile of trash headed for the dump, a collection of resources that cannot be reclaimed.

However, as I pointed out in chapter 3, our modern product-oriented system has in fact created the opposite effect: a cavalier attitude toward our planet's finite resources that has created an entrenched and sinful practice of waste. As alternative builders, then, our job is not to look for radical new structural concepts but to take what's out there, whether modern, traditional, or something else, and put it into sensible practice. Keeping an open mind is an important part of that process.

FOUNDATIONS

Foundations often set us dreamy idealists squarely in the modern world, whether we like it or not. The fact is that your hip eco-natural building might be best served with a foundation made using heavy machinery and some amount of poured concrete. If you look at the majority of popular alternative building approaches you'll see a lot of thick walls, some of them very heavy. For example, straw bales are wide and need to be lifted well off the ground. The same goes for cob and cordwood—and those materials are heavy, to boot. These wall systems usually need wide foundations, which means a lot of digging, attached to wide water-resistant walls, called stem walls, that will lift organic wall materials off the ground. (See the discussion about foundations in chapter 2.)

Stone foundations are sometimes seen as the natural answer. If you have enough appropriate stone around your site, and also some skill and a lot of time, you can make a wonderful stone foundation. However, stone has its drawbacks. For example, it's both difficult to insulate and to water-proof, a real problem for designs calling for floors on grade (sitting on the ground), which includes most buildings that incorporate passive solar heating. One interesting substitute for stone sometimes used in alternative building is chunks of concrete salvaged from sidewalk or building demolition sites. The concrete, often called *urbanite*, is squared up and stacked like stone. Other alternatives include rammed earth tires, earth-filled bags, and others, many of which use some amount of concrete when all is said and done.

Personally, I'm an advocate for not throwing the baby out with the bath water. Concrete is a versatile material that's been used for thousands of years by humans in different parts of the world. There are several good reasons why it's used for foundations: (1) it can be made to order, creating a variety of structural strengths; (2) it can be formed to almost any size and shape, acting almost like a poured-in-place rock; (3) it employs widely available, naturally occurring materials; (4) it's relatively easy to learn how to use; and (5) it can be incredibly strong and durable. The downside, and it's a big one, is that concrete has a high embodied energy (the amount of energy required for its production, transport, and use) and causes pollution.

Find the foundation. Wood posts and stones work together to carry the weight of this log building. By my definition, only the first course of stones and the rock on which the post stands are the foundation, which distributes the loads of the building to the ground beneath. The rest of the stones comprise a stem wall, the functions of which are to lift the log walls away from water and insects and to distribute loads to the foundation.

Glass also has a high embodied energy, but I've yet to hear anyone suggesting that it shouldn't be used. The main problem with concrete is simply the obscene amount that's produced worldwide each year. Sometimes it seems that we're covering the whole world with the stuff. To my mind, concrete isn't evil; it's just abused. It's a wonderful, versatile material that should be respected and used carefully. For builders, that means two things: (1) design intelligently and (2) build smaller. In the end, the main factor influencing your foundation's impact, both in terms of dollars from your wallet and resources from our planet, is its size. The smaller the building you construct, the smaller your foundation will have to be.

Salvaged concrete. The stem wall for this small, round building is made of salvaged concrete, often called urbanite, from old sidewalks that had been broken up and were on their way to the dump. The urbanite pieces were shaped and then laid with mortar on a gravel trench foundation. The building's walls will be built from load-bearing adobe bricks.

New and Improved Concrete?

I don't want to minimize concrete's horrible environmental record. I'm a realist, however, and have to admit that in our modern context in many building situations, concrete remains a sensible choice when used carefully.

Wouldn't it be great, though, if we could improve it? Scientists claim they have. The main ingredient (about 60 percent) in Portland cement is limestone, or calcium carbonate. A new cement has been developed that replaces the calcium carbonate with magnesium carbonate, with the following positive results:

1) Lower embodied energy. Both cements are produced by burning materials in kilns. The magnesia-based cement can be burned at considerably lower temperatures, requiring less energy.

2) Less CO_2 in the atmosphere. Massive quantities of carbon dioxide, one of the main gases responsible for global warming, are produced in the manufacture of Portland cement. The lower kiln temperatures of magnesia-based cements reduce these emissions. What's more, magnesia concretes, through a process called *carbonation*, can actually

absorb CO_2 from the air during their manufacture and application, resulting in a net reduction of the gas in our atmosphere. In other words, rather than adding to global warming, this concrete could conceivably help to alleviate it.

3) Fewer virgin resources used. Magnesium carbonate is a naturally occurring mineral and, like its conventional limestone counterpart, has to be mined. However, because of their much lower alkalinity, magnesia concretes have the ability to incorporate a wide variety of waste materials into the mix while still maintaining strength. These bulking additives can include waste plastic and rubber, as well as organic materials such as rice husks, wood chips, and sawdust, all of which could add insulation value to the cured concrete.

The jury's still out, of course—only time and experience will ultimately deliver a verdict—but this new concrete could help solve one of our most urgent environmental problems. It's something to keep an eye on, at least.

WALLS

Most alternatives to modern construction are identified by their various approaches to walls, simply because walls are where the most obvious differences occur. That's why people call the complex interaction of many different materials, including straw bales but also often a wooden skeletal structure, a "straw bale house." However, when thinking about walls, it's wise to forget about labels and to focus on how various approaches fulfill the actual structural function of walls, which is to transfer building loads to the foundation. Let's take a quick overview of the alternatives.

Monolithic Alternatives

As we discussed in chapter 2, walls that distribute loads throughout their volume are said to be "monolithic." Many popular alternatives to modern construction, including cob, cordwood, tires, and even straw bales, can be configured as monolithic walls.

One advantage to this approach is that locally scarce or environmentally destructive materials often can be replaced with sensible, abundant alternatives. For example, earth-filled tires, an abundant urban waste material, can replace structural concrete. This is the case with the tire walls of Earthships, described at the end of this chapter. Similarly, locally harvested firewood, or cordwood, stacked to create thick monolithic walls can replace mass-produced, truck-transported, store-bought lumber used to create a skeletal wall structure. Going a step further, clay and sand, usually at least partially from on-site subsoil, can be mixed with straw and water to make cob, which then can be used to create thick structural walls—sometimes completely without the use of wood.

A possible disadvantage of monolithic walls is that the same materials installed to carry loads must also resist the flow of heat; in other words, they must be insulative. In general, though, structural materials are dense and heavy while insulative materials are light and airy. This physical law tends to translate into monolithic walls having a relatively low thermal performance compared to skeletal walls with insulative infill. One exception is monolithic straw bale construction, also called "Nebraska style." But using straw bales structurally presents its own unique set of challenges. We'll discuss these issues and compare the insulation value of our different wall systems in future chapters.

Skeletal Alternatives

Most modern buildings use some form of skeletal framing in their walls. Even the monolithic wall systems mentioned above usually utilize at least some degree of wood framing. For example, the south walls of Earthships are conventionally wood-framed. Monolithic cob and straw bale construction generally incorporate wood framing for doors and windows, and often provide only infill within a wooden skeletal structure.

We've already identified the basic strategy behind the skeletal option: take up only a small part of the volume of your walls with the materials that are holding the weight and then fill the rest with a light, airy material that will slow the movement of heat: insulation, in other words.

When it comes to skeletal framing, there are a variety of terms floating around that need sorting out. The phrases "post-and-beam," "timber frame," and "stick frame" all refer to skeletal wall systems using columns and beams. "Stick framing" refers to walls built using thin wooden columns, called studs, and beams, called top and bottom plates, that span the distance between columns. These members can be thin—usually 2x4s or 2x6s—because they're spaced closely together, usually 16 or 24 inches apart.

"Post-and-beam" refers to walls built using larger columns, called posts, and beams that, because of their greater size and consequent load-bearing capacity, can be spaced more widely apart. Post-and-beam structures are built using any of a wide variety of materials such as round logs, milled lumber, masonry blocks, and steel. Wide, strong members can also be built from components, including 2x4s and plywood. This technique is sometimes called "modified post-and-beam," and can be used to create extremely wide structural members needed in some forms of straw bale and clay-slip straw construction, both of which will be discussed in later chapters.

"Timber framing" is a type of post-and-beam construction distinguished by the use of careful wooden joinery instead of exterior metal fasteners. In a timber frame, the columns, beams, rafters, and joists are all similar, solid wooden members joined together by skillfully executed, interlocking notches cut in the wood. Timber frame structures are usually built with massive timbers, allowing very wide spans between columns, and the exposed interior structure is often highlighted with decorative flourishes, such as ornate truss designs.

As a builder, keep in mind that the line between these phrases describing skeletal wall structures can be quite blurry, and that your choices are not limited to one specific definition or another. Someone might build a structure using round posts and mechanical fasteners and still call it a "timber frame," for example. I would call the structure of our little building "post-and-beam." Definitely our exposed porch posts and beams are a textbook example. However, the "beam" spanning between the corner posts of our west wall is actually a "stick-framed" wall. On the other hand, that framing varies considerably from conventional "stick-framing," so it's perhaps misleading to use that term, too.

In the end, as usual, the labels aren't really important. Once freed from the strictures of a predefined system, skeletal framing is very flexible and can be adapted to fit the situation at hand. That's one of its inherent strengths, and one of the reasons why I favor it in many applications, and particularly for beginning builders.

Defined by connections. Both post-and-beam and timber frame structures use large posts set far apart. The clearest distinction between the two is often in their connections. *Top:* Mass-produced metal fasteners and diagonal bracing are used to tie the members together in this post-and-beam frame with straw bale infill. *Bottom:* Components of this timber frame are cut, notched, and pinned together so that they interlock, a technique called *mortise and tenon joinery*.

Thinking about Materials

Building is a process of assembling materials, whether you buy them, grow them, dig them, or find them. We're finally ready to collect a bunch of stuff to mix, nail, screw, smear, and tie together into the little building we've been slowly preparing to construct throughout this book. Let's take a quick look at the various sources we'll be tapping for materials.

Self-Produced

Far from being a spontaneous exercise, gathering and processing raw materials takes a lot of preparation and planning. For example, as we'll explain in more detail in chapter 9, we needed to start turning trees into cordwood many months before we intended to stack our cordwood wall. Similarly, as you'll see in chapter 8, we needed to make soil composition and cob mix tests long before actually building with cob. In addition, as with any other resource, site-harvested materials need to be used wisely as part of a sensible design. For example, we had enough stone on site to build solid stone walls for our building. However, stone has almost no R-value, so stone walls would be an irresponsible green building choice in our climate, creating the need for huge energy expenditures to heat the building through its entire life.

Salvage

Salvaging materials requires a unique mindset. Rather than going out and choosing things as you need them, you have to be on the lookout constantly for things that you might eventually need. Armed with this frame of mind and the two basic salvaging tools, a truck and ample storage space, the world will quickly become your oyster. The main raw material the modern world produces is trash. For that reason, the main salvaging skill to develop is a selective eye. If you collect a bunch of junk that you never end up using, all you've accomplished is trash relocation and pollution from the gas you wasted driving around. If you don't have a dry place to store delicate materials, don't pick them up in the first place. Remember also that finding and storing the stuff is just the beginning. You also have to install it. As we'll discuss in chapter 15, using salvaged doors and windows can sometimes actually cost more money and do more environmental damage over the life of the building than using new materials.

Locally produced

Depending on where you live, some materials that you can't gather or salvage may be produced locally. For example, there's a tiny lumber mill five miles from our site where we bought some of our structural lumber. The straw bales we bought at the local huge hardware/nursery chain store were produced about 200 miles away, which is close by modern mass-production standards. By getting to know the regional economy and asking the big chain stores where a particular material originated, you should be able to find a lot of local and therefore environmentally superior replacements for mass-produced materials.

Mass-Produced

As modern green builders we've decided that our building needs to have a low construction impact while being energy efficient, long lasting, nontoxic, and beautiful. Sometimes mass-produced materials seem to be the right choice to serve that complex goal. All modern materials are not created equal. For example, some lumber companies carefully manage forests while others don't. Increasingly, there are sustainability and energy-efficiency criteria and certification systems being developed to compare modern building materials. Don't just buy the cheapest material or what happens to be sitting on the shelf in front of you at the building supply. Ask questions about where and how materials are produced and put your money where your green building mouth is by paying more for responsibly produced, quality materials.

ROOFS

How's this for an alternative builder's dream: Take a renewable resource, combine it with an ancient technique for using triangles to manifest strength, and create a beautiful, lightweight structural sculpture that can easily be configured to form a roof. Well, those structural sculptures are no dream. They're called *trusses* and they make up the roofs of most of the residential construction you see today. They're usually combined with a long-lasting surface such as modern metal roofing, a popular choice in both conventional and alternative circles. A conventional truss roof is often sheathed with plywood before the final roof surface is attatched. However, if you replace the plywood sheathing with some wood planks, called *purlins*, and hang a sun-shaped wind chime from an eave, you've basically got the roof that graces many of the cob cottages and straw bale houses you'll come across.

Sure, if you have a mill nearby, you can use rough-cut material to build your own trusses or rafters, though I hope you don't have powder post beetles in that non-kiln-dried lumber. Yes, you can cut small round trees from your site and make a roof structure, but it's going to be uneven and harder to work with, which means a greater chance of leaks. If you have a leaky roof, it's not really a roof at all. Unchecked, that leak will slowly make the house unpleasant and will eventually cause structural damage. Yes, you can try bamboo or something else. On a small building in temperate climates, the amount of wood you'll be saving will be burned in one month of winter wood stove use, or the equivalent energy expended in burning natural gas or propane.

If you're a beginner, cut yourself some slack and conscientiously and aesthetically build a conventional roof. It doesn't have to be boring. The living roof for our little building is basically just a conventional roof with site-built trusses and a lot of stuff piled on it.

TWO SIMPLE RULES

This quick overview of structural alternatives has been heavily infused with my own opinions. As I've advised repeatedly, however, you shouldn't let yourself be swayed to any particular approach by any one person's opinions, including mine. Whatever the materials or techniques you choose, I'm confident that you'll create a solid, dependable structure if you follow two simple rules:

1) Think holistically. A structure is only as good as its weakest component. Strong walls and a weak foundation add up to weak walls. Similarly, a strong roof attached weakly to strong walls equal a weak structure. The most important thing about a structure, trumping materials choices and aesthetics, is that it must work together as a unit. If it doesn't, then it won't be a structure, at least not for very long, and without a structure, you don't have a building.

2) Use our collective history. Humans have been building strong structures for eons. Incredible, elegant solutions have already been worked out for myriad climatic situations and material combinations. Just look around you and use the ideas that have been proven in your area. If there's a plethora of buildings made of load-bearing marshmallows in your neighborhood that have stood the test of time, and if there's someone who can show you how to build the same, then go for it. On the other hand, unless your goal is careful, pure research, the load-bearing structure of a building is no place to experiment. Don't stray too far from proven practice, especially if you're a beginner.

Truss-worthy approach. The best and only really plausible structural choice to hold our little building's heavy living roof was this conventional wooden truss framing.

STRUCTURE APPLIED: OUR LITTLE BUILDING

Fortunately, when it came time for us to decide exactly how to support the loads exerted on our building, there were a lot of things we already knew. We knew that we needed a skeletal structure, because we'd decided to choose a different system and materials for each of the four walls. Trying to connect these different materials so that they worked together as a load-bearing, monolithic unit wouldn't make practical sense. We also knew that three of our walls would be very thick, and that all four walls—like any walls made from wood, cob, cordwood, or straw—would be susceptible to water damage. That meant we'd need to set them on wide, waterproof stem walls that would lift them off the ground.

The inherent thickness of cob, cordwood, and straw bale construction also meant that we'd need to use large posts that could be set far apart, so that we could keep the majority of the wall volume open for our wide infill materials. In addition, we planned to collect solar energy in our little building's floor as a major source of winter heat. This meant our stem walls needed to be well insulated to prevent heat loss.

The only remaining piece of the general structural puzzle was the issue of roof surface. We'd been thinking of installing either a metal or living roof. A metal roof would allow us to collect rainwater for use in and around the building. It'd also be less expensive, much easier to install, and much lighter, which meant our roof structure wouldn't have to be as stout. On the other hand, a living roof would be insulative and last much longer—at least theoretically—and could be beautiful, really tying together the building and the site.

We decided to go with the living roof, which we'll discuss in detail in chapter 13. In terms of structure, our decision meant we'd need to create support strong enough to handle the considerable extra weight that's inherent in a living roof.

THE FOUNDATION

As you read in chapter 2, a foundation's job is to access dry, solid, unfrozen ground and to disperse building loads to that ground. The specific site determines how deep you need to go to both access solid ground and reach below the frost line. The specific building design determines how wide and thick the foundation needs to be to distribute building loads over a broad enough area for the ground below to support it. Of course, it's important to get below the frost line so that no water or dampness that gets under the foundation will be able to freeze, expand, and push up on the building. This "frost heave" can cause major structural damage.

The conventional modern approach is to dig trenches as deep and wide as they need to be and then to basically fill them with concrete. The first step is to pour a foundation, commonly called a *footer*, that covers the entire surface of the trenches and is deep enough to distribute building

Figure 1
FRAMING AND INFILL CHOICES

Post-and-beam framing (top) creates a wide, uninterrupted open volume that's well suited to bulky infill materials such as cob and straw bale. Stick-framing (bottom) allows the use of much smaller "posts" and "beams," but the narrow spaces between all of those vertical members are perhaps best suited to a loose-fill insulating material such as recycled newspapers.

Post-and-beam framing with straw bale infill

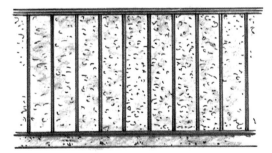

Stick-framing with recycled newspaper (cellulose infill)

loads. At this point, you can start building the walls, except at that level the footer is probably considerably below the surface of the ground—in cold climates, possibly 3 or 4 feet below—and many insulative wall materials need to be raised above the ground in order to keep them away from water. The conventional residential solution is to install concrete stem walls to create a surface above the ground on which to build the insulated walls. These stem walls are usually made by pouring concrete into temporary forms made of wood or metal, or into permanent forms, such as concrete blocks, made with more concrete or some alternative, such as the recycled wood chips and clay used in some composite blocks (see page 210).

Conventional concrete foundation and stem walls. First (left), trenches are dug as wide and deep as the desired foundation and steel rebar reinforcement is added. Then concrete is poured into the trenches, filling them, with rebar left protruding in places measured to fit inside the cavities of the hollow concrete block to come. Then, concrete block stem walls are laid on top of the concrete footer (right) and poured solid with concrete. The process makes a very strong foundation, but uses a large amount of concrete and steel.

Our Pier Foundation

The foundation we planned—four corner piers connected by gravel-filled trenches—would use the same concepts and principles as the conventional approach, but only a fraction of the concrete. First, we'd pour four concrete foundation footers, each 12 inches thick by 24 inches long and wide. Given the concrete's load-bearing rating of 3,000 psi (pounds per square inch), we knew that this would be plenty of concrete to carry the loads from our corner posts. Then, we'd build concrete-block piers atop the footers, and pour them solid with concrete. Finally, we'd create the connecting trenches.

We started by cutting and shaping a reinforcing grid of steel rebar for each of the footers, using the techniques shown in the photos below. Then, using plywood forms to define them, we poured the footers. It would've taken 24 bags of concrete mix to create our pads. Instead, we had a mixing truck deliver and pour the concrete. Even with the delivery fee, it was only a bit more expensive and saved us about a day of work. We ordered a relatively dry mix, because the drier the concrete, the stronger it will be.

Because our site's east and west sides were at different levels, we had to plan carefully before we dug and poured the footers so that all four finished piers would end up at the same height, as shown on page 152. We used our transit to help us keep an eye on our goal: the line that defined the desired level of the top of the stem walls.

▲ **Step 1.** Our first job was to make four grids like this one. Rebar cut to length and wired together in this overlapping square pattern would provide the tensile reinforcement for each of our four concrete footer pads.

▲ **Step 2.** First, we measured the rebar and marked the lengths using a piece of soapstone.

◄ **Step 3.** A manual rebar cutter and bender, available at most rental stores, is a great tool. It both cuts and bends steel.

Optional tools. If you can't find a rebar cutter, you can use an inexpensive metal-cutting blade on a circular saw. *Always* wear goggles when you're using a power saw! You can use wire and pliers to bind rebar pieces together, but ready-made rebar ties and this simple twisting tool work much better.

▲ **Step 4.** After we'd cut the rebar to length we simply laid out the squares and bound the rebar together with the wire ties.

Is Rebar Green?

Foundation materials redistribute to the ground all the varied loads that push and pull on a building, so they have to be extremely durable and strong. The concrete in footers is inherently strong when pushed (compression) but weak when pulled (tension). A thin steel rod, on the other hand, is very strong in tension—in other words, you can't pull it apart—but weak in compression. If you embed a grid of steel into wet concrete, the combination dries into a material with the strengths of both. The thin, ribbed steel rods used to reinforce concrete in this way are called *rebar*.

Many green builders avoid using rebar because it's a nonrenewable resource that requires a lot of energy to manufacture. On the other hand, rebar is usually made of close to 100 percent recycled steel, and steel is readily and often recycled. On this project, our intent was to create a building that would last a very long time. In that context, using a bit of rebar to guarantee the strength of our vital footers and stem walls, which would be virtually unrepairable after the fact, made sense to us. In some countries bamboo is widely used to reinforce concrete, and it's being incorporated for that purpose in some projects in the United States. I plan to experiment with bamboo as a reinforcement someday, but the concrete footers for our building seemed too critical a place for such an experiment. This is just another example of the many difficult, and seldom black-and-white, decisions a green builder must make.

▲ **Step 1.** We used salvage plywood to create forms for our foundation pads, or footers.

▲ **Step 2.** The rebar stake is called a *grade stake*. We drove one into the center of each of the four pads and used the transit to set them to the desired height. We then leveled off of each stake to set our forms.

▲ **Step 3.** Next, we installed the rebar reinforcement grids. We used wire stands called *rebar chairs* to lift the rebar a couple of inches off the ground.

▲ **Step 4.** We wire-tied two lengths of vertical rebar (bent at a right angle on their bottom ends) to each grid. The vertical rods would tie our pads into the concrete-filled block piers we'd build on top of them.

▲ **Step 5.** We ordered a dry mix and poured the footers. Notice the vertical rebar already in place and protruding above the forms.

▲ **Step 6.** Next, using a trowel, we smoothed out, or *screeded*, the concrete to create a level surface on which to stack our pier blocks.

▲ **Step 7.** After the concrete had stiffened, we wet it two or three times a day for a few days. This slows the cure and creates a much stronger concrete.

Fun with excess. With concrete, the only thing worse than ordering too much is ordering too little. It's wise, then, to order a bit more than you expect to need and then have some plans to use the leftovers. In conventional construction, the excess is often just dumped on the ground. We decided to make pavers from our excess, and built these reusable forms to do the job. Tim's kids helped us decorate the pavers.

◀ **Step 8.** Our footers are ready to go.

The Piers

Next, using concrete blocks, we extended our piers far enough above grade, or ground level, to protect our vulnerable wall materials, and poured them solid with concrete. To compensate for the height difference between our site's east and west sides, we'd poured our east footers to sit one block's width higher than the west. This allowed us to use standard 16 x 16 x 8-inch chimney flue blocks in combination with 16 x 8 x 4-inch "half blocks" to produce piers that would be level with one another. We stacked one flue block and a pair of side-by-side half blocks to create the east side footers, and used the same combination plus one additional flue block to make the west side footers (see figure 2 and photo, below).

Before pouring our piers solid with concrete, we had to make sure we'd positioned them correctly. In other words, we needed to lay out the same building rectangle with the same four corners that we'd laid out on the ground, but this time on top of the blocks, using the same measurements and triangulation process I described in chapter 6 (see page 133). Ideally, if everything we'd done to this point was dead-on, each corner post would sit in the middle of its respective pier. But this is seldom the actual case, so we'd made our footers large enough to allow us to shift any of the piers

Figure 2
KEEPING IT ON THE LEVEL

The purpose of our piers is to raise our building sufficiently above the ground to lift sensitive materials away from water. Because the east side of our site is higher than the west, we needed to build taller piers to the west than to the east to provide a level surface for the rest of our building. Using our trusty transit to guide us, we carefully poured our west footers one concrete flue block's thickness lower than our east footers. This allowed us to bring all four piers to the same height by simply adding an extra flue block on the west footers.

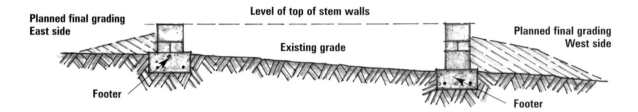

Planned final grading East side · Level of top of stem walls · Existing grade · Planned final grading West side · Footer · Footer

"Block head" thinking pays off.
Here, we're checking each of the piers one last time with the transit to confirm that all four are indeed at the same elevation. Sure enough, our thinking had allowed us to bring the piers even with each other by simply stacking an additional block on each of the west-side piers (in the foreground, right).

a few inches in any direction until we brought our rectangle into square. We also designed the piers to be large enough so that they could support our building loads even if a post ended up being set a bit off center on any given pier. This is always a good idea in real-world foundation work, because it's difficult to be exact when digging holes and pouring concrete is involved. In our situation, we were using irregularly shaped and sized log posts with no easily defined center, so having some wiggle room was important.

Keeping all of those variables in mind, we pulled tape measures between the piers, measured the diagonals across them, and shifted the piers as necessary until we'd positioned our rectangle so that all four corners were square and gave us room atop each pier to install the posts and brackets (see figure 3). Then we pulled chalk lines between the four piers and repeated the triangulation/diagonal measuring process, shifting the strings' positions as needed until they outlined the precise dimensions of our rectangle. The point where two strings intersected at each pier marked that exact corner. We planned to place each post's squared-off corner at that point and install its bracket flush up against it.

Finally, we poured the piers solid with concrete and embedded a pair of anchor bolts set in a temporary wooden holder into each pier's fresh concrete, using the chalk marks left by the chalk lines we'd pulled to help us align them.

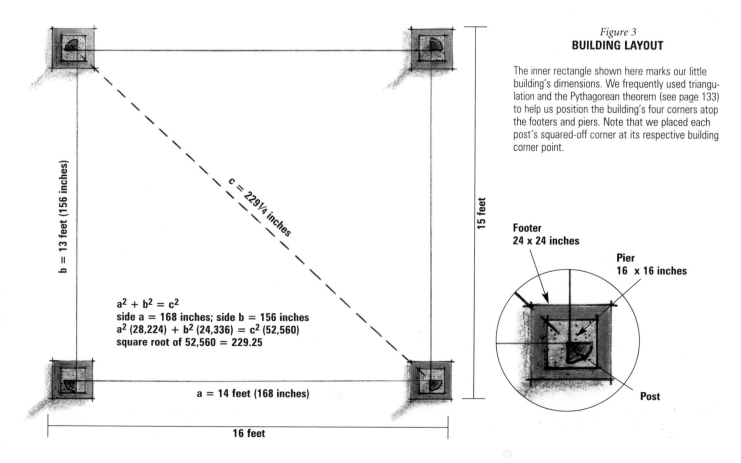

Figure 3
BUILDING LAYOUT

The inner rectangle shown here marks our little building's dimensions. We frequently used triangulation and the Pythagorean theorem (see page 133) to help us position the building's four corners atop the footers and piers. Note that we placed each post's squared-off corner at its respective building corner point.

b = 13 feet (156 inches)

c = 229¼ inches

15 feet

$a^2 + b^2 = c^2$
side a = 168 inches; side b = 156 inches
a^2 (28,224) + b^2 (24,336) = c^2 (52,560)
square root of 52,560 = 229.25

a = 14 feet (168 inches)

16 feet

Footer
24 x 24 inches

Pier
16 x 16 inches

Post

▲ **Step 1.** After checking to make sure that we'd placed our piers correctly so that the building's four corner posts and their brackets would rest properly on them, we pulled chalk lines between the piers and again used triangulation to lay out the building's rectangle and four corners, as outlined by the strings.

▲ **Step 2.** We adjusted the chalk lines and rechecked the diagonals as necessary to fine-tune the position of all four corners and create our building's exact rectangle. The point where two strings met at each pier marked that corner and determined the positions of the corner posts and their brackets. This pier's post will sit in the lower left quadrant, with its squared-off corner aligned at the intersection of the chalk strings. Its bracket will be placed in the lower right quadrant, directly across from the post and aligned along the vertical line at the intersection.

Our goal. Ultimately, here's how the corner post and bracket will be positioned and installed on the pier. Notice the anchor bolts extending upward from the pier.

▲ **Step 3.** Here you can see the blue chalk that marks the two lines that intersected to form the corner position of the post, as shown in step 2. We used those same lines to help us place our anchor bolts relative to the corner. For each pier we cut a small length of scrap plywood that would hold two bolts in position after we'd poured concrete into the piers. The plywood's edge has been placed along the line where this pier's post will be positioned. The pencil line on the plywood marks the distance from the post to the holes in the bracket. Tim is marking the spots where he'll drill holes for the bolts, spacing them to match the bracket's holes.

Deep reach. This photo shows how deeply each pier's anchor bolts will extend into the concrete. We made four of these wooden bolt holders, one for each pier.

▲ **Step 4.** At last, it was time to fill our piers with concrete. Because we needed only a relatively small amount, we hand-mixed bagged concrete in a wheelbarrow and shoveled it into each pier.

▲ **Step 5.** We tamped the concrete as we filled the pier, to get rid of air pockets. Then we troweled the surface smooth.

▲ **Step 6.** Finally, we aligned each wooden bolt holder along the blue chalk line marking the post's corner position, and used a hammer to knock the bolts through the drilled holes and into the wet concrete.

▲ **Step 7.** We left the wooden holders in place until the concrete had stiffened considerably. With the boards removed, our piers were finished, and after curing for several days they'd be ready to support the loads we had planned for them.

Foundation Drain

Once we'd finished our piers we installed a foundation drain of perforated pipe to drain away any water that might make it to the foundation by somehow bypassing our other defenses, such as the retaining wall, site grading, and gutters. Of course, it's essential for any drain to slope gradually downward from the highest point to the lowest, so as we laid the pipe we checked frequently, using a spirit level or a transit, to make sure the pipe fell consistently toward the exit point.

The Foundation Drain

Swamped. In case you're wondering why we need a foundation drain, here's what our footer and trench excavation looked like one day during a furious rain storm. I had to use a garden hose to siphon out the water. Though ultimately most rainwater will be directed away from our building by its roof overhangs and final grading, I think you get the point.

▲ **Step 1.** First we cleaned out our trenches, removing debris and clumps of soil. Notice the dirt that we've banked against the footers. The idea is to direct all water toward the drains, leaving no areas where it might pool up.

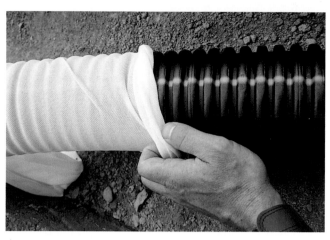

◀ **Step 2.** We used 4-inch perforated plastic pipe. It has little slits cut in it to allow water in. Here, we've temporarily installed the pipe to check the grade. We'd carefully graded our trenches to fall from the highest point, at the northeast east footer, to the lowest at the southwest footer.

▲ **Step 3.** This fabric is designed to allow water to flow through the perforated pipe but to keep out soil or anything else that might clog the pipe's holes.

▲ **Step 5.** We attached a junction fitting at the lowest corner where the two sides of our drain come together. In the top right of this photo you can see the trench we've started to take any water away that makes it to the drain.

▲ **Step 4.** Our drain falls away on both sides from this highest (north-east) corner and meets at the lower (southeast) corner. We checked often to make sure that our drain was falling toward the exit point.

▲ **Step 7.** Here's our foundation drain installed. Notice the exit trench at the upper left.

▲ **Step 6.** We finished digging the exit trench and checked its slope with a spirit level. We'll use solid plastic pipe here to carry water away. The rounded shovel made a nice seat for the round pipe.

The payoff. Here's the reward for all our work: Storm rainwater running out of the drain, safely removed from our building's site.

▲ **Step 8.** We carefully covered the drain with gravel, making sure that the stone didn't lift the pipe as we shoveled it into the trench.

▲ **Step 9.** We knew some water would come through our stone retaining wall, so we decided to add a second foundation drain outside of our trench to catch this water, just in case. The decision meant more digging, more pipe, and more gravel, but it may well also help avert some damage and lengthen the life of our building.

Tim's Take
On Sizing Up Holes

Until someone invents a precision-cutting laser version of a shovel or backhoe, holes and trenches dug into the earth for footers or other construction purposes will always be at least slightly irregular in shape and/or depth. Trying to determine how much concrete, gravel, or some other material I'd need to fill an irregular cavity such as a trench used to fill me with dread. What if I ordered too much or, even worse, not enough? Even slight irregularities can make a big difference in a trench more than a few feet long. Then I hit on the system below.

The basic formula for volume is W X L X H; width times length times height. That makes things easy enough when you're working with a uniform space. If I know, for example, that the interior of a room is 8 feet by 8 feet at the floor and the room has 8-feet ceilings, calculating the volume is simple: 8 X 8 X 8 equals 512 cubic feet.

Things get trickier when you're calculating the volume of a trench undulating through the earth. For the sake of this exercise, let's say the trench is roughly 2 feet wide by 40 feet long by 1 foot deep. I can measure the length with reasonable accuracy, but the trench's width and depth will vary significantly from point to point. If I assume that the trench has a volume of 2 X 40 X 1, or 80 cubic feet, I will almost surely be wrong.

Enough's enough? Or too much? Ordering the right amount of gravel or concrete to fill an irregular space such as a foundation trench can be tricky.

Here's the trick for estimating an irregular shape's actual volume more closely.

1) Divide the irregular shape into smaller, even sections and measure their widths and depths in inches.
Lay one measuring tape along the length of the area you need to fill. Starting at one end and proceeding at two- to four-feet intervals (we'll say every 4 feet in this example) use another tape to measure each section's width and depth in inches. Write those numbers down in your handy pocket memo pad.

2) Calculate the average width and depth of the sections.
In our 40-feet trench, we measured at 4-feet intervals, so we now have 10 different measurements each for width and depth. Let's say that when we add all the width measurements and divide by 10, we get an average width of 25.25 inches. When we add all the depth measurements and divide by 10, we come up with 13.50 inches.

3) Calculate the volume using the average width and depth, and convert the volume to cubic feet or cubic yards (the units of measure most often used when ordering concrete, gravel, or other fill materials).
One cubic foot = 1,728 cubic inches (12 X 12 X 12 inches)
One cubic yard = 27 cubic feet or 46,656 cubic inches.
Given that our trench is 40 feet, or 480 inches, long, our volume calculation would be:
25.25 inches X 480 inches X 13.5 inches = 163,620 cubic inches
163,620 cubic inches ÷ 1,728 = 94.68 cubic feet
94.68 cubic feet ÷ 27 = 3.50 cubic yards

The beauty of this approach is that all measurements are made in small units—manageable inches, instead of awkward feet and fractions of feet. Only at the end do we convert to cubic feet and cubic yards. Note that there is a nearly 15-cubic-feet difference in volume between our theoretical uniform trench and the real-life uneven trench. Sometimes the difference will be great, sometimes not, but taking a few minutes to use this method can help save you from costly over- or under-orders.

The Gravel Trench

To complete our foundation, we filled the volume of the trench between the four footers with gravel. This approach, aptly called a "gravel trench foundation," replaces the usual continuous concrete footer in a conventional foundation with gravel, a much more locally available and much less polluting resource that's easy to install. Any water reaching the gravel will trickle down below the frost line to the bottom of the trench and be carried away by the drain. No water will accumulate above the frost line, so frost heave is avoided. Gravel trenches won't work in all situations, so check with an engineer or knowledgeable builder before using one.

The Gravel Trench

▲ **Step 1.** Gravel takes on a structural role in replacing concrete in our foundation, so after filling the trench we compacted the gravel by tamping it.

◀ **Step 2.** Even though we went to a lot of trouble to install a foundation drain, our first line of defense is still to keep water away from the trench. We placed about half of this filter fabric's width overlapping our trench and covered it with gravel. We'll pour our stem wall over the covered portion of fabric, then pile dirt against the wall and over the remaining fabric. The dirt will create a slope to direct water away from the building, and the fabric will keep that dirt from entering the trench and possibly clogging our drain.

▲ **Step 3.** Here's our finished "gravel trench foundation," complete with filter fabric skirt. While we had our shovels and wheelbarrows out, we went ahead and covered the interior of the building space with gravel. This prevented rainwater from washing dirt from that area into the trenches, and created a nice, mud-free workspace. Because the first layer of our floor would be gravel, this initial gravel was also the beginning of our floor.

THE WALL STRUCTURE

With our foundation completed, it was time to create the structure for our walls. At last, our building would begin to rise above ground!

Stem Walls

We built our stem walls on top of the gravel trench. As I've said, their function is to create a surface on which to place water-sensitive wall materials, such as wood, straw, and cob.

Our first challenge was to find a material that could accommodate the thickness of our wall materials *and* provide good insulation. A conventional narrow, continuous concrete stem wall can do neither. Concrete has almost no insulation value. If it's used for stem walls in passive solar, floor-on-grade designs, it's usually covered on the inside or outside with some form of rigid insulation. One problem with this approach is that rigid insulation is fairly fragile stuff. Ants love to chew it up to form nests, and termites can go through or behind it to access the walls above.

Figure 4
STEM WALLS: A HOLE IN THE DAM?

Everything is right about this foundation, except for the stem walls. Conventional concrete or stone stem walls have essentially no insulation value. As a result, the advantages of your passive solar design and of those carefully chosen, highly insulative materials such as straw bales are greatly diminished. We solved this problem by using a lightweight concrete containing vermiculite, which gave our stem walls integrated insulation, thus plugging this thermal leak.

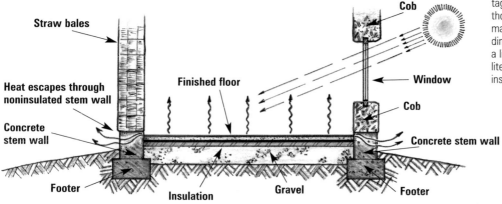

After some deliberation we decided to use a poured mix of vermiculite and Portland cement. Vermiculite is a mineral, similar to mica, that expands when heated, creating airy flecks that can replace the normal stone and sand aggregate in conventional concrete. The resulting mix has far less structural strength, but much greater insulation value. We chose a mix of six parts vermiculite to one part Portland cement, which according to manufacturer specifications, yields a wall with an R-value of about 1.5 per inch and a compressive strength of 125 to 225 psi (pounds per square inch). This is a decent R-value, about the same per inch as straw bales. However, the compressive strength is about one-fifteenth that of typical poured concrete for residential foundations and stem walls. For this reason, we had to carefully consider the structural characteristics of each infill wall. We'll go over these specific challenges and decisions as we discuss each wall in following chapters.

Before making the final decision to use this concrete we did careful research, including reading fact sheets from several sources, crosschecking compressive strength figures, and finally talking with an engineer from the vermiculite supplier. We also made test blocks using several different ratios of vermiculite to cement, and subjected the blocks to our own unscientific but reassuring compression tests, such as hitting them with a hammer, dropping them, and throwing them around. This is the bane of the alternative builder. When you're designing specific to your situation, you may come up with solutions that have few precedents for your chosen application. If you're going a slightly different route than the norm, make sure that you read up and make careful tests before committing. It's really worth it.

Preparing to Pour

To install the stem walls, we first had to build forms in which to pour our mix of vermiculite and cement. We used salvaged wood and forms already built for other projects. Concrete is heavy and can exert a lot of force on formwork when poured, so we had to make strong connections and brace everything carefully. All of the wood we used lived on to fill other functions in our building process; for example, a lot of the plywood was used in our modified stick-frame wall. To strengthen our concrete and ensure a good connection between our stem walls and piers, we added steel reinforcement inside the formwork.

Before pouring our mix, we made some final decisions about anything that needed to be piped into or out of the building—water, propane, and greywater, for instance—so that we could create forms specifically to incorporate these pipes and bring them through the stem wall instead of running them underground, beneath the wall. We also needed to make exact decisions about the size and placement of our doors, so that we could adjust our pour to accommodate them.

This extensive formwork preparation was a lot of extra work up front, but the work invested in the forms was tiny compared to what it would take to stack stone stem walls. Plus, we got great insulation and an ability to accommodate pipes and chases with ease as part of the bargain. It was a better alternative than trying later, for instance, to install a drainpipe with the correct fall by digging a trench under the foundation. And it would also help us avoid potential problems. For example, because our pipes are encased in the insulated stem wall, they won't freeze.

Preparing to Pour the Stem Walls

◀ **Step 1.** Tim marked the outside edge of the stem walls on their respective piers.

◄ **Step 2.** Next, we attached our forms made of salvaged plywood and 2x4s to the piers. In the photo at left I'm using a *ramset*, a hammer-activated gun that attaches wood to hard materials such as cured concrete.

▲ **Step 3.** We were careful to brace our formwork well and often so that it would hold up to the considerable weight of the concrete.

◄ **Step 4.** Before installing the steel rebar reinforcement for our insulated concrete, we tamped our gravel smooth one last time.

Bend steel with your bare hands. A piece of plastic water pipe makes a handy tool for straightening rebar.

▲ **Step 5.** Then we used a ½-inch hammer drill and a sledgehammer to install a pair of rebar pegs into the piers at each stem wall end.

▲ **Step 6.** In each trench, we laid two parallel lengths of rebar set several inches above the gravel on wire rebar foundation chairs, like the ones used in our footers.

▲ **Step 7.** Then we wire-tied the rebar lengths to the pegs we'd installed in the piers.

▲ **Step 8.** It's always important to think way ahead when you're building. Because we'd decided beforehand where our sink would be, we were able to install our water supply and drainpipes inside the stem wall. The wood blocks on top of the form would hold the pipes in place during the pour.

◀ **Step 9.** We also installed a plastic-pipe "chase," or hollow cavity, for our propane line to the cookstove and backup heater. We put in a similar chase for electrical wires, just in case we ever decide to add a photovoltaic system to our little building.

Figure 5
PLANNING AHEAD

It's a good idea to lift wall materials off the interior floor by setting the finished floor level a bit below the top of the stem wall. This not only looks better, but will protect your walls if you ever have a leaking water pipe, for example. You'll be able to visually check for any termites that might make it around your termite barrier, too. However, setting the floor lower also means that the section of the stem wall at the door must be poured lower than the rest of the stem wall, to allow the threshold to lie level with the floor. This requires planning ahead (where will the doors be? how thick will the threshold be?) and creating forms to accommodate those plans before the concrete is poured. You can't adjust that stem wall once it's in place. See photo, below.

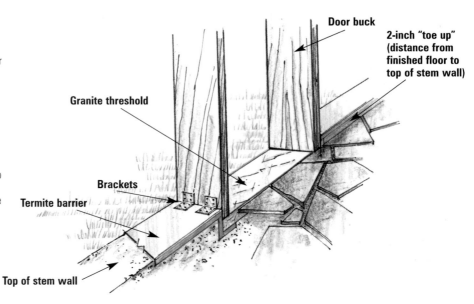

Door buck

2-inch "toe up" (distance from finished floor to top of stem wall)

Granite threshold

Brackets

Termite barrier

Top of stem wall

Future notch. This may look complicated, but it's really just a box dropped partially into the form to keep concrete below it, creating a big notch in the poured stem wall where our doors will be.

Pouring the Stem Walls

With our forms set, we were ready to pour our insulated concrete—but we couldn't, because we didn't have the vermiculite we needed. Our innovative stem walls turned out to be a good example of the ups and downs of trying to find and use alternative building materials. Vermiculite is sold in different forms for different uses, including as a soil amendment and as a dry insulation infill for concrete blocks. By doing some research, we found out that the block-infill type, though readily available, is sprayed with a silicone coating to prevent it from taking on water—a property that isn't desirable if you're trying to bind the stuff with cement.

We also discovered that there's a vermiculite product that's designed specifically for use in making insulated concrete. It includes an air-entraining agent that causes the mix to be permeated by tiny air bubbles, thereby increasing its insulation value.

Unfortunately, this material had to be special ordered, and a minimum quantity was required. We ended up having to buy twice as much as we needed, and lost construction time waiting for delivery. (We made good use of the waiting time, though, by going ahead and building our roof trusses; see page 179). Still, there was no way to know how the quick solution, the more widely available block-infill type, would perform. And once installed, our stem walls would be literally set in stone. I'm sure we made the right decision.

The logistics of working with insulated concrete also turned out to be different. Insulated concrete is supposed to be mixed for only a short period before placement, so it can't be delivered premixed like conventional concrete. We had to order a concrete truck with a specific amount of water and nothing else. We then poured bags of cement and vermiculite into the truck's tumbler on-site, mixed it for five minutes, and then placed it in our forms.

Here's the good news for anyone used to dealing with conventional concrete: vermiculite concrete is a dream to work with. It's much lighter and spreads like butter. In fact, because of its lightness we probably didn't need to build our forms as strong as we did. However, if you've ever experienced a form blow-out during a concrete pour, you know that taking a chance really isn't worth it.

One closing caveat: this was the first time we used this concrete mix in this context. Theoretically, it should create the insulation that we planned, but in reality we have to acknowledge that it's an experiment. Only the performance of the finished building over time will tell us if this approach has merit.

Pouring the Stem Walls

▲ **Step 1.** We checked our finished forms carefully to make sure everything was in place and ready to go, with good, secure connections and solid bracing.

▲ **Step 2.** After mixing the cement and vermiculite with water on-site, we transferred the concrete to our forms both directly, using the truck's hopper, and by the wheelbarrow load.

◄ **Step 3.** Vermiculite concrete is very light and easy to move, but it doesn't flow like conventional concrete, so filling the forms required a lot more pushing around and patting down.

Like buttah. Containing a special vermiculite that entraps tiny air bubbles, the insulated concrete mixture was light and airy, with a consistency more akin to butter or whipped cream than to conventional concrete.

◄ **Step 4.** Insulated concrete cures slowly and while curing can be damaged by rain, so we covered it to protect it.

◄ **Step 5.** We removed the forms after three days. Notice that the structural, noninsulative, conventional concrete piers are placed to the outside and are therefore surrounded by the insulative stem wall concrete.

Tim's Take
On Moving Heavy Things

"Give me a lever long enough and a place to stand, and I will move the world."

Archimedes, 230 B.C.

One of my first construction jobs was in the summer of 1973, when I was in what my parents liked to refer to as "your mountain man phase." I worked for a company that made custom log cabins. We bought lengths of timber from a guy named Bob, who had a chain saw and a cherry picker (a truck with a long hydraulic arm). He kept us supplied with the logs that we milled into parts for cabins.

Moving all of that wood was no easy feat. Once off of the truck, it had to be stacked and sorted. I was about 19 years old at the time and rather full of myself, and I was able to throw the logs around like matchsticks—at least for a little while. Early in my employment, the company's owner came up to me and told me in simple terms what he thought of my brute-strength efforts. To put it politely, he thought I was a #*&$# idiot. *Don't use your back, you #%^$! Use your head!* he ever-so-delicately counseled. It was the best advice he could've given me. He proceeded to teach me how to move 300-pound logs effortlessly by rolling them and using their balance point to lever them wherever I wanted to put them. I was able to move just as many logs as I had before—in one-tenth of the time and with one-tenth of the effort.

Building almost anything involves lifting or moving weighty stuff—beams, blocks, posts, and lots more. So I offer the same advice to you that my old boss passed along to me: don't use your precious back to move heavy things. Use your head—plus, perhaps, the help of a few handy devices.

Lever

One of the simplest and most powerful tools for moving heavy things is the basic lever. A pry bar is a lever used to pry two pieces apart. A crowbar is a longer lever designed for heavier prying or lifting. Today, I used a 4-foot piece of 2x4 to flip over 600-pound beams with one hand, and I was able to do it not because I'm that strong, but because I let the lever multiply my strength.

The whole idea with levers and other devices is to create a mechanical advantage. If I can exert 200 pounds of force and want to move something that weighs 600 pounds, I need a mechanical advantage of at least three to one, or better yet four or more to one, so that I don't end up with a hernia or ruptured disc.

As you can see from the illustrations, the distance between the lever's ends and the fulcrum is the key. There's a direct correlation between the ratio of lengths and the force required to move a given weight a certain distance. For example, in the sketch of the 2:1 lever, the ratio of 20 inches to 10 inches produces a 10 to 5 (or 2 to 1) relationship. If you push the right side of the lever down 2 inches with 5 pounds of force, the left (10-pound) side will rise 1 inch.

LEVERS AND PULLEYS

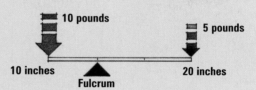

2:1 LEVER

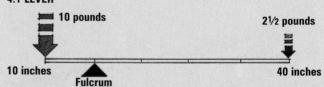

4:1 LEVER

Block and Tackle

Generally, while levers are used to move things apart; a block and tackle—a configuration of rope and pulleys put together to achieve a specific mechanical advantage—is used to lift, or bring items together. Pulleys have the capacity of multiplying your effort much like a lever. Not accounting for friction, I can raise 10 pounds with just over 5 pounds of force because the line I'm pulling with 5 pounds of effort will

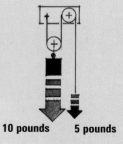

BLOCK AND TACKLE

move 2 feet for every foot the 10 pounds goes up. The more pulleys you add to the configuration, the higher the mechanical advantage. I have an assortment of pulleys that allow me to pull, or lift, up to 2,000 pounds by myself.

Rope and Knots

Whether you're using a block and tackle or simply need to haul a heavy item a few feet up or along the ground, you'll need rope and the ability to tie it into a secure knot. For good all-around rope, I suggest a minimum ½-inch-diameter braided line. A "yacht weave" braid is most comfortable on the hands. Avoid three-strand rope; it'll make a mess of your palms in short order.

In my opinion, you cannot work safely in construction if you don't know at least a few fundamental knots. At the very least, learn to tie a bowline and a clove hitch quickly and correctly.

For general all-around use, the bowline is the easy-to-tie knot of choice. It creates a tight, secure loop that you can tie around objects or simply tie at one end of a rope to slip over a pole, peg, or nail.

The best time to use a clove hitch rather than a bowline is when you want the rope to grip tightly around the object. Clove hitches cinch themselves down and don't allow the object to slip out (see photo, below).

Both kinds of knots are not only easy to tie, but also easy to *untie*, even after being subjected to heavy loads.

Common Sense

Finally, don't forget to put plain old common sense to work.

When you absolutely have to lift a heavy (but not too heavy!) object without mechanical help, squat down, get a good grip on the object, and—while keeping your back and neck straight, as perpendicular as possible to the ground or floor— stand straight up, lifting with your legs, not your back.

If you have a large amount of material to move from one place to another, and you have to do it by hand, do it sensibly: rather than carry all you possibly can at a time in 20 trips, carry half as much at a time in 40 trips. Pace yourself, in other words. The job will still get done, and you will still be intact.

Above all, regardless of the situation, never forget my boss's simple advice. Make it your construction-site mantra: brain, not back; brain, not back; brain, not back. There is nothing that can be accomplished with brute force that cannot be done more safely and expeditiously by applying a bit of brain power.

CLOVE HITCH

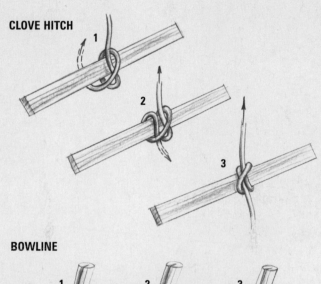

BOWLINE

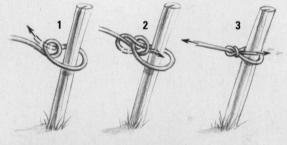

Know your knots. A basic knowledge of knots can make many construction tasks easier. Here, we're using a clove hitch and sturdy rope to hoist a heavy roof truss into place.

Our Termite Barrier

So far, so good. We'd not only built a good, solid foundation and stem walls, but in the process we'd improved on conventional approaches by using a lot less concrete while creating waterproof stem walls with integrated insulation. Up to this point, we'd used only materials that are highly durable in the face of the forces of decay. From here on up, though, we'd be building the basic framework of our walls using a variety of damage-susceptible forms of cellulose, such as wood, straw, and recycled newspapers. It was time to think about how to protect them.

Water wasn't an immediate concern, because we'd built our stem walls to lift materials out of that particular form of harm's way. Termites, however, were another matter. The kind in our area live in the ground and dig tunnels outward from their nest in a constant search for cellulose to eat. The insects can't survive very long in sunlight, but that doesn't stop them from finding food aboveground in the face of a barrier such as, say, a stem wall. They simply build hollow dirt tubes and crawl through them to take their search for cellulose higher.

We've already discussed physical termite barriers in chapter 3 (see page 61). Unfortunately, neither of the alternative methods I mentioned there—an impassable fine-mesh screen and a special-size sand that termites can't carry away or use to build tunnels—is widely available in the U.S. We couldn't find either in our part of the country, so we chose the next best thing: a termite shield on top of the stem wall.

The concept behind a termite shield, or barrier, is to bring termites out into the open so that they have to build tunnels, thus revealing their presence. Our main barrier, then, is the height of the stem wall. In order to crawl up the stem wall in search of food, termites will be forced to create dirt tunnels that we'd be able to see. There exists, however, one possible chink in the armor: termites can make their way through tiny cracks in concrete, so conceivably they could go right into the stem wall and up through it to the building's cellulose without anyone ever seeing them. We solved that problem by installing our metal shield over the top of our stem wall and down around both edges, to force any termites searching upward through the concrete to build a visible tunnel around the shield.

This approach allows you to do nothing until you see evidence that termites are around; then you can take steps to deal directly with the bugs. Destroying their tunnels could conceivably work, or you could install bait stakes that trick termites into carrying a substance back to the nest that will sterilize the queen and eventually eradicate the nest.

A termite barrier is a huge improvement over the conventional approach of broadcasting a coating of chemical treatment everywhere termites might conceivably gain access to the building. Conventional termite shields, however, are usually made of overlapping thin sheet metal, a code-approved practice that nonetheless leaves open the possibility that termites could pass around the lap seams completely undetected. As I've said, the whole point and only reason for a termite barrier is to force the termites out into the open.

That's why we decided to take the extra steps of soldering any and all seams when installing our barrier. Because it requires using some special techniques, such as soldering stainless steel, our termite barrier may be too advanced for the beginner. On the other hand, if you choose to try using a barrier like ours and don't have the necessary skills yourself, you can probably get help from someone who does; just show that person the how-to sequence that follows.

Before you take any measures, however, do some research. Termites may not even inhabit your area, which, of course, would allow you to forego all of this. On the other hand, termites might be epidemic and unavoidable in your climate, in which case either anti-termite sand or metal mesh barriers are likely to be available in your area and are probably advisable.

Perhaps the most important point of this entire discussion is that, in building, almost right is often just as bad as completely wrong. Termites need only a single gap, such as the seam in unsoldered overlapping barriers, to get in and create the problem you're working to avoid. In other words, whatever you do, be sure to do it right.

Installing Our Termite Barrier

◄ **Step 1.** First, we prepped the stem wall surface by scraping a brick across the top to smooth any rough spots. We used a hammer to carefully straighten any bolts that had fallen over during the curing process.

▲ **Step 2.** A termite barrier needs to be perfect, with no gaps. Our barrier's main weakness was the punctures we had to make to accommodate anchor bolts and pipes. At these critical points, we used a gasket made from a scrap piece of EPDM (synthetic rubber) and silicone caulk to seal the gaps.

Machine-shop help. We had the basic parts of our barrier cut and bent at a machine shop. Each piece was cut to overlap the next. After fitting the barrier to the stem walls, we soldered all the joints.

◄ **Step 3.** Because the piers jut out beyond the stem walls, they each needed a separate cap. We drilled holes for the anchor bolts and installed the cap.

◄ **Step 4.** We used a rubber gasket and caulk around these holes cut to accommodate water and drain pipes.

▲ **Step 5.** We also needed to bend some custom pieces ourselves. The device that bends metal in a shop is called a "break." We used a homemade version onsite to create components such as the one shown on the right, which folds down underneath what will eventually be a granite door threshold.

Soldering the Barrier

Soldering necessities. These are the tools we used to solder all the joints, creating a single seamless barrier. *Left:* a hot hand-held torch, flux, solder, a tinning block, muriatic acid, soldering irons. *Right:* a hot propane flame for heating the irons.

▲ **Step 1.** Before soldering a joint, we carefully cleaned it with muriatic acid (the chemical is extremely caustic; always wear a mask, protective eyewear, and gloves). Then, after the acid had dried, we brushed on some flux.

▲ **Step 2.** Next, we heated the joint with the torch.

▲ **Step 3.** Then we took an iron off the hot flame and rubbed it, along with a small piece of solder, in the tinning block. This prepares the iron and encourages a smoother flow of solder.

▲ **Step 4.** We touched the hot iron to the joint and solder stick at the same time until the solder ran, joining the seam.

▲ **Step 5.** Our joints weren't pretty, but they're solid. No termite will get through there.

Applying Structural Stucco

The concrete and vermiculite mix we used for our stem walls cured much more slowly than conventional concrete and never got so hard that you couldn't easily scratch it with a nail. For that reason, we decided to cover the stem walls with a stucco mix that contains small fiberglass fibers for strength. These mixes are often called *structural stuccos* and are commonly used to cover concrete block walls that have been laid without mortar. One coat of structural stucco is reportedly seven times stronger than a typical mortar joint. We figured it would protect our stem walls and help improve their compressive strength.

Protecting the Stem Walls

▲ **Step 1.** First, we filled any large voids in the stem wall with a standard concrete patcher.

▲ **Step 2.** Then we applied an even coating of structural stucco. The stucco goes on with conventional stuccoing tools such as a trowel, but it's very stiff, almost like peanut butter.

▲ **Step 3.** Here's our finished, stucco-protected stem wall later on in the construction process. Note the termite barrier between the wall and the horizontal board, or bottom plate.

Preparing and Setting the Posts

We were ready to install our walls' main structural posts. We used some black locust from our land that I'd cut and stacked several years ago for just such a project. Black locust grows like weeds in our region. Resistant to water and insect damage, it tends to be straight, grows quickly, and is incredibly hard. By raising them off the ground and partially protecting them with roof overhangs, our locust posts should last indefinitely.

We prepared the posts by cleaning up the locust logs and having them milled on two sides. Then, because we'd carefully constructed our stem walls and piers to create a level surface from corner to corner, we were able to simply cut each post to the same length.

Before attaching our posts upright to the anchor bolts we'd placed in their concrete piers, however, we decided to go ahead and frame and temporarily brace the stick-frame wall we'd planned for the west side. That would give us a solid, plumb structure to which we could attach our first posts.

I'll cover the details of how we framed that wall in chapter 11. For the purposes of our discussion now, suffice it to say that we framed up enough of the wall to create a surface on which to start our posts and build our roof.

Prepping the Posts

▲ **Local postage.** These locust logs were cut on our land and had been stacked outside for years. Sturdy, straight, and resistant to weather and insects, locust can make excellent structural posts.

▲ **Step 1.** We took the logs to a local sawmill and had them squared off on two sides.

◄ **Step 2.** Using a wire brush attachment on a drill, we cleaned up the wood's weathered outer layer.

◄ **Step 3.** We marked both milled sides of each post and cut through as far as possible with a circular saw.

◄ **Step 4.** Then we finished the cut using a reciprocating saw. We could've used a handsaw, but that would've been a tough job on wood as hard as locust.

◄ **Step 5.** Finally, because our posts would be exposed to the elements, we treated the bottom of each with an insect-repellant borax solution.

Setting the Posts

▲ **Step 1.** Before installing the posts we used scrap EPDM and caulk as a gasket to shore up any possible chinks in our termite-barrier armor.

▲ **Step 2.** Next, we installed metal brackets made from angle iron to connect our posts to the foundation. We trimmed away any excess gasket and tightened the nuts down on the bolts.

Step 3. We attached our posts to the brackets using thick lag bolts. Always use stout, quality fasteners. After all of our careful planning, we'd have been in real trouble if our lag bolts had snapped as we were setting our posts.

▶ **Step 4.** Use it while you've got it. Notice that we hadn't quite finished the termite barrier installation when we installed the posts. We had impromptu volunteer help on that day, so we changed our schedule to accommodate the free labor, much needed when setting heavy timbers.

▲ **Step 5.** After bolting a post to its pier, we moved the upper end as necessary until the post was plumb from top to bottom, then attached temporary bracing to hold it in position. This fancy Japanese plumb bob (left) holds a string 2 inches out from the surface. We simply pushed the post around until the bob hung 2 inches away at the other end (right). Notice the diagonal bracing in these photos. The horizontal 2x10 attached to the top of the post in the left photo is the temporary "header," or support, that we installed between posts on the east side to hold our roof until the wall's cordwood infill could take over the job.

Braced west wall. This is the beginning of our stick-framed west wall, which we created at this stage to provide a supporting structure for our first posts and for the roof's west side. We'll cover this framing, and our method for distributing loads evenly across the stem wall, in chapter 11.

Load-Bearing Walls

Our building's simple gable roof design distributes almost all of its loads onto only two (the east and west) walls (see figure 7 on page 182). We knew that our insulated stem wall didn't have the compressive strength to accept a concentrated load on one spot, also called a *point load*, so we could place load-bearing posts only in the corners where we'd poured conventional concrete. We needed either to install a large beam to span the entire distance between the corner posts of the load-bearing walls, or devise some way of distributing the load evenly across the stem walls. Our east load-bearing wall wasn't a concern. It would be filled with stacked and mortared cordwood, creating a monolithic infill wall that would distribute roof loads evenly over its stem wall without creating any point loads. All we needed to do was install a strong temporary beam, or *header*, to carry the roof loads until we could build the cordwood wall to permanently accept those loads.

The west wall, however, demanded more attention. We'd framed it up so that each roof truss would be supported by a thin column. In this configuration, the heavy living roof load would be transferred to our stem wall at two concentrated points—the middle two columns, made of double 2x6s (see figure 7)—thus putting more compressive pressure on that wall than it could likely stand. Our solution, which I'll describe in detail in chapter 11 when we discuss the specifics of our stick-framing, was to make the entire wall into a truss that would transfer all of the applied loads to the strong concrete piers on which our corner posts stand.

THE ROOF STRUCTURE

Our roof structure had to serve roles of both form and function. On the one hand, it had to be very strong to carry the weight of our heavy living roof. On the other hand, it would play a major role visually: its huge overhangs would dominate the building's profile, and the roof's structural members would be exposed both on the interior and exterior, requiring that their configuration be aesthetically pleasing.

Our solution was to create simple, elegant trusses that are very stout, so that they could be spaced far from each other. We chose a low 1.25:12 pitch, which means that our roof rises 1¼ inches in height for every 12 inches of its length. We knew that this low pitch would make it easier to hold our living roof materials in place, and would allow more water to soak into the growing medium.

Building the Trusses

One of the main selling points of a living roof is its longevity. Once it's in place, you hope never to have to mess with it in your lifetime. For that reason, we chose to build trusses on-site with the most stable materials available to us locally: store-bought, kiln-dried southern yellow pine. We used conventional framing techniques to create trusses designed specifically for our structural situation (see figure 6).

Building the Roof Trusses

▲ **Step 1.** Long pieces of wood often bend. The high side of this bend, called the crown, should be placed upward, since this is the stronger structural orientation. Tim marked the crowned sides of these roof members.

Horse power. We knew our trusses would be large and heavy. We only wanted to move them once, so we set up a series of saw horses next to the building as a work bench and storage rack. Once they were all done, it took only a single movement to lift each truss into place.

◄ **Step 2.** Tim used a framing square to measure and mark the proper pitch (1.25:12) on each rafter end, and then cut it.

◄ **Step 3.** We used a template, also called a jig, to mark the notch we'd cut in each rafter to accommodate the roof's ridge beam.

Step 4. For each truss, we nailed a collar tie to one pair of rafters (upper left), attached a center support block (upper right), and then nailed the second set of rafters in place (lower left) to create two strong right triangles on each side. Look back at our discussion of triangles in chapter 2, especially figure 4, to see how the collar tie acts as a strong tension member to balance out the compressive forces pushing down on the rafters from above.

Step 5. After making sure all the components lined up properly, we drilled holes for and installed a carriage bolt at each end, through both pairs of rafters and the collar tie, for extra strength. Later, we decided to add a second bolt next to the first at each end, just to make sure the trusses would hold up under the living roof's considerable weight.

A finished truss. Notice that we hadn't even poured the stem walls at this stage. We were waiting for our order of vermiculite to come in, so we went ahead and built our trusses and stored them here for easy installation when the time came. If you get stymied on one front, you have to move on to another.

Figure 6
ROOF TRUSS

Our trusses consist of a collar tie and a center support block sandwiched between two pairs of 2x8 rafters. Each truss can be seen as two trusses combined to permit a wider span from one roof truss to the next. Notice the strong triangular design. Notice, too, the "crown faces up" arrow. Long pieces of wood often bend, making a sort of shallow arch. The high side of this arch, called the crown, should be placed upward, so the roof will push down on it. Why is this the stronger structural orientation? See chapter 2's discussion of the strength of shapes for the answer.

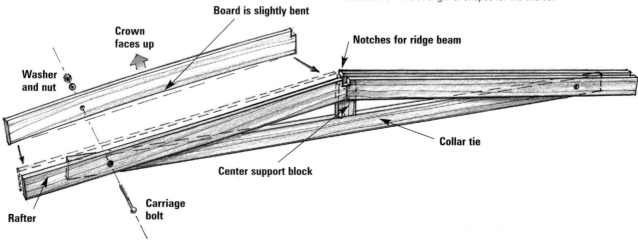

Framing the Roof

In conventional roofs, trusses are most often placed 16 or 24 inches apart. The combined strength of our heavy trusses and the stout 2x6 decking that we planned to install over them allowed us to space our trusses about 4 feet apart. This gives the exposed ceiling on the interior a more expansive feel, which is important in this small building.

Hoisting the trusses into place and positioning them properly, with all the trusses aligned and set at the same height, took patience and care—as did installing the ridge beam and boxing off the trusses' ends. But the result was well worth it: a truly strong and visually attractive roof structure.

Installing the Trusses

Figure 7
OUR BUILDING'S STRUCTURAL FRAMING

This is the basic permanent structural framing of our little building. Not shown here, but certainly present at the stage of construction discussed in this chapter, are the temporary cordwood wall header and all the temporary braces (visible in this chapter's photos) that we used until they could be gradually removed as our structure was further solidified by wall infill materials.

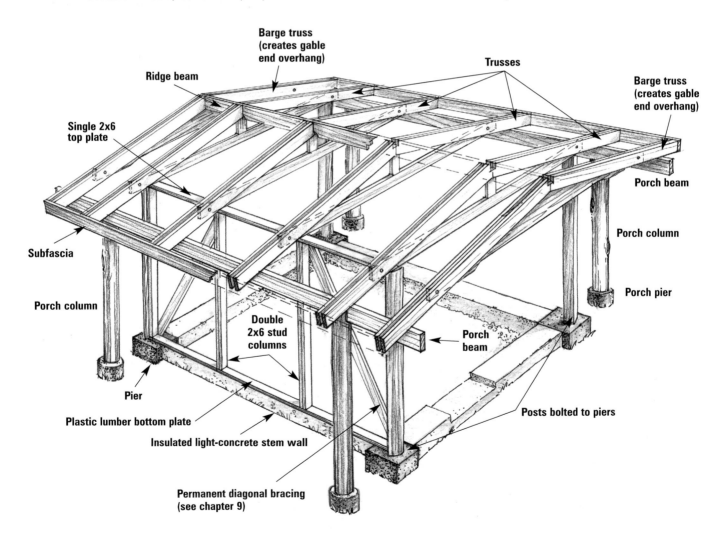

◄ **Step 1.** We hefted our heavy trusses into place one at a time, using a combination of muscle power and mind power. *Left:* We used rope to lift this truss onto a temporary header on the east (eventually cordwood) wall. *Right:* Tim used a 2x4 to skid the trusses along into position. *Bottom:* Placing the trusses was definitely a two-person job.

◄ **Step 2.** We used temporary braces to hold the trusses upright.

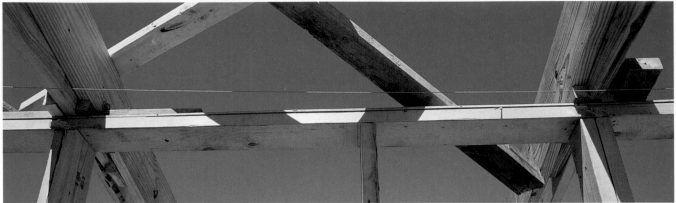

▲ **Step 3.** A string pulled between the two end trusses helped guide us in bringing all the trusses to the same height.

Wedge wood. We placed wedges under each rafter to hold each truss at the desired level.

◄ **Step 4.** Once we had the trusses spaced correctly and parallel (left), we temporarily attached them to their respective post, top plate, or temporary header (middle and right).

Installing the Ridge Beam

▲ **Step 2.** Tim cut the ridge beam to lock into the truss notches. The portion of the ridge beam above the squared-off top section of this cut will fit down into the notch in its corresponding roof truss. The curves on each side will not only add a nice decorative accent to the exposed interior roof structure, but will also help avoid the splitting that might occur over time (from normal expansion and contraction of the wood) if the cut extended straight down, tight over the full width of the truss members.

▲ **Step 1.** Before installing the ridge beam, we had to make sure the notches were lined up.

▲ **Step 3.** We set the ridge into the notches. *Left:* Here, Tim is placing the ridge beam at one of the gable ends. Note the half-curve notch and the decorative shaping at this end of the ridge beam. *Right:* Here's that end of the beam as it looks beneath the overhang in our finished building.

▲ **Step 4.** We could've used a hammer to pound the ridge beam into place, but loosening the joint with a thin-bladed saw allowed the beam to slide into position, avoiding the risk of cracking the joint.

▲ **Step 1.** We'd left our trusses long so that we could cut them to length in place. We measured down from the ridge at each end, marked the ends with a chalk line, and cut each rafter tail at the correct length using a circular saw.

▲ **Step 2.** Next, we proceeded to connect all the tails of the trusses with an outer board, sometimes called the *subfascia*.

◄ **Step 3.** Because our roof is over 17 feet long—longer than we could purchase a single 2x8 board—we needed two boards on each side to make our subfascia. We used a short board to splice these two boards together. This is a much stronger connection than the common technique of nailing the ends of two butting boards to the same rafter tail.

◄ **Step 4.** We completed the framed box of the roof.

▲ **Step 5.** Finally, we removed any irregularities, such as very large crowns, to create a uniform surface for the decking. Here, Tim uses a power planer to even out a truss member.

Roof Decking

Because our trusses were spaced so widely apart, we needed a very strong decking material that could span the 4-feet distance between trusses and still bear the weight of all of that living-roof material we were going to pile on top. We chose 2x6 southern yellow pine tongue-and-groove planking. This material both structurally ties the trusses together, replacing plywood in conventional construction, and serves as a beautiful interior ceiling.

Decking the Roof

◄ **Step 1.** Our decking had picked up some mold from getting wet in storage, so first we sanded it.

◄ **Step 2.** Next, we sealed the decking with tung oil, first rolling it on and then working in the excess with a rag.

◄ **Step 3.** We measured down equal distances from the ridge at both ends and snapped a chalk line between those points. We used this line as a reference to lay our first decking course, to ensure that it would start square to the ridge.

◄ **Step 4.** We laid our first course with the tongue of the decking flush to the outside of the chalk line. Then we ripped (cut lengthwise) the outside edge of the decking so the portion overhanging the subfascia board would be flush to the drip-edge board we would soon install beneath it (see page 192).

A time for power. Many books on alternative building wax poetic about using hand tools, but power tools definitely have their place. *Top:* When quick, accurate cuts are important, this miter saw with a finish blade works great. *Bottom:* This power nailer allowed us to accurately nail the decking in a fraction of the time needed using a hammer. Notice the tongue of one board pulled tightly against the groove of the next.

▲ **Step 5.** As we continued laying courses of decking boards, we left the ends long, knowing that we'd cut them all off together later.

◄ **Step 6.** Often we needed to close up gaps between the decking caused by minor differences in the boards' straightness. Sometimes we used a clamp (left) and sometimes a hammer did the trick (right).

▲ **Step 7.** The final course of boards at the ridge needed to be ripped to fit the width of the remaining space. Then we simply slipped those decking boards into place and nailed them down.

▲ **Step 8.** Once we'd completed one side, we repeated the process on the other side until all the decking was installed.

Minimal waste. This small wheelbarrow load of cut-off pieces represents almost all of the waste generated in decking our little building's roof.

▲ **Step 9.** We'd set all courses a bit longer than necessary on the gable ends so that we could simply mark and cut the edge in one even stroke. The small pieces beginning every other course were the result of careful calculations to waste as little wood as possible by utilizing cut-off lengths from each preceding course.

Tim's Take
On Tools

Tool (tool) n. 1. A device, such as a saw, used to perform or facilitate manual or mechanical work. 2. Something regarded as necessary to the carrying out of one's occupation or profession.

I don't know about other occupations or professions, but for any builder, and for any building project, tools most certainly are necessary. The question is, which ones do you really need? Given the vast variety available today, and the apparent human tendency to acquire tools in quantity, it's all too easy to end up with a collection that is unnecessary, or at least ill-chosen.

Resist the temptation to buy every tool you think you might need, all at once. Instead, keep in mind the old adage, "use the right tool for the job," and let each task at hand determine your tool requirements. Erecting a steel structure requires a different tool kit than what you need to cut a timber frame or to lay up cob walls. As you gain experience working on different kinds of projects, you'll accumulate not only a variety of tools, but the knowledge of which tool really is right for a given job—in other words, the one that will best help you achieve the results you want, which is the real issue when it comes to tools.

Having said that, there are nonetheless several tools that are indispensable in any builder's kit. Here are the ones I can't imagine doing without.

Level-and-Plumb Tools

Having tools to determine whether your building's components are level and plumb as you build them helps you create a structure with walls that don't lean and floors that don't make you walk uphill from one side of a room to the other.

A common spirit level is a stick that has a fluid vial with a bubble inside. These come in various lengths, from 6 inches to 8 feet. They're capable of providing good information on the degree to which a horizontal surface, such as a floor, is level or a vertical surface, such as a wall, is plumb. Less expensive spirit levels, however, tend to go out of adjustment if you look cross-eyed at them, so don't skimp on this tool.

You can determine whether a spirit level is accurate: Put it on a surface and note the bubble reading; then turn the level 180 degrees and see if you get the same reading. If it's not the same, either have the level adjusted, or bend it in two and toss it in the trash. Building with a bad level is asking for trouble.

In cases where you need to establish a level point over long distances, you'll want to use a transit or a water level (see pages 121 to 123).

Establishing plumb over a long vertical distance can be accomplished with near-absolute accuracy using just a bit of local gravity and a plumb bob, a pointed weight on a string (a deluxe version is shown in the photos on page 195). This simple tool can be helpful in hanging doors, framing walls, and transferring reference points from a high place to a low place and vice-versa.

Manual Building Tools

A good hammer is a must. I prefer a hammer with a straight claw because you can use it to pry apart wood that's been nailed together and it's much better for use in demolition and digging, among other things. (It's amazing how often a hammer comes in handy for a bit of digging: to clean up a footer hole, for instance.) The sole advantage of a curved claw is that it's sometimes better for pulling nails. I always carry a small pry bar, called a cat's paw, as a nail puller. Whatever hammer you choose, do not go cheap. A hammer is literally an extension of your arm. It should feel good in your hand. And don't think that a heavier hammer is necessarily a better hammer: In many cases, a 22-ounce hammer will do more work than a 28-ounce hammer because you can swing it faster and it will actually deliver more force to its target than its big brother. It's a lot easier on your arm, too.

Buy a 25-foot tape measure with a stiff metal blade. This may cost you twice as much as a flimsy-bladed unit, but I suggest that you buy it anyway. The sturdier tape will extend much farther before it "wilts."

Choose either a three-, six-, or eight-pound sledgehammer for those times when you need some extra oomph (driving stakes, nudging framing members, etc.).

Don't build your home without at least a couple of saw-horses. You can either buy a pair or cobble together your own—a good beginner's building project.

Those tools are only the bare-bones basics, of course. There are many other key building tools that you may or may not need for a given project: pliers; a saw with a short, stiff blade; a socket wrench; and more. As I said, let the task at hand decide the tools you need to acquire next. And when you do buy tools, get the best you can afford.

Power Building Tools

When I was studying guitar making, we had to create our first instruments using no power tools whatsoever. The training was excellent; it helped me develop a sensitivity to different woods and their characteristics, and gave me a deep appreciation for the plane and chisel. But, oh, let me tell you—when I finally got to employ some power tools, I was able to cut the time it took to make a guitar in half. I'm not saying that power tools are superior, but they certainly can play a crucial role in getting the job done. Generally, no matter what sort of project you may be tackling, the following two tools are indispensable:

Circular saw. In almost every application where power is available, a circular saw is more efficient than a hand saw. Get a 7 1/4-inch model with a carbide blade that has at least 24 teeth.

Drill motor (more commonly called a plug-in drill). Cordless drills are very handy, but if you have electricity where you're working and can afford only one drill, use a good 3/8-inch electric drill (4 amp minimum). It may not be as convenient as a cordless, but it will last longer and will deliver more torque, or turning power.

Other power tools. If you're going to be doing much with wood boards, a power planer is invaluable. You can shave, trim, fit, smooth, and shape with ease. A disc sander, miter saw, router, table saw, mortar mixer, nail gun, 1/2-inch drill—all are also very handy power tools. You can probably put most of these off until you really need them, but that may be sooner rather than later if you work on many projects. Remember, too, that most such tools can be rented—a more sensible option if you don't anticipate using the tool often. A network of generous friends who own such tools can be a valuable resource, too.

Thinking About Our Living Roof

Because we'd decided to build a living roof, which would require installing a waterproof membrane, we needed to make sure that our roof decking would be smooth, with no jutting nails or other possible puncture points. Now was the time, too, to work on the edge of the roof, to prepare for the day when we'd wrap the membrane down over it. And because that day wasn't going to come immediately, we also had to install some temporary waterproofing over the decking to protect it in the meantime.

Preparing for the Living Roof

◀ **Step 2.** Then we sanded the entire roof surface to remove any rough edges.

▲ **Step 1.** To smooth the way for installing a waterproof membrane, we carefully set all nail heads that were sticking up.

▲ **Step 3.** To prepare the edges of our roof, we first needed to make and install drip edge beneath the roof's overlap. We rip-cut lengths of composite-lumber decking to fit under the overlap, and cut a groove down the middle of each piece using a circular saw. The groove, or drip edge, would stop water from running back along the underside of the decking to the building. We chose composite lumber because this drip edge will often be in contact with water. Natural wood would be difficult to maintain and would quickly rot, but composite lumber (made from plastic and wood waste) is virtually unaffected by water, sun, and insects.

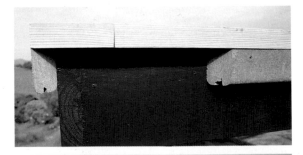

▲ **Step 4.** Then we installed the drip edge under the decking overlap.

Right screw for the job. I recommend these special screws designed specifically for composite lumber. You can sink them flush without predrilling or using a countersink bit.

▲ **Step 5.** We'd intentionally set the decking a bit long (left) so that we could route the edge (middle) to create a smooth surface (right).

◀ **Step 6.** We also used a router to round the top edge of our decking, so that the waterproof membrane could be pulled smoothly over the edge without the danger of slow abrasion by a corner.

▲ **Step 7.** Our roof was ready for the membrane.

▲ **Step 8.** Because there would be a time lag between finishing the decking and installing the living roof, we temporarily protected our decking from rain using tarpaper and boards.

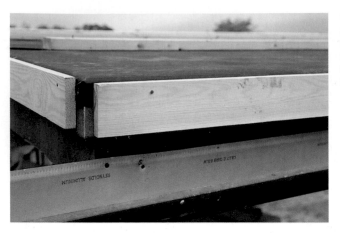

◀ **Multitasking with wood.** One good way to use wood wisely is to plan multiple jobs for the same boards. The 2x4s shown here holding down tarpaper on top of our roof were first used as temporary diagonal bracing when we were setting our trusses. Later, they ended up permanently installed as part of the structure. The 1x4s keeping the tarpaper tight around the roof's edges eventually were used as part of our straw bale wall's pinning system.

THE PORCHES

Porches are outdoor rooms connected to buildings. They often have their own roof. The porches we planned, however, would be created by the two huge overhangs of the roof of the building itself, on the east and west sides. Those overhangs would need to be supported, and because of the added weight of our living roof, that support would have to be substantial. We decided to build a stout, open, post-and-beam wall structure for each overhang using locust posts from our land and large pine beams rough-cut and green (in other words, not kiln-dried) from our local sawmill.

Pier Foundations

To build our porch structure, we first poured small concrete piers to support the locust posts and lift them off the ground, away from moisture. We poured each pier to extend roughly 8 inches above what we anticipated to be final grade (or ground level) at that particular pier's location after we'd finished adding fill dirt, gravel, and general site repair.

◀ **Goal: outdoor room.** Our next task was to create an outdoor porch/room on the east and west sides using the building's own roof overhangs as porch roofs and simple, open, wall-like support structures made of two locust posts and a pine beam. This is a view of the finished building's east porch.

◀ **Step 1.** To mark the position of our post footers, we dropped a plumb bob from the spot on our trusses where the posts would be placed.

▲ **Step 2.** Then we dug the four footer holes and placed a wired grid of rebar in each.

▲ **Step 3.** Next, we wired a long piece of vertical rebar to the grid (the rebar was L-shaped at the bottom end, as shown in the section on pouring our corner piers on page 148) as close as possible to the footer's center. Then we poured hand-mixed concrete into each hole.

▲ **Step 4.** After letting the footers cure for a couple of days it was time to make the piers. We used cardboard forms made specifically for pouring piers. We marked the form at the desired height of the pier using black duct tape, and then followed the edge of the tape to cut the form accurately.

◀ **Step 5.** We hung a plumb bob again from the truss, as in step 1, to locate the precise center of the pier, and marked that spot by driving a masonry nail into the concrete. Then we placed the form onto the footer and measured out from the center nail to make sure that the form's perimeter was spaced evenly all around.

◀ **Step 6.** Masonry nails driven into the concrete were enough to secure the shortest forms while we poured the concrete and let it cure.

▲ **Step 7.** We added bracing to support the form for the southwest pier, which was the tallest because the final grade level would be raised substantially here during final site work.

▲ **Step 8.** After the concrete had cured for two days we simply cut off the cardboard forms, and our piers were ready to go.

The Porch Posts

Though using local materials whenever possible is a fundamental concept in green building, it's important to understand that working with raw wood such as rough-cut green (not kiln-dried) lumber and logs is usually more difficult than using milled, planed, and kiln-dried store-bought lumber. Green lumber splits and moves as it dries out, and logs are irregular both in width and contour, which makes for complicated cutting and measuring. As you'll see in the following photo sequences, we had to grapple with these challenges as we set our porch posts.

Installing the Porch Posts

◄ **Step 1.** Though log posts are beautiful, they're more difficult to work with than milled lumber. In order to cut them to fit, we had to be conscious of how they deviated from straight.

◄ **Step 2.** To make our irregular logs fit between their respective piers and trusses, we had to do more than just measure and cut. First, we cut each post a bit longer than needed.

◄ **Step 3.** Next, we held the post in place on its pier and marked where it met the roof truss. Then we took the post down and cut it to length along the mark. This clumsy method allowed us to take into account the post's less-than-straight length and the slope of the roof truss. However, it required lifting our heavy posts into place at least a couple of times to make sure the fit would be just right.

Step 4. We cut the rebar extending from each pier so that it was long enough to add some stability to the post, but short enough to allow us to fit the post in place. The roof is already fastened to the building's corner posts, which are anchored to concrete. Those connections, and the heavy living roof, will prevent wind uplift at these porch posts. The rebar pins here are a safeguard against a huge one-time lateral load, such as a truck running into a porch post, that could knock a post off its pier.

▲ **Step 5.** While holding the post in position on the pier again, we transferred its outline onto the pier in an attempt to accurately determine where to drill the peg hole into the post.

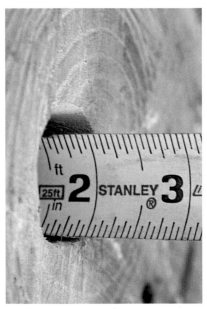

▲ **Step 6.** We drilled the hole oversized and off center to match the rebar's position, and checked the depth to make sure that the post would fit all the way down over the peg.

▲ **Step 7.** After we treated the bottom of the post with borax solution, it was ready to install.

◀ **Step 8.** It sometimes took several tries to get it right, but we hoisted each post over its peg and, after making sure that it was seated properly and snug against the truss, we drilled pilot holes and drove galvanized nails through the post and into the truss members.

Plumb difficult. *Top:* Here you can clearly see this post's curving profile. The natural contours of the locust logs we used are aesthetically pleasing but made installation tricky. *Bottom:* Even with all of our careful work, this irregular log didn't bear evenly on its pier.

▲ **Step 9.** To fill in any gaps at a post's bottom end, we drove in a shim cut from the same material and chiseled off the excess. Though it was a lot of work, getting our posts tightly installed, well off the ground, was worth it. They should last indefinitely.

▲ **Step 10.** As a final nod to longevity, we painted all of our posts, including the four corner posts, with borax preservative.

Time Out for Site Repair

Building can become a steam engine moving you from one detail to the next. The goal, though, is to create an entire place, so you have to constantly remind yourself to step back and consider the bigger picture. For example, with our porch piers and posts set, we were ready to install a long beam between each pair of posts to help support the living roof. On the other hand, our porch piers were the final bit of grade-level work we needed to do, so we decided it'd be a good time to turn our attention temporarily to grading and site repair. By choosing to go ahead and create much of the final grading now, we could ensure that the land was sloped properly to keep water away, and we could also get a jump on planting, so that we'd have our grass growing and protecting the soil sooner. Because we planned to create a patio around the entire building eventually, including a large courtyard to the north, we could also go ahead and put down a gravel substrate for the patio that would eliminate mud from the building site and make the whole process of construction easier and more pleasant.

Grading and Site Repair

◄ **First things first.** With the porch posts set we were ready to install supporting beams between them, but we decided that final grading was a more pressing matter. Earlier, we'd had to dig a temporary trench to remove water pooling around the northwest footer.

◄ **Step 1.** All around the building we added dirt to make sure that water flowed away from the structure. Here on the north side, you can clearly see how the dirt is higher at the east end (background) than on the west (foreground).

▲ **Step 2.** Because we intended to build a workshop someday on the north side, to the left in this photo, we graded the site so that water would flow away from both buildings into this little ravine that we fashioned by hand.

▲ **Step 3.** On the building's west side , we surrounded our water pipes with a cinder block before covering them with dirt, so it would be easy to access them when we're ready to hook them up to a source of water.

▲ **Step 4.** We added dirt from our original site excavation to create level areas where needed, such as here, under our west porch roof. We borrowed our neighbor's tractor again to move the dirt, and then tamped it solid by hand.

▲ **Step 5.** Next, we prepared to install a tiny brick retaining wall that would hold our gravel and act as a splash block for rain coming off of the roof. There's a good slope away from the house here, so we didn't plan to install rain gutter on this side of the roof.

▲ **Step 6.** We simply lined up a single row of bricks lengthwise to make the little retaining wall. The holes in the bricks allow any water that may blow under the overhang to drain out. Notice that we also added dirt on the other side of the bricks, to continue a gentle slope away from the building.

▲ **Step 7.** To keep weeds from growing on our outdoor work and patio space, we covered the ground with landscape fabric.

◀ **Step 9.** We repeated the process, laying down landscape fabric and spreading gravel, around the entire building.

▲ **Step 8.** Then we spread gravel over the fabric.

Site for sore eyes. Notice the sloping ground. If you compare it to earlier photos of our site, you'll see how much we changed the grade.

◀ **Step 10.** Finally, we added some topsoil that we'd stockpiled, and seeded it with grass and clover. A couple of weeks later, you wouldn't have known that it ever looked any different.

The Porch Beams

The final step in our basic structure was to finish the open walls of our porches by installing a beam between each pair of porch posts to help support the roof overhang. Using our estimations of how much the living roof was likely to weigh at its heaviest, after a steady downpour or substantial snowfall, Tim consulted beam-span tables and applied his own encyclopedic knowledge of post-and-beam framing to determine the size of the beams we'd need. (Most experienced builders have developed a good, reliable feel for such matters. If you're a beginner, it's always best to ask a veteran builder for advice on these structural decisions.)

Like installing the posts, setting the beams solidly beneath the already-in-place trusses required careful effort. If you're thinking that constructing our post-and-beam porch wall structures first and then installing the roof directly on top of them would've been easier, you're right. But it also would've made other tasks more difficult. For example, it would've required placing the piers very accurately in relation to the foundation of the little building. It seemed a surer thing to us to base the location of our porch structure on where the roof trusses actually ended up rather than where they theoretically should be. In the real world of construction, tasks don't always progress in linear order, and decisions aren't always black or white. You have to be flexible.

The Porch Beams

◀ **Step 1.** We picked out a couple of pine beams at the local mill.

◀ **Step 2.** An experienced timber frame builder, Tim skillfully shaped elegant "shoulders" where the beam would rest on notches cut into its supporting posts.

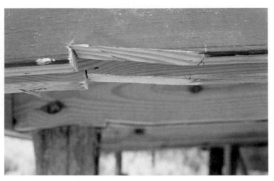

▲ **Step 3.** Next, we used a little jig to mark and notch our trusses. The angle of the notch compensates for the pitch of the roof trusses, so that when the beam is installed it will sit level to the ground, with its upper surface seated tightly against the trusses.

▲ **Step 4.** We knew the beams were going to carry a lot of weight, so we notched out a strong seat in each of the posts. We used a chain saw to make the cuts.

▲ **Step 5.** We installed the beams. The process was made much easier because we'd notched out a little extra in each post, giving us some room to set the beam in place. Then we used a shim to tighten the seat. Later, we replaced this wooden shim with a metal one that doubles as a hanging-plant holder.

◀ **Step 6.** We finished the installation by fastening the beams to each post with a pair of sturdy lag bolts.

WHAT WE'VE ACCOMPLISHED

At the beginning of this chapter, I offered some structure-related green building advice. Let's see if we practiced what I preach. Through carefully selecting materials and designing a foundation that's strong only where it needs to be, we created a well-drained, sturdy foundation with insulated stem walls that fit our passive solar design while using a reasonable, resource-conscious amount of materials. We employed a mixture of store-bought and site-harvested materials, and even used some stick-framing to create a structure that places strength only where it's called for, and redirects loads to take some pressure off of our nicely insulated but compressively challenged stem walls. We protected these efforts by carefully installing a foundation drain and a well-built termite shield that benignly redirect the forces of decay. We were neither afraid of nor slaves to modern tools, materials, and approaches, while always thinking about our specific situation and the effects of our building on the local environment and beyond. As a result, our structure is not only strong and protected, but is also aesthetically connected to our site and design.

Already, our building was starting to reflect the overall feeling that we'd planned for this place. We were off to a good start.

Our Building's Structure and Siting

These photos on this and the next two pages, taken just before we installed the porch beams, clearly show our little building's basic structure and how it works to create a commanding feeling, a presence that reflects our vision of this place.

North view. The wide, low-pitched roof gives the building a hunkered-down, embracing feel. Here, you can see clearly how the north and south walls (foreground and background respectively) won't be carrying any of the roof loads. Compare this photo to the foundation layout photos on page 134, and you'll see how much we've raised the ground to the west (right). It looks like it's always been this way.

Southwest view. The comfortable, useable flat space around the building transitions nicely into the surrounding land. You'd hardly know that we've moved any dirt.

East porch from north side. The nice exposed ceiling and locust posts combined with the retaining wall give this porch a private, sunken-garden feel.

Northwest view. Already, our grass "bandage" has speeded the site's healing and slowed any possible erosion. We'll cover the details of how we framed this (west) wall in chapter 11.

Northeast view. As you can see here, we've already installed the insulation, plastic, and gravel for our living roof. We'll cover that process in detail in chapter 13.

Southeast view. The top of the retaining wall blends nicely into the landscape. You can stand there and touch the roof, which shows how successfully our siting has incorporated the building into its environs. You can also easily see how water has been redirected away from the building by our site work.

VARIATIONS

Our structural design feels right because it fits our situation so exactly. What are some situations that would mandate a completely different approach?

SIMPLE STRUCTURES

To be frank, I don't recommend that a beginner try constructing a living roof, or perhaps even something like our wide porch overhangs, as a first building experience. What if you just want to build something simple to get your feet wet in construction—a playhouse for your kids or a one-room office in the backyard?

The first difference you might want in your design is a framed floor. This would allow you to simplify your foundation—you wouldn't need a gravel trench, for instance—and probably forgo major grading.

You could, for example, simply dig four corner post holes, set your posts directly in them, and frame the floor to the posts. Pouring some concrete in the holes before backfilling them would give you more stability and protection against wind uplift, but

Three foundations. *Left:* This cedar post sits directly on a foundation of solid ground at the base of a 1-foot-deep hole. Cedar resists water and insect damage, so it's a good choice for direct ground contact. *Middle:* A small shed's heavy floor framing has been sitting on this simple foundation of stacked stones for at least 50 years. The building's weight has been enough to hold the structure in place in the face of strong winds. *Right:* This porch floor rests on concrete block pier foundations similar to those we used in our little building. The framing is securely fastened to bolts set in concrete. This approach is more expensive and uses more materials, but it pretty much guarantees that the structure above is going to stay put in the face of reasonably foreseeable forces.

you could also do without it in some situations. Of course, the problem here is that wooden posts in the ground will eventually rot. In my experience this can be true even of pressure-treated wood if there's enough water around. However, locust fence posts in my area last 20 to 50 years and sometimes longer, a respectable life span for a temporary structure. Any dense hardwood might produce similar results.

Another possible approach is to build piers with stones or bricks and just frame a floor directly onto the piers. The problem with this is that you can't attach the building to the piers, and even if you could, the piers aren't attached to the ground, so you must rely on the weight of the building to resist lateral and uplift wind loads. You can, however, get just a bit fancier and pour concrete piers, as we did, and attach the framed floor to anchor bolts protruding from the piers. This would get your framing off the ground and protect against wind loads.

All of these methods would allow you to forgo the gravel trench and stem walls, and even the foundation drain, too. If drainage is a problem, you can always dig small trenches to redirect water away from the building, much like we did as a temporary measure before completing our grading. And if you didn't need to control the interior temperature—in other words, if you don't intend to heat or cool the building—you can build very simple walls using any of a variety of materials. In this situation, the roof, too, can be very simply framed. This would give you an opportunity to try round poles or something else fun. If you get a leak in a building with a metal roof and without insulation, it's usually easy to find the source and fix it.

No digging. The framed floor for this small timber frame was leveled by building up brick piers of different heights in each of the corners. This technique allowed the building to be sited without moving dirt. The huge weight of the timbers should be enough to hold the building in place without physical attachment to the piers. Frost heave, however, could conceivably be a problem.

Simple structure. This little building's structural design is simple and direct. The foundation consists of wooden posts set directly into the ground. The framed bamboo floor is lifted well above the ground, allowing rainwater to flow under the building—no dirt moving, gravel trench, or foundation drains were needed. The very light roof structure framed with bamboo allows for the use of thin bamboo posts to create the wall structure, and doesn't require supportive stem walls. This structural approach works well for the people it's meant to serve, but of course won't translate into all situations. For example, it'd be difficult to insulate this building to maintain a temperature much different inside from that outside. In addition, this building isn't really built to last. Strong winds could destroy it, and the exposed cellulose materials, such as bamboo, palm thatch, and rough-cut wood, will deteriorate relatively quickly in this wet climate.

MONOLITHIC STRUCTURES

I know that I've come down heavy on the side of skeletal structures for beginners, but I've also emphasized the concept of a building as a specific expression of your particular situation. The fact is, I know nothing about you, so definitely don't let me tell you what to do. This book is intended to give you information, not make decisions. In that spirit, let's look at some monolithic structures.

Monolithic Mud

Mud in various mixes and incarnations has been used for thousands of years all over the world to produce strong monolithic walls for buildings. Soil containing clay, sand, and some form of reinforcing fiber such as straw are often the core ingredients, but there is wide local variation in mixes and techniques. We'll cover this option in detail in our chapter on cob construction, so for now just keep in mind that it's possible to build mud walls very capable of carrying roof loads.

Composite Block

An approach that combines some of the qualities of modern and traditional monolithic construction is the use of composite blocks. The idea here is to make permanent concrete forms, much like conventional concrete blocks, but out of materials that provide integral insulation and other benefits. One incarnation makes the forms out of recycled polystyrene bound with Portland cement. Another uses Portland cement to bind clay-treated wood chips. Still another utilizes aerated concrete, making blocks with properties similar to our poured insulated stem walls. In general, all these blocks can provide insulation in a form that's highly resistant to sun, water, wind, and insects.

Composite blocks. *Left:* Clay-treated wood-chip blocks are designed to lock together, which allows them to be stacked without mortar. *Middle:* These composite blocks can be used much like conventional concrete blocks to create stem walls. Note that because of their locking feature, the blocks can be stacked unstaggered. *Right:* The walls of this home are made of Durisol, a wood-chip/Portland cement composite block that's manufactured in Canada. The wood chips provide some resistance to heat flow, and additional insulation can be inserted into slots in the block, thus allowing a wall's R-value to be adjusted based on the demands of the situation.

Another structural advantage is that these blocks have an interlocking design, which allows them to be stacked dry, without mortar, before being poured solid with concrete. I know of a project in which some block cavities were poured solid with concrete and others packed with rammed earth.

Nonstructural benefits include the fact that these blocks are reportedly hygroscopic—as we discuss elsewhere, this helps keep the air at a more constant humidity level, which discourages the growth of molds and fungi, thus helping to maintain good indoor air quality. These walls also have integrated skins, meaning that they don't necessarily require any covering inside or out, though they're often plastered.

Monolithic mud. This intriguing little building (yet to be roofed) is made of cob and adobe, both of which are load-bearing. A ring of cob, called a bond beam, was installed on top of the stone foundation and at the top of the wall. The bulk of the wall is built of adobe bricks. The sculptural designs, applied after the walls were up, were formed from wet cob mixed with lots of straw. The whole building is covered with an earth plaster. See chapter 8 for more about making cob and adobe.

Earthships

I really can't use the words "alternative" and "monolithic" together without mentioning Earthships. This innovative, integrated building design, the brainchild of Taos, New Mexico architect Michael Reynolds, is a movement toward a modern, indigenous building system. The design harvests an abundant modern resource—used automobile tires—to serve as permanent forms for rammed earth walls (see chapter 8 for more on this). The tires are stacked like bricks and tamped full of earth to form self-buttressing, U-shaped walls. The U's are built side by side and bermed into the ground facing south, creating a long, thin building. These features, combined with angled glass (to maximize winter sun exposure), indoor planters, solar power, and integrated rain catchment and greywater treatment, create a textbook passive and active solar design that nestles these buildings into their native arid environment.

Here, once again, we run up against our modern dilemma. The Earthship is a wonderful building because it's connected to a particular climate. A dedicated group of people have carefully designed, experimented, built, redesigned, lived in, built some more, etc. in a specific place for a number of years. The result is a phenomenal rate of improvement and success, creating the effect of an indigenous culture developing in fast forward. The climate in question is that of northern New Mexico, a very dry and very sunny place. Albuquerque, for example, receives about 9 inches of rain per year and gets sunshine about 75 percent of winter daylight hours.

The climate where I live, in contrast, is very wet and fairly sunny. We get around 48 inches of rain per year and the sun shines during about 55 percent of our winter daylight hours. It's a distinctly different climate than northern New Mexico's, yet I'm starting to see Earthships popping up around here. In principle there's nothing wrong with that. However, the devil is in the details. For example, the irregular surface of tire walls is difficult to water-proof. Obviously, that's not a huge problem in a dry climate, and the standard waterproofing method in the Earthship construction texts is to drape the tire walls with thin plastic sheeting before backfilling with dirt. That's not going to be adequate in a wet climate like mine, especially here in the mountains where underground springs are common. This is just one example of problems that could arise as a result of applying an approach that's native to one region to an area that has its own unique combination of conditions.

If you're going to transplant a climate-specific system such as the Earthship to a different climate, you immediately lose the benefits of much of the experience that went into the development of that system. It's not at all like trying to build an igloo in the desert, but there's something to be learned from that image. If such a transplant is attempted, it's up to the transplanter—that's you—to think it through completely and make all of the necessary adjustments. That's often a tall order, one to be taken seriously.

Tires as structure. Remember our discussion in chapter 2 of the strength of different shapes? Bermed Earthship tire walls are curved, thus using the intrinsic strength of the arch to withstand the mass of dirt that will be placed against them. Here, two tire U's have been capped with a concrete bond beam that will provide a level surface for the roof framing while also equally distributing roof loads to the top of the tire walls.

Classic Earthship design. This building faces south, with glass set to the appropriate angle to maximize winter solar gain for the given latitude. Tire walls, like those shown in the photo on the previous page, are bermed on their north side to key into the stabilizing thermal mass of the earth and to protect the building from cold winter winds. The long, thin panels at left are part of a solar hot-water heating system, and the panels mounted to the top of the roof produce electricity. The cylindrical shape next to the door at right is a cistern for storing rainwater collected from the roof.

Earthship hybrid. This building has many features of an Earthship but within a more conventional aesthetic. It faces south and has bermed tire walls on its north side (shown under construction on the previous page). Southern glass is placed for solar gain, but isn't angled. This reduces the amount of possible winter solar gain, but also reduces nighttime heat loss and makes it much easier to shade the glass during hot months. This feature, as well as straw bale kitchen walls and other adjustments, distinguish this building from the classic Earthship design.

PART TWO: BUILDING

Temperature

Just like the human body, a house has to maintain a stable temperature inside in the face of fluctuating temperatures outside. Our next focus will be laying the groundwork for creating this stable indoor temperature. To accomplish this, we need to surround the building interior with a cocoon of materials that are resistant to the flow of heat. Though we'll be working on this throughout the construction of our building (for example, in the floor, roof, and skin), the core of our stable temperature will come from filling the volume of our walls. In the next four chapters, then, we'll introduce each of the materials that we chose to fill our walls, give you insight into why we chose them, and, of course, show you in detail how we installed them.

Chapter 8 - **Cob and Other Earth Mixes**

Chapter 9 - **Cordwood**

Chapter 10 - **Straw Bale**

Chapter 11 - **Modified Stick-Frame**

215

Chapter 8

Cob and Other Earth Mixes

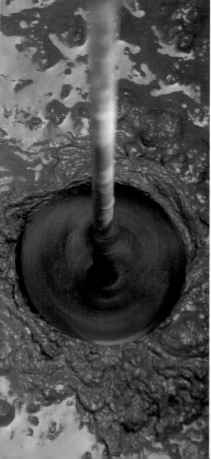

Before the advent of the hardware superstore

with attached cappuccino bar and playground, humans were stuck building houses from materials they could gather themselves. In those days, a popular building product was called dirt. You could find it almost anywhere; in fact, you spent a lot of time standing on it. By mixing this stuff with a handy material that fell from the sky, called water, and maybe some other ingredients lying around, such as the straw left over after grain harvesting, you could create a muddy mixture that could be formed into walls and that later dried to a rock-hard consistency.

Earth can be used as a building material in a variety of ways. It can be fashioned into blocks, packed between forms, or molded by hand to create thick, strong walls. It can be air-dried or kiln-baked. Additives such as straw can make it stronger or more insulative. It's this flexibility that has allowed people for thousands of years from diverse cultures and climates all over the world to find earth-building solutions appropriate to their needs.

In dry climates, a common method of choice is to mold a mud mix, sometimes containing straw as a strengthener, into blocks that are allowed to dry in the sun before being stacked into walls. This method, usually called adobe, can create amazingly durable buildings. In Egypt, for example, self-supporting arches of mud brick built 2,000 years ago to store grain behind the Temple of Ramses II still stand today, the finger marks of the masons showing in many of the bricks. Fired earthen blocks, durable in a wider range of climates, also have been used in construction for thousands of years. We use basically the same materials and technology today to make the common brick.

In wetter climates, perhaps partly because it's more difficult to air-dry bricks there, mud mixes are often placed wet, directly by hand, either to make load-bearing walls or as infill. In Europe and European-influenced countries, many earthen structures built using local soils combined with water and straw, mixed by foot, and placed by hand hundreds of years ago are still in use. These hand-molded earthen mixes are sometimes called monolithic adobe, but usually go by their English name, *cob*. Yet another technique is to weave sticks between the posts of a skeletal structure and then cover them with a mud mix. This method, called wattle and daub, is what creates the wall volume of many of the Tudor-style timber frame structures that have become the stereotypical image of Medieval Europe.

Far from being a historical curiosity, earth building is still thriving throughout the world. For example, in Africa, earth construction runs the gamut from single-family houses and simple granaries to multistory apartment buildings and expansive mosques. In the United States, adobe construction has been a fixture in the Southwest for hundreds of years and is a code-approved, mainstream housing choice today. In fact, earth building approaches such as cob and clay-slip straw (which we'll explain later in this chapter) are finding their way into a widening array of building projects in modern industrialized countries, often in places where they have no historical legacy.

International dirt. Earth has been used to create buildings all over the world for many thousands of years. *Top:* This ancient mosque in Timbuktu is made mostly from a mixture of water, millet straw, and local soils containing clay—a concoction commonly called *cob. Bottom:* Meanwhile, halfway across the world, the common bricks forming the second story of this building are made from earth, kiln-baked clay to be specific. The stones creating the first floor are closely related, since clay is produced when certain types of stone weather slowly over time and are broken down. Even the concrete blocks at right, made primarily from a mixture of limestone, clay, and other minerals, are an example of earth processed to create a building material.

Adobe. The buildings of this sprawling neighborhood in Mali are made of sun-dried adobe bricks. An earth plaster is used to protect the roofs and some of the walls.

Fired brick. The common bricks making this arch aren't a modern invention. In fact, intact kiln-baked clay bricks have been discovered that are more than 6,000 years old.

Wattle and daub. The spaces between the skeletal wood structure of these old half-timbered, or Tudor-style, buildings are filled with wattle and daub, a network of interwoven sticks covered with a thick clay-rich mix of mud. The waddle and daub is in turn covered with a white lime plaster, creating the "Old Europe" look that has become a stereotype.

Rammed earth. This building, built in the mid-1800s in New Zealand, is made of rammed earth, probably consisting simply of local clay/sand soils mixed with a small amount of water and tamped between forms.

GENERAL CONTEXT: COB

Of all the many viable forms of earth building, cob—in which soil containing clay and sand are mixed with water and straw and formed by hand into walls—made the most sense for use in our building. Because of this, and because the technique provides a good, direct example of how earth in general can be utilized in building, we cover it in depth in this chapter and then compare it to other methods, showing how you can adjust earth-based building materials to fit different specific situations.

ADVANTAGES OF COB

Cob is presently working its way into the modern green building vernacular for a number of good reasons. The most obvious is that the materials used to make it are readily available, inexpensive, and often can be found on-site. In addition, cob wall construction is also straightforward and conceptually simple: using very few tools and no formwork, you make some thick, sticky mud and pile it up.

The result, perhaps contrary to the instincts of the uninitiated, is walls that are strong and durable even in the face of substantial rain. When designed intelligently for their specific site, cob walls can withstand pretty much any punishment that nature can dish out.

In addition, cob walls are hygroscopic, which means that they'll take on and give off water vapor from the air in response to humidity changes (see chapter 3). This trait helps keep humidity levels more consistent inside a cob building, which discourages mold growth and in turn fosters good indoor air quality. Thick cob walls also are virtually fireproof and muffle outside sound nicely.

Perhaps cob's main allure is its creative flexibility and intrinsic beauty. Thick, curved cob walls with built-in niches, shelves, and benches can create a space with a personal subtlety and uniqueness of character that most of us recognize, even long for at some deep level, but have perhaps forgotten even exists. For this reason, a first encounter with a cob building can be something of an epiphany for many people, like finding something wonderful that you didn't know you'd lost.

Cob cottage. Cob mixes can be molded into sculptural shapes that often give finished cob buildings a whimsical feel.

Earth interior. Cob buildings can vary in feel from wild and free-flowing to stoic and stately. The simple curves and clean arched openings of this cob interior covered in lime plaster are at the conservative end of the cob pallet. The thickness of cob walls creates a feeling of coziness and security that's very homey. Notice the wooden steps built into the cob wall and the stone floor.

DISADVANTAGES OF COB

After that glowing description, why would you ever choose *not* to use cob? To my mind, there are two possible reasons.

First, building with cob is a team sport. Mud-building evolved at a time and in cultures where groups of people worked together to create housing. Large families or whole villages built together, with children growing up learning the techniques and gaining the experience as part of daily life. These days, however, we're often either working alone as relatively inexperienced owner-builders or paying skilled labor to construct our homes. In the first case, building with cob can become a Herculean individual marathon; in the second case, ironically, it can be cost prohibitive. This is simply because building with cob is hard manual labor, and lots of it. Of all the wall systems we used in our little building, cob was by far the most physically demanding and time-consuming. I did most of the cob work on our project alone, and came to jokingly call the process "chain gang with beer."

A second possible reason not to build with cob, at least in some situations, is that it's a poor insulator. Cob's main components—dirt and sand—have little resistance to conductive heat loss. The fibers added for tensile strength—straw, in most cases—*are* good insulators. But how effective are they in a cob wall? That's hard to say because, as far as I know, cob hasn't been tested for relative resistance to heat flow (called R-value). We're left, then, only with personal experience and theory as guides.

Of course, the percentage of straw to other materials should have a large effect on the actual R-value of a given mix, but it's hard to know exactly what effect because there are many variables involved. For instance, we used five straw bales in our cob wall and 27 bales in our straw wall to fill the same volume. If we say our straw wall is R-28—the current accepted best estimate for straw bale walls configured like ours —then the straw in our cob wall might provide an R-value of around 6, and the clay and sand probably wouldn't bring that up to more than R-8 for the whole wall. In fact, the R-value might be even lower, because the straw in cob doesn't act as a unit; it's spread out and separated by the noninsulative clay/sand mixture. On the other hand, some argue that cob buildings possess a "mass-enhanced R-value" (see the sidebar) that reflects much better thermal performance.

My advice, as always, is to do your own research and draw your own conclusions. Read different sources and, more importantly, check out some actual cob structures in your climate at different times of the year. I've done both of those things and have come to my personal conclusion that cob is a wonderful building material, but a poor insulator.

Poor insulation. Earth is dense and heavy, making it a good thermal mass but a poor insulator. Though you can hem and haw about it, and many people do, I believe this fact often makes earth-based mixes such as cob poor choices for cold climates.

Mass-Enhanced R-Value

Light, airy things make good insulation; dense, heavy things don't. This is a widely accepted truth, and it puts dense wall materials such as logs, cordwood, concrete, and cob at a distinct thermal disadvantage compared to all the airy cellulose-based infills such as straw bales, cotton, and recycled newspapers. However, the argument is often made that thermal mass materials are the victims of a laboratory testing procedure that doesn't reflect their real-world performance.

R-value—the measure of resistance to heat flow through a material—is usually tested in the laboratory by creating a constant temperature on one side of a material and then measuring how much energy needs to be expended to keep the other side of the material at a different constant temperature. Materials in the real world, however, usually face another

situation entirely, in which the outside temperature is in a state of flux. If this flux creates outdoor temperatures that fluctuate both above and below desired indoor temperatures during a relatively short period of time—say, a single day/night cycle—a material with a high thermal mass can actually perform significantly better as insulation than the steady-state R-value test described above would indicate. In this case, the material is said to have a *mass-enhanced R-value*.

Here's how it works. Let's imagine that you've built a house with thick adobe or cob walls in a hot, arid climate. On a summer day, temperatures might rise above 100°F. Because heat is always seeking equilibrium and moves toward relative cold, that 100°F outdoor heat will start moving through your thick walls toward the cooler air inside. Think of this heat as a force pushing inward. After the sun goes down, however, the

How dense can you get? *Top left:* Conventional concrete, like the mix that produced these blocks, is very dense, and therefore makes a great thermal mass, but has little resistance to heat flow. A typical mix has an R-value of about 0.1 per inch. *Top right:* Wood is a middle-of-the-road material. It's dense with a lot of thermal mass, but its structure is also airy enough to give it some R-value. These poplar logs have an R-value of about 1 per inch, or at least 10 times that of concrete. *Bottom:* This same wood fiber can be processed to make a very light, airy insulative material with almost no thermal mass. Recycled newspaper insulation, usually just called cellulose, has an R-value of about 3.5 per inch. Here, cellulose is being blown into a wall cavity.

outside air quickly begins to cool, thus robbing the force pushing inward of some steam. If the outside temperature falls below the indoor temperature, then the heat force turns around and starts pushing toward the outside. Effectively, then, the mass has prevented the flow of heat into the building and has acted as a dynamic form of insulation.

Using this property of mass walls is most feasible in climates where daily temperature swings rise above and fall below the desired indoor temperature. This rise and fall causes the push of heat movement through a wall to change directions on a daily basis. If a mass wall is thick enough, then, this movement could theoretically bounce back and forth within the wall and never actually "reach" one side or the other. The end result would be a stable interior temperature buffered from the constant fluctuations of outdoor temperatures.

Without these fluctuations above and below desired interior temperatures, however, the situation simply reflects the standard steady-state model used in R-value tests. For example, in a climate where outdoor winter temperatures often remain below the desired indoor temperature for a full day and night, the mass effect is of no value during that period. In fact, in this situation, a wall mass in contact with outside air can actually be a detriment, because once it cools down it will take a lot of energy to heat back up. If outside temperatures remain cold, this energy will have to come from the building's internal heat source. In other words, you'll be burning fuel to heat not only the indoor air but also the mass in your walls. In these climates, then, the postulated low R-

value of mass materials such as cob would likely be an accurate, or possibly even high, estimate of the walls' real-world insulation value.

Ambient outdoor temperature is not the only factor at work here, however. On a clear, sunny winter day, for example, the southern face of a building receiving direct sunlight can experience temperatures above the ambient outdoor temperature. If the southern wall contains thermal mass, the wall can become a heat sink for the sun's energy, creating a mass-enhanced R-value for that part of the building. This effect would be enhanced by an energy-absorbent wall surface color such as red, which coincidentally is the natural color of cob and earth plasters. The overall impact of the mass would depend on several factors, including how much the outside temperature dropped at night, the thickness of the wall, and the amount of heat the mass could store in a unit of volume, also called its *specific heat*. In any case, mass walls facing other than south in a climate where outdoor temperatures don't rise above the desired indoor temperature during the winter would most likely not experience a mass-enhanced effect at this time of the year.

Conclusion: In certain climates, with correct solar siting and design, mass walls can perform better than would be expected based on standard steady-state R-value tests. Similarly, other climate types and solar siting and design features can create a "mass-*reduced* R-value" in those same mass walls. In plain English: "Mass-enhanced R-value" is not a property of a given material, but, if possible at all in a given situation, the result of careful design. For the owner-builder, unless emulating local buildings that clearly exhibit the effect, depending on creating a "mass-enhanced R-value" is probably a crapshoot at best.

When mass becomes insulation. The thermal mass of these thick adobe walls helps keep interior temperatures cooler in this desert climate because outside temperatures go through a predictable daily cycle: very hot during the day and cool at night. As a result, these walls are probably providing a mass-enhanced R-value—a real world R-value that's higher than would be measured if they were tested in a lab. Other factors, such as the shade created by the clustering of buildings, very low regional rainfall, the fact that earth is the main building material available in the area, and cultural acclamation to higher indoor temperatures, also contribute to the efficacy of this building approach in this particular situation.

DOES COB FIT YOUR SITUATION?

Cob and other mud-building techniques are historically most prevalent in hot, dry climates where the mud mixes are not exposed to constant rain and where their mass can more easily be a helpful part of creating a desired interior temperature. (See the sidebar Mass-Enhanced R-Value, page 221). On the other hand, cob has been widely used in very durable buildings in wet, cool European climates. Building roofs with good overhangs, lifting cob off the ground, and covering it with protective plaster can shield cob from rain and make it durable. In fact, well-constructed, well-designed cob is, in my mind, the most durable wall material we cover in this book. The question remains: Is cob right for you?

The cob renaissance is populated with dedicated, wonderful people who disagree with what I see as possible disadvantages connected with using cob. In fact, they express the opposite belief: that working with cob is fun and accessible to all, and that the end result is a low-impact, energy-efficient, immensely comfortable, incredibly inexpensive home. I think we're both right.

All building techniques have pros and cons. The measuring stick for choosing is simply to be fanatically realistic about your situation. If you're going to be working alone and are unaccustomed to rigorous manual labor, or if you need a large building, cob might not be for you. On the other hand, if you enjoy physical work and live in a cob-appropriate climate, building a small cottage with cob made of soil from the site might be the perfect choice. There's really nothing like making your own materials and shaping them into a building, and cob can create a whimsical space that's literally molded to your exact specifications. In addition, if you have an extended family or friends with time on their hands, then a cob building project might also be a wonderful social experience. It is, after all, playing with mud, a childhood pastime to which, I hope, none of us are too old to relate.

Victory over the sun. Cob is basically oblivious to the sun, but susceptible to water damage, so a hot, dry climate is a perfect match for these cob buildings.

Cob umbrella. Large roof overhangs protect the cob walls of this building built in a wet climate.

Same materials, different results. If your climate is too cold to make solid cob walls practical, why not mix things up, or should I say "unmix" things. Cob is a mixture of earth and straw. Since straw is good at preventing heat flow and earth is good at holding heat, why not use straw to keep cold outdoor air out and earth to hold the indoor heat in? That's exactly what's going on in this house in a sunny, cold climate. The adobe partition wall soaks up heat from the sun and the nearby woodstove, then slowly gives it back to the room when the sun goes down and the fire goes out, while the straw bales in the exterior walls do a great job of holding that heat in.

Still, there's the problem of insulation, which in my opinion makes cob a poor choice for cold climates. The best test is to find cob construction in your area. Talk to the owners about how the building performs, and try to visit cob buildings a few times in different weather—including at least once when it's cold. If no one is building with cob in your area, the burden is on you to figure out why. Maybe people haven't caught on yet, or perhaps cob just isn't right for your climate or region. If you design carefully, are sure your cob will keep you warm when it's coldest in your area, are up for the physical challenge, and have a good source of clay, sand, and straw, then cob most definitely can serve you well.

WHAT MAKES GOOD COB?

In the context of building, "mud" is any mix of aggregate, i.e., various sizes of rock and sand, with a strong, earth-based binder. The different sizes of aggregate fill most of the volume, and the binder holds this aggregate together. Once the mix has dried, the result is usually a material that's strong in compression, but not so strong in tension.

Concrete and cob are both mud mixes of this sort with an ancient history. In modern concrete, the aggregate is usually gravel and sand, and the binder is Portland cement, which is made from lime, usually from limestone, and other minerals that are baked in a kiln. In cob, the aggregate is sand of different sizes and the binder is clay. Though it wasn't always true in the past, the modern versions of both concrete and cob tend to have long thin members added to increase tensile strength. In the case of concrete, the additive is steel rebar. In cob, it's strands of straw.

Traditionally, cob was made mostly from soils and additives available on or very close to the building site. In other words, you had to take what you could get. Today, because of the availability of truck-delivered sand, straw, and even clay, your choices aren't so limited. You can start with your site's soil and then, if necessary, add off-site ingredients to achieve the desired mix.

There are differing opinions on precisely what proportions make a good cob mix, and testing the exact materials to be used is a necessity because the properties of the materials themselves vary widely. However, a conceptual starting point is a lot of sand, enough clay and water to bind it, and as much straw as you can comfortably stuff in. A good numerical starting point is roughly 75 percent sand and 25 percent clay.

If you were going to run down to the Clay and Sand Superstore to get your materials, that information would be immediately useful. But because you want to build green, and thus understand the merits of using on-site rather than

Is Cob Green?

In this book, we've defined green building as a dynamic practice that's closely tied to the specifics of the project at hand. How "green" a given material will be, then, depends, to a large degree, on the specific context within which it's used. Still, in chapter 1, we defined five topics that should be considered when attempting to build green. Let's take a quick general look at cob, and by association, other earth mixes, in those terms:

1) Low Construction Impact. In many locales, the basic ingredients to make cob are readily available and don't need a lot of processing that creates pollution and requires a lot of energy. Cob, then, often has a low construction impact in terms of resources used and pollution created.

2) Resource Efficiency through the Life of the Building. As we've said, cob does a poor job of resisting heat flow. For that reason, in some climates more energy will be needed to keep a stable indoor temperature behind cob walls than would be required for many other materials. In some situations, this will mean that cob is not an energy efficient choice. In others, though—especially hot climates, or areas with relatively mild and sunny winters—cob will be a sensible choice in terms of energy conservation.

3) Long Lasting. Well-built cob that's protected adequately from water should be incredibly long lasting.

4) Nontoxic. Cob is made of naturally occurring, non-toxic materials that can work together to keep indoor humidity levels stable, thus helping to prevent mold growth and keeping indoor air cleaner.

5) Beautiful. Cob is an incredibly flexible material that lends itself to personal expression. Building with cob encourages people to be playful and create spaces that

Personally grounded. The flexibility of earth as a building material lends itself to personal expression. In this single room, clay-rich earth was used to make the bricks in the vaulted ceiling, the coils in the wall to the left, the bumpy relief in the wall at right, the tiles on the floor and on the wall detail, and even the flower vases on the table. The result is a room of vivid personal expression and singular beauty. Once built, a room like this becomes a part of you, making it difficult to give up.

match their personality; in other words, spaces that they find beautiful in a deeply personal way. This kind of synergy between home and inhabitant is important because it can convince the builder to stay put long enough to allow the inevitable intricacies of a comprehensive green building design to come to fruition. Trees, gardens, and meaningful human relationships all take time to grow to maturity. Cob construction has the potential to spawn that kind of growth.

Mud reinforcement. Mud mixes start out wet and dry to become hard, monolithic materials that are usually strong in the face of compressive forces and weak in response to tensile forces. For this reason, mud mixes often require structural reinforcement. *Top:* These long thin pieces of steel rebar will add tensile strength to the concrete that will be poured in this foundation trench. *Bottom:* Long thin pieces of straw add tensile strength to this unplastered cob wall.

trucked-in materials, you probably want to get as much of your clay and sand as possible from soil dug on or near your site. That means you'll need to figure out what's in your soil before you can determine what needs to be added to it.

IS YOUR SOIL SUITABLE?

Generically, soil is a mixture of crushed rock and humus, or organic matter. The humus is basically a thin layer on top (quite logically called topsoil), which is good because you don't want it in your cob—for three reasons. First, topsoil is precious as a growing medium and shouldn't be wasted in a wall. Second, organic matter in cob will decay, which can cause settling that might result in structural cracking. Third, the organic matter also can attract pests.

There are two basic kinds of crushed rock in soil: water-absorbent and non-water-absorbent. The nonabsorbent stuff falls into three size categories, which, in declining order, are rock/gravel, sand, and silt. Rock and gravel work great in cob, but are difficult to deal with, especially if you mix cob the traditional way, by walking on it and smooshing and stomping it with your feet. For that reason, the main aggregate in your cob needs to be sand of various sizes—basically any nonabsorbent crushed rock particles from ¼ inch down to the smallest size you can see with the naked eye. All particles of nonabsorbent rock smaller than sand are silt. Silt particles are too small to be of structural use. If they make up too much of your cob volume, they'll weaken it.

The water-absorbent stuff is called clay, and, as I said earlier, it's the binder for a cob mix. Clay, in fact, is made of even smaller particles than silt, but these tiny, flat particles absorb water, swell, and connect, becoming the ocean in which the mix's sand swims. When that ocean dries, the connected clay shrinks and locks the aggregate together. Adding straw helps to bind these many individual unions into a larger whole, linking them throughout the wall's volume, creating a single structural unity. (An important note: Remember that we're talking here about straw, not hay. Straw is the skeletal husks left over from cereal grain harvesting. These husks are rigid, resistant to decay, and unattractive to insects as food. Hay, on the other hand, is cut meadow grass that's used as livestock feed.)

The long and short of all this is that you'll have to test your subsoil, the stuff below the topsoil, to see how much of each material it has. If it turns out to have a lot of silt, you may have to look elsewhere. If it's made up mostly of clay and sand, you should be able to add one or the other ingredient to make good cob. It's even possible that you'll luck out and find a subsoil that's the perfect ready mix.

In any case, you'll need to find out well before you intend to actually do any cob building. Testing your soil, and then evaluating various cob mixes based on those tests, requires some time, and the outcome can have a major influence on your approach (see The Shake Test, on page 228). In fact, testing your soil's "cob-ability" is a good thing to do during the design phase, when you're still weighing all your options. You're not building anything yet, so you can take the time to play around and have some fun testing and getting to know your soil better.

COB APPLIED: OUR LITTLE BUILDING

DESIGNING WITH COB

Throughout the process of creating the design for our building, cob kept coming to mind. We wanted to create a homey little nest that would convince guests to nestle in and relax. If you look at children's books depicting woodland elves, talking badgers, and bearded wizards, you'll notice that a lot of these creatures are living in cob cottages. As we've already mentioned, cob just has a special aura about it that most of us relate to on some deep level. In addition, we felt certain that our site excavation would yield some wonderful clay that would make great cob.

Practically speaking, though, there were a couple of problems with cob. We had only one person working full-time on the building, and we knew from previous experience that building with cob means a lot of physical work. Also, our climate seemed a bit too cold for an all-cob building. The north, shaded, side of our building, for example, might not see temperatures above 40°F for months at a time. A north cob wall would always be cold in the winter, and the mass, once cold, would constantly be pulling heat from the inside. Cob is wonderful, but it's not worth the work if you're going to place it somewhere that doesn't take advantage of its physical properties.

We decided that the best approach would be to limit our cob use to the south wall where it would be exposed to the low winter sun's warmth, creating a situation, we hoped, that would yield a mass-enhanced R-value as discussed on page 221. Cob here would serve our important outdoor room, the front patio. It'd be nice to sit on the south patio on a sunny, cool winter day and lean against the sun-warmed cob wall.

We also had to decide how much of that south wall would be devoted to door and window glazing, since a cornerstone of our design was that the building be heated as much as possible by direct solar energy. As we pointed out in chapter 3, the surface area of south-facing glazing needs to be matched to the amount of mass in the building that will be storing solar heat. There are different ways to calculate this ratio, but we went with window and door glazing representing 12 percent of our floor area, which would be made up of a 4-inch-thick thermal mass consisting of salvage slate over sand. We derived this percentage from information adjusted to our climate that we'd gotten from the state-funded solar energy center for our region. These calculations may sound too technical for what you've envisioned as a whimsical building process, but the long and short of it is that you're almost certainly going to tend to put in too much glass unless you do calculations that force you to go against your instincts. Too much glass means overheating during the day and quick heat-loss at night.

Because we planned four different wall systems for our little building, we needed to think, too, about the order of construction and how the different systems would integrate with each other. One important consideration was that we wanted to plaster all of the walls at the same time. Cob needs to dry quite a while before being plastered. Straw bales, on the other hand, are better plastered immediately after installation. So we decided to build with cob first and straw bale last.

TESTING OUR SOIL

Long before committing to using cob in our building, we tested the soil on our site to make sure it had sufficient clay content. In our location, as in most, sand is easy and inexpensive to purchase, but clay is not, so we knew it was important to find a good source of clay that we could access ourselves. Our first soil test was very simple: we dug up some dirt where we intended to excavate and looked at it. We found a very thin layer of black topsoil on top of red, hard-yet-creamy subsoil. It sure looked like clay, which was good news and enough information to warrant more testing.

The Shake Test

For our next test, we took a sample into the lab. Our soil-testing laboratory consisted of a glass jar, some water, and a spoonful of dish soap. With this equipment we performed a simple analysis, often called the shake test, to get a rough determination of our soil's composition. The goal of this test is to separate the gravel, sand, silt, and clay in the soil to get an idea of what percentage of each the soil contains.

Here's how it works. We put a well-crushed sample of soil in a jar, soak it in water, then shake it vigorously. After shaking, soil particles will settle by size. First, the particles useful as aggregate—small rocks and sand—will settle out. The particles too small to use as aggregate, silt, will settle next, with the tiny clay flakes finally coming to rest after that.

However, these layers can be hard to distinguish because particles of both silt and clay are too small to see with the naked eye. In some soils this isn't a problem because the clay is a distinctly different color than the sand and silt. In this case, after everything has settled, the sand layer will be the visible particles, the silt will be the next layer that is probably the same color but without visible particles, and the clay will be the different-colored layer on top.

If your soil doesn't have this convenient color difference, then you'll have to resort to very rough estimates. In general, the sand particles will settle after about 5 seconds, all the silt will have settled in about 15 minutes, and the clay will be everything that settles after that. If you make marks on your jar recording the settling at those time intervals, you'll have a rough graphic estimate of the percentage of each material in your soil sample.

Obviously, this procedure won't get the Nobel Prize for science, but it *did* provide an easy test to decide if our soil was worth messing with. We knew that silt is too small to be of use as structural aggregate, so if it took up too much of the volume of the soil, it could severely weaken our mix. If there wasn't a lot of silt and there was a decent amount of clay, we figured we ought to be able to adjust our soil by adding sand to make a good cob mix. If the result had been unclear, we'd have done another shake test. We could also have compared soils from different spots on our site by doing a series of tests. Any soil that isn't clearly a washout is probably worth graduating to the next series of tests.

Based on our shake test, it seemed our soil had about 30 percent sand, very little silt, and around 70 percent clay. As we said before, a good starting point for a cob mix would be 75 percent sand and 25 percent clay, so these results indicated that our soil would need sand, but had enough clay to make good cob. Our first test, the visual inspection, had told us the same thing, so we were starting to become confident that we were on the right track.

▲ **Step 1.** We filled our jar about one-third full with a sample of subsoil. The whole point of this test is to separate all of the soil's sand, silt, and clay particles, so we didn't want any lumps remaining in the jar after it was shaken. Our soil was very clumpy, so we had to break it up quite a bit before putting it in the jar.

▲ **Step 2.** Next, we poured in enough water to fill the jar almost completely. We also added a teaspoon of liquid soap to help the clay in the sample settle out more quickly. A spoonful of salt has the same effect. We let the soil soak for a while to soften it up before performing the test.

▲ **Step 3.** We put a lid on the jar and shook it vigorously for at least a full minute, and then set the jar down immediately on a level surface. Here, you can already see the sand layer settling on the bottom.

◄ **Step 5.** After everything had settled out, we made an estimate of the relative proportions of the materials in our sample. The sand line we'd marked with a pen on the jar seemed to represent about 30 percent of the settled material and, since we had decided that we had little silt, we assumed that the rest, or about 70 percent, was clay.

▲ **Step 4.** After about five seconds, we marked the level of the particles that had come to rest. This line will roughly represent the sand content of our soil sample. After about 15 minutes, very little else had settled out, so we assumed that we had little silt and that almost everything above our mark would be clay. Since the clay is so fine, it can slowly sift down into the sand layer, obscuring the visual divisions between the materials. That's why the mark on the jar will be a more accurate yardstick of the amount of sand in the sample than a visual inspection. It can sometimes take days for all of those tiny flakes of clay to finally come to rest.

Playful Research

Next, we left the lab and went out into the field. This took intense concentration and a highly analytical approach … well, actually we just had fun messing around. Since clay is extremely moldable, we knew a wet sample of high-clay soil would be fun to play with, but a low-clay soil wouldn't hold together well. This wasn't rocket science: We simply used our intuitive feel for clay derived from our extensive experience with kindergarten art projects. We tapped into that well of knowledge and got to know the soil. We wet a sample and then rolled it around in our hands to see how sticky it was. We made a soil ball, pressed it into our palm, and then turned our hand over to see if the soil was sticky enough so the ball would hang suspended from our downturned palm. We tried rolling the soil into a long, thin column. We squeezed it through our fingers. We played, and in the end, we were thoroughly convinced that we had the makings of a good cob mix.

FINDING THE RIGHT MIX

Now that we knew we had good soil, our next step was to make some test batches to determine a good cob mix. (See photos on pages 232 and 233.) We knew that clay shrinks and is sticky and that sand doesn't and isn't. If our mix were to contain too much clay, it would shrink excessively in the wall and cause cracking. If there were too little clay, on the other hand, the sand wouldn't bind together sufficiently and the mix would crumble. By creating test mixes, we were looking for the perfect balance between the two.

Regardless of our soil composition estimates from the shake test, it was possible that our subsoil would make the best mix without adding any extra sand, so we first tried a test batch using just plain soil. That mix cracked badly, so next we tried a variety of mixes made up of measured amounts of subsoil, store-bought sand, and enough water to allow everything to be dispersed evenly. We bought mason's sand because it has a wide variety of sharp-edged sand-grain sizes. The sharp edges bind much better than rounded edges, like those in beach sand, and, as we've said, we want a variety of aggregate sizes.

These tests really aren't much work and the ramifications are substantial, so it's smart to test a wide variety of mixes. From our testing and the fact that our pure soil mix cracked, we knew we had a lot of clay, so we made test mixes with increasing amounts of sand. The first mix had one part sand to one part soil (1:1), the second was 2:1 (sand/soil), and the third was 3:1. If we were less sure of our clay content, we'd have tried some mixes with more soil than sand also. Since the main mechanism that makes cob strong is clay particles surrounding sand particles, we wanted access to all of the clay particles in our soil. For that reason, we broke up clumps and then soaked our soil to separate the clay particles before making a mix.

First, we made small test mixes that we formed into balls, being careful to keep track of which ball came from which mix. Each ball was small enough to fit into a palm and just wet enough to hold together. Next, we played catch with each ball while standing a few yards apart. A good mix won't break or crumble (those that do are too dry or have too much sand) and won't squish or dent (those that do are too wet or have too much clay). We also tried dropping the balls from waist height onto a solid surface. The balls made from a very good mix came away relatively unscathed.

We set the balls that more or less passed the test aside and let them dry. In our case, this took a couple of days. We were looking for a mix, that once dry, made a ball that was hard as a rock and that, when hit lightly with a hammer, would either break cleanly or not break at all.

All of our mixes performed well enough to move onto the next level of testing, which entailed making two bricks from each mix, one with and one without straw. After testing these bricks, we felt very confident that the 1:1 mix was clearly superior.

It may seem like this was a lot of fuss to make over choosing a mix, but let's look at the results. On visual inspection, our soil seemed to have good clay content. In fact, it held together quite well on its own, pointing toward the possibility that it could make good cob without the addition of any sand. Based on the generalized ideal of 75 percent sand and 25 percent clay, however, the results of our shake test indicated that we would need a 3:1 (sand/soil) mix to create good cob. Only after making a variety of test bricks did we discover that our soil performed best when mixed with an equal amount of sand. In other words, our preliminary test suggested a possible 0:1 mix, our intermediate test pointed to a 3:1 mix, and our final, most accurate test indicated a 1:1 mix. That's quite a difference. I'm glad that we subjected our materials to the full barrage of testing before making our decision.

Handmade rock. A good cob mix produces a ball that dries rock-hard. This ball broke with a medium hammer stroke, but it didn't crumble.

▲ **Step 1.** After our simple ball tests, we made more small test mixes, this time dividing each batch in half. We made bricks out of one half of each mix...

▲ **Step 2.** ...and clearly marked each brick for identification.

▲ **Step 3.** We let the samples dry completely. These bricks were made with three, two, and one part sand to one part subsoil, respectively. We kept our bricks in the shade while drying. Too much sun can cause an otherwise good mix to crack badly due to quick drying.

◄ **Step 4.** Next, we tested the bricks. We dropped them, tried to break them, scratched them, and cut them. In all cases, the brick from the one part sand to one part soil (1:1) mix faired better than the others. *Left:* The 1:1 brick was hard to scratch. *Middle:* The 2:1 brick scratched a bit easier (notice how it crumbled slightly). *Right:* The 3:1 brick didn't hold up to the nail; it probably contained too much sand.

▲ **Step 5.** We added straw to the second half of each mix, working in as much straw as the mud would reasonably hold, and then made more bricks, marking them as we'd done the others.

◄ **Step 6.** We also let these bricks dry in the shade. The process took several days. Just a visual inspection of the dried bricks gave us more information. The 1:1 mix (on the right) was easy to shape and kept its form while drying. The 3:1 mix (on the left) didn't even have enough body to allow a clear mark with the nail.

▲ **Step 7.** Finally, we put the straw-mix bricks through the same tests as before—and then some. Because the straw increases their tensile strength, these bricks were able to stand up to even more rigorous treatment. The 3:1 brick was a dud. It scratched easily and crumbled when broken with bare hands. The other two bricks seemed solid. They didn't break when dropped and weren't easy to scratch. *Left:* We cut our two best bricks with a masonry blade on a circular saw. In the 1:1 brick the straw was well integrated and there was no cracking or crumbling. This brick was impossible to break by hand. *Right:* After comparing the two cross sections, we were completely convinced that the 1:1 mix was superior. The section from the 1:1 brick (on top in the photo) looked like a single, integrated unit. The section from the 2:1 brick (below in the photo) displayed cracks and uncoated straw.

PREPARING TO BUILD WITH COB

Probably the biggest shock to inexperienced builders is simply the mind-boggling number of steps involved in accomplishing any task. It may seem that, with our tests completed, we were ready to jump right into mixing and building with cob, but there was actually still much to do.

Gathering Materials

As I've said, we had done all of our soil and mix testing well in advance of any actual cob construction. As we neared the time to actually start building with cob, it was time to get all of our materials together: the clay, sand, and straw we'd need to make our wall. First we figured out the volume of wall we'd be filling with cob. Then, based on the proportions of our chosen mix, we figured out how much of that volume would be filled with store-bought sand. Since a good proportion of sand's cost can be delivery, we made sure that we thought of all the uses for sand on the project before making an order. We knew we'd be using sand in our plaster and as a base for our floor, so we ordered enough for everything.

Next, we had to figure out how much straw we needed. In our experience, a rough estimate of straw usage is one to two bales for every cubic yard of mix. Since our building was going to have a straw bale wall and we have a dry barn for storage, we went ahead and bought all the bales we'd need for the whole project. Check out chapter 10 for more details on choosing and buying straw bales.

Finally, of course, we also needed a steady supply of mix-ready soil, the same stuff we'd tested. In anticipation of cob construction, we'd already separated our topsoil from our subsoil during the excavation of our site (see chapter 6) and had stockpiled the subsoil just above the building site for easy access.

Prepping the Wall

We had all our materials ordered and gathered, but we weren't ready to start mixing cob. We still had to prepare the wall, including finishing our termite barrier, installing a door threshold, building and installing a door buck, and building a window buck.

At this point, we also had to think carefully about how our cob would integrate with its neighbors, cordwood to the east and modified stick-frame with wooden lath to the west. (See figure 1.) The cordwood connection seemed easy enough: we'd just square the cob off and let the cordwood fill in around it. However, logistics dictated that we'd have to install the lath on the west wall before we installed the cob. (Here, dear reader, we run up against the limitations of such pre-hypertext technology as books. Although in the real world we installed the lath at this point, for ease of reading, this book will cover that step in chapter 11, where we discuss modified stick-framing.)

Figure 1
CONNECTING DIFFERENT WALL SYSTEMS

When combining different wall systems, it's important to think of the building as a whole. How will the different materials connect? What's the correct order of installation? In our situation, for example, we wanted to build our cob wall first to give it a chance to dry before plastering. That was no problem on the east side—we just built our cob square and then laid cordwood around it. On the west, though, it made much more sense to install the basic stick-framing and interior lath first and then push the cob tight up against it.

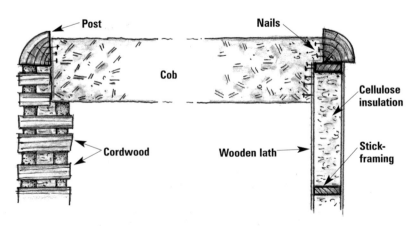

Post — Cob — Cordwood — Nails — Cellulose insulation — Wooden lath — Stick-framing

The Door Threshold

Any exterior door threshold needs to create a durable surface that will withstand years of foot traffic, provide a smooth walking transition between the ground outside and the floor inside, and redirect water that falls on the door and threshold away from the building. For durability, we made our threshold out of a piece of salvage granite. To create a smooth transition, and to allow for easy sweeping, we designed our threshold to be set at the same height as the interior finished floor and a standard step height above our exterior patio. To redirect water away from the building, we installed our threshold so that it sloped slightly away from the door. We also cut the granite to extend about an inch over the stem wall and cut a drip edge into the underside of this extension. (See chapter 3 for a photo and description of a drip edge.)

The Door Threshold

Set in stone. As you'll remember, we had to carefully plan our door threshold before pouring our stem walls, because that act would literally set our decision in stone. Here's the slot we'd built into our stem wall to allow our threshold height to be the same as the finish floor.

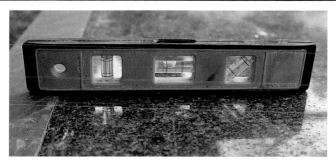

▲ **Step 1.** Using thinset mortar, we set our threshold, being careful to pitch the granite away from the door so that rainwater falling there will be directed away from the building.

◄ **Step 2.** We placed the threshold so that it extended beyond the stem wall and cut a drip edge into this extension so that water will fall off the granite, therefore redirecting it away from the joint between the threshold and stem wall. Notice also that the termite barrier wraps underneath the threshold. This is so there will be no exposed joint between the door buck and termite barrier, which would create a possible entry point for termites into the wooden buck.

▲ **Step 3.** Before installing the door buck, we sealed the gap between the stem wall and the granite with silicone caulk.

Details, details. Salvage materials are wonderful, but they often entail extra work and some creative problem solving. Our salvage granite wasn't wide enough to be the entire threshold, so we installed a piece of black slate to form the interior threshold edge. Notice also the little metal clips attached to the stem wall. We soldered these in place to tie the cob to the slick surface of the termite barrier. That might have been overkill, but it just took a few minutes and some scrap leftover from the barrier.

Figure 2
LINTEL LOADS

The ends of a lintel protruding into cob, or any monolithic wall material, help to balance downward loads.

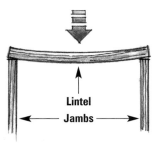

a. There's nothing to prevent this lintel from bending other than its own inherent strength.

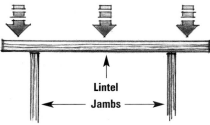

b. The load pushing down on the center of the lintel wants to push the ends up, but the lintels ends are already being pushed down by the cob itself, making bending much more difficult.

The Door Buck

When you buy a new window or door, it's usually set into a box that is designed to be attached to a skeletal structure (such as a stick-framed wall) that's already handling all of the loads the wall must bear. This box, usually called a "frame," isn't designed to carry loads. In a monolithic, load-bearing wall, such a weak frame won't work. Instead, windows and doors need to be set into a strong, self-supporting structural box capable of redirecting building loads around the opening that the window or door creates. Such a box is usually called a "buck."

Though our building has a skeletal structure, we only have posts in the four corners, and therefore there is no structure to which we could attach a doorframe in the middle of our cob wall. We couldn't depend on the cob itself to structurally support the door because there's no way to create a truly secure connection between cob and wood; in other words, you can't nail into cob. In addition, cob tends to shrink somewhat as it dries, thus pulling away from things such as doorframes, making connection even more difficult. For these reasons, we wanted to build a structural door buck that would hold its shape both in the face of any building loads pushing down from above and through the daily abuse of heavy doors swinging open and closed, regardless of what the cob around it was up to.

If our buck were to shift or sag over time, our doors would very possibly stick. In the worst-case scenario they could become impossible to open or close. To prevent these problems, we built the buck out of sturdy lumber, fastening the components firmly together. We bolted the two sides, or *jambs*, to the foundation, and planned to use quality hinges to eventually hold the doors resolutely to the jambs. We attached a heavy lintel to span across the top of the jambs, securing them. The protruding ends of the lintel will help redirect loads pushing down on the door opening from above. (See figure 2.)

Although we couldn't depend on the cob for steadfast structural support for our buck, we still wanted to tie the buck to the cob as best we could. To accomplish that, we attached wood blocks and nails to our jambs to key them into the cob. We knew the wings of our lintel embedded in the cob would also help tie the two materials together.

The Door Buck

Imagining a door. Since we had decided to build our own doors, we had the freedom to choose an exact size that seemed right for this situation. Before building our buck, we mocked up a door with some 1x4s and clamps to make the final decision about the height of our doors. This is yet another instance where having extra lumber on hand proved useful.

◀ **Step 1.** This buck needs to survive a long life of heavy wood and glass doors slamming shut, so we want it to be very sturdy and long lasting. We used heavy rough-cut, air-dried lumber. I found the white oak lintel piece laying around in the barn, and the jambs are red oak that a neighbor gave us. As we've said, connections are the weak point in any structure. In order to create a solid connection between the components of our buck, we cut a seat into the lintel for each jamb. First, we cut grooves into the lintel with a circular saw.

Step 3. Finally, we used heavy lag bolts to connect the lintel to the jambs.

▲ **Step 2.** We removed the excess wood with a chisel to create the groove to accept our jambs.

◄ **Step 4.** We hoped to create a buck that would be able to do its structural job of redirecting loads and holding the doors plumb regardless of the state of the cob around it. To accomplish that goal, we firmly bolted the buck to the brackets we had set in our stem wall before we poured it…

◄ **Step 5.** …and fastened our lintel to the roof framing. After the cob had dried and shrank all it was going to, we removed these blocks to make room for clay-slip straw installation. I don't foresee any problems, but in retrospect, I wish we'd left this connection intact and just plastered over the wood blocks along with the clay-strip straw. Why remove structural strengtheners if they can be incorporated into the finished design?

Too much sometimes isn't enough. Here's the buck in position, mimicking the placement of the mockup we'd done. Check out the strong diagonal bracing we'd added as yet another measure to keep our buck rock steady during installation of the cob. Even with measures that I considered to be overkill, our jambs still bowed quite a bit, a mystery we'll solve for you at the end of this chapter.

Connections

Wood has the incredible ability to grab things that are pushed into it, like nails and screws. And you can embed a fastener in concrete and be sure that it won't move because concrete doesn't tend to shrink when it dries. Cob, on the other hand, doesn't grip like wood and it *does* shrink when it dries, so connecting things to it can be a challenge. Luckily, its stickiness makes initial connections easy, and its general massiveness causes most shrinkage to be downward, controlled by gravity. This means that cob tends to settle down on things embedded in it, therefore, holding them in place with its weight.

It is possible, though, for cob to shrink away from wooden window frames causing them to loosen, or for the constant pounding of a door in its wooden frame to create a separation. One strategy for preventing this kind of movement is to embed nails into the wood that will protrude into the cob. This won't prevent the cob from pulling away, but it can create a physical pin that will prevent the wood from being able to completely free itself from the cob. That's probably all you really need, because gaps and cracks can be filled in with a sticky mix that will help reset the wood. If you're installing very heavy doors, on the other hand, a smart strategy is to build a buck that is truly structurally independent from the cob surrounding it. (See figure 3.)

Connecting to cob. *Left:* Even though we wanted our buck to be able to do its job alone, we still made every effort to connect it to the cob. Toward that end, we had installed a vertical piece of wood on each jamb and attached blocks and nails to it that were intended to lock the jamb to the cob, much like the anchor bolts we'd used to hold our brackets to the concrete piers and stem walls. The vertical boards were installed directly behind the spot where we intended to attach the doors to the jambs; therefore, they served a double purpose as stiffeners to keep the jambs from bowing. None of these efforts was completely successful (see the sidebar Construction Blunders, page 282). *Right:* Cob engulfs nails added to a post and window buck in a post-and-beam, cob-infill wall similar to ours.

Figure 3
CONNECTING HEAVY DOORS

When installing heavy doors in a cob wall, it's a good idea to create a self-supporting buck that won't move and will remain plumb regardless of what the cob around it is doing. Here, the buck is connected strongly to both the stem wall with angle brackets and the roof truss with small wooden studs. If the cob shrinks and pulls away from the lintel, or even cracks, the buck will still be able to do its job of holding the doors firmly as they open and close.

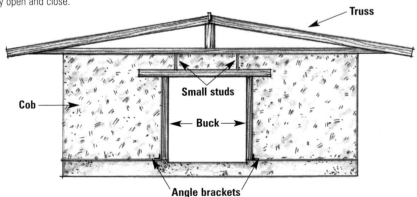

The Window Buck

A great feature of cob is that it can be molded to create openings with a variety of contours. As we discussed in chapter 2, an arch is an intrinsically strong shape. With cob, you can sculpt a structurally sound arched opening, something that would be much more difficult to do with wood or straw. For that reason, we chose a salvaged arched window for our cob wall.

Window bucks are usually a basic box with two side jambs, a head piece, and a bottom piece. Like door bucks, they're often built to be very stout because they need to be structurally strong enough to transfer loads coming down from above around the opening that they create in the wall. This wasn't the case with our arched window buck because the cob arch will do the job of redirecting loads around the opening. The real function of our cob buck, then, is to create a firm structure that will hold our window plumb in the opening so that it will open and close smoothly.

The Window Buck

▲ **Step 1.** We used old salvaged oak boards to create our buck. After cutting our jambs to length, we mortised them with a chisel.

▲ **Step 2.** Then, we installed the hinges that were already on the window. We had to clean them up a bit first and oil them, but in the end they worked fine.

▲ **Step 3.** If you look at any closed window or door, you'll find it resting against a sort of frame within a frame. The pieces of this frame, usually thin strips of wood, are called *stops*, and they do two things: prevent the window or door from swinging freely (hence the name "stop") and create a more or less air-tight seal around the window or door. We caulked our stops in place to help prevent air infiltration behind the wood.

▲ **Step 4.** Then, we nailed them in place with galvanized ring shank siding nails. We used some cedar we had salvaged from trimming a house exterior to make the stops. Cedar heartwood holds up well to rain and bugs tend to not like it, so it's a good choice for exposed exterior wood details.

Three-sided buck. Notice that the jambs of our buck stop where the window starts to arch. From here on up the cob itself will act as the rest of the buck. The 2x4 spanning the top of our jambs is a temporary brace. We installed blocks on the bottom and sides to key the buck into the cob. Here, unlike with our door buck, we installed the window in the buck before laying the cob so it could act as a movable form for building the cob arch. You'll see how this works a little later in the chapter.

MAKING COB

Finally, the time came when we were ready to mix our cob. As we've said, the basic goal of cob mixing is simple: surround as many sand particles with clay as you possibly can, then cram in as much straw as the mix will hold. However, even simple goals can be approached by many different roads, and making cob is no exception.

Cob is an ancient technique that can be accomplished with few materials and simple tools. That's because in many places earth building is a community activity. Groups ranging from families to villages have mud construction as part of their social fabric. In parts of the world today, adobe and cob builders work together to grow cereal grains as food and use the leftover stalks, or straw, along with local soils dug by hand to create earth mixes without the use of machinery.

For many cob builders in industrialized countries, this paradigm seems within reach. I often read reports of modern cob construction in which lots of adults volunteer to help each other, children are diligent, focused workers, and a pit full of mud is a venue for intimate dancing. In this world, modern complications—things like deadlines, worker's compensation insurance, and power tools that need polluting electricity—can be downplayed.

I honestly wish I lived like that, but the situation in which I find myself is very different. In my world, all of my friends are busy people I rarely see, children enjoy playing in mud until they realize that you want them to, and my pit full of wet clay has sharp rocks in it. On top of that, I usually have fairly tight project deadlines and time often means money. In my world, machines are attentive, obedient workers, loudly buzzing stand-ins for the volunteers who never come. They help me do alone what would otherwise take a group to accomplish.

In the context in which we found ourselves, it simply made sense to use power tools to make cob. We had electricity near the site, already owned the tools, and we didn't have the large crew and self-sufficient lifestyle that underscores cob construction in other parts of the world.

Both as an illustration of exactly how a little machinery makes things easier and in an attempt to represent common, power-tool-free practice, we made cob mixes both with mechanized help and *au naturel*. Here's how it went.

Soaking Clay

Before making a cob mix, we had to prepare our soil. As we've said, clay works as a binder for sand in cob, filling voids between the sand particles to create a matrix of clay that sticks to itself, holding the sand in place. To accomplish this connection, the clay particles must first be suspended in water; this clay soup then seeps between the sand particles, coating them. When they dry, the little clay flakes lock together.

Making a Mixing Pit

If you're not using our electric drill/paddle mixer technique, you'll need something to hold your cob mixes during their initial wet stage. For this purpose, we made a multipurpose cob-mixing container out of straw bales and a plastic tarp. This easy-to-make pit is a common sight on cob construction sites. Sometimes you can use such a pit for clay soaking also, but that didn't work with our clay, as we'll discuss in a bit. This little mixing pit is a great example of practical green-building design. We'll be able to reuse these bales as part of our clay-slip straw and plaster mixes. At the same time, we're not ashamed of using a distinctly modern, often vilified material: plastic. I don't think I've seen a rustic homestead or natural building construction site that didn't have at least one plastic tarp in use. They are durable, easy to store, and useful for many tasks around the building site.

▲ **Step 1.** Without the aid of our electric drill/paddle mixer, the initial stages of cob mixing were very wet. We had to create some kind of pit to contain our wet mix. First, we made a box out of six straw bales.

 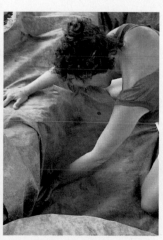

▲ **Step 2.** Then, we covered the straw-bale box with an 8 x 10-foot plastic tarp, being careful to tuck the tarp around the base of the bales. We created our pit under the roof of our building to protect it from rain and allow for shaded mixing.

Plastic-coated straw box. This finished pit will hold a wet mix, is a comfortable place to sit while resting between mixing forays, and—as we'll explain later—the tarp can work double time as a mixing partner.

Soaking Clay without Power Tools

Some clay soils are already very fine, and therefore are easily suspended in water simply by being soaked. The finest soils can even be mixed with sand first and then wetted to create the suspension. If you have a clay soil that fits this description, you're in luck.

If, on the other hand, your clay won't break down completely in response to soaking, another approach is to leave some of your clay in clumps. Cob likes aggregates of different sizes, and any little clumps of clay that aren't functioning as binder will be good aggregate. If you have abundant clay on site, but it's clumpy and hard to break down completely, then your time might be better spent just adding more soaked clay to get enough separated flakes as binder and leaving some clumps for aggregate. If, instead, clay is more scarce or hard to access in your situation, it'll make sense to take the extra time to really break up the clay, even grinding it if necessary. (See chapter 12 for a discussion of grinding clay.)

If you decide to leave a good percentage of your clay in clumps as aggregate, try to do the same as you conduct your tests, so that your test mixes will match your actual mixes.

Soaking Clay without Power Tools

▲ **Step 1.** There are various methods for soaking clay. The simplest is to dig a hole, put some clay in, and add water. We tried this method, starting with the pile of clay we'd excavated during our site work.

▲ **Step 2.** We simply dug a pit in the pile and filled it with water.

▲ **Step 3.** Then we added clay and let it soak.

◀ **Step 4.** Unfortunately, we found that in *our* soil the water in the pit seeped away before the clay was substantially broken down. Covering the pit with a tarp before adding clay and water solved the seepage problem.

◀ **Step 5.** After soaking the clay for several days we drained out the water.

▲ **Step 6.** It's possible to drag the whole tarp to the mixing area, but we moved it in 5-gallon buckets.

▲ **Step 7.** To save the work of carrying heavy buckets of wet clay, we also tried soaking our clay in the mixing pit. The problem with this approach was that it took more water to soak the clay than we needed for the actual mix. Therefore, when we added sand and straw to the soaked clay pictured here, we ended up with a mix that was much too wet.

▲ **Step 8.** In the end, our clay simply didn't respond well to pit soaking. Here's a sample of our clay after soaking in a jar for a full month! If we'd been dedicated to the idea of mixing without power tools, it would have made more sense for us to leave lumped clay in the mix as aggregate and just add more clay to get enough in suspension for binder. Of course, if that had been our strategy, we would have left our clay chunky in the test mixes also.

Soaking Clay with Power Tools

Our soil was very tough and chunky. It didn't respond well to traditional pit-soaking. I've been told a good remedy for chunky soil is to leave it exposed for a winter so that it can be subjected to freezing and thawing, which breaks up the chunks. We didn't have that option, and leaving a building site excavated for a full winter would have potential downsides, like possible erosion.

Alternately, we could have left the clay clumps in our mix and increased the clay percentage to get enough suspended clay for binder as mentioned before. However, though we had a lot of clay in our soil, our excavation was small and we needed soil not only for cob, but also for earth plaster and to finish the grading around our site.

We chose instead to break down our clay using 55-gallon barrels and the help of an electric drill with a mixing blade. The selfless cooperation of the electric drill and paddle mixer made it possible to get a high percentage of our clay particles suspended in water, allowing us to divide our excavated clay among our various projects.

Soaking Clay with Power Tools

▲ **Step 1.** We put several bucketfuls of clay soil in the bottom of a 55-gallon drum and added enough water to cover it.

▲ **Step 2.** Next, we mixed the clay and water using a paddle mixer attached to a powerful electric drill.

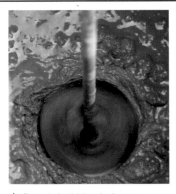

▲ **Step 3.** It didn't take long to make a creamy mixture; we added more clay and water and continued the process.

Mixed results. These two kinds of drill-driven paddle mixers are commonly sold for mixing drywall joint compound. The curved mixer on the right worked nicely for mixing cob. The one on the left was a flop.

▲ **Step 4.** Once we had basically filled the barrel, we topped it off with water to continue soaking. With this method, we could create really nice clay for mixing with only a day's lead-time. In a pinch, we could use it directly after paddle mixing.

Mud reserve. It's a very good idea to stockpile soaked clay. Mixing and laying cob is enough work for a day; you don't want to have to mess with digging, moving, and paddle mixing it for soaking at the same time. Here, two barrels are happily soaking away while waiting their turn.

Mixing Cob

The first step of our cob-mixing procedure consisted of combining measured proportions of soaked clay and sand to create a homogenous concoction in which, hypothetically, each individual particle of sand was surrounded by clay. Just as with any mortar or concrete mix, we were careful to add only as much water as we needed. From experience with a wide variety of wet building materials, we knew that we could always add more water if the mix was too dry, but we couldn't remove water if the mix was too wet. A couple of times, we made mistakes and our mixes ended up too wet. We found that adding some vermiculite soaked up the excess liquid quickly.

Our goal here was to create finished clay/sand mixes that were as firm as possible, both because they are easier and more stable to build with and because firmer mixes dry faster. Finally, we added straw, lots of it, and worked it in until, again hypothetically, each strand of straw was surrounded by the clay-sand mix.

Mixing Alone

On this project, most cob mixes were made by one person. Though it's hard work, if you're in good physical condition, mixing cob alone can be more efficient than mixing in a group. If you put on some music and get into a groove, it can become a fun, rigorous, trancelike workout. Still, to make the most of your finite muscle power, stage your materials as close as possible to the mixing pit. Buckets of clay and sand get heavy fast, and the less you have to move them around, the better.

Remember, our tests told us that a 1:1 mix (sand/clay) was what we wanted. Our basic mix size was four buckets of soaked clay soil, four buckets of sand, and as much straw as we could comfortably stomp in. Personally, I find this mix size to be about right. It is small enough to keep the materials shallow on the tarp, which makes mixing much easier, but large enough to give you a good amount of cob to build with. Other cob builders I know make smaller mixes. Experiment for yourself.

Though jumping around in mud is fun, it can get old fast if you're working alone, especially after you've brought your foot down on one too many sharp rocks. Remember the electric drill and paddle mixer we used to break up our clay for soaking? Well, the same set-up dramatically sped up the process of mixing our clay and sand together. In addition, with this method the mix was already pretty dry before we got our feet into it. This allowed us to forgo the straw "pit" altogether and just mix directly on a tarp. Another perk was that the stiff mixture resisted the movement of our feet through it which made encounters with rocks much more pleasant. In fact, when using this method, we left the rocks in the mix, which created a wider range of aggregate sizes. We've already pointed out why that's good for structural strength.

Even this method was a lot of work, and I would imagine that a mortar mixer could speed things up even more. Mortar mixers, unlike concrete mixers, have spinning blades that come close to the sides of the stationary drum. This action creates a crushing, smooshing action that, it seems to me, would work well with cob mixing. I haven't personally gotten a chance to try one out on cob, but my experience with them in other contexts leads me to believe that they would be a great benefit to the solitary cob worker. However, mortar mixers are expensive to buy, and renting one for the time period needed with cob would probably be cost prohibitive. I certainly wouldn't suggest buying one without trying it out first—I may be wrong about how well they'd work with cob.

▲ **Step 1.** First, Lisa took four buckets of soaked clay and poured them into the pit. You can see that there are still a lot of lumps in it.

▲ **Step 2.** Our soil had some nice sharp rocks in it, so Lisa went through the clay with her hands and took out as many rocks as she could find before stomping around. As we'll explain later, with machine-enhanced mixing we could leave these rocks in as aggregate without damaging our feet.

◄ **Step 4.** Next, Lisa placed all of the buckets of sand she'd need for this mix next to the pit so she wouldn't have to get out to reach them. She then added sand a bucket or two at a time, mixed it thoroughly into the clay with her feet, then added more sand. She added water as needed, but was careful not to add too much because she wanted her final mix to be as dry as possible.

▲ **Step 3.** Next, she squished around in the clay, breaking down as many lumps as she could. Again, the clay we mixed with the electric drill/paddle mixer before soaking didn't have these clumps. If we'd used that clay, Lisa could have skipped this step. We also could have left the lumps as aggregate; however, we'd done our test mixes using well-broken-down clay, and we wanted to use the same mix proportions here as we had in our tests.

▲ **Step 5.** To get an even mix, she had to keep turning her materials to get access to what was at the bottom. *Left:* To do this, she grabbed one side or corner of the tarp and pulled it toward her while walking toward the opposite side or corner. This consolidated the mix into a tall pile with some of what had been on the bottom now sitting on top. She then mashed the pile out with her feet. She repeated this tarp-pulling and feet-mashing process until she had a uniform mix. *Right:* This is a good-looking sand/clay mix.

▲ **Step 6.** After mixing the dry sand with the wet clay for a while, the mix became dry enough to push the bales out of the way to make more room for tarp pulling. Next, Lisa took an armload of straw and shook it over the sand/clay mixture.

◄ **Step 7.** She mixed the straw in with her feet by jogging, jumping, or dancing around.

◄ **Step 8.** She used the same tarp-pulling procedure to integrate the straw in the mix.

▲ **Step 9.** As she kept adding straw, the cob started becoming very structural, taking on a shape when she turned it. She kept adding straw and turning the mix until it was difficult to work any more straw into the cob. Since the straw is both structural reinforcement and insulation, she didn't want to skimp when it came to straw.

◄ **Step 10.** A good cob mix will look like a big burrito or cigar when turned. If the straw sticks to the tarp as it's pulled back, then the straw isn't integrated enough, there's too much straw, or the mix is too dry. This was Lisa's very nice finished mix.

War wounds. Not only do I find paddle mixing to be much more efficient, it's proven to be a lot safer in my experience. I cut my big toe badly on a rock while mixing clay using the common pit-mixing technique.

◀ **Step 1.** First, Lisa filled a 5-gallon bucket half full with soaked clay. She used our trusty paddle mixer to whip it up one last time before adding sand.

▲ **Step 2.** Next, she added an equal amount of sand and mixed it into the clay with the paddle mixer, adding water as needed.

◀ **Step 3.** This process took only a couple of minutes. The end product was sort of like chunky cake frosting.

▲ **Step 4.** Eight buckets of this stuff made a full mix. Lisa dumped it on a tarp, integrated it together a bit with her feet, and then added straw and also mixed that in with her feet. The integration of the straw is the only step that is the same in both approaches.

◀ **Step 5.** The end result was a superior mix. More clay flakes were suspended in the soaked clay, creating thorough binding; the clay and sand were more thoroughly mixed by the drill than by the feet; and small rocks were left in the mix, creating more aggregate variety. In addition, the whole process was much faster.

Group Mixing

As we got close to starting our cob work on this project, it seemed that everyone I knew or met was intrigued by the idea of cob and was interested in giving it a try. In the end, no one ever actually followed through and came out to do a mix. Such is our busy modern world.

As a result, the group-mixing on this project was limited to one day when Tim brought his two daughters, Shannon and Natalie. Everyone had fun, though the kids started whining pretty quickly about this and that. We spent a beautiful sunny day outside together doing physical work, and that in itself is valuable. However, on this project at least, it wasn't a scenario that could be sustained over the long run, and from a completely "let's get this building done" point of view, mixing together on a single tarp is not as efficient as mixing alone.

In my estimation, if you had a crew of four or five hard-working, experienced cob mixers in good physical condition, the way to get the most cob mixed would be to have each person mixing alone on his or her own tarp with one person keeping the materials coming.

Group Mixing

▲ **Step 1.** Since we had a group, we decided to forgo the paddle mixer and go old school instead. With all of those feet working, we also decided to make a double batch.

▲ **Step 2.** To mix the sand into the clay, one pair danced while the other rested.

No accounting for taste. Some like squishy clay, while others find it "icky."

▲ **Step 3.** Then the next couple took over.

▲ **Step 4.** And then everyone jumped in together.

▲ **Step 5.** They added water with the hose as needed. Here, the mix was at a good consistency to start adding straw.

▲ **Step 6.** Then more dancing commenced to integrate the straw.

Extracurricular activities. *Top:* Shannon loved jumping off the nearby retaining wall into the soft mix. *Bottom:* There had to be at least one mud fight.

▲ **Step 7.** The double mix turned out to be a bear. *Left:* It was hard to turn with the tarp, so it was difficult to get all the materials evenly distributed. *Right:* That's a lot of cob.

▲ **Step 8.** Still, the finished mix was very dense.

Cob consciousness. We haven't said a whole lot about how to tell when a mix is done. After a bit of practice, it's easy to tell when a mix is ready just by how it feels under your feet, or how it looks after being turned. *Left:* As a physical test, though, take a handful of your mix and try to pull it apart with a friend. *Above:* The mix should resist your tugging, and should stick to the straw and not crumble when you do pull it apart.

Proud parents. In the end, everyone had a good time and the result was superb cob. This is a much better way to spend time with the family than in front of the television, but I don't want to sugar coat it. These photos don't show how often the kids left to do other things, they don't depict how inefficient a mixing technique dancing is, and they don't show me back at it the next day mixing alone when everyone else had other things to do. On our project, group mixing turned out to be more of a fun break than a way to really get much work done.

LAYING COB

We've worked very hard to create cob in which all the ingredients are mixed evenly together with the clay coating the sand and the clay/sand-mix coating the straw. We've done this because cob gets its structural strength from all of these materials acting together in a matrix. However, we couldn't just mix one big batch of cob and roll it into the wall. We had to make many separate batches, and each individual batch, in turn, had to be broken up into manageable handfuls. As we laid our cob then, we needed to weave these handfuls and separate mixes back together into a strong, homogenous mix.

There are several methods of laying cob, basically all variations of the same idea: integrating the cob into a single mass. In the method we used for this project, cob was laid on the wall in thin (about 6-inch) horizontal layers that we'll call *courses*, since that's the conventional masonry term for a horizontal layer of brick or stone. The English derivation of cob means "a rounded mass or lump" and that's a good description of how we brought our cob to the wall: we pulled hunks off our finished mix (the big burritos pictured on the previous page), loosely molded them into a "rounded lump or mass," and then placed them on the wall. These small tight units kept their shape and allowed us to maintain a flat surface on the wall as we laid. Loose blobs, on the other hand, would have tended to settle toward the outside creating a hump in the middle, which would only have gotten worse as we continued up the wall.

To create the homogenous unit mentioned above, we worked each lump (also simply called a cob) that we set onto the wall into the lump next to it as well as the course of cob below it. We did this both with our fingers and with the aid of a simple tool called a *cobber's thumb*, basically a blunt stick that can be easily pushed into the cob.

To keep our progress orderly and to help the interior of the cob wall dry more quickly, we used a specific pattern for laying. We began each course by laying a series of cobs down the middle of the wall, like a spine and then attached cobs along each side of the spine like ribs. The next course just fills in the holes between the ribs, creating a flat surface on which to start the next spine and rib pattern.

This method gave us a lot of organized points where cobs were touching each other, which made it easier to pinch and thumb them together. It also left the center of the wall more open for a time, which gave it a chance to dry out a bit. We always planned our day so that we'd finish with a spine and rib pattern, which left the center of the wall exposed for the night, giving it some time to dry. Since our wall was 18-inches thick, it seemed a good idea to try to help that center dry as much as we could.

Pacing was important once we started laying cob. If we had laid too much in a day, the wet portion of the wall could have slumped under its own weight. If we had let the cob sit too long before laying another course, it could have become too dry, thus making it very difficult to weave the new course into the old. For this reason, we tried to do at least one course a day. Skipping one day was never a problem, but if we skipped two days we sometimes found the cob very set up and difficult to weave with the new batch. We made sure we never skipped three days between cob mixes on this project.

As our wall continued to grow, we needed to be conscious of the overall contour that we were creating. If we'd been building a load-bearing cob wall designed to carry roof loads, we would have created a definite taper in the wall, making it wider at the bottom than at the top. (See Variations on page 285.) This is a typical strengthening strategy for monolithic structures: Think of the trunk of a tree.

▲ **Step 1.** We started each course by laying a "spine" of cobs down the middle of the wall.

▲ **Step 2.** Next, we laid a staggered pattern of cobs along the spine. These were the "ribs." We tied each cob into the one next to it by pinching and poking with our fingers...

▲ **Step 3.** ...or with a sturdy stick called a cobber's thumb. This one is a piece of dowel.

▲ **Step 4.** Next, we filled the gaps between the ribs of our previous course, always integrating the new cob to the old...

▲ **Step 5.** ...and then started the whole process over by building another spine on top. By the way, the kids pretty quickly lost interest in actually trying to lay cob, which was fine because they didn't have the strength to make good cobs.

▲ **Step 6.** As we moved up the wall, we always tied our courses together by using a cobber's thumb to push straw from the new layer into the course below it, therefore, causing different layers to share some of the same structural reinforcement.

▲ **Step 7.** We planned our days so that our last course ended up in the rib and spine configuration. This sped up the drying time of our wall by exposing at least parts of the interior to a full night of drying.

Peace of mind. We'd never laid cob on a metal termite barrier before and we weren't sure if the slick metal and cob would like each other. As we said earlier, we decided to solder metal clips onto the barrier to help secure the cob in place. They probably weren't necessary, and I'm sure some cobbers out there will laugh at them, but somehow it just didn't seem right without them. In new situations, I like to err on the side of overkill if only for peace of mind, which on a construction site is worth a lot.

▲ **Step 8.** We molded the surface of the cob with our hands to fine-tune contours and shapes.

▲ **Step 9.** After the cob had set up for a couple of days, we poked holes in the surface with a piece of rebar. My thinking was that this would make a better key for the plaster and help speed the drying of the wall.

In our situation, this wasn't as important because we were using cob as infill inside a skeletal structure, which meant that the cob needed only to carry its own weight. Still, cob is heavy, so we created a small amount of taper to add structural strength. In many situations, it's best to use a 4- or 6-foot level to keep track of how things are shaping up. Within our small wall, there was only a short expanse of cob between two plumb columns, the locust posts and the door buck, so we did pretty well just eyeballing things.

Creating an Integrated Wall

One of the wonderful aspects of cob is its exactness. You can decide exactly where that window is going just before you put it in. You can make that sill exactly as wide as you want it. You can place a bottle pattern right here and a shelf just there. What's more, you can work slowly on a non-structural sculptural design, adding to it, messing with it, changing it until it's right. Except for obeying the laws of physics, there are really no limits to contours, shapes, and features of your cob construction. In this way, more than any wall system with which I am familiar, you can truly create a wall that integrates all of its features into a single entity. Dare I say it? I think this might be art.

This feature of cob also has its downsides because it means that the finished space is less flexible. For example, once a cob wall is completed, you can't just nail up shelves anywhere you want, or lower a shelf two inches to accommodate some larger books that you just bought. Adjustments to cob require cutting into dense, hard walls, mixing mud, and, often, creative problem-solving skills. As a comparison, though stick-framing is a much more rigid, less playful medium, it creates an interior wall space that is easily adjustable because it is designed to have things attached to it.

All this really means is that you need to know a lot about how you want to use a space before building with cob. That wasn't a problem for us because we had already spent a lot of time imagining the space we wanted in detail through a fairly rigorous design process. We knew clearly what our cob wall needed to accomplish and what basic elements it needed to contain. That clarity gave us the mental space to be playful as we actually built our wall, making it possible for us to create an integrated sculpture.

Simple scaffolding. Cob is heavy. As you move up the wall, make sure that you take the time to create a sturdy work surface. We used cinder blocks and a strong, rigid walk board to create simple, adjustable scaffolding.

A Delicate Balance: Doors and Windows

This is our first wall and our first window. We've definitely reached another moment to step back and check in on the big picture. Remember our design discussions in chapter 4? Our perspective is that we're not just building a building, we're crafting a feeling. We know from earlier discussions that the true function of a house is to create a delicate balance of separation from and connection to the outside. To feel that connection, we need more than a view. In a very real way, windows and doors are an agreement between the part of us that wants to be outdoors and the piece of us that would rather be inside. A subtle, powerful, functional, and emotional portal between the two worlds can make both sides happy. As a result, everything about your doors and windows will have a huge effect on the feeling your building creates.

Each opening in a building should have a clear purpose or series of purposes. A given window may be designed as both part of a ventilation strategy and as a special place that frames a specific view. It might be placed to give access to the scents of a flower garden, or to open up onto a frequently traveled path to allow for easy communication between those inside and out. Windows and doors need to be accessible to allow fresh air in, a way to quickly change the temperature when it's a bit too hot, and an easy exit from the building. In short, they need to be carefully, consciously, and loving placed, and, for the most part, they need to be able to open wide to the world.

Fixed vs. operable glass. *Above:* To me, the fixed glass in this cob wall isn't much better than the inoperable windows of city skyscrapers. *Top right:* The arched window in our cob wall, on the other hand, can be opened, creating a real connection between the inside and outside. *Bottom right:* Our window helps create a beautiful place that will draw people to it.

For this reason, I'm genuinely surprised to see how many cob buildings use mostly fixed glass for windows. Sure, fixed glass is easier to install and allows the use of odd pieces of salvage glass, but does it make a window? I promise you that careful thought and soul searching, as well as a bit of extravagance in your choice of materials, will be well worth it when it comes to filling openings in your buildings.

The thickness and sculptability of cob give you a lot of options when it comes to windows and doors. Should the window be on the inside, middle, or outside of the wall? How big do you want the sill to be? What shape should the wall take around the opening? Windows and glass-covered doors will let in more sun if they are set to the outside of the wall, which is important in passive solar designs. This configuration also gives you a large useable niche or even a potential window seat on the inside. On the other hand, inset windows create a certain feel from the outside that's very appealing, almost archetypal.

Window shopping. In thick walls, you have a lot of choices when it comes to window placement. Where the window rests relative to the inside and outside wall surfaces affects light quality, solar gain, and sill type. *Above:* This is a view of our finished cob window from the inside. We set it in the middle of the wall, which allowed us to install granite sills to serve as shelves on both sides of the window. The curved reveals create a slow transition from light to dark, which cuts down on glare. *Right:* These windows are set in from the outside wall, creating a sill to the outside.

Corbelling

In order to create structurally sound sculptural shapes, we used a technique called corbelling. Corbel literally means "bracket." In masonry it refers to a process of creating contour by offsetting progressive courses of a material. By corbelling, you can make arches, vaults, domes, brackets, shelves, and any number of decorative protuberances. To corbel with cob, we made special cobs that contained lots of long straw all oriented in the same direction for extra structural strength. Corbelling allowed us to integrate into our cob sculpture both an operable arched window and a heavy protruding exterior sill.

Overlapping strength. These bricks are corbelled. Each course cantilevers over the supporting course below it.

▲ **Step 1.** To make corbel cobs, we first pulled some long, strong straw strands from a bale.

▲ **Step 2.** Then, we took some finished cob complete with straw and formed small tight loaves.

▲ **Step 3.** Next, we spread out our long straight straw…

◄ **Step 4.** …and rolled a loaf into it. We wanted the straw all oriented in the same direction along the length of the cob to create consistent reinforcement in one direction, much like steel rebar in concrete.

◄ **Step 5.** We worked the straw in with our fingers.

▲ **Step 6.** Based on where we were using the corbel, we either shaped it further with our hands, bent it in half for added strength, or flattened it out with a foot.

Strong, yet flexible. Our finished corbels were firm and bulging with straw (left), but flexible enough to be adjusted to the need at hand (right).

Installing the Window Buck and Sills

As we had done with our doors, we elected to set our cob window in a bit from the outside. We planned to create a curved reveal that would let in more sun. The first step to installing our window buck was to hold it up at various heights and positions in the wall to get a good general idea of where it would go.

Since the outside of our cob wall would be the backdrop for our outdoor patio room, we decided to make the exterior windowsill into a small table. To do this we needed to corbel a protruding seat for the sill. Any feature that protrudes from a building needs to be installed with care because it will most likely collect water. Little details like sloping the sill away from the wall and installing a drip edge can make all the difference.

Installing the Window Buck and Sills

◀ **Step 1.** About a foot below our sill height, we started corbelling a seat for our granite sill, cantilevering each successive course of corbel cobs a couple of inches beyond the one below it. We were careful to tie our corbels to the mass of the wall with a cobber's thumb.

▲ **Step 2.** With the corbelled sill seat in place, we set the window…

▲ **Step 3.** …and temporarily braced it firmly to the building structure—another perk of having a post-and-beam structure.

▲ **Step 4.** Next, we used a trowel to smooth out a seat for the sill…

▲ **Step 5.** …making sure that it sloped away from the building, so that rainwater would be directed away from the window.

▲ **Step 6.** We chose a piece of salvaged granite as a sill. We cut it to length using a mid-grade masonry blade on a circular saw. We cut the groove in two passes, taking only half the depth out on the first cut. This put a lot less stress on both the saw and the blade.

▲ **Step 7.** Next, we cut a drip edge in the bottom of the sill. We'd marked the cut with a soapstone marker, being careful not to set the groove so close to the edge that the stone might break.

▲ **Step 8.** We set the saw to cut about a ¼-inch groove. When water rolling over the sill hits this groove, surface tension will be broken and the water will be induced to fall away from the wall.

▲ **Step 9.** Next, we set the sill in its seat…

▲ **Step 10.** …pushed it into place…

▲ **Step 11.** …and checked to make sure we had the slope we wanted.

Sill and seat. Here's the installed sill. The strong corbelled seat allowed the sill to be large enough to make a nice little table (see photo in the sidebar A Delicate Balance: Doors and Windows, page 256). Notice also the drip edge we cut into the bottom of the sill.

◄ **Step 12.** We followed the same procedure for installing the interior sill, except we didn't need to install a drip edge. Also, since our interior sill was a little smaller and the window was set slightly toward the outside of the wall, this sill didn't cantilever as far out over the wall, so we didn't need to corbel a seat for it. Notice also how this sill is notched around the window buck. We did this to get more stone bearing on the cob.

▲ **Step 13.** We also supported this sill with a "stiff leg" until we had set enough courses of cob above to hold it in place.

Building the Arched Window Opening

We continued up the wall sculpting a curved reveal as we went. Finally, we used our window frame as the form for the corbelled arch that became the top of the window opening. This worked wonderfully because it allowed us to move the form temporarily out of the way, by opening the window, so that we could shape the cob into an integrated window stop and attend to other details.

A hole in a wall is a structural weak spot. The lintel of our door buck was designed to redirect the loads around the hole created by the doors. Our arched window has no lintel; the arch itself has to redirect those loads around the opening. For that reason, we were careful to build a strong, structural arch with corbel cobs that were conscientiously tied into the rest of the cob wall. We also shaped the arch to be thinner in the middle, therefore reducing the weight that needed to be supported at that crucial spot.

If you aren't installing an operable arched door or window that can be used as a form, there are other options. For example, sometimes people build sturdy forms that are left in place throughout the entire construction of an arch. The downside of this approach is that it slows drying and makes detailed shaping difficult. It's also possible that you'll use the form as a crutch and not mold an arch that will be structurally sound once the form is removed. Alternately, you could make a template out of some rigid material and hold it up often to check your work as you build. This approach allows you to build to a desired shape while keeping the cob easily accessible for shaping and drying.

Creating the Curved Window Reveal

▲ **Step 1.** The shape created around openings will determine the quality of light coming inside. We rounded the cob around this window on both sides to let in more light and cut down on glare.

▲ **Step 2.** Since the window opens on this side, this reveal will also be the place where the window comes to rest. As such it will take some abuse. For that reason, we were extra careful to tie the reveal thoroughly into the rest of the wall.

◄ **Step 3.** We also carefully shaped the reveal to let the window open as far as it could. We checked our progress by opening the window often. This was another advantage of having the window already installed in the buck.

Corbelling the Arch

▲ **Step 2.** Next, we added corbel cobs to each side of the central cob and, as usual, tied everything together.

▲ **Step 1.** We made long corbel cobs that extended far back into the existing cob and wrapped over the course below to create the center of each layer of the arch. We tied these into the mass of the wall with a cobber's thumb.

◀ **Step 3.** Since our arch opening needed to match our arched window, it made sense to use our actual window as the form. This technique worked wonderfully because it allowed us to swing the form (window) open, and closed at will. *Left:* We closed the window to place the cob, thus allowing us to create a shape that matched the window. *Right:* Then we opened it to fine-tune the shape and weave the cob. We always left the window open at night to let the arch dry.

◀ **Step 4.** *Left:* We created a built-in window stop in our arch by wrapping our corbel cobs about an inch over the window when it was closed. *Right:* This created the groove at the base of the arch that you can see in this photo. The window nestles tightly against this groove, or "stop." Notice also that we rounded the arch so that it was thinner in the middle. This made the most-suspended portion of the arch lighter and therefore easier to support.

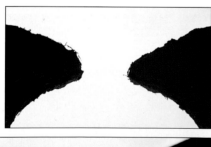

Coming together.
Top left: Using these methods, the two sides of our arch slowly came together. *Bottom left:* This cob seems to be defying gravity, a testament to the incredible strength of a well-built corbelled arch. *Right:* In the end, the window fit perfectly.

Shaping Niches and Installing Shelving

Built-in niches and shelves were another piece of our cob sculpture. We chose to add a large built-in wooden shelf above our arched window, three recessed shelves above what will eventually be a kitchen counter, and a block for attaching a coat-hanging hook by the door. Of course, these were permanent fixtures, so we had to think hard about the finished building in order to make good decisions. Again, all of our earlier design work and focused imagining really paid off when we got to this point.

Installing the Wooden Shelf

▲ **Step 1.** First, we created a nice flat surface for our shelf using a concrete finish float…

▲ **Step 2.** …and checked to make sure that our shelf bed was level.

▲ **Step 3.** For our shelf, we used a weathered, old piece of milled oak and fitted it with these little cleats.

◀ **Step 4.** *Top:* We tapped the shelf into place. *Bottom:* The cleats helped the shelf grab the cob. Before installation, we had hammered in a few nails to help the shelf tie into the cob. We marked where we planned to stop our cob with a pencil line.

▲ **Step 5.** We braced our shelf temporarily until the cob on top of it had dried enough to support it.

▲ **Step 1.** We decided to build a three-shelf sunken niche above the kitchen counter. After leveling out a place at the bottom of the niche, we placed the shelf. *Left:* We used a carpenter's trim hammer to level the shelf, which allowed us to bang pretty firmly to adjust its position without worrying about breaking it. *Right:* Unlike exterior shelves or sills that need to slope away to repel water, interior shelves are better off level so that objects won't roll off them.

▲ **Step 2.** We temporarily attached this block to our west frame wall and used a shim to get the shelf just where we wanted it. This way, if the cob were to shrink, our shelf would still be held level and we could just fill in the gap created beneath it with a bit more cob.

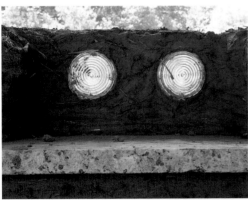

◀ **Step 3.** *Top:* We recessed our cob to make the niche. *Bottom:* Here's the back of the niche seen from the outside. These bottles will let in light to illuminate the shelves. We'll show you how to make these bottle units next.

▲ **Step 4.** We continued up the wall using the same procedure to install the other shelves and shape the niche.

Using Bottles

Bottles can be added to cob to create effects that you really have to experience to appreciate. Using the method described here, an incredible amount of light is captured and transferred through a small hole in the thick wall. Colored bottles are lovely, but transfer much less light. A subjective word of caution: It's easy to start just messing around with the fun things you can do with cob. I've seen some beautiful uses of bottles, and some that seemed like absent-minded doodles.

We spent a lot of time designing our use of bottles in this wall. Lisa, our resident visual artist, made a lot of sketches before choosing a pattern, and spent time choosing just the right glass and bottles. You may or may not like what she came up with, but the important thing is that we like it because we had a very good idea of what it was going to look like before installing it. We suggest you take the same care.

Making Glass Bottle Blocks

◀ **Step 1.** Lisa made a lot of drawings before deciding on a design. This was not only important aesthetically, but also necessary to make sure that we had the bottles we needed prepped and ready to go when it was time to install. The drawings on the left are the exterior view and those on the right are of the interior. The two bottom drawings in the photo depict the design we chose to install.

▲ **Step 2.** To make her bottle designs, she needed to make long "glass bottle blocks" that would collect and transfer light through the wall. First, she chose two bottles whose combined length would span the width of the wall.

▲ **Step 3.** She connected these with duct tape.

▲ **Step 4.** Next, she wrapped the bottles in reflective metal. We chose thin aluminum flashing for this purpose. Lisa cut a piece of thin aluminum flashing…

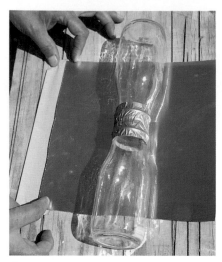

▲ **Step 5.** …and set a piece of tape on each end.

▲ **Step 6.** She attached one side of the flashing to the bottles…

▲ **Step 7.** …then rolled the flashing tightly onto the bottles and taped it securely.

▲ **Step 8.** *Above:* Next, she taped both ends of the flashing to the bottle. *Right:* The finished product was a solid unit, a "glass bottle block" that could be quickly mass-produced and stockpiled for use in the wall. By the way, all of that taping served the double purpose of creating a unit and sealing the bottles so that water in the cob or surrounding air wouldn't get inside, condense, and cause fogging.

◄ **Step 9.** Using the same method, she made a wide variety of bottle blocks. Here, Lisa made one by combining a blue wine bottle and a salsa jar.

Bottle block bazaar. On the left, a gallon apple juice jar was combined with a bathroom light fixture globe. Next to that are two outdoor light globes. The rest were made of wine bottles, salsa jars, and other common glass from the recycling bin.

Installing Glass Bottle Blocks

▲ **Step 1.** First, we set the bottle blocks with a thin bed of pure, sticky clay.

▲ **Step 2.** Then we leveled the bottles, both relative to the wall (left), and to each other (right). Here, Lisa used our trusty trim hammer to tap the bottles into place.

◀ **Step 3.** Since the cob patches between our bottles were so thin, we were always careful to weave them in. Lisa used a piece of rebar here both because it was thinner than our wooden thumbs and because the cob beneath had set up a bit and needed a little more persuasion.

◀ **Step 4.** Our bottle design called for a uniform spacing between bottle blocks. *Left:* Here, Lisa used the width of a 2x4 as a spacer. *Bottom:* Here, a 2x4 cut to length kept the different parts of her design a uniform distance apart.

Majestic mud. Here's the finished design installed. I think it gives our little building a bit of majesty.

Trimming

We did most of our shaping as we laid our cob. However, every couple of days, we'd step back and look over our progress. At this point, the cob a few layers below our present work was firm, but still wet enough to be shaved off in flakes, much like carving a bar of soap with a knife. We mostly used a machete, but a spud, basically a flat blade attached to a handle, is handy to have around for certain cob-shaving situations. (See page 310 for a picture of a spud.) When the cob had become very dry, or for tight spots and exact shaping, we had good luck with an electric grinder and grinding wheels on electric drills.

We trimmed our cob to correct small amounts of slumping, tweak sculptures, and adjust our window opening after settling. Trimming can fix bulges made during lapses of concentration or by some absent-minded volunteers who stopped by; however, it's a not an efficient way to create the overall shape of a wall. If you get way off—you don't pay attention to your contour and the whole wall starts getting wider as you go up, for example—then you're in for some arduous trimming work.

Trimming

▲ **Step 1.** We used our machete to smooth rough spots…

▲ **Step 2.** …and to clean up around sculpted shapes. By the way, we saved these cuttings. They work great for sculpting since they tend to have smaller pieces of straw.

Cobber's tools. This machete was our main trimming tool. Also pictured are two incarnations of a cobber's thumb.

▶ **Step 4.** For fine-tuning after the cob was too dry for the machete, we found that a masonry wheel on a small grinder did a good job. We always wore a mask and goggles! The dirt really flew when using this baby.

▶ **Step 3.** As our cob dried and settled, we had to trim our arched window opening on several different occasions so that the window still fit.

Sculpting

As we've said, we were careful to create most of our shaping as we laid our cob, and we added many sculptural elements through that process. However, another wonderful feature of cob is that you can add non-structural sculptural elements at any time, even after the wall has dried.

Taking advantage of this fact, we did some of our subtler shaping after the cob wall was completely laid. Without the stresses of creating a full mix and laying cob, we were able to step back and take a calmer look at the shapes we wanted to create. At this point, our cob work had moved clearly out of the realm of construction into the world of art. By that I mean that we had only aesthetics to guide us. These sculptures can be adjusted and played with forever, which can be both a blessing and a curse. As with any art form, part of the discipline of cob is learning to recognize when you are done.

Sculpting with Cob

▲ **Step 1.** To make a sculpting mix we first collected some dried cob remnants off our mixing tarp and poured them in a bucket. We then added water and some short straw. We wanted this mix to be stickier than our normal cob, so we added some more clay as well.

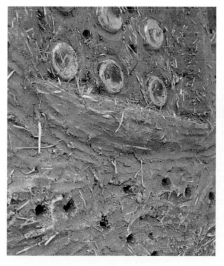

▲ **Step 2.** We had started the shape we wanted as we were building the wall (left). Now we just needed to flesh it out. First, We used a hatchet to rough up the area for better adhesion (middle), and added some nails to tie the sculpture into the wall (right).

   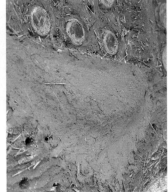

▲ **Step 3.** Next, Lisa took handfuls of the wet sculpting mix and worked them onto the wall, shaping the mix with her hands.

 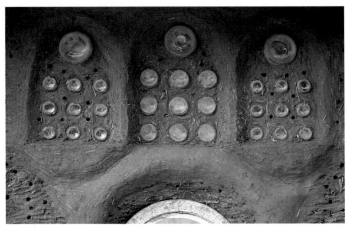

Mud makeover. This is the full sculpture before (left) and after (right).

Thinking about Structure

Structural design is based on worst-case scenarios. We knew it didn't matter if our building structure functioned perfectly 99 percent of the time. If it can't withstand that once-every-15-year windstorm or that rare blizzard snow load, then it's not good enough, plain and simple. For this reason, as we built, we kept an eye toward structure, always asking ourselves questions like "Does this seem strong enough?" or "Should we beef that up a bit here?"

What are the structural demands on our cob wall? As we said in chapter 7, the simple gable design of our roof puts almost all of the dead loads from the heavy living roof onto our east (cordwood) and west (stick-frame) walls, and almost none onto our cob wall. This means that our cob wall needs to deal mostly with lateral loads, in addition, of course, to carrying its own weight.

Before we starting building our cob wall, we had installed temporary diagonal braces across the space that the cob would occupy to help prevent the building from twisting or even collapsing in response to lateral loads. By filling the volume between the walls that will bear the roof loads, our cob is taking over the job of this bracing, and it would probably be enough. However, once a building is done, it's difficult to beef it up structurally. Especially with the great potential to amplify lateral loads that will be created by our heavy living roof (see the sidebar Lateral Loads). Why take a chance? We decided to install braces imbedded in the cob that attach the locust corner posts to the roof truss.

Structural retrofit. Unfortunately, after this building was basically finished, the building inspector decided it wasn't structurally sound. At this late date, these permanent external log braces were the only available solution.

Better safe than sorry. When it comes to structure, I always try to err on the side of caution. *Left:* In that spirit, we installed small braces between the corner posts and the roof truss as just that much more structural insurance against lateral loads. *Right:* We then surrounded the braces with cob.

Lateral Loads

In construction texts, lateral loads are often almost exclusively associated with wind pushing sideways against a building. However, the picture is more complicated than that. In our little building, for example, the heavy living roof potentially creates a top-heavy structure that will amplify the effect of almost any lateral load.

To understand this, let's imagine a simple structure: four bricks set on end, each supporting the corner of a thick, rectangular piece of plywood. This simple structure has no trouble supporting its own weight. Now, imagine standing on the plywood. If you're careful to center your weight in the middle, the structure will hold you easily. However, if you introduce even a small lateral load, by rocking gently back and forth for example, the top-heavy structure will quickly collapse.

The bricks and plywood are similar to a building with a skeletal structure topped perhaps with a light roof of trusses covered with metal roofing. Standing on the plywood is like adding the weight of a living roof.

We'll put a similar stress on our little building by placing a very heavy living roof onto an open skeletal structure consisting of four posts and two beams. By itself, this setup would be structurally unsound, and the building could very possibly collapse. However, by using a combination of some heavy wall infills and careful structural bracing, we intend to create a dense, stiff structure that will avoid this top-heavy state.

Thinking about Water

The first thing to say about cob and water is that your common sense is wrong. Well-built cob can actually be very resistant to water. Unlike our straw bale wall, for example, our cob wall doesn't have a hard exterior with a soft vulnerable interior, so there's really no place for water to go. If it wears down the outer layer of cob, water will just find more cob that will do a pretty good job of shunning it.

On the other hand, cob *can* absorb water over time. If a cob wall ever soaks up enough water so that the clay particles start loosing their hold on each other (in other words, start reverting to mud), then the wall could potentially collapse. A consistent roof leak directing water onto the top of the wall, water pouring off an unguttered roof and splashing onto the base of the wall for an extended period, or consistently wet soil below the building constantly wicking moisture through the foundation into the wall are all situations that could potentially introduce too much water into cob.

Our first line of defense against such problems was to prevent water from hitting the wall in the first place. Toward this end, we lifted the cob off the ground on solid stem walls, created a good-sized overhang on the roof, and cut drip edges into our window- and doorsills. Together, these steps will keep most falling rain and snow from ever hitting the wall. Most of the water that does reach the cob will be easily repelled by a durable lime-based plaster. We'll cover that process in detail in chapter 12.

The only vulnerable spots remaining are the joints where cob meets another material. Joints like these are places where flashing usually comes in handy. Flashing, though, is really designed to prevent water from seeping behind a hard building skin and being trapped to damage the interior framing of a wall or vulnerable infills, such as fiberglass, recycled newspapers, and straw bales. It also protects external trim pieces, and causes water to be directed away from window and door openings and prevented from running down exterior wall skins.

As mentioned above, the hard outside/soft inside scenario doesn't apply to cob. A cob wall really has no void inside for the water to reach. If flashing is used with cob, then, it's to protect embedded wood pieces like our lintel and to keep water away from window and door openings and from running down the outside of the wall. In our situation, we didn't need to install flashing on our door lintel because it's high enough in the wall to be completely shielded from rain by the roof overhang.

Cob of steel. This clump of cob has been sitting out in the open air for more than a year. That means it's been baked by the sun, blown by the wind, and pelted with close to 50 inches of rain and snow. Though the outer surface of the clay and sand has worn away a bit, this clump is still a very solid structural unit.

Think like water. Since our arched window has no protruding head jamb with a drip edge, more water will hit our window and roll down toward the base of our window buck. This isn't great because the buck is wood, and therefore susceptible to water damage and also because this water could work its way into the cob. Our solution was to install something equivalent to the head jamb with drip edge, but at the base of the window. Now, water that rolls down the window will be pushed out over this trim piece and fall from the drip edge away from the buck and onto the granite sill which is slanted away from the wall. It, in turn, has a drip edge to direct water away from the lower portion of the wall.

Shrinkage

I suppose the perfect cob mix wouldn't shrink perceptibly. All of the different sizes of sand would fit together so well that they'd be touching, and the clay would just fill the tiny gaps between. When the clay dried, it wouldn't really have much room to shrink, and the effect would be to lock the already touching pieces of aggregate together.

In my experience, though, cob does shrink. It certainly did in our wall. Theoretically, the more clay a mix has, the more it will shrink. It's possible that our mix was a bit clay-rich, but you'll remember the detailed testing we did to find the right mix. We didn't get enough shrinkage to cause any cracking, and our cob is incredibly solid, so I'm very happy with our mix.

In any case, shrinkage is to be expected and usually no problem if it's within reason. We filled larger shrinkage gaps with more cob. We stuffed thin gaps with straw and—yes, you're reading this right—spray foam insulation. We went to this trouble because these small gaps, though no structural threat, would certainly let in a lot of cold air in the winter. We've gone to a lot of trouble to design this building to be energy efficient, but the design won't mean much unless we follow its intent through into the details of construction.

On the other hand, shrinkage can be a problem at structural junctures such as lintels. A lintel installed on cob that's still very wet, for example, can be pulled away from the cob subsequently set on top of it as the cob below dries and shrinks. This can cause cracking. If the lintel isn't part of a full window frame (in other words, it sits on top of a bare piece of fixed glass), the shrinking cob could cause the lintel to settle downward, pressing on and potentially breaking the glass. (Another reason, in my opinion, to avoid fixed glass windows.)

To avoid these kinds of problems caused by shrinkage, we had to strike a balance. We laid cob up to the bottom of the lintel and let it dry a bit longer than usual, to give it a chance to shrink, but not so long that it would be impossible to structurally integrate the new cob with the old. Of course, the best defense against shrinkage problems is to carefully craft a good mix by making adequate tests.

Dirt shrinks? Cob tends to shrink as it dries. Our cob shrank somewhat, pulling away from the locust corner posts (top) and the door buck (bottom). We stuffed the biggest gaps with our regular cob mix and smaller gaps with straw.

Ancient and modern materials working together. Though I'm sure this will freak out some cob enthusiasts, we used a nontoxic (at least it said so on the can), water-based spray foam insulation to fill some of the shrinkage cracks that were too small to stuff with straw. From my point of view, this is a sound green building choice. We've designed this building to be able to last for hundreds of years, and I'm not averse to using some modern materials to make it as energy efficient as possible for that long tenure. We later covered all of these joints with earth plaster to create a seamless finish.

Cob Math

I took detailed notes on the size and number of mixes it took to fill our wall. The volume we filled, accounting for windows and bottles, was about 100 cubic feet. Each mix contained four 5-gallon buckets of sand and four buckets of clay, which adds up to a wet volume of about 5 cubic feet per mix. We did 28 mixes, which means we put about 140 cubic feet of wet material on the wall. If I include a bit of volume for the straw integrated into the mix, I come up with about 50 percent more wet mix volume than finished dry wall volume.

A bit of this difference is shrinkage, but most of it comes from the fact that the clay fills in a lot of space that already exists between the sand, therefore creating a volume that is smaller than the sum of the parts. In other words, one plus one doesn't equal two. The message: If you are reading about or discussing cob volumes, especially estimates about how much cob you can expect to lay in a day, be sure you're clear on what's being talked about: separate wet ingredient volume, wet volume on the wall, or dried cob wall volume.

How Long Did It Take?

Before getting into this topic, let me make something clear about myself. I may have been called a lot of things, but lazy isn't one of them. While some people who know me might use the word "maniac," I prefer "driven worker." I'm fit, strong, obsessive, and experienced with a wide variety of construction techniques. I love hard physical work. Okay, now read my lips: Building with cob is very slow going.

At the beginning of this chapter, I listed the amount of time and physical effort required as a possible disadvantage of cob construction. To put some numbers behind that claim, I took careful notes on our cob-laying progress on this project (see the sidebar Cob Math). We filled about 100 cubic feet of wall volume with 28 mixes of cob. That means that each hard-fought cob mix covered an area about 6 inches tall, 1½ feet wide, and 5 feet long.

Now, I think that's slow progress by anyone's standards. In addition, it's important to remember that there's a lot more going on in cob construction than mixing and laying cob. On any given day, we found ourselves replenishing clay in the soaking barrels, making final decisions about the placement of a window, prepping a granite slab for a sill, installing bottle designs, doing a little carpentry, and, of course, cleaning up when the day was done. The long and short of it is that our cob wall took longer to complete than any of our other wall infill systems.

I've tried to drive this point home throughout this chapter because, to be frank, many people I know are just plain out of shape. In my experience, the average American, for example, has limited knowledge of real physical work. If you're not in that group, then take what I've said about the hardships of cob building with a grain of salt. Sure it's hard work, but so are a lot of very worthwhile endeavors.

Building with cob is like creating a huge clay sculpture that can follow your imagination pretty much anywhere it wants to go. In fact, the main thing that separates a cob sculpture from those commonly labeled "art" is that once the cob is finished, you can move in. As long as it's appropriate for your climate as discussed above, I think the work inherent in cob is a small price to pay for something that can provide personal expression, enduring beauty, and a living room couch!

Good honest work. At the end of a day of cobbing everyone is exhausted.

CLAY-SLIP STRAW

As we neared the top of our wall, we started thinking again about the issue of mass enhanced R-value. Because of our roof overhang, we realized that no sun would ever hit the cob above the door, thus there would be no possibility of a mass-enhanced R-value in our climate for the material installed in that spot. In addition, whatever filled that space wouldn't need to hold any weight. In fact, something light would take pressure off the lintel over the door, and, let's face it: we were getting sick of mixing and hefting that heavy cob high up onto the wall.

Then it hit us. We own this factory, so let's just change the mix. We could up the straw and cut back on the clay and sand to get a higher R-value and a lighter material. It's a good idea and, like most good ideas, we're not the first to have had it. It's an ancient technique, but people using it today can't seem to agree on what to call it. I've seen it referred to as straw-clay, clay-straw, light straw-clay, *leichtlehm* (light loam), slip-straw, and, the name that seems most descriptive to me, clay-slip straw.

Whatever you want to call it, the stuff is made by mixing a slurry of water and dissolved clay, called clay-slip, with lots of loose straw. This wet mix is then placed between temporary forms. After that mix dries, the forms are moved up the wall and another mix is added. After the whole wall dries, the result is a surprisingly hard wafer of straw bound together with clay.

Same materials, different proportions. On the left side of this post is clay-slip straw, on the right side, cob.

Faster Cob: Another Perspective

I don't know anyone who claims that cob is quick and easy. Still, I have friends who are experienced cob builders who use faster methods than I practice. Here are some of their suggestions:

1) Unless you are really hurting for clay content, don't worry about breaking down all of the clay clumps. Just adjust your mix so that the clay that readily breaks down in water will be enough to coat the sand. The leftover clumped clay will simply function as larger aggregate, filling more volume with less work. Also, don't get paranoid about having some topsoil in your mix. It doesn't seem to hurt anything.

2) Don't get hung up on the idea of coating every piece of sand with clay. Historically, people used the soil at hand, added some water and straw, stomped on it, flipped it a couple of times, and built walls. Be thorough in your mixing, sure, but use your common sense.

3) Don't worry so much about tying layers of cob together with cobber's thumbs or planning for interior drying with spine patterns or poking holes in the exterior. Layers of cob create a strong wall without careful interconnection and will dry over time without special techniques. Go ahead and relax if you need to take a break while building. You can add wet cob to part of the wall that has dried considerably without pushing some of the new down into the old.

Here's the fine print: Though cob is an ancient technique, no one I know has sufficient experience with it to really know the long-term performance of the buildings they're creating. Will adherence to more careful mixing and laying allow a cob building to last an extra hundred years? Will it be the difference between surviving an earthquake or being destroyed? I simply don't know.

In that context, my approach is to be thorough and careful in my methods. At the same time, experience with a material creates knowledge and confidence, and my friends simply have more cob building experience than I do. Over time, I may find myself altering my methods. Again, the broken record: You'll have to decide for yourself what seems like a sensible approach to cob construction, given the materials at hand, the results of your tests, and your own personal temperament.

Clay-slip is basically a wetter version of the soaked clay that we'd been using. How wet is open to debate. The wetter the slip, the easier it will be to mix with the straw, but the longer it will take to dry. A wet mix can slow progress because it has to dry out somewhat before the forms can be moved. Also, mold and insects can be a problem until the mix dries. On the other hand, some mold on the surface of drying clay-slip straw is normal. After the water has evaporated, there'll be nothing for the mold to feed on and it will die off, as long as the area stays dry. The most important feature of a mix is that the slip be spread evenly throughout, evenly coating the straw. At first, it's hard to imagine that this wet, sloppy stuff could dry into a hard, monolithic wafer, but then it does.

The advantages of clay-slip straw over cob have already been mentioned. It's much lighter (though messier) work, and the result is what I intuitively assume to be a huge increase in R-value. One disadvantage is that you need a skeletal structure as thick as the finished wall on which to attach the forms. Our simple locust post columns wouldn't be enough by themselves, for example. In addition, clay-slip straw is a true infill that cannot be trusted to handle any significant structural loads because it essentially has no aggregate. It's basically a way to make loose straw into a moldable, self-supporting unit.

Since the materials are the same, cob and clay-slip straw are great companions and are a good example of ways you can tweak things to fit the specifics of the situation at hand. In our situation, clay-slip straw worked perfectly over the door because, as you'll see, existing building elements served as most of the necessary formwork.

Mixing Clay-Slip Straw

▲ **Step 1.** To make clay-slip straw, we started with a slightly wetter version of the clay we had been paddle mixing and then leaving to soak. Ideally, each individual flake of clay should be suspended in the water.

▲ **Step 2.** Clay-slip straw can be mixed on a tarp on the ground or on some sort of platform. First, we laid out some loose straw…

▲ **Step 3.** …then poured slurry over the straw…

◄ Step 4. …and mixed everything together. *Left:* One advantage of platform-mixing is that it allows the use a pitchfork and is easier on your back. *Right:* But I find that hand-turning on the ground is faster and creates a more even coating, although it is definitely very messy work.

Sticky straw. *Left:* A finished mix looks like dirty straw. *Right:* The goal is simply to coat all the straw with slurry.

Straw brick. For anyone skeptical that this stuff works, I suggest making a test brick. Let it dry and then try to break it with your hands. It ain't easy.

Prepping the wall. *Left:* The area above our door lintel was ideal for clay-slip straw because already-existing building elements would act as permanent forms: the door lintel below, cob on two sides, the roof truss to the outside, and the ceiling above. *Right:* On the outside of the wall, all we had to do was cover the hole between the roof truss and the door lintel with a temporary form, and we were ready to go.

Building with Clay-Slip Straw

To build with clay-slip straw, you need some form of thick box to stuff it in. Generally, at least two sides of the box are permanent. The bottom is the stem wall and the top is the ceiling. The sides perpendicular to the surfaces of the wall can be made up by doorjambs, another wall, or some kind of temporary or permanent form (see Variations, page 285). The outside and inside surfaces of the box are generally made from temporary forms. The space above our door lintel was an ideal place to install clay-slip straw because our formwork was already almost completely in place.

Clay-slip straw is laid in courses, also called "lifts." A single lift is the amount it takes to fill the formwork. After a course has dried enough to support a mix laid on top, the formwork is detached and moved upward in preparation for another lift. In our clay-strip straw installation, we only needed a single lift and, therefore, didn't have to move our formwork.

Building with Clay-Slip Straw

▲ **Step 1.** We pushed handfuls of our wet mix against the back of our form and filled as much volume as we could without a front form piece.

▲ **Step 2.** We tied the clay-slip straw mix into the adjacent cob as best we could.

▲ **Step 3.** Next, we installed a front form piece to finish our "box."

▲ **Step 4.** Then we stuffed the space behind the form with our clay-slip straw mix.

Stuffed. We were careful to push the mix all the way back against the roof truss to fill the entire volume. Notice the cleat at left. We used it to temporarily fasten our form to the ridge beam of the roof. In this small space, we only needed to install a single "lift" of mix; in other words, we didn't need to move the formwork up the wall. After a couple of days when the mix had dried enough to stand up on its own, we pulled the form off to let the mix dry completely.

Shrinkage. We only installed about 20 inches of clay-slip, and it shrank about an inch as it dried. If you think about it, that makes sense because the mix is all clay and water with no sand as aggregate. We stuffed this gap with loose straw before plastering.

Memo from the real world. Though we define straw as the skeletal stalks of grass without seed, there's always some seed in straw, and this seed can sprout in clay-slip straw, creating a vertical lawn effect. Far from something to worry about, I see this as a positive. First off, the grass roots will add a bit more tensile reinforcement. Second, when the clay-slip straw has dried completely, the grass will die from lack of water, and you'll know that the wall is ready to be plastered.

Construction Blunders: Too Much, Too Early—Problems with Our Door Buck

Our door buck gave us some problems that in retrospect could have been avoided. I'd mentioned to our neighbor that we were getting ready to build this buck, and she gave us some beautiful red oak boards expressly for the purpose. The wood had been cut off her family land and had been air-drying for about eight years. The boards were over 11 inches wide and a full 1 inch thick. Normally, we'd build a buck with wood at least 1½ inches thick, but here was this beautiful, sturdy, sustainably harvested wood plopped right into our laps. To make up for the thinner thickness, we really beefed up the buck. We installed a stiffener along the back of these sides at the place where the doors would sit, and attached wood blocks perpendicular to the brace, figuring these measures would lock the cob to the buck, preventing movement.

Unfortunately, after we were well into the process of laying cob, we noticed that these oak buck sides were cupping badly. We tried to solve the problem by adding more blocking to the buck, but our reward was the only crack to appear in our entire wall.

Of course, after it was too late, the problem was obvious. The wood cupped in response to the water in the cob, and it was precisely at that moment, while the cob was still wet, that the cob had no strength to prevent the wood from cupping. To put it another way, all of our stiffeners and blocking would only be of use when the cob was structurally strong, i.e., dry, but it was really when the cob was wet that we needed them most.

Door buck problems. Our door buck seemed like a fortress. It was braced and temporarily tied to the roof structure. We installed a vertical board running the entire length of the jambs at the spot where the doors will be attached. With the horizontal cleats attached to the stiffener, as well as nails hammered in all over the buck, it was hard to imagine it going anywhere.

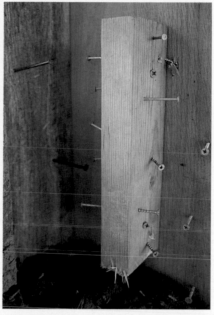

...and installed more blocking with protruding nails and screws...

But it did. You can see the gap developing between cob and buck here. This was caused by the buck cupping badly, curling away from the cob. We tried to brace the buck with boards pushed between the jambs...

In retrospect, there were several things we could have done to prevent this problem: (1) we could have used kiln-dried lumber; (2) we could have used lumber that was much thicker and hence more stable; and (3) we could have primed the back of the buck with a waterproof sealing paint to prevent water from the cob from penetrating the wood and causing it to cup. Any of these measures might have been enough, and a combination of all three would probably have been best.

In the short term, since we hadn't built our doors yet, there wasn't any real harm done, except making door installation more time-consuming. In the long term, however, I'd definitely prefer to have beefier, straighter doorjambs.

...but the result was the only crack in the wall where the cupping door buck simply ripped the blocking through the drying cob. This is an example of a shrinkage crack as described in Shrinkage, page 275.

WHAT WE'VE ACCOMPLISHED

At the beginning of this chapter we touched on the long history of earth building around the world and made the claim that it's earth's adaptability to different situations, along with its obvious general availability, that has given it a long and varied career in the world of building. The design flexibility of good old dirt is expressed in the earth wall we've just built.

The main section of our wall, cob, is dense and incredibly strong. It can support roof loads and, given the proper maintenance and building design, should be able to withstand pretty much anything the world can dish out. The downside is that it's heavy, labor-intensive, and a poor insulator in the context of our particular climate. To deal with those shortcomings, we made the wall thick and installed it on the south side of the building to expose it to winter sun in an attempt to take advantage of its thermal mass to hopefully create a "mass-enhanced R-value." As for the hard work, we thought it was worth it for such a beautiful, durable wall.

In the same wall and using the same earth-based materials mixed in different proportions, we installed a section of clay-slip straw that has basically the opposite characteristics of the cob section. It's lightweight and should be very insulative. However, it has little structural strength, requires formwork to install, and will be, in the long term relative to the cob, a more delicate material. For these reasons, we used clay-slip straw instead of cob in a place where insulation value and lighter weight were a real plus: the shaded area above our door. This spot is also very protected, has virtually no structural loads bearing on it, and easily accommodated formwork, all of which made it even more ideal for this particular earth mix. In other words, in a single wall, we've demonstrated the two poles of the earth-building continuum and how earth's flexibility can be used in building design.

In addition, we kept a focus on the overall feeling we were looking to create, which caused us to carefully plan and execute all of our various wall features, including doors, window, bottle designs, shelves and sculptural shaping. We strove to integrate all of this into a sculptural whole that could serve the complex purpose of inviting entrance, cozy interior, and embracing back wall to the outdoor room of our front patio. The result is that, even with only one wall in place, a strong sense of the feeling we're seeking is taking shape, something that started as only a dim glimmer of need in our imagination.

Live-in sculpture. Our finished cob and clay-slip straw wall is strong, beautiful, and very practical. It utilizes the adjustability of earthen mixes to maximize the energy efficiency potential of the materials involved while integrating functional features such as storage, a table, doors, and a window into a single stately-yet-whimsical sculpture.

VARIATIONS

In this chapter, we've focused on cob and clay-slip straw, but the world of dirt building is huge and varied. For example, clay soils aren't always mixed with sand and straw. They can be used alone, stabilized with Portland cement, or mixed with everything from cow dung to asphalt emulsion. A given mixture can be formed into blocks, packed into forms, poured into bags, pumped into fabric tubes, pounded into tires, or molded by hand. Let's take a quick survey of this smorgasbord of dirt.

ADOBE

One frustrating aspect of cob building is that you have to both manufacture your building material and install it at the same time. As we've said, this makes for slow going in the wall-raising phase. Another approach to using the same materials is to form your cob mix into individual blocks that you then allow to dry before installing.

This technique is called adobe and has been used all over the world for thousands of years. As with cob, adobe mixes vary widely with available soils and local custom. In general, though, the principle is the same: a soil mix blended with water containing a sand aggregate of differing sizes and enough clay to bind it. Sometimes straw is added to increase tensile strength and perhaps increase R-value, but adobe is also made without straw.

Adobe worldwide. Adobe has been used around the world for millennia. *Top:* These unplastered adobe barns are in New Zealand. Notice how the adobe is raised high off the ground on stone stem walls. *Left:* This adobe building covered with earthen plaster, the St. Francis of Assisi Church in New Mexico, is about 200 years old.

◄ **Step 1.** Adobe blocks are usually made in wooden forms. The small form in this photo makes four adobe blocks at a time. It's lined with thin sheet metal to keep the bricks from sticking as the form is pulled off. Another approach is to oil wooden forms to help the bricks slide out easily. First, the form is placed on a relatively level, flat surface and the earth mix is stuffed in.

◄ **Step 2.** As soon as the mix is in place, the form is removed. This mix is wetter than our cob mixes. The added wetness makes it easier to fill the form without gaps.

▲ **Step 3.** The form is set down and filled again.

◄ **Step 4.** The adobe bricks are allowed to dry. These adobes are being made under a tent, which will allow airflow to help them dry but will keep rain and harsh sun away.

◄ **Step 5.** After the blocks dry sufficiently to be moved, they are stacked and allowed to dry more thoroughly before use.

Mobile mud. One advantage of adobe is that you can make it one place and install it somewhere else. Here, a human conveyor belt is moving bricks from a drying area to a truck and having fun doing it. All of the adobe block-making and moving pictured here was done at a workshop hosted by the nonprofit organization Kleiwerks.

◀ **Step 6.** Meanwhile, other folks are mixing a simple earth mortar by foot in plywood boxes lined with plastic tarps. *Left:* At this point, the mix is very wet. It will have a lot more clay and sand added before it's ready. *Right:* Adobe blocks will be set in a thin bed of this finished mortar.

Modular cob. After a supply of adobe blocks has been made, wall construction can progress very quickly. *Bottom left:* This adobe building was built at a workshop in Thailand in conjunction with Kleiwerks and the Baandin Team, using adobe bricks made with the techniques shown in the photos above. Notice the bamboo pieces sticking out of the middle of the building. This is a bamboo sub-floor structure that was covered with an earthen floor. Notice also the two adobe buttresses. The one on the right is being covered with cob. To review the function of a buttress, see chapter 2. *Bottom right:* Here's the building nearing completion.

RAMMED EARTH

Rammed earth construction is simply the process of compressing soil into a structural mass to make up the walls of a building. This is usually accomplished by compacting a soil mix within some kind of form. There are a large number of variations on the technique.

Modern rammed earth buildings often are built using large plywood forms very similar to those used in conventional concrete wall construction. The soil mix is placed in the forms in layers, or "lifts," a foot or so at a time and compressed with hand or pneumatic tampers. After the walls are finished, the forms are removed.

Another approach is to use a small form to make compressed soil blocks that are then stacked into walls like bricks or any other masonry units. Usually a mud-slurry mortar is used between blocks. Rammed earth blocks can be made with a manual block press (you'll usually see it referred to as the CINVA-Ram) or a gas- or electric-powered hydraulic press capable of mass-producing blocks quickly right on the construction site.

Yet another approach is to use permanent forms that stay in place after the earth mix has been tamped into place. The tire walls of Earthships, for example, are simply permanent forms for rammed earth. Tires are stacked in overlapping courses like bricks, each tire being tamped full of dirt, again using either manual or pneumatic tampers, before the next course is laid on top. (See pages 211 to 213 for more on Earthships.) Another permanent form system is "earth bag" construction, wherein bags, such as polypropylene feed sacks, are filled with soil and again laid in courses like bricks. Each course is tamped in place before the next course is laid. Reinforcement in the form of barbed wire can be laid between the courses. Another interesting form system, pioneered by architect Nader Khalili, is called *superadobe*. In this approach, very long fabric tubes are pumped full of damp soil and coiled into domes.

Rammed earth. *Left:* Damp soil was mixed with a small amount of Portland cement and then tamped between sturdy temporary formwork to make the walls of the first floor of this building. *Right:* Like most earth-based construction techniques, rammed earth can conform to a variety of styles. This rammed earth home near Tucson, Arizona, was built to look like the traditional adobe buildings native to the region.

Permanent form systems are able to utilize a wider variety of soil types. Rammed earth tire walls, for example, can usually be built using the soil on site as is. Stand-alone rammed earth, either as blocks or formed walls, requires a more carefully considered soil mix because, unlike cob, it doesn't have the advantage of the tensile strength provided by straw. Clay, sand, gravel, water, and Portland cement are all potential additives to a given local soil to create a mix that will produce the desired result: walls that will hold a roof over your head. Put simply, you must test a rammed earth soil before committing to building with it. Tests vary from intuitive probing of sample blocks to full-fledged engineering analysis of blocks or core samples. Don't build until you're sure of your soil.

Depending on the system, soil mix, and climate, rammed earth buildings can either be plastered or not. Earthships and earthbag structures are almost always plastered. Mixes stabilized with Portland cement will be much less vulnerable to moisture and can often be left unplastered. Dry climates and building design elements, such as large overhangs, can allow non-stabilized mixes to remain unplastered in certain situations.

MONOLITHIC EARTH WALLS

There are many, many earthen buildings that use thick mass walls to carry roof loads. Rammed earth, adobe, and cob all are completely capable of forming such walls. In fact, most of the buildings with earth walls with which I'm familiar have load-bearing earth walls, not infill within a skeletal structure as is the case with our cob and clay-slip straw wall. Look over the photos of the adobe, rammed earth, and cob buildings in this variations section and you'll see that they all have load-bearing earth walls.

You'll remember from chapter 7 that we don't advise beginners to start out creating monolithic, load-bearing walls. However, if my perception is correct, we are in the minority of those interested in earth building these days who suggest that beginners start with a skeletal structure. If you live in an area with a strong local tradition in monolithic mud building and scant resources for creating skeletal structures, then our previous generalized sage advice may be of little value to you.

If you happen to live in the southwestern United States, for example, load-bearing construction using sun-dried adobe blocks has a long, proven history in your area. There are many examples to study, experienced craftspeople to learn from, and building projects from which to gain hands-on experience. The huge amount of sun, cold winter nights, low rainfall, and lack of trees make this geographical area a perfect fit for mud building. The high thermal mass can work well in a sunny, cold climate. The low rainfall is kind to the water-sensitive blocks, and the local availability of materials makes practical and environmental sense.

Permanent formwork. This building is being constructed out of long fabric tubes pumped full of damp dirt that are then coiled like a huge coiled-clay pot. The tubes act as permanent formwork for an earth mix that wouldn't be able to hold together structurally on its own. This amazing technique is called *superadobe* and was pioneered by architect Nader Khalili.

Strong dirt. This little building has load-bearing cob walls. Thick, rounded walls and a lightweight roof structure combine to create a very sound structural package.

Whether you are interested in using cob, adobe, or some other earth-based technique to create load-bearing walls, here are a few basic pointers you might want to consider:

1) Quality Control. Mass-produced materials tend to cause pollution and are often not matched to the specifics of the situation. On the other hand, they're usually of very consistent quality because of uniformity of content, stringent testing, and careful quality control mandated by a very litigious society. Put simply, you know what you're getting.

Handmade materials, on the other hand, begin and end with you. You have to be your own factory, government testing laboratory, and angry class action suit lawyer. In other words, quality, testing, and accountability are up to you. Just because that adobe block or cob mix looks good now doesn't mean it will withstand the constant and ever-changing stress of being part of a building. If installed as load-bearing components, these materials will be suspending heavy weights over your (or someone else's) head, so the stakes are high.

Make sure that you're very confident of the quality and long-term performance of your materials before building. At the very least start by building a test wall, maybe a little garden wall or even a dog house, before moving forward.

2) Think Strength. Modern concrete cheats. Inside that monolithic poured mass is usually a skeletal structure of steel that greatly increases the tensile strength of the material. Mud building doesn't have this advantage, so structural design concepts such as buttressing are extremely important.

First, make sure that your wall is thick enough to support the necessary loads. Read other books on cob to get guidelines. Remember, though, no one can really give you this information in general terms. It'll be a function of the strength of your mix. Second, make sure that you start wider on the bottom and taper to thinner at the top. If you like, you can make the inside surface straighter, and put most of the taper on the outside. This shape is structurally stronger than a straight, perpendicular wall.

Concrete vs. cob. *Left:* Steel-reinforced concrete is very stable against lateral forces. This long retaining wall is connected into a concrete foundation with steel rebar. You couldn't build a freestanding wall this long, tall, and thin out of cob. *Right:* Strong earth walls take a different avenue to structural integrity. The load-bearing adobe walls of this building are tapered, in other words, much wider at the bottom than at the top. Notice also the extensive buttressing around the door and along the wall to the left.

A curved wall is also structurally stronger than a straight one, and there's no reason you have to build straight walls with cob. Finally, if it's your first building, don't install a living roof. That's just too much weight to mess around with in this situation without experience.

3) Focus on Connections. As we are repeating perhaps *ad naseum*, a building is a system. Modern monolithic buildings are standardized systems complete with specialized fasteners to connect different materials. As we pointed out in chapter 2, places where materials connect are often the weak point in a structure. This is definitely true of monolithic mud construction. Connecting a roof to a cob or adobe wall can be a challenge. The process sometimes starts as the wall is being built, requiring forethought and experience and making repairs or the correction of mistakes much more difficult than in a skeletal structural system. Be sure you are confident and clear about your methods for connecting the roof, doors, and windows before you begin construction. (See figure 4.)

4) Prepare for Rain. Working in the rain is never fun, but it can be a real bummer in the context of monolithic mud building. If you are building in a wet climate, make sure your walls can be protected from rain during construction. You can accomplish this with a temporary roof or careful covering of walls when it's raining. Both of these options can, frankly, be a pain in the butt. In unskilled hands, temporary tarped roofs are often just an opportunity for the wind to make a fool of you, or should I say "me." I've never had much luck creating a temporary tarp roof that lasted very long. The alternative of trying to keep things dry by covering them with tarps can end up being a thankless, almost full-time job.

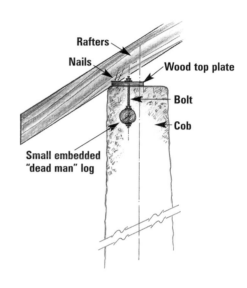

Figure 4
CONNECTING A FRAMED ROOF TO A LOAD-BEARING COB WALL

One approach to attaching a roof to load-bearing cob is to install horizontal pieces of wood, called *dead men*, at appropriate places in the wall. These are then attached to the roof framing with wires or bolts. Although some might find it unnecessary, I'd also install a top plate to distribute roof loads.

Temporary roof. If you do it right, a temporary roof can be a great solution to the problems of building monolithic earth walls in a wet climate. Here, the wall structure and fabric roof of a yome, an inexpensive yurt-dome hybrid manufactured by Red Sky Shelters, has been set up to create a protected area to erect adobe walls.

CLAY-SLIP STRAW WALLS

We used clay-slip straw to fill only a small portion of our earthen wall. However, since our building has a skeletal structure, we could have considered using clay-slip straw to infill the entire volume of the wall. The advantages here would be greatly increased speed and ease of construction and a superior insulation value allowing the energy-efficient use of an earth mix in a wider variety of climates and solar orientations. In addition, clay-slip straw requires far less clay than cob construction, so less excavation is required. The main disadvantage would be the hassle of creating a wide formwork box to hold each lift of clay-slip straw.

The formwork box can be created in a number of ways. You can build a permanent box of desired width whose interior and exterior surfaces consist of a lath used as a plastering surface. For example, the modified stick-frame structure we discuss in chapter 11 could have been filled with clay-slip straw instead of recycled newspaper insulation.

Another approach would be to create wide structural columns out of concrete-filled blocks to serve as two sides of the box and as a surface for affixing temporary interior and exterior forms (see figure 5a). Replacing conventional concrete blocks with insulative composite blocks made from wood chips bound with concrete would be a more energy-efficient choice for the columns.

Yet another method would be to forgo the wide columns and create a more conventional thin post-and-beam structure. Forms could be held together with pieces of wood spanning the width of the wall (see figure 5b). After the clay-slip had dried enough, the forms would be unscrewed from the wood ties, which would stay embedded in the wall and be covered with plaster. The forms would be moved up and fastened to new wood ties in preparation for another lift of clay-slip straw. The forms themselves can be made of salvage plywood and scrap lumber.

Full wall clay-slip straw infill. In this situation, the formwork for clay-strip straw consists of 2x6 framing covered on the exterior with plank siding. The interior side of the formwork box, removed at this point, was a piece of plywood attached between 2x6 studs, like the one visible in the photo. After clay-slip straw was stuffed into the box and allowed to dry enough to be stable, the form was moved up and the process repeated. Vertical lines in the cured clay-sip straw show where each wet course of material was set on top of the drying layer below. The cavity to the left will be filled next using the same sequential forming technique. The finished wall will be covered with plaster. This is a convenient system, but clay-slip straw walls need to be made much thicker than in this example if they are to rival the R-values of such conventional insulation infills as cellulose or fiberglass.

Permanent clay-slip straw formwork. To achieve a decent R-value with clay-slip straw, you need to create thicker walls than a conventional skeletal frame alone will provide. The walls of this little round building consist of two separate frames separated by spacers to create a deep cavity for infill. This configuration looks somewhat like a ladder, so this technique is sometimes called a "ladder truss." Here, the ladder truss is covered with lath made from waste strips created by milling lumber. The cavity will be filled with clay-slip straw and then the wall will be covered with earth plaster.

a

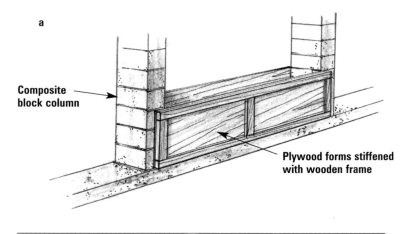

Composite block column

Plywood forms stiffened with wooden frame

b

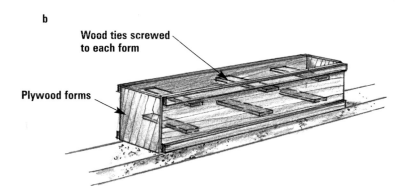

Wood ties screwed to each form

Plywood forms

Figure 5
CLAY-SLIP STRAW FORMWORK

a. Composite Block Columns. This is the formwork for a clay-slip straw wall utilizing the width of insulative composite blocks as structural columns. The plywood form will be temporarily attached to the columns, and then simply moved up when it's time for the next course.

b. Wooden Ties. If your structural supports are thinner than your desired wall thickness, as is the case with most post-and-beam wall systems, you can use stand-alone formwork. Here, plywood forms are stiffened with 2x4s on the top and bottom and screwed together with pieces of wood that create the desired wall width. When it's time to move the forms up, just unscrew the ties and leave them embedded in the wall to be covered with plaster. Another set of ties would connect the forms for the next course above. This drawing doesn't show the structural posts of the wall to which the formwork would need to be attached. These posts could either sit to the inside or outside of the clay-slip straw infill.

Clay-slip straw whimsy. Don't let all of this technical talk of formwork fool you into thinking clay-slip straw has to lose the flow and whimsy of cob. *Left:* The walls of this beautiful cottage in the Texas hill country are a timber frame infilled with clay-slip straw. *Right:* The cottage's 18-foot cathedral ceiling, exposed framing, and undulating clay-slip straw infill covered in rich lime plaster create a simultaneously cozy and almost regal atmosphere.

OTHER USES FOR EARTH MIXES

The wonders of earth construction go far beyond walls for buildings. Earth mixes can be used to build covered benches, garden walls, bread ovens, outdoor sculptures, and…well, just use your imagination.

Versatile cob. Here cob covered in earth plaster is used to create a beautiful, whimsical garden wall. Notice the stone foundation lifting the cob off the wet ground and the simple wooden shingle roof protecting the vulnerable top against rain. This wall is at the home of Linda Smiley and Ianto Evans, two of the pioneers of the modern cob renaissance in the United States and elsewhere.

Earth oven. This fanciful cob bake oven has a kiln-baked brick firebox surrounded by an interior layer of cob without straw for thermal mass, covered in turn by a layer of cob with lots of straw to keep heat in the oven. The whole thing is covered with an earthen plaster. The oven sits on a broad bed of cob, the top layer of which also has lots of straw for insulation. The oven was built as a community project in Portland, Oregon.

Dirt bench. This beautiful cob bench built by Janell Kapoor and Kleiwerks is incredibly strong, and the gentle curves make it comfortable to sit on. Corbel cobs, similar to those used in our little house, were built up to create the huge cantilever. When the bench started to sag during construction, straw bales were set under it as temporary forms. A wash made of casein and borax was applied to the bench to seal the earth plaster, making it more waterproof and preventing it from "dusting," i.e., sloughing off in response to abrasion. If you're skeptical about the structural strength of cob, sitting on this bench will make you a believer!

Tim's Take *Getting It Done: Cob*

Let's talk straight about actually getting something built. Although it is possible, and on occasion accomplished, it is rare that an owner-builder truly builds a house alone. In most cases, there comes a point when help is needed. And cob, while often billed as a do-it-yourself system, is not an exception to this rule. Cob walls for a modest house require an outlay of physical effort and time that few modern people—or even families—are able to muster alone. Let's consider realistic options for getting cob done.

The Workshop

One approach to gathering a cob crew is to construct your building as part of a workshop. The concept here is that experienced cob builders guide students through the construction of part of your building. The students pay tuition, which the professionals keep as their fee. The hosts, i.e., owners, of the building, provide food and lodging for the participants in exchange for the work done on the building.

Though such a set-up can be advantageous for everyone involved, there are lots of things to consider. First, to really get anything done, the workshop needs to be lengthy—a week to 10 days is a common time frame. Second, you can't build a house in 7 to 10 days, so such a workshop will only partially solve your labor problems. Third, if any real work is going to come of a workshop, it has to be very well organized. Everything has to be ready well in advance: the foundation finished, permanent or temporary roof in place, all materials on site and ready to go, clear design decisions made, etc.

Finally, though cob isn't rocket science, it still requires focus, hard work, and some level of physical coordination. Students coming to a workshop simply may not have these prerequisites, and, though they may learn a lot, you may not end up getting enough work out of them to justify the time, effort, and expense of putting on the workshop in the first place.

Hiring a Crew

Although making and laying cob is not hard to master, a paid cob worker would need to be both strong and motivated, have stamina, and be willing to mix materials with his or her feet. In addition, unlike plastering for example (which could potentially be completed in a couple of weeks), building cob walls for a modest house would take much longer. In other words, we're not talking about grabbing some college kids on spring break here, but something resembling a true construction crew.

To be honest, I'm not sure how I would go about finding a group of people like that to hire. If I did find them, the slow pace of cob construction would insure that a cob wall laid by a hired crew would not be inexpensive. And at this level of commitment, you have to start considering things like worker's compensation and injury insurance, an expensive proposition.

Once you start hiring people, the efficient use of time becomes paramount. Cob offers a few unique challenges in this area. First, you can only add so much height to a cob wall at a time. Wet cob piled on top of wet cob will eventually slump. This means that you would need to carefully tailor the size of your crew to the size of the job. There's nothing worse than writing checks for people who are sitting around with nothing to do. At the same time, you start loosing good employees if you can't offer them steady, clearly defined work. In addition, remember that cob is definitely a warm weather pastime. Asking employees to put their hands or, even worse, their bare feet into wet stuff is not an option when it's cold. Try it and watch your efficiency plummet and your costs skyrocket.

Hiring Subcontractors

Of course, building cob walls will be only part of the construction process. If you're an inexperienced builder, you may find yourself needing help with the foundation, stem walls, roof, electricity, plumbing, or other aspects of your building project.

In general, it will be more difficult to find skilled subcontractors who can integrate into a cob project. For example, a professional framer who has built hundreds of roofs on stick-framed buildings may have no interest in trying to put one on top of your load-bearing cob walls. This is true even assuming that you have the proper permits and code approval for your building, a completely separate but equally important issue.

You can't overestimate the advantages of a building system that's well known and supported by the local economy. Even if you don't hire professionals for anything major, it's great to have knowledgeable people around who'll answer your questions or whom you can hire in a pinch. In many places, cob isn't established enough to have that kind of technical support. On the other hand, cob construction is on the rise and professional builders are starting to appear on the scene. If cob is popular in your area, there may be experienced crews available for hire. You'll just have to do your research.

Chapter 9

Cordwood

Controlled fire, and the wood that fuels it, is perhaps

the archetypal image of human civilization. Fire could even be considered the first house. It defines a space by creating a temperature different from the surrounding air and establishing some degree of separation from marauding predators, and, of course, the connection to the outside is unrivaled around a campfire. All that's lacking is a real structure to underpin the other three elements a house provides.

It's not hard to imagine the pulsing cerebellum of a little human sitting out of the wind against a neatly stacked pile of firewood and staring into the fire. Suddenly, DING! An idea surges into that big brain. Why not get more sticks to burn and just leave this nice windbreak of stacked wood here? Eventually, he or she might have expanded this wood wall to encircle most of the fire, added more sticks and perhaps leaves as a simple roof, and voila! firewood construction was born. Of course, no one took the time to update their blogs in those days, so we don't really know the origins of building with firewood. But in our era there are numerous examples of firewood buildings built in the last couple of centuries in the United States and other parts of the world.

Duh. It doesn't take much imagination to see this stack of covered firewood (left) becoming this little building (right).

GENERAL CONTEXT: CORDWOOD

Firewood is measured in units called "cords," one cord of wood being a stack 4 feet tall, 4 feet wide, and 8 feet long. *Cordwood masonry construction* is the name given to the modern incarnation of the practice of using firewood to build walls. In this technique, short pieces of air-dried round or split wood are laid in a double bed of mortar. This mortar is usually Portland-cement based, but cob has also been used. The space between the two mortar beds is usually filled with some form of loose insulation, such as sawdust or vermiculite. This technique can be used to construct monolithic (load-bearing) walls or as an infill within a skeletal structure.

ADVANTAGES OF CORDWOOD CONSTRUCTION

I live in a wooded mountainous area where lots of people heat their homes with wood. Around here, you see huge piles of cordwood stacked like fortresses on the porches or in the yards of small, poorly insulated houses. I can't help but think that some of these folks could build a nice little energy efficient cordwood cottage with the firewood that they burn in one winter, move into it, and burn a lot less firewood the next year. Herein lies the central allure of cordwood construction. If you heat with wood, those piles of neatly stacked firewood look a lot like walls already. Why not harvest a major building material from your own land that you're already harvesting and storing for another purpose?

Where firewood is abundant, cordwood can be an inexpensive, low impact, renewable, and easily accessible material. In addition, wood is a good thermal mass and a decent insulator. The infill insulation between mortar beds and the addition of insulation to the mortar itself in the form of sawdust create a wall whose entire volume has uniform resistance to heat flow. This feature, combined with the fact that cordwood can easily be cut to any size to allow walls of any desired thickness, makes cordwood an adjustable system that can usually deliver the insulation value required by a given situation.

Also, though cordwood construction is hard work, the end product has an integrated skin, meaning that no plastering or other wall finish is required. Once you've laid the cordwood, your walls are basically done, thus avoiding a number of steps inherent in other wall systems. The exposed log ends and the inherent thickness of the walls give cordwood a unique aesthetic, creating a feeling to which a lot of people respond.

Finally, like cob, cordwood walls are hygroscopic, which, as we've said, means that they can take on and give off water vapor from the air in response to humidity changes. On the outside, this means that water soaking into the exterior surface of the wood from rain exposure and humidity changes shouldn't cause rot, so long as the wood is able to dry out in a timely fashion. On the inside, the exposed end grain of the wood will be able to take on and let off water in response to humidity changes, therefore keeping indoor air at a more consistent humidity level. As we've pointed out before, this mechanism should discourage mold and fungus growth and help keep indoor air cleaner.

DISADVANTAGES OF CORDWOOD CONSTRUCTION

Wood and mortar are very different materials. They both have distinct characteristics that can clash when combined in the same wall.

For example, wood is dynamic and flexible, but mortar, once it cures, is steady state and rigid. As wood dries, it shrinks. This shrinkage can cause cordwood pieces to split, or "check," pulling away from the rigid mortar in which they sit. This can cause gaps that allow air infiltration. If enough shrinkage occurs, cordwood pieces can even become loose in the wall. Far worse, it's possible for the wood to expand, which could cause the wall to heave (much as a poorly built foundation can experience frost heave), which could in turn cause cracking or even severe structural damage.

What is Mortar?

In conventional building, the word "mortar" usually refers to a mixture of Portland cement, hydrated lime, sand, and water used to bond building units such as stone, brick, or concrete blocks into a structural whole. In green building, the word "mortar" isn't as clear-cut. For example, adobe blocks can be laid with an earthen mortar and cordwood can be laid with a cob mortar. Unless otherwise specified, the word "mortar" in this chapter refers to the mortar we used in our cordwood wall— a mixture of sand, hydrated lime, sawdust, Portland cement, and water.

Shrinkage. When wood shrinks it can crack (left) or simply leave a gap between the wood and mortar in a cordwood wall (right).

However, different species of wood respond to the loss of water with different levels of shrinkage, so with conscious wood choice and preparation, the danger of heaving can be avoided and the nuisance of shrinkage can be minimized.

Another problem with the marriage of these two materials is that their intrinsic strengths are so different. As we've already pointed out, Portland cement has a high embodied energy and creates pollution in its manufacture and transport. On the other hand, correctly mixed and placed mortar can last a very, very long time, and this longevity can overstep the negatives of its manufacture in certain situations. The small pieces of green (not kiln-dried) wood used as cordwood have the opposite traits. They are readily and quickly replaceable, but, relatively speaking, not very durable.

Even considering its hygroscopic nature, wood is susceptible to water infiltration and is a popular food for molds, fungus, insects, and even some mammals. Wood such as cordwood that's exposed on its end-grain is even more susceptible to this problem, just as an exposed cut is more susceptible to infection. In a cordwood wall then, these two materials can hold each other back. The lifespan of the mortar is limited by the wood, and the environmental sensitivity of the wood is counteracted by the mortar.

This effect is exacerbated by the fact that cordwood construction uses a fair amount of mortar. In fact, the word *mortar* usually refers to a thin layer of bonding agent laid between whatever units actually make up a wall, be they bricks, stones, or whatever. The shapes of the pieces of cordwood, which generally are either completely or partially round, create a lot more empty space that needs to be filled. Cordwood guru Rob Roy estimates that mortar makes up 40 percent of the surface area of a typical cordwood wall. That's a lot of mortar.

However, this apparent conflict between materials is really only a design challenge. As we'll discuss below, the inherent strengths of cordwood and mortar can be brought together through careful selection of wood and a good water-protection strategy, such as lifting the wood off the ground on stem walls and covering it with ample roof overhangs. These steps will both extend the life of the wood, bringing it closer to the lifespan of the mortar, and help prevent shrinkage and expansion.

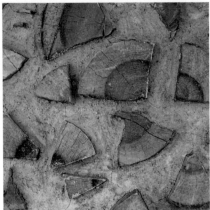

Is it mortar? Compare the thin bed of mortar that binds these concrete blocks (top) to the huge amount of mortar between these pieces of cordwood (bottom). If a wall is around 40 percent mortar, it's probably not accurate to call it mortar anymore.

There are other design options including covering the mortar with a flexible chinking compound, covering the entire wall exterior with plaster, and replacing the Portland cement-based mortar with cob. Personally, I think the cob option may be the best direction for cordwood construction in general. Cob is well matched to cordwood with a low embodied energy and a flexibility that allows easy repair for mortar cracks and shrinkage gaps. We'll touch on all of these options in this chapter and in chapter 12. The point here is that apparent disadvantages of cordwood can be overcome through careful, conscious design.

CHOOSING WOOD

Regardless of the overall design strategy, wood selection is a central part of the cordwood construction process. The general criteria for choosing cordwood are, in no particular order, availability, durability, estimated insulation value, and shrinkage factor. Let's take a look at each one.

Availability

Having a ready, local source of cordwood is paramount. Trucking cordwood long distances misses the point of this material. On the other hand, not having wooded property at your disposal shouldn't take cordwood out of the picture. Many kinds of salvage and "waste wood" could make good cordwood. Trimmed edges or ends left over from milling, a variety of cut offs from log home manufacturing, and the completely useable "trash" left around after a piece of land has been logged are all possible sources.

Trash or treasure? A sawmill or logging operation can sometimes be a source of cordwood for building.

Durability

Wood's durability can be a measure of its structural strength, rot resistance, or unattractiveness to insects. In terms of strength, pretty much any wood species is adequate for the purposes of normal cordwood construction. Rot refers to decomposition caused by bacterial or fungal action. For any wood, the main factor that affects rot resistance is exposure to moisture. If wood is kept truly dry, it shouldn't rot. If wood *is* exposed to water, dense woods with a tight grain, such as hickory, locust, or maple, will be more water resistant. This is especially true if the end grain is exposed, which is the case in cordwood construction. As for attractiveness to insects, again water content is paramount. Wood-eating insects, such as termites, like wet wood. The heartwood of some wood species, such as cedar, contains oils that are unattractive to some insects. However, this property probably isn't that important in this context, because cordwood construction uses both the sapwood and heartwood of the tree.

Shrinkage

When alive, wood is water-rich. If it's cut and stacked to dry, it will loose water and consequently shrink. Wood shrinks *across* growth rings ("against the grain") at different rates than it shrinks *along* growth rings ("along the grain"). The outer part of a log (the sapwood) dries faster than the inner part (the heartwood). All these factors combined cause milled lumber to crack, cup, and bow. Cordwood also cracks for these reasons, but just as importantly its overall volume changes. As mentioned above, this means that installed cordwood gets smaller as it dries, which can create gaps that will allow air infiltration. It also swells as it takes on water, possibly pushing up on the wall, causing cracking and even structural damage.

To make an educated guess as to how a particular piece of cordwood might perform in a wall, we need to answer three questions. First, what is the volumetric shrinkage potential of the wood being used? In other words, what percentage of its volume will it loose as it goes from being green (water saturated) to kiln-dried? This information is available for a large number of species of wood. (See figure 1 on page 302.)

Next, we need to know how dry the wood is as it is set into the wall. For example, if the wood has the potential of loosing about 10 percent of its volume in shrinkage and its water content is about halfway between green and kiln-dried, it could continue to loose about 5 percent more volume, potentially causing some gapping. Likewise, it could potentially gain about 5 percent of its volume in certain situations, which might cause cracking or even heaving of the wall.

This brings us to the third thing we need to know: how much water will the wood be exposed to after it's set in the wall? If for example, our wood in question is in a wall that's covered by a roof overhang in an arid climate, it would be safe to assume that the wood will never expand in the wall, and in fact, it will probably slowly dry out and consequently shrink. However, the same wood in a very wet climate with little protection from rain, might expand in the wall. Again, in the worst case, this expansion could cause structural damage.

Comparison shopping. This stack of firewood is made up of a variety of species, each with unique R-value, shrinkage, and durability characteristics.

Insulation Value

Dried specimens of different woods having the same volume will weigh different amounts. That's because some woods have a more open cell structure and are therefore "airier." As we've said, in general terms, the lighter a wood is, the more insulation value it will have. We've also mentioned that wood resists the flow of heat across the grain much better than along it. (The amount of difference depends on factors such as species type, moisture content, and size of the wood sample.) In any case, there seems to be less consensus as to the R-values for different woods along the grain, partly because we have fewer and less-conclusive test measurements for along the grain. It's difficult, then, to make accurate estimates of the R-values of a given specimen of cordwood. Still, if we use measured across-the-grain values to make relative comparisons, the differences are striking. For example, western red cedar's across-the-grain heat resistance is more than twice that of white oak. (See figure 1.) Across an 18-inch-thick cordwood wall, that would make quite a difference.

Figure 1
SHRINKAGE AND INSULATION VALUES OF WOOD SPECIES

The following chart is adapted from *Wood Handbook: Wood as an Engineering Material*, published by the United States Department of Agriculture. I've included just a few species for general comparison. Remember that the R-values are across the grain and cordwood is oriented along the grain. According to this source, along-the-grain measurements vary from 1.5 to 2.8 times less than the across-the-grain measurements for different species, though specific test results have varied widely.

Notice that in general terms, lighter woods are more insulative and (counter-intuitive to my mind) denser woods shrink more. If you're serious about making these comparisons, I advise looking at the complete chart and reading the associated material in the *Wood Handbook*. It's available online at http://www.fpl.fs.fed.us/documnts/fplgtr/fplgtr113/fplgtr113.htm.

	% Volumetric Shrinkage from Green (Saturated) to Kiln-Dried Moisture Content	R-Value Across the Grain	
		12% Moisture	Kiln-Dried
Western Red Cedar	6.8	1.5	1.7
Eastern White Pine	8.2	1.3	1.6
Yellow Poplar	12.7	1.1	1.3
Sugar Maple	14.7	1.0	1.2
Black Locust	10.2	not available	not available
White Oak	16.3	0.7	0.9
Shagbark Hickory	16.7	0.7	0.9

The Bottom Line

If all of this sounds both complicated and inexact, it is. Actual wall shrinkage is a function of things that are hard to know, like the actual water content of your wood on the green-to-kiln-dried continuum. Furthermore, as we've said, actual R-values for the wood you choose really aren't possible to discern.

Still, we can be fairly confident of our ability to make relative comparisons. The smartest approach is to pick the wood you can get your hands on that has the lowest measured shrinkage values, because it's the wood with the least likelihood of expanding in the wall. Chances are, this wood will also have one of the higher R-values. Look at figure 1: Oak has a high shrinkage rate and low across-the-grain insulation value. It's also slow growing, and therefore not as quickly renewable. Eastern white pine doesn't shrink much, has twice the insulation value as oak, and grows quickly. Given access to both, it's obvious which is the smarter choice.

The only reason someone might argue for choosing oak is that it would be more durable in the wall. It's true that pine would fare poorly if exposed to a lot of rain, and oak would be more durable in that situation, but it would also be in danger of expanding when exposed to that same rain. In other words, setting either pine or oak cordwood in a wall exposed to a lot of rain probably isn't a good idea.

The bottom line is that the exposed end grain inherent in cordwood construction is best protected from direct rain, regardless of the wood type used. In a wall protected from rain, low-shrinkage, high R-value woods—in other words, softer, less durable woods—are the better choice for cordwood construction.

MORTAR

Cordwood mortar has different demands placed on it than mortar in most other masonry situations. In fact, the huge mortar joints are perhaps better thought of as a mortar wall in which large pieces of wood aggregate are randomly embedded. A conventional mortar asked to span that kind of distance and put up with the movement of a flexible embedded material like wood, would almost certainly crack. Too much cracking could cause structural problems, so cordwood mortars need to be reengineered to make sure they are less likely to shrink and crack.

In addition, most conventional masonry walls make no attempt to resist heat flow through their volume, relying instead on insulation applied to the wall's exterior or interior surface. The volume of a cordwood wall, on the other hand, needs to be resistant to heat flow on its own. Since cordwood mortar is a considerable component of that volume, it would be nice to make it more insulative than its conventional counterpart.

To make a long story short, cordwood builders have developed a variety of mixes that include a water-absorptive, insulative component, usually sawdust. Mortar shrinks and cracks mostly either from being too wet or from drying too quickly. If sawdust is soaked in water and then added to a mortar mix, it will give that water back slowly to the mix, thus keeping the mortar wet longer, slowing the cure, and (it's hoped) preventing cracking. In addition, once the mix has dried, the airy structure of the sawdust should enhance the R-value of the mortar. Perlite and vermiculite have also been used to similar effect.

Due to the situation-specific nature of a number of variables, including how your particular cordwood species responds to wet mortar and the nature of the type of sawdust or other additive you choose, the best mortar mix for your project is something probably best discovered through experimentation and tests. The ideal situation would be to get your wood to the desired level of dryness and then build a few tiny test walls with different mixes and let them cure for a few weeks to see how they fare. This would also be a good chance to practice a little cordwood masonry. These practice walls could be designed to be useful, as an outdoor seat or short garden wall perhaps.

Concrete wall with wood aggregate?
The huge mortar bed required by the irregular shapes of cordwood pieces puts unique demands on a mortar mix. Additives like soaked sawdust and vermiculite can help prevent the mortar from cracking while possibly adding insulation value.

How much of each? It's not really possible to make an accurate measurement of exactly how much of the volume of this wall is going to be wood, mortar, or insulation.

Figure 2
POSSIBLE R-VALUE RANGE OF CORDWOOD CONSTRUCTION

Wood (Poplar)

	Width (inches)	R/inch	R-Value
HIGH	16	.85	13.6
LOW	16	.5	8

Mortar and Infill

		Width (inches)	R/inch	R-Value	Total
HIGH	Mortar	10	.5	5	20
	Infill	6	12.5	15	
LOW	Mortar	10	.2	2	14.6
	Infill	6	2.1	12.6	

Total Estimates

	Cordwood (60% of wall)	+	Mortar (40% of wall)	=	Total
HIGH	13.6 (.6)	+	20 (.4)	≈	R-16
LOW	8 (.6)	+	14.6 (.4)	≈	R-11

WHAT'S THE R-VALUE OF A CORDWOOD WALL?

Cordwood is an integrated system with variable parts that make accurate estimates of R-value difficult. The first issue is the species of wood you choose. As we've said, light, airy woods are more insulative than dense hardwoods. Generalized across the grain per inch, R-values for softwoods are usually listed as R-1.25 and for hardwoods as R-0.9. For cordwood construction calculations, we of course need along-the-grain numbers, but we've already learned that these are hard to come by.

The next nebulous material we have to think about is our mortar. Conventional mortar has no R-value worth mentioning, but our cordwood mortar contains sawdust, which should give it some insulative value, although how much is just a guess. Moving on to our infill insulation we run up against similar problems. If we are using vermiculite, for example, there are measured per inch R-values to which to refer, but how much of the volume of our wall is taken up by this infill? The random nature of cordwood makes each wall different and accurate estimates of the volume of infill impossible to make. If we use sawdust as insulation, we can't even start with an accurate per inch R-value measurement of the insulation because wood type, particle size, and other variables would make R-value vary between sawdusts.

Obviously, then, any number we come up with is basically a guess, though it can be an educated one. Let's look at the wall we built for our little building as an example. We chose poplar cordwood, specimens of which have been measured to have an across-the-grain R-value of 1.2 per inch. We can plug in a couple of possible along-the-grain values to get a range, let's say 40 percent and 70 percent of the measured value, giving us per inch values of 0.5 and 0.85.

Next, we have two 5-inch-wide mortar beds with sawdust. According to my sources, typical sawdust has an R-value in the 2- to 2.5-per-inch range. Our sawdust makes up about 20 percent of our mortar, so we might be safe in claiming an R-value of 0.4 to 0.5 per inch of mortar joint. As with the straw in cob, though, this may be a mistake because the sawdust is spread out and surrounded by the very heat-conductive mortar, so let's arbitrarily make up a lower value to create a range, say R-0.2 per inch of bed. As infill insulation, we chose vermiculite, which has a measured R-value ranging between 2.1 and 2.5 per inch. For our final bit of vital information, the relative volume of cordwood to mortar, let's go with Rob Roy's 40 percent mortar estimate.

Using this information, we calculated that the absolute worst performance of our cordwood wall we could imagine is around R-11, and the best we could hope for would be around R-16. (See figure 2.)

DOES CORDWOOD FIT YOUR SITUATION?

The only way cordwood construction makes sense is if you have easy access to cordwood. Though this may seem obvious, apparently it isn't a widely accepted concept, because there are as many wood-based buildings going up these days in the desert as in the forest. If cordwood is locally available, then it should be an option in a wide variety of climates because it has a decent resistance to heat flow.

Since building a thicker cordwood wall is as easy as building a thinner one (all you need is longer cordwood), it's theoretically possible to get pretty much whatever R-value your situation demands. In severe climates, people sometimes build two cordwood walls separated by an insulation-filled space to create a super-insulated wall. That's a lot of wood and a lot of work. Based on available information, cordwood's insulation potential is only mediocre. When put in terms of the amount of material and work needed to gain a specific R-value, it lags behind straw bale and well-designed stick-framing.

In very wet climates, the exposed end-grain of cordwood construction could severely limit its durability, though good design and wood selection could go a long way toward easing that worry. All of our other wall systems are covered with a plaster mix that not only protects the wall against direct attack from weather, insects, and woodpeckers, but can be also be adjusted for various climatic conditions. I don't see any reason that cordwood couldn't be plastered to gain the same benefits, therefore alleviating any concern about exposed end grain whatsoever.

All in all, then, I believe that cordwood construction could be engineered to be appropriate in most situations where cordwood is easily available.

Good planning. This beautiful cordwood wall is protected nicely from rain by a generous roof overhang and a graveled perimeter that's sloped to direct water away from the wall. We recommend taking the further precaution of lifting the cordwood off the ground on a stem wall, as we did with all of our wall systems.

Is Cordwood Green?

Let's run cordwood up the green building flagpole and see who salutes.

1) Low Construction Impact. In wooded areas, especially where wood is burned as heating fuel, cordwood and sawdust are readily available with little embodied energy. If trees need to be cleared to make room for the building, then the cordwood could even be considered to have no embodied energy since the wood needed to be removed regardless of the building system chosen. However, conventional cordwood techniques use a fair amount of lime and Portland cement, both high-embodied-energy materials. The kilns that produce these materials release pollutants into the air, affecting the environment at large. Replacing Portland cement-based mortar with a cob mortar would greatly reduce the construction impact of building with cordwood. Still, assuming site-harvested or local wood, cordwood can be considered to have a fairly low construction impact, regardless of the type of mortar used.

2) Resource Efficiency through the Life of the Building. Since the thickness of a cordwood wall is easily increased, theoretically, cordwood can be adjusted to fit the energy requirements of the situation. However, the likelihood that shrinkage will occur between wood and mortar (causing cracks that allow air infiltration) makes me wonder about the real-world R-value of any given cordwood wall. The present absence of reliable testing leaves my questions unanswerable. Consequently, I'll limit my completely subjective resource-efficiency rating to: good.

3) Long Lasting. Like all cellulose-based building systems, cordwood is susceptible to decay. The exposed wood end-grain inherent in the system might make cordwood more at risk, though, as we've said, this problem could be solved through plastering. If wood is kept dry through good design and maintenance, then it can last indefinitely. Still, point for point, I can't put cordwood in the same class as cob in terms of longevity.

4) Nontoxic. An installed cordwood wall should give off no toxins, and, given correct design, should help improve indoor air quality through its hygroscopic nature.

5) Beautiful. There's almost nothing more beautiful than a stack of firewood that you've collected and cut yourself. It embodies the unique satisfaction of turning healthy, physical work using raw materials at hand into a basic necessity required for your personal survival. That's one reason why people who already collect wood to burn for heat can be drawn to cordwood building. The construction method is immediately familiar and graspable (a stack of firewood made permanent with mortar), and the finished product is a constant, physical reminder of your self-sufficiency. That's the kind of beauty I'm talking about being important in a green building. For the right person, then, cordwood construction can result in a deep personal connection between building and inhabitant. It's this intangible connection that's needed to bring a truly green building to fruition.

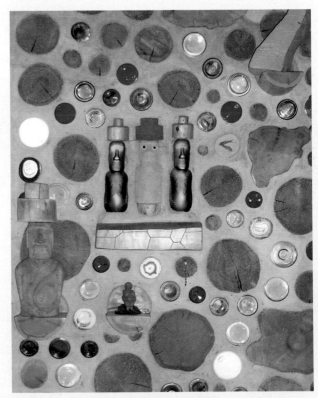

Bond between builder and building. Personal mementos, both embedded in mortar and set on integrated cordwood shelves, combine with vivid color supplied by bottle patterns to make this wall a very personal expression of the people who built it.

CORDWOOD APPLIED: OUR LITTLE BUILDING

DESIGNING WITH CORDWOOD

As we were creating the pattern language for our little building, cordwood was never far from our mind because we were already storing firewood on the site. Since a couple species of trees grow like weeds around here, we knew we'd have easy access to plenty of either one. Our first design step, then, was to compare the characteristics of these two abundant trees.

Tulip poplar is a very light wood, giving it good insulation value. However, it is susceptible to damage from water and insects if left exposed. Locust, on the other hand, is the wood we used for our structural posts. It is very dense and hard, characteristics that make it very durable, but less insulative. However, its density also gives it a higher thermal mass than poplar. Interestingly, both of these woods have similar shrinkage values, not great, but not terrible. Therefore, our comparison can be very direct: do we want more insulation or better durability and thermal mass?

As we've learned from previous discussions, the answer to that question depends on where we plan on placing the wood. The locust would be a good fit for a relatively exposed wall that gets good winter sun. It could take the exposure to the elements because it's very durable in the face of water and insects. Its middle-of-the-road shrinkage value would mean that it could take some water exposure without expanding. The winter sun exposure would allow this wood to possibly take advantage of the mass-enhanced R-value effect discussed in the last chapter. It's perhaps surprising to learn that many woods actually hold more heat per unit volume than concrete or adobe. The denser the wood, the higher the specific heat and, consequently, the better thermal mass it will be. Dense locust, therefore, would be an excellent thermal mass.

In the last chapter, though, we determined that in our climate only the south wall of our building would possibly experience this mass-enhanced R-value, and we've already filled that wall with cob. We're, of course, very happy with that beautiful wall, but it's interesting to note that a locust cordwood wall in that position would have probably performed better thermally than our cob. At least according to measurements taken from charts, it would have both more heat storing capacity and more R-value.

On the other hand, the poplar wouldn't have been the best choice for the south wall. Poplar's weakness is its vulnerability to the elements. Though the roof on that side has a two-foot overhang, it's a gable end, so that wall has some exposure to rain and sun. Poplar would work well on a protected wall where it would be out of the weather. Our east wall has a 4½-foot porch overhang that would keep the wood well protected. In addition, its superior R-value would come in handy there, where it's often shady.

We decided, then, to make a cordwood wall of poplar on our east side. In this way, we greatly reduced one of the disadvantages of cordwood construction that we'd identified: its incompatibility with mortar. With our wood so protected, we'll be able to let it dry considerably (so that it won't shrink or move away from the mortar significantly) without fear that enough liquid water could ever access it to cause expansion. In addition, this protected spot most probably will bring the lifespan of the wood closer to that of the mortar, therefore better justifying the use of this material with a high embodied energy.

PROCESSING CORDWOOD

The first thing we had to do was calculate how much wood we needed. To really be accurate with such a calculation would take a lot of work. However, since we burn wood for heat, we knew we could always use any excess, so our main concern was getting enough. For that reason, we simply calculated the volume of the entire wall, not concerning ourselves with areas that wouldn't be wood, such as the mortar matrix and window openings. We gathered enough wood to more than fill this entire volume, knowing that we'd end up with some extra.

Next, we had to take the bark off. Anyone who has worked much with firewood knows that insects and little critters of all kinds like to get between the bark and the wood, a situation you don't want to encourage in your wall. Bark also slows drying and will eventually pull away from the wood, which could cause the cordwood to loosen in the wall. The best time to remove bark is when the sap is rising in the tree. This can vary based on species and local climate, but spring is a good bet. In any case, it's always best to debark a tree as soon after felling as possible. If you catch it at the right time, the bark just falls of the wood of some species. At the wrong time, it sticks like white on rice.

Believe me, we know from experience. For this project, we broke both rules and paid for it. We decided to use some trees that just happened to come our way. The only down side was that they'd been felled a few months earlier, which meant they were cut in late autumn. By the time we started removing bark, it was fastened snug and tight against the wood. I spent a full, long day of hard labor debarking logs that could have lost their bark almost effortlessly given the correct timing (see page 310.)

After the debarking ordeal, we cut the wood to consistent lengths so that we could create an even wall surface. Way back in the design phase, we'd decided to make our wall 16 inches wide. We'd poured our stem wall to that width and now we cut our cordwood to that length.

Next, we split our wood. Some people like the look of round log ends in a wall, however, split cordwood has a number of advantages. First, drying time is greatly reduced because more wood surface area is exposed to air. Second, the smaller pieces of wood will shrink less in the wall and won't tend to split or check as much. Third, the squared sides of the split pieces allow for smaller mortar joints and therefore greatly reduce the amount of mortar needed while actually increasing structural strength. (See figure 3.)

To make laying easier and more aesthetically pleasing, we made sure we split our cordwood into a variety of sizes. It's an option to leave some round pieces to add visual variety to your wall, though we chose not to. We put aside curved or wildly irregularly shaped pieces because they can cause difficulties in laying.

Figure 3
ROUND VS. SPLIT CORDWOOD

If you compare round and split cordwood in a wall, you'll notice several clear differences. For one thing, the interlocking pattern of the split pieces creates much smaller mortar joints in comparison to the round. This tighter-fitting pattern also gives the split-piece wall more structural strength. In addition, given the same species of wood, split pieces will split, crack, and shrink less, thus creating fewer gaps for air infiltration over time. Finally, the split pieces will have dried faster, allowing for a quicker construction cycle.

a. Round   **b. Split**

Finally, we put our cordwood up to dry. We'd chosen a sunny spot open to the breeze, and had processed our wood close by so that we'd only have to move it a short distance to stack it. To facilitate drying, we built what was in essence a makeshift building, lifting the wood off the ground and covering it with a roof to protect it from water.

Since we'd chosen a wood with a moderate shrinkage factor and were installing it in a very protected place, we weren't concerned about in-the-wall expansion. Therefore, we were comfortable letting our wood be as dry as possible before installation. In the end, our schedule allowed our cordwood to dry about six months before we used it. A light wood like poplar sitting covered and in the breeze for that period of time can do a lot drying, and our wood definitely felt very light as we were laying it. However, I imagine that it would have lost even more water given more drying time, so I wouldn't be surprised if we ended up with some shrinkage in our installed cordwood over time. We'll just have to wait and see, and deal with it if and when it happens.

▲ **Step 1.** Because we brought our logs close to where we intended to cut and stack them, we only had to move them once.

Cordwood processing tools. *Above:* We used a picaroon (left) to turn the logs and spud (right) to peel their bark. You can also make a spud by cutting the end off the blade of a square shovel. *Right:* We used this cool tool intended for grabbing and turning logs that Tim had from his days as a timber framer. You may not want to invest in something this elaborate, but don't try to turn logs with brute force. The result might be a damaged back, crushed hand, or both.

▲ **Step 2.** We wedged the spud between the bark and wood (top), then pushed off layers of bark much like skinning a potato (bottom).

◄ **Step 3.** If you've chosen the right time to debark, large pieces of bark should just fall away with a little nudge from the spud, as shown here. This was a rare occurrence for us because our logs had been sitting too long after being felled. Most of our bark was tightly fused to the wood beneath it.

◀ **Step 4.** Once they were bark-free, we clearly marked the logs with a lumber crayon and cut our cordwood to uniform lengths with a chainsaw. We'd chosen a 16-inch thickness for our wall.

▲ **Step 5.** After splitting the wood with a maul (a heavy, broad-headed axe), we stacked it to dry. *Left*: To help keep rain water away, we raised the wood up off the ground on some old wood scraps and bricks, then built a simple shelter with cinderblocks and a piece of metal roofing. *Right*: Plenty of air got to each piece in the stack to help speed drying. Splitting our wood allowed us to use less mortar between pieces and also reduced the amount each piece might crack and shrink in the wall.

PREPPING THE WALL

Before actually laying cordwood we still had some work to do to get the wall ready.

Tweaking the Structure

A typical, textbook post-and-beam structure creates a framework of posts and beams that hold up a roof. The larger space between structural members is then filled in with some material. Our situation is a little different. (Look back at the drawing of our building's structure on page 182 to better understand this discussion.) We have two tiers of posts. The outer tier is the four porch posts. A beam spans the two posts on the east side and another spans the two posts on the west side of the building. All of the roof trusses sit on these two beams. This setup alone wouldn't be enough to support our heavy roof, so we have an inner tier consisting of the four corner posts of our building. However, we don't have traditional beams spanning between these posts. On the west side, our "beam" is going to be a stick-frame truss, which we'll describe in chapter 11. On the east side, our "beam" will be the cordwood wall itself. In other words, the entire volume of the cordwood itself with help to carry roof loads.

We had this all worked out nicely when we started the building. Our porch posts and beams would be plenty strong to carry the weight of our roof structure without all of the living roof materials in place, so we'd be able to build our cordwood wall under the cover of the roof. Once the cordwood was in place to take its share of the loads, we could install the living roof. However, as often happens in construction, "something" came up. The something this time was that we got behind schedule and realized that we needed to get the living roof installed before laying cordwood, so that the plants would take hold in time for us to shoot the photos we'd need for this book. Before putting that heavy load up there, we had to shore up the structure of our west wall to take the extra weight. Toward that end, we installed strong temporary posts under the two roof trusses that our cordwood wall would eventually help support.

We also installed diagonal bracing between our porch posts to handle lateral loads until our cordwood wall could take on that role.

Temporary support. Because we had to install our heavy living roof earlier in the construction process than expected, we supported some of the weight with temporary posts placed under the two roof trusses that will rest on the volume of the cordwood wall. Also, notice the diagonal bracing between the porch posts. Once the cordwood wall is completed, the bracing and temporary posts can be removed.

Building the Window Bucks

We chose two matching salvaged windows to flank the couch/bed that we planned to install inside along the cordwood wall. Since we knew this wall would have to carry some of the huge weight of our living roof, we definitely needed to build strong, structural window bucks to be part of its load-bearing volume. For our cob wall, we had built window and door bucks that were thinner than the wall and then installed cob to curve around and meet them. We didn't have this option with cordwood. Our bucks needed to be as wide as the wall so we could set mortar between the buck and the adjacent cordwood.

You may remember that we had problems with our cob door buck cupping in the wall. To avoid similar problems here, we used kiln-dried lumber a full 1½ inches thick to build our cordwood bucks.

Building the Window Bucks

▲ **Step 1.** We used kiln-dried 2x10s to make our bucks. We started by screwing together the rectangular box shown here.

▲ **Step 2.** We then cut two 2x10s to match the length of the longest sides of the box. *Left*: We attached these inside the box, so their widths overlapped the inside of the box's long sides by 2½ inches and extended out 6¾ inches. (If our math seems off, remember that 2x10s are actually 9¼ inches wide.) Now our long sides were 16 inches wide, which is the width of our wall. (You can see these overlapping sides more clearly in the photo for step three.) We then capped the box's short sides with 2x10 pieces that were not set into the box but rather butted up to the sides. These created a sill and headpiece that are each 18½ inches wide, and so will protrude 2½ inches from the wall. *Right*: Before installing the sill, we cut a drip edge into it.

◀ **Step 3.** Remembering our cob door buck's cupping problems, we sealed the back of these bucks with a water-resistant primer to keep water from the mortar from penetrating into the buck.

▲ **Step 4.** After making sure our bucks were square (top), we braced them before installation (bottom). This is an important step to keep the bucks plumb throughout the installation of the cordwood. If we don't have plumb bucks, our windows may not open and close well.

Figure 4
OTHER OPTIONS FOR VERY WIDE WINDOW AND DOOR BUCKS

There are a number of ways to create a wide buck. We chose the overlapping method because it was easy to construct and created a reveal that broke up the wide buck visually. Here are a couple of other options:

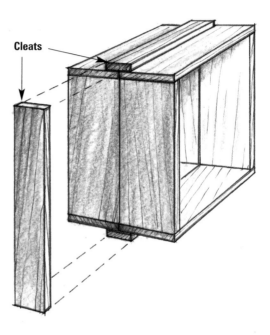

Cleats

a. Two boxes with butted joints
This buck is basically two identical boxes butted against each other and attached with boards overlapping each. These connecting boards will also sit between mortar beds and act as a cleat to help lock the buck into the wall.

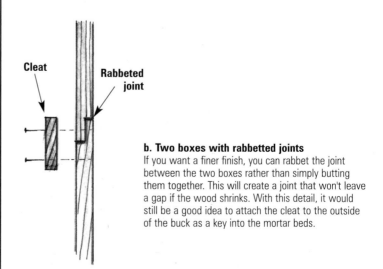

Cleat

Rabbeted joint

b. Two boxes with rabbetted joints
If you want a finer finish, you can rabbet the joint between the two boxes rather than simply butting them together. This will create a joint that won't leave a gap if the wood shrinks. With this detail, it would still be a good idea to attach the cleat to the outside of the buck as a key into the mortar beds.

MIXING MORTAR

Due to the high embodied energy and inflexibility of mortar, we considered embedding our cordwood in cob. However, you'll remember the care we took to weave our cob wall into a monolithic unit. As mortar, the cob would be only several inches thick and splayed out in a thin matrix broken up by cordwood, a material that could expand and contract slightly. Having no direct experience with cob as cordwood mortar, we simply didn't know for sure how it would respond. The fact that this was a load-bearing wall and that we had a very heavy living roof gave us further pause.

If we'd used cob as a complete infill between the wood, I would have been much more confident of its strength. However, that would have meant forgoing the loose-fill insulation and, therefore, probably a considerable loss in R-value. Intuitively, I think a cob mortar would be strong enough, even in our situation, but we decided to wait for another project to give it a try.

After making a few tests trying different proportions and additives, the mortar mix we chose was taken from Rob Roy's book *Cordwood Masonry Housebuilding* and consisted of 9 parts sand, 3 parts soaked sawdust, 3 parts lime, and 2 parts Portland cement. There are a variety of different materials out there being sold under the general name "lime," so make sure you are getting the right stuff. Crushed limestone will not work. You want lime that has been burned and rehydrated. (See the sidebar What Is Lime? page 318.) It comes in bags, usually 50 pounds, and I've seen it called *builder's lime*, *autoclaved mason's lime*, and *hydrated lime*.

Remember that all sawdust isn't the same. It can't be too fine, like that from a table saw, or too large and hard, like hardwood chips from a milling operation. The ideal is probably sawdust from a softwood with a low shrinkage value that has been cut at a mill or with a chainsaw. We used what we were told was poplar and pine sawdust from our local mill, but it seemed a bit hard and may have had some other woods mixed in.

Mortar tests. We did a series of mortar tests before committing to a mix. The mixes we made using vermiculite instead of sawdust were brittle and easy to break with our bare hands. Our sawdust mixes, on the other hand, were much stronger.

Preparing sawdust. *Left:* First, we sifted our sawdust through a ¼-inch screen to cull out bark and larger pieces of wood. *Right:* Then we soaked the sawdust. The idea is for the sawdust to slowly give moisture back to the mortar, rather than wicking moisture out of it, thus allowing the mortar to cure more slowly, which helps prevent cracking. (By the way, we sifted and soaked this little bit of sawdust for our tests. For our actual construction, we filled a 55-gallon barrel with soaked sawdust and used all of it in our wall.)

We primarily mixed mortar in an inexpensive, electric cement mixer. The deluxe tool would be a mortar mixer, which we didn't have, and, of course you can always mix in a wheelbarrow. The great thing about using a powered mixer, though, is that cordwood can be laid at the same time mortar is being mixed. If working alone, you can always have a batch mixing while you're laying the present batch, which really allows you to get into a rhythm. If working with a partner, one person can just focus on laying cordwood, while the other can keep the mixer going and then jump in with laying when the mixer is in action. The one advantage to wheelbarrow mixing, in my mind, is that wheelbarrows are easier to clean than cement or mortar mixers. If I were only going to do a batch or two of mortar, for example, then I'd probably mix in a wheelbarrow.

Mixing Mortar in a Wheelbarrow

◄ **Step 1.** First, we gathered all our materials and organized them so that we could keep track of how much of each we'd added.

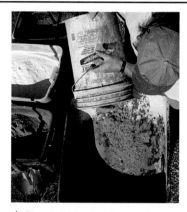 

▲ **Step 2.** We'd put 3 shovels of sand in each of 3 buckets for a total of 9 shovels of sand. Then we added a portion of each dry ingredient in sequence: 1 bucket (3 shovels) sand, 1 shovel lime, 1 shovel soaked sawdust, 1 shovel cement. We continued that pattern until all dry ingredients were in the wheelbarrow: 9 parts sand, 3 parts lime, 3 parts sawdust, and 2 parts Portland cement.

◄ **Step 3.** We then dry-mixed the ingredients with a hoe. Adding materials in sequence created layers that made dry mixing much easier.

◄ **Step 4.** Next, we added water. We had no regular measured amount we knew to add because of the variables of soaked sawdust and damp sand. We simply added water slowly, focusing on not adding too much. As we've said before, you can always add more water to a mix, but once it's in there you can't take it out. Finally, we mixed the ingredients with a hoe, adding more water if needed.

Finished mortar. Because they are laid in such a wide, thick bed, cordwood mortars need to be stiffer than conventional masonry mortars. After laying cordwood for a while, you get a feel for the right consistency. Until then, a good test is to throw a ball of mortar a couple of feet into the air (left). A good mix only deforms slightly when caught (right).

Powered Mortar Mixing

◀ **Step 1.** We found a cheap, electric cement mixer to be a great help if we were doing a full day of cordwood laying. We set it up under the cover of our roof only 5 feet from the wall we were laying. *Left*: We used the same layering technique for adding materials, but we started with a bit of water in the mixer to keep the blades wet in an attempt to prevent our mix from sticking to the mixer. *Right*: Plastic tubs with tight-fitting tops are a great place to store lime and cement. They're a lot easier to shovel out of than the bags these materials come in. When not in use, we closed the lids to keep the materials dry and clump free.

◀ **Step 2.** After adding water, we could go back to laying cordwood using the previous batch of mortar. When we needed more mortar, there was always a batch ready in the mixer.

What Is Lime?

Limestone is a sedimentary rock usually formed from the skeletons of marine microorganisms and coral. Thousands of years ago, humans discovered that if you burned limestone at high temperatures, and then added water to the resulting powder, you would produce a putty that could be used to make plaster, mortar, and even structural concrete mixes that seemed much like the original limestone: hard and durable. It was as if, through this processing, you could mold the actual stone to the shape of your whim.

Modern chemistry has explained that, in fact, this is very much what's happening. When burned at high temperatures, limestone releases water and carbon dioxide, while its main ingredient, calcium carbonate, becomes calcium oxide, which is known as *quick lime*. If water is added to quick lime (a process called *slaking*), over time calcium hydroxide is formed along with a huge amount of heat. In this form,

our lime is called *lime putty*. After this putty is installed as part of a plaster, mortar, or other incarnation, it begins to react with carbon dioxide in the air and slowly returns to its original state, calcium carbonate, i.e., limestone.

The longer lime putty sits without drying, the more complete will be its transformation to calcium hydroxide, and, consequently, the more complete its eventual return to calcium carbonate. I read somewhere that an ancient Roman law prohibited the use of lime putty less than six years old. In Europe, aged lime putty is readily available. In the United States, however, a powdered form is all that's commonly manufactured. This product is slaked in a factory, and the heat produced is used to turn the putty into a powder. It's sold in bags and called a variety of names, *autoclaved lime* and *hydrated lime* among them.

LAYING CORDWOOD

To lay our cordwood, we simply placed a bed of mortar on each side of the wall, filled the space between these beds with insulation, and then embedded cordwood into the mortar. But there was more to it than that. Before starting, we decided on an overall aesthetic that we liked. Though some people lay pieces of very similar size in even rows, we preferred a more random effect that juxtaposed large against small so as not to create any linear, horizontal courses in the wall. Even so, we were careful to take time to think about the overall visual effect of our wall as we were laying, stepping back often to admire our work.

We also chose to let our log ends protrude quite a bit (from ½ to ¾ inches) past the mortar. This highlighted the cordwood by creating a shadow around each piece. Other options would have been to have the log ends flush with the mortar or even to create random protrusions. You can choose the look you like by studying the photos in this book and elsewhere and, if possible, by observing some actual cordwood walls.

We needed to be conscious of our overall contour as we built. Our intent was to build a plumb wall. If we wanted to be very accurate, we could have pulled a string between our two corner posts at the point that would mark the outside edge of our wall. This is the technique used by brick- and stonemasons. However, the random layout, large mortar joints, and short length of our wall made this step unnecessary. We used both a four-foot and a six-foot level to check our work. Eyeing down the wall from one post to the next was an effective double check.

Laying Cordwood

◀ **Step 1.** We started with a stem wall cleared of all dirt and debris. In this photo, the diagonal bracing we installed while building our roof structure is still in place. We moved this out to the porch posts to make room for cordwood installation.

◀ **Step 2.** First, we plopped down double handfuls of mortar (top) and smoothed them together into a mortar bed of uniform width and depth (bottom).

▲ **Step 3.** We did the same things on both sides of the wall to create a double mortar bed. Our goal was two beds about 5 inches wide with a 6-inch space in the middle for mortar. We made a template stick to gauge our bed widths at the beginning.

▲ **Step 4.** Next we poured loose fill insulation to fill the space between the beds. This is vermiculite.

Optional brightening. Some species of wood darken as they cure. If you don't like this look, an option is to brush on a small amount of chlorine bleach before installation. The wood will usually brighten instantly. Chlorine, though, is a harsh chemical, so you might decide it's better to just let things be. The dark color doesn't signal impending damage. If anything living caused the darkening, it should die out as long as the wood stays dry.

▲ **Step 5.** Then, we laid the cordwood as close together as possible while still leaving room for a bed of the stiff mortar.

▲ **Step 6.** We pushed the cordwood pieces into the mortar and jiggled them side-to-side a bit to seat them. (A rubber mallet sometimes came in handy for seating pieces into the mortar in tight spots.)

▲ **Step 7.** We continued with the same sequence for the next course. We'll push the pointed side of a piece of cordwood into the thick sections of mortar, so this bed won't end up as thick as it looks.

◄ **Step 8.** *Left:* The challenge of insulating cordwood is that there are lots of little spaces that need to be filled. An infill insulation, then, has to be able to flow into a lot of tight spaces. Often the access to a large area below is through a thin throat between two pieces above. *Right:* We tried various materials. Perlite (white stuff at bottom) and vermiculite (see previous photos) are very fine and do a great job of filling all voids. Our sawdust coated with lime as a preservative (top) was bulkier and didn't flow as nicely. One downside to the lighter, finer materials is that they can blow onto your mortar in the wind. We didn't have much of a problem with that, partly due to the big roof covering we already had in place.

◄ **Step 9.** We wanted a random look, so we didn't lay in uniform courses but instead used different sized pieces to break up the rows. Notice the two smaller pieces in the middle flanked by two larger ones.

◄ **Step 10.** As we moved up the wall, we checked for level often to make sure that we were building plumb.

◀ **Step 1.** We had laid cob flush up against the locust corner post so that it covered the full width of our stem wall; this left a small column about 1 foot long and 6 inches deep at the southeast corner of the building. We laid mortar beds to surround this juncture...

▲ **Step 2.** ...then laid small pieces of cordwood that we had cut with our electric miter saw.

◀ **Step 3.** We continued this method up the wall, creating a small cordwood column in this corner.

◀ **Step 4.** We laid full-length cordwood next to the column to wrap around the cob wall.

◀ **Step 5.** Since our straw wall wasn't there yet to build a similar cordwood column against, we decided to install full-width cordwood against the northeast post. *Left:* We used a temporary form made of scrap plywood to hold the mortar until it dried. *Right:* We attached this form to the locust post with a 2x4 cleat (top of photo), moving the form up as the mortar dried. Notice also that we had to fill the final cavity between form and cordwood completely with mortar to prevent the insulation from pouring out. Our straw bales will be pushed up against the cordwood and loose straw will be stuffed to fill the small gap between the bales and the locust post.

Pointing

Once the mortar was firm, but not rock hard, it was time to clean up the joints. This process, called pointing, was usually done either at the end of the work day or the first thing in the morning on the next day, depending on how quickly the mortar set up. Though pointing has a lot to do with how the final wall will look, that's not its only function. Pointing also pushes the curing mortar tight against the cordwood, creating a better bond with the wood as well as filling gaps.

We mostly used a conventional pointing knife designed for the smaller joints of brick and concrete block masonry. It's true that many common metal implements lying around the house can make good pointing tools, though for really compressing the mortar tight against the wood, the heavy gauge, curved metal of a commercial pointing knife is hard to beat, in my opinion. I suggest buying a pointing knife and then supplementing it with whatever doodads you want to try.

There were times when we couldn't be around to point our work at the right time. In those instances, we found ourselves staring at some rock-hard, unpointed mortar joints. We dealt with this by using a wire wheel or brush on the end of an electric drill. This worked well for cleaning up the rough surface area. As for pushing the mortar tight against the wood, there was really nothing that could be done about that at this point, aside from filling any gaps with fresh mortar and compressing those spots.

Pointing

◀ **Step 1.** The process of pressing and jiggling our cordwood to seat it caused mortar to ooze around the wood in a number of places (left). The first step of our pointing procedure was to clean off these areas of excess with our pointing knife (right).

◀ **Step 2.** On the other hand, sometimes installation had left gaps around the wood. We filled these by hand with a little mortar.

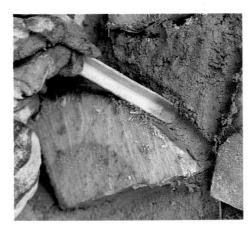

◀ **Step 3.** Next, we compressed the mortar around each piece of cordwood by pushing the knife into the joint and, while applying some pressure, dragging it along the piece of wood. This tightened the bond between mortar and wood while also creating a smoother surface.

▲ **Step 5.** In some cases we wanted to do a bit more cleanup after the mortar had dried. We used a wire brush attachment on a cordless drill. It worked especially well for cleaning up our protruding log reveals.

▲ **Step 4.** The large areas of mortar between cordwood pieces tend to be uneven. For aesthetic reasons, we evened these out by scraping off the excess with the pointing knife. You can see here that we've already done that at the bottom of the photo, but not at the top.

Installing Our Window Bucks

Since our couch/bed will be on this wall, we'd decided in the earlier design process to set our windows low so that someone sitting on each end of the bed could read by the light coming through the window and use the deep sill as a small table. To get a general idea of how high that should be, we sought out windows we liked in other buildings and sat next to them to see how they felt. We asked ourselves if the sill was a good height for setting a drink or leaning with our elbow. From that research, we decided that about 27 inches was a good sill height.

As the height of our laid cordwood got near this planned sill height, we measured up from the existing floor and decided where to stop our cordwood for the buck installation. We were careful to measure based on the eventual finished floor height, not where our floor existed now, which was a full 8 inches lower. Next we needed to decide exactly where the windows would be placed. To do that, one of us held the actual window (the bucks would have been too heavy) while another looked on from different places inside the space. Once just the right place was found, we made pencil marks on the cordwood to mark the spot.

We don't have a door in our cordwood wall. If we did, we'd have built the buck just like the window bucks but without a sill. It would have been installed on the stem wall exactly the same as the door buck in our cob wall, except we would probably have either lengthened the angle bracket or included another one on each side so that we had a connection near each outer edge of the buck.

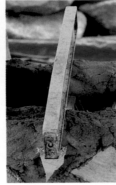

◄ **Step 1.** We wanted our windowsills to be at the same height, so we created a level bed for both windows at the same time, making sure to check that they were level both along and across the wall.

◄ **Step 2.** We made sure that our mortar mix was stiff for this application. These bucks were heavy and we didn't want all the mortar to just squeeze out under their weight. We pushed the bucks into the mortar to set them and checked the level again.

◄ **Step 3.** Immediately after installation, we built up some cordwood around our bucks to lock them into place.

Thoughtful placement. We were careful to place the windows in relation to the entire building. This sill height meshed well with our cob window. Referring back to our careful design discussions, we also left room for the partition that will create a backrest for someone reading by the light of this cordwood window.

Buck details. Though our huge porch overhangs won't let much water reach it, this protruding sill with drip edge will direct any that does get here away from the wall.

Connections

One advantage of cordwood over cob is that you can easily attach things to it. For that reason, we didn't have to be as thorough in our preparation of this wall for its end use. In fact, this flexibility is another reason we chose to place cordwood on the east side of our building where it forms the back wall of an outdoor room under our porch overhang. This space is designed to be both a place to store garden tools and a place to hang out, with the possible addition of a built-in sleeping nook for kids next to the windows mirroring the bed on the inside. We'll be able to attach hooks for tools and any framing for our outdoor bed directly to the cordwood.

As for connecting the embedded materials in the wall, such as the window bucks and shelving, we are relying on the weight of the cordwood and the bond of the mortar to hold them in place. Using nails to tie into the mortar, like we did on the cob wall, didn't seem like a good idea because we felt it could cause the mortar to crack as it dried. In any case, it turned out that everything is set very tightly into the finished wall, and we have no worries about anything coming loose.

Cordwood connections. The log ends of our cordwood wall are like a big pegboard for attaching shelving, tools, or whatever we want.

Shelving and Bottles

Though their appearance is strikingly different, in many ways cob and cordwood are quite similar. Many of the same techniques apply to both. Though it takes more careful planning because of the less flexible nature of the wood pieces, interesting bottle designs can be realized in cordwood similar to those possible in cob. Also, the technique for creating built-in shelving is similar. Corbelling can also be used in cordwood, though you'd need to think about this in advance in order to cut and dry some longer cordwood pieces in preparation.

We used similar stone shelving and bottle blocks in our cordwood wall as we did in the cob wall. I think they work as a visual connection between the two different wall systems, helping to tie them together.

Installing Shelving and Bottles

▲ **Step 1.** To install a shelf, Lisa first laid two level mortar beds...

▲ **Step 2.** ...and filled the void with insulation.

▲ **Step 3.** Then she installed the shelf and leveled it.

Filling tight spaces. This little tool is called a "tuck pointer" and is great for pushing mortar into tight spaces like the one between our shelf and the window buck.

▲ **Step 4.** Using bottle blocks identical to those we used in the cob wall, Lisa installed a bottled design directly on top of the shelf. First, she laid a bed of mortar that overlapped the back of the shelf, then she set the first bottles in place.

▲ **Step 5.** Next, she used the tuck pointer to push mortar between the bottles.

▲ **Step 6.** Since the bottle blocks are thinner than the cordwood wall, Lisa capped them with a second stone shelf as a sort of lintel for the cordwood above, allowing the wall to return to its original thickness. The shelves and bottles together create both a functional little niche and a beautiful detail. As the sun rises to the east in the morning, the bottles light up.

Coat bolts. Your imagination is pretty much the only limit to what you can stick in a cordwood wall. We found these big old bolts next to a railroad track and installed them in the wall as coat pegs. You can just barely see the wire that we wrapped around each and embedded in the mortar to enhance the bond.

Thinking about Structure

Unlike our cob infill, our cordwood wall has to handle a lot of weight from our massive living roof. For that reason, we needed to take a completely different structural stance as we were building this wall. In the last chapter, we mentioned that holes in monolithic walls, such as created by doors and windows, are structural weak-points often strengthened by a spanning member called a lintel. Our window bucks are very strong and, in some situations, would have been strong enough. However, in this situation we felt it was a good idea to install strong lintels over our bucks. In our design, we had decided to create the feel of a small room in the area of these windows by somehow creating a lower ceiling here. Thinking of that now, we decided to create a single large combination lintel/shelf that would span across both windows and cantilever out into the room. This single piece of wood, then, provides an important structural function while creating storage space and the protected feel of a lowered ceiling we'd been looking for in our design.

As we've pointed out, monolithic structures like cordwood walls distribute loads throughout their volume. However, places where heavy loads are focused in small areas, called point loads, are still areas of weakness in monolithic walls. Perhaps a layperson's way of thinking about this would be to say that at that place, the wall hasn't had a chance to disperse the load yet, and therefore there's a lot of pressure on that little area. Huge point loads will be exerted on our cordwood wall where the roof trusses come to rest.

In cordwood construction, there are a couple of ways to deal with this load. For one, you can install a small block under the truss that will act much like a lintel, and disperse the load to a wider area. A variation on this approach is to install a member that spans the entire wall, called a top plate. This approach should create the most even distribution of the roof load over the wall. Again because of our uncertainty about the effect of our large roof load, we decided to install top plates on our cordwood wall.

Installing the Lintel

◄ **Step 1.** We carefully laid cordwood to the top of our window bucks without going beyond. To accomplish this we had to think ahead, choosing cordwood pieces of the right size to create a level seat.

▲ **Step 2.** We laid a mortar bed and made sure it was level.

▲ **Step 3.** Then we lifted the lintel into place.

▲ **Step 4.** After checking for level again, we temporarily braced the lintel in place with a 2x4 column (in front of window buck to the right). We bought the piece of wood for the lintel at our local mill. Tim shaped it with a gentle curve and sanded the edges before we installed it. Notice also that the lintel/shelf extends far beyond the window toward the cob. That was an aesthetic decision and not necessary structurally.

▲ **Step 5.** We compressed mortar tightly into the joint between the bucks and the lintel to fill all gaps and create a dense, solid bed at the edge. We left the brace in place until the mortar had set.

▲ **Step 6.** We pushed mortar into the joint between bucks and lintel on the outside of the wall also. (Here, you can clearly see the temporary posts supporting the roof trusses that we discussed earlier.)

▲ **Step 1.** Instead of laying our cordwood almost to the roof and then trying to cram our heavy top plates into place in a tight space, we attached the top plates to the roof first and then built the cordwood up to meet them. We installed two top plates, one flush with the face of the outside wall (left), and the other flush with the face of the inside wall (right).

◄ **Step 2.** The top plates were cut to span the entire length of the top of the wall. We had to notch the exterior top plate around the cob wall to allow it to stretch all the way to the locust post.

▲ **Step 3.** We used simple 2x4 brackets to hold the top plates snugly against the roof. These brackets are placed to also serve as the nailer for our blocking above the top plates. (See next section for more on this.)

◄ **Step 4.** Finally, we installed cordwood up to within an inch or two of the top plates and pushed mortar into the remaining space. This allowed a very tight fit, and the top plates are resting directly against the roof trusses instead of having a mortar joint between them.

Thinking about Water

As we've pointed out several times in this chapter already, cordwood is potentially susceptible to water damage. The exposed end grain in a cordwood installation is much more vulnerable to water penetration than the side grain of a log cabin or our structural locust posts, for example. However, as long as wood has a chance to dry out well between soakings, it can be very durable even in exposed locations. We nipped this problem in the bud, however, by installing our cordwood wall under a huge porch overhang so that almost no precipitation will ever contact the wall in the first place. Even so, we still cut drip edges into our windowsills as a precaution.

Let's imagine, though, that our wall had been in a very exposed location. What steps could we take to protect it? First, I'd waterproof the log ends with linseed oil or some other water-resistant-yet-vapor-permeable coating. Next, I'd want to limit any areas where rainwater might be able to collect or pause before falling. To accomplish that, I'd set the ends of the cordwood flush with the mortar so that there was no protruding edge. I'd also be very careful to push the face of the wall just past the face of the stem wall, so that there wasn't a lip there for water to rest on.

We'd still want the tops and bottoms of our window bucks to protrude out past the wall so that we could cut drip edges into them that would cause water to fall away from the window. The tops of windows and doors create a long horizontal joint that, in combination with a slightly shrinking window or door buck and cracking mortar, could create a nice avenue for water infiltration. I'd install flashing here. Since there is no exterior skin, such as plaster, to lap over the flashing, I'd cut a thin notch in the cordwood pieces being installed over the door or window. The notch would be placed so that a bend in the flashing would fit inside it. This isn't a common practice among cordwood builders, but I think it would be well worth the effort in a wall exposed to a lot of rain.

Finishing the Top of the Wall

Perhaps the hardest area to deal with on a cordwood wall is the area between the roof members, in other words the space between the top plate and the roof. These spaces can be filled with cordwood, but that creates incredibly tight working conditions, and it's difficult to insulate the final cavity. Another option would be to leave off the roof decking until the space around the roof trusses were filled with cordwood. Not only does this require finishing the cordwood at the perfect height to fill in the space and not get in the way of the roof, it also means that we wouldn't have any roof cover while building our walls. Our solution was simply to stop the cordwood at the top plate and install blocking between the plate and roof as is often done in conventional stick framing. This allowed us to snugly span the opening with custom-cut wood while also easily filling the entire width and height of the space with insulation.

◀ **Step 1.** Instead of messing with laying cordwood in the tight area near the roof, we decided to sandwich insulation between two blocks of wood. First, we installed blocks to fill the spaces between the trusses on the outside of the wall, attaching them to nailers connected to the roof trusses.

▲ **Step 2.** Next, we installed a layer of scrap 2-inch foam insulation against the blocking on the inside. The insulation wrapped around the cob in the south cavity.

▲ **Step 3.** We then installed 2x4 blocks on the inside to act as nailers for our blocking. *Left*: Notice that the bracket attaching the top plate to the truss at right was placed so that it could also act as one these nailers. *Right*: We didn't attach any blocking to the roof because we didn't want to chance accidentally puncturing our roof membrane. (See chapter 13 for more on this.)

▲ **Step 4.** Next, we filled the rest of the cavity with loose straw...

▲ **Step 5.** ...and installed the interior blocking to finish off our wall. These blocking pieces required some carpentry skills because we needed to cut the wood to match the pitch of the roof and notch it around the truss.

How Long Did It Take?

Cordwood construction is a form of masonry, and, like all masonry, it's hard, messy work. We worked long days, and usually found ourselves cleaning out the mixer in the dark. However, with one person working fulltime and a second helping on two days, we finished this wall in a week. Our cob wall, in comparison, took about a month. In addition, we won't be plastering the cordwood wall, so we're saving a lot of work that we're going to be putting into our other three walls.

On the other hand, as we've said, cordwood's integrated skin has weaknesses. Wood shrinkage may allow eventual air infiltration and the exposed log ends are vulnerable. We may find ourselves having to spend more time on this wall later than we will on our other three walls. Still, from the standpoint of time spent from start to finish, our cordwood wall required less time to complete than any of our other walls.

Construction Blunders: Don't Let Stress Push You Around

No matter how carefully I plan or how many books I read on Zen, the process of construction always creates a level of stress. There is a lot to organize and keep track of, and sometimes you can swear the weather is conspiring against you. The backdrop is always the specter of finite available time or money. In this mindset, it's really difficult to calmly move forward, always just doing the next thing, always doing the completely sensible thing.

Our cordwood pressures started pretty much immediately. By the time our cordwood had dried enough to make a small test wall, we were ready to start building the actual wall, and we were already seriously behind schedule. If we'd really been able to step out of the moment, we probably could have found a way to make little test walls and allow the mortar to cure while doing something else on the project. Instead, we did a couple of quick mortar tests with scraps of 2x4. These tests allowed us to find a mix that cured to a strong mortar but didn't let us see how it would fare when surrounding our chosen cordwood in a wall.

The result is that our mortar cracked more than I'd hoped. If my memory serves, we didn't have any cracking until after the wall had been completed, so it took at least a week of curing for the cracks to materialize. To be honest, the cracking is minimal and very fine, and I'm not sure I could have improved upon our good results with testing. Definitely, I have absolutely no structural worries. If the small cracks bother me aesthetically, I can use a log cabin chinking compound to cover the mortar, or even have fun with the mortar in some other creative way. Luckily, then, no real harm was done, but the lesson still remains: Take your time, do the necessary tests, think things through, and don't let stress push you around.

Cracking under the stress. This section of small cracks is about the worst we experienced. They aren't a problem structurally or for water or air infiltration, but I'd still rather not have them. I think we could have avoided these cracks if we hadn't cracked under the pressure of time constraints.

WHAT WE'VE ACCOMPLISHED

By analyzing the properties of the types of wood we had readily available, we were able to make a choice that was well suited to the shaded, well-protected wall we wanted to build. We carefully considered the specific structural situation of our wall and installed strong reinforcement where needed in the form of bucks, lintels, and top plates to guarantee that our wall could handle any loads that might come its way. We placed our windows carefully and made our structural lentil work triple duty as a shelf and space divider, thus keeping in close contact with our overall plan and the pattern language behind it. We now have two beautiful walls, each of which snuggle into their intended use and are already creating a powerful, very specific feeling.

A feeling taking shape. The elements of our building are starting to come together to create a special place. *Above:* Notice that the temporary roof bracing is gone and our cordwood wall and the porch beams are now carrying all of the roof loads on this side. Our wall is strong and beautiful. *Right:* Our cordwood and cob walls balance each other nicely.

VARIATIONS

Though nowhere near as fluid and malleable as cob, cordwood is a very flexible material. Curved walls and corbelled or cantilevered sections are common and not much more difficult than basic cordwood construction. These techniques and others are really just extensions of the basics we've presented here, and, to a large degree, are limited only by your imagination. Let's look at a few options.

STACKED CORNERS

In our building, the cordwood wall was created by first setting timbers vertically as structural posts. We then cut similar timbers into shorter pieces that were laid horizontally to fill the space between the structural posts. Another approach would have been to make posts out of stacked cordwood, also called "stacked corners." Stacked corners can be constructed from a wide variety of materials including cordwood, 4x4 posts, 2x6 cut offs, or logs that have been milled on two sides like the locust posts we used for the corners of our little building. The corner pieces are usually laid in sets of two in a repeating pattern that alternates from course to course in a process that creates structural stability. This is basically the technique you'd use to stack a pile of bricks to prevent them from collapsing.

The first step is to build up two corners a couple of feet, and then fill the space between them with cordwood. (See figure 5.) This process is simply repeated until the top of the wall is reached. With this technique, when all is said and done, you've basically created structural corner posts that fill the same role as our locust posts. The only difference is that you built them up from small members a little at a time.

Combination stacked corner and post. This corner starts out with wide, solid, milled timbers arranged to create a stacked corner. At window height, longer timbers are oriented horizontally to make a post that continues the structural duties of the stacked corner below.

Figure 5
STACKED CORNERS

In a stacked corner, members are laid in overlapping courses with an alternating pattern: one course with the length oriented along one wall, the next with the length oriented 90 degrees to the first. Two corners and the wall between them are built at the same time. A small section of each corner is built, then the wall is filled in between. This process is continued straight up the wall. It's probably best to use squared lumber on stacked corners because the outer members of the corners might have more of a tendency to pop out if they're round.

This technique requires more skill and precision than our infill did. One trick will be to build all of the corners to exactly the same height. In conventional masonry, the consistent size of the units, bricks and concrete blocks for example, makes this much easier because each course is the same size. By checking each course with a stick level along with a string and line level (a small level attached to your string), it's not difficult to make sure you are plumb and level. One solution would be to build your stacked corners using milled lumber of a consistent width and thickness, such as 6x6s, so that equal-sized courses could be built and checked using conventional masonry techniques.

Figure 6
TOP PLATES FOR STACKED CORNERS

Just as posts need to be tied together with beams, stacked corner columns need to be tied together with top plates. Illustrated here is a typical double top-plate from conventional stick-framing that's been widened to accommodate the width of a cordwood wall. You can see how the first top plate configuration ties the two corners in the foreground together with unbroken pieces of wood. The second top plate configuration attaches each of these corners to an adjacent corner at the other end of the building with unbroken pieces of wood. In this way, all of the columns are tied together, creating a unified structure. These top plates also create a level surface on which to build and attach the roof.

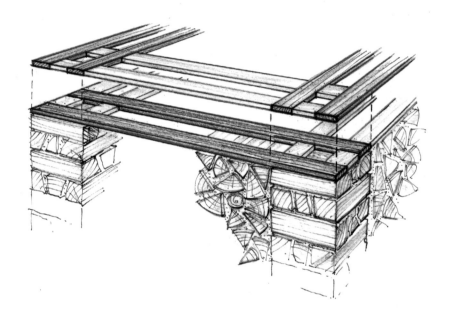

ROUND BUILDINGS

Another popular cordwood option is to build round. All other variables being the same, a cylinder is stronger than a cube, so a round building makes sense structurally. Also, a round building has no exterior corners, and can therefore be constructed as a single wall. The cordwood is laid in the same fashion, the only difference being that the exterior mortar joints will be wider than those on the interior. Since there are no corners, you don't need any milled corner pieces, so you can build the whole wall with the same cordwood. Without the ability to pull a string or to eyeball down the length of the wall, you'll need to use a level more frequently to make sure you are building plumb. To my mind, the main complication for the beginner is that round buildings require round roofs, and a round roof is much more complicated to build than a simple gable or shed. Cordwood enthusiast and author Rob Roy is really into round buildings with living roofs, so check out one of his books if you're interested in this option.

Cordwood in the round. *Top:* This cool little round building with a living roof has no corners and is therefore basically a single cordwood wall. Notice also that cordwood fills the space between the roof rafters, a technique we chose not to use in our wall. This building functions as a library at Rob and Jaki Roy's Earthwood Building School. *Bottom:* The Roy's home at the school is a round cordwood building with a protruding southern wing. The earth-bermed section of the lower floor is constructed of dry-stacked concrete blocks covered with structural stucco and filled with sand. The small round building at lower right is a sauna.

CORDWOOD WITH COB MORTAR

Although we decided against it in our situation, cob can be used as the mortar for a cordwood wall. The high embodied energy of lime and Portland cement, along with the associated air pollution created, makes a cob mortar well worth considering. As I mentioned earlier, this is a structurally weaker application of cob for two reasons: (1) the cob is broken up into a web of small interlocking pieces by the cordwood, and (2) this web of cob is much thinner than in a monolithic wall. In fact, cob mortared cordwood is actually two very thin webs of cob separated by a space filled with some form of insulation and connected by the cordwood pieces. If you decide to try a cob mortar in a load-bearing situation, I'd make a little test wall first and see how it holds up.

Having said that, I imagine that a good cob mortar would be plenty strong for most common cordwood applications, and it would come with some real advantages. First, cordwood shrinkage would be no problem. A little smear of an earth plaster mix (see chapter 12) would easily fill any shrinkage cracks. Second, any cracks that appeared in the mortar could be easily sealed using the same method. Third, the materials involved have a low embodied energy and would therefore improve the "green building" index of cordwood construction greatly. Aesthetically, nicely detailed cob mortar in a cordwood wall can be very beautiful!

There are a couple of potential disadvantages to using cob mortar. First, there's the problem of rain exposure. Unprotected cob mortar might be damaged by rain. In most cases, I don't imagine a structural problem would result, but it might require a fair amount of maintenance. On the other hand, we're talking about cob maintenance, so it would require time, not money. Of course, this problem could be solved with large roof

Adjustable mortar. The cob mortar of this cordwood wall will be easy to repair if it cracks. If the wood shrinks, a mix of clay, sand, and chopped straw, basically an earth plaster (see chapter 12), will do an excellent job of filling any gaps.

overhangs, like we used over our wall. The second disadvantage would be that cob mortar would slow the cordwood laying process down a good deal. With our little electric concrete mixer, we were able to whip out a batch of sand/lime/sawdust/Portland cement mortar in no time. As we learned in chapter 8, the process for making cob is more involved.

Another way of looking at the same situation, however, would be that using cordwood could considerably speed up the typical cob construction process. Cordwood could be seen as giant aggregate in a cob wall, replacing a huge portion of the volume that would normally be filled with cob. Creating two separate thinner cob walls connected by cordwood with infill insulation between would also greatly increase the R-value of a cob wall. Cordwood mortared with cob, then, would greatly improve the two main weaknesses we identified for cob: labor intensity and poor thermal resistance.

Tim's Take
Getting It Done: Cordwood

Cordwood construction is an interesting mix of locally harvested and readily available commercial materials. It's also a very straightforward infill technique that meshes well with conventional post-and-beam construction. As such, I think the careful, realistic, inexperienced builder has a good chance of success because he or she can easily turn to a variety of people for help.

1) Getting wood. Even if you live in town and have never split a piece of firewood in your life, cordwood construction could still be an option. If you live in an area where wood is burned for heat, people often sell firewood by the pickup truck-load at a reasonable price. The only problem with this wood is that it might not be of consistent length or of an appropriate species for use as cordwood. If you make clear your needs, you should be able to order custom cordwood cut and split to your specifications. All you'll need to do is stack it under cover to dry.

2) Getting help. Cordwood is basically a masonry wall system that replaces concrete blocks with pieces of wood. That being the case, anyone familiar with conventional masonry would have the requisite skills to efficiently build a cordwood wall. By the same token, unskilled labor, a healthy teenager, say, could be quickly trained to be the brawn to complement your brain. The main physical labor of cordwood is the mortar mixing. A good system would be to train a helper to mix mortar while you lay cordwood. A motivated mortar mixer could quickly learn to keep two cordwood-layers in mortar. This three person crew could really make some progress.

3) Getting it done. My major piece of advice is to use cordwood as infill between a skeletal structure. There are a number of reasons I say this. First, if you're a novice, this would allow you to hire a professional to erect a strong structure that you could then infill with cordwood at your leisure, over a period of years if you so desired. That kind of schedule flexibility is like gold to the owner-builder. Second, unlike other forms of masonry, uncovered partially completed cordwood walls are vulnerable to rain and snow. Imagine a three-day torrential rainfall thundering down onto your partially finished cordwood wall. Water will soak deep into your insulation cavities and may pool against the wood at the base of the wall, especially if there's a concrete slab or other floor already in place. Both situations could lead to serious problems. You've carefully covered your cordwood to dry for all of those months, why would you leave it out in the open during the actual construction process? Finally, as we've said, laying up cordwood as a structural system takes a lot more skill than laying it as infill. Since it's all wood anyway, why not just make your life a whole lot easier by using some as structural posts and beams?

Chapter 10
Straw Bale

You remember the story of "The Three Little Pigs."

One really stupid pig makes a house out of straw, another almost-as-dumb pig builds a house out of sticks, but, luckily for all involved, the third pig is a genius and builds with bricks. After the Big Bad Wolf opens a can of whup-ass on their houses, Stupid and Dumb have to seek refuge with their brother the mason. Whoever wrote that story must have been a lobbyist for the brick industry. We've already shown that you can build strong walls out of sticks of cordwood, and now it's time to set the record straight about straw: You can build sturdy, beautiful, durable buildings by using straw bales for walls.

GENERAL CONTEXT: STRAW BALE CONSTRUCTION

Though straw and hay of one kind or another have been used by humans in building for thousands of years, *baled* straw and hay are recent arrivals dating to the invention of horse- and steam-powered balers in the late 1800s. Farmers living in the arid, hay-rich and timber-poor Sand Hills of Nebraska were quick to see the building potential of baled hay, and some buildings constructed there during this period still survive. Though the technique apparently didn't catch the mainstream imagination, straw or hay bale houses were definitely built in the first half of the twentieth century in Nebraska, South Dakota, Wyoming, and Alabama. Today, straw bale building has experienced a revival, and you can find straw bale construction in many different climates in many parts of the world.

Bale inheritance. There's a legacy of building with bales in the United States. *Left:* The walls of this building, built in 1908 in Purdum, Nebraska, were made of baled meadow hay. These bales were load-bearing; in other words, they carried all roof loads. A number of similar buildings, some documented and others still standing, were built in Nebraska around this time. Today, buildings that use straw bales to carry roof loads are sometimes called "Nebraska style." *Above:* Though from a distance you'd never know it, this modern house is part of the same lineage. Built about 500 miles away and 90 years later, its walls are formed from baled straw wrapping a timber frame structure.

TWO TYPES OF STRAW BALE CONSTRUCTION

There are presently two distinct categories of bale construction: infill and load-bearing.

Straw Bale Infill

You can use straw bales to fill the spaces between columns in a skeletal structure. In this context, the bales carry very limited loads and are acting simply as insulation. There are more variations for creating structural skeletons for straw than you can shake a bale at. They range from wrapping the inside or outside of timber frames with stacked bales to filling the spaces between studs in a fairly conventional stick-framed structure with bales

Straw or Hay?

We mentioned this in our cob discussion, but it bears repeating. Hay is dried grass, loved by cows, molds, and fungus alike. Straw is the skeletal husks left over after the harvesting of cereal grains such as wheat, rye, and rice. Straw is hollow, hard, decays slowly, and is of much less interest to anything as food. Both hay and straw can be baled, and both have been used in different situations in the history of housing construction. Though there is talk of other scenarios, such as baling the dead stems of non-native, invasive species, right now you are probably going to have the choice between hay baled for animal food and straw baled for animal bedding and mulch. If you're looking to build with either of these, the straw bales are definitely what you want.

Hay, That's Not Straw! Though both hay and straw are part of the huge world of plants generically called "grass," they don't show the same promise as building materials. *Left*: Straw is made up of tough, hollow strands left over after the harvesting of cereal grasses such as wheat. Because the seed, i.e., "grain," is what was harvested from the plant, straw is mostly free of seeds. *Right*: Hay is meadow grass that's been cut, seed and all, usually for the purpose of feeding animals. Though its stalks are hollow, they are much thinner and less rigid than the stalks of cereal grains. As a result, hay is not very tough and things like to eat it, including mold, insects, and mammals. This hay hasn't completely dried, so it's still somewhat green in color.

standing on end. In any of these situations, however, the bales remain constant: large, fairly rigid, modular units. Obstructions like windows, doors, framing, and bracing can require bales to be custom sized and shaped, which takes time and effort. The more of these obstacles you have, the more difficult it becomes to infill the structure with straw bales.

Load-Bearing Straw Bale

Straw bales can be stacked in an interlocking pattern like bricks to form walls with sufficient compressive strength to carry roof loads. This is the technique known as Nebraska style, mentioned earlier. The concept of stacking up some bales, throwing up a roof, and moving in captures the imagination, but, of course, the reality is somewhat more complicated. For example, bales beneath roof loads compress over time, so bale walls either need to be pre-compressed or allowed to settle for a period of time with the roof attached before being plastered. This issue and others create some interesting construction details unique to load-bearing straw bale construction. We'll discuss some of these in the Variations section at the end of this chapter.

Straw bale infill. Straw bales are being used to infill the spaces between the load-bearing skeletal framing of this building.

Structural hybrid. On the first story of this building, the straw bales are wrapped around a wooden load-bearing frame capped with a framed floor. On the second story, the bales are stacked alone on this floor platform and are carrying all roof loads without the help of a structural skeletal framework. Notice also the hip roof that provides equal protection from rain to all four sides of the building.

PROS AND CONS OF STRAW BALE CONSTRUCTION

As we've just pointed out, the term *straw bale construction* can refer to two completely different approaches. A look at the pros and cons of building with bales, then, needs to be both a general discussion and a comparison of the two types.

General Advantages

Straw has some incredible points in its favor. First, it's excellent insulation. Though its per inch R-value is sometimes debated, the best estimate available puts it at around R-1.5 per inch when laid flat and R-2 per inch when laid on edge. (See figure 1.) These rates are far less than the values of R-3.1 to -3.8 per inch given for commercial cellulose insulation. However, there's simply a lot more insulation in a straw bale wall because bales are so thick, anywhere from 14 to 24 inches. What's more, straw bales tend to engulf the structure, therefore eliminating the thermal bridging that occurs in conventionally stick-framed and infilled walls. (See the sidebar Thermal Bridging.) These factors combined make straw bale walls by far the most insulative system we are covering in this book. Depending on thickness, these walls rate between R-28 and R-35.

Figure 1
ESTIMATED R-VALUE OF STRAW BALES

Laid flat. Estimated R-Value = R-1.5/inch. The hollow, long thin strands of straw are oriented to give air and heat an easier conduit.

Laid on edge. Estimated R-Value = R-2/inch. In this orientation, the hollow ends of the strands aren't as open to air infiltration and don't give heat those nice long straight paths from one side to the other.

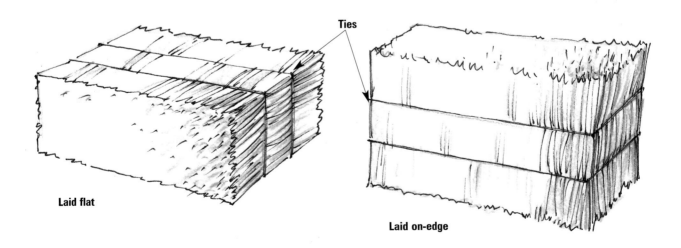

Ties

Laid flat

Laid on-edge

Thermal Bridging

In comparisons of different wall systems, you'll often hear the term "thermal bridging" or "thermal break" come up. This is usually a reference to the difference between the R-value of the insulation in a wall and the R-value of the other components, such as the structure, doors, and windows. For example, a 2x4 stud in a conventionally framed wall has an R-value of around 4, whereas the fiberglass insulation next to it has an R-value of 13. In this wall, then, the stud could be considered a thermal bridge because it's allowing heat to flow through it more easily than the insulation on either side of it is. Likewise, the stem wall in figure 4 in chapter 7 is a thermal bridge.

The broader issue here is that the thermal performance of a building is the sum of its parts. For example, if you insulate well, but put in too much glass, you are lowering the overall R-value of your wall. Likewise, if someone claims a wall has a given R-value, you have to ask yourself whether they're talking about the whole system or just the insulation tested alone in a laboratory.

Energy-efficient straw. Straw bales are a good match for energy-efficient passive solar design. In this building, the windows in the long southern face allow the low winter sun's heat to be collected by an interior mass floor, and clerestory windows allow that sun to reach deep into the building. Limited glass on other walls (such as the east wall visible to the right in the photo) and the superior insulation of straw bales help keep that heat gain from escaping. In the summer, the thick, insulative bale walls do a good job of buffering the interior from the sun's heat. The panels at right are using the sun's energy to heat the building's water.

Another possible advantage of straw is its sustainability. Straw is a byproduct of food production and, hence, is a resource renewed on an annual basis. In fact in our modern context, it's really a waste product of industrial agriculture that's often burned for want of a better use. So, in areas where grains are grown, straw is abundant, easily replenished, and can actually prevent pollution if used in walls instead of being burned.

Perhaps the factor that most draws people to straw is spending a bit of time in a bale building. The thickness and contour of plastered straw bale walls is incredibly beautiful. The deep sills and soft shapes create a unique feeling that many people find profoundly relaxing and nurturing. The thick walls and plaster are also great sound-proofing, creating a sense of quiet and privacy.

Though the method is sometimes touted as "easy," "owner-builder friendly," and "inexpensive," I can't bring myself to include these traits as advantages of straw bale construction. There's a lot of complexity inherent in building with bales. They're big, cumbersome, fuzzy blocks that shed a lot, can't get wet and can only be shaped in limited ways. You can cut a common brick in half or angle it with a couple of taps of a hammer on a chisel; to get the same results with a bale takes a number of steps, as we'll explain later in this chapter. Lifting bales away from water and condensation, attaching them to each other and the structure, as well as designing, building, and connecting appropriate window and door enclosures are all procedures that take a fair amount of time and ingenuity to do well.

A tale of two bales. Straw bale construction attracts a wide variety of people. In my experience, the one thing they all seem to have in common is an enthusiasm for the finished product. *Top left*: This luxurious straw bale home in Texas is full of deluxe features (including a three-story tower) and came complete with a high-end modern price tag. *Bottom left*: The tall ceilings, deep, rounded window reveals, and details like this rough flagstone floor give this modern house a timeless feel. *Above*: This funky, owner-built straw bale cottage situated in an intentional community in the woods in North Carolina was created with a tiny amount of cash and a lot of sweat. The result isn't regal like its uptown cousin, but this home is cozy, energy efficient, and paid for.

Environmental Arm Wrestling: Straw vs. Wood

Though the focus of this book is green building, we hope first and foremost it's simply an introduction to good building. In our opinion, the key to really sensible building is a healthy skepticism. When it comes down to it, the only thing that is real is an actual building and how it performs through its life. All the rest of it—the sustainability arguments, the mass enhanced R-value discussions, the embodied energy calculations, and everything else that attempts to create general abstractions out of complicated specific realities—needs to be held at arm's length.

As an illustration, let's look at a seemingly obvious claim: straw is more sustainable than wood. It's a no-brainer, right? Straw will be produced yearly as a byproduct of food production whether it's used in construction or not. Trees, on the other hand, must grow for years before they can be harvested; as a result, the deforestation of the planet is a crisis of epic proportions. If that wasn't bad enough, those 2x4s or that log home kit may end up being trucked thousands of miles to find their home.

Yet, there is another side to the argument. It says: If straw were truly sustainably managed, as part of a sustainable agriculture, much of it would probably be composted so that its nutrients could be returned to the soil. On the other hand, the straw you buy to build with will almost certainly be the product of industrial agriculture. As such, it will most probably have been grown in huge, monocropped fields with the aid of chemical pesticides and fertilizers. In fact, the clear-cutting deforestation and its companion topsoil erosion mentioned above might have taken place to make room for the agribusiness megafields that produced your straw. To top it off, cereal grains are only grown in certain areas, so your bales may need to be trucked quite a ways to get to you. Wood, on the other hand can be locally, sustainably, and even site harvested. Its production requires no crop dusters or plant Viagra. Keep yer stinkin' genetically modified, toxic Frankenstein straw away from me!

Which argument is right or even closer to being right? Don't ask me. I'm going to stick to consciously creating the best building I can given my specific set of circumstances. Trying to construct a building that truly serves its inhabitants without harming the environment is a humbling experience.

Eco-wrestling: straw vs. wood. Which is the more sustainable uber-material?

General Disadvantages

There are three major stumbling blocks for the straw bale builder: water, water, and water. As with all alternative techniques, straw bale builders are often very dedicated to their chosen approach, and, as such, they have a tendency to kick and scream when this weakness is pointed out. You'll hear arguments that straw and wood are both cellulose, so they carry the same risk of water damage. You'll also hear that, like cordwood and cob, straw bale walls are hygroscopic, so they're able to take on and let off water. In other words, they dry out after they get wet.

Both of these arguments are half true. Yes, wood and straw both can rot in the presence of water. However, lay a locust log and a straw bale on the ground exposed to rain and snow and watch the straw bale be destroyed before the wood even flinches. Wood can be chosen and placed so that it can withstand being exposed in wet climates. Straw really cannot. In any case, both straw bale construction and conventional stick-framing don't intend to allow liquid water access to their cellulose, and in this capacity, stick-framing out performs straw bale construction. (See our discussion of drainage planes and hygroscopic walls in chapter 3.)

The fact is that typical straw bale construction is inherently vulnerable to liquid water. It has a plaster coating that is physically bonded to thousands of hollow strands of cellulose, a wonderful conduit for liquid water. To make matters worse, the plaster is often a more water-permeable earth- or lime-based plaster and, therefore, will take on liquid water. Any water absorbed by the plaster will most likely wick into the straw. As we've said, these plasters are used as part of a strategy to allow the straw to take on and let off water vapor in response to humidity changes. Plaster mixes that might reduce transmission of liquid water, such as conventional Portland cement stucco, are often avoided because they are less vapor-permeable and therefore can trap water that gets behind them, and cause the straw to rot. However, a hygroscopic strategy works only if the wall is dry enough often enough to prevent mold, mildew, and the connected decay of the straw.

In some climates, such as that of parts of New Mexico, with lots of sun and small amounts of rain, these issues are little if any problem. However, straw bale construction in wet climates needs to be carefully designed. High stem walls, large overhangs, and good drainage—including gutters and proper grading—can go a long way toward keeping liquid water off walls. However, even without contact with liquid water, a straw bale wall could get too wet if it's taking on more humidity from the surrounding air than it has a chance to give back in a timely fashion. If you live in a very wet, very humid climate, it might just be better to steer clear of straw bales, or at the very least carefully research other bale buildings in your area. You could build a test wall and craft different plaster mixes based on your local humidity and temperature. Cutting into that wall after a year or two would provide great information for you and a wonderful gift of information to others working with bales in your area. I guess I can sum it up by saying that there are many ways to protect straw from water, but ignoring its vulnerability isn't one of them.

Desert design. This straw bale structure sits in an area of Colorado that averages less than 10 inches of rainfall per year. It was built to mimic a traditional adobe building with a flat roof, no protective overhangs, and uncovered log roof framing, often called vigas, puncturing the earth/lime plaster mix of the wall surface. Such a design could only work in an arid climate where rains are few and far between, giving the walls ample time to dry out between soakings. Personally, I wouldn't build this way even in the desert. Roof overhangs would serve the double purpose of providing precious shade in a hot climate while also protecting the walls from rain and snow.

Infill vs. Load-Bearing

We've identified vulnerability to water damage as the main disadvantage of straw bale construction. For a well-designed straw bale building, the only real threat of water damage should come during construction, when the bales are exposed to the weather. From that point of view, infill construction wins easily over load-bearing. First of all, you keep infill straw in a completely dry storage area until the roof is on the building and the door bucks (and, in some systems, even window bucks) are in place. Bales can be efficiently installed and kept dry for the most part. As soon as they're in place, preparations for plaster can commence.

With load-bearing walls, on the other hand, bales are installed without a protective roof cover. Though door bucks will be installed, window bucks never are. Bales need to be stacked, resized, and pinned while potentially exposed to rain. This stacking process needs to be done carefully and without the aid of a skeletal structure as a reference for keeping plumb. Next, the top plate assembly needs to be installed. At this point, the walls either need to be pre-compressed, a process whose success is debated in the literature, or a roof needs to be installed and the walls allowed to settle under the roof load, a process that takes weeks. Only now can the wall be prepared for plaster. During all this time, the bales are exposed to whatever weather happens to rear its ugly head.

Dry bales. A tarp attached under the roof overhang creates complete protection from rain for these infill straw bales. These bales were taken directly from storage and immediately installed here, so they had no chance of being exposed to rain during the construction process. This is something that's impossible to guarantee in load-bearing bale construction.

What about Fire?

Perhaps contrary to initial common sense, straw bale construction consistently performs extremely well in fire-resistance tests, and these tests have been conducted in a number of countries around the world. In every test of which I'm aware, plastered bales easily surpassed code requirements set for stick-frame construction. This makes sense when you remember that fire needs air. A plastered bale wall contains little air to feed a fire. However, loose straw (and to a much lesser degree, unplastered bales) can burn, so precautions should be taken during the construction process.

Another advantage of infill is that it gives you the option of creating a thinner wall with essentially the same R-value. This is because, as mentioned above, bales placed on end are more insulative per inch, and it's easier to stack them in this configuration when using them as infill.

The one real advantage of load-bearing construction is that it saves some structural lumber. However, since roofs and window and door bucks for both systems are usually framed in wood, the only lumber saved will be any structural posts and beams, which can be minimized in a well-designed skeleton. Even this comparison isn't completely fair because structural door and window bucks, as well as top plate assemblies, in load-bearing construction use more wood than their infill counterparts. Still, infill straw bale definitely uses more lumber, so load-bearing straw bale construction can make sense in very dry climates where structural lumber is scarce and construction can take place with the confidence that rain days will be few and far between.

ABOUT BALES

There are all sorts of grains out there whose skeletal stalks might be baled, including barley, rye, wheat, and rice. In my experience, the most common is wheat, so if you're getting something else it might be a good idea to do a bit of research on its success as a building material. Straw bales are held together with wire or twine, and come in a range of sizes. (See figure 2.) Two-string bales are generally around 14 inches tall, 18 inches wide, and 32 to 40 inches long. Three-string bales are generally 14 to 17 inches tall, around 24 inches wide, and 32 to 47 inches long.

Most straw isn't going be baled with wall building in mind; therefore, it can be difficult to get bales with exactly the features you're looking for. The one variable that's absolutely crucial is that your bales be very dry. Though you can tell something about the amount of water in a bale by its weight, you can also check moisture levels with a moisture meter. You may want to own such a meter anyway to periodically check moisture levels in your walls over the years, so why not buy one now to get an accurate measurement of the moisture content of your building blocks? Some building codes require you to measure bale moisture levels before building.

In addition to being dry, bales need to be tightly packed and of consistent size. Though most bales from a single source tend to be of the same width and height, they can vary in length, which can be a pain if you have carefully designed your walls to accommodate bales of a specific size.

Figure 2
BALE DIMENSIONS

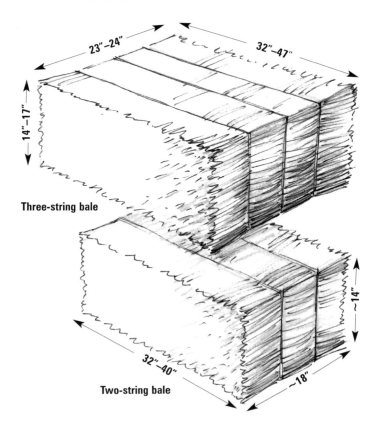

23"–24"

32"–47"

14"–17"

Three-string bale

~14"

32"–40"

~18"

Two-string bale

If you live near grain farmers, you might be able to convince them to make bales to your specifications. If not, at least you can make sure that the bales haven't been left in the rain, and you can handpick them at the time of purchase. In some parts of the country where straw bale construction is popular, people bale straw for the purpose of selling to builders. Most of us, however, have to be more resourceful. If you're buying bales from a nursery or "feed and seed," you have to make it very clear to them what you need and why you need it. Don't order any bales delivered unless you've seen them or have made it clear that you'll refuse bales that don't meet your reasonable expectations. If ordering directly from the source, you have to plan ahead and be ready for bales when the grains are being harvested, which might mean you'll need to store them for some time. Straw bales take up a lot of space, and they need to be kept dry through transport and while being stored on your site, so plan and prepare carefully.

Call me a straw bale dork, but I ended up buying bales for this project at the local hardware/nursery mega-chain store. They had a constant supply of dense, two-string wheat straw bales that were both delivered and stored in a closed-cabin semitrailer. When it was time to get bales, I just rented a truck with an enclosed cargo area, drove up to the trailer, handpicked my bales, paid, drove home, and unloaded directly into the barn. For the relatively small number of bales needed on this project, it was a great way to go.

DOES STRAW BALE CONSTRUCTION FIT YOUR SITUATION?

I know I sound like a broken record, but it can't be said too often: The main issue to think about is water. Straw bale construction had its genesis in a dry climate, and much of its renaissance seems to be centered in drier climates, too. That is absolutely not to say that you can't build with straw in wet climates, but you do have to be more conscious and careful in wet situations. Just because somebody in New Mexico has a wonderful story about how swell their building project went, that doesn't mean it will be the same for you in Seattle.

I live in a wet climate and I've visited a straw bale building in my neck of the woods that almost knocks me over with the stench of mold every time I walk in it. At the same time, I've been in beautiful straw bale homes around here that appear to be perfectly dry and have wonderful indoor air quality. If you spend objective time looking at the literature, you'll see that there's a debate between experts about how well straw bale construction performs in different climates. Check out straw bale buildings in your area during different seasons. If you can't locate any bale buildings, ask yourself why. Above all, take your time, do your research, and trust your own conclusions. I can tell you one thing: The difference between success and failure will lie in the construction details. Careful, thoughtful design is always of the utmost importance, but doubly so for straw bale buildings in wet climates.

Buying bales. If you're picking up your straw yourself, look for outlets with dry storage that will allow you to handpick your own bales. Remember, for most people straw is going to end up as mulch or in some other application that doesn't require that it be dry. You're the exception, not the rule. This is the straw trailer at my local hardware store where the straw is kept snug and dry.

Is Straw Bale Construction Green?

Let's hook straw bales up to our green building analyzer for a diagnostic.

1) Low Construction Impact. In our modern context, straw is a byproduct of commercial agriculture and, as such, is part of an environmentally destructive industry. However, since straw is often burned in the field as "waste," using straw in construction can actually prevent pollution. That's what I call a low construction impact! But there's a lot more that goes into a straw bale building than the bales themselves, so a true discussion of construction impact would need to consider the building as a whole. Still, the bales themselves are a very good start.

2) Resource Efficiency through the Life of the Building. Of the four wall systems covered in this book, well-built straw bale performs the best at holding temperature. There are some complications in accommodating plumbing, electrical, and other systems, but these can be overcome through thoughtful design. A well-constructed building that uses straw as insulation and successfully stops airflow with a good skin should be very energy efficient.

3) Long Lasting. As with all cellulose-based building systems, the secret to straw bale longevity is protection from water. However, this mantra is the gospel for straw. If straw gets wet and stays that way for even a relatively short period of time, it starts to rot. As long as straw stays dry, however, it can last indefinitely, as historical straw bale buildings have proven.

4) Nontoxic. Straw bales are, of course, natural and give off no synthetic toxins. However, human-made compounds aren't the only toxins we need to be concerned about. More than any of our wall systems, straw bales are the most susceptible to mold and fungal growth, which, if left unchecked, can create serious indoor air quality problems. The solution is the same broken record: Keep straw dry and allow it adjust to humidity changes. If these steps are taken, straw bale construction should create a cozy, quiet indoor environment with excellent air quality.

5) Beautiful. Though not as flexible, moldable, and potentially whimsical as cob or even cordwood, the thick, gently undulating walls of plastered straw bale construction have a mesmerizing beauty. This reaction, in addition to the energy efficiency and sustainability of straw as a building material, tends to make people who choose straw bale construction very proud of their homes. They often feel they've done the world a good deed and, in return, gotten a cozy, quiet, beautiful place to live. This kind of love for a building is the sort of personal connection that might break our modern concept of a house as a financial investment and turn it into a real home, a place around which a life is built. That's the kind of beauty I'm talking about in the context of green building.

The beauty of bales. *Left:* Though less sculptural than cob or even cordwood, bales still allow for a lot of personal expression, as the whimsical spiral of this straw bale house and integrated garden wall demonstrate. *Right:* The thick, undulating surfaces of plastered straw bale walls create a quiet, calming, secure interior atmosphere.

STRAW BALE APPLIED: OUR LITTLE BUILDING

DESIGNING WITH BALES

If you'll remember back to our design discussions, this little building was a real challenge because we wanted to create a very private getaway/guesthouse in the midst of a fairly public space that includes car parking, a workshop, and outdoor work area. The only way this could work was to create a real physical barrier, both visual and aural between the inside of the cottage and the workshop courtyard behind it. Due to space limitations, this barrier had to be the actual north wall of the cottage. This north wall, like all north walls in the northern hemisphere, is perpetually shaded by the building itself; in addition on our site, it's exposed to cold winter winds, which usually come from the northwest. Therefore, we needed a material with excellent insulation value that could also block sound and provide an imposing visual barrier.

Straw bales seemed to fit the bill perfectly. They have the highest insulation value of any wall system in our repertoire, have excellent sound-absorbing qualities, and provide a wall thickness which, when viewed through the deep sill of a small window, will create a real feeling of separation. Our only concern was, surprise! water. We get a lot of rain and snow around here, and we knew this north wall would be slow to dry out when it got wet because it would never receive direct sun. In addition, it will be a gable end wall, so it will receive less benefit from the roof overhang. Also, to come clean, our bales will only be six inches above grade, which is a bit on the low side. To be completely honest, using straw bales in this situation is going to be an experiment. We decided to be very careful in our design and detailing and see what happens over time.

It's important to point out that, for the sake of continuity, we're describing this design process now, whereas in fact, all of this work was done before the building ever got off the ground. Remember that straw bales are like huge bricks. Though they can be cut and angled, they really can't be shortened. Therefore, wall height has to be planned as a multiple of the bale height. In an infill wall, there's some wiggle room here. You can, for example, stuff a little bit of loose straw to fill a gap at the top of the wall. However, the point remains the same: if you're using bales, it's important to design with their rigid nature in mind. We based the wall height of our entire building on the size of our bales.

Straw bale experiment. This is the northeast corner of our finished bale wall already plastered. This is the spot where ground level, or grade, is closest to one of our wall infills. It's normal practice to lift bales higher off the ground than this, but I think all of our design details working together will keep our wall safe from damage.

THE SILL PLATE

Our basic building design has already gone a long way toward protecting all of our wall materials from water damage by lifting them off the ground both inside and outside the building. Still, there is the possibility of condensation coming up through the termite barrier. To combat that possibility on this wall, we created a sill plate out of an essentially waterproof composite lumber made from recycled plastic and wood chips, and we insulated it with rigid foam insulation. This sill will both lift the bales away from possible condensation and also be a place to attach the wooden strips we'll use to pin our bales to the structure.

The Sill Plate

▲ **Step 1.** Our waterproof sill lumber comes in boards 1¼ inches thick and 5½ inches wide. It's as easy to cut, drill, and shape as wood. In order to stretch this expensive material further, we first ripped boards in half with a circular saw. We then had to drill and notch the ends (top left, top right) to accommodate the brackets attaching our locust posts to the structural concrete pads (bottom).

▲ **Step 2.** Instead of puncturing our termite barrier to fasten our sill, we soldered on brackets made from scraps of the barrier (top). Since composite lumber isn't very rigid, we pulled a line between our posts as a reference to keep our sill straight as we fastened it to the barrier (bottom).

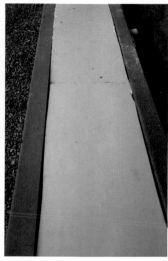

◄ **Step 3.** After installing a second sill plate on the interior of the wall using the same technique, we insulated the cavity in the middle with 1-inch-thick rigid foam.

▲ **Step 4.** Next, we covered the whole assembly with tarpaper (left) and stapled the paper to the sill (middle), notching it around obstacles (right) to create a second layer of protection from condensation rising up from the stem wall.

THE WINDOW BUCK

Windows and doors can be installed in straw bale infill walls in various ways. For example, sometimes people frame out structural openings for them that are attached to the skeleton, making the window frame itself non-structural, similar to the case in conventional stick-frame construction. Another very common approach is to build structural bucks similar to those we used for our cob and cordwood walls. In an infill wall, these bucks don't need to be as strong since they'll be carrying only the weight of the bales above them, not roof loads. This absence of loads also means that gravity won't be much help holding the buck in place. We decided to combine these two approaches to get the benefits of both. First, we created a lighter structural buck capable of supporting the bales above it. Then, we attached this buck to the structure of our building to prevent it from moving around.

Figure 3
THE WINDOW BUCK

We used ¾-inch finish plywood for all four sides of the buck, which allowed us to create a 20-inch-wide sill with a single piece of wood. We also attached an integrated exterior cedar sill and head piece as part of our strategy to keep water away from our bales. Our straw bales will be connected to the building's structure by being sandwiched between thin wooden strips attached to the sill plate and roof structure. We designed our buck to be attached to two of these strips, thus locking it into the structure of the building.

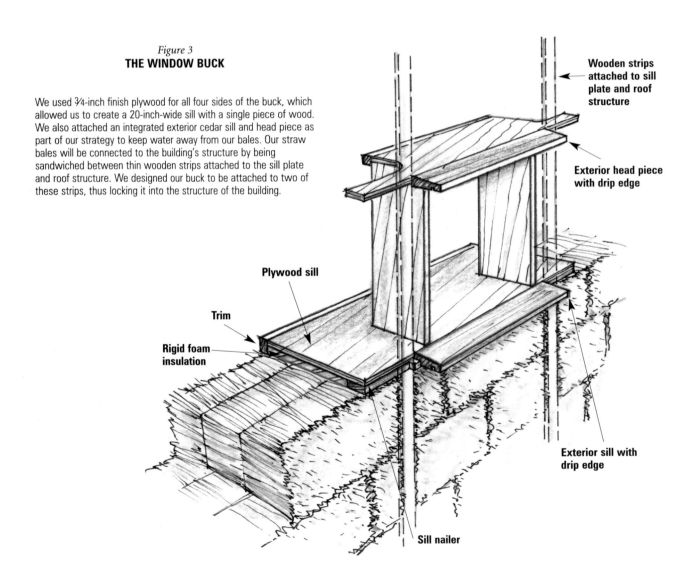

Wooden strips attached to sill plate and roof structure

Exterior head piece with drip edge

Plywood sill

Trim

Rigid foam insulation

Exterior sill with drip edge

Sill nailer

PLACING THE WINDOW

Cob and cordwood both allow for the careful placement of windows as you fill in the wall. According to the specific technique being used, this is more or less true with straw bale construction. In our situation, we had decided to attach our buck to the wooden strips we'd be installing to connect our bales to the building structure. That meant that we needed to decide where the buck would sit before installing the strips. Therefore, before actually laying bales, we did a mock-up of the wall by stacking bales temporarily and trying different window locations. We then placed wooden strips based on both our window placement decision and the bale layout (we'll explain this later). When it's time to actually install the buck, the wooden strips will be exact markers of where we chose to place the window.

As with all window and door decisions, we find ourselves at a crucial moment for the feel of our building. Since this window will open out onto our courtyard, its placement will have a big effect on how the inside of the cottage interacts with the "public" space. Of course, we could have gotten maximum privacy by including no window at all. However, a desk will sit against this wall. North light is more consistent and glare-free, so it's great for a workspace like a desk. Putting a window here will permit someone to work most of the time during the day by sunlight and will keep a connection to the outdoors by allowing a breeze and the sights from the outdoors in when desired. Right now, not in the design phase, is the only moment when all of the subtleties of this important window placement can be assessed.

Though this mock-up process allows us to fine-tune our window placement, it also exposes an inflexible aspect of straw bale construction: window sizing and placement is most practical if based on the size of a bale. For example, our buck is two bales tall, allowing it to fit within the regular bale-course sequence. It would have complicated things quite a bit if we'd wanted to make it 2¼ bales tall. Similarly, our possible sill heights were limited to setting the buck on the second course or a full 14 inches higher on the third course. Anything in between wasn't really an option within our system. Though there are ways around these limitations, they aren't completely straightforward or they have their own inherent complications. In our situation, then, we were fairly limited as to the size of the window and the height it could be installed in the wall.

Straw bib. Before bringing bales onto the scene, we covered the ground with plastic tarps to catch loose straw. This was especially important on the inside of the building because we didn't want any straw rotting under our floor.

Placing the window. We stacked bales to different heights and tried the window in different places. Since the bales can support the buck, we were able to leave it in place as we walked all around checking the placement from different perspectives. Once our placement was clear, we took note of how many bales-courses high the buck was sitting and made marks on the sill plate to designate where the wooden strips needed to be placed to hold the buck.

THE DRAINAGE PLANE

We've already explained that the typical straw bale wall doesn't need a drainage plane other than its plaster skin. However, we decided to create one on the first course of this particular wall (see figure 4) because it will be the least protected by the roof and will get the most backsplash from rain. For this purpose, we used a piece of conventional building wrap, which is very strong and tear-resistant and reportedly repels liquid water while allowing water vapor to pass both ways. Still, let's be clear that this is not a standard straw bale construction detail. Some experts would disagree with our decision. As I've said repeatedly: do your research and make your decisions based on your specific situation.

Installing the Drainage Plane

◀ **Step 1.** First, we installed small blocks as nailers for the wooden strips that will tie our bales to the structure of the building. *Left:* With blocks this small, we predrilled to prevent splitting. (A general tip: Tim and I have sworn off Phillips-head screws. We always use the more expensive deck screws that take square bits because they never strip.) *Right:* We spaced the blocks carefully so that the vertical strips would lie as close to the middle of the stacked bales as possible. (See figure 8 on page 369.)

 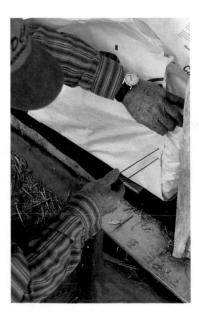 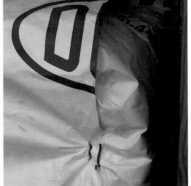

▲ **Step 2.** Next, we laid our building wrap over the sill so that it would be able to wrap around the first course of bales entirely.

◀ **Step 3.** After the first course was in place, we pulled the outer side of the wrap over the top of the bales. We used staples made from fiberglass insulation supports (left) to tie the paper tightly to the bales (right). Notice that we also took a small piece of building wrap and capped each end bale.

◄ **Step 4.** Next, we installed flashing with a drip edge at the base of the wall, then pulled the other side of the building wrap over the bales from inside the building so that it overlapped the flashing, completing the drainage plane. (See figure 4.)

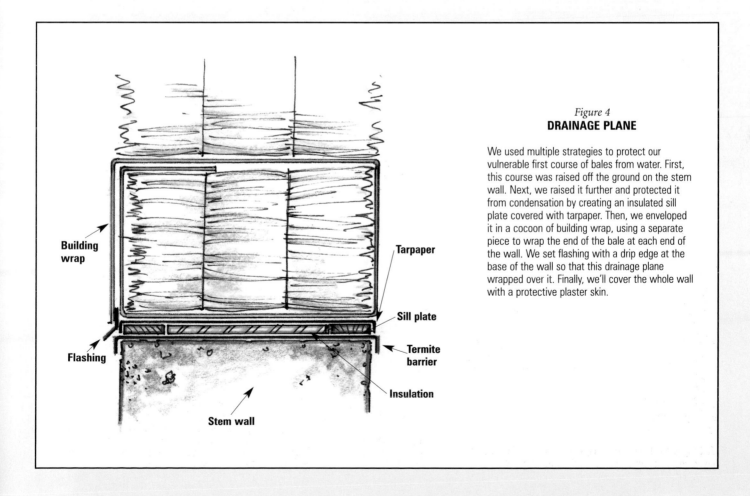

Figure 4
DRAINAGE PLANE

We used multiple strategies to protect our vulnerable first course of bales from water. First, this course was raised off the ground on the stem wall. Next, we raised it further and protected it from condensation by creating an insulated sill plate covered with tarpaper. Then, we enveloped it in a cocoon of building wrap, using a separate piece to wrap the end of the bale at each end of the wall. We set flashing with a drip edge at the base of the wall so that this drainage plane wrapped over it. Finally, we'll cover the whole wall with a protective plaster skin.

TYING THE BALES TO THE STRUCTURE: PART I

Though the bales in our wall will be carrying few loads, it's still a good idea to tie them together and to the building structure to create a solid unit. There are various methods to do this. We chose to sandwich the bales between wooden strips attached to the sill plate and roof structure. This method is straightforward and doesn't require puncturing our termite barrier or the cocoon we wrapped around our first course of bales. (See figure 5.)

There are two possible sequences with this method. We chose to install the wooden tie strips on one side of the wall only, groove and stack the bales against them, wrap a tie wire around each strip, then continue with the next course. When all the bales were in place, we then installed the wooden strips on the other side and attached the tie wires. The advantage of this approach is that it's easier to lay and groove the bales, but the disadvantage is that the bales will have to be muscled into place when it comes time to install the interior strips. The other option would be to install the strips on both sides of the wall first and then to wedge the grooved bales between them.

Installing the Wooden Tie Strips

▲ **Step 1.** We used ½ x 1½ inch wooden strips, which are pretty flimsy, so we predrilled them to prevent splitting.

▲ **Step 2.** We screwed the strips to the blocks we'd installed on the sill plate.

▲ **Step 3.** After making sure the strips were plumb, we attached their tops to a nailer we'd installed on the bottom of the roof truss. (See figure 5.)

Don't use tarpaper. We first tried tarpaper instead of building wrap as a drainage plane, but it was too rigid and ripped where the strips pushed against it.

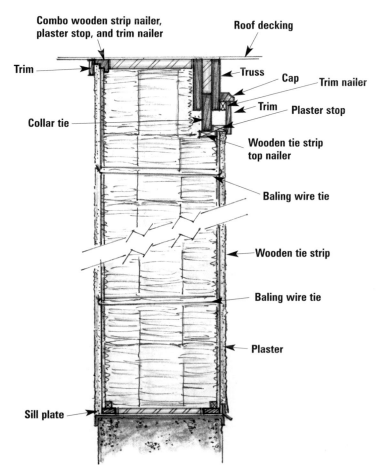

Combo wooden strip nailer, plaster stop, and trim nailer

Roof decking

Trim

Truss

Cap

Trim nailer

Collar tie

Trim

Plaster stop

Wooden tie strip top nailer

Baling wire tie

Wooden tie strip

Baling wire tie

Plaster

Sill plate

Figure 5
DEVIL IS IN THE DETAILS

This drawing outlines some of the details we needed to install in order to attach the bales to our structure and to prepare the wall to receive plaster. This is the part of building that takes a lot of thought. Notice how we set the sill plate in a bit on the interior so that the termite barrier could function as the bottom plaster stop. On the outside, we needed to push the sill plate to the edge of the stem wall so that we could install our drip edge flashing. Also notice that we had to be thinking about laying bales way back during the framing of the roof—we had to position our roof truss to allow us to attach our wooden tie strips to the structure. In other words, we had to be thinking about all of these details long before we actually purchased our bales.

▲ **Step 1.** Before laying a course of bales, we bent pieces of baling wire around each wooden tie strip, cutting them long enough to extend past the inside surface of the bale wall. We'll use these to tie the interior and exterior wooden strips together and snuggle the bales up to the framing of the building. (See Tying the Bales to the Structure: Part II, page 369.)

◀ **Step 2.** We wanted the wooden tie strips to pull in tight to the plane of the bales, so we cut a groove in each bale with a large bit on a router (left) and pushed the grooves up against the strips (right). A grinder with a wire brush or cutting wheel also works well for this job.

BALE-LAYING BASICS

Commercial baling equipment produces bales with one cut and one folded side. The cut side consists of stems that have been sliced with a sharp knife, creating a fairly regular surface. The other side of the bale has a lot of folded stems that tend to make it uneven, almost fuzzy. Since the cut sides are easier to plaster, the decision needs to be made as to how to orient the bales.

Some people lay one course of bales with the cut side to the outside and the next course with the folded side to the outside. This way, the fuzzy, difficult-to-plaster bale portions get divided evenly between the two sides of the wall. Since we were concerned about water, it made more sense to create a very even surface for plaster on the vulnerable, outer side of the wall, so we placed all the cut sides in this direction. Other than this decision, basic bale laying isn't rocket science. We inspected each bale before laying it, setting aside loose or really wonky ones. These didn't go to waste because there's always a use for loose straw, for example, in plaster or as garden mulch. We stacked the bales in staggered courses like bricks so that the joints between them didn't line up through the wall. We pushed the bales tight against one another and kept them plumb. Bale laying tip: Don't be shy. Kicking, shoving, and whomping are all officially sanctioned techniques.

Two Sides to Every Bale. Here are two sides of a single bale. *Left*: This is the cut side. You can see the hollow ends of the cut stalks creating a fairly level surface like the bristles of a brush. This smoother, stiffer side of the bale takes plaster well. *Right*: This is the folded side. It's more unruly with lots of long, slippery stalks running along its surface. This side doesn't take plaster nearly as well.

CUSTOM-LENGTH BALES

We needed to make bales of custom sizes. For starters, since we wanted to stack the bales with offset joints, we knew we'd need two half bales to place at each end of every other course. In fact, since our bales didn't all turn out to be the same length, we usually ended up using a half bale on one end and then a custom-length bale to fill the gap at the other end. Also, since our window isn't exactly a single bale wide, we had to make bales to fit around it.

Straw bales are held together with two or three strings of twine or wire. Making custom-length bales simply entails tying new sets of strings around the sections of the bale you want to separate and then cutting the old strings.

Making Custom-Length Bales

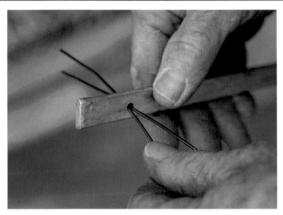

▲ **Step 2.** We chose baling wire to make our custom bales, though polypropylene twine also works well. We threaded the needle with two wires (left), and folded them over so they wouldn't come off in the bale (right).

▲ **Step 1.** We made this needle (which we used to push wire through the bales) by drilling a hole in a chainlink fence tensioning bar (available wherever chainlink fence is sold). Just about any thin stiff piece of metal would work. (We eventually figured out that cutting a point on the end, as seen here, helped the needle move through the bale. In the photos to come, our needle tip is still squared.)

▲ **Step 3.** Next, we measured off the amount of straw we needed in our new bale, then pushed the needle into the bale next to an existing string (left) and through to the other side (right).

▲ **Step 4.** We then pulled enough wire through to wrap around each new small bale. You can see that in this case we're splitting this bale in half.

▲ **Step 5.** After wrapping the wire around the new bale, we pulled up the slack and made a single twist by hand.

◄ **Step 6.** After a few twists with a pair of pliers, the wire was tight against the bale (left). Using the same pliers, we cut off any excess so the wire won't get in the way at some future point (right).

▲ **Step 7.** We then used the other wire we'd pushed through to the tie up the other half of the bale. Next, we repeated the process by pushing two more wires through next to the bale's other original string. After tying these wires, we were ready to cut the old strings (left) and pull the old bale apart (middle), to create two new half bales (right).

OTHER CUSTOM BALES

There may be times when you'll need to use other kinds of custom bales. You can use angled bales around doors and windows to make a splayed reveal that lets in more light or to create another visual effect. (See figure 6.) Bales of different widths may also be required; for example, as we neared the roof, our roof truss took up part of the volume of our wall, so we had to create some thinner bales to fill this space.

Figure 6
TWO TYPES OF ANGLED BALES

a. Angled lengthwise
This bale has been retied to create an angle along the full length of the bale. The new string, colored red, has been pulled up and tied close to one of the old strings on one side. After that, the other old string was cut and removed to allow the straw to be cut away at an angle with a chainsaw, handsaw, or a tool made specifically for the purpose called a "straw knife." This bale would work well on top of a window buck to create an angled reveal above the window. The new, shorter side would sit on the buck, as shown in figure 7.

b. Angled widthwise
This bale has been retied to create an angle across the bale's width. The new string, colored green, has been threaded through, following the same procedure we used to create our half bales. It was then secured with the new red string before the old string was cut. This bale could be placed at the side of a window buck to create an angled reveal

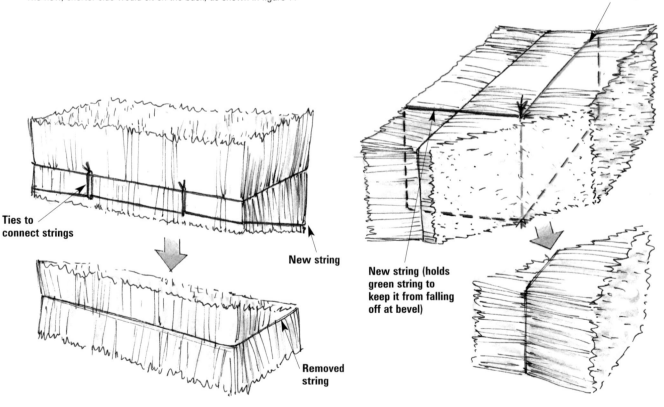

Ties to connect strings

New string

Removed string

New string

New string (holds green string to keep it from falling off at bevel)

Making a thinner bale. *Top:* We used a chainsaw to make thinner bales. With this cut, we were able to keep both string ties intact, so we didn't need to retie. When cutting near a string, be careful not to hit it with the chainsaw! *Middle:* This is the finished bale. *Bottom:* We'll install our thinner bale in this space at the top of the wall where the roof truss (to the right) takes up part of the width of the wall. To the left you can see the top plate, blocking, and insulation at the top of the stick-frame wall. Also, notice the combination wooden tie-strip nailer, plaster stop, and trim nailer (and the rigid insulation packed behind this nailer) that will fill the space between the final bale course and the ceiling. (See figures 5 and 7.)

Figure 7
WHERE WE USED CUSTOM BALES

We needed custom bales on top of the window buck and at the very top of the wall. The bale at the top of the wall (which is pushed against the truss) is a thin bale like the one we made with the chainsaw in the photo at left. The bale on top of the window buck creating the reveal is an angled bale like the one in figure 6a.

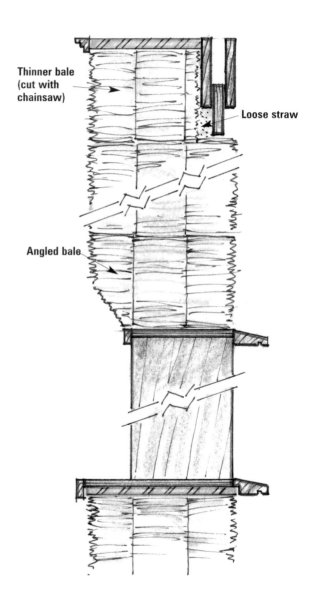

Thinner bale (cut with chainsaw)

Loose straw

Angled bale

INSTALLING THE WINDOW BUCK

For windows to open and close properly, their frames need to be installed level and plumb. In stick-frame construction, for example, window frames are set inside of structural openings, called *rough openings*, adjusted to plumb and level with wooden shims, and then fastened tightly to the framing of the rough opening. It can be difficult to adjust a freestanding buck in a straw bale wall because it has nothing to shim against or fasten to.

We solved this problem in our wall by attaching our window buck to the wooden tie strips we're sandwiching our bales between. This allowed us to adjust the buck and then fasten it in place. You'll remember that we had mocked up our wall, chosen a window placement, and then placed two of our wooden strips so that they could be attached to our buck.

We don't have a door in this wall, but if we did it would need to have a strong buck attached to the stem wall in a similar fashion to the door buck in our cob wall. Straw bale builders have come up with lots of design permutations for door buck construction. See Variations, page 384, for a few examples.

Installing the Window Buck

▲ **Step 1.** In our mock-up we'd chosen to place our window on the third course of bales and placed two wooden tie strips in position to be attached to our buck. After we'd stacked three courses of bales, then, we set our buck in place and checked it for level and plumb.

▲ **Step 2.** Next, with an eye on the level, we fine-tuned the placement and screwed the buck to the wooden strips.

▲ **Step 3.** With the buck firmly attached to the structure, we could continue laying bales, pushing and shoving them into place, without worrying whether we were knocking the buck out of level or plumb.

Thinking on our feet. It's often hard to see a problem until it materializes physically in front of you. Once the buck was in place, we could see that the wide top flanges wouldn't work with our plans to create a splayed window reveal (described below), and we also noticed that we hadn't cut drip edges into the head piece or sill. So, we removed the buck, cut most of the top flange out with a jigsaw, and cut drip edges into the cedar head piece and sill. Some people would call these mistakes; I call them part of the design process. When building, you have to keep your eyes open and have the presence of mind to adjust things as you go.

TYING THE BALES TO THE STRUCTURE: PART II

Once all of the bales were stacked, it was time to tie them to the structure of the building. To do that, we installed wooden tie strips on the inside of our wall directly across from those on the outside and then tied them together with the wire we had judiciously set in place while stacking the bales. (See figure 8.) We attached the interior strips at the bottom to blocks installed on the sill plate and at the top to the combo nailer/ plaster stop as shown in figure 5. We cut a groove in the bales as a seat for the wooden strips just as we had on the outside. However, we found it easier to use a grinder with a wire brush attachment on the fuzzy, folded side of the bales.

Figure 8
A SIMPLE CONNECTION SYSTEM

We installed wooden tie strips on the inside of the wall directly across from those on the outside and tied them together with wire that we'd laid on top of each course of bales. Notice how we carefully planned the placement of the strips so that they didn't cross any bales at a joint.

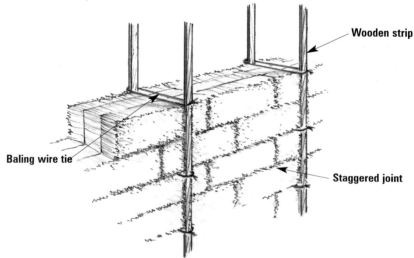

Wooden strip

Baling wire tie

Staggered joint

A tight bale sandwich. By pulling on the wire we'd set in place earlier and pushing on the wooden strips, we squeezed the interior and exterior strips tightly against the bales and then locked the wire in place with a few twists from a pair of pliers (left). After repeating this process with each wire, the end result was a very solid wall (right).

Unruly bales. At this point, our bales were in place, but they weren't pulled tight to the structure.

Rain poncho. As soon as we started stacking bales, we covered our wall at night with a tarp, and we left it in place while working if rain was threatening.

PREPPING FOR PLASTER

At this point, our wall volume was filled. However, there was still a lot to be done to prepare the bales for plastering.

Trimming Bales

The undulating contour of a plastered bale wall is a subtle part of its beauty. However, wild undulations or patches of loose or protruding straw can make plastering difficult. There are various ways to trim unruly sections of your wall. A grinder with wire brush or cutting wheel, a weed-eater with a nylon string, or even a chainsaw all work. The advantage of the weed-eater is that you can reach a lot farther and it doesn't get clogged up with straw. The chainsaw is very accurate, but also very dangerous. The grinder is better for small areas and for reaching into tight sections.

Trimming

▲ **Step 1.** We used a chainsaw to give our bales a haircut. Though this method was fast and accurate, we often had to stop, remove the cover, and clean out loose straw that was clogging the bar. Please, only use this method if you have a lot of experience with this incredibly dangerous tool.

▲ **Step 2.** We used a grinder with wire brush attachment for smaller areas. This tool is also wonderful for creating little niches or pockets for electrical outlets.

Covering Wood

As we'll learn in chapter 12, the Achilles heel of plaster is its tendency to crack. The chance of cracking becomes more pronounced if something that the plaster is covering moves. In chapter 9, we discussed the fact that wood can expand and shrink as it takes on water and dries out. This movement could cause the plaster covering the wood to crack.

As a preventative measure against this possibility we decided to cover all wood surfaces in our wall with tarpaper to isolate them from water. Unfortunately, plaster adheres best when it has something to grab. The bristly ends of straw work well for that purpose, but the smooth surface of tarpaper doesn't. Therefore, we in turn had to cover the tarpaper with metal lath to provide a rough surface to which the plaster could adhere. It's possible that this extra work and use of mass-produced materials was unnecessary. Looking ahead, I can tell you that our stick-frame wall is covered with plaster over wooden lath and we've had no problems with cracking on that wall. On the other hand, we've also had no problems with cracks on our straw bale wall, so we did something right.

Covering Wood

▲ **Step 1.** Before covering any wood, we stuffed loose straw into all voids between bales.

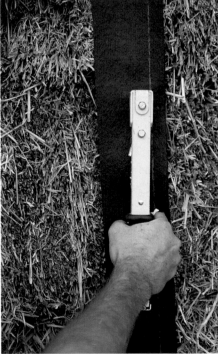

▲ **Step 2.** We cut thin strips of tarpaper (left) and stapled them to any exposed wood in the wall (right).

▲ **Step 3.** Next we cut strips of metal lath, also called diamond stucco mesh. We ripped several strips of lath at a time, using a metal cutting blade on a circular saw and being careful to use ear and eye protection! You can use tin snips instead if you have a couple of days to spare and the forearms of Hercules.

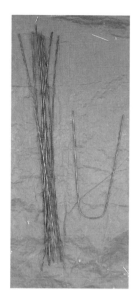

▲ **Step 4.** To attach the mesh to the wall, we made staples out of very rigid wire. Supports for fiberglass batt insulation work great (left). These staples need to push flush against the straw, so they must have a flat head. To accomplish this, we bent the wire around a scrap of wood held in place with a clamp (middle and right).

▲ **Step 5.** We then placed a piece of metal lath over the tarpaper and attached it with these homemade staples. To get a good grip, the staples needed to be pinched in a bit (left). That technique, in combination with a good flat head, usually succeeded in pulling the lath up tight to the bale (right). If not, we pulled it out and tried again.

Mice aren't nice. Our plaster will stop at the top of the wall just below the roof truss. We'll eventually protect the truss and these exposed triangles of straw with a piece of trim. However, right now these openings could make this wall party central for mice, so we temporarily covered them with plywood scraps to keep critters out.

Integrating Our Wall Systems

After all our bales were stacked and tied to the structure, we needed to make the final connections to our adjoining walls. You'll remember that we laid our cordwood wall all the way to the corner post, creating a small void between the post and the stacked bales. The stick-frame wall (discussed in chapter 11) creates a similar but smaller void on the west side of our straw bale wall. We stuffed these voids with loose straw, then stretched a piece of lath between the corner posts and the first wooden tie strip on each side. This held the loose straw in place and structurally tied the wall to the corner posts.

Figure 9
CONNECTIONS TO ADJACENT WALLS

Since they are connected to the wooden tie strips and these strips are attached to the corner posts, our bales are held tight to the structure and wedged between the two adjacent walls, creating a very snug fit.

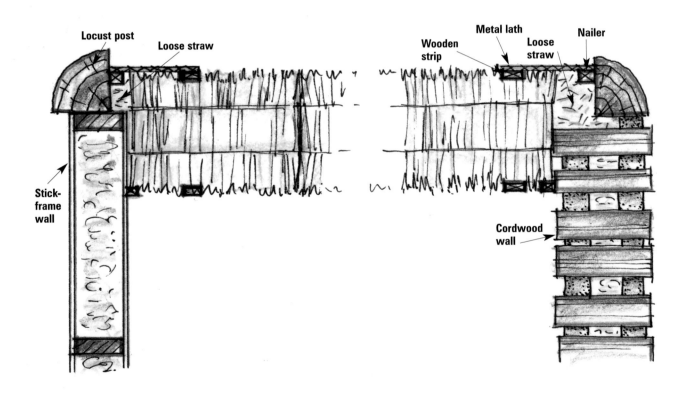

▲ **Step 2.** Now, we stuffed loose straw into the void between the posts and the bales at each end of the wall. We held the straw in place with metal lath attached to the nailers on the posts and the first wooden strip at each side.

▲ **Step 1.** Before installing our bales, we had attached nailers on each locust post.

Tight fit. On the inside, the bales simply butted up against the two adjacent walls.

The Window Reveal

We decided to build a curved reveal on three sides of our window to create a nice variety of light and a beautiful contour in our wall. You can make a reveal in a bale wall either by shaping the bales next to the buck or by using a combination of metal lath and stuffed loose straw. We used both methods.

We installed angle-cut bales above our window buck, but on the sides we chose to stop the bales at the wooden tie strip, stuff loose straw into the gap between the bale and the buck, and then stretch a piece of metal lath from the buck to the wooden strip, creating a nice deep, angled reveal.

The Window Reveal

◀ **Step 1.** As we stacked the wall, we installed angle-cut bales above our window buck (see figures 6a and 7).

◀ **Step 2.** We had stacked bales on the sides of the window only as far as the wooden strip to which the buck was attached. We now installed nailers for lath on the sill, jambs, and head of the buck, seen here already covered in tarpaper.

◀ **Step 3.** On the outside, we installed mesh on both sides of the buck (left) and stuffed loose straw against it, filling the space between the last bale and the buck (right).

▲ **Step 4.** Next, we stapled a piece of mesh to the nailers on the jambs (left) and to the wooden tie strip next to the buck (middle), enclosing the loose straw, and creating the side reveals (right).

◄ **Step 5.** Because we had stuffed loose straw to fill the gap above the last bale course at the peak of the ceiling, we attached one end of a piece metal lath to the top of the window and the other to the nailer on our roof truss. This also helped hold the straw in the angled bale, which can tend to loosen up where the angle has been cut. Our reveal is now ready to be plastered.

THINKING ABOUT WATER

Of all the walls in our building, this one is the most vulnerable to water, so we carefully planned a holistic water strategy: lift the bales off the ground on a stem wall, lift them away from condensation on an insulated sill plate, block much of the rain and snow with a good roof overhang, carefully install flashing, cover the wall with a consciously designed plaster, and, finally, seal any remaining vulnerable joints with trim.

We've already completed many of those steps. Of those remaining, we'll discuss plaster and trim in chapter 12. Let's focus here on the flashing. We had two long horizontal joints that needed to be protected with flashing: the base of our wall and the top of our window. Since we knew the base of the wall would be the place of highest water exposure in the wall, we'd already installed a double drainage plane with integrated flashing here. To finish this detail, we now added metal lath over the drainage plane to give our plaster a surface to which it could adhere. Any water that might get behind the plaster near the base of the wall will still hit the building wrap and be deposited on the flashing, which will direct it to the sloped ground and therefore away from the building.

Our other vulnerable horizontal joint, the top of our window, required a different approach. To repeat our double drainage plane here would require covering the entire top of the wall from the roof to the window with building wrap. That would be difficult to accomplish and would go against our strategy of creating a hygroscopic wall that allows water vapor to move in and out. (See chapter 12 for more on this.) Without a second drainage plane, any water that gets behind the plaster will likely go behind the flashing, too. Since our window is set high in the wall, the roof overhang will keep most of the water off that portion of the wall. The plaster itself will do the job of directing the little bit of water that does reach this high onto the flashing. We decided then that the flashing alone was enough protection in this situation. Its sole function here is sealing the vulnerable joint between the plaster and the window buck, not stopping liquid water that's worked its way behind the plaster. (See figure 10.)

Finishing the drainage plane. We'd already installed the very important flashing and drip edge at the base of the wall. We now cut and installed a piece of metal lath to fit over the entire drainage plane as a rough surface for plastering. Notice how both the building wrap and the lath are over the flashing, preventing any water that rolls down the wrap from getting behind the flashing.

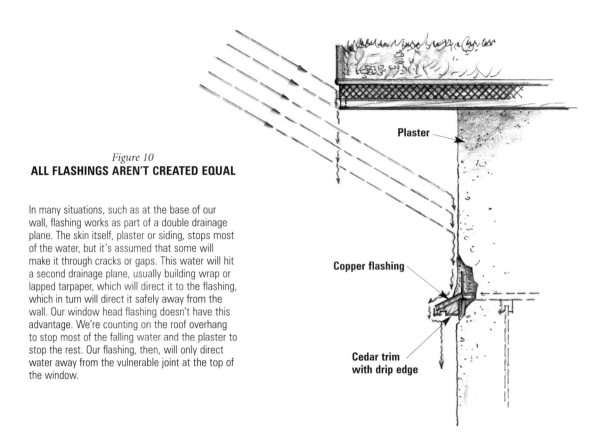

Figure 10
ALL FLASHINGS AREN'T CREATED EQUAL

In many situations, such as at the base of our wall, flashing works as part of a double drainage plane. The skin itself, plaster or siding, stops most of the water, but it's assumed that some will make it through cracks or gaps. This water will hit a second drainage plane, usually building wrap or lapped tarpaper, which will direct it to the flashing, which in turn will direct it safely away from the wall. Our window head flashing doesn't have this advantage. We're counting on the roof overhang to stop most of the falling water and the plaster to stop the rest. Our flashing, then, will only direct water away from the vulnerable joint at the top of the window.

Plaster

Copper flashing

Cedar trim
with drip edge

Flashing the window. *Left:* We capped our window head trim with copper flashing. In addition to being beautiful, copper is soft and a dream to work with. This simple flashing detail could be the difference between a short, moldy death and a long, dry life for our straw bale wall. *Right:* We installed plaster mesh over the window flashing to give the plaster something to grip at this crucial joint. Notice also the drip edge cut into the bottom of the cedar head piece and how far this piece extends beyond the window. This acts like a little roof directing water away from the long joints between the straw and the sides of the window.

Connections

It's difficult to attach things to straw bales. In an infill wall, the easiest solution is to have the skeletal structure exposed to the interior and make all attachments to it. Our skeleton is exposed to the outside, so that wasn't an option on this project. Our solution was to leave the beautiful undulating surface of our wall alone, and place all of our shelving, counters, vents, and pipes in other walls more hospitable to connections. On the other hand, straw bale builders have found all kinds of interesting ways of attaching things to straw, most of which involve embedding wood into the wall in one way or another. (See figure 11.)

Figure 11
ATTACHING THINGS TO STRAW BALES

People have come up with lots of creative ways to make attachments to bale walls. They can vary from the light duty that require no planning to the heavy duty that have to be carefully placed before plastering.

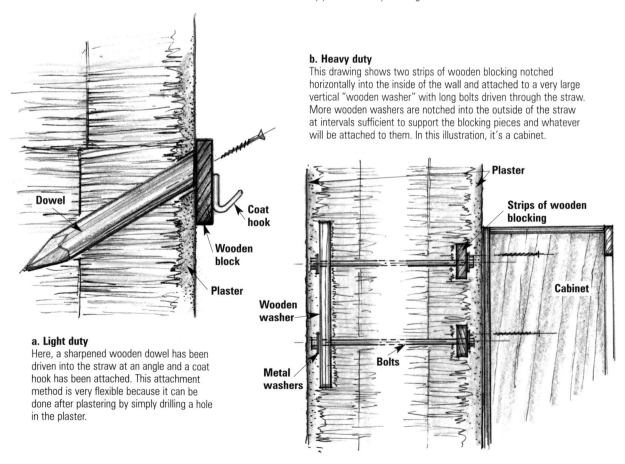

b. Heavy duty
This drawing shows two strips of wooden blocking notched horizontally into the inside of the wall and attached to a very large vertical "wooden washer" with long bolts driven through the straw. More wooden washers are notched into the outside of the straw at intervals sufficient to support the blocking pieces and whatever will be attached to them. In this illustration, it's a cabinet.

Dowel

Coat hook

Wooden block

Plaster

a. Light duty
Here, a sharpened wooden dowel has been driven into the straw at an angle and a coat hook has been attached. This attachment method is very flexible because it can be done after plastering by simply drilling a hole in the plaster.

Plaster

Strips of wooden blocking

Cabinet

Wooden washer

Metal washers

Bolts

THINKING ABOUT STRUCTURE

In most post-and-beam or timber frame structures, it's common practice to include diagonal bracing between posts and beams to create the classic triangular strength that we've discussed often in this book. However, such braces cause complications in straw bale infill walls. If they're inside the volume of the infill, then bales need to be altered to accommodate them. If they're inside or outside the bales, then they cause plastering complications. (If they are on the outside, there's the additional problem of exposure to the forces of decay.)

To avoid these problems, we were able to make our other walls strong enough to take some pressure off our straw bale wall. Our cordwood infill, for example, acts like one big brace because it fills the full volume of the wall with a heavy, solid mass. In other words, there's no open, structurally weak space to strengthen with a triangular brace in that wall. Our cob wall also fills the entire space with heavy mass, but you'll remember that we added bracing inside the volume of that wall anyway. We decided to do that partly because it was easy to do—the cob just wrapped right around it—and partly because the combination of our door and the clay-slip straw above it created a large vertical gap in the mass filling the wall. As for our stick-frame wall, we'll learn in the next chapter how it acts like a powerful truss that's internally braced. It's basically built like a bridge.

All of this incredible structural strengthening allowed us to forgo diagonal bracing in our bale wall. We were able to create adequate strength with the combination of tightly stuffed bales tied into the skeletal structure by wooden strips and the eventual application of a strong lime plaster on both sides of the wall.

Before and after. *Top:* Back when we only had the basic structural framework in place and none of our infill systems were as yet taking on their structural roles, we needed a large diagonal brace from top to bottom across our north wall. *Bottom:* By the time we started stacking our bales, the infill of our other three walls had added so much strength to the building that we didn't need a brace of any kind on this wall. In fact, we could have left this end of the building open indefinitely without having any structural worries.

Construction Blunders: Think Twice, Install Once

Stacking straw bales is such satisfying, seemingly easy work, that it isn't difficult to forget what you're really doing as you happily throw up bales without a care in the world. In a work party setting that includes novice volunteers and perhaps a few beers, I've heard the ensuing chaos called "bale frenzy." The results can include, but are not limited to, windows left uninstalled and sloppy, out-of-plumb work.

Our version of bale frenzy was installing three courses of bales, wooden tie strips, and our window buck before realizing that we'd forgotten our drainage plane on the first course. We were so excited to finally be laying bales that we forgot a basic element of our design. We had to take everything out, including the wooden strips, and start again!

The lesson: There's an old carpenters' saying that goes, "Measure twice, cut once." In other words, think about what the hell you're doing before you do it. That sounds easy, but it's one of the hardest parts of construction.

Think once, install three times. *Left*: What's wrong with this picture? There's no drainage plane on the first course. Once we realized that fact, we had to dismantle this work, including the wooden tie strips, and start again. *Top:* Not again! Next, we reinstalled everything using tarpaper as a drainage plane, only to find that it ripped where the wooden tie strips pushed against it. *Bottom:* The third time's a charm. We finally got it right.

HOW LONG DID IT TAKE?

Straw bale construction is sometimes billed as an incredibly fast construction method. In my book, that's inexperience, wishful thinking, or straight ahead lying. As we've said, stacking full bales is easy, but that's almost none of the work involved. In our wall, the sill plate assembly, wooden strip installation, bale sizing, lath attachment, and other details were time-consuming. As we'll see, the deep contours and peculiar surface of straw requires a more labor-intensive first plaster coat than our cob or stick-frame wall (and, of course, cordwood gets no plaster at all). Unless logistics are carefully considered, the added worries about rain can really slow down straw bale construction in comparison to other techniques. In our building, I'd estimate that our straw bale wall was installed and plastered in about the same amount of time as the stick-frame wall.

WHAT WE'VE ACCOMPLISHED

We started our wall with a dilemma. Straw bales were both perfect for and vulnerable to the design realities of our north wall. Their superior insulation was a good match for the coldest side of the building and their sound-deadening qualities would create privacy from the eventual workshop, public courtyard, and car parking to the north. However, the permanent shade and less-protective gable-end roof overhang would also make this the wettest wall on the building. We solved this problem by creating a careful design for the situation, including a first-course drainage plane cocoon, thoughtful flashing, and our still-to-come plastering decisions. Just as importantly, we realized that design through careful and painstaking consideration in the actual installation.

Mind over matter. Through careful planning and conscientious attention to detail in installation, we were able to maximize the benefits of straw bales while protecting their weaknesses.

I have a confession to make. I've been a straw bale skeptic for over a decade.

Why? Well, it's the same old story Clarke has pounded on pretty hard. There are lots of inherent pressures that come to bear on the construction process: deadlines, money, the inevitable people squabbles, and the constant sparring match with the weather. I just could never get my head around bringing a material into the mix that seemed as vulnerable to water damage as a straw bale. More headaches I don't need.

Admitting to that prejudice, I must say that I really liked making this wall. In our case, the benefit of working under an existing roof made me feel reasonably secure, and I knew that we were going to give considerable thought to the potential of moisture problems. Preparing it for plaster involved a lot of tricky details, but the end result seems well worth the effort. The deep sill and gently curved reveals of the window, along with the eventual warmth and undulation of the finished plastered wall, warms my Irish heart. I'm happy to be able to say, "I was WRONG—I like this stuff!"

VARIATIONS

Our straw bale wall consists of infill between two posts with no intervening obstructions. This is a very simple layout as straw bale walls go. Let's take a quick look at some other bale-laying possibilities.

STRAW BALE INFILL OPTIONS

Any common skeletal structural system can utilize straw bales as infill insulation. Conventional stick-framing, for example, can be slightly modified to create a space between studs in which bales can be stacked on end, leaving the stud in the middle of the wall or flush with either the interior or exterior surface. The tiny void between bales created by the studs can be infilled with loose straw. Bales can also be stacked on either side of a stick-frame structure. An advantage here is that the studs provide many places for attaching both bales and anything else, such as shelving and cabinets, to the structure.

As we've seen in our wall, post-and-beam or timber frame structures can also accommodate bales. If stacked between posts, the bales need to be notched to engulf the structure, so that their insulative cocoon isn't interrupted. (See photo at left.) Also, as mentioned earlier, a complication here is that these structures tend to have diagonal bracing that gets in the way of bale infill. One solution to this problem is to wrap the bales around either the inside or the outside of the structure. The inside option recesses the bales further under the roof, offering them more protection from rain (see photo at top, next page.) Wrapping bales around the outside protects the skeleton from exposure to water, freeze/thaw cycles, and critters such as insects and woodpeckers. This approach also makes the potentially beautiful frame visible from the inside, which also makes it available as a surface for attaching shelves, electrical boxes, and other fixtures that the bales themselves have trouble accommodating.

Notched bales. Bales set between the posts in this post-and-beam structure are notched to accommodate framing members, bringing the bales flush with the outside of the structure. Thin metal bracing, T-shaped for strength, replaces triangle braces, typical of timber framing, that would get in the way of the bale infill.

Another method is to create a load-bearing structure designed specifically for straw bale construction that spans the width of the wall. Since they match the width of the bales, such structures, often called *modified post-and-beam*, put wood on both the interior and exterior face of the wall, allowing for easy attachments on either side. Modified post-and-beam frames can be built out of readily available commercial materials such as 2x4s and plywood or particle board. (See photo at lower right.)

Each of these approaches offers its own unique challenges in the process of construction. Consider, for example, the installation of doors and windows. Though there are two basic approaches, either creating a free-floating structural buck or attaching a frame to the structure, the details for actually installing the bucks or frames vary for each skeletal system. The same applies, to some degree, to attaching bales or applying plaster.

The main point to glean from this basic introduction is that the wide array of possible infill structures for straw are a kind of double-edged sword. On the one hand, they extend the possible situations, budgets, and skill levels that straw bale construction can accommodate. On the other hand, they each have unique design and detailing complications that make generalized comments about construction technique only so helpful. In other words, it's going to be up to you to consider the ins and outs of a given approach, insuring the need to use both your research and creative problem-solving skills. The success of your walls will depend on it.

External structure. This internal bale wrap is separated from the post and beam structure by several inches, simplifying the plastering process among other things. Large plywood "washers" are held tight to each side of the bales by nuts on a piece of threaded rod that extends through the wall and the post. This set-up both ties the wall to the structure, providing lateral bracing, and allows for vertical alignment of the bale walls through adjustment of the nuts on the plywood "washers." One possible downside to this technique could be that the water vapor will have a tendency to condense on the metal bolt within the wall.

Windows and doors in an infill wall. In this infill bale wall, self-supporting bucks are made by creating the tops and sides out of strong boxes, often called box beams. Structural posts are placed on each side of these bucks so that plywood extending past the jambs can be attached to the posts, and hence, the structure of the building. Notice also that the window buck at right extends to the floor. This was done so that the window can become a door in a planned future addition to the building. The bucks in this wall will be incredibly strong and long-lasting; however, there are other approaches that would have used far less wood.

Modified post-and-beam. In this wall, the same materials used in conventional stick-framing are rearranged to create a thick structure to efficiently accommodate straw bale infill. Rebar embedded in the concrete slab will impale the first course of bales that will be lifted off the slab by treated wood sill plates. Lightweight columns made from 2x4s and oriented strand board (OSB)—which is often used to sheath stick-framed walls—are strong and able to be spread wide apart to get out of the way of stacked bales. The wall height was sized so that the final course of bales laid flat will stop at the base of the double 2x12 beam. A course of bales laid on edge will fill the space between this course and the roof framing, wrapping the beam with insulation without having to cut bales as we did in this same situation.

LOAD-BEARING STRAW BALE CONSTRUCTION

There is no doubt that straw bale walls can carry roof loads. There are buildings that have been standing for at least 100 years that prove that point elegantly. As far as I can tell, though, the only argument for using bales to take on these loads is to save wood. However, since the roof framing is the same for both systems, and the top plate and window/door framing actually uses *more* wood in a load-bearing bale system, the amount of wood saved seems relatively small. If the building is going to be heated by burning wood, then the logic of this argument goes out the window altogether.

If it seems as if I have a bias against using straw bales to carry roof loads, it's because I live in a wood-rich, very wet climate. In our straw wall, for example, the only wood we would have saved by choosing load-bearing construction was two deadwood locust posts found in the woods above our site. If we'd wanted to build all four of our walls out of infill bales, we could have done so with a few more of these posts and two green rough-cut beams purchased from the tiny family-owned mill 5 miles away. Our straw bales, in contrast, were trucked in from several hundred miles away. On top of that, we get about 50 inches of rain per year around here. In that context, the idea of leaving straw bales intended for building sitting around without a roof over them to save a little bit of wood just doesn't compute for me.

At the same time, I acknowledge that there *are* situations where load-bearing bale construction makes sense. In the United States the dry areas of New Mexico, Arizona, and Nebraska, with their sunny, cold winters and limited local forests, are good fits for this technique. In addition of course, wood is being terribly mistreated and overused in our modern world, so efforts to save even small amounts have an inherent logic. My mindset is created by my context, and it's simply hard to wrench yourself free from the ocean in which you swim. You may find yourself floating in completely different waters. If so, don't listen to me. Seek out bale buildings and builders in your area and see what they have to say. In that spirit let's look at some of the basics of load-bearing straw bale construction.

Free-range wood. This locust tree had lived a long happy life, died of natural causes, and fallen over of its own accord years before we found it laying here on the forest floor and cut it up to use as a couple of posts for our little building. In our case, going through the hassle of building load-bearing straw bale walls to avoid using a couple of these dead trees really made no sense.

Bales

Infill bales fill a defined space; however, load-bearing bales define the space itself. If precut roof members are going to fit properly, then that definition of space needs to result in the top of the walls being a level surface of a predetermined perimeter. This means that accurate stacking of bales is crucial. If the bales get seriously out of plumb or square, the roof might not fit the walls.

There are several ways we can assure that this doesn't happen. (See figure 12.) For example, temporary plumb corners can be installed as guides to build against. These guides can also be used to pull taut strings from corner to corner as reference points for keeping the wall plumb while stacking. This is the same technique used in conventional brick masonry. Similar guides can be placed in the middle of long walls, helping to keep bale-stacking plumb and temporarily buttressing the wall against bulging. A limited bond between bales can be accomplished by some form of pinning, such as impaling bales horizontally with rigid stakes or connecting corners with U-shaped pieces of rebar. As it goes up, the wall should be checked for level every couple of courses and shimmed where necessary with loose straw.

As for the bales themselves, our desire to find dense, compact bales of regular size becomes more urgent when we imagine them actually holding up the roof. In addition, if they're available in our area, it makes sense to use the wider, usually denser, three-string bales because they'll make a more stable unit with which to build.

Permanent buttress. A temporary brace in the middle of a wall can help keep bales plumb during the stacking process and perhaps add structural support until the bales are further secured. Another approach is to install interior partition walls as permanent buttresses to brace long load-bearing straw bale walls. The wall in this photo is being structurally strengthened with plywood sheathing and is attached to the bales with a plywood washer system like the one used in the exterior post-and-beam infill system described earlier.

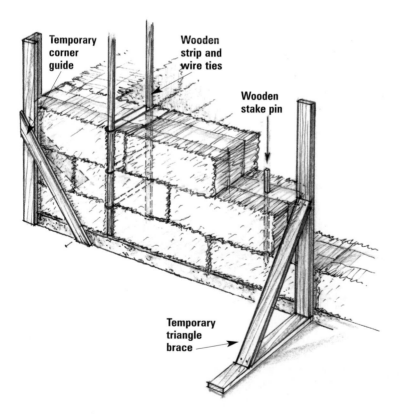

Temporary corner guide

Wooden strip and wire ties

Wooden stake pin

Temporary triangle brace

Figure 12
LAYING BALES IN A LOAD-BEARING STRAW BALE WALL

The main goal is for the finished wall to be plumb and solid, with bales sitting tight together. To help keep things plumb, firmly install temporary corner guides and wall braces to the stem wall. The braces act as both a protection against bulging and as a guide to plumb stacking. To create some level of connection between bales, pin them with wood or bamboo stakes and tie them together with wooden strips, using the same technique we used in our infill wall.

Doors, Windows, and the Roof

In a skeletal wall, the roof and the straw are relatively unrelated, and the openings created by doors and windows need only deal with the weight of the bales above them. In a load-bearing wall, all of these elements work together as a structural whole. As a result, bucks need to be stronger and the roof needs to be physically tied to the straw. The focal point of this system is the roof bearing assembly (RBA).

There are two basic approaches to RBA construction. The first is to create a rigid RBA that acts much like a structural lintel, spreading out roof loads to take pressure off of window and door openings below it. Another approach is to build a more flexible RBA. This assembly requires stronger window and door bucks beneath it, but it's easier to adjust and make level. Regardless of construction type, RBAs are attached both to the foundation, usually with cables or straps, and to the roof framing, thus creating a structural system that works as a unit.

Anatomy of a roof. A box beam made of 2x8s and plywood caps this load-bearing straw bale wall. The rafters are conventional TJI beams made of 2x4s and particle board and are attached to the RBA with conventional roofing hardware. Horizontal 2x4s, called purlins, add rigidity to the roof structure and will serve as nailers for the metal roofing. A 2x4 block supports the upper edge of the sloped rafter, allowing it to bear on both the inside and outside edges of the RBA, creating an even load. Polyester banding ties the RBA to the stem wall. Thick cardboard pieces set under the banding protect the corners of the RBA from being crushed.

Structural buck. All four sides of this large window buck in a load-bearing straw bale wall are box beams. The top and bottom boxes extend the full width of the opening, therefore using the strength of the boxes, not the fasteners holding them together, to transfer loads. These two boxes are of identical construction because they are dealing with the same loads; in other words, the top box is transferring all of its loads through the sides to the bottom box. This buck was also sized so that there's a bit of space between the bales stacked on top of it and the RBA, thus allowing for settling of the wall without putting undo pressure on the buck. The open space inside all of the box beams was filled with insulation, an important detail to remember. Straw, commercial cellulose, or rigid foam all can be used.

Figure 13
STRUCTURAL MEMBERS IN LOAD-BEARING STRAW BALE WALLS

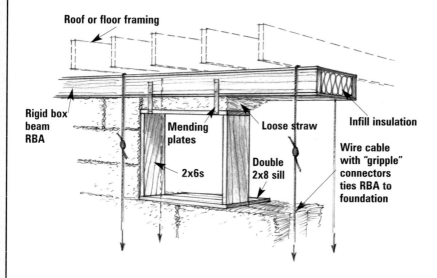

Roof or floor framing

Rigid box beam RBA

Mending plates

Loose straw

Infill insulation

2x6s

Double 2x8 sill

Wire cable with "gripple" connectors ties RBA to foundation

a. Box beam RBA

The roof bearing assembly (RBA) of this wall is a strong box made of dimensional lumber and plywood. This configuration is often called a box beam. The advantage of the box beam is that it's rigid and therefore strong enough to preclude the need for beefed up window and door bucks below it. The disadvantage is that it's more difficult to adjust and level in installation. The window buck under this RBA is simply a box of 2x6s with two 2x8s making a wide sill. The top of this box is attached to the RBA with thin metal plates called mending plates. The space between the top of the buck and the RBA is stuffed with straw or other insulation, and a piece of lath is stretched across the opening, similar to the technique used in our wall. A similar detail can be used to create a beveled reveal on the sides of the window.

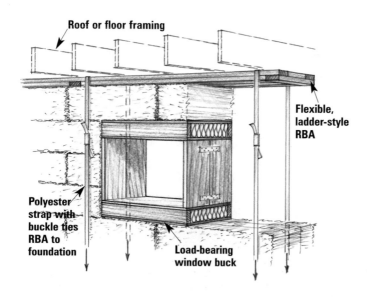

Roof or floor framing

Flexible, ladder-style RBA

Polyester strap with buckle ties RBA to foundation

Load-bearing window buck

b. Ladder-style RBA

This wall is capped with a ladder-style RBA very similar to the top plates for load-bearing cordwood walls illustrated on page 336. In its straw bale incarnation, it's a flexible top plate that's easier to adjust and level in place than a rigid RBA. However, it requires structural, load-bearing lintels or window and door bucks below it. The top and bottom of the window buck pictured are formed by box beams, and the sides are made of double 2x8s connected with mending plates. The disadvantage of this type of buck is that it doesn't easily allow a beveled reveal to the inside.

The Construction Process

The goal of any construction project is to be efficient. However, that mandate takes on a new urgency when building with bales without a roof over your head. Once you start laying bales, you want the whole construction process to move forward like clockwork until the roof is on and covered. It's very important then, that everything that can be prepared and all decisions that can be made be completed before the bales poke their heads out of storage. This means that all window bucks need to be built, and all door bucks built and placed. The roof bearing assembly needs to be assembled and rafters or trusses have to be cut and/or built and ready to go. Tarps need to be at the ready to cover installed and waiting bales in case of rain. Any people helping have to be reliable and briefed on their role before they show up to perform it.

Anatomy of a Bale Raising

In load-bearing straw bale construction, the goal is to get bales covered with a roof as quickly as possible. The bale walls and roof of the building pictured here were raised in a single day. This impressive feat was accomplished through meticulous planning and careful attention to detail.

Careful attention to detail. Hundreds of construction details need to be attended to before bales should ever see the light of day. Let's look at all the work that had to be done in just this single spot before bales were ready to be installed. First a conventional monolithic foundation, stem wall, and concrete slab were poured. The perimeter of the slab was then waterproofed to prevent water migration into the wall. Rebar was embedded in the slab as a pinning system for the first course of bales. Anchor bolts were also embedded in the slab to hold the treated wood sill plates that will lift the bales off the concrete to help prevent condensation. Pea gravel was poured into the gap between sill plates also to prevent condensation. Pieces of metal that will tie the roof bearing assembly to the foundation were threaded under the sills plates. Metal plates were attached to the sill to prevent this banding from crushing the wood when tightened. The door buck (at right) was built and then installed, extending into the sill plate assembly, where it was bolted to the slab.

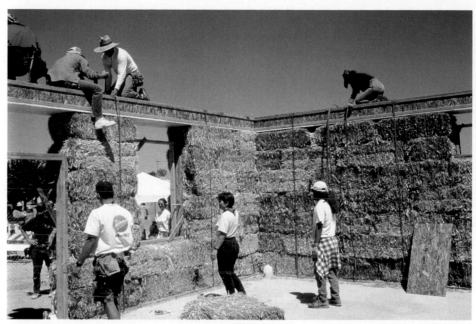

Meticulous planning. A week before the public wall raising, organizers held a workshop in which 20 wall leaders were trained. At this time the box beam RBAs and all the bucks were built. The door bucks and strong corner guides for laying bales were also installed and braced. On the day of the wall raising, the bale stacking started at 7:30 am. By 11:00 am, the RBAs were in place, fastened together, and tied to the foundation with metal strapping. Notice that the door buck at left is framed out of 2x6s. It doesn't need to be very strong because the RBA above is acting like a lintel and equally distributing the roof loads throughout the wall.

The payoff. By about 3:30 pm, all the roof trusses were in place. By 6:00 that evening, the roof was decked and the bales were basically covered and protected. After several weeks under this roof load, the straw bales had compressed, leaving the original metal banding loose. This banding was cut, new banding was installed and tightened, and the walls were ready for plastering.

Compression

One issue that's unique to load-bearing straw bale construction is wall compression. Once the roof is in place on the walls, the walls will tend to compress under its weight to differing degrees depending on the properties of the bales and the weight of the roof. This process usually takes a number of weeks. Since plastering can't take place until the walls have settled, it would be great to be able to manually compress the bales, so that plastering can proceed immediately. Though there are various approaches aimed at achieving this pre-compression, it doesn't seem that a good system that's practical for the owner-builder has been invented yet.

However, since the roof is already in place at this point, the bales should be fairly well protected, especially the top of the bales which would be the most vulnerable to serious infiltration. You can further protect bales through the time required for them to compress by attaching some plastic tarps to the roof and tying them off to stakes in the ground. Such a tarp set-up is a good idea to have in place for the plastering process anyway.

The most common procedure, then, is to tie the RBA securely to the stem wall once the roof has been installed. After the bales have had time to compress (usually a period of several weeks), the ties should be somewhat loose. At this point, these ties are either cut with new straps spliced in and cinched up or the original ties are tightened, depending on the system used. The final result should be a roof firmly connected to the foundation, hopefully completing a very solid structural system.

Tying the top to the bottom. *Top left:* Metal cable wraps under the sill plate assembly and over this RBA to tie the roof structure to the foundation. A metal angle bracket has been installed under the cable to protect the RBA, and mass-produced "hurricane clips" attach the roof framing to the RBA. Notice also the blocking filling the space between rafters. This is the same detail we used at the top of our cordwood and stick-frame walls. *Left:* After the bales had compressed under the roof loads, this piece of metal tensioning hardware called a gripple was used to cinch the cable tight. *Right:* On this building, polyester banding replaces metal cable as the material tying the roof to the foundation. In this system, the bands are first tensioned with the red-handled tool, and then fastened with metal clips that are crimped in place with the tool being used in the photo. After the bales have compressed under the roof loads, the now loosened bands are cut, new pieces are spliced in, and the bands are retensioned and finally crimped again.

Who's Carrying the Load?

Now that we've had a quick introduction, it's time for a pop quiz: What material is carrying the roof loads in load-bearing straw bale construction?

Of course, common sense would say it's the bales. However, according to Paul Lacinski and Michel Bergeron in their excellent book *Serious Straw Bale* (White River Junction, Vt.: Chelsea Green, 2000), engineering research indicates that, in fact, the plaster skin covering the bales is taking on most of the loading. The concept here is that plastered straw bale walls work like Structural Insulated Panels (SIPs). A SIP is a structural unit made up of an insulative core sandwiched between two thin rigid outer layers. As a unit, this sandwich acts structurally like a steel I-beam, with the rigid outer layers being the flanges and the insulation being the web. (See figure 14.) In the case of load-bearing straw bale, the plaster on both sides of the wall would be the structural panels and the straw would be the insulated core.

Figure 14
STRUCTURAL VOLUME

a. Monolithic volume
Most thick walls carry loads through their entire volume. These materials, like the bricks shown here, are strong but not very insulative.

b. Structural insulated panels
SIPs are a way to create a well-insulated volume without thermal breaks that has the required structural strength for a given situation. A low-compressive-strength insulative core is sandwiched between two structural membranes that carry the loads. The SIP in the drawing has a core of foam insulation sandwiched between two pieces of plywood and capped with a top and bottom plate of dimensional lumber. Units like this are often used to fill in the volume of modern timber frame buildings. Some engineering data supports the notion that a straw bale wall plastered on each side is a SIP with the plaster (like the plywood in the drawing) taking most of the loads. The bales' job in this scenario is to hold the plaster to keep it from buckling.

Engineering studies aside, the commonsense way to understand this might be to imagine that the straw will always have a tendency to settle. If, after the walls have been plastered, the straw settles just a touch more, then the plaster would be taking on a good bit of the load. In any case, a compressive live load such as snow would surely compress the straw more than the plaster, thus causing the plaster to take on the load.

Who cares exactly how a straw wall works? Well, the way we conceive of the loads being carried will affect our decisions on how to construct the wall. Obviously, if we think that our plaster is going to be carrying loads, then we'll design it to have the most structural strength possible. We'd probably be less likely to go with an earth or lime plaster and would choose a metal reinforced Portland cement–based plaster. (See chapter 12 for a discussion of these plaster mixes.) In addition, if we see our bales' structural role being mainly to keep plaster from buckling, then their strength as an interlocking matrix would be less important. This would allow us to lay our bales on edge which would leave them less vulnerable to water damage because the hollow, water-wicking straw ends would be oriented away from our plaster and possible water infiltration. In addition, this orientation creates more insulation value, a thinner profile, and, according to the engineering studies mentioned above, is actually more stable against vertical compressive loads.

What's the right approach? Again, I must confidently assert that I have no idea. The point here is that bales are relative unknowns as structural units. Until they become as well understood and ubiquitous as wooden members in a skeletal frame, there isn't any "common sense" that you can trust. If you decide to build load-bearing bale walls, always consult experienced builders and engineers familiar both with load-bearing bale construction and your specific climate.

Best of both worlds? An interesting hybrid of infill and load-bearing construction is the building within a building. *Left:* This post-and-beam structure will carry all roof loads and create an 8-foot porch overhang all around the building. Straw bale walls will be stacked on the stem wall (visible in the picture), completely separated from the load-bearing structure of the building. In this approach, you get the advantages of infill, including building under the cover of a roof, along with the simpler plaster details and aesthetic of load-bearing straw bale walls. *Right:* Here's the finished building. The huge overhangs keep the walls dry and allow for the use of an earth plaster that might not be protective enough in a more exposed application. One downside to this method is that the huge overhangs wouldn't allow much exposure for solar gain in a cold climate. This approach would be ideal in a very hot climate where shade and cooling are highly desired and winter solar heat gain isn't.

Tim's Take
Getting It Done: Straw Bale

My basic advice to the inexperienced owner-builder contemplating a straw bale project echoes a theme that has carried through this chapter: Use the infill method. Clarke has already amply discussed the problem of exposure to water in the construction process that a load-bearing bale system presents. On a personal note, I can add that the notion of using straw as a load-bearing form makes the voice of my inner builder scream, *Noooooooo!*

Let me give you some other compelling arguments for infill. First, as common sense tells us, a great way to make a complex task easier is to separate it into manageable chunks. Infill straw bale construction allows you to divide the project into two distinct stages: before bales and after bales. In the first phase, you focus solely on creating a strong skeletal structure that fits your design. Personally, I'd go with the option of modifying a conventional stick-frame to accept bales. However, a simple elegant post-and-beam designed to accept an exterior bale wrap could be straightforward to build and would create a beautiful exposed interior structure.

In either case, the main challenge will be to adapt the conventional structure to accept bales. How wide is the stem wall and where should the posts sit on it to accommodate the bales? How will the bales be raised off the stem wall? What kind of diagonal bracing will you use and how will the bales interact with it? How will windows and doors interact with the framework? How will the area between the beams and roof be dealt with? How will the bales fill gables ends in the roof? How will plumbing, electrical, heating and cooling systems be adjusted to work with the bale wall system? Answering these questions and many more will be the difference between an elegant and an awkward finished building. That's enough work to focus on for now without having the distraction of a bunch of fuzzy straw sponges sitting around.

This brings up another advantage of infill. Adapting a very common conventional structural system for bales will make the entire professional residential building world available to you: framers, roofers, plumbers, electricians, and, most importantly, building inspectors should be able to see the logic in increasing the amount of infill insulation installed within a common skeletal frame. Therefore, even if experienced bale builders can't be found, conventional professionals can be called on to help. Again, though there is much to deride in the world of modern commercial construction, creating a building that isolates you from its expertise can be a lonely task. No builder can be an island. A cost-effective approach might be to hire a professional crew to erect the entire structure with your role confined to deciding how that structure needs to be modified to accept the bales.

Once this stage is completed, you'll have a self-supporting structure covered by a protective roof that can sit there without bales for years if need be. That's a nice relaxing feeling. Now, by looking at the actual structure, you'll be able to plan specific solutions to detailing problems that weren't obvious on paper. At your leisure, you can mount sill plate assemblies, build window and door bucks, and install any framing you'll be using to attach them to the structure. You can use the area under the roof as a workshop, organizing tools and leaving them set up, so that you can do the work as time permits.

Meanwhile, have a party or two under the roof. Eat dinner there or go there just to relax. It's during these moments of play and repose that you'll discover exactly where a window should go or how to solve that little problem that's been nagging you. It's an incredible luxury, reserved for owner-builders, to be able to stop the construction process and allow time for reflection. By keeping your vulnerable bales out of the picture until the end of the project, you can take full advantage of this wonderful option. Finally, organize and prepare your plastering operation. Decide on your mix, order materials, schedule plaster work parties or a paid crew, and plan a tarping system to protect bales from rain and plaster from sun. In other words, do everything that can be done before the bales ever reach the site.

Now, finally, get your bales and install them. If you've prepared well, you'll find this step to be fun, fast, incredibly rewarding, and only a tiny proportion of the work required to complete the building.

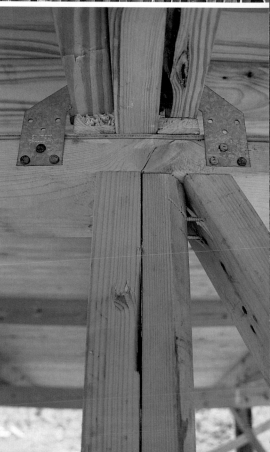

Chapter 11
Modified Stick-Frame

We've already introduced stick-framing in chapter 7 as a

variation of post-and-beam construction using very thin wooden posts, called *studs*, spaced closely together and capped by equally thin beams, called *plates*. In the United States at least, stick-framing has taken over as the prevalent residential construction method. The technique is used to make everything from mobile homes to mansions. In this incarnation, stick-framing is part of a building system that's eating our forests while simultaneously swallowing up farmland as part of urban sprawl. Environmental activists and thoughtful builders sometimes portray it as an idiotic material feeding frenzy serving only short-term commercial gain, almost as if the devil himself lived in a stick-frame split-level ranch in the pits of hell. Why, then, is a book on green building bothering with stick-framing?

To answer that question we need to talk about the human love affair with wood. For thousands of years, human cultures all over the world have been frantically using…and running out of…wood. For example, the ancient Greeks depended on wood for cooking, heating, smelting, and the construction of ships and homes. This heavy reliance led to wood shortages as early as the fifth century B.C. The Romans experienced shortages for similar reasons several centuries later. It's theorized that the Polynesian society on Easter Island and the Norse communities on Greenland both perished due to complete devastation of the wood resources that were pivotal to their survival. There are other examples of this scenario repeated by different cultures in different places at different times throughout history. The only thing that's changed today is that the world economy makes it possible for our next wood shortages to be on a global scale. Forestland is being lost worldwide at alarming rates, and the destruction of huge tracts of forest, such as the Amazon jungles, is changing the climate of the entire planet.

This recurring problem comes about not because wood is an inappropriate material, but, quite the opposite, because it is very appropriate for so many things. It is dense cellulose and therefore a convenient package of Btu's to burn for heating and cooking. (Can you envision how much straw you'd have to burn in a stove to keep a house warm?) Wood is strong yet flexible, very workable, and can take on a mind-boggling array of forms. It's hard to imagine that a sheet of paper, sailboat, cardboard box, guitar, and house can all be created using the same raw material.

In building terms, wood is very strong in response to both compressive and tensile forces, yet it's very easy to cut and even easier to fasten. A given volume of wood has a thermal mass comparable to the same volume of concrete and an insulation value in the ballpark of an equal volume of straw. What's more, wood is a completely replenishable resource. Money doesn't grow on trees, but wood does. In other words, it's an incredible building material. If someone discovered wood today, it would be heralded as the greenest of the green building materials, destined to revolutionize the environmental impact of housing construction.

Good vs. evil. This mild-mannered stick-frame building looks harmless enough—is it part of a major worldwide environmental crisis or just another potentially sensible choice for the conscious green builder?

A SHORT HISTORY OF BUILDING WITH WOOD

Stage 1: Cutting to length. The simplest wood construction can be accomplished by collecting wood and breaking it to length, either by hand or with a simple cutting tool like a stone or metal hatchet. *Left:* This building uses the crook created between limbs to hold simple floor joist logs that have been roughly cut to length. Notice the sticks protruding near the top of the building—these form a platform for branches that are covered with mud plaster to create a roof. *Right:* Other than the door, all of the wood on this building consists of logs, sticks, and branches collected, cut to length, and connected with simple fasteners.

Stage 2: Notching and splitting. Tools capable of chopping, notching, and splitting expanded the options for wood building. *Left:* Fairly large trees were felled, shaped, and notched by hand to create the walls for this building. *Right:* Tools allowing wood to be split into small squares, called shakes, allowed the manufacture of a fairly waterproof roofing and siding material.

Stage 3: Ripping, joining, and carving. The development of hand and power drills and saws as well as metal tools of all kinds allowed complicated joinery and carving. *Left:* Wood lends itself to the creation of incredibly intricate designs under the hands of a skilled carver. *Right:* Exacting cuts and the ability to drill holes for pegs make possible the connection of very large timbers into large skeletal structures.

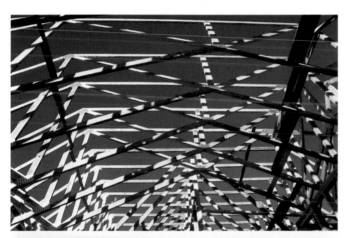

Stage 4: Mass-production and composites. Modern machinery and technology allow for the production of massive quantities of uniformly sized wood components, many of which use waste products and small-dimensioned, fast growing trees. *Top Left:* Modern stick-framing usually consists of a dizzying array of mass-produced wood units. *Left:* A microlam (at left in photo), a structural beam made up of thin strips of wood laminated together with strong glues, holds up I-beam floor joists made of chipboard sandwiched between small strips of wood. This floor framing, in turn, holds up a subfloor of more chipboard panels. *Above:* Both the decking and framing of this walkway are constructed of "lumber" that's made of recycled plastic and wood chips.

I submit, then, that the recurring human problem with wood isn't inherent in the material, but is the result of poor management and short-sightedness. If we stopped using wood today without adjusting our thought process, consumption patterns, and priorities, then some other material would just take its place on the endangered species list. The broader answer lies in matching our demand to our resources regardless of the materials we use. In that context, stick-framing as a case study becomes the perfect topic for a book on green building.

Though it may cause me to loose my membership in the Angry Woodland Elves Society, I'll state for the record that there is simply nothing inherently wrong with stick-framing as a building method. In fact, as a structural system, it is in some ways an environmental improvement over older wood-based techniques. Underneath all of that expendable vinyl siding, formaldehyde-glued particleboard, and vapor barriers made of plastic sheeting is just thin little sticks of plain ol' natural wood. Let's see if we can take a technique that's part of the world-crushing industrial building machine and recast it as a useful method for the conscious green builder.

GENERAL CONTEXT: STICK-FRAMING

STICK-FRAMING BASICS

As a structural system, stick-framing essentially takes the loads carried by the large, widely spaced posts of timber framing and post-and-beam construction and splits them up among a bunch of much smaller columns spread throughout the wall. (See figure 1.) These basic columns are called studs and they're attached on top and bottom to thin beams called top and bottom plates. Just as in our other wall systems, holes in the wall created by windows are structural weak spots that need lintels. Lintels in stick-framing are called *headers*, and they sit in a structural assembly made up of special studs called *jacks*, *kings*, and *cripples*. (For some reason, there's no queen—don't ask me why.)

In conventional construction, this skeletal structure is given a monolithic component by attaching structural plywood sheathing to the outside surface of the framing, which helps to distribute loads throughout the wall and acts as powerful bracing. The structural role of plywood can be, and historically was, accomplished with diagonal bracing. A stick-frame wall assembly is usually built laying flat on the ground and then lifted into place where it can be attached equally well to a concrete slab, stem wall, or framed floor.

CONVENTIONAL STICK-FRAME CONSTRUCTION

As we've said, humans have been building with wood for quite a while. The stick-framing structural system just described is simply another version of what we've been doing for millennia. It came about because saws were invented that allowed wood to be efficiently ripped into thin boards of consistent width and thickness. In many ways, this innovation simplified the process of making a strong wooden structure. Once they were milled, the small sticks were light and easy to move. They could be cut quickly with a handsaw and hammered together with simple nails; therefore, no complex joinery was needed. Though it may not have been on anyone's mind at the time, these small sticks were a step in the right direction toward sustainable forestry stewardship because they allowed the use of younger, smaller diameter, quickly replenishable trees.

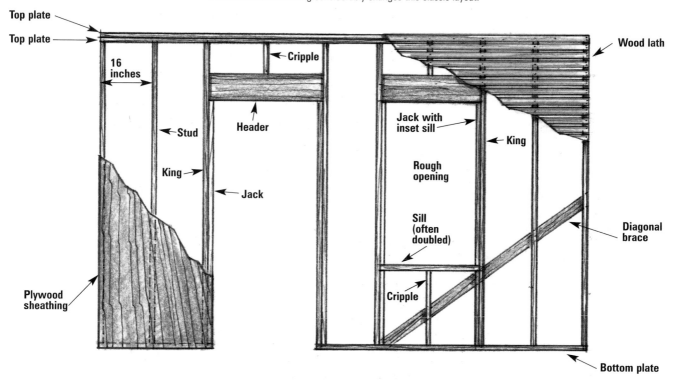

Figure 1
STICK-FRAMING BASICS

This drawing shows the basic components of stick-framing. On the right, diagonal bracing and wooden lath provide the structural strength that plywood does on the left. Our modified version of commercial stick-framing considerably changes this classic layout.

If this system doesn't seem so bad on the surface, it's because it isn't. The problem with stick-framing today isn't the method itself but the inefficient and irresponsible practices of the modern construction industry and the consumer culture that fuels it. Conventional stick-framing is a system driven by inflexible mass-produced components and an economic context that promotes incredible waste, as well as a rigid division of labor that doesn't encourage a cohesion between design and construction. Huh? Let me show you what I mean.

As part of the modern conventional stick-framing system, products like plywood, drywall, and fiberglass batt insulation are packaged in standard sizes that make them easy to transport and sell. However, these materials are immediately cut up into custom-sized pieces on site, creating an incredible waste of products that took a lot of energy and resources to produce and transport. For example, plywood is often used as a substrate for the final skin on the exterior of the building. The wall is framed on the ground as described above and then 4 x 8-foot sheets of plywood are attached to the entire surface of the frame. The plywood covering window and door openings is then cut out and thrown in the trash! Later, the same procedure is followed in covering the interior of the wall with drywall, creating more offerings for the god of the trash pile. This same approach is repeated with a variety of materials, so that by the time the building is finished there's a mountain of trash consisting of brand new, virgin materials ready to be taken to the plastic-lined hole that is the local dump.

Brand new trash. The wood in this plywood went through an incredible amount of processing and travel before it finally ended up on a building site only to be immediately cut up and thrown on this trash pile headed for the dump.

To make matters worse, these modular materials force a standardized layout for the stick-frame lumber to which they're attached. In conventional stick-framing, 2x4 studs are placed 16 inches apart. Modular materials are manufactured to be multiples of that 16-inch increment in length and width. For example, plywood sheets are 96 (6 X 16 = 96) inches long and 48 (3 X 16 = 48) inches wide. Fiberglass batt insulation comes in rolls 14½ inches wide, which is the width of the cavity created by 1½-inch-wide 2x4s spread 16 inches apart.

The problem with this system is that it only increases the waste described previously. For example, if you want to create a 104-inch-long wall, full sheets of plywood will leave 8 inches of wall uncovered. This difference will have to be made up by ripping small strips off of a full 4x8 sheet of plywood. Maybe you'll find a use for the now stunted sheet, or maybe it will end up as waste. Similarly, in order to fill the small cavity between studs created at the end of the wall, you'll need to custom cut your modular fiberglass batts, most likely creating more cut-offs for the trash.

Perhaps the major waste created here is in the framing itself. In timber framing, posts and beams are spaced based on the loads they'll be called upon to carry. In conventional stick-framing, instead of placing precious wooden structural members where they are needed to carry loads, these members are placed based on how they'll accommodate plywood, drywall, fiberglass and other modular materials. As a result, an eave wall (like our cordwood wall) that's carrying major roof loads will be framed in the same manner as a gable end wall that is carrying minimal loads, which in turn will be framed the same as an interior partition wall carrying basically no loads at all. This is an extremely frivolous use of resources.

Wood overload. A large amount of the wood in this frame for a modern residential house is serving no structural function. It's there to accommodate other materials. The roof rafters, for example, are sized large and spaced close together to accommodate fiberglass batt insulation. Collar ties are large enough to do their structural job if installed only every third or fourth rafter pair but are attached instead to each pair to accommodate drywall.

Why is industry being so wasteful? It's especially baffling because a major lament of homeowners and contractors alike is that lumber and other materials are too expensive. Obviously, they are, in fact, too cheap if they can be so carelessly misused. I suppose the explanation may be that the real money is made in our modern world through mass production. Though this approach to stick-framing is a waste of wood and other resources, it allows for the production of massive quantities of modular materials. This economy of scale creates lower prices.

In addition, the complete standardization of the stick-framing system allows the design and construction of these buildings to be similarly standardized. Therefore, all the materials needed to construct a building or entire subdivision can be ordered and delivered in a bundle. In modern residential construction, where passive solar heating and cooling strategies are almost unknown, houses that are more or less exactly the same can be built in a wide range of climates by using heating and cooling systems that burn fossil fuels. Though this approach wastes nonrenewable resources and creates a lot of pollution, it allows the same mass-produced building materials to be sold in a wider market. This scenario, of course, is the model for success in our present economic system. In other words, in the context of our economy, an incredibly wasteful building approach makes sense.

As if all of that wasn't enough to break the back of poor little stick-framing, we, in the United States at least, are building larger and larger homes. A 5,000-square-foot second home for a vacationing retired couple isn't a rarity. We're building too much, too big. It would be too much cob, too much straw bale, too much cordwood, too much Earthship, or too much of anything!

The problems don't end here. The products of this industrial approach, everything from mobile homes to apartment complexes to subdivision spec houses to McMansions, often don't feel like complete buildings. There's just something missing. On the other hand, many stick-frames that I've come across that are 40 or more years old don't suffer from this malady—they somehow feel right. What's changed?

Window waste. As we'll discuss on page 405, stick-framing is a flexible system that can be adjusted to save wood. Given a different mindset, this flexibility can result in the considerable waste of wood and other materials. For example, in the real world, windows are rarely sized or placed to fit neatly within the standard 16-inch stud layout. In commercial stick-framing, their placement often creates extra framing and lots of irregularly sized cavities, as is the case with this window. Modular fiberglass batts will need to be custom cut to fill most of this space. Notice also the bizarre framing under the window. This happened because the owner decided to raise the windowsill height after the rough opening had been framed, requiring reframing and more wasted wood.

Thinking inside the box. This concrete block wall is poured solid with concrete and supports the floor above it. The stick-frame wall in front of the block wall is serving no structural function. Its sole purpose is to hold drywall as a finish surface. Nonetheless, studs are spaced 16 inches apart, as they would be in a structural wall, to accommodate the modular size of the drywall sheets. The exact same function, a smooth white wall, could have been accomplished with a single coat of plaster, saving time, money, and materials. This is an incredible waste of precious resources that could have been avoided with a little thought.

Again, the answer it seems to me is the mass-production mindset. Stick-frame construction is easily divided into distinct construction phases. Modular materials and specialized tools have created specialists, workers that do only one small job on each building. One crew puts in the foundation, another frames, another puts up the siding, another insulates, another installs drywall, and yet another surfaces the roof. This division of labor creates a factory mentality with few people knowing or caring about the true goal of the building.

This situation is exacerbated by the fact that in the United States many people working in construction have never been trained formally. There are almost no guilds, no apprenticeships, no masters, and no students. Generally speaking—though there are, of course, many exceptions to the rule—construction has truly become an "industry," and the artisans have become mere workers installing components on a residential housing conveyor belt.

Stick vs. stick. *Above:* This brick-faced modern stick-frame house in the United States is trying hard to be interesting with different roofs, arched windows, and a covered entrance. It's also large, expensive, and in a nice neighborhood. In the end, though, it just falls flat. It's got no soul. *Left:* In contrast, though run down, boarded up, and abandoned, this old stick-frame still has a wonderful feel. The proportions, roof pitch, big overhangs, and simple, creative trim details work together to create a truly complete building. With the same basic materials and a much lower budget, this little house succeeds where the other fails.

RECLAIMING THE STICK-FRAME

Obviously, I agree with environmental activists that modern stick-framing is a disaster. However, I maintain that all we have to do to solve the problem is stick to our alternative building mantra: Design specifically for your situation.

First of all, there's no need to use sheet materials like plywood or drywall. You can replace them with wooden lath and plaster. With inflexible modular materials gone, you can place structural lumber only where structure is needed, therefore vastly reducing the amount of wood used. Look back at figure 1. Through conscious design in the stick-frame wall in our building, we were able to do without the second top plate, structural headers, jack and cripple studs, plywood sheathing, and 16-inch stud spacing. These adjustments result in different-sized cavities between studs, which can be filled with a non-modular insulation such as cellulose made from recycled newspapers that creates no waste in its installation and performs better thermally than fiberglass batts. Another approach creating the same effect would be to adjust our stick-frame structure to accommodate straw bale infill. The bales would serve as both incredible insulation and the interior and exterior plastering surfaces.

Wood from a different side of the tracks. Stick-framing doesn't have to mean mass-produced lumber trucked and trained thousands of miles to the local building supply. *Left:* We used a combination of store-bought/kiln-dried, locally milled, salvaged, and site-harvested woods to create our stick-frame wall. *Right:* The wood for this stick-frame was cut and milled on site.

Since you're not part of a system trying to supply wood to a huge industry, you can purchase the small amount of wood you'll need to build your single, consciously sized building from sources that sustainably manage their forests, or you can even process it yourself if wood is available on site. You can do the work yourself, therefore taking away the waste-producing panic of expensive labor and reuniting the realms of design and construction. Finally, as we've done in our little building, you can use stick-framing only where it makes sense and combine it with other techniques to create a sensitive design that truly fits your specific situation. In other words, you can return to your idealistic pursuit of crafting a feeling and molding your dreams.

ADVANTAGES OF STICK-FRAME CONSTRUCTION

Now that we've reclaimed stick-framing as a potentially sane building approach, what are some of its strengths?

First, a popular claim of enthusiasts for many building alternatives is that their chosen technique is the easiest. Of the four wall systems described in this book, however, I think a group of beginners given a basic text and left to their own devices might actually have the best results with stick-framing. There are lots of reasons for this claim, a few of which include: (1) the structural system is very graphic and easy to grasp, (2) the walls and roof are built using the same tools and techniques, (3) lots of light pieces come together to make a strong whole, (4) structural strength is easy to access and fortify at any point during construction, allowing the beginner peace of mind, (5) materials are relatively unaffected if left in the rain, allowing construction lulls and creating a fairly forgiving atmosphere for neophytes unfamiliar with the ups and downs of building, (6) the wide array of mass-produced fasteners, flashing pieces, and other custom accessories designed specifically for conventional stick-framing are a resource that can make problem solving far easier for the beginner, and (7) everybody and their dog knows how to stick-frame, so there's always someone around to ask for help if you get stuck.

Light pieces combine to carry heavy loads.
If you get rid of the plywood and drywall, the basic components of stick-framing are relatively light and easy to move. These big roof trusses are made of 2x4s and are light enough to be installed by two people.

All of these traits contribute to making basic stick-framing a relatively quick, comparatively less stressful building method. In addition, good ol' wood is widely available. As we've said, the thin sticks required can be milled from smaller, fast-growing trees, so the variety of trees available for stick-framing is wider than for some other wood-frame systems. If you have trees on site, that means you have a better chance of being able to use them, perhaps even those that need to be cleared anyway to make room to build. On the other hand, people living in cities often have no choice but to truck in building materials. For that reason, the piles of neatly stacked, kiln-dried stick-framing members already waiting at the local building supply may end up being the most practical resource in some situations.

Another advantage of stick-framing is that it can be adapted to most climates and design strategies successfully. It can deliver a good R-value even given its small width when its cavities are filled with an appropriate insulation. This R-value can be adjusted to the situation by using wider studs, such as 2x6s or even 2x8s set more widely apart to create walls with more space to accomodate insulation for very cold or very hot climates. Actually, walls of basically any width can be built using what is sometimes called "ladder truss" stick-frame construction. (See photo at right.) By adjusting the type of skins used (see chapter 12), the height that the wall is lifted off the ground, and the size of the roof overhangs, stick-framing can work in the wettest, cloudiest climate. Since it can accommodate almost any size or placement of window and door opening, it's a good fit for passive solar strategies or designs that depend on good ventilation for cooling. Though it's perhaps not the most elegant system to fit any of these climates or strategies, stick-framing can work well in all of them.

DISADVANTAGES OF STICK-FRAME CONSTRUCTION

As with all construction methods, stick-framing definitely has its inherent disadvantages. First, wood burns easily. In fact, humans through history have probably used wood to burn for cooking and heat as much as they've used it for anything else. The thin wood sticks of this framing system are simply great firewood, and, as such, stick-framing can be almost ridiculously susceptible to catching fire. Second, though it's true we can adjust the width of the wall, stick-framing tends to be on the thin side, which means we don't have as much space to insulate. What's worse, each stick creates a thermal break, a concept we introduced in the last chapter. For example, a 2x6 spruce stud is probably about R-7, while the infill insulation on either side can rate up to R-20 or more. The stick-framing structure itself, then, isn't very insulative and brings down the insulation value of the wall as a system. To be fair, though, as far as I can determine, this thin wall would be far, far better insulated than our thick cob wall and at least as well, if not much better, insulated than our cordwood wall. (See our R-value estimates in the previous three chapters.)

Ladder truss framing. This wall is a variation of stick-framing that's sometimes called a ladder truss because it involves assemblies of two studs separated by wood blocks that look like the rungs of a ladder. This system allows you to use stick-framing to create walls of basically any thickness. The wood in this wall is mostly uneven rips from the outer edges of logs that would normally be waste in the milling process. It was milled on site and is being used here in combination with salvage rough-cut lath strips to create a wide box to hold clay-slip straw infill. (See chapter 8 for a discussion of clay-slip straw.)

A Building Puzzler

Imagine two tiny cottages built side by side a year ago in an idyllic clearing in the woods. One is made of monolithic cob. All the wood needed for the roof, window frames and doorframes was carefully salvaged from various demolition projects. The second cottage was stick-framed with 2x6s purchased at the local hardware store and insulated with commercial cellulose insulation. Otherwise, both cottages are identical. After braving a winter that was severe even for the cold, forested northern climate where they're situated, they both seem to be holding up very well. The owners of each cottage have kept exact records of the amounts of virgin wood used on their project. When they compare notes, it turns out the stick-frame building used less wood. How can this be?

The answer is that both buildings are heated with firewood from the surrounding forest. Though the cob cottage used no virgin wood during construction, we learned in chapter 8 that its weakness is thermal resistance, so the superior insulation of the stick-frame cottage requires less wood to be burned to heat it. In this cold climate, the cob cottage has already burned more wood in a single winter than the stick-frame used both for framing and for heating combined. This wood gap will continue to grow over the lifetime of the two buildings. In the end, the wood-framed cottage will have used a miniscule amount of wood compared to its cob neighbor.

Cob lost this contest not because it's an inferior system to stick-framing, but because it was a poor choice for the given situation. One of the goals of this chapter is to shake up your preconceptions. Materials are only tools. They can only become a good building if they are appropriate to your climate and used in a conscious, creative way.

Wood burns. In fact, of course, it's often burned to heat houses. Why build a house out of firewood? In today's world, with fire hazards such as electrical wiring and gas piping as common building components, it's an even better question to ask. In a way, the fact that people have been willing to overlook its combustibility for thousands of years underscores the convenience and workability of wood as a building material. Still, I can completely understand anyone's decision to forgo wood construction based on its susceptibility to burning.

Another problem is that the fast-growing softwoods that make the most sense to use in stick-framing are particularly susceptible to insects, fungus, and mold. In other words, wood is food and will probably eventually be eaten. If it's kept dry, though, this fate can be postponed almost inevitably. Still, roofs eventually leak and buildings get neglected. A stick-frame building with a cellulose (newspaper, cotton, or straw) infill will quickly deteriorate in the presence of liquid water. When it comes to wood, termites are in a category unto themselves. Though interesting nontoxic remedies have been developed (see chapter 3 for a discussion), probably the best approach to dealing with termites where they are very prevalent is simply not to build with wood. The modern advance of kiln-drying makes wood much less attractive to insects and mold, and it also makes it more stable, because it twists, bows, shrinks, and expands less than green or air-dried wood. Kiln-drying, though, adds embodied energy to wood, and isn't usually an option for site-harvested lumber.

Perhaps the main disadvantage of stick-frame construction is that even careful, considerate use of wood may be too much for a world crowded with billions of people. Though wood is replenishable, it grows more slowly than straw, for example, which is a yearly crop. This makes it more difficult to manage sustainably. What really are the best materials to use in housing? Clearly, they'd be those that created the most energy-efficient, long lasting buildings with the least invasive, most replenishable materials. As I hope this book is making clear, this isn't a simple black or white question. In this context, though, it's obvious that stick-framing makes sense only if used as part of a very conscious design. Again, the answers, if there are any, lie within the give and take of a conscious building process that takes the specifics of each situation into consideration.

Finally, a common argument against stick-framing is that its boxy, angular nature and thin-walled profile creates unnatural, psychologically oppressive, and creativity-stifling spaces. Nature, it is argued, doesn't build with straight lines. I'm sympathetic to the feel of this argument, but have been in too many wonderful, old, creatively crafted stick-frame buildings to give it too much credence. It seems to me that good buildings come from the human first and the material second. Still, I will agree that stick-framing is a more rigid, less whimsical medium than any of our other wall systems. Its thinner profile and sharp edges can be harsh, but these characteristics can be softened with thoughtful design.

DOES STICK-FRAMING FIT YOUR SITUATION?

I'm not arguing that your dream house should be a modification of conventional stick-framing. As a whole house building system, it's probably in the end just a middle-of-the-road technique. There are most likely approaches that will more elegantly fit your specific climate and needs. Still, I can imagine the day in a couple of hundred years when building straw is a genetically modified monocrop and everyone is complaining about the shoddy workmanship and high price of their cob contractor. Perhaps then sensible modified stick-framing will be the hot topic at food co-ops and in intentional community brochures.

Until then, though, the fact remains that stick-framing skills are invaluable on most projects. Wooden roofs, partition walls, and outbuildings are often stick-framed regardless of the main construction approach of a building project. The basic tools and techniques of stick-framing are useful whether you're constructing the window and door bucks for a cob or cordwood wall or banging together a small shed for storing straw bales. Once you get over stick-frameaphobia, you may find yourself drawn to build a sweet little stick-frame outhouse or wood shed next to your wonderful little cob cottage. You may even decide to sensibly design a stick-frame skeleton to be infilled with straw bales as the core approach for your house design.

So, though I support and defer to your probable inclination away from stick-framing as the overall structure of your house, I strongly recommend that you learn how to do it and be open to incorporating it in your design when it makes sense. Just ignore those whispered insults at the organic cappuccino bar. Well-designed stick-framing, after all, is a quick, flexible method of using an organic material to create a light, strong, well-insulated structure that will function admirably in most climates.

Wood rots. Once the metal roofing on this old barn was ripped off by the wind, the pine and poplar framing started getting wet regularly. This led to mold and eventual insect infestation, both of which slowly ate away at the wood until it failed.

Sticks for straw. Once you know the basics, stick-framing can be an incredibly flexible system. Remember this photo from the last chapter? Looks a lot like stick-framing, doesn't it? This is just one of many ways that people have come up with to adjust the basic stick-framing system to accommodate straw bales. Another interesting option is to keep the basic stick-framing stud layout but adjust the distance between studs so that bales can be laid on end to fill each stud cavity.

Is Stick-Framing Green?

In general terms, how does stick-framing stand up to our five-point green building test?

1) Low Construction Impact. I live in an area of the United States that's a picturesque combination of farmland and forest. However, I can't buy locally grown produce at the area supermarket chain or locally grown lumber at the nearby mega hardware store. Instead, both businesses purchase products grown thousands of miles away on huge, monocropped farms and shipped by train and truck to my neighborhood. In this context, stick-framing materials have a high embodied energy, contribute to soil degradation, and cause pollution in their manufacture and transport. In addition, this wood and associated materials are used wastefully on the construction site. If you build as part of this system, stick-framing has a high construction impact. On the other hand, if you break this cycle by finding locally grown, sustainably harvested lumber and use it sensibly in your design, stick-framing can have a very low construction impact. The only difference between the two scenarios is you, and which alternative you choose.

2) Resource Efficiency through the Life of the Building. Part of the reason for stick-framing's present popularity in some areas of the world is that it's a good match for modern heating, electrical, and plumbing systems. Ducts, pipes, conduit, and wires are easily installed in its open cavities and attached to its structure. This fact, along with the potential for the second highest R-value of our four wall systems, makes stick-framing an energy-efficient choice, especially in combination with modern heating, water, and electrical systems.

3) Long Lasting. Like all cellulose, stick-framing materials and the insulations that fill them are susceptible to water and insect damage. If correctly designed by being lifted off the ground and protected by good roof overhangs and an appropriate skin, stick-framing can last a very long time as long as the roof and skin are maintained.

4) Nontoxic. Modern stick-frame buildings can be crawling with synthetic materials such as vinyl siding, plywood with formaldehyde glues, fiberglass insulation, plastic vapor barriers, high VOC paints, and acrylic carpeting, not to mention all the furniture, appliances, and other mainstays of industrialized life that fill the space. However, the actual sticks that make up the structure are just plain old natural wood and all the synthetic materials mentioned above can be replaced with natural, nontoxic alternatives.

5) Beautiful. We chose stick-framing as part of our little building partly to make a very simple point: it's not the materials but the builder that makes a building green. Using the same material base and financial resources, stick-frame buildings run the gamut from mass-produced, impersonal, poorly constructed, short-lived commodities for storing people and their televisions to energy-efficient, beautifully designed, whimsical yet practical owner-built expressions of personality. This contrast is proof that, in some situations at least, we really do make our own reality. With the right frame of mind, even a typically wasteful, conventional system can be adjusted to create a space that connects you and your site in a deep and lasting way.

Beauty or the beast? All of these buildings are conventionally stick-framed. The mobile homes at left were mass-produced at a factory; the house at right was the product of the owner's imagination—it was built to serve his specific needs and personal vision.

STICK-FRAMING APPLIED: OUR LITTLE BUILDING

DESIGNING WITH STICK-FRAMING

As we developed our pattern language design, various zones of activity began to take shape. The west side or our building was becoming the main utility area. On the outside, our west wall had a large porch overhang and plans for shelving and a utility sink. The inside of our west wall would house both the tiny kitchen, including a sink, stove, and storage shelves, and our small wall-mounted, direct-vented propane heater. Therefore, this wall would be covered on inside and out with things attached to it, and would need to allow water pipes and a vent to go through it. This situation just isn't a good match for some wall systems. For example, both cob and straw bale construction, with all of their strengths, are difficult to attach things to, and each has separate inconveniences in accommodating pipes and vents.

In addition, the generally shady location of this wall combined with short bouts of intense low western setting sun required that it be a good insulator without requiring thermal mass, since the mass would be of no value here in the shade. Finally, this wall would have to take on a considerable weight from the living roof above it, so it needed to be of unquestionable strength. All of these variables added up to an obvious choice: stick-framing. Stick framing effortlessly accommodates attachments like shelving and is easily adjusted to house vents and pipes. Unlike its wasteful modern cousin, our approach puts structural members only where they need to be, allowing us to create a strong wall with a small amount of lumber. In addition, there's no reason to be limited to conventional 2x4s, so we can achieve higher R-values with wider framing if we so desire.

THE BASIC STRUCTURE

As will become obvious by following the photo progression in this chapter, our stick-frame wall took shape slowly. We did the initial framing as part of the basic skeletal structure of the building before any of our infill walls had been installed. However, we didn't insulate this wall until after plastering was well under way and the building was almost finished. In the chronology of our building, then, our stick-frame wall was started first and finished last. In our minds, it just made sense to present it as the last wall system in the book.

Our wall puts into practice the principles that we outlined for reclaiming stick-framing from the jaws of wasteful industry. By avoiding the use of modular materials like plywood sheathing, drywall, and fiberglass batt insulation, we weren't forced to create a uniform distance between studs. This allowed us to place structural members only where we needed them. In our situation, that meant a stud at each end of the wall; two thin columns (double 2x6 studs) spaced 52 inches apart and set directly beneath our trusses; a single 2x6 top plate; a composite lumber (recycled plastic and wood chips) bottom plate; and a final stud to finish our window framing. This simple structural system will eventually be further solidified by thick wooden lath salvaged from old siding; therefore, our wall system used very little virgin wood.

However, our particular situation presented an even greater opportunity to show off the inherent structural flexibility in the stick-framing system. The poor compressive strength of our stem wall combined with the huge weight of our living roof created a unique structural twist. Luckily, we were free to design to fit our situation, so we dusted off our big brains and opposable thumbs to come up with a simple wall truss that elegantly dealt with our specific structural situation. (See the sidebar The Wall Truss, on page 413.)

▲ **Step 1.** We used conventional framing techniques to create our basic structure. First, we cut our top and bottom plates to length and laid them side by side. We measured over from one end and marked where our stud columns needed to be attached to both plates so that they would be positioned directly under our roof trusses.

◄ **Step 2.** The bottom plate needs to be water-resistant because water could potentially condense between it and the termite barrier. In conventional stick-framing, some form of wood treated with poison is the common water-resistant material used for bottom plates. We chose instead to use a composite lumber made from recycled plastic and wood chips. This lumber was designed as deck flooring and can be cut, ripped, shaped, and fastened much like wood. Here, we're nailing the bottom plate to one of our studs. We also used it for our straw bale sill and part of our living roof trim.

▲ **Step 3.** We used the same salvaged EPDM gasket and caulk detail around our pipes that we used when installing our termite barrier and corner posts (see chapter 7). This sealed the only possible passageways for termites through the barrier. At this point, we also drilled holes in the bottom plate to accommodate our water and drain pipes. Since the bottom plate will rest flush with the outside of the stem wall, all we needed to do was measure over from the locust post and in from the edge of the stem wall to find where each pipe would need to penetrate the bottom plate.

▲ **Step 4.** After nailing our studs to the top and bottom plates, we lifted the very light wall into place and braced it. There's about 3½ feet between each locust post and the double stud. There's over 4 feet between the two double studs. Conventional framing would have placed a stud every 16 inches and would have included a window header, a king and jack on each side of the window, a double sill with a cripple below it, and a double top plate.

Water in a blanket. Our water pipes are now safely installed within the volume of what will be an insulated wall cavity. This will help prevent them from freezing during cold winter nights. The large pipe at left is the drain. The two smaller pipes are water supplies, one for the inside kitchen sink and the other for the outside garden sink. We'll plumb separate cut-off valves to each supply so that we'll be able to turn off water to the outside sink in the winter.

Tim's Take
The Wall Truss

The basic shape of most skeletal frames is rectangular. In chapter 2, we discussed the inherent structural weakness of rectangles and the different approaches to strengthening them. Using these simple techniques, we adjusted our stick-framing to fit our unique situation.

Look back at figure 5 in chapter 2. The triangular braces in the second drawing are both creating rigidity against lateral loads and supporting the beam by giving roof loads a more direct avenue to travel to the posts. In fact, you can think of them as little diagonal posts that transfer loads to another post instead of to the foundation. The plywood in the third drawing is taking a different approach to the same problem. It's connecting every inch of all four sides of the rectangle, thereby causing lateral and downward loads to be distributed evenly, in essence creating a monolithic wall out of this skeletal structure.

In our wall, it made sense to combine these two approaches. Here's our situation: we have a huge roof load that we want to transfer with small stick-frame members. Therefore, rather than creating a large open span with a big beam supported by triangle braces connected to posts, we needed to put smaller columns

Structural diagnosis. With our roof framing in place, it's easy to understand the basic structural system of our wall. The loads from four roof trusses are transferred directly by individual posts. The locust corner posts at each end transfer their loads to structural 3,000 psi concrete, and the double 2x6 posts in the middle transfer their loads to our 125 psi vermiculite concrete stem wall. We were concerned that this much weaker concrete couldn't handle these point loads from our very heavy living roof.

Figure 2
POINT LOADS

Our basic structural framing created point loads that our
insulated concrete stem wall might not be able to handle.

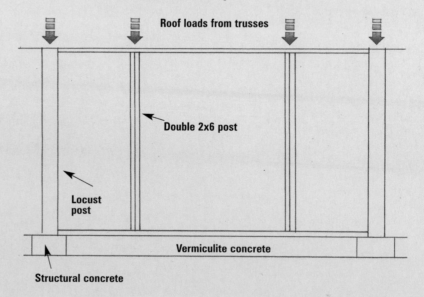

Roof loads from trusses

Double 2x6 post

Locust post

Vermiculite concrete

Structural concrete

under each truss to prevent our thin beam, or top plate, from bending. However, this transferred the loads of our trusses directly to specific points on the stem wall. Our weak insulative concrete probably couldn't handle these point loads, so we needed to find a way to more evenly distribute that weight.

To do this, we first installed diagonal braces from the top of our 2x6 columns to the structural concrete footer pads. These function like the triangle braces in the drawing from chapter 2 except they're redirecting roof loads to the foundation instead of to another post. Next, we firmly attached strips of salvage plywood to the top and bottom of the wall. This created a truss that's very similar to what you may have seen in bridge construction. The plywood unitizes the wall, which now functions as a beam, with the top in compression and the bottom in tension. The result is that the significant weight of our living roof will now be distributed throughout the wall and across the entire foundation, thereby alleviating the point loads that concerned us.

▲ **Step 1.** To adjust our structural system to fit the situation, we first cut diagonal braces to span between the bottom plate at each corner post (left) to the double stud under each roof truss (right). These diagonal braces, basically angled posts, transferred some of the roof loads from the middle trusses to the stronger structural concrete under the corner posts.

Figure 3
LATERAL THRUST

Diagonal bracing reduced the point loads on our stem wall but also introduced a force pushing out on the base of our locust posts. This force is called a "lateral thrust."

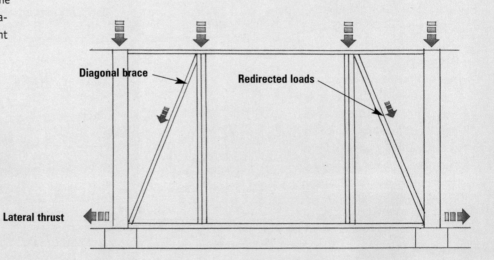

Diagonal brace

Redirected loads

Lateral thrust

◀ **Step 2.** However, we still had considerable point loads on the stem wall and we'd introduced a lateral thrust to the base of our locust posts. We then used both a strong glue (top left) and nails (bottom left) to attach salvaged plywood strips to both the top and bottom of our wall (above). These plywood pieces were veterans of a number of concrete pours, including our stem walls. The finished wall truss spread the roof loads evenly across the stem wall, taking away the point loads and the lateral thrust at the base of our corner posts.

Figure 4
EVEN DISTRIBUTION OF WEIGHT

We've transformed single columns working alone into an
integrated system that evenly distributes roof loads.

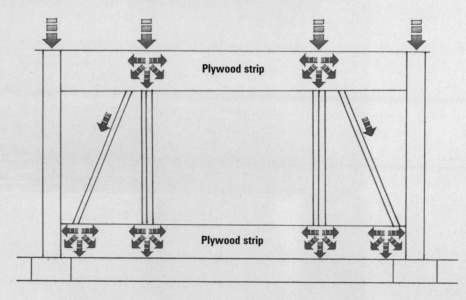

THE WINDOW ROUGH OPENING

In our cob and cordwood wall, the window bucks were structural frames floating freely within the volume of the wall. This allowed us to fine-tune their placement as the wall was being built. In stick-framing, window frames are attached to specially prepared holes in the skeletal framing called *rough openings* (see figure 1, page 401); therefore, decisions about placement of window and door openings usually take place as the wall is being framed lying flat on the ground. This sequence doesn't allow for exact window placement to frame that particular view or create just the right height for a sill shelf.

Though our photos don't capture the chronology, we improved on this situation by waiting to install our window opening after the basic wall structure was in place. Initially, we attached only the double stud columns and the studs at each end of the wall to our plates and lifted this assembly into position. One of us then took the window we'd chosen for this wall and held it at different locations while another moved around to experience the placement from different angles. We traded places and went back and forth until we found a location we both thought was right. In the end, we compromised by a couple of inches so that we could use one of our double stud columns placed under a roof truss as one side of the opening. We then framed out the opening using a minimum of wood. All of this was only possible because we didn't sheath the wall exterior with plywood, a step taken in conventional stick-framing as the wall is laying on the ground.

Only wood where it's needed. Once we'd chosen a window placement, we minimized the wood used in framing the rough opening. The double stud column at right serves as one side of our opening, and a single stud and cripple make up the other side. Since our window opening has no roof loads pushing down on it, we don't need a structural header, so a single 2x6 boxes out the top of the rough opening.

Superfluous structure. By contrast, in conventional stick-framing, structural headers are usually added whether they're called for or not. This door header is over 14 inches tall, yet you can see that the floor truss above isn't even resting on it. In other words, there is no weight for this header to bear. In fact, most of the framing in this interior partition wall is completely superfluous. Notice the double jacks below the header and the double cripples above it, not to mention the double top plate, all structurally completely unnecessary.

LATH

As we've said, a conventional stick-frame skeleton is usually covered on the outside with some form of sheet material like plywood or particleboard and on the inside with gypsum board, also called drywall. In and of themselves, these materials actually aren't bad by modern standards. Drywall is gypsum, a naturally occurring mineral, covered in paper. Plywood is thin strips of wood laminated together with glue, and particleboard is a generic term for chips of wood glued together into sheets. Still, these products usually aren't produced locally and must therefore be transported, sometimes thousands of miles, to get to the building site. Also, as discussed previously, sheet materials usually end up creating a lot of waste when connected with stick-framing. In addition, many plywood and particleboard products contain formaldehyde glues that can off-gas potentially harmful fumes.

Before sheet materials were popular, stick-frame buildings were covered with wooden lath, which was then covered in plaster. We decided to use lath on our wall, partly to avoid plywood and drywall, but also because we wanted to give our cellulose insulation the chance to breath; in other words, we decided to create a hygroscopic wall instead of one with a double drainage plane. (See chapters 3 and 10 for a discussion of these topics.) Historically, wooden lath was usually only about ¼ inch thick by 1½ to 2 inches wide. Since our studs are so widely spaced, we decided to make our lath thicker to create a more stable surface for our plaster. We used ¾-inch strips ripped down from some old yellow pine siding that a friend had just pulled off a house he was remodeling. We nailed these lath strips horizontally across our studs, leaving a small space between each row to give the plaster something to grip.

Installing Lath

▲ **Step 1.** I'm a fan of exposed water pipes. If they start leaking you know immediately rather than after water has soaked through the wall. Before installing our lath, we framed out a box around our water pipes at the base of the wall. We'll stop the lath at the framing, creating a permanent opening for the pipes to enter the room.

Raw materials. Our lath came from siding salvaged from a house renovation. It was moldy from sitting in the rain after being torn off the building. Wood stands up very well to water; it just can't stay wet. We took all the nails out, and then we stacked it in a barn to let it air dry. After the mold died off, we ripped it down on a table saw into strips about 2 inches wide.

▲ **Step 2.** We used small temporary shims to hold the lath pieces about ¼ to ⅜ inch apart as they were nailed in place with small galvanized ring-shanked nails.

▲ **Step 3.** We created this space between the rows of lath to allow the plaster to ooze through and hook over the back, making a strong connection. Notice how the first row of lath is lifted slightly off the stem wall to protect it from condensation. This section of the wall will eventually be wrapped in cob (see chapter 8).

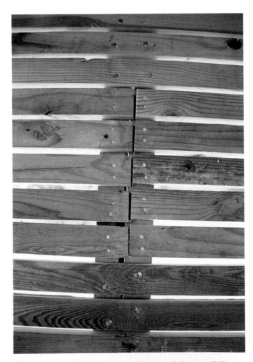

▲ **Step 4.** In chapter 10 we discussed the possibility of wood under plaster moving, and, thus, causing the plaster to crack. Our lath has more chance of moving through expansion and contraction at the joints, so we staggered our lath joints about every five rows to help prevent plaster cracks.

Large span. Traditionally, lath was ¼ inch thick and attached to studs every 12 or 16 inches. Our lath is spanning much farther, over 3 feet in some cases, so we used ¾-inch-thick material to create a more solid surface. Notice also the boxed out water access at the base of the wall.

▲ **Step 5.** We installed the exterior lath using the same methods. Again, notice the spacers. The lath was often bowed, so we had to push it down on the spacers as we were nailing. Once one row was done, we removed the spacers and used them on the next row.

▲ **Step 6.** Our locust posts create a reveal that separates each wall system (left). We left a space between lath and the posts at each end to allow for expansion and as a key for the plaster (right).

Lathed. I think the finished lath wall was beautiful in itself.

FINISHING THE TOP OF THE WALL

In the space between our top plate and the roof, we installed blocking similar to that over our cordwood wall. The width of this wall is much thinner, so we didn't feel loose straw would be adequate insulation. Instead, we tried two insulation methods, filling two cavities with rigid foam scraps and a third with blown cellulose.

▲ **Step 1.** In a detail similar to that used on our cordwood wall, we boxed out the space above our top plate between the roof trusses with blocking and filled the cavity with insulation. First, we attached nailers (left); then we installed the exterior blocking (right).

▲ **Step 2.** To prevent air infiltration, we sealed small gaps with caulk (top of blocking) and larger gaps with spray foam (bottom of blocking). Some green builders may shy away from these mass-produced materials, but I'm betting that we'll quickly regain their embodied energy with the increased energy efficiency their installation will add to our building.

▲ **Step 3.** We shaped 2-inch rigid foam insulation scraps to fit in the cavity between trusses. First, we cut the foam with a straight edge and a utility knife (left); then we used a serrated bread knife to cut an angle along the top of the foam to match the pitch of the roof (right).

◄ **Step 4.** We installed two layers of these custom-sized foam pieces in the cavity, giving it an R-value of 20. Here, we've installed the first layer.

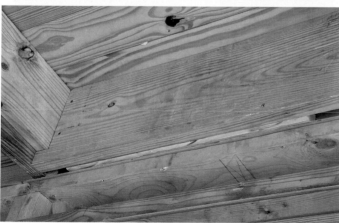

▲ **Step 5.** After installing the second layer of foam, we attached interior nailers (top), and installed the interior blocking (bottom). The blocking extends beyond the plane of the wall so that it can act as a plaster stop (see Prepping for Plaster). Notice also that we left out the final two rows of lath. We did this as part of our cellulose insulation procedure (see Installing Cellulose Insulation, later in this chapter).

Cut to fit. In order to fit well, this blocking required a fair amount of carpentry. Due to the roof pitch, the interior blocking had to be slightly taller than the exterior. We also had to rip an angle along the top of each piece to match the roof pitch, cut notches (also matching the roof pitch) on each side to fit the truss assembly, and, in some cases, we even had to carve out a space for the metal hangers that held the trusses to the wall (seen here above the notch). This piece of blocking was cut to fit on the interior of the wall.

THINKING ABOUT WATER

Our stick-framing is under a huge porch overhang, so it is, for the most part, protected from liquid water. However unlike our east-facing cordwood, this wall will be exposed to driving rains since we get a lot of strong westerly winds on this site. The most vulnerable spot will be the bottom of the wall, where rain could possibly make its way behind the plaster where it hits the stem wall. For this reason, we installed a tarpaper drainage plane at the base of the wall complete with flashing and drip edge. In addition, we had already installed a plastic lumber sill and attached our scrap plywood wall truss piece so that there is a ½-inch gap between it and the stem wall. Therefore, if a bit of water gets behind our drainage plane to land on the stem wall, it won't find anything there to rot.

Since our window is high in the wall, it will probably be completely protected by the porch overhang, and therefore really doesn't need flashing. However, window flashing doesn't take a lot of time or materials (we actually used salvage flashing collected from another project), so we went ahead and installed some. When it comes to water infiltration, better safe than sorry is wise advice.

PREPPING FOR PLASTER

In chapter 12, we'll discuss plaster and the plastering process in detail. For now, all we need to know is that it's a seamless covering that's spread onto a wall. Exposed edges of plastered walls are vulnerable, so they're usually fitted with raised surfaces that cradle the plaster, called *plaster stops*. In addition to protecting the edges, stops ensure that plaster edges are thick enough while also providing a surface for the plaster to be compressed against, which helps insure a good bond between plaster and wall. By considering these details while constructing our wall, we were able to place elements we were already installing so that they could double as plaster stops. Examples are the blocking at the top of the wall and our window frame. In other situations, a small piece of trim here or there did the trick.

In addition to stops, plaster needs a rough surface underneath it to grip. For the most part, our wooden lath serves as the gripping surface. The plaster squeezes between the lath pieces and actually oozes around the back, gripping the lath in a process sometimes called *keying*. The plywood on our exterior that's part of our wall truss will need an applied gripping surface. We used diamond metal stucco lath, the material employed in commercial stuccoing, to fill this function. This is the same metal lath we used in spots on our straw bale wall.

Drainage plane. We installed flashing with an integrated drip edge at the base of the wall and lapped it with tarpaper to create a drainage plane over the plywood of our wall truss. Any water that gets behind the plaster will flow down the tarpaper, hit the flashing, and be directed out to fall on the gravel that's sloped away from the building.

Keying. In a wooden lath system, plaster is pushed onto the wall where it squeezes through the gaps between lath strips and oozes over the wood. When the plaster dries, this ooze grabs the wood like a hook in a process called keying.

▲ **Step 1.** Unlike the freestanding window bucks in our other walls, we built a structural window rough opening into our stick-framing. We installed a window frame inside this opening made of 9-inch-wide rough-cut oak boards that extended 1 inch past the lath on both sides of the wall. These extensions will create a plaster stop around the entire window and will also allow the window to be set so that it can clear the plaster when it hinges open.

▲ **Step 2.** At the top of the wall, we'd set the blocking to protrude past the top plate so that it could double as a plaster stop. We also added tarpaper and metal lath over the plywood strip of our wall truss to give the plaster something to grip. I installed flashing at the top of the window frame and wrapped it under the tarpaper. Tim laughed at me for doing this, saying that water will never reach there because of our huge roof overhangs. It only took a few minutes, and I figured better safe than sorry.

◀ **Step 3.** At the base of the wall, the flashing serves as the plaster stop. At each end of the wall, the protruding locust corner post will serve as a stop. The trim that looks like a picture frame in the center of the photo will serve as stops to hold plaster out of the area where our heater vent will eventually puncture the wall. The small, ¾-inch plywood blocks painted grey are plaster stops that will allow us to attach ledgers and brackets for shelving without having to puncture the plaster. This should prevent cracking and will keep the shelves from abrading the plaster. As we'd done at the top of the wall, we installed metal lath over the drainage plane to give the plaster a rough surface to grip.

▲ **Step 4.** We attached this piece of plywood to the inside of the exterior lath directly behind the plaster stop box for the heater vent. We installed an identical piece directly across from this one on the inside of the interior lath. This will allow us to cut through the wall to install the heater vent without severing our lath structure or disturbing any plaster.

▲ **Step 5.** We took similar measures to prep the interior. These plywood strips are plaster stops to which we'll attach ledgers for kitchen shelving. (On the exterior our small plywood blocks serve the same purpose.) Notice also how the window frame is creating a plaster stop on the interior of the wall as it did on the exterior. (For more on our interior plaster stops, see chapter 12.)

CONNECTIONS

We've already stated that we chose stick-framing for this wall mainly because it's so good at making connections. We'll connect two sinks and numerous shelves to both sides of this wall as well as a heater on the interior and a bench on the exterior. We'll also send a heater vent through the entire wall and bring water in and out through an access door in the wall's interior. I wouldn't want to try this density of attachments and punctures in any of our other wall systems.

Our stick-frame wall was also connection-friendly to the other adjacent wall systems. You'll remember that on the cob side, we had simply pushed the cob into the gaps between the interior lath, creating a interweaving of the two materials much like the keying we expect to achieve when plastering. The only other thing we did was add a few nails to help lock the stick-framing to the cob. The result was a strong connection that created no gaps after the cob had dried. On the straw bale side, the bales were squeezed tightly against the framing and a piece of metal lath was stretched between the bale wall and the west corner post. The result here was also a strong bond, and we've experienced no cracking plaster or other signs of movement.

Connection frenzy. The various blocks, strips, and trim pieces that we installed in preparation for plaster are a map of the places we'll be making connections on this wall's exterior. There's a similar maze of points on the interior. Connection friendly stick-framing allows us to use pretty much every square inch of both sides of this wall for some functional purpose.

Cob connection. You'll remember that we wrapped cob around our interior lath. Notice the nails installed in the locust post to give the cob a little more grip. For the same reason, we also added a few nails on the section of the lath that the cob covered.

Straw connection. The bales of our straw bale wall were pushed tight against the wooden lath at this corner. The small gap between the post and straw bales was filled with loose straw; then a piece of metal lath was attached to the post and to a wooden tie strip attached to the bales. This both covered the gap and created a strong connection between the two walls.

Cellulose vs. Fiberglass

Cellulose and fiberglass insulations are both products manufactured by industry to insulate stick-frame buildings. If you want a crash course in the dark world of modern marketing, follow the debate between representatives of these two competitors. Each side makes a convincing case for their product over the other. Of course, to do that they have to use only those sources that support their point of view. Government studies are conveniently ignored if they don't help the given case. Even supposedly hard numbers like laboratory-measured R-values vary quite a bit from one side to the other. I guess this could all be chalked up to an honest difference of opinion...or maybe someone's just lying. If we want to make an educated choice, we simply have to look at the available information ourselves. Here are some highlights from my personal research institute:

1) Embodied energy. Simply put, fiberglass is made from glass melted at very high temperatures and spun into thin fibers. My research indicates that it takes quite a bit more energy to produce an equivalent volume of fiberglass insulation compared to cellulose. At the same time, the claim made by cellulose representatives that it takes 40 to 500 times as much energy to make fiberglass appears to be based on comparing equal weights of the two materials, not equivalent insulating masses. That's a meaningless comparison.

2) Materials used. Though the borax added as a fire retardant does have to be mined, cellulose insulation is made mostly from recycled newspapers, so its manufacture reduces the already existing waste stream. In addition, cellulose installation methods create little waste on the building site. Both dense packing and damp-spray techniques involve blowing cellulose from a hopper through a tube into cavities. Any over-blow can be sucked back into the hopper to be used on another wall or on another job. We've already discussed how fiberglass tends to create waste in installation. In addition, though there are versions now available that don't, most fiberglass insulation is bound with formaldehyde glues that off-gas toxins after installation.

3) R-value. Weeding through the many different R-value claims listed for both materials, it seems that cellulose has a slightly higher per inch R-value rating than fiberglass batts. In addition, several studies, including one conducted by the United States Department of Energy, seem to document that fiberglass insulation looses R-value significantly as the temperature drops. In the DOE tests, for example, an exterior temperature only 25°F lower than the interior temperature resulted in almost a 10 percent drop in R-value. When the temperature differential increased to 88°F, the fiberglass R-value was reduced to less than half of its rated value. In the same test, the R-value of blown cellulose was unaffected as it got colder. For some reason, this study seems to be absent from fiberglass industry literature.

4) Fire resistance. The fiberglass industry claims that fiberglass isn't flammable and cellulose is. Well, first of all, cellulose is treated with borax and boric acid and has passed stringent fire-rating tests. In my own "scientific" study involving a blowtorch and a small sample of fiberglass and cellulose, I couldn't get either material to ignite. Interestingly, the fiberglass quickly

The same only different?
Cellulose and fiberglass insulations are both mass-produced products manufactured by large companies to serve exactly the same purpose. Is there a difference? *Left:* fiberglass comes as loose fill for attics or in batts of standard widths. *Right:* Here, loose cellulose has been blown through holes in thin fabric attached to a stick-frame wall.

gave way to the flame, melting like cotton candy. The cellulose on the other hand just became charred on the surface and kept its shape. In any case, this line of thought is only part of the story. Of course, the wood structure of a stick-frame is a considerable fire hazard, so the real question is how the building as a complete system reacts to a fire. Some studies seem to indicate that a stick-frame building with well-installed cellulose might outperform fiberglass in this regard. To my mind, this makes sense because cellulose is packed more tightly around wooden members, giving fire less access to air, which of course it needs in order to spread. Of course, the fiberglass industry hotly contests this claim. I just don't know on this one.

5) Real world performance. The above tests were done in a laboratory. The performance of fiberglass is even further diminished in real world installation. Fiberglass batts are presized and pushed into cavities. Any obstructions, such as water pipes or outlet boxes compress the batts, lowering their effective R-value. In addition, the batts don't flow into every little nook and cranny and don't necessarily rest tightly against all wood members. Cellulose, on the hand, is either stabilized with a bit of glue and blown damp into open wall cavities or pumped into

closed cavities by a process called "dense packing." Both of these approaches fill small irregular spaces more thoroughly. Though I have found studies cited that support it, the following claim is mostly based on my personal experience working with the two materials: Cellulose responds better to real world complications in installation.

6) Design flexibility. We've already criticized fiberglass as a modular material that forces structural studs to be placed in a rigid pattern. Blown or sprayed cellulose, on the other hand, conforms to the cavity, allowing wood to be placed where needed. This feature also permits cavities of any desired width to be built, allowing the creation of a variety of R-values. Cellulose, then, allows for considerable design flexibility.

I could go on. Obviously, I like cellulose better. However, the point I'm really making here is that it took a combination of skeptical research and personal experience to reach this opinion. If I had based my conclusions on written information alone, there's no telling what I'd believe. This lesson holds as true for cob construction as it does for rigid foam insulation. Without personal experience, reading will only give you enough information to be dangerous.

Installation. *Left:* Stabilized with a little glue and water, this cellulose was blown through a hose into the open cavities of this wall. A special roller was then used to trim the insulation flush with the plane of the walls. All the trimmings and over-blow were sucked back into the hopper by the same hose to be used again. *Right:* Modular fiberglass batts usually create waste that ends up headed for the dump. The only thing wrong with these cut-offs of brand new insulation is that they don't fit the standard-sized stud cavities.

INSTALLING INSULATION

Of all our wall systems, stick-framing is the only one in which insulation is a completely separate installation step. In conventional stick-framing, walls are usually insulated after the roof is on and the doors and windows are in place but before the interior drywall has been installed. Though fiberglass batts are still the main conventional choice, there are many other options. For example, recycled cotton insulation comes in rolls like fiberglass, but is much more pleasant to install, like a big, fluffy blanket. There are also a range of contractor installed sprays including polyicynene foam and aerated cementi-tious insulations. Cellulose insulation can also be installed by contractors. In one application, a damp mix of cellulose stabilized with a small amount of glue is sprayed into open wall cavities. The result is a soft but firm blanket that will stay in place until the interior wall surface is applied. In another technique, called *dense packing*, cellulose is installed in cavities already enclosed on both sides. Small access holes are cut in the wall and cellulose is blown under pressure into the cavities.

For our wall, we chose cellulose because it has a good R-value and can take on and give off water vapor as our design strategy requires. As outlined in the sidebar Cellulose vs. Fiberglass, we also feel it's a very decent mass-produced product. Finally, it's inexpensive and available at building supply stores right next to the fiberglass.

Cellulose is easy to install, but you need a bit of machinery: a blower and a long hose. We rented a blower from the store where we bought the insulation. If you buy enough, they'll usually let you use the machine for free. This set-up is designed to install loose cellulose into attics. In that application, you just blow insulation in as thick as you want to get the desired R-value. If you're worried that the insulation will settle over time, just blow in a bit more to make up for it. In a closed wall cavity, the amount of insulation installed is dependant on the amount of pressure the blower exerts. The attic blower isn't as powerful as the type used by contractors who do dense packing, so we weren't able to push in as much insulation as a contractor would have. As a result, I'm not sure what our finished R-value really is. In addition, our more loosely packed insulation may settle a bit over time. We'll be able to take off the trim pieces at the top of our wall to check in a year or two. If we've experienced any significant settling, we can just install more insulation.

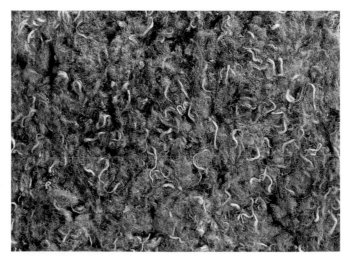

Fabric insulation.
Cotton insulation comes in cut rolls much like fiberglass and is made mostly of recycled fabric fiber. It's much firmer than fiberglass and doesn't compress as easily. It's also soft as a pillow—unlike the sharp little fibers of most fiberglass insulation.

▲ **Step 2.** We then covered these holes with removable blocks made from a piece of baseboard trim left over from a house project. Notice also that we added metal lath over plywood as a gripping surface for the plaster.

▲ **Step 1.** In order to create access to our wall's interior for our blown-in insulation, we left off the last couple of rows of lath and installed plywood with holes big enough for the insulation hose.

▲ **Step 3.** Before insulating, we had to close in our box by applying the first coat of plaster to both the inside and outside surfaces of our wall. The blocks covering the holes served as plaster stops and then were temporarily removed to blow in the insulation.

▲ **Step 4.** Cellulose insulation comes in bales packed in plastic bags. The equipment required for installation is simple, consisting of a blower and a long tube. The machine has a hopper on top that's equipped with paddles that push the insulation into the blower.

▲ **Step 6.** When little bits of insulation started puffing out around the rag and the blower's operating pitch got higher, we knew the cavity was full. This blower isn't powerful enough to create a dense pack, so our insulation may settle some over time. We'll be able to pull these blocks off after a year or so to see if the insulation has settled.

▲ **Step 5.** We removed our hole covers one at a time, inserted the tube, and blew in the insulation. As it turned out, we only needed to access one hole between each set of studs to fill the cavity with insulation. We used a rag to fill gaps around the hose and an outlet strip with an on/off button (sitting on top of ladder) to allow the operator to cut off the flow when the cavity was full. These measures really cut down on excess cellulose being blown into the air. Still, we were careful to wear masks.

▲ **Step 7.** We pulled off a couple of our interior shelf plaster-stop/nailers just to make sure we were filling all the voids. It looked good!

▲ **Step 8.** To fill the cavity below the window, we blew insulation into a hole we had drilled in the framing.

Planning ahead. If you're paying close attention, you'll have noticed that the hole for insulation in the rough opening framing meant that we actually hadn't installed a sill as part of our window frame. *Top left:* Instead, we'd installed pieces called extension jambs that brought the base of our rough opening flush with sides of the frame and acted as plaster stops. *Top right:* Then we troweled on some thinset mortar. *Left:* Finally, we installed a granite sill to cover the insulation hole. The sill was installed sloped slightly to the outside in case any rain reaches it. The outside edge of the sill extends beyond the jamb and has a drip edge cut into it.

Top plate cavity insulation. As mentioned earlier, we tried two methods for insulating the cavity above the top plate. We have already filled two cavities with rigid foam. We blew cellulose into the third through a hole drilled in the blocking. In this photo of the finished wall, that hole has been covered with a diamond block trim piece.

HOW LONG DID IT TAKE?

Creating the structure of our stick-frame wall was fast and relatively easy. A few cuts, a few nails, and we had the framework of our wall. Things slowed down a bit after that. Ripping and installing the lath took some time, as did plastering. However, plaster removes the need for a lot of trim that's necessary when you're using plywood and drywall. The insulation installation went quickly, but we did have to drive to town, rent the machine, and then return it. I'd say that, all told, we spent about the same amount of time to build, insulate, and cover our stick-frame as we did creating our straw bale wall. To review the time factor for our four walls, then, cordwood, the fastest, came in first; straw bale and stick-frame were neck in neck for second and third; and cob was definitely fourth.

Construction Blunders: New Materials = New Problems

This little building marks our first foray into insulated concrete work. As such, we are very happy with, even proud of, our stem walls. However, we're used to strong conventional concrete, so we designed our stick-frame wall to deliver point loads to our stem wall, just like in conventional construction. We didn't mention this before, but we'd already framed up this wall and had moved on to other tasks before Tim stepped back and realized that these point loads might cause problems. He quickly devised the cool wall truss described previously to alleviate the problem. The moral of this story is that it's really difficult to envision all the implications of a material or technique that you're using for the first time. In such situations, step back often and scrutinize what you're doing with fresh, critical eyes. If you make that a habit, you have every chance of catching mistakes before they fester into catastrophes.

Adjustable structure. With the interior lath installed, you can clearly see the wall truss we built after rethinking the structural loads on our stem wall. One advantage of wood framing is that you can step back, look at it, and beef up the structure as you see fit. That's much harder to do with other wall systems, especially monolithic load-bearing walls.

WHAT WE'VE ACCOMPLISHED

By keeping our minds open to all options, we were able to realize that the much maligned practice of stick-framing was actually a perfect fit for this wall. By freeing ourselves of conventions like plywood sheathing and fiberglass batts and by using a lot of salvage and recycled insulation, we were able to create a strong wall while using only a small amount of virgin materials. The result is a resource-sensitive wall crawling with shelves, vents, and pipes that would have been difficult to realize with the building's other wall systems. In other words, our wall is not simply a demonstration of how stick-framing can be improved, it's the right green building choice for this particular situation.

Working together. Far from being a simple demonstration project, each of our wall systems was chosen for specific reasons to support the building as whole. Even lowly stick-framing can proudly take its place, uniquely serving a purpose that would be difficult for the other materials to handle.

VARIATIONS

SIMPLE STRUCTURES

Most of the wall systems we're covering in this book only really make sense when used in houses—buildings that will house people. For example, is it worth the work to create thick, heavy cob walls to build a structure to store wood? Why would you go to the trouble of installing and protecting all of the delicate insulation inherent in straw bales for a tool shed? Do you really want to build a cordwood wall just to hold up a little porch roof? All of these systems usually only make sense if you need to create a different temperature inside than outside. There are a lot of building needs that don't require such a separation, and these are often most sensibly fulfilled with some kind of simple framing.

Stick-frame storage. Simple wood framing makes sense for open structures like this little firewood storage area.

Porch wall. Minimal materials create a wonderful outdoor room off of this old log cabin. The thin locust posts are acting as studs with a deck plank as the bottom plate and a rough-cut 2x4 as the top plate to create an open stick-framed wall for the porch.

Right for the job. This large barn is a sort of hybrid post-and-beam/stick-frame structure that was built to cure tobacco. A series of wooden poles extend to the ceiling in horizontal rows, allowing the entire structure to be filled with hanging tobacco. The wooden siding is set with gaps between each row similar to the lath in our wall. In this case, the gaps aren't to accommodate plaster but to allow wind free passage through the structure to dry the tobacco plants. Wood framing is the right choice for this job, especially since it was all cut from the farm on which the barn stands. Creating this huge open structure with any of the other methods covered in this book just wouldn't make sense.

Green Building for Chickens

This stick-frame chicken coop took only a few hours to build from start to finish. Let's see how it rates as a green building:

1) Low Construction Impact. No site work; built completely of salvaged materials.

2) Resource efficiency through the Life of the Building. Heated on occasion with a single light bulb; occupants hang out elsewhere if it gets too hot.

3) Long Lasting. Should provide many years of roosting pleasure, provided of course that the chickens take care of it.

4) Nontoxic. It may be full of chicken crap, but there's nothing toxic in this building. Big windows and the fact that chicken door is always open allow for ample air circulation.

5) Beautiful. This building was specifically crafted based on its site and the exact needs of its inhabitants. Though they had nothing to do with its construction, they moved in the second it was finished. They just *knew* it was for them. They use it every day and show no signs of wanting a bigger place or a better neighborhood. This building has become a part of their identity, and they'll stay here for life. For me, that's what green building is all about!

BAMBOO

Stick-framing is really a structural concept and isn't married to any single material. Commercial construction often replaces wood members with steel in the standard stick-framing layout. On the other end of the spectrum, bamboo is widely used in many parts of the world to create strong stick-frame structures. In Asia, bamboo is lashed together to make multi-story scaffolding for building projects and forms the walls, roofs, and floors of many buildings. There are over 1,000 species of the grass generically called bamboo. Some grow quickly and are very strong, durable, and flexible—all properties that make bamboo extremely useful in construction.

Versatile grass. Like wood, bamboo can be shaped for many purposes. Bamboo artisan Michel Spaan created this elegant arched bamboo awning.

Bamboo framing.
Left: Bamboo creates both the lightweight roof structure and plays a major role in the walls of this little building. *Right:* Of course, though the concepts are similar, bamboo construction is a world away from wood. For one thing, you can't use nails. Here, bamboo is lashed together with strong cord as part of a roof structure.

A split bamboo fence. Michel Spaan uses split bamboo lashed to a combination of living trees and log posts to create an elegantly curved fence (above). The outside (top left) and inside (bottom left) each have a distinctive look that adds to the beauty of this outdoor wall.

Tim's Take
Getting It Done: Stick-Framing

I don't need to say much about the real world issues of building with stick-framing. In much of the United States, at least, stick-framing *is* the real world. You can't throw a rock in most neighborhoods without hitting a stick-frame building. As such, there are hundreds of books outlining all aspects of the technique, many people (probably including your neighbor's teenagers) know how to do it, and the materials to make it are neatly organized at your local hardware store. You've got plenty of resources at your disposal, so I'll confine my comments to a few things that I don't see mentioned enough.

One thing that makes stick-framing easy to grasp is that it's a very graphic system. One of the best ways to learn about it is to closely examine examples under construction. Try to organize your own field trip by politely asking a builder if you can hang around at strategic moments while a building is going up. If you promise to stay out of the way and show up with donuts and coffee, chances are you'll be able to find a crew that will tolerate you.

The first thing you'll learn is that framing walls is easy and fast. Once you understand the basics of window/door openings and corners, you've basically got it. Roof framing is a different story because it incorporates a lot of angles and requires creating a symmetrical structure over open space, like a bridge. Most likely, you'll be using a stick-frame roof structure regardless of the wall systems you choose, so this part of the field trip applies to everybody. A good strategy for beginners is to keep the roof design basic and use pre-assembled trusses. Even these measures will backfire if you haven't carefully shaped the walls to create a symmetrical surface of even elevation.

This is where the apparent simplicity of stick-framing walls can actually be a problem. It's very easy to get way off as you happily slap your walls together. If your walls aren't plumb, level, and of consistent elevation, the roof will be difficult and time-consuming to frame, windows and doors will be a hassle to hang correctly, and the interior will be difficult to finish. To avoid these problems, don't get in a hurry. Use the old carpenter's motto "measure twice, cut once." Most of all, use geometry. Almost every aspect of stick-framing can be conceived of as a combination of triangles. If you look for those triangles and use geometry to determine lengths and angles, your measurements, diagnostics, and cuts will all go more quickly and be more accurate.

For example, I often see people using a 2-foot-long L-shaped ruler called a "framing square" to check if a wall, say 8 foot tall and 16 foot long, is square. This really only measures a tiny corner of a big assembly. Instead, you can use the Pythagorean theorem to check the complete wall, just as we did to lay out our building on the ground in chapter 6. (By the same token, a plumb bob measures the plumbness of the entire height of a wall, while a level can only really check the section on which it rests.)

One final advice tidbit: take photos of the framing layout before closing up your walls. This is especially true if you are using irregularly sized stud cavities like we did in our wall. You'll thank me later when you're trying to hang shelving or make other connections. If you ever need to demo a wall to open up the building for an addition, or if you just want to add a door or window, the whole process will be made that much easier if you know where your framing, plumbing, and electrical wiring are located. With that information, stick-framing would definitely be the easiest of our four walls to add onto and renovate. Can you imagine trying to cut out a large section of a cob or cordwood wall? Cutting into bales would be easier, but I can envision all kinds of complications. In comparison, stick-framing is tailor-made for renovation.

PART TWO: BUILDING

Separation

In order to survive, a house needs to be protected from a number of forces bent on its destruction. We've already made a good start in separating our building from these forces of decay by constructing a well-drained foundation, strong raised stem wall, well-made termite barrier, and large roof overhangs. In the next three chapters, we'll focus on completing this separation by covering our walls, roof, and floor with a protective skin. If we do a good job, this building should last a very long time. If we don't, it won't, so we're going to put careful thought into our materials and methods. Along the way, we'll round out our treatment of other housing elements, including major work toward creating a stable temperature by insulating the floor and roof.

Chapter 12 - **Covering the Walls**

Chapter 13 - **Covering the Roof**

Chapter 14 - **Covering the Floor**

Chapter 12
Covering the Walls

No matter how well built, no matter how thick and strong,

walls are vulnerable to the incessant meddling of the outside world. You need to do your best to protect them, but you don't want to go overboard, either. In chapter 3, I pointed out the modern tendency to take a good vs. evil approach to separating a building from the outside. In this approach, the forces of decay play the role of the devil, and separation is created by any means necessary. The result is a constant stream of supermaterials appearing on hardware store shelves. The fact that this paint may leach a toxic ingredient or that pesticide may do harm to more than termites is seen as a necessary concession to the greater good. Ironically, what this mindset has created is a strange overconfidence. It's now common to see modern housing without roof overhangs or even properly installed flashing, but covered in high-tech paints or wrapped in vinyl coverings.

GENERAL CONTEXT: COVERING THE WALLS

The alternative to this perspective is to try to redirect forces of decay rather than eliminate them. Large overhangs, solid stem walls, and good flashing are important parts of this strategy. Another component is a wall skin that serves not as a fortress but as a repairable sacrificial layer. For the entire life of the building, you don't want to ever have to replace or repair the material creating the volume of your walls. That's just too much work, and, besides, these materials are tied into the structure of the building. Damage to them is like damage to internal organs: difficult to treat, likely to spread, and possibly malignant. At the same time, you must realize that the forces of decay are omnipotent and *will* eventually win out. Your strategy, then, should be to give them something to damage that you can repair in a potentially never-ending cycle. The law of entropy is obeyed, yet your building lives on.

WORKING WITH THE WALL

When you stop and think about it, this sacrificial concept isn't unique to our alternative perspective—it's accepted that modern paints and sealers are only temporary coverings. Pigments and UV-protection additives are basically elements that are slowly eaten away by the sun's radiation. They sacrifice themselves so that the material beneath can survive. You replace them when necessary through periodic maintenance. However, even this inconvenience is only begrudgingly accepted. I'm sure that there are labs busily inventing materials that will put up a better and better fight until victory is ours. The alternative strategy, on the other hand, welcomes this cycle of decay and has no illusion of a victory over the sun.

Working together. In most buildings, many components work together to protect against the forces of decay. Here, the wall is covered with a plaster mix containing large stone aggregate, called pebble dash, the floor framing is covered with a piece of wooden trim, and the stem wall is faced with brick. All of these skins, in turn, are covered with a thin protective sacrificial layer commonly called paint.

Sacrificial layer vs. supermaterial. *Top:* This earth plaster doesn't try to defeat water. Its life cycle will be one of slow erosion and periodic renewal through reapplication. As long as someone cares about this building, it should survive with only occasional maintenance. *Bottom:* This vinyl is intended to defeat water. It's designed to keep water out with no consideration of the possibility that water might break its defenses. Its intended life cycle: last as long as possible and eventually, after fading and cracking, be replaced and sent to the dump.

The more delicate topic is water. The modern approach is only marginally sacrificial when it comes to water. Some paints and caulks may slowly be eaten away, but vinyl, for example, is for all practical purposes indifferent to water. Scientists can, then, imagine a coating that water cannot penetrate. *Imagine*, however, is the operative word, because in the real world, if there's a way in, water will find it. When water does get behind a "waterproof" membrane, it's often trapped there and, over time, causes damage. For this reason, sensible systems try to keep water out while at the same time allowing a means of escape for any water that does make it in. There are two basic approaches to this goal: creating multiple drainage planes and creating hygroscopic walls. (See chapters 3 and 10 for discussions of these concepts.)

The point here is that you need to understand the theory behind your wall skin's interaction with the forces of decay. This may sound too scientific, but remember that you're experimenting. Chances are good that your exact location doesn't have a long heritage of using the alternative techniques outlined in this book. Even worse, if you're using modern products, you're constantly experimenting with materials and approaches that haven't withstood the test of time. In either scenario, disastrous mistakes can be made. The only substitute for generations of indigenous trial and error is some kind of conscious theory.

Don't worry, it's usually not all that complicated. For example, if you plan to let some form of cellulose in your walls act hygroscopically, don't cover your building skin with a waterproof paint or sealer. Here's another "complicated" theory: Avoid the issue of water infiltration by using large overhangs to keep water off your walls in the first place. These concepts may seem obvious, but look around you at how seldom such basic measures are utilized in modern buildings to see how easily they are ignored. Ultimately, your goal is simple: to create a skin that works with the wall material at hand.

Finally, it's important to realize that skins often aren't just for protection—they can also play an important role in completing a wall's heat-flow strategy. Straw bales, for example, are used for their great insulation value, but an unplastered straw bale wall is a sieve for air and therefore has only a fraction of its potential insulation value. It takes a skin of several coats of plaster to seal a straw bale wall from air infiltration and allow it to become an effective resistor to heat flow.

TYPES OF SKINS

In chapter 2, we introduced the idea of integrated and applied skins. Stone and concrete are examples of materials whose integrated surface is a durable exterior skin. We identified applied skins as coming in two flavors: lapped and seamless. Skins made up of units, such as milled lumber siding or slate shingles, need to be lapped in order to create a homogenous surface that will repel water. The advantage of this technique is that the individual units can move a bit, swell and shrink without cracking and, thus, without allowing water to enter. A lapped skin is a drainage plane and can be used in combination with a second drainage plane such as lapped tarpaper installed behind cedar shakes. Lapped wall skins have a long history and include such wide-ranging examples as palm leaves and vinyl siding.

Another approach is to avoid all of those lapped surfaces by creating a seamless coating (called plaster or stucco) that covers the entire wall. Though they don't have pesky seams, a disadvantage of these coatings is that they *can* crack, creating an open avenue for water. For that reason, stuccos and plasters are often applied in multiple coats. If cracking does occur, it's generally in a single coat, so the crack doesn't penetrate all the way to the interior wall surface.

Laps and seams. *Left:* These lapped cedar shakes have the advantage of being able to expand and contract without cracking, but their installation creates numerous seams which, over the years, may become more and more vulnerable to water infiltration. *Right:* This plaster only has seams where it intersects projections, such as this window. However, its limited ability to move in response to changes in temperature and humidity may cause it to crack and slowly let water into the wall's interior.

Plaster

In general, plaster can be defined as a seamless coating that's applied wet and dries to a hard, consistent surface. In building, countless different mixes can produce a plaster. Common ingredients in our context are clay, sand, lime, Portland cement, and water. However, many others exist, including wheat paste, blood, urine, cactus juice, vegetable oil, and on and on. Some traditional plasters are simply animal dung. Popularly these days though, plasters are placed into three basic categories: earth, lime, and cement.

"Plaster" or "Stucco"?

I look at all plaster mixes as parts of a spectrum. They're all seamless, applied wet, and dry to a hard coating. Once installed, they all have some level of strength, flexibility, durability, and water absorbency, and it's in comparing these traits that mixes are tweaked and particular materials are chosen for a given situation. Be that as it may, two names are commonly used to describe these mixes: *plaster* and *stucco*. What's the difference? As far as I can tell, in common usage stucco is a mix that contains Portland cement, and plaster is everything else. Perhaps this is because Portland cement is unique as a *hydraulic mortar*, which means that it hardens chemically, even when under water. But to my mind, Portland is just one of many materials sometimes added to plaster mixes in different proportions and in different combinations. In this book, then, I just call everything plaster.

Earth plaster. While not especially durable, earth plasters have a low embodied energy, are repaired easily, and are extremely attractive.

Lime plaster. Although they have a high embodied energy, lime plasters are more durable than earth plasters and more hygroscopic than concrete-based plasters.

Concrete plaster. Fun tile designs have been set into the plaster containing Portland cement that covers this stick-frame building.

Earth Plaster

Plasters created from local clay soils might be the most common mixes historically. If monolithic mud buildings are plastered at all in dry climates, they are usually covered with an earth plaster mix. This is the ultimate example of a sacrificial skin: the surface is covered with a thin coating of essentially the same material as makes up the wall. Sun, rain, and abrasion will slowly eat this layer away, but more can be easily added. The end result is that the wall proper remains unchanged. Most of the interesting additives listed above (blood, urine, etc.) are used in earth mixes to create a desired characteristic: more water resistance, more flexibility, or what have you.

Earth plasters aren't particularly strong or durable in the face of rain or constant abrasion, which means they shed dirt readily through regular wear. They are, however, very hygroscopic and quite flexible, which makes them easily repairable. In addition, they're usually made from locally available materials, have a low embodied energy, and are beautiful.

Lime Plaster

In chapter 9, we described the interesting phenomenon called "lime." Basically, it's a mineral that can be changed through a chemical process into a malleable form that then slowly hardens back to its original form. Because of this, plaster mixes containing lime will slowly harden into a big smeared-in-place rock. This technique, used for thousands of years, is still the plaster approach of choice in many parts of the world.

In general, lime plasters are both stronger and more durable than earth plasters. Though they're fairly flexible and hygroscopic, they're less so than earth plasters. Lime also is a high embodied energy material, requiring temperatures higher than those needed to produce Portland cement. Lime plasters are popular in alternative construction as a middle ground between earth and concrete-based plasters because they're durable and don't abrade like earth plasters but are more hygroscopic than cement plasters.

It's hard to say just what constitutes "lime plaster" since a range of lime products may be used to create plaster. In the U.S., for example, only pre-slaked powdered lime is available. Some traditionalists consider this material vastly inferior to traditional lime putty; however, other plaster aficionados claim there's little difference between plasters made with traditional or pre-slaked lime.

Cement Plaster

All plaster mixes contain some kind of cement, the ingredient that binds everything together. When people refer to "concrete" or "cement stucco," they're usually talking about a mix that contains Portland cement, which is made up of lime and other naturally occurring minerals. As I've said, Portland cement is a hydraulic mortar, which means that it can harden under water.

Portland cement is mixed in various proportions with other materials, including lime and sand, to create plasters that are generally stronger and more durable than lime plasters. However, the addition of Portland cement tends to make a mix less flexible and less hygroscopic.

Portland cement plaster mixes have gotten a bad name in part because they've been used to replace lime plaster mixes on mud walls in historic buildings with horrible results. Apparently the mixes used didn't allow the cob or adobe beneath to release accumulated moisture quickly enough, and, in some buildings, deterioration and even collapse have been the result. This tragic misuse of concrete in plaster seems to have snowballed into a general trashing of the material as water trapping and sinfully high in embodied energy. It's true that Portland cement has a lot of embodied energy, but it probably has less than lime. In addition, it's simply not true that Portland cement will completely prevent a plaster from absorbing water, a statement that can be easily tested by hosing down most any unsealed, unpainted plaster mix containing this ingredient. Portland cement is just what it is, another of many possible additives in the continuum of mixes loosely called plaster.

Applying Plaster

Regardless of the materials used, plaster is applied wet. In commercial construction, it's often sprayed into place with a gas-powered pump. In our context, plaster is spread on by hand using a hawk and a trowel, though earth plasters are often applied directly with the hands. A *hawk* is a flat, hand-held surface used to bring the plaster close to the wall. *Trowel* is a general term referring, in this context, to any flat, smooth tool used to spread plaster onto a wall.

Plaster is usually applied in multiple coats to deal with one of its potential weaknesses: cracking while curing. The thicker the application of plaster, the more likely it is to crack while curing. Therefore, several coats of thin plaster will crack less than one thick coat. In addition, if a coat of plaster does have cracks, multiple coats will guarantee that those cracks won't go through the entire plaster skin. A common approach to plastering is to use three coats. The first coat is designed to completely cover the desired surface and create a good substrate for the second coat. To increase adhesion between coats, the first coat is often roughed up, or "scratched," and is hence often called the "scratch coat." The second coat, called the "brown coat" in conventional plastering, covers cracks in the first coat and fine-tunes the surface, smoothing out rough spots if so desired. The final, or "finish coat," is the thinnest and, therefore, least likely to crack. It creates the desired final look and covers any cracks in the second coat.

FINISHING THE SKIN: TRIM

Covering walls requires more than simply designing and applying a durable coating. We pointed out in chapter 2 that the weakest structural areas of a building are often those places where different materials are connected together. Well, the same axiom applies when dealing with the forces of decay. The places where materials join are the most vulnerable and require special attention. In the building vernacular, the materials and techniques deployed to protect these vulnerable joints are generically called trim. The function of trim is to cover gaps and joints in the building that might let water, air, insects, or animals into places where they aren't welcome such as the interior of walls. Aesthetically, trim can play a large role in the overall feel of your finished building.

Exterior trim. The function of exterior trim is the same in most situations: keep water, air, insects, and animals from gaining entry. Here, naturally water- and insect-resistant cedar has been used to cover the joints created by an exterior door.

Interior trim. Interior trim also closes gaps against water, air, and insects, but since it tends to have less of those elements to deal with, its focus is often aesthetic. *Top:* This baseboard trim covers the seam between the drywall and the flooring, but it also adds shape and color. *Bottom:* Trim can be very expressive. Here, the top of a window is animated by the addition of a few small pieces of wood.

COVERING THE WALLS APPLIED: OUR LITTLE BUILDING

DESIGNING A SKIN

This book's core theme is that by taking responsibility for your own shelter and designing for the exact specifics of your situation, you can overcome many of the problems inherent in modern, mass-produced construction. Nowhere was this concept clearer than in our freedom to customize the wall skins of our building. We had four very different wall infills, each physically separated from the other on the outside by a locust post. Each wall, then, was a panel that could be treated, on the exterior surface at least, as a separate entity.

Since we'd already decided earlier in our design process that the cob, straw bale, and stick-frame walls would be plastered and the cordwood wall would be left alone, the only question remaining was what materials and mixes we'd use to make our plasters. As we've said, the wonderful thing about plasters is that they're adjustable, so we got our basic raw materials together, did some tests, and then approached each wall separately, determining our exact mixes as we went along.

PREPARATIONS FOR PLASTER

The basic ingredients we planned to work with were straw, sand, clay, lime, and perhaps Portland cement if we felt the need for a boost in strength and a quicker curing time. We already had all of those materials on site from other cogs in our construction wheel; however, some of them needed to be prepared for use in plaster.

Clay

We used the same clay in our plaster that we used in our cob. However, this time we had to process it more carefully because we didn't want any stones at all in this clay. Also, since we were going to apply thin layers of plaster, we really needed the clay to do its job as a binder. For those reasons, we took extra care to break the clay down as finely as possible.

Preparing the Clay

▲ **Step 1.** To create plaster-quality clay, we first built a box covered with ¼-inch mesh and set it on top of our clay-soaking barrel.

▲ **Step 2.** Next, we ground the clay with a brick or piece of wood. (We discovered that wood doesn't tear up the mesh as fast as a brick does.)

▲ **Step 3.** The undesirable rocks were left behind...

▲ **Step 4.** ...and the fine clay was deposited in the barrel.

▲ **Step 5.** Finally, we added water to the clay and whipped them together with that trusty paddle mixer attached to an electric drill that we'd used extensively in mixing cob. We wanted our clay wet enough to be easily scooped into and poured out of buckets, but not so wet that it forced our final plaster mix to be soupy. As I've repeated numerous times throughout this book: Remember that you can always add more water when needed, but you can't take it out once you've added it. Add water slowly! Once you've experimented a bit, you'll get the feel for the right consistency.

Lime

A quick review of the lime cycle: Lime (calcium carbonate) is burned to form quick lime (calcium oxide), which, when soaked in water, slowly becomes calcium hydroxide. It's the calcium hydroxide that reacts with CO^2 in the air to become calcium carbonate again, i.e., nice hard lime. So, the more calcium hydroxide, the better our plaster is going to be. That's why lime putties are left to sit as long as possible, sometimes years, before being used.

We, however, used the same autoclaved hydrated mason's lime for our plaster as we used in our cordwood mortar. On the bag, the sole ingredient is listed as calcium magnesium hydroxide, which is claiming that all of the calcium oxide is now calcium hydroxide, which could mean that longer soaking periods wouldn't produce a better plaster. I've never soaked a bag of lime for a year to find out. We made sure that our lime soaked for at least three days, and our first barrel was soaking for several weeks before we used it in a plaster. All of our mixes using this lime worked very well.

To make lime putty, we filled a 55-gallon drum with water and slowly poured in about six 50-pound bags of lime. (See photos on page 448.) Lime is very fine and tends to clump up as it hits the water. We tried to remedy this by covering the soaking barrel with a fly screen and then pouring the lime through that. But the lime is so light that it easily blows in the wind, and the screen only encouraged this. We found it worked better if we poured the lime directly into the barrel and then dispersed the clumps with the paddle mixer before adding sand. (Whatever your technique, always use a mask and goggles when working with dry lime.)

Preparing the Lime

Preparing lime: soaking. *Left:* To prevent the lime from clumping, we tried pouring it through a fly screen, but that turned out to be a hassle. An alternative method, which worked well for us, was to forgo the fly screen and simply break up any clumps with a few spins of the paddle mixer before adding sand. *Right:* Since air starts lime's setting process, we covered our soaking lime with a thin layer of water and sealed our barrel tight.

Sand

As we stated earlier in discussing mud mixes such as concrete and cob, the more varied the aggregate size, the stronger the mix. The same holds for plaster; however, though plaster does need a degree of structural strength, it also needs to be smooth and fluid. We adjusted these variables by controlling the sizes of the sand particles in our mix. For a strong first coat we wanted a wide variety of sand sizes in addition to some chopped straw, while the fine finish plaster contained only very fine sand and no straw.

Preparing the Sand

Preparing sand: sifting. *Left:* To adjust the size range of sand grains going into our plaster, we built a box we could cover with different sizes of metal mesh. We built this box so that it could fit over a 55-gallon drum and just inside the rim of a wheelbarrow. *Right:* Even for rough first plaster coats, it's nice to have sand particles no larger than 1/8 inch. It's difficult to find 1/8-inch mesh, though, so we used two overlapping pieces of 1/4-inch metal screen, often called "hardware cloth," to approximate a 1/8-inch mesh for sifting sand. When we wanted to limit the aggregate size even more for fine finish coats, we placed a piece of metal fly screen over the mesh.

Straw

The function of straw in a plaster mix is to provide tensile strength and to create integrated *control joints* in the mix. A control joint, also called an *expansion joint*, is a break in a plaster coat that prevents a crack from spreading. The straw fibers in a plaster mix act like hundreds of tiny control joints that localize the effects of shrinkage and expansion in the mix. Our goal, then, when adding straw to our plaster mixes, was to strengthen the mix without hindering its ability to be applied smoothly and fluidly. For that reason, we needed to shred our straw before using it in the plaster.

Control joints. *Left:* The lines in this plastered wall are called control or expansion joints and are actually little double plaster stops with a space in between. They divide the wall into sections and create small spaces that allow each section to expand and move independently of the others. If a crack does start somewhere, it won't spread across the expansion joint. *Right:* The chopped straw in this earth plaster is acting like thousands of little control joints.

Preparing the Straw

▲ **Step 1.** Our friends Chuck Marsh and Mollie Curry turned us onto the neat trick of using an inexpensive mulching leaf blower as a suburban straw-chopper! On the mulch setting, our chopper sucked up straw and chopped it…

▲ **Step 2.** …then blew the bits into the attached canvas bag. For some uses, just one trip through the chopper would be enough.

▲ **Step 3.** For our plaster mix, we chopped the straw two or three times to get this finished product.

Plaster Tests

Our little building offered a smorgasbord of surfaces and situations for plaster, so after gathering and prepping all of our materials, we conducted some tests reflecting the scope of our needs.

 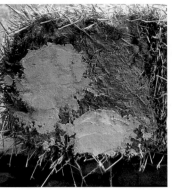 

Plaster tests. *Left:* We did a number of plaster tests. Here, we used metal plaster lath on a board and tested mixes using different proportions of ingredients. *Middle:* It's also important to test mixes on the surface where they'll be used. Here, we tested two different earth plasters on the same side of a bale, and then we tested two lime mixes on top of the earth plaster. *Right:* This is a test of a lime mix directly on straw. You can see that it didn't work too well. We also did small test patches on all of the actual walls.

Water Vapor and Plaster

Water vapor moves into a wall in various ways. Of course, it can move through holes and cracks, which is why we need to carefully apply flashing to breaks in our plaster. Water vapor, or any gas really, can also move into a wall due to differences in vapor pressure between one side of the wall and the other. Wind is one mechanism that can create this difference; another is temperature variance. As we've said, air seeks equilibrium. If, for example, the air is warmer inside a building than outside, the molecules in the warmer, inside air will be moving faster than those in the cooler, outside air and, therefore, will push on the interior surface of the wall in the direction of the lower pressure zone outside. If this warm air hits a surface that will bring it down to the dew point, condensation will result. (See chapter 2, Water and Air: The Issue of Condensation.) This fact forces us to choose one of the following strategies.

1) Block the movement of water vapor into the wall.
This strategy uses a water vapor barrier, such as plastic sheathing, installed in the path of the most vapor, in other words, the side of the wall that is warmest most of the time: inside in cold climates, outside in warm climates. This is the common modern construction strategy.

2) Encourage water vapor entering the wall to move through the entire wall volume to exit on the opposite side. This strategy applies skins that have different vapor permeability rates to each side of the wall. The less-permeable skin is placed on the "cold" side of the wall so vapor that's pushed through by higher pressure on the warm side can theoretically move right through the wall and exit through the more permeable skin on the other side.

3) Assume that the pressure differences will balance out, so that water vapor that enters on one side of the wall due to a pressure difference will eventually be allowed to leave the wall the same way it came in because of a reversal in this pressure difference. This strategy utilizes skins of roughly the same vapor permeability on the inside and outside. It assumes that vapor will enter a wall, penetrate only so far, and then dry back out in time. An equilibrium is created that will never produce enough interior wall moisture to encourage the growth of mold or create structural damage.

PLASTERING THE STRAW BALE WALL

Our straw bale wall was definitely our biggest plastering challenge and also the wall we knew we needed to protect first. As we've already pointed out, our straw is vulnerable in this perpetually shady, somewhat exposed north wall. One approach would have been to cover the bales with a drainage plane and cover that with a less-permeable skin, such as wood siding. However, intuitively that didn't seem right. The rough surface of straw would be difficult to fit with a drainage plane, and we didn't like the idea of water condensing behind siding in front of bales even with a drainage plane in between. It just sounded moldy. So, we went with the more common approach that treats straw as a material that needs to be able to take on and let off water vapor. In any case, this particular situation cried out to us that we needed to be sure to create a plaster that would allow water vapor to move freely without allowing liquid water in.

There is no clearer example in this book of where our lack of an indigenous building system required that we take a theoretical stance. In the case of straw bales, the third option from our sidebar Water Vapor and Plaster seemed to make the most sense. First off, there is no "warm" or "cool" side of a wall—both sides will, at some point, experience a higher vapor pressure. Second, I have trouble believing that water vapor would enter a straw bale wall on the inside, move through the entire 18 inches of volume, and then continue on out through the exterior plaster, as is the theory in the second option. Finally, the second option would require a more permeable plaster on the outside than on the inside. Outside is where the rain and snow is, so it doesn't make sense to me to create a skin that will be more vulnerable to these very real outside threats. After thinking all of this through, we decided on basically identical skins on the inside and outside of this wall.

Before starting to plaster, we carefully checked that all flashing and plaster stops were in place.

Earth Plaster on Straw

We chose to use an earth plaster for the first coat on our straw bale walls for several reasons. First, as our tests clearly showed, our lime plaster mixes don't key into straw particularly well. Second, studies have shown that for any given relative humidity, clay will always have a lower water content than straw. This means that clay will always wick moisture out of the straw it's coating, therefore helping to keep the straw drier. Third, earth plasters are cheaper and workable by hand, which makes them great for stuffing holes and irregular shapes in straw bale walls.

As we've said, one of the advantages of plastering is that the mixes are adjustable to the situation. Our single straw bale wall had a lot of different surfaces: the cut side of the bales on the exterior, the folded side on the interior, deep pockets between bales, metal lath over felt paper, and metal lath over building wrap. It was a simple matter to adjust our mixes to work with the different surfaces. If a mix wasn't adhering well in one place, we just applied it somewhere else and tried a different mix on the trouble spot. In some situations, we applied an earth plaster with our hands, in others with a hawk and trowel. Since our shaded earth plaster coats dried slowly, we plastered both sides of our straw bale wall and then moved on to other things while they dried.

▲ **Step 1.** Though we adjusted it for various situations, our basic earth plaster mix for the exterior straw wall was 1:1 (sand/clay) with as much chopped straw as we could comfortably add. First, we mixed the ground, soaked clay and plain unsifted sand with our paddle mixer.

▲ **Step 2.** We put the clay/sand mix in a wheel-barrow and then added dry straw.

◄ **Step 3.** We started off mixing with a hoe, but found our hands were the best tool for really getting the straw spread evenly throughout the mix.

◄ **Step 4.** This was a nice mix for a cob wall or a fairly smooth straw bale wall. It had a lot of straw and therefore resisted cracking while having a lot of strength. The bumpy surface of the interior of our straw bale wall called for a wetter, stickier mix.

Applying Earth Plaster to the Straw Bale Exterior

▲ **Step 1.** To really tie the earth plaster into the straw bales, we smeared some on with our hands (left) and worked it in with our fingers (right)...

▲ **Step 2.** ...and then smeared on some more.

Ouch. You may want to use gloves when applying plaster to metal mesh—we didn't and we paid for it with lot of little cuts on our hands.

▲ **Step 3.** As we moved up the wall, we set up some simple sawhorse scaffolding.

▲ **Step 4.** We were careful to push plaster tight into the joints around our window and over the flashing.

◀ **Step 5.** We needed to let the mix dry completely before applying the next plaster coat. *Left:* Here's the finished coat a few days after application. You can see that our mix was drying slowly. *Right:* Here's our wall after about a week. It seems dry and ready for the next plaster coat.

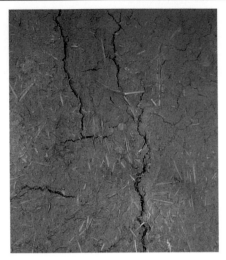

▲ **Step 1.** Wherever metal lath covered the straw on the interior, we used a mix with straw, much like the exterior mix.

▲ **Step 2.** However, on the rest of the interior, we used a clay-rich mix, usually without straw, because it was much harder to get the plaster to adhere to the folded side of the bales. We pushed it into any deep pockets by hand, but troweled on most of the rest.

▲ **Step 3.** The uneven wall caused us to lay it on thick in some places. This fact, as well as the shady interior, caused the coat to take a couple of weeks to dry. We got some big cracks, especially where the mix was thick. This was expected and no problem. This mix did its job of creating a good substrate for the second coat.

Prepping for the second coat. We wanted the best seal we could get at all plaster stops because imperfections in our plaster here could let water in. For that reason, it was important to cut away any excess earth plaster at these stops to allow the next coat complete access to the joint (left). We also ran over the wall lightly with a stiff brush to knock off any loose pieces of plaster (right).

Lime Plaster on Straw

Our tests showed us that the earth/lime plaster mixes were quite a bit more water permeable than the lime/sand mixes. We tested both over earth plaster on straw with good results, so we decided to go with the sand/lime/straw mix for our second coat to guarantee that more liquid water would move unimpeded down the plaster drainage plane, i.e., wouldn't be absorbed.

Our first step was to clean up the earth plaster to prepare it to accept the next plaster coat. We then mixed a 3:1:½ (sand/lime/straw) plaster batch (using sand that had been screened through a ⅛-inch mesh) and applied it to the wall with a hawk and trowel. It's important that lime plasters cure slowly to prevent cracking. We knew the fact that this wall is shaded and faces north would help prolong cure time, but to be safe, we added pre-soaked straw to our mix and then hosed down each coat of plaster with water for the first couple of days after application.

Lime tests. We tested both lime/sand (on the left) and earth/lime/sand (on the right) plaster mixes over the earth plaster. Both did well, but we went with the lime/sand because it proved less permeable to liquid water.

Mixing Lime Plaster

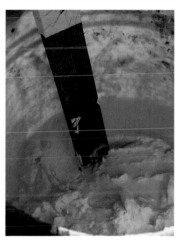

◄ **Step 1.** We wanted to make sure that our mixes had the same proportions of materials as our tests. Our unit of measure was "X number of 5-gallon buckets." *Left:* These sticks allowed us to accurately measure partial buckets. *Right:* Believe me, a 5-gallon bucket is deceptive because it's larger at the top than the bottom, so this measuring technique is worth the trouble.

▲ **Step 2.** We used the handy paddle mixer again to mix the 3:1:½ (sand/lime/straw) plaster batch. We soaked our straw in lime water before adding it to the mix to help slow the drying time of our mix, and in turn, diminish cracking.

▲ **Step 3.** This is a good finished mix. It's wet enough to spread easily with the trowel, but firm enough to stick to the wall.

▲ **Step 1.** First, we painted on some lime water to wet the wall and help create a bond between the two coats.

▲ **Step 2.** Using a conventional hawk and trowel, we applied a thin coat, probably an average of ¼-inch thick, though we definitely went thicker where we wanted to fill contours.

▲ **Step 3.** We started plastering at the bottom, but you can also go from the top down. Try both approaches because each has advantages.

▲ **Step 4.** Here, the finished first coat is drying. At the right moment in the curing process, we worked the entire surface with a sponge to create a rough surface for the next (finish) coat to grab. When is the plaster ready to be sponged? You really just have to get a feel for it. Try it often on a little test area. If you're actually moving plaster instead of just roughing up the surface, it's too wet. If it gets a bit too dry, don't be afraid to put some pressure against the plaster with the sponge. We were able to apply the second coat after about five days.

The finish coat. This is the finished second coat of lime plaster. It made it through a very cold winter with absolutely no cracks.

We retrowled the lime plaster coat after it had set a bit to really compress it. We had to hit the wall at just the right point in the cure to accomplish this. Common wisdom says to retrowel when the plaster is still soft enough so you can press your fingernail into it, but hard enough so you can't dent it with your knuckle. How long this will take depends on a number of variables, such as the amount of sun hitting the wall and, most importantly, the specific plaster mix. It could vary from an hour or two to several days or even longer with some lime mixes. Our mixes still did fine in the spots where we couldn't manage a retrowling.

It's common practice to use straw in the base coat only and to increase proportions of lime to sand in successive coats. On our exterior wall, however, the section next to the northeast corner post had been infilled with loose straw to fill a gap between cordwood and straw bales. As a result, this section was somewhat spongy even after our first coat of lime plaster had cured. This caused a few cracks, and we were concerned that this would be a weak spot in the wall. As a result, we applied another coat of sand/lime/straw mix to this area as a kind of structural patch. This really solidified the spongy spots. We decided to use the same mix with course sand aggregate and straw in our final coat to further strengthen the entire wall. We wonder if the straw in this mix will suffer in exposure to rain and shade. If so, we can always add another coat of plaster without straw at a later date. For the time being though, this mix seems to have really stiffened up that area and we have no cracks anywhere on the wall.

Since our interior wall surface undulated quite a bit, we used slightly different techniques on the first interior lime plaster coat. We had filled in some of the huge contours with the earth plaster coat, but the wall was still more uneven than we wanted. We decided to add more sand to the first lime mix, so that we could apply it unevenly—thicker in some spots than others—without it cracking. Our 4:1:½ mix worked wonderfully, and absolutely no cracks appeared even though we probably had areas that were 1½-inches thick.

Finished interior plaster. The light color of the lime plaster really brightens up the inside of our building.

We learned a lesson while applying our final coat of lime plaster—a 3:1 (sand/straw) mix—on the interior. It had rained torrentially the day before, and although we'd covered our sand with a tarp, it was totally soaked. Wet sand and wet lime putty make a very wet mix. Even without adding any water, the mix was soup. We tried adding dry lime, but it didn't help. We ended up having to let the mix dry overnight before applying it. Even then, we had to use some sand that we'd baked overnight in a friend's pottery kiln to make the mix dry enough to use. Moral: Keep your sand dry.

PLASTERING THE COB WALL

Compared to the straw bale wall, designing a plaster system for our cob wall was a snap. We knew that cob is really incredibly durable, as evidenced by a clump of it we'd left out in the weather for many months (see photo on page 274). And we also knew that clay wicks moisture away from straw, so we felt confident that the straw in our cob wall was snug and secure. With our generous roof overhang and the cob wall's sunny southern exposure, we probably could have gotten away without any plaster. On the other hand, you could knock clay and sand off the surface of the wall just by running your hand down it, so it would be messy, especially on the inside, to leave our cob unplastered. In addition, further protection from rain would definitely prolong the life of our wall and make maintenance easier, so we decided to plaster it.

Earth Plaster on Cob

Our first step was to clean up the wall and prep it for plaster. This entailed smoothing rough spots, cleaning up around the bottle designs, trimming the edges near the posts, completing the final shaping of the window opening, and cutting off any long, protruding pieces of straw.

Next, to increase our bond to all the contours, we mixed a clay-rich $1:1\frac{1}{2}$ (sand/clay) batch of plaster, added lots of chopped straw, and applied it to the wall. This mix dried crack-free in just a couple of days in good sunshine. We applied a batch of the same mix to the inside of the wall, but this time we put the sand through a $\frac{1}{8}$-inch screen to make it easier to navigate the contours.

Our earth plaster coat on the cob wall was incredibly beautiful. Still, our mix, though crack free and well bonded to the wall, gave up clay and sand easily in the face of light abrasion. Since this is a guest cottage, we'll tend to focus on it less than our own house, which means that available maintenance time for the cottage will be somewhat limited. Mostly for that reason, we decided to apply a more protective,

Prepping the Cob Wall for Plaster

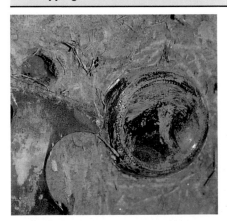   

▲ **Step 1.** We knocked and scraped all excess cob from the bottle designs.

▲ **Step 2.** Then we used a brick to create a smooth transition to all plaster stops.

▲ **Step 3.** We also ran the brick over the entire cob surface to knock off loose material.

▲ **Step 4.** Finally, we used a wire brush wheel on a cordless drill to fine-tune the shape of our window arch and create a bit of space for plaster.

longer lasting coating of lime plaster. One down side to this decision is that the deep red of the earth plaster is perfect for absorbing solar heat in the winter and would be the right choice for our strategy of using mass to enhance the R-value of our cob wall. We feel fine about this decision, though, because we can always use a colored lime wash or some other permeable pigment to coax the wall into absorbing more solar heat at some later date. On the other hand, the light color will help the building stay cooler in the summer.

Earth Plaster on the Exterior Cob Wall

▲ **Step 1.** We wanted a very sticky mix, so we added more clay than we did for our exterior straw bale plaster.

▲ **Step 2.** Perfect! Our plaster sticks like glue to an upturned trowel.

▲ **Step 3.** Spreading earth plaster on cob is a sensual experience. Just grab some and smear it on with the palm of your hand.

▲ **Step 4.** Let dry. Though it's not a good idea with lime plasters, our earth plasters weren't affected adversely by drying in the sun. It took this earth plaster coat just a couple of days to dry, and we had absolutely no cracking.

Done. The earth-plastered cob wall, ready for the next coat

Earth plaster on the interior cob wall.
We used the same mix and technique to apply earth plaster to the interior of the wall. *Left:* We used the surface of each adjoining wall as our plaster stop. *Right:* Our finished interior earth plaster coat. Again, it was so beautiful that we were tempted to leave it as the finished surface. However, especially inside, this plaster is just too easily knocked off. It would be a real mess. In addition, the white lime plaster will really help to lighten up the interior.

Lime Plaster on Cob

We intended to use an earth/lime plaster for the protective coat, but once we made a full batch of a 6:1:1:1 (sand/clay/lime/straw) mix and started applying it over the earth plaster, we didn't like the way it was going on. It was clear that we'd have trouble navigating all the shapes and contours of this organic wall with this particular mix. We quickly shifted gears and applied this mix to the interior of our stick frame wall instead. For the cob wall, we then tried a 3:1:½ (sand/lime/straw) mix over the earth plaster. This was much more plastic, conforming and bonding to the contours of the wall very nicely.

For the finish coat, we tested a 2:1 (sand/clay) mix with the sand sifted through a fly screen, but it set up very quickly and cracked badly. We adjusted to a 3:1 mix with the same fly-screen-sifted sand. It went on smoothly and sponged out nicely. (Pushing the sand through a fly screen is a big pain, by the way; I'm not sure it was worth it, since we went with a slightly textured, sponged finish anyway.) On the inside we applied a single coat of 3:1 (sand/lime) mix with mostly fly screen–sifted sand. This covered the flaky earth plaster and brightened the building's interior considerably.

Lime Plaster on Cob

▲ **Step 1.** First, we gave the wall a quick brushing to knock off loose material.

◀ **Step 2.** Next, we brushed on lime water to increase the bond.

◀ **Step 3.** Then we troweled on the lime mix.

▲ **Step 4.** Lime plaster must cure slowly to prevent cracking. The soaked straw in our mix helped with this, but we were also careful to protect the wall from the sun for a couple of days and to hose down the wall often during this period to keep it wet.

▲ **Step 5.** When the plaster was stiff but not hard, we used a sponge to create a rough surface for the next (final) coat to cling to. When we could push a fingernail but not a knuckle into the plaster, we knew it was time to sponge.

Rub out cracks. You can also use a sponge to close cracks. As soon as you see a crack, just rub the sponge over it and work the area smooth. Keep an eye on the wall because after a certain point in the cure, this technique is no longer effective.

Almost done. Our first lime coat was now ready for the finish coat.

The finished cob wall. We used the same basic technique to apply the finish coats to both sides of the cob wall, being careful to make any final fine-tuning adjustments to the sculptural shapes. *Left:* After a couple of months, the exterior finish coat had no cracks. As of this writing, like all of our finish coats, it still has none. *Middle:* Our finished window arch with snow on the sill. *Right:* The finished interior plaster.

Working with lime plaster. Lime plaster is very plastic, i.e., moldable, but applying it around our wall's bottles, curved windows, and sculptural designs was tricky. Here, we're using a plastic putty knife. A collection of finish, margin, and pointing trowels comes in handy for these situations. After the finish coats had dried, we used a small soft wire brush on the cordless drill to clean the plaster off the bottles.

Details. *Left:* The design of our arched window opening with an integrated stop allowed us to apply a seamless plaster coat from outside to inside. This protects the cob very well because no joint is created that could allow water to get behind the plaster. *Right:* We sealed the bottom of the wall with plaster. If I'd thought to push the cob back a bit during its installation, we could have used the termite barrier as a plaster stop. If this joint cracks, theoretically, water could slowly work on the cob underneath, but it should be fine—I'll just keep an eye on it.

PLASTERING THE STICK-FRAME WALL

In some ways, this wall is similar in composition to our straw bale wall. Both are made up of cellulose infill insulations combined with structural cellulose in the form of wood. However, the huge porch overhang protecting the stick-frame wall takes a lot of pressure off that wall's plaster mixes. Still, we knew we needed to take a stance on how the stick-frame wall would handle water vapor. We decided, as with the straw wall, to create comparable interior and exterior skins on the assumption that water vapor will move only so far into the wall and then leave from the same side. Nevertheless, this wall was an interesting experiment because the lath in some spots spanned quite a distance between structural supports. It seemed possible that this lath would move around a bit as it expanded and contracted in response to the wet plaster. We tried combating that possibility by installing spacers between the lath in strategic locations. In case the suspense is killing you…it worked great!

Spacers. *Top:* You'll remember that we'd left gaps between our lath to give the plaster a surface to grab. However, the wide spacing between our studs in this wall resulted in our lath pieces sometimes warping together to close the gap. *Bottom:* To stop this from happening and to prevent possible movement of the lath after plastering, we installed little wooden spacers between the lath pieces at various vulnerable spots in the wall.

Tim's Take:
Gypsum Plaster

An alternative to interior earth and lime plasters is gypsum plaster. Gypsum is an abundant naturally occurring mineral that is the main ingredient in both drywall and drywall joint compound, also called drywall mud. In fact, the easiest route to a gypsum plaster is to buy premixed buckets of drywall mud and apply them directly to a wall with a hawk and trowel. A couple of years ago, my daughters and I had an evening of mudness, smearing and shaping drywall mud onto a block wall in our house. We all had a great time, and we turned a boring wall into a nice textured surface that we've used for subsequent expressions of artistic abandon and as a kind of large "canvas" that has now been painted and repainted many times.

Premixed joint compound, however, is expensive compared to our other materials and has artificial additives, such as vinyl acetate polymer, to increase elasticity and to speed set time. Gypsum is also packaged as a powder in bags specifically as a plaster. Some of these products are available without or with fewer additives. The advantages of gypsum plasters are that they are readily available, set hard, and resist cracking. The disadvantages are the expense, quick set times which force a level of organization sometimes difficult for beginners, potential for off-gassing from some additives, and poor resistance to liquid water. Gypsum plasters are very vapor permeable, which could either be an advantage or disadvantage based on the situation.

Gypsum can be extended and therefore made cheaper by adding sand and even straw for texture. However, as I've tried to point out in my comments throughout this book, cost is relative to the situation. If you need to plaster a small interior area, or find yourself in a situation where clay or lime are unavailable, it might end up being cheaper to use a good, easily available option like gypsum rather than spend a lot of time pulling your hair out trying to locate materials.

Earth/Lime Plaster on Stick-Frame

Our friend Chuck Marsh does a lot of plastering and swears by a clay/lime/sand/straw mix that we tried on this wall. The idea behind adding clay is to create a plaster that can wick water away from the cellulose more efficiently.

Mixing Earth/Lime Plaster

▲ **Step 1.** First we mixed our clay, lime, and sand with our trusty paddle mixer.

◀ **Step 2.** We added dry straw for the mix that we used on the first coat. We added pre-soaked straw instead for subsequent coats and had far less cracking.

◀ **Step 3.** Here's our mix ready to go. Once again, we knew our mix was sticky enough when it stuck like glue to an upturned trowel.

For our first coat, we chose a 4:1:1:½ (sand/lime/clay/straw) mix that had tested well. It went on wonderfully and dried very hard but with many hairline cracks. This didn't concern us on a first coat; we were happy with the solid connection and fact that the lath seemed very stable within its plaster cocoon. However, we knew we didn't want subsequent coats to crack that much, so we tested two different mixes for the first coat on the inside of the wall. The first was a 6:1:1:1 mix with unsoaked straw like we'd used on the outside, and the second contained the same proportions with soaked straw. The results were dramatic—the plaster with unsoaked straw cracked badly, while the soaked-straw plaster cracked only slightly. My explanation for this is that the clay in the plaster really pulls water out of the mix and can cause it to set up too quickly. The soaked straw can give up its water to the clay, allowing the plaster to set more slowly so it doesn't crack. You'll remember we used soaked sawdust in our cordwood mortar for the same reason.

▲ **Step 1.** The clay made the mix a bit stiff, but it troweled on pretty nicely.

Filling the gaps. Here, you can see how the plaster is squeezing between the gaps in the lath. It's actually oozing over the back and gripping the lath.

▲ **Step 2.** We knew our dry wooden lath might soak up water from the plaster, accelerating the drying time and potentially causing cracking. To combat this problem, we let our lath take on some water before applying the plaster by gently spraying it with a hose, repeating the process whenever it seemed to be drying. Notice also that the plaster adhered equally well to the metal and wooden lath.

Once around the block. It was time-consuming to work around the blocking, but in the end it was great to be able to attach our shelves without breaking into our beautiful plaster.

Undercover. Our porch overhang allowed us to plaster in almost any kind of weather.

◄ Step 3. We left our finished plaster to dry for several days. When the sun was low to the west in the late afternoon, we hung a tarp from the roof overhang to protect the plaster from drying too quickly. We still got a lot of cracking, but the plaster adhered really well and seemed to key tightly into the lath.

▲ Step 4. After the plaster had cured for about a day, it was stiff enough to scratch with a wire brush. Don't do this too soon. You don't want to be pushing plaster around—just rough up the surface so that the next coat will adhere well.

Okay, so we lied. It makes sense to tell the story of our skins as if we plastered each wall separately from start to finish. The reality is that we had to keep moving around the building from coat to coat. Some of our mixes took up to two weeks to cure and others were ready to receive another coat after a day or two, so we had to be flexible if we wanted work to continue.

Interior plaster stops. *Left:* Both our window trim (just barely showing at right in the photo) and the blocking over the top plate above were installed to extend far enough out to act as plaster stops. Our cob wall (left in the photo) will serve as the stop. Notice also the line of spacers between the lath to the left. *Right:* We installed a metal drywall plaster stop at the base of the wall and trimmed around our water pipe chase to create a plaster stop for that opening.

Lime Plaster on Stick-Frame

In any case, we switched to a lime/sand plaster for the remaining coats, mainly so that all of the walls would end up the same color. The second exterior coat was a 3:1:½ (sand/lime/soaked straw) mix, and the finish exterior coat was a 3:1 (sand/lime) mix without straw and with the sand sifted through an ⅛-inch screen. We used this same mix for the final coat on the interior.

Lime plaster over earth/lime plaster. *Left:* Our lime plaster spread more easily than the earth/lime mix did. Here, Tim applies the first lime coat over our scratch coat of earth/lime plaster. *Right:* The lime plaster adhered nicely to the coat below.

Tools of the trade. *Left:* Plastering the interior lath walls, we ran into many tight spots. Here a credit card makes a great small flexible trowel. *Right:* A small flat trowel, called a margin trowel, was handy in small areas such as this one between the windowsill and the shelf blocking.

Outside and in. *Left:* This photo was taken months after our finish coat was applied. The freeze thaw cycles of the winter produced no cracks. *Right:* Meanwhile, our inside stays cozy and the finished interior sand/lime plaster has a nice warm glow.

Our Plaster Mixes

We adjusted our plaster mixes quite a bit from coat to coat. This chart doesn't even represent the full story because we sometimes made adjustments from mix to mix within a single coat of plaster. For example, in our first coat on the straw bale interior, we added straw for some sections and not for others. As we've said, once you get the hang of plastering, this on-the-spot design flexibility is one of its real strong points.

Plaster Mixes for Our Building		1st coat*	2nd coat*	3rd coat*
Straw Bale Wall	outside	1:0:1:S	3:1:0:½	3:1:0:½
	inside	1:0:1½:S	4:1:0:½	3:1:0:0
Cob Wall	outside	1:0:1½:S	3:1:0:½	3:1:0:0
	inside	1:0:1½:S	3:1:0:0	
Stick-Frame Wall	outside	4:1:1:½	3:1:0:½	3:1:0:0
	inside	6:1:1:1	3:1:0:0	

* sand/lime/clay/straw; S = some amount of straw

Tim's Take
Getting It Done: Plaster

Getting started in plastering doesn't require a big invest-ment. All you need to do the most basic work is a hawk, trowel, hoe, and wheelbarrow. Any dexterous person can learn the basic technique of plastering, and it can be fun and rewarding. All these traits make it a good candidate for do-it-yourself status, even if you aren't doing a lot of the other work on your building.

However, plastering is an ambitious project and can quickly overwhelm one person. Remember also, that most plaster mixes will crack if they freeze while curing. As your inevitably overly optimistic building schedule recedes into the distant past, you may find yourself in a plastering race with winter. In a bind, you may end up hiring a plaster crew when you thought you'd be doing it yourself, and this unex-pected expense could be a shock. The moral: Plan ahead and be realistic about your schedule. Long before you ever start plastering, determine if you'll need help and, if you will, where you're going to get it.

Recruiting Friends and Family

The first group of workers to consider is friends and family. A two-day plastering frenzy disguised as a party can actually accomplish a lot. Motivated novices can be trained fairly easily. The secret here is to be organized. First off, your walls need to be completely ready before the party begins, with all stops, flashing, and other details in place. All tools and materials should be on site days if not weeks before the party is scheduled. Make sure you have enough hawks and trowels to go around.

For this to work, you'll have to take on the role of a boss. That means carefully overseeing that the mixes are right and keeping an eye on quality control. Without over-sight, such a plaster party can quickly degenerate into, well...a party (especially if beer is part of the incentive). The hardest job for the plaster party boss is firing volun-teers. Make no mistake, plastering takes a certain amount of strength, stamina, and dexterity. You don't want to end up with more plaster on the ground than on the wall. And you want to make sure that what does end up on the wall has been applied with enough force to create a good bond. If, in the end, you're cleaning up a mess and replastering the wall, that's no party.

Earth plastering is a possible happy exception here. Earth plaster applied to cob, for example, is almost impossible to mess up. Since it's usually applied with the hands, it takes less skill and strength to apply than other plasters. As long as someone with experience is generating a good mix, almost any group of unskilled family, friends, and children can have fun applying earth plaster and actually get a lot done.

Hiring Unskilled Labor

If you need more help than a weekend party or two can pro-vide, a variation would be to find some strong, young helpers eager to earn a bit of cash, such as high school kids in the grip of a long summer. With a little training and supervision, you might quickly find you have an efficient plaster crew. Once you start paying people, of course, organ-ization and efficiency become even more important.

Hiring Skilled Labor

Unlike many of the other materials and techniques we cover in this book, plastering is well represented in both the "conventional" and "green" building worlds. If you need it, skilled help shouldn't be hard to find. Though plaster crews in your area may be mostly familiar with Portland cement–based plasters (or "stucco"), the mixing and application techniques for most plasters are similar, so their skills should translate well. In addition, you should be able to find old-time plasterers around who work on historic renovations or repair plaster in older houses. They'd be great resources.

However, the problem is that many skilled professionals aren't going to be willing to have you work with them. They'll often either want to do the whole job, or have noth-ing to do with it. The choice, then, might come down to either doing all of your own plastering or hiring someone to do it. If you do end up hiring professionals, make sure that you have the wall completely prepped before they come on site. If they aren't experienced with the given substrate, straw bales for example, then it's up to you to install stops, flashing, and everything else that's part of your water redi-rection strategy.

PLASTER WRAP UP

All these different mixes and wall types probably don't provide the clearest introduction to the basics of plastering. Let's sum up our discussion with a few key pieces of advice:

1) **Buy quality tools.** Good plastering tools are a bargain and will last a lifetime. Don't be afraid to buy a variety of trowels and finishing tools—you'll thank yourself once you're working on your precious walls. I know, I know, people will tell you that you can build a hawk out of a piece of plywood. Please, just shell out the few bucks for a nice aluminum hawk. It'll be light and have a wonderful rubber rest for your hand. Believe me, you're worth it.

2) **Always prepare your materials well in advance.** Lime needs to be soaked, clay needs to be screened, and straw needs to be shredded. If you run out of one of these materials, especially lime, it can really put a crimp in your schedule.

3) **Keep your sand dry.** In lime and earth plasters, sand is often the only dry ingredient. If your sand is wet, it may be hard to create a plaster with the consistency you need.

4) **Conduct tests.** Clays will vary widely. Limes may also. Different substrates interact with plasters in different ways. Try to test each mix in the situation in which you plan to use it.

5) **Make sure that all plaster stops and flashing are in place.** Look long and hard at your wall before mixing any plaster. No matter what material you're covering, you don't want liquid water to be able to get behind the plaster.

6) **Plan your day.** Plastering is a lot of work. On walls with complicated details (like our cob wall with all of those bottles and curves) plastering can move forward at a snail's pace. It's a good idea to apply a full coat in one session; otherwise, it can be hard to cleanly combine a plaster coat that's been curing for a day with a fresh one. Because of this, if you're not careful, you may find yourself plastering late into the night. Have lights handy just in case.

7) **Shade your lime plasters.** The worst enemy of any plaster containing lime is drying too quickly. The result will be cracking. If at all possible, don't expose your plaster to any direct sunlight while it's still setting up. Our earth plasters didn't crack in the sun, but if yours do, shading them during drying should help.

8) **Check your curing plaster often.** Regardless of the finished look you want, there's going to be a moment that's just right to achieve it. If you sponge too soon, for example, you can get a smeary mess; sponge too late, and you won't get consistent results.

CORDWOOD SKIN

Our cordwood is the only wall we didn't plaster. That's because cordwood construction is typically seen as having an integrated skin—the cordwood and mortar make up both the exterior and interior skins. In our situation, this concept works very well because our wall is so protected by a large roof overhang.

However, as we've said previously, the exposed end grain of cordwood can make it vulnerable in some situations. In cases where that's a concern, let's say in a very exposed wall, I don't see any reason why cordwood couldn't be plastered as a protec-

Construction Blunders:

Last Minute Changes

At some point after the stem walls were in place, we carefully figured out the best construction sequence and exactly how each material should connect with the next. We decided to have both the straw bale and cob walls go all the way to their respective posts on the sides where they intersect the cordwood wall and then to build a small cordwood column to fill in the gap. We did this on the cob wall. As we started laying the cordwood wall, however, we made the abrupt decision to take it all the way to the post on the northeast corner. The gap created was only about 4 inches deep and it seemed that would be easy to stuff with straw.

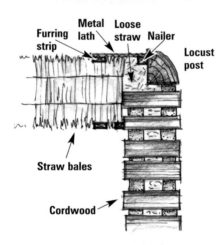

Furring strip · Metal lath · Loose straw · Nailer · Locust post · Straw bales · Cordwood

Figure 1
POOR BACKING FOR PLASTER

As soon as we pulled the lath across this loose straw column, it was obvious that it would have been better to take the straw bales all the way to the locust post instead of creating a space that had to be infilled with loose straw.

When we installed the straw bale wall, we discovered it was easy to stuff that space, but the resulting 4-inch-deep by 8-inch-long column of loose straw covered in mesh was very spongy. The first coat of earth plaster adhered nicely and didn't crack at all, but you could easily push the wall in about an inch at that spot. It's a testament to the incredible flexibility of earth plaster that even this much movement didn't produce any cracks. However, the first coat of lime plaster with straw didn't fare as well—you couldn't press in as much, but it cracked a bit in this area. We tried a second coat of lime with straw and, luckily, this seemed to do the trick. The wall still appears to be very solid there, but I'm not sure how it will hold up under extreme stress, like a 10 year old throwing a football against it. If we'd left our original plans intact, our straw bales would have been tight against the column and we wouldn't have created this possible weak spot.

The lesson: Though many people extol the virtues of designing as you build, there's a lot to be said for the quiet solitude of an office or kitchen table. If you've carefully thought something out in peace, don't be too quick to make changes on a whim during construction.

Second Thoughts

If there's one detail on the whole building that concerns me it's this spot at each corner of the straw bale wall. The bales are only about 8 to 10 inches off the ground at this corner, which means that rainwater both falling directly from the sky and splashing off the ground can access this area. The flat protruding termite barrier allows this water to pause here before rolling to the ground. This is also the shady, north face of the building, which means this area will be slow to dry out. All of this makes me wonder about what's going on behind the plaster here.

You'll notice the plaster has flaked a bit at the bottom corner. That happened during a cold snap not long after I'd finished plastering; I think water in the plaster froze and expanded, causing the flaking. It's been almost a year since then and no further flaking has occurred. We've had no cracks here or anywhere on the building. Still, next time I'd think of a different design than the flat protruding termite barrier for this spot. On the other hand, I'm very glad that we carefully covered our first course of bales in building wrap and installed a piece of flashing. Though you can't think of everything, careful, conscious building at every stage will encourage you to add in multiple safeguards like these that will help you overcome those inevitable little design mistakes.

You can't think of everything. In retrospect, I think this spot was a design mistake. However, other design elements took up the slack, so I think we won't have any problems.

tive measure. Plastering might also be a good repair for a wall in which the cordwood has shrunk badly after a number of years of humidity and temperature changes. The advantage would be that the plaster would become a sacrificial layer that could be periodically repaired, considerably lengthening the lifespan of the cordwood. Of course, you'd need to experiment with the mix. It seems to me that a semi-permeable lime plaster like we've used on our other walls would work well with cordwood.

FINISHING THE SKIN: TRIM

I'm amazed by how many construction books, especially ones about green/natural/alternative materials and techniques, don't take the time to discuss trim details. It's probably because trim and flashing are very situation specific. Doing them right takes skill and creativity. It's impossible to describe even a fraction of the different scenarios you might encounter in your quest to seal all the joints in your building.

At the same time, neglecting the topic altogether is a big mistake. Details on the level of trim and flashing may be small in the scope of the entire building, but they're often some of the most important steps you'll take in the entire construction process. I'll even hazard to say that the origin of most building problems can be traced to some tiny construction detail involving the joints in the building skin that trim, flashing, and related procedures are meant to address. The hardest thing about trim is that, functionally speaking, good trim and bad trim can look almost identical. The ability of a particular trim installation to keep water, air, insects, and animals out rests solely on the conceptual understanding, skill, and care of the installer. Trim carpentry can be tedious and frustrating. It can also be challenging, creative, and rewarding. If you don't want to wrap your head around it, then find somebody who does. Whatever you do, don't neglect it.

As I've said, I can't begin to catalog the array of joints in need of covering that you'll come across in your building odyssey. However, a quick tour of some of the trim in our little building will at least give you some insight into the thought process. The variety of wall materials we used and our assorted window- and doorframes created a lot of different situations to consider.

A trim expert could look at our trimless building and instantly identify a shortcoming that all of our walls share: The joints between our locust corner posts and the wall materials are theoretically vulnerable to water infiltration. This is an instance where both aesthetics and the fact that we were building in the context of a how-to book led us to choose a detail that wasn't the best functionally. In order to make a clear division between our different wall systems, we decided to keep the locust corner posts exposed to the outside, thereby creating joints between post and wall materials at all corners. Long vertical joints like this are difficult to trim out, especially when using undulating materials such as cob, straw, and cordwood. We could have chosen instead to wrap our wall infill materials around the outside of the posts, thus alleviating the vertical joints and the potential problem. In actual practice, though, the joints at the posts aren't a problem for most of our walls because of other factors that we'll explain below. Let's take a look at each wall individually.

Vulnerable joint. This exposed locust corner post will be very resistant to rain and insects and creates a beautiful division between our different wall systems. However, the long plaster joint is vulnerable to water infiltration and would be difficult to cover with trim.

Skin over skeleton. The beautiful timber frame of this building is completely wrapped in a plastered clay-slip straw box, therefore no vulnerable joint is created between skeleton and skin. As a result, the structural frame of this building is completely protected from water, and the exposed wood adds a wonderful feel to the interior.

Trim for Our Cob Wall

You don't see too much trim on cob walls. One reason is that cob is a freeform material, so in many spots the trim can't lay flat and create a seal. Also, since cob walls are thick and the material is so moldable, window and door bucks are often set into the wall a bit and the cob is curved around to meet them, usually covering the edge of the buck that would normally be trimmed. Another reason may be that lots of folks who choose cob are trying to minimize their wood use, and wood is the most common trim material. Perhaps the main reason is that cob is a solid mass, so it won't allow water to flow into its core easily the way other materials, such as straw bales, will. As a result, the main function of trim on cob walls would be to protect wood window and door bucks, not the cob itself.

In any case, we found a couple of places on our cob wall where trim was a good idea. As for the vertical joints at the locust posts mentioned above, I'm not really concerned about them with our cob wall. Our overhangs will keep most of the rain off the joints; this wall gets lots of sun, so any water that hits the joints will have ample opportunity to dry out, and, as we've said, cob is a monolithic mass, so the water really has nowhere to go if it does access those joints.

Cob truss trim detail. *Top:* Our cob and clay-slip straw wrap around the back of the roof truss at the top of our wall (see upper left in photo). We figured the truss would move slightly over time. Therefore, if we plastered over it, the plaster would probably crack. We decided instead to use the bottom of the truss as a plaster stop while installing trim over its exposed exterior. *Middle:* Notice in this close-up of the truss how the clay-slip straw in the left triangle hasn't shrunken as much as the cob in the right triangle has. We filled these gaps with a wet cob mix and let them dry before attaching the trim. *Bottom:* Here's the trim in place. It not only seals the truss and cob/clay-slip straw packed between its members, but it also adds a beautiful detail to this wall. Notice the curved trim over the door. Since the door is so high in the wall, the roof overhang will protect it from rain, so this piece of trim has no head flashing or drip edge—it's simply a plaster stop and decorative addition.

Moldable trim. We set our thin cob window buck in the middle of the wall. As we built cob around it, we curved the wall in toward the buck, creating a sensuous reveal both inside and out. We then plastered over the edge of the buck, leaving only the inner face exposed. This inner face of the buck is covered by the window on the outside, which is the only place it would be vulnerable.

Trim for Our Cordwood Wall

Trim for our cordwood wall was an interesting case because the juncture between every piece of cordwood and the mortar that surrounds it creates a joint that, theoretically, is susceptible to water and air infiltration. The matter is made worse by the fact that the cordwood pieces could shrink slightly over time, creating a gap between the wood and the mortar. As we discussed in chapter 9, using cob as mortar would be one solution because then we could just fill all of those gaps as they appear with a simple smear of an earth plaster mix. But it seems to me that the best solution, regardless of mortar type, is to use large overhangs above cordwood walls to keep water off. We used this strategy, and, as a result, we didn't need to add any trim to this wall. Our huge porch overhangs are also the reason the joints at our locust corner posts aren't vulnerable to water infiltration.

However, this approach doesn't solve the potential problem of air infiltration through gaps between wood and mortar. There are several solutions. If our wood shrinks only a tiny amount, we may do nothing. If we get a few larger radial splitting cracks or gaps between wood and mortar, we'll just caulk them. However, if we experience a lot of gapping, then caulking would be a crude, time-consuming, and ugly solution. A better cure for this malady would be to cover all of our mortar joints with a flexible chinking material like those developed for log cabin joints. This material bonds to the wood and is flexible so that it should expand and contract with the wood, preventing gaps. It would also give a smoother finish to the mortar joints.

A final fix would be to plaster over the entire exterior wall. This would not only cover the gaps but, as we mentioned above, would also cover the exposed end grain of the wood. However, our protruding log ends would force us to lay the plaster on pretty thick in order to cover them. If we were going to plaster this wall, it would have been better to set the cordwood flush with the mortar. In any case, we'll just keep an eye on our wall for a couple of years and see how it does. If, after that point, its skin seems to need some improvement, we'll decide what to do then.

No trim needed. The long vertical joints created by these two window bucks in our cordwood wall would have created an interesting trim challenge in some situations. The uneven surface of the cordwood and mortar would have been difficult to seal with trim. Our solution was to cover the wall with huge roof overhangs so that rain can't reach these joints; therefore, no trim was needed.

Shrinking skin. *Left:* This tiny amount of cordwood shrinkage is probably not a problem. The insulation between the mortar beds should prevent air infiltration. *Right:* The mortar joints of this wall have been covered with a log cabin chinking compound. This material should expand and contract with the wood and stop air infiltration in situations where larger gaps have developed between cordwood and mortar.

Trim for Our Modified Stick-Frame Wall

Our stick-frame wall is covered with the same huge overhang as our cordwood wall, so our functional need for exterior trim is greatly diminished. On the interior however, we found several trim opportunities.

Stick-frame wall exterior trim. Here, our trim-less window's exterior jamb is integrated into our exterior shelving (we'll learn more about the shelving in chapter 15). Our huge roof overhang keeps water away from the wall, probably making trim unnecessary. It's possible a gap could develop between the window jamb (the outside edge of which is painted blue in this photo) and the plaster. If that happened, air infiltration might be a factor, but it's very unlikely since there's a stud behind this joint and cellulose next to that. In any case, we could always add trim later if it seemed necessary.

Stick-frame wall interior trim. Let's start at the top of the wall and move down. The diamond-shaped trim piece at the top left covers a hole we used to blow cellulose infill into the cavity above the top plate. We filled the other top plate cavities on this wall with rigid foam and those on the cordwood wall with a combination of rigid foam and straw, but we added these trim diamonds to all cavities for symmetry. Moving down, the white trim blocks (in a row below the level of the truss) cover holes that we used to fill the wall cavity with cellulose. The bowed piece of trim over the window is pure aesthetics. Finally, the tile pieces above the sink act as both a backsplash and trim cover for the joint between the window jamb and plaster.

Trim for Our Straw Bale Wall

As we've brought up several times, our straw bale wall is something of an experiment. It's on the building's shaded, north side in a very wet climate, sits pretty near the ground, and is under the less-protective, gable end of the roof. The joints between our straw and the window in the straw bale wall are probably the most vulnerable places in the whole building. All of these facts make water infiltration more of a possibility in this wall than in the others. For that reason, we've been especially careful with water detailing on this wall all along. The final step in that process was to diligently apply trim.

Trim for Our Straw Bale Window

Since we knew it would be a critical spot, we had carefully planned our window installation with water in mind. First, our plans for the interior space made it make sense to set the window high in the wall. This maximized the protection of the gable end roof overhangs. Next, our window buck has integrated head and sill drip edges and a custom copper head flashing to redirect any water that does reach the window. We also carefully tested our plaster and chose a mix that we're pretty sure won't crack. The last step in this whole process was to carefully install trim that will protect the joints at the sides of the window.

▲ Step 1. We used a table saw to fashioned our trim pieces from a single piece of water-resistant cedar so that they wrap around the buck and the plaster without creating a joint. Here, we check the fit.

▲ Step 2. We aren't averse to using silicone caulk when it's appropriate. We knew the trim wouldn't sit completely flush against the undulating wall plaster, so we applied caulk as an added level of protection to seal this joint against water- and air-infiltration. You can clearly see the different layers of our wall skin in this photo: felt paper, metal lath, earth plaster, and lime plaster.

▲ Step 3. We put a double bead of caulk along the plaster, a bead at the top and bottom, and another one along the side of the window buck, which is the wood covered with white primer in this photo.

▲ Step 4. Next, we pushed the trim into place and snugged it up with a hammer.

▲ Step 5. We predrilled the trim before nailing with galvanized trim nails.

▲ Step 6. Then we repeated the procedure on the other side.

From top to bottom. *Left:* At the top, our trim intersects the head piece, which has an integrated drip edge and copper flashing. *Right:* At the bottom, it intersects the beveled sill, which also has a drip edge.

Interior Straw Bale Window Trim

▲ **Step 1.** Our interior trim wasn't as critical since water wasn't a factor. However, the plaster joint at our sill was exposed, vulnerable, and aesthetically unappealing. We decided to cap our interior plywood sill with a single wrap-around piece of trim similar to the side trim pieces on the exterior. We used a scrap piece of oak from one of the window bucks and ripped it on the table saw to create this L-shaped trim piece. (We had installed a temporary plaster stop, which has already been removed.)

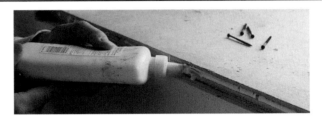

▲ **Step 2.** We used carpentry glue because this piece of trim is so narrow and thick. Also, since screwing into plywood doesn't create the strongest connection, we wanted the glue's extra strength.

▲ **Step 3.** We set the trim in place. Remember, trim carpentry requires patience—you may have to go back to the saw several times to get that perfect fit.

▲ **Step 4.** We had predrilled the piece before setting it. Here, I'm using thin screws with small heads, called "trim screws," to attach this piece.

▲ **Step 5.** The final fit was snug.

Trim for Our Straw Bale Truss

The issue of covering the roof truss at the top of our straw bale wall is a good example of how complicated simple things can be. Mice and other critters, including all kinds of insects, love to nest in straw. After plastering, the only possible entry point left in this wall was the gap between the truss rafters and the collar tie. In order to cover this entry point properly, we had to rip, cut, shape and install a number of custom pieces of blocking and trim.

In need of trim. Here, straw has been stuffed into the hole between the collar tie and the truss rafters at the top of our straw bale wall. At bottom, you can see the blocking attached as a plaster stop.

Figure 2
Straw Bale Truss Trim Detail

Look at all of the pieces of wood we had to install to finish off this section of our straw bale wall. First, we had installed a piece of blocking on the bottom of the truss collar tie so we could attach the furring-strip bale supports. Next, we installed a strip of wood on top of this collar tie blocking to use as a plaster stop. Later, we had to attach strips of blocking along the bottom of the truss to create a surface in the same plane as the plaster stop, so we had someplace to attach our trim piece that would cover the loose straw between the collar tie and truss rafters. Then, we capped the top of the trim to cover areas where we hadn't installed blocking at the bottom of the truss rafter. Finally, we filled the small hole at each end of this assembly between the plaster stop and the blocking on the rafter. Phew! If that's confusing to read, you get my point. You'd never know just by looking at the wall how many steps it took to seal it well.

Trim at work. Here's the trim piece and cap in place. Notice how this trim piece overlaps the plaster stop, thereby covering another joint in the wall and preventing wind-blown rain (a frequent occurrence on this north side) from ever landing on top of the stop and perhaps working its way into the straw.

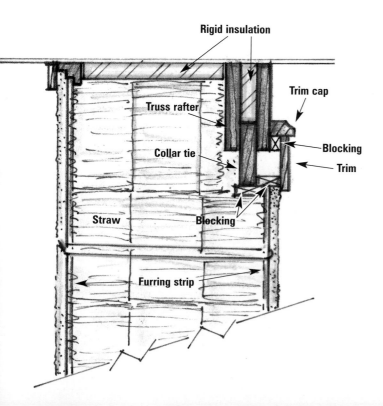

Rigid insulation

Trim cap

Truss rafter

Blocking

Collar tie

Trim

Straw

Blocking

Furring strip

Making waves. My last comment on trim: have fun. This piece of trim at the top of our straw bale wall interior covers the plaster stop. We could have left it off, or installed a straight board, but I think little details like this can add a lot to the feel of a room.

WHAT WE'VE ACCOMPLISHED

Throughout this book, we've tried to tie our real-life construction decisions into the building fundamentals and alternative strategies that we laid out in our earliest chapters. We can share our process of design and decision-making and the basic techniques for using various materials, but it's important to remember that your actual decisions will be different from ours. For that reason, we've tried at the end of each chapter to sum up our specific construction accomplishments in the context of these bigger issues. In previous chapters we summarized how each wall contributes to two of the four basic elements a house must provide: structure and stable temperature. Now we're ready to recap how each of our four walls provides a third element: separation from the forces of decay.

The story of the wall skins for this building is basically the story of water, both liquid and vapor. Because of our huge porch overhangs, the sun is really only an issue on our south wall, and cob is, for all intents and purposes, indifferent to sun. Just about any plaster would protect our lath and straw bale walls from wind, and cob is essentially oblivious to wind. Though, as we've discussed, wind pushing through gaps between wood and mortar might cause heat loss in our cordwood wall, the structure of the wall itself will be very resilient to wind. That leaves only water as a possible force of decay, because without water, life has no chance of gaining a foothold, or should I say toothhold.

Our first step was to try to understand how water vapor would interact with each wall, and our second was to develop a theory of how best to accommodate that vapor in each situation. We took advantage of the fact that plaster is very adjustable to create custom mixes that were designed to deal with each wall's specifics. In addition, our plaster mixes worked with previously installed flashing and other strategies to create a formidable barrier against the intrusion of liquid water into the volume of our wall infills. Since our water strategies have been slowly put into play throughout the whole book up to this point, it seems worthwhile to summarize our approach for each wall here. (See figure 3).

VARIATIONS

A casual survey of any group of buildings will reveal an array of approaches to covering walls. It's beyond the scope of this book to even scratch the surface of those possibilities. Just in the realm of plaster, the options are endless. Even on our single little building, we used a variety of plaster mixes. Let's take a quick glance at a few other options we could have considered in the realm of plaster.

NATURAL COATINGS FOR EARTH PLASTERS

We decided to cover our base coat of earth plaster with more durable lime/sand mixes to avoid dust and to create a lighter interior color. However, we could have used other materials and approaches. *Lime washes*, for example, are watery mixes of lime putty, water, and (if desired) a pigment that can be brushed onto earth plasters to create color and add a level of protection against abrasion. Lime washes can also be used as

Lime wash. The walls of this building are protected by coats of lime wash, a paint made of diluted lime putty.

Figure 3
WHOLE BUILDING WATER REDIRECTION PLAN

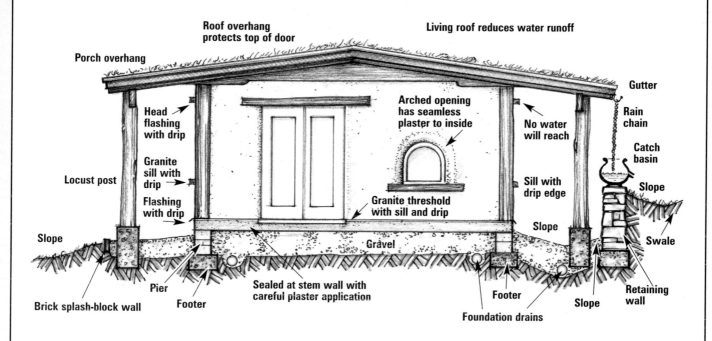

All Walls
- Gravel trench and foundation drains
- Raised stem wall
- Careful sloping of grade away from building
- Locust posts resistant to water
- Good overhangs all around
- Living roof reduces and slows rain runoff from roof
- Drip edge on all roof fascia
- Carefully designed plaster mixes specific to each wall

Cob Wall
- Plaster carefully sealed to termite barrier
- Granite threshold and windowsill with drip edges both carefully sloped away from building
- Arched window has seamless coat of plaster from outside to inside, so no seam for water to get behind
- Roof overhang protects top of door, so no flashing needed

Cordwood Wall
- Huge porch overhang and retaining wall block almost all rain access to wall
- Windowsills with drip edges
- No way water will reach window head pieces, so no flashing
- Gutter with rain chain and catch basin to direct rainwater to swale

Stick-Frame Wall
- Porch overhang keeps most rain off wall, though heavy weather comes in from the west
- Plastic-lumber sill plate
- Flashing with drip edge at base of wall
- Granite windowsill with drip edge
- Metal window head flashing with drip edge
- Ground slopes quickly away from building, so no gutter needed
- Brick splash-block wall with built in drainage to stop roof run-off from creating erosion

Straw Bale Wall (not shown)
- Flashing with drip edge at stem wall
- Building wrap drainage plane "cocoon" around first course of bales
- Wide windowsill and head piece extend past window. Each has integrated drip edge
- Custom copper flashing at top of window
- Window high in wall, so roof overhang blocks a lot of water headed toward it

Homemade paint. Both the interior and exterior of this cob building are covered with an earth plaster containing clay, sand, finely chopped straw bits, and vegetable oil to make it more water resistant. The interior earth plaster has been covered with a homemade paint that was applied with a sponge. It was made on site using Kaolin clay, silica sand, mica, flour paste, milk powder, and a little vegetable oil. The thin flakes of mica have a lubricating effect that makes the paint easier to apply and gives it a beautiful luster.

a periodic maintenance coat for a lime plaster, or, if pigment is added, to change the color of a lime-plastered wall. *Alis* paints are mixtures of water, wheat paste, colored clays, and often other additives such as mica and finely chopped straw. They're usually used to seal interior earth plasters and can be incredibly beautiful and colorful. A more durable and water-resistant covering for earth plaster can be made using milk protein as a binder in a paint containing pigments and lime putty or clay. Such mixes are generically called *casein paints*.

PORTLAND CEMENT

Though we didn't use Portland cement in our plasters, we're going to be unhip and state that we don't necessarily have anything against it. Portland cement is sometimes used to tweak more traditional mixes. It's often added, for example, to soil mixes in modern rammed earth buildings to create a stronger and more consistent mix. It can also be added to traditional lime plaster mixes using true lime putty to speed up the incredibly slow cure times. Conversely, vermiculite and lime can be added to conventional concrete stucco mixes to create a more cost-effective, vapor-permeable plaster. Portland cement is also being used to make an extremely durable concrete siding board that comes with a 50-year guarantee. This material can be cut with a saw and attached with conventional fasteners.

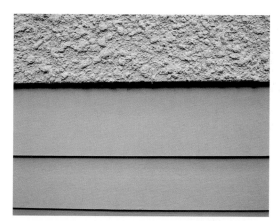

Cement skins. *Left:* This lap siding is made of sand, Portland cement, and cellulose fibers. The plaster above it is made of sand, Portland cement, and lime. *Below:* Perlite was added to a plaster mix with Portland cement to create a more hygroscopic skin for this house insulated with straw bales. This plaster was then covered with a lime wash, giving the building its white color.

EVERYTHING ELSE

We've focused on plaster in this chapter because it's by far the skin of choice for most popular alternatives to conventional construction. Earthship, earthbag, rammed earth, cob, clay-slip straw, straw bale, and adobe walls, if covered at all, are usually covered with plaster.

There are exceptions. For example, straw bale walls can incorporate a rainscreen into their skin. In such a system, the straw bale wall is first sealed against air infiltration by a single coat of plaster. Then, a siding material, such as wooden lap siding, is attached to nailers on the straw bale wall. The siding stops almost all liquid water from reaching the plastered bales while the nailers create an air space between the plaster and the siding, allowing both to dry out in response to humidity changes.

Of course, stick-framed buildings are usually not plastered in modern construction, but we'll leave discussions of the myriad options for covering framed buildings to that wall of books on conventional construction at your local library.

Chapter 13
Covering the Roof

The surface of a roof takes an incredible pounding.

Between the sun's baking, the wind's tugging, and the rain's pelting, the daily life of a roof is filled with tribulation. As we pointed out in chapter 2, the forces of decay are impetuous and pervasive in combination, and nowhere are they more prevalent than on the roof.

First, the UV radiation in sunlight has the ability to break down an impressive array of materials. In fact, as we pointed out in the last chapter, most paints and sealers are just a temporary coating sacrificed to the sun and water gods. The sun's daily cycle is responsible for differences in temperature between night and day, and on the roof these swings are much more pronounced. A roof surface will tend to expand as it bakes during the day and then shrink back as the temperatures cool at night. This constant push and pull can be very stressful to a roof skin, causing cracking, bending, or separation of different components.

It can be a downhill road from there. In cold climates, for example, water can make its way into tiny cracks in the roof surface and then freeze as the temperature drops, causing expansion and widening the cracks. The water then thaws, more water gets in, freezes again, the crack widens more, and around we go. These freeze/thaw cycles can eventually do a lot of damage. Once water has a way in, there's no stopping it. Since water is so mobile, it can be hard to find where a leak originates, which can make it difficult to fix. Even a small leak in a roof can do incredible damage to the structure of a building over time.

All of the above factors can contribute to loosening the fasteners that hold a roof skin in place. This action only helps the wind to get a foothold, and the result can be pieces of skin torn off during a storm. As if all of that weren't enough, our poor, beleaguered roof may also be accosted by falling tree branches and the occasional football. These forces will eventually defeat a roof skin. Generally in relatively few years, roof surfaces need to be repaired or replaced if the building below is going to have any hope of survival.

GENERAL CONTEXT: COVERING THE ROOF

TYPES OF ROOF SKINS

As with walls, roof skins can be either lapped or seamless.

Lapped Roof Skins

Lapped roof skins include all types of metal roofing, shingles, and thatch. Metal roofing, usually made of aluminum or steel, comes in sheets that run uninterrupted vertically from the peak of the roof to the bottom. Each sheet overlaps the previous, therefore covering the joint. Shingles are small units that are laid in overlapping courses to cover a roof. They can be made of ceramic or concrete tile, slate, recycled plastics, tar-impregnated organic felt, or other materials. Thatch is basically a form of shingling in which bundles of straw or wetland reeds are tied with metal hooks in overlapping courses to steep pitched roofs.

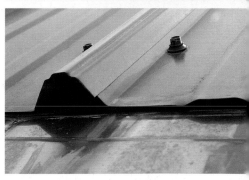

Lapped roof skins. *Top:* Overlapping layers of palm thatch make up this roof. *Middle:* Each course of slate laps the previous one to create a drainage plane to repel water. *Bottom:* The seams in this metal roof are vertical joints running from the top of the roof to the bottom where each piece of metal overlaps the next.

Seamless roof skins. *Top:* The plaster on these adobe buildings covers the roofs and walls in one seamless coat. *Bottom:* These domes are covered with a plaster containing paper pulp and Portland cement.

Seamless Roof Skins

Seamless roof skins are represented by a grab bag of examples, from fabric tents, to plastered domes, to living roofs. The roof of a parking garage usually consists of the last parking deck, with the seamless concrete skin performing the function of the roof. Earthbag structures (domes made of dirt-filled bags) are covered in seamless plaster. Modern "living," or "green," roofs are usually a variation on commercial flat-roof applications wherein some form of waterproof membrane is laid down on the roof deck. As we'll discuss in detail in Designing Our Living Roof, page 490, this membrane is then covered with a series of layers of insulation, drainage, growth medium, and plants.

FINISHING THE ROOF SKIN

Let's be blunt. While many aspects of a house allow some room for error, a roof basically has to be perfect, at least as far as water infiltration is concerned. As we've said, over time a tiny roof leak left unchecked can wreak havoc on a building. In other words, a roof is only as good as its weakest point. As with other aspects of building, these weak points are the joints created by breaks in materials.

Punctures

As we mentioned above, lapped roof skins, such as shingles and metal roofing, cover joints by overlapping each new course of material over the previous. But there are other joints created in a roof. For example, any puncture, such as those made by chimneys, vents, or skylights, creates a hole that must be carefully sealed. This technical marvel is usually best accomplished with flashing. We've tried our best to drive home the importance of flashing throughout this book. However, there's no way for me to introduce here all the possible roof-puncture scenarios and the variety of approaches to flashing them. All I can say once again is that you have to take flashing seriously. If there's a hole

Fixing a hole. This is the top of a skylight set into a roof covered with asphalt shingles. Notice the molded metal cap that protects the hinged top of the window and the curved piece of flashing that fits under this cap at one end, under the shingles at the other, and wraps around the side of the skylight. This is just a small part of the elaborate flashing kit installed with this window. The kit was manufactured to go specifically with this skylight using this particular roofing material. When you punch a hole in a roof, you have to go to pains to seal it back up.

in your roof, you have to seal it PERFECTLY. There are short cuts, like smearing tar all over the place and hoping for the best, but don't heed that siren call. Learn how to flash, carefully think through each situation, and be vigilant in your installation.

Roof Edge

The biggest joint on a roof is the one between the roof and the air around it, in other words, the roof edge. If this joint isn't properly detailed, our old friends gravity and capillary action will conspire to suck water into all sorts of places where it's not welcome. Often some combination of trim and a drip edge are used to direct water that's flowed down the roof away from this vulnerable edge. (See figure 1.)

Gutters

Okay, let's assume that we've designed and installed our roof skin extremely well. All the water that hits the roof is flowing along the surface past well-flashed punctures and is directed safely over the edge. We're still not finished. We have to make sure that all of this water is directed away from the building. This is the job of another often neglected housing detail: gutters.

Gutters catch roof water and redirect it to wherever you want it to go. In some situations this might be just onto a splash block at the bottom of a downspout. In others it might be into a buried pipe that deposits the water somewhere safely away from the building. In still others, the water may be directed into a reservoir where it's collected for later use. The choice of if, when, and how to use gutters is specific to each building and the terrain around it. The goal of all guttering, however, is the same: to keep the huge amount of water that falls onto the surface area of your roof from falling where you don't want it to go.

Redirecting water. A luscious sedum living roof covers this little adobe cottage in New Zealand. Manufactured flashing with integral drip edge wraps a wooden box installed to keep living roof materials in place. The flashing protects the wood from the wet world of the living roof around it and the drip edge makes sure that no water is allowed to roll under onto the roof framing. To the right at the low end of the shed roof, a gutter is directing roof runoff to a downspout and safely away from the building.

Figure 1
ROOF EDGE DETAIL

Here, shingles, tarpaper, flashing with drip edge, fascia trim, and gutter all work together as a water redirection system.

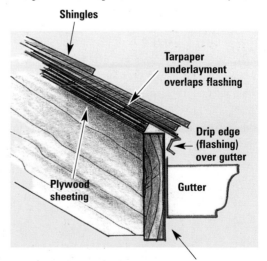

Shingles

Tarpaper underlayment overlaps flashing

Drip edge (flashing) over gutter

Plywood sheeting

Gutter

Fascia trim seals spaces between rafter tails and provides surface for gutter attachment.

Water highway. This copper downspout system on an old stone building takes water from the gutters and directs it to the ground and away from the walls.

Are Living Roofs Green?

Compared to other roof surfaces, living roofs are a lot of work, require a much stronger supporting structure, and are conceptually nerve-wracking. Just thinking about trying to find a leak in a living roof gives me the creeps. With all of that hassle, why did we bother with a living roof? Well, because they're green (no pun intended). To prove it, let's go down our usual checklist:

1) Low Construction Impact. Modern humans have a bad habit of replacing naturally occurring water-absorbent soil and plant systems with impervious surfaces such as roads, parking lots, and roofs. Especially in the city, this drastic alteration of the terrain causes a bunch of problems. Rain run-off chokes city sewers. Reflected and reradiated heat creates a "*heat island effect*" that plagues many cities with higher air temperatures than the surrounding countryside. And, of course, habitats for birds and other animals are destroyed. A living roof, on the other hand, acts much like natural terrain. It absorbs water, reducing run-off; the plants use the sun's heat for photosynthesis rather than reradiating it to the air; and the little ecosystem can be a habitat for insects, birds, and other small animals. With the addition of a patio or other recreation space, a living roof can become a habitat for humans, too. Living roofs take the greenspace lost by the footprint of a building and put it on the roof, resulting in practically no net loss. In the city, a living roof retrofit can actually add greenspace that's been lost. Now, that's a low construction impact!

2) Resource Efficiency through the Life of the Building. The layers of a living roof system create an incredible combination that will resist many kinds of heat transfer. *Radiant heat*, the main source of heat transfer in many roof systems, is absorbed by the plant cover and therefore isn't transferred as readily to the building. The plant layer also isolates the roof from "*wind chill*"—the loss of heat through moving air. The huge thermal mass of the plants, growth medium, and gravel creates a stable buffer zone between the insulation below and the outside. This means that daily temperature fluctuations often don't reach the insulation itself. Finally, the plant layer creates *evaporative cooling* through transpiration, as described in chapter 2, which acts like a built-in air conditioner on the roof. All of these traits add up to a roof system that should significantly lower the energy requirements of the building below it.

3) Long Lasting. The real skin of a living roof is the waterproof membrane. The roof will last as long as the membrane. In a well-designed system this membrane is protected from the pernicious combinations of the forces of decay that prey on roof skins. First, of course, wind isn't a factor because the membrane rests under heavy cover. Second, the sun will never hit the membrane, which means that destructive UV radiation is neutralized. Third, at least in our design, the membrane is well-protected from freeze/thaw cycles because it's situated below the rigid insulation as well as the other layers of the roof. The living roof membrane, then, is in a warm and shaded cocoon, well protected from its enemies. This should make it last a very long time.

4) Nontoxic. "Toxic" basically means "harmful to life." Since a living roof is alive, it would seem to be the least toxic part of a house. Its plants are giving off oxygen, and its little ecosystem is creating a cycle of decay that is creating more topsoil. You can even grow strawberries or other foods up there. On the other hand, the membrane is made of synthetic rubber. I don't know if it gives off anything harmful over time. Still, compared to other roof skins, I'm confident that living roofs rate very low on the toxicity meter.

5) Beautiful. Last but by no means least, living roofs are simply beautiful. We want our little building to feel part of the site and be an inviting, whimsical place that will soothe our guests and convince them to come back again and again. As you'll see, our living roof is the icing on the cake, putting the finishing touches on our little hobbit house.

All shapes and sizes. *Top:* This large meadow is on the roof of a building in the middle of a city. It should last a long time, help the building save energy, reduce run-off to the city's sewers, release little reflected heat to the surrounding air, and provide a beautiful place to enjoy the out-doors to boot. *Bottom:* At the other end of the spectrum, this tiny meadow covers the roof of a little building in the country. Though it won't have the impact of its city-dwelling sibling, it will provide a durable, beautiful, insulating cap that connects this building to its surroundings.

COVERING THE ROOF APPLIED: OUR LITTLE BUILDING

DESIGNING OUR LIVING ROOF

The idea behind a living roof is simple: a roof with plants on it. However, as is so often the case in life, there's a big divide between concept and realization. There are a number of elements that need to come together to make such a roof work, including a very strong roof structure, an absolutely waterproof membrane, adequate integrated insulation, good drainage, and the right growth medium and plants for your specific climatic situation. In addition, of all the techniques addressed in this book, the living roof seems to be the hardest to find in practice, at least in the small-scale residential incarnation that is of interest to us. Add all of that together and you're left with an interesting design challenge. As a result, we spent a lot of time carefully considering the details of our living roof. Figure 2 illustrates all the elements of our system, so refer back to it throughout our discussion.

PREPPING THE ROOF

Way back in chapter 7 we completely prepped our roof for installation of the skin. We used a router to smooth the edges of the decking and set all nails so that there would be nothing to snag or puncture the membrane. Since we weren't going to put on the living roof immediately, we installed a protective layer of tarpaper over the decking. Since it was already there, we just left the tarpaper in place, but it's not necessary as a permanent part of the roof. In fact, it could be a hassle if it crumpled in the process of installing the membrane. If you do use paper for temporary or permanent protection, I'd install it with furring strips as we did. Staples or other fasteners might abrade and puncture the membrane.

Roof prep. Back in chapter 7, we rounded the edges or our decking and set all nail heads in preparation for installing our waterproof roofing membrane. We also installed a small fascia trim piece with drip edge under the outside edge of the decking.

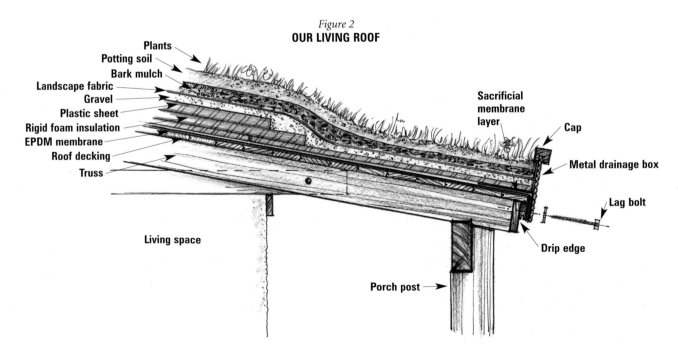

Figure 2
OUR LIVING ROOF

Plants
Potting soil
Bark mulch
Landscape fabric
Gravel
Plastic sheet
Rigid foam insulation
EPDM membrane
Roof decking
Truss

Sacrificial membrane layer
Cap
Metal drainage box
Lag bolt
Drip edge

Living space

Porch post

THE WATERPROOF MEMBRANE

There are various membrane products available that are designed specifically for application on roofs. We chose an EPDM (synthetic rubber) membrane because we could buy a single piece large enough to cover our entire roof; thus, we didn't have to deal with seams. There are various kinds of EPDM available, it's commonly used as a pond liner, but the one we bought is specifically designed for roofing.

EPDM is very heavy. It took three people to lift our 20 x 25-foot membrane onto the roof. We had the convenient access provided by our retaining wall. Without that, we definitely would have needed a piece of machinery to get it up there. It's also not the easiest thing to drag around, especially on tarpaper. We were careful to position its folded form carefully on the roof, so that unfolding it was most of the work of placing it. We found that we could adjust the final placement pretty easily by grabbing both ends and flopping it like we were shaking off the sheets on a bed. It's amazing what a current of air under sheet materials will do!

Installing the Membrane

Check that membrane! This was actually our second membrane. The first was delivered with a hole in it. Remember to check your materials before the delivery truck leaves!

▲ **Step 1.** We hoisted the heavy membrane onto the roof and unfolded it.

▲ **Step 2.** We temporarily attached it to the side of the roof with wooden cleats. We ordered a bit extra to cut off and use as a sacrificial layer (described in step 2, next page).

THE DRAINAGE BOX

One tricky aspect of living roofs is finding a good way to keep all of that stuff up there. We needed a box that would hold gravel, dirt, and plants while allowing water to drain away freely. It had to be pretty strong and very durable in the face of sun and water. Our solution was to build a box out of heavy metal grating.

The Drainage Box

▲ **Step 1.** We had metal grating cut into 6-inch widths by the supplier. The sample in the showroom had a slightly different profile than the metal they cut, so we had to deal with these razor sharp edges. This won't be a long-term problem because we'll cap them, but it meant we had to be very careful during installation.

▲ **Step 2.** The edge of the roof is the only place where the sun will be able to access our membrane, so we lapped a 1-foot strip of EPDM over the actual membrane as a sacrificial layer at the edge. (Refer again to figure 2.) The sun will have to eat through that entire piece before even starting on the actual membrane. Here, we cut a hole in the membrane…

◀ **Step 3.** …and attached the grating with a lag bolt through the hole. When we didn't cut a hole, the membrane twisted around wildly as the lag bolt screwed in.

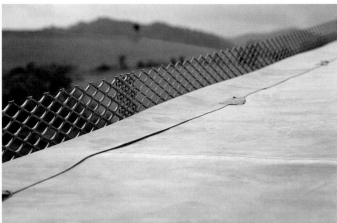

◄ Step 5. We overlapped pieces of grating for extra strength at the joints. Notice the sacrificial layer taped to the actual membrane.

◄ Step 6. Finally, we trimmed off the excess membrane at the roof edges.

▲ Step 4. We used rebar ties to connect the intersecting pieces of grating.

Waterproof. The installed membrane lay very smooth against the decking, creating a seamless waterproof skin (left) that immediately started doing its job (right).

INSULATION

We placed 5 inches (R-25) of rigid insulation over the living space, and stepped it down to 1 inch over the overhangs where it functions as freeze/thaw protection and a barrier between the gravel and the membrane (see figure 2, on page 490). As discussed earlier, our actual thermal performance should exceed the measured value of the insulation. There's a surprising array of types of rigid insulation available. Dow makes a product specifically for roofs that has a higher compressive strength, but we couldn't get it around here. Whatever you do, make sure that your insulation is rated to withstand exposure to water. (See the sidebar, Construction Blunders: Read the Fine Print, on page 505.)

Roof Insulation

▲ **Step 1.** We cut strips of landscape fabric to line our drainage box. This protects the edge of the insulation from sun and bugs and hides it from view as well.

◀ **Step 2.** We wanted 5 inches of rigid insulation over the interior space, but only 1 inch over the overhangs as a protection against freeze/thaw. To achieve this, we used 4x8 sheets of both 2-inch and 1-inch-thick rigid insulation (top) and installed it using a stepped pattern (left) that allowed us to stagger the joints (right). Thus, though this insulation could move a bit over time, creating a gap, there's no joint beneath it to continue the break. Therefore, there won't be any serious thermal bridges through gaps in the insulation. (Refer again to figure 2.)

▲ **Step 3.** We lapped the insulation over the landscape fabric…

▲ **Step 4.** …and trimmed it to get a tight fit.

▲ **Step 5.** We filled the gap at the ridge with a latex foam sealant.

▲ **Step 6.** Finally, we weighed the insulation down with some 2x4s to keep it from blowing away before we installed the next roof layer.

THE DRAINAGE LAYER

We used two inches of pea gravel for our drainage layer. This was the same stuff we used for our foundation, so we were able to order it all at once. Pea gravel is rounded and is much easier to shovel than some other forms of crushed stone. We could also have used broken brick nuggets, which are sold at nurseries. They're much lighter than gravel. They're also porous, so they'll absorb water. This is a real plus because we want to keep as much water up there as we can for the plants. However, for the size of our roof, that would have been a lot of bags of the more expensive brick nuggets, so we stuck with the gravel.

The Drainage Layer

◄ **Step 1.** We covered the insulation with plastic, both to help prevent movement and to protect it during gravel installation. The plastic also functions as an initial water-repellant membrane.

◄ **Step 2.** We once again borrowed the tractor from our kindly neighbor to help get the gravel to the roof.

▲ **Step 3.** It was still a lot of work to shovel it all into place (left). In the end, we tried to get about a 2-inch cover over the whole roof (right).

CAPPING THE DRAINAGE BOX

To cap our drainage box, we turned once again to composite wood-chip/plastic lumber. We've already used some as the sill plates for our stick-frame and straw bale walls and as the fascia/drip edge for our living roof.

Capping the Drainage Box

◄ **Step 1.** To create our cap trim, we started with a full piece of composite lumber decking (left), and ripped it into four pieces with a circular saw and rip fence (right).

Technological marvel. This stuff is really pretty amazing. It can be worked like wood and is incredibly flexible. This thin strip didn't break when bent.

▲ **Step 2.** We routed the edges of our rips…

▲ **Step 3.** …and cut a groove (top) into which we set the razor sharp top of our drainage box (bottom).

◄ **Step 4.** We tapped the pieces with a hammer to impale them a bit onto the sharp metal edge and mitered the pieces to create nice-looking joints.

▲ **Step 5.** At corners (left) and the ridge (right), we used little brackets to make connections.

Capped. The finished cap covered the sharp metal and created a nice finish detail at the top of the roof.

Draining. Here, you can see our completed drainage box in action. Notice how the metal acts as a drip edge for most of the rain. The drip edge on the composite lumber fascia trim piece (under the bottom of the metal grating) catches the rest.

▲ **Step 6.** We installed rebar ties here and there to make a mechanical connection to the grating.

THE GROWTH MEDIUM AND PLANTS

Lisa and our good friend Christopher Mello designed the living portion of the roof. They chose to use a variety of sedum plants because sedums are very hardy, love direct sun, and don't need much water or soil. Christopher had a large garden of sedums that he graciously agreed to relocate to our roof.

Sedums need a very fine, thin layer of soil into which to tie their roots. The challenge, then, wasn't getting enough soil on the roof to support our plants but designing a system that would drain well and give the plants the soil they needed now and as they continued to grow and spread over the years.

Here's what Christopher and Lisa did. First, they covered the gravel with landscape fabric to prevent the soil from clogging up the drainage layer. Next, they installed about 3 inches of inexpensive pine bark mulch. This layer will slowly decay and turn into more soil for the sedums to use. For now, it's a drainage layer. On top of this, they laid a 1-inch layer

Propagating Plants

▲ **Step 1.** The sedums we chose for the roof like to live in sparse soil on and around rocks (left). Christopher harvested mature plants (middle) and collected them for transplanting (right).

◄ **Step 2.** The plants were then separated into smaller specimens and planted on paper-covered flats in the soil we will use on the roof (left). They now have room to spread out (middle). The flats were left outside and watered. When the roof surface was ready, we took these flats (right) directly to the roof and transplanted them.

of fine potting soil as the growth medium for the plants. They bought topsoil because we didn't have any to spare around the site. To be honest, the bags sure made it easier to transport the soil to the roof. Finally, after transplanting the sedums, they added a thin layer of small river stones and shells. This mimics the natural situation where sedums thrive. Water will tend to condense on the underside of the stones keeping the plant roots moist. On our roof, the stones have the added advantage of holding our soil in place until the sedums knit their roots into it.

The Growth Medium and Plants

▲ **Step 1.** The whole reason we have a layer of gravel is to insure good drainage. If our soil fills in between the gravel pieces, drainage will be severely curtailed. To prevent that, we laid two layers of felt landscape fabric over the gravel.

▲ **Step 2.** We ran the first layer vertically and the second horizontally so no joints lined up. (By the way, the difference in color between the two layers doesn't mean anything; it's just what our supplier had.)

▲ **Step 3.** With the felt in place, we moved our bags of bark mulch onto the roof.

◄ **Step 4.** We poured the mulch onto the roof (left) and spread it around to create a layer about 3 inches deep (right).

▲ **Step 5.** Then we trimmed the excess fabric around the edges of the roof.

▲ **Step 6.** Next, we added some pelletized lime to bring down the acidity of the soil.

▲ **Step 7.** On top of that we installed our primo topsoil (top) and spread it around in a thin layer, about 1 inch thick (bottom).

▲ **Step 8.** We transferred the flats of plants to the roof.

▲ **Step 9.** We transplanted each group of plants, trying not to disturb the root systems.

▲ **Step 10.** Finally, the small river stones and shells were brought onto the roof in buckets (left) and carefully placed around the plants (right).

▲ **Step 11.** The sedums were rounded out with a variety of plants including thyme, roof irises (top), and fire lilies (bottom).

Plant painting. Far from just a bunch of plants thrown together, what Christopher and Lisa created was a carefully planned garden. Plants cascade over the sides and combine to create a kaleidoscope of shapes, sizes, and colors.

FINISHING THE ROOF SKIN

Our roof skin is almost finished. We've carefully installed a multi-layered skin that will direct all water to the roof's edge. We've installed a drainage box and trim with an integrated drip edge to make sure that the water falls away from the roof. Now, all we have to do is redirect the water safely away from the building.

The ground slopes quickly away from our building's west side. Our huge porch overhang and carefully sloped grading to the west (see chapter 7) allow us to forgo a gutter on this side of the building. On the east side, a hill directs water directly at the building, so we built a retaining wall to create a slope away from the building. Now, we need to use a gutter to direct our roof water onto this slope.

Our gutter system. Our gutter is attached to our wooden sub-fascia so that it hooks under the drip edge on our composite lumber fascia piece. The water falls into the gutter, down our rain-chain "downspout," and into our catch basin. The spout on the back of the basin empties the water onto a broad stone that directs it to the sloped ground, which carries it away from the building.

Rain chain. A conventional downspout hanging out here in space would have looked horrible and been very susceptible to damage. We chose instead a version of an old Japanese technique: the rain chain. Though rain chains can get pretty elaborate, ours is simply a piece of heavy steel chain suspended from the hole in our gutter. At first, all the water wasn't falling on the big chain, so we attached the smaller chain and moved it around until it was sucking up every drop. It's incredible how the water sticks to the chain almost like glue.

Beam flashing. Our aesthetic choice to have our porch beams extend past the roof edge exposes these beam ends to rain and runoff from the roof. We protected each end with lapped copper flashing. Notice how the ends of the flashing are rolled back to create a drip edge.

Construction Blunders: Read the Fine Print

We were shopping around for rigid insulation for our roof when our contact at the local lumberyard told us he had some with a 20 percent higher R-value than other rigid insulations. It was also made of "greener" materials than its competitors. The only problem was that we'd have to special order it. We told him what we were using it for, he said it would work, so we ordered it. When the stuff arrived, we read a piece of packing material that cautioned to store the insulation out of the rain. That didn't sound good to us because we were planning on installing this stuff on top of the roof where it was likely to see plenty of rain.

After some research on the company website and a bit of emailing, we learned that (1) the company had lowered its R-value claims because of new testing requirements, and (2) we absolutely shouldn't use this insulation in applications where it was going to get wet. Clearly this stuff wasn't going to work for us. After a lot of hassles, we finally got our money back … as a credit minus a 20 percent restocking fee (despite the fact that we returned it ourselves). The moral: Don't rely on what salespeople tell you. Do the research yourself, and don't buy until you're sure of what you're getting. At the very least, don't install anything until you're sure it's right for the job.

The wrong stuff. We're storing this insulation to be returned. A salesman had told us it was the right stuff for our needs. After special ordering it, we discovered it wouldn't work for our application. Even after borrowing a truck and returning it ourselves, we still had to pay a sizeable restocking fee.

WHAT WE'VE ACCOMPLISHED

Our living roof is an example of something that looks simple on paper, but was actually pretty tricky to install. Small details like the sacrificial layer of EPDM on the edge will probably be an huge help in extending the life of the roof. Because we took the time to think these details through and were willing to absorb time and money losses, like our misordered insulation, we feel as if we came away with a really wonderful roof that will perform better than any metal or shingled roof we can imagine. In addition, this roof really fits our original pattern language and design thought process by helping to nestle our little building into the site. More than probably any other element, our roof helps create the feeling we're trying to engender. Now that it's in place, I can't imagine the building having any other roof surface.

Habitat. We created a small path and patio on the roof. It's a nice place to hang out (top) and attracts the interest of a variety of visitors (left).

A living thing. Our roof anchors the building to the ground. It almost makes it seem as if the whole building sprouted and grew or some extinct river carved it out of bedrock.

VARIATIONS

As you can tell, we love this roof. However, of all the techniques we describe in this book, the living roof is perhaps the one I'd be least likely to advise a beginner to undertake. You have to be incredibly careful in your installation because basically any puncture in that membrane would most likely be a pretty big disaster down the road. Also, engineering a roof to hold that much weight isn't a beginner's job. I guess it just comes down to how much you trust your skills. Of course, there's the added expense (at least compared to a basic metal roof) and a lot of extra work. If you want to pass on the living roof this time around, there are plenty of other options.

METAL ROOFS

Compared to a living roof, a metal roof is easy to install. If the surface is of a galvanized metallic or light reflective color, it can be effective at preventing solar energy from penetrating through the roof, especially if an air space is created below the skin by raising the metal above the decking. Metal roofs are durable, but not immortal. A good quality metal skin can be expected to last up to 40 years, perhaps more.

All metal roofs aren't created equal. *Left:* This "standing seam" metal roof is designed so that all fasteners puncturing the roof are covered and, therefore, not exposed to rain. *Right:* The screws holding this metal roof are out in the open. Spongy neoprene washers fill the holes that the exposed screws have made in this roof. These washers tend to degrade over time, which will eventually make the punctures vulnerable to water infiltration.

SHINGLES

As mentioned at the beginning of the chapter, the term *shingles* refers to a wide variety of materials. Those at the high end of the spectrum— slate, concrete, and terracotta tiles—are very durable. Slate shingles, for example, can last almost indefinitely. It's the metal fasteners that eventually fail and need to be maintained. All of these types of shingles, however, are quite expensive. Thatch, too, while perhaps of humble origins, is expensive to have professionally installed. On the other hand, these roofs are incredibly beautiful and durable, so I think they're worth the money if you can afford them.

The lower end of the spectrum, the much maligned asphalt shingle, is perhaps the easiest and definitely the cheapest of the conventional roofing options. Asphalt shingles are made of either a felt or plastic mat covered in asphalt and small stones. Good quality shingles can be very durable, some of them approaching the life expectancy of metal roofs. However, when torn off the roof, they usually end up at the dump, though they're starting to be recycled in some places.

All thatch isn't created equal. *Left:* These thatch roofs are made of durable Norfolk reed installed in overlapping rows much like shingles. Created by master craftsman Colin McGhee, these roofs are a perfected art from a long tradition and should give many years of faithful service. *Right:* These beautiful thatch roofs are made of a relatively thin, single layer of straw. They're covering grain storage huts in a dry climate. Also part of an ancient tradition, they don't need to be as durable to do the job asked of them.

All shingles aren't created equal. Shingles run the gamut from very thin, cheap, short-lived asphalt varieties to very durable and expensive slate and tile versions. *Top left:* These shingles are made of recycled plastic. *Top right:* Tile shingles grace the roof of this elegant building in China. *Bottom left:* Both the walls of this building and the roof of its little porch are covered with cedar shingles, sometimes called shakes. *Bottom right:* These shingles are made of asphalt-impregnated felt paper covered with tiny gravel. They are much thicker than standard asphalt shingles and have a life expectancy equivalent to some metal roofs.

RAIN CATCHMENT SYSTEM

We've already pointed out that a typical roof causes water run-off problems because it creates what's called an *impervious cover*, a surface that doesn't allow water to be absorbed. One solution is to create a living roof that will, in fact, absorb water; another is to use this impervious cover to collect water for use in and around the building. On a small building, a rain catchment system can be a very manageable enterprise.

If you want to drink the water, then you need to make sure your roof skin isn't leaching anything into it. Cedar shingles, for example, may leach oils into water that you wouldn't want to drink. You'll also need to be careful to keep the water cool and out of the sun. Often, water storage cisterns are buried to slow the inevitable arrival of life forms such as algae. In addition, you'll have to take various measures to purify the water, culminating in an expensive filtering system. On the other hand, if you're willing to limit your rain catchment water use to non-drinking applications, like watering gardens, washing tools, etc., then you can greatly simplify your system. Pretty much any roof skin will do, you can avoid expensive filtering, and your cistern placement options are more flexible. In figure 3, we outline a simple system that we could have used on our building.

Figure 3
SIMPLE RAIN CATCHMENT SYSTEM

Before we decided upon the living roof, we considered this rain catchment system in combination with metal roofing. Downspouts from two gutters catch all the water coming off the roof and dump it in a raised cistern. A spigot and basin give you access at the cistern for cleaning or watering. A hose can send water anywhere downhill. An overflow, plumbed into a buried drain, takes excess water away from the building. Though we'd probably need a rough filter to keep out larger particles, there's no reason we couldn't use this system with our living roof.

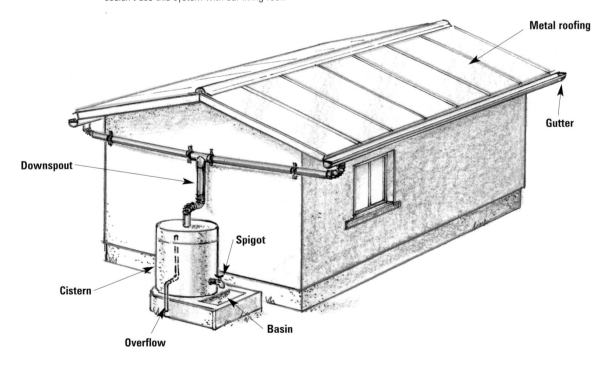

From the sky to your sink. Here's an example of a similar rain catchment system on a little house at Earthaven intentional community in North Carolina. The cistern was made on site from a wire cage covered in a lightweight concrete mixture, a technique called ferrocement.

INSULATION FOR NON-LIVING ROOFS

Most roof skin systems don't have integrated insulation like our living roof. Instead, insulation is installed either between the rafters in cathedral ceilings or on top of the ceiling on the floor of the attic. Blown cellulose insulation made from recycled newspapers, like we used in our stick-frame wall, is perhaps the best available material for these applications. People do use alternatives like loose straw or clay-slip straw, but both of these options would give a considerably lower R-value per inch than the blown cellulose. Since newspapers and straw are both industrial byproducts in the modern world, I'd go with the cellulose.

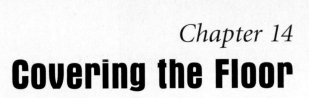

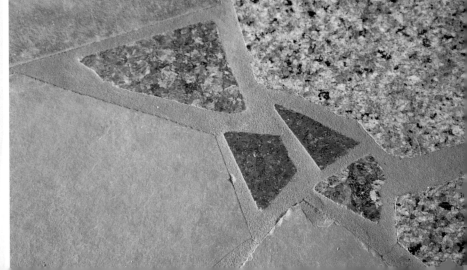

The basic showroom model floor is the earth itself.
It has some good features, such as being very solid, but sometimes it's wet, cold, and bumpy.
Human innovation has improved on nature to create floors that are solid, dry, warm, level surfaces.
How do we do it?

GENERAL CONTEXT: COVERING THE FLOOR

A floor improves on the ground beneath it by creating the balance of separation and connection that we've discussed throughout this book. On the most basic level, the earth is the structural support for any floor, so every floor has to be firmly connected to the ground below it in some fashion. At the same time, the ground is often uneven, and human indoor activities, across cultural divides, require flatness. Floors, then, need to be separated from the unevenness of the earth. In addition, a floor must interact with two other major aspects of the ground.

INTERACTING WITH THE GROUND

First, the earth is a huge source of water. Of course, we know that water flows under and on top of the ground, but the earth, just like the air, also holds water. The ground is constantly giving off this water to the surrounding air through evaporation as part of the hydrologic cycle that continually recycles water throughout the planet. A building can act like a terrarium and capture this moisture as it evaporates from the ground beneath. This evaporation can create humid indoor air and be a source of the water that's deposited as condensation (see page 40, Water and Air: The Issue of Condensation). Humidity and condensation can lead to mold, fungus, and insects such as termites. We need to separate our floor from this water and the damaging life forms it can foster.

Second, the earth is a huge thermal mass and as such it takes a long time to heat up and cool down. In fact, if you go below the frost line, you'll quickly access an area that's always about the same temperature. In many places this zone is 55° to 60°F. The temperature above this zone will fluctuate slowly throughout the year. Daily changes in air temperature have little effect on the temperature of the earth. This huge mass, then, is a powerful temperature sink that will pull things in contact with it into the envelope of its temperature.

That's good and bad news. On the one hand, the earth maintains a temperature that's often only slightly lower than human comfort zones. In other words, it can be a free, basically infinite source of 55°F temperature. However, a building whose inside (also called the "thermal envelope") takes advantage of this free temperature will have to struggle against that leviathan mass to create temperatures above it. Therefore, we have to choose a conscious strategy for our building that will either separate it from or connect it to this imposing thermal force.

What's a floor for? You want your floor to be solid, level, dry, durable, and comfortable to walk on. To accomplish this feat, your floor has to carefully interact with the ground beneath it.

TYPES OF FLOORS

These features of the ground beneath a building have spawned two basic approaches to creating floors: raised and on grade.

On-Grade Floors

A floor on grade is a floor whose entire mass is supported by the earth. In other words, it actually rests on the ground. The goal of a correctly designed floor on grade is to create a level surface that ties the inside of the building into the huge thermal mass of the earth. However, as we pointed out before, we're most likely tying into a stable temperature below the human comfort zone. This is one reason why most basement concrete slab floors are cold to walk on. We can deal with this problem by installing insulation between the earth and the floor surface. This will let us use the stable mass of the earth as a buffer against wild temperature fluctuations, while also allowing us to raise the floor temperature through passive solar or radiant floor heating. Such a floor on grade is like an insulated wall with no windows set against a constant outdoor air temperature of around 55°F (see figure 1). That's a pretty mild climate.

In some applications, people decide not to include insulation in an on-grade floor. This makes sense if you're only concerned with cooling your building or if you're confident that the earth you're accessing will consistently have a stable temperature at human comfort levels. If in doubt, however, I don't suggest taking a chance. (See the sidebar Should We Use Modern Materials? on page 522.)

Figure 1
OUR FLOOR

This is the floor we installed in our little building. Compare this to the raised floor in figure 2, page 516. Both designs enclose the entire living space in a box of insulation, but our floor only needs to combat a constant 55° F temperature, so we don't need as much insulation under it as we would with a raised floor (which would be dealing with much colder air temperatures in our climate). The energy of the sun entering our insulated box is stored in the slate and sand mass and slowly given back to the room.

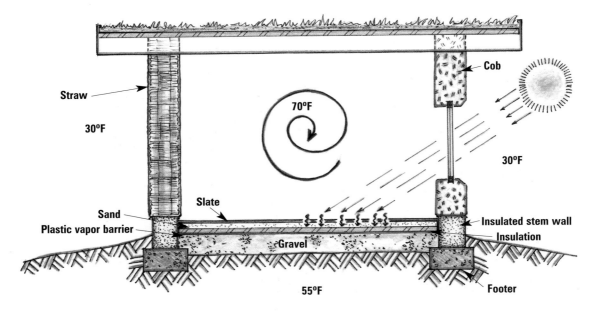

Slabs on grade. Probably the most popular modern floor on grade is the concrete slab. It comes in many flavors. *Left:* A floor doesn't have to be inside to be part of a room. This painted concrete slab makes up the floor of a cozy patio. *Middle:* This beautiful floor is a concrete slab covered with salvaged granite pieces laid in thinset mortar. *Right:* This floor is—you guessed it—a concrete slab. This time it's covered with ceramic tile set in thinset mortar. In most climates, a slab on-grade floor should have insulation installed under it to create a buffer from the temperature of the earth beneath.

Since this floor is sitting on the ground, creating a separation from water is an important issue in all but the driest climates. First and foremost, grade floors need to be coupled with careful grading and foundation drains (see chapter 6) to keep liquid water out of the picture. In addition, some measure needs to be taken to prevent moisture held in the earth below the building from loading the interior air with water, causing high humidity and condensation. For example, a vapor barrier, such as plastic sheeting, placed somewhere below the floor surface will simply block the water's movement. Another strategy is to use a material containing a lot of air space (such as a gravel bed) to break up the direct route water would take through capillary action.

A floor on grade can be made using pretty much any dense thermal mass. Examples are concrete slabs, puddled adobe, and stone or brick set in sand.

New, improved earth. Adobe floors are sublime. They take materials from every building's real floor, the earth, and refashion it to serve human needs. Like concrete slabs, they can be designed to be durable, dry, insulated, and used as thermal mass for passive solar designs. Unlike concrete, they have a natural warmth and softness and a low embodied energy because they're made primarily of soil.

Raised Floors

A raised floor attempts to isolate the interior floor surface from the earth. This is accomplished by suspending a framed platform above the surface of the ground (see figure 2). In modern residential construction, the framing is usually wood covered with plywood sheathing, and it's installed on stem walls connected to a foundation. Framing on piers to create an area under the floor open to air circulation is another option. The space below the floor is commonly called a crawlspace if it's shallow and a basement if it's deep. This strategy allows for the creation of a level floor that's solidly supported by the earth through a foundation while at the same time separated from surface water and the cooler-than-human-comfort thermal mass of the earth. In most climates, insulation is integrated into the raised platform to work with wall and roof insulation to completely encircle the building, thus allowing the interior to maintain a temperature separate from the air surrounding it.

Figure 2
RAISED FLOOR

The strategy here is to lift the entire living space away from the cold, wet, insect-ridden ground and surround it with insulation. Without significant mass in the floor, passive solar heating becomes more difficult, so some other primary heat source needs to be called upon.

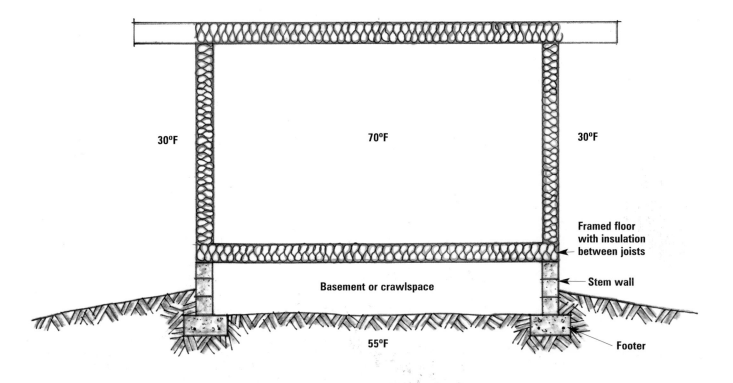

30°F   70°F   30°F

Framed floor with insulation between joists

Basement or crawlspace

Stem wall

55°F

Footer

Even though it's physically separated from the ground, water can still be a big problem in a raised floor. In fact, in most cases, both raised and grade floors have essentially the same relationship to water. Liquid water needs to be graded away, and water vapor held in the earth needs to be prevented from accessing the air in (and with a raised floor, under) the building. We'll discuss raised floor strategies for dealing with water at the end of this chapter.

Finish floor. Wood flooring, like these tongue-and-groove pine boards, is a common surface for raised floors.

Living floor. This side of the floor of a little building in the woods was raised above the ground by tying a floor joist log to a living tree. Raised floors can be the fastest, easiest way to create a flat surface and rise above water.

Cocoon of insulation. The raised floor of the first story of this house is level with the porch. It's framed on the stem walls of the basement, therefore separating it physically from the ground. Cellulose was blown between the floor joists to combine with the wall and roof insulation to surround the living space with a cocoon of insulation (see figure 1, page 514).

COVERING THE FLOOR APPLIED: OUR LITTLE BUILDING

DESIGNING A FLOOR

We've already talked at length in chapter 3 about the mandate that each of us has to use passive solar design. In our particular climate of fairly cold winters and pretty hot summers, that means collecting the winter sun and buffering our building from the summer sun. Most of the sunlight that enters a building hits the floor, so the floor is the logical choice to put mass that will collect the sun's energy. In our climate on a sunny site such as ours, a thermal mass on-grade floor was really the only sensible choice. Not only will it collect the winter sun's heat, but this mass will also serve as a shaded heat sink for warmer summer air.

We've already gone to great lengths to set the stage for passive solar collection. We've carefully placed our building in the path of the winter sun, chosen a great thermal mass material—cob—for our southern wall, installed insulation materials that fit the particular situation in all of our walls and the roof, and calculated the right amount of glass to feed the sun's energy onto a mass floor of our choice. All that's left is to install that floor.

Real World Passive Solar

As we've discussed, the basic idea of passive solar heating is to let enough winter sun enter through south-facing glass to be stored in the floor mass to keep the room warm. Too much glass or too little mass means overheating during the day and quick heat loss at night. Too much mass or too little glass means a building that responds slowly to temperature change. Therefore, it was important for us to match the amount of floor mass to south-facing wall glass in our little cottage.

However, to create a truly effective solar design, we needed to consider many factors. Everything from how often the sun is likely to shine in the winter (ratio of shady to sunny days) to the thickness of our walls (thick walls block more sun coming in at an angle than thin walls) will affect the actual amount of sun passing through our glass to hit the floor mass. In addition, passive solar heating and cooling needs often conflict in the same building. For example, windows set to the east and west for summer ventilation will mean more heat loss in the winter. These and other variables complicate solar design and make it difficult for the owner-builder to rely solely on general recommendations found in books. Therefore, the best research you can do is to find passive solar buildings in your exact climate and investigate their particular strategies and how well they're working.

Combining this information with whatever theory you've learned in books will give you the best chance of creating a passive solar design appropriate for your situation. Be sure, however, that you use it as part of a complete design approach. In other words, use passive solar design to enhance your building; don't let it control it. In our building, for example, we used a bit less glass than was optimum for solar heating with the mass in our floor. We did this because it seemed more glass would compromise the feeling of privacy that was very important to our overall design. In the end, a building based solely and rigidly on passive solar principles runs the danger of becoming an energy-efficient yet soulless place.

THE BASIC DESIGN

The details of creating an on-grade floor designed to collect solar heat can be tricky. On the one hand, you need the area surrounding the mass to be insulated. If it isn't, a lot of that solar heat we worked so hard to collect will simply leak right back out of the building. On the other hand, most insulation materials need to be lifted off the ground and therefore away from the floor, as is the case with all four of our wall systems. They are generally lifted up on some sort of masonry stem wall, made either of stone or concrete. Neither material has any insulation value to speak of. A common modern solution is to install rigid insulation on the outside of the stem wall, though in this position it's vulnerable to ants and can be a hidden access area for termites. Our solution was to create insulated stem walls out of concrete with vermiculite aggregate (see chapter 7 for details). These stem walls create an insulated box within which we can install the layers of our floor: leveling bed of gravel, vapor barrier, insulation, sand, and, finally, grouted slate.

The Gravel Bed

Our gravel bed serves two purposes: It creates a level surface and slows down the movement of water from the ground through capillary action. To install it we figured out the collective depth of the layers of materials we would need above it, and then poured in, leveled, and tamped gravel to the appropriate height on our stem wall. You may remember from chapter 7 that we planned on having our finish floor end about 2 inches below the level of our infill wall materials. This is called a toe-up and it helps protect the vulnerable infills. For example, if a water pipe were ever to break, the whole building would have to be flooded with more than 2 inches of water before the walls were in danger.

Figure 3
GRAVEL BED

To install the gravel bed, first we had to determine how far below the top of the stem wall the top of the gravel bed should sit. To do that, we simply figured out how thick the combined layers of our floor were, not including the gravel bed. (By the way, figure 1 on page 514 shows the concrete footers at the corners of the building. Figure 3 is a cutaway showing the middle of a wall, so the gravel trench is visible here.)

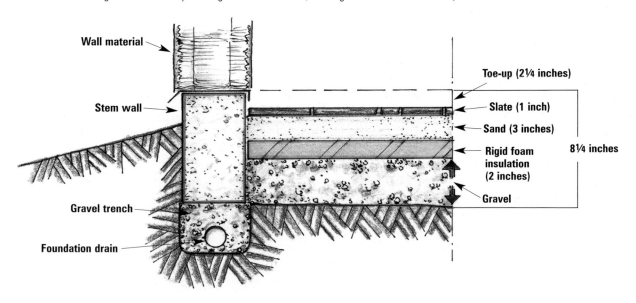

▲ **Step 1.** Remember way back when we built our stem walls and created the initial frame of the building? At this point, we started the floor by installing most of the gravel bed. First, we figured how far from the top of the stem wall the top of the gravel bed should be (see figure 3). Then we placed a straight board on top of the stem walls and moved it around to check the gravel elevations at different spots with a tape measure. We added gravel until it was approximately at the correct depth all around the space.

▲ **Step 2.** The finished floor is often the last element installed in a building so that it won't be subject to the foot traffic, dropped tools, and dragged ladders common in construction. After we'd installed all of our walls, doors, and windows, we resumed work on our floor by finishing the gravel bed. First, we used a magnet attached to a broom handle to pick up any loose nails and other metal that might have fallen into the gravel over the course of construction. This is important because we don't want to puncture our plastic vapor barrier. At this point we also removed any small stray wood pieces, straw, or other cellulose that might attract termites.

▲ **Step 3.** After double-checking the depth of our gravel bed relative to the top of the stem wall, we raked it level...

▲ **Step 4.** ...and compacted it with a hand tamper.

The Vapor Barrier and Insulation

A gravel bed should slow water movement from the ground toward the floor, but is it enough to keep the floor dry by itself? A simple test is to lay a tarp over an installed gravel bed. If, after several days, there's condensation on the tarp when it's turned over, the gravel is still letting considerable water pass up from the earth. (Of course, this test only works if you have a roof over your gravel.)

We installed our gravel many months before we were ready to install the floor, so we had the opportunity to do this tarp test several times. We consistently found a lot of condensation on our tarp. As a result, it was a no-brainer that we needed a vapor barrier. After carefully sealing the barrier to the stem wall, we placed our rigid insulation.

The Vapor Barrier

Condensation test. Throughout the building process, we kept our gravel bed covered with a tarp. Every time we pulled the tarp back, we found a fair amount of condensation below. Here, you can see the damp gravel and droplets of condensation on this tarp that has just been pulled back. These tests were clear evidence that we needed to use a vapor barrier over our gravel bed.

▲ **Step 1.** First, we laid our barrier on our clean, level gravel bed. We used 6-mil polypropylene sheeting as a vapor barrier. We were able to use a single sheet off a 14-foot-wide roll, so we only had joints at the edges of the floor.

◄ **Step 2.** A vapor barrier is supposed to prevent condensation from moving from the earth into the flooring materials. It doesn't make sense to go to the trouble of installing one and then leave a huge joint open for water movement all around the edge of the barrier. For that reason, we sealed the edges of the plastic to the stem wall by applying a bead of roofing cement with a caulk gun (top), and pushing the plastic into it by hand (bottom).

Dry. Since we were also careful not to puncture the plastic, there should be very few, if any, avenues for water to move up from the earth below.

◀ **Step 1.** We laid 2 inches of rigid insulation over the vapor barrier. We used both new sheets…

▲ **Step 2.** …and any scrap we had leftover from the roof as well as pieces we'd collected from other projects. If we didn't have a tight joint, as is the case here, we laid scraps of ½- or 1-inch foam over the gaps.

Should We Use Modern Materials?

For someone who's being environmentally or even financially conscious, choosing modern mass-produced materials can seem like a sin. Often, though, if we look at the embodied energy in a material and then consider the energy it's likely to save over its lifetime of service to the building, we can make an intelligent, responsible decision to use these materials in specific situations.

For example, let's look at the use of rigid foam insulation in the floor of our little building. First of all, unlike foam placed outside of stem walls, our foam should last a very long time in this application because it's protected from UV, abrasion, and insects—the three forces to which it's vulnerable. By using published embodied energy estimates, we figured that the foam in our floor would take about 900,000 Btu's to produce. The little direct-vent propane space heater that we plan to install in the building is rated at 10,000 Btu's per hour. That means that our foam would have to help store enough solar energy in the floor to prevent our heater from having to come on for 90 hours before it would recoup the energy made to use it.

Our building is small and well insulated, so our propane heater is tiny—its output is basically equivalent to that of a single burner on a typical gas cook stove turned all the way on. Based on my experience with passive solar in my climate, I believe that our foam will help recoup that energy in the first winter, and probably in the first month of the first winter. If my estimation is correct, then, it would be environmentally irresponsible NOT to use the foam. By the way, according to our calculations, the embodied energy of our plastic vapor barrier is about 175,000 Btu's or 20 percent of the embodied energy of our foam. We also feel that energy expenditure will be recouped many times over.

Of course, we're basing our estimates on someone else's calculations of a very complex concept, embodied energy, so maybe our numbers are wrong. I don't like doing anything based on numbers alone. I'm also relying on experience and that infinite 55° F heat sink under the floor to give me confidence that adding insulation will save energy in the long run.

Installing the Mass

The mass for modern passive solar floors is most often provided by a concrete slab, either left plain or covered with tile or some other massive finish material. The other end of the spectrum is an adobe or earthen floor that consists of a number of layers of a cob-like mix that's then usually sealed, often with oil and wax. We chose to treat our floor much like an outdoor patio. First, we installed a 3-inch layer of sand mixed with a bit of dry Portland cement. We leveled and smoothed this layer by running a long straight board, a screed board, over it. This is a technique that's often used to level poured concrete. We laid large pieces of salvaged 1-inch-thick slate and granite over this sand layer. The result is 4 inches of total mass, which should be a good amount for our passive solar needs. The final floor is incredibly beautiful, very durable, and quite inexpensive, with a low embodied energy.

Installing the Sand Layer

▲ **Step 1.** We were now ready to install our sand layer. We had some old bags of Portland cement that had gotten wet on another job, so we decided to use what we could salvage from them to stabilize our sand a bit. We dry-mixed about 1 part Portland cement with 6 parts sand.

▲ **Step 2.** Before installing our vapor barrier, we'd measured down from the stem wall and marked where the top of the sand layer would sit. We used a level to draw a line around the perimeter of the building (see arrow in photograph). We now spread about 3 inches of our sand/Portland cement mix on top of the insulation, using the line as a guide.

◀ **Step 3.** We then compacted the mix with our ever-faithful tamper.

▲ **Step 4.** Before leveling the surface, we carefully installed supports for screed boards on the north and south edges of the floor. These supports were leveled to be flush with the line we'd drawn on the stem wall to represent the top of the sand layer. We used some thin slate pieces as supports, but we could also have used strips of wood because they'll be removed before laying the finish floor.

▲ **Step 5.** We placed a long straight board on the supports and pulled it slowly back and forth, a process called "screeding," to create a level surface at the height we wanted. We took out excess or added sand as needed.

▲ **Step 6.** We worked from both sides toward the middle and doubled-checked things on occasion with a level.

Ready for the finish floor.
To use up the old Portland cement, we ended up filling the final little voids and skimming the surface with a Portland-rich mix. That's why the surface of our finished sand layer is grey.

Installing the Finish Floor

◄ **Step 1.** We dampened the sand mix with a hose before laying the stone; this water and ambient moisture should eventually harden the sand/cement layer enough to prevent any settling of the floor over time. Since we'd made a mock-up of our floor on the ground outside, we knew our approximate layout before beginning to set the floor.

▲ **Step 2.** We cut the stone when needed with a masonry blade on a circular saw.

▲ **Step 3.** Then, simply set it into place.

▲ **Step 4.** The sand mix was generally flexible enough to allow for a bit of adjustment with a few light taps of a hammer if necessary.

▲ **Step 5.** We checked for level often and also used a straightedge, such as a 2x4, to make sure that the edges of all adjacent pieces were in the same plane.

Stone puzzle. Here you can see some of the variety of shapes and joint sizes. We'll add smaller pieces to the larger joints before grouting. One word of caution if you're using salvaged stone: Make sure that everything is the same thickness. Some of our granite was a full ¼-inch thicker than other pieces, which created lots of headaches in installation after we'd gone to the trouble of making such a wonderfully smooth sand layer.

Grouting

Since our stone isn't cemented to a sub-floor, as is usually the case with modern tile and stone floors, gravity and the grout filling our joints will be called upon to hold the pieces in place. We used a sanded grout and applied it as with any tile or stone floor.

Grouting

▲ **Step 1.** At this point, our floor was like any other tile or stone installation. Here, Lisa grouts the joints…

▲ **Step 2.** …and sponges off the excess.

▲ **Step 3.** Some of our joints were large enough to be in danger of having the grout crack. We reduced the grout span with small decorative granite chips.

Construction Blunders: Look before You Lay

As we'll discuss in the next chapter, salvage materials sometimes bring hidden costs in time, materials, and poor energy performance. For the most part, though, the salvaged stone we've used all over our building hasn't been like that. However, we did make a mistake by installing a polished granite door threshold. It seemed like a good idea at the time. We found a piece that was the right size, and we knew it would be very durable and would add an elegant beauty to our entrance.

Polished stone, though, is very slick when wet, something we remembered the first time we stepped on our threshold after a rain. We fixed the problem by covering the stone with a couple of coats of polyurethane with a bit of sand mixed in. The sand creates a rough enough surface to create foot traction. If this solution isn't durable over time, we may decide to cover the threshold with a rough tile. The lesson: It's great to be creative with resources; however, you also have to keep the practical side of your brain engaged to make sure that what you're installing will actually do the job intended.

Great material, bad application. This piece of salvaged granite is both durable and beautiful. Unfortunately, it's also slippery when wet, which makes it a poor choice for an exterior door threshold.

WHAT WE'VE ACCOMPLISHED

Our floor is the culmination of a careful passive solar design strategy. By creating an insulative box with our stem walls and using a combination of salvaged and mass-produced materials, we've created a beautiful surface that has all the characteristics we look for in a floor: It's flat, level, durable, dry, and warmer in the winter while cooler in the summer.

Solid beauty. The finish floor is solid, level, and quite striking. You can't tell that it's sitting on sand rather than a concrete slab.

Solar floor. On sunny winter days, our large, south-facing glass doors will bathe the mass of our floor in the sun's heat. In the summer, our large roof overhangs and thick walls will shade the floor, keeping it cool.

VARIATIONS

RAISED FLOORS

Though floors on grade are much easier to incorporate into most passive solar strategies, there are plenty of situations in which a raised, framed floor is the best choice, the most obvious example being the floors of multistoried buildings. You can't build a floor on grade 10 feet in the air.

A wet, hot climate is another place where floors on grade often don't make sense. The ground is damp and there's no need to collect the winter sun's heat, so why not get your floor up and out of the way? In this situation, a floor on piers would keep the area under the floor open, allowing ventilation and also creating storage for outdoor items like ladders and bicycles.

If the climate is right, then, it's probably best to leave the area under a raised floor open. In colder climates where floor insulation is required, the space beneath raised floors is often encased in a stem wall box, creating an area called a crawlspace. This frequently leads to a conceptual incongruity: Though framed floors are trying to get away from the ground, they now have a damp, dark useless piece of ground directly below them that attracts mice, snakes, mold, and anything else that likes to live in a cave. If you live above such a zoo, its inhabitants will eventually give you plenty of opportunities to crawl around on your stomach in a feeble attempt to convince them to leave.

Ventilation and storage. This building is raised up on mortared stone piers. It was built in a cold climate, so insulation was placed between the floor joists as a part of a cocoon of insulation surrounding the living space, as illustrated in figure 2, on page 516. The space underneath the floor is left open, allowing for air circulation, which will help keep the area dry and, hopefully, mold free. This open space is also being used for organized storage, something that's often in short supply, especially in and around a small house.

Open floor plan. A raised floor was obviously the only option in this situation. Even if built over land instead of water, open raised floors make sense in this hot, wet climate. The open framing allows plenty of air circulation to help keep the bottom of the floor cooler and also drier and less susceptible to mold and other growth. Since there's no winter heating season, nothing would be gained from connecting to the ground or closing in the raised floor and insulating it.

If your building calls for an enclosed crawlspace, your main concern needs to be to keep water out because water is what attracts everything else. Water can enter a crawlspace by several avenues: as liquid moving on top of or through the ground and as vapor moving through the air or evaporating from the ground. First, you need to deal with the liquid water. If it's coming up through the ground (a spring, for example), you're in trouble. The only real solution is not to build where this is a possibility. Surface water, on the other hand, can be redirected by shaping the ground around the building, a process called grading that we covered in chapter 6. So much for liquid water.

Now, on to vapor. The dirt floor of crawlspaces can be a huge source of water vapor. The most obvious step is to cover the ground with a vapor barrier. Be sure to seal the edges of the barrier against the building as we did with our floor. Hollow concrete block walls are another avenue for moisture. As water evaporates off the surface of the ground, it can pass through the open block cavities and be deposited directly onto floor framing. If you need to use hollow block or are trying to fix a moisture problem in a building that already has them, stuff the open cavities with something waterproof, like plastic bags, to prevent air movement and hence vapor movement through the block.

Having sealed all other avenues, the only way water can enter your crawlspace now would be in damp air. As we know, when damp warm air hits a cooler surface, condensation is the result. This is exactly what happens when warm damp summer air passes through foundation vents into a cool crawlspace. Though they are installed to help remove damp air, in a crawlspace where liquid water and water vapor evapo-

Misguided crawlspace. The raised floor for this house doesn't sit on the stone but was framed on a ledger attached to the post at right and others like it. Stone was added later to surround the building as an aesthetic choice, creating an enclosed crawl space below the floor. This was a mistake for several reasons. First, the ground around this building isn't well graded, so some liquid surface water ends up under the building after big rains. Second, the ground under the building is irregular, so a vapor barrier would be difficult to install. Third, the stonework wasn't done well enough to keep animals out. The result is a dark, very wet, moldy crawl space that's home to a variety of creatures. There's so much condensation that the fiberglass batts between the joists are damp and falling down. Eventually, this building will suffer structurally from water damage because of this situation. The interior air quality is suffering now.

rating off the ground have been eliminated, these vents may be the only remaining source of moisture getting in. In that case, closing foundation vents, or never installing them in the first place, should be the final measure that will allow your crawlspace to stay dry.

Basements are just giant crawlspaces, usually with concrete slab floors, so the same techniques apply to them. An added problem with basements is that they have dirt piled against their stem walls, so liquid water and condensation in the earth need to be prevented from moving through the wall and into the space. Therefore, in addition to the measures already described, a well-designed and carefully installed waterproofing system is important on the outside surface of basement walls.

HYDRONIC FLOOR HEATING

Regardless of the type of floor you choose, hydronic floor heating (sometimes called radiant floor heating) is something to consider. In this system, tubes that carry a heated liquid are installed within the heated envelope of the floor, i.e., above the insulation.

Hydronic heating is a good backup for passive solar floors because the floor mass already in place will absorb heat from the tubes in much the same way as it will absorb the heat from the sun. Therefore, on shady winter days, the heated liquid in the tubes simply replaces the sun, heating the floor mass, which then slowly radiates the energy into the room. What's more, by running it through roof-mounted solar collectors, the liquid in the tubes can actually be heated by the sun part of the time.

Hydronic heating can also be used with raised floors. A thin slab incorporating the tubing can be poured over a framed and sheathed floor system, or hardwood flooring can simply be installed over tubes attached to a wooden subfloor.

HYDRONIC FLOOR HEATING

▲ **Step 1.** In this system, roof-mounted panels collect the sun's energy to heat liquid…

▲ **Step 2.** …which is circulated to a storage tank that's hooked up to a pump, sensors, a back-up heat source, and all sorts of apparatus that send thermostatically controlled amounts of heat …

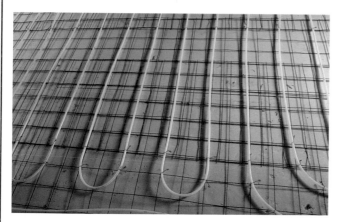

▲ **Step 3.** …to tubes like these embedded in insulated concrete slabs…

▲ **Step 4.** …under both hardwood and tile floors, creating an even, very comfortable heat for the building.

PART TWO: BUILDING

Connection

The secret to making a small building big is to connect it intimately with the outside. In chapter 15, we'll flush out our indoor and outdoor rooms while finishing the doors and windows that serve as transitions between the two. More fundamentally, everything we need comes from the outside: sun, water, air, and food. Although features such as natural ventilation and passive solar design allow for direct access to much of what we require, most houses augment these direct connections (for example, plumbing brings in water and wood stoves bring in heat). These efforts are collectively called "systems." In this section, we'll also discuss the simple systems that will round out our building.

Chapter 15

Creating a Connection:
Inside, Outside, Transitions, and Systems

At this point, our building is a self-reliant entity that can deal with gravity, snow, rain, wind, sun, insects, animals, molds, fungi, and probably earthquakes on its own. Yet it's clearly not done. It's still just a shell of the dream we started out to fulfill. What's left to do? How do we finish it? In order to get to the bottom of that question, let's take a moment to review where we started and how far we've come.

GENERAL CONTEXT: CREATING A CONNECTION

We humans are in an interesting predicament. We need to be constantly and intimately connected to the outside world, but we can't actually live there. Our local environment is too cold, too hot, too wet, too windy, too dangerous, or some combination of these for us to survive outside—or at least be as comfortable as we'd like to be. Housing to the rescue. A house divides the world into two zones, an inside and an outside, with the dividing line being the house itself. The goal of a house is to make the inside a more stable and comfortable environment than the ever changing outside while still keeping a constant connection to the basics of survival that the outside world provides: sunlight, water, air, and food.

In this book, we've been intimately involved in trying to understand how to create this separation with constant connection. Toward that goal, way back in chapter 1 we defined a house as a building designed to sustain human life. We then outlined four elements a house needs in order to do its job: a self-supporting structure, the ability to create a stable indoor temperature, an effective separation from the ever present forces of decay, and a constant connection to and exchange with life-giving elements of the outdoor environment. In terms of these four elements, then, where does our building stand at present? We've carefully constructed an incredibly stable structure, including a strong skeletal framework buttressed by structural infill materials. We've encouraged a stable indoor temperature through careful passive solar design that includes both heating and cooling strategies. We've gone to great lengths to create an exterior skin that will separate our building from the forces of decay, and, we hope, insure it a long, fruitful life. All that remains, then, is for us to focus on the final element: connection to the outside.

To do that, we need to return to the image of a house separating the world into two zones—an inside and an outside. To finish our house, we must set up both the inside and the outside around the building to match our needs, while also creating a strong connection between the two spheres.

Connecting inside to outside. The connection between an indoor and outdoor living room becomes complete when these large doors are swung open.

THE INSIDE

For most modern people, a building is all about the inside. They rent an apartment or buy a spec house, and the only thing they can control is the decoration of the interior. Unfortunately, much of the true character of the building's interior isn't created by furniture or artwork but by the way that the physical building has been designed to allow a connection to the outside.

The way sunlight enters a room, for example, almost single-handedly defines the space. But once a building has been sited and the windows and doors placed, little can be done to change this pivotal characteristic of the interior. The same is true of how fresh air moves through a building and many other variables that create the feel of an interior space. In other words, by the time you're ready to hang that painting or place that couch, most of the character of the interior has been determined.

The only way to really get the interior you want, then, is to consider the connection between the exterior world and the interior of the building carefully throughout the design and construction process. If you do this, then finishing the interior is a process of putting the final touches on the creation of a feeling you've been crafting for some time.

That's not to say that these finishing touches aren't incredibly important. In chapter 4 we pointed out that any place, including a single room in a house, is identified by the repeating actions it encourages. The details of the steps you take to finish the interior of your building will have a huge effect on this.

Take, for example, something as simple as a light switch. I've lived in houses where the light switch was set on the hinge side of a door opening into a room. This meant I had to walk into the room and close the door before turning on the light instead of just reaching for the switch as I walked through the door. No matter how many times I did it, this awkward action drove me crazy. Put a bunch of details like that together, and you've got yourself some grumpy inhabitants.

Of course, the opposite is true for the other side of the coin. Thoughtfully conceived details, such as color combinations, shelves in the right places, or a private seating niche connected to a public room, can add up to encourage a feeling of ease and contentment. In fact, careful consideration of all the small details of your building will have a huge effect on your happiness.

Forcing an interior on an unwilling building. Somebody really tried to make this shopping mall a nice interior space. They created the façade of a medieval market, including wooden shingled arcade roofs complete with dormers brimming with plastic greenery and bay windows protruding into the "street." In the end, though, the big ugly box of a building preordained a drab, soulless interior.

Building and interior created together. The interior of our little building, on the other hand, was an integral part of the design from the beginning. The wall surfaces have built-in shelves and hangers, windows were placed carefully to illuminate specific activities with their sills constructed to be useful, and many other small features have come together to create a complex, complete environment in a tiny space.

THE OUTSIDE

Though it may sound corny, it's simply true that our real home is the earth itself: the outside. Everything that sustains us comes from the earth: food, water, warmth, and air. We need to bring these things into our houses, true, but we need more than that. A prison, after all, has food, water, heat, and ventilation. The modern human has still not lost the need for outdoor spaces such as gardens, patios, open-air workshops, and plots of open space to throw a Frisbee or fly a kite. Consequently, a successful house has both indoor and outdoor rooms.

As a project gets to this stage, the outdoor rooms, if considered at all, are often neglected in favor of finishing the interior. Money, time, and patience are all waning, and something has to give. That's understandable, but it's important to do at least some work on the outdoors at this point. First of all, the act of construction has most likely been disruptive, and there might be ailing areas that simply need immediate attention. Second, some elements of outdoor rooms can take quite a while to install. For example, those deciduous trees that you want to plant for summer shade are going to take many years to grow into their job. The same goes for gardens, berry bushes, and firewood groves. Unless you're immortal, it's important to get started on these things now so that you can enjoy them in their fullness during your lifetime. Another reason to get started is that finished outdoor rooms encourage people to spend more time outside. That translates into a lot of positive things: less electricity used, more fresh air breathed, more muscles moved, more neighbors met, and a closer connection to what's going on outside in our real home, the earth.

Growing a room. Building outdoor rooms can take a lot of time. This is the north side of a partially bermed, passive solar house soon after construction (left) and two years later (right). Deciduous trees have been planted that will eventually shade the roof and porch in the summer as part of the building's cooling strategy, but it will be a number of years until they're really doing their job.

TRANSITIONS: DOORS AND WINDOWS

The line between indoor and outdoor rooms is the building itself. Openings in that line, windows and doors, create transitions between these spaces. At this point in the process, we've already gone to great lengths to meticulously create and prepare these transitions. We've carefully designed their locations to create the best ventilation, just the right views, the correct amount of solar heat gain, the right kind of illumination for the task at hand, and the most natural flow of movement between inside and out. In the act of construction, these openings have required a lot of work, including careful structural reinforcement as well as trim, flashing, and other measures to seal the joints created in the protective skin. Even after all of this preparation, what we've accomplished functionally is to create strong weatherproof holes that render all of the painstakingly installed insulation in floor, walls, and roof basically useless.

It's now time to carefully fill these holes. We're not going to go into great depth about doors and windows because it's a topic amply covered in numerous sources, and, in fact, doors and windows are one area where I think modern construction has made great strides. Let's just go over a few basics.

Glass

Though it blocks the wind, a single pane of glass is still basically a hole in the wall as far as thermal performance is concerned. Luckily, modern glass technology has developed ways of creating multiple-paned glass units. Basic double-pane glass (two pieces of glass separated by a sealed air-space) has a base R-value at least double that of single-pane glass. This can be improved with special coatings and by replacing the dividing air with other gases to make the glass unit four or more times more energy efficient than a single pane. Triple pane glass units go even further.

One thing to think about, though, is that more panes, coatings, and the like can also drastically cut down on the amount of sunlight that passes through the glass. This isn't a good thing if the glass is supposed to be part of a passive-solar collection system. If you're going to be collecting solar energy in a mass (and you live in the Northern Hemisphere), then I suggest using windows and doors with air-filled double-pane glass to the south and fancier glass units with higher R-values in windows facing the other compass directions.

Connection between indoor and outdoor rooms. A beautiful entrance doorway creates an easy transition between the comfortable shaded outdoor patio and the interior living room of this little house.

Single-pane glass. In this window, thin strips of shaped wood, called mullions, separate four single panes of glass.

Double-pane glass. Two panes of glass placed on top of each other are separated by a sealed air-filled space in this window.

Salvage vs. New

There are pros and cons to using salvage windows and doors. The pros are that they reuse resources, are often cheap or free, and can add a beauty and feeling that can be hard to accomplish with new construction. There's nothing quite like the light that comes through old wavy glass. Perhaps contrary to common sense, the main con is that installed salvage windows and doors are often more expensive than new construction. Oh yeah, and they're also commonly covered in toxic lead paint.

Salvage can be more expensive than new because it usually has to be repaired, cleaned, fitted with hardware, and custom installed. This all takes lots of time, a fair amount of skill, and sometimes not a little bit of money. What's worse, as we pointed out above, the single-pane glass in most salvage is almost like a hole in the wall as far as heat loss is concerned. Over the life of your building, this can translate into a lot of energy literally flying out the window, which means more money spent. There are, of course, also environmental costs when energy is wasted. It seems silly to go to the trouble of making a thick insulated straw bale wall, for example, and then install a big energy-sucking single-pane window. This incongruity can be remedied at least partially by installing insulated shutters or some other form of movable insulation to cover the glass on winter nights. Windows that aren't collecting solar heat can also be covered during the day in unused rooms.

New doors, old look. These doors are commercially made. They have double-pane glass and come installed in the doorjamb with stops, weather-stripping, a deadbolt to lock one door in place, and an integrated threshold. Mullions applied to both sides of the glass give the impression of multiple panes.

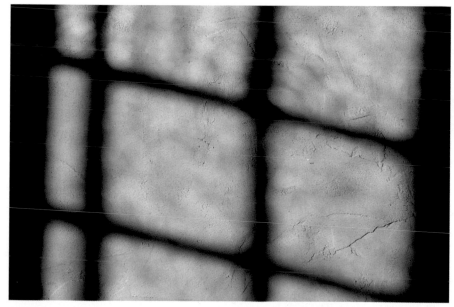

Glass makes light. Humans have been making glass for more than 4,000 years and using it in windows for about 2,000 years. Over that time, glass has been made in a variety of ways. Modern technology has developed techniques for very strong, very clear glass. Older glass-making techniques resulted in less symmetry and perfection, but more character—both in the glass itself and the light passing through it. Here, light shining through old, wavy glass creates a complex pattern on a plastered wall.

If you include your labor in the price, you can most likely build better windows for the same price with new double-pane glass than you can salvage windows with single panes. Custom-sized double-pane glass is reasonably priced, and making an energy-efficient, long lasting door or window is, to my mind, a very sensible use of wood. Another option, of course, is just to buy new windows and doors. In fact, many commercial units are well made, easy to install, energy efficient, available in a wide range of styles, and reasonably priced. I'd definitely check out all your options before committing to a protracted salvage, or make-it-from scratch, adventure. In my own house, I bought high-efficiency windows and doors for the exterior and used salvage and homemade on the interior. Interior doors and windows don't need to be hung as tightly or sealed against rain and air. This means that interior salvage is a lot easier to install. In addition, poor energy efficiency isn't an issue for interior glass.

Interior salvage. *Top:* This old transom window is installed between two interior rooms. Since it's indoors, the wood can remain exposed and even a missing pane can go unreplaced. When closed it provides privacy. *Bottom:* When open it provides natural ventilation as part of an open floor plan/passive solar design.

SYSTEMS

It used to be that most of the necessities of life, the connections to the outside, came in through the front door: water in buckets from the well, vegetables in baskets from the garden, and firewood by the armload from the woodshed. Fresh air came through open windows, and friends had to physically be there in order to have a conversation. In modern housing, these necessities are provided more and more through tubes: electricity through wires in conduit, water through copper or plastic plumbing, gas through steel piping, voices through telephone wires, and warm or cool air through ducts. Collectively these components are called the house's "systems."

In chapter 3, we went over the basics of what I consider to be a sensible approach to systems. It basically boils down to being your own municipal service as much as possible: collecting your own water when possible and purifying it yourself if necessary, producing your own electricity, and manufacturing your own temperature with locally available fuels, such as the sun. The secret to success in this realm is two-tiered: (1) design your building to be energy efficient and (2) create a lifestyle that uses less of everything. For example, rain catchment systems and greywater recycling become a lot more practical if your water use is reasonable. Photovoltaic systems become affordable if you're able to use less electricity. Passive solar design becomes more encompassing if you're willing to wear a sweater inside in the winter and sleep on a shaded north porch in the summer.

A thorough discussion of systems is beyond the scope of this book. However, it's important to at least point out that they aren't all created equal. Sensible systems conceived as an integral part of your design can result in a building that uses less energy than its historical counterparts. On the other hand, systems called upon to provide all life support to a building and to maintain an unconscious lifestyle of energy squandering are a large part of our present environmental crises.

Having our cake and eating it too.
Sensible, efficient systems don't preclude comfort. In my house, we have a combination roof-mounted solar hot water heater (left) with tankless propane backup (white box on wall in photo at right). In the summer, this simple homemade solar heater usually gives us all the hot water we need. In the spring and fall, our tankless propane heater kicks in when we need to supplement the sun. In the winter, the tankless does most of the work. The result is a very low-energy system that provides as much hot water as we want whenever we need it. Notice also our sawdust composting toilet at bottom left of the photo at right. Our house doesn't create any sewage and we drink spring water directly from the ground, so we aren't part of the modern chlorine machine.

CREATING A CONNECTION APPLIED: OUR LITTLE BUILDING

Remember all of that talk back in chapter 4 about places not being things and how the process of building was about slowly crafting a feeling that you imagine? Maybe it sounded esoteric back then, but now we can show you how concrete and straightforward those concepts really are. Since in our design the interior, exterior, and the building itself were always considered together, the process of finishing our building is like placing the last few pieces in a jigsaw puzzle. The whole works together, and it's obvious where those last pieces fit. The interior of our building is tiny, but it doesn't feel small because it's so well connected to the outside. The area around the outside of the building is inviting and will be used because it isn't cut off from the inside. The building itself creates the separation we need (for example, allowing the interior to be much warmer than the exterior on a cold winter night) but also acts as a comfortable, seamless transition between the two related worlds of inside and outside.

TRANSITIONS: DOORS AND WINDOWS

The following short discussion is intended as just a brief introduction to a huge topic. Our goal is to give an inkling of what it's like to both work with salvage and build new doors and windows. Once you get a bit of experience, much of the existing literature and expertise on doors and windows can easily be adapted to fit your specific needs, regardless of the wall system you choose.

Working with Salvage

We used a combination of built-from-scratch and salvage doors and windows in our building. After my spiel on salvage above, it would be fair to ask why we used any salvage at all. There are several answers. First of all, the thick walls of our building will easily accommodate thick insulative shutters which, when closed, will correct the poor energy efficiency of our salvage windows. Second, our building is tiny, so it will be easy to heat and, therefore, it can afford a bit of heat loss in the name of aesthetics. Our salvage windows have beautiful old wavy glass that creates a wonderful interior light and multiple panes that match the feel of the building. Third, and perhaps most important, we had a wonderful collection of salvaged windows stored in a barn about 100 yards from our site. In other words, they were sitting right there.

Even with all of these good reasons, Tim and I occasionally questioned our decision to use salvage. After we'd trimmed them to fit, repaired rotten spots, safely stripped paint (don't forget the issue of lead paint), replaced broken glass, and sealed every pane, we still had to hang them in the jambs, put in stops, and install weather stripping. Store-bought units have all of these pieces already in place along with energy-efficiency ratings several times that of our old windows. Still, the finished salvage windows are really beautiful and add a lot to the feel of our little building.

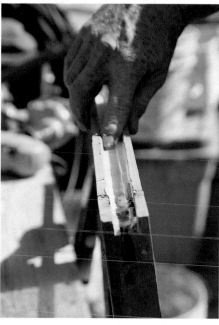

Repairing damaged wood. Creating tight fitting, solid windows or doors out of salvage often requires some honed carpentry skills, store-bought materials like glass and glazing compound, and not a little time. Here, Tim is replacing a rotten piece of wood in an old window. After removing the rotten wood, he evened out the surface with a router (left), then spread some glue in the groove (middle), and installed a new piece of wood that had been ripped to the correct dimension on the table saw (right). Next, he'll trim the new piece to fit and sand the sides to make it blend in with the old.

Repairing glass. *Left:* First we replaced a broken pane with this new glass that we had cut at the local hardware store. We've already installed glazer's points, small metal clips that hold the glass in place. Now, we're sealing the pane with glazer's compound to prevent water and air infiltration. Traditionalists still use putty in a can, but I find this caulk-type tube applicator much easier. *Right:* Next, we used a putty knife to smooth out the compound. Any excess compound on the wood or glass can be easily scraped off with a putty knife after the joint has sufficiently dried. This particular window for our west wall had twelve panes—all of which needed to have the old cracked glazing compound removed and new compound installed. It took quite a while.

Beveled arch. We found this beautiful arched window in the barn. I don't know where it came from. Notice the delicate bevel of the glass around the perimeter of the arch.

Operable. Many arched windows in cob walls are fixed glass. I think it was well worth the effort to make this one operable.

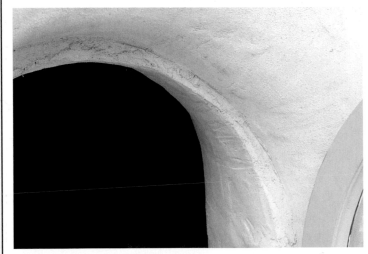

Molded stop. You'll remember that we created an integrated window stop out of cob and covered it in plaster.

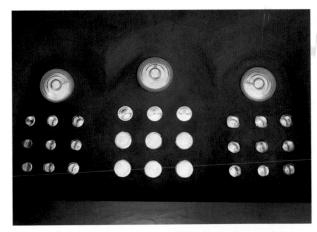

Salvage glass. Don't forget that these bottle units are also salvage. The light they contribute to the interior is very special.

FINISHED SALVAGE: STICK-FRAME WALL WINDOW

Weighted window. We want to use the sill inside this window as a shelf over the interior sink, so we didn't want the window opening in. Opening out would have put the window in the way of people walking by or using the work area under the big porch overhang. *Left:* We decided instead to hang it at the top and have it open up. The window glides open and closed with the help of the counter weight and pulleys seen in this photo. *Right:* When fully open, ventilation is maximized.

Fully adjustable. A jamb cleat from a sailboat, a remnant from Tim's boat-building days, allows the window to be opened as much or as little as we want.

Awning window. In the summer when the hot western sun is a problem, the window can be covered with a piece of fabric and partially closed to act as an awning, blocking sun but allowing ventilation. Notice the wooden stops (the green strips) installed around the window. Stops hold the window in place and help seal against water and air infiltration. We'll eventually install weather-stripping against these stops, as well as those on our other windows and doors. When the window is closed it will compress the weather-stripping and fill any small gaps and irregularities between window and stop, therefore further preventing wind infiltration.

Closures. We used these simple casement window closures to secure all our windows.

Neighborhood salvage. Our neighbor had collected a number of these salvage windows to use as cabinet doors in his house. He was kind enough to let us use these that were leftover.

Old hinges. We used the original hinges, but had to soak them in turpentine and clean them up so they'd move smoothly.

Sill tables. By hanging the windows on the outside of the buck, we created wide sills that can serve as tables for people sitting on the couch.

Building from Scratch

We built our little north window and double doors from scratch. Again, the question might be asked, why didn't we buy commercial units? Well…we originally designed the opening in our north wall for a salvage window. You'll see it if you look back to the plastering photos earlier in the book. When it came time to actually install the window, we realized that it was a complete piece of junk. It was pretty and quaint but would have required way more repair than it was worth. At this point, though, the buck was set and the trim was on. We had no choice but to build a window to fit the opening.

As for our doors, store-bought ones come in standard widths, and they're usually 6 foot, 8 inches tall. For aesthetic and passive-solar reasons, we'd decided to make our doors taller, so off-the-shelf doors weren't really an option in our case. Custom sizes are usually very expensive. Also, you'll remember that our cob door jamb warped quite a bit, so our door was going to need some customizing to fit the opening anyway. For these reasons, site-built doors seemed to make sense.

Still, if it's possible in your design, I recommend buying new windows and doors. If you go that route, remember that they aren't all created equal. Do yourself a favor and buy quality. Good windows will last a lifetime. The only advantage of bad ones, on the other hand, is that they won't last a lifetime, therefore allowing you to replace them sooner with units that actually open and close well. Also, be sure that you choose your windows and doors before building bucks and walls. They need to be designed to work together with the exact specifications of your wall system. There will be sizing and trim details particular to your approach that may vary slightly from the typical stick-framed opening that these units are designed to fill. Plan ahead.

BUILDING WINDOWS FROM SCRATCH

Outside. The window in our straw bale wall was built from scratch in the same manner as the doors, though it was installed using the more sensible approach of hanging the hinges on the exterior edge of the trim. With the applied mullions, I think it looks like an old window, but it has the energy efficiency of double-pane glass, especially important on this cold, shaded north side. **Inside.** On the interior, our thick straw wall, beveled reveals, and deep sill make a beautiful and useable space.

BUILDING DOORS FROM SCRATCH

Simple, sturdy doors. Our doors are thin, tall, and mostly glass—a possible recipe for warping. Luckily, Tim is an experienced door builder. He used kiln-dried southern yellow pine two-by framing lumber off the local hardware store shelf and some simple yet effective joinery to build the doors.

Glass. *Left:* Tim had cut an integral stop around the entire perimeter of each frame as a seat to hold the glass. *Right:* Here the glass has been installed after the window was painted. We added trim and thin mullion strips to make the large pane of glass seem like a number of smaller pieces. Alone it seemed like too much glass for such a small building.

Bowed buck. This bow in our door buck made installation more difficult. We could have put another frame on top of this to create a plumb and even surface on which to hang our doors. This is standard procedure in conventional stick-framing. In our situation, however, each door panel was already only 24 inches wide, which is about the minimum for comfortable movement in and out for most people. We didn't feel we could make the opening any smaller.

Checking for square. Tim checks the squareness of the opening. If it's off, he'll have to trim the door bottoms down to fit.

Hinge complications. We wanted our doors to open inward, which meant we should set our hinges on the inside edge of our buck. However, if you're trying to collect solar heat through glass set in a thick wall, the further toward the outside of the wall that you set the glass, the less the wall will shade it. We decided to set the hinges close to the outside and have the door open in. This complicated the installation.

Installed doors. Even with the frustrating installation complications, everything turned out fine in the end. I think the mullions make our new doors fit with the feel of the salvage windows and the building in general. We bought the brass hardware at an architectural salvage store.

THE OUTSIDE

If you look back at our design discussion in chapter 4, you'll remember how important the area all around the building is to the place that we're trying to create. This tiny guest cottage is supposed to feel like a complete home for our guests, and our outside space needs to be subtly crafted to serve many overlapping functions. We need to make comfortable outdoor spaces that will augment the indoor space, thereby increasing its size. We also need to construct outdoor work areas, places for kids to play, gardens, pathways, and, perhaps most of all, a delicate interplay between privacy and community. It will take a number of years to realize the full dream and create a complete place that's fully integrated with the site and has all the features that we imagine. For example, much of the feeling of privacy will come from plantings that can't just be erected, but have to grow at their own pace. That's all the more reason to get started now. Let's look at a few of the things that we chose to do right away as part of the initial building process.

The Workspaces

Outdoor workspaces are wonderful. Many activities, such as potting plants, require storage shelves and work surfaces but don't really make sense to do indoors. Also, if you're outside working or playing, it's great to have a place to wash hands or soak something without having to take off your dirty shoes to go in the house. The combination of our porch overhang and our "easy to attach things to" stick-frame wall was perfect for creating an outdoor workspace. On the other side of the building, the cordwood wall is easily adapted as an outdoor tool shed.

Installing the Outdoor "Potting Shed"

▲ **Step 1.** You may remember that we'd screwed blocks to the lath before plastering so that we could make attachments later without puncturing the plaster. Here, we've begun attaching strips of wood to these blocks to act as ledgers for our shelving. The metal bracket to the left is going to hold the sink.

▲ **Step 2.** We then screwed our shelves and other attachments onto these ledgers. Here, the shelves, braces, sink, and a little bench are all installed.

Comfortable workspace. *Left:* The completed "potting shed" has ample shelving, a large sink, and a seat below the window that offers a nice view of the surrounding countryside. *Right:* The thickness of our cordwood, cob, and straw bale walls gives them a special feeling that's missing in most modern buildings. The shelving on both the inside and outside of our stick frame wall gives it a similar feeling of thickness.

Salvaged shelves. We used old oak boards for the shelves and ledgers, round "tobacco sticks" (pieces of wood used to hang tobacco for curing) as supports between the shelves, and an old sink. All of these resources came from our pile of salvaged materials collected over the years.

Outdoor tool shed. Our cordwood wall under the other porch overhang is presently an extension of the outdoor workspace—a tool storage area. The log ends are kind of like a big pegboard, allowing us to easily customize hangers for each different tool. By the way, we predrilled before screwing into log ends to prevent splitting.

The Patio

We've said that the area immediately around our cottage needs to serve many functions simultaneously. The workspace that we just installed, for example, is also going to be the path to the cars, or "car connection" in our pattern language vernacular. For the time being, our east side is going to have some tool storage and may eventually be a children's sleeping porch. It's also going to be the path to the eventual composting toilet and the communal courtyard between the shop and the cottage. The area to the south in front of the cob wall is designed to be an extension of the indoor space and to eventually become a private outdoor room for cottage guests. In order for all of these outdoor rooms to be complete, they need to have some kind of floor. It could be grass or even dirt, but we decided to create a more defined patio surface out of slate pieces.

Unlike an indoor floor, an outdoor floor doesn't need to be concerned with condensation or heat loss, but it does need to be able to withstand surface water. An outdoor floor, then, needs to be basically waterproof and sloped slightly to redirect water away from the building. As with indoor floors, there are both on-grade and raised outdoor floors. Raised floors outdoors are usually called decks, and on-grade floors are called patios. Most patio floors are made of some kind of stone set on a substrate that both levels the ground and creates a cushion. Probably the most common substrate for gravel patios is sand. In fact, the interior floor of our building was laid like a conventional patio. We chose to use pea gravel as the substrate for our patio and installed it over landscape fabric early in the construction process so that we could use it as a temporary mud-free work area. (See chapter 7 to review the installation of the gravel base.)

Installing the Outdoor Floor

▲ **Step 1.** After grading the gravel to create a smooth surface that sloped gently away from the building, we laid slate as we had to create the interior floor. It was important that the gravel beneath each piece supported it evenly, so we often had to add a bit of gravel and smooth it out by hand to create the bed.

▲ **Step 2.** The slate pattern was determined by the pieces we had. We occasionally cut a piece with the circular saw or broke off an end with a mason's hammer to get a nice fit before setting it in place.

◀ **Step 4.** Next, we took fine river stone (the same stuff we used as a top layer on our living roof) and poured it into the joints between the slate.

▲ **Step 3.** Once the piece was in place, we slid it back and forth a bit to settle the gravel and help level the slate. Often we had to take pieces out and rework the gravel. This was more tedious than if the substrate had been sand, but it was worth it to get a subfloor that worked double duty as a dry, mud-free workspace throughout the construction process.

◀ **Step 5.** We didn't fill the joints with the pour so there would be room for the excess, which we swept into the gaps by pushing the broom at an angle across the joints.

◀ **Step 6.** We tried to keep the finish "gravel grout" just below the surface of the slate so that feet passing over the area wouldn't pull gravel out onto the patio floor. It still happens sometimes, but it's easy to sweep up.

Outdoor floor. Our finished patio creates a clear transition from the outside (grass at far upper left), to the outdoor living space, to the interior living space. It more than doubles the effective size of the building.

Future Outdoor Rooms

As of this writing, we still have many outdoor rooms to create in order to bring the complete vision of our guest cottage to the light of day. These projects will be spread over a period of years. Good building—building that seeks to create a complete place that integrates the outside with the inside—is a huge commitment. It requires patience, pacing yourself, and the ability to enjoy always having another project on the horizon.

Plant plans. We used gravel in the joints because we plan to introduce mosses and other low growing, shade loving plants that we hope will slowly fill the joints. Our intent is to have the south patio be a very private shady, summer retreat. To that end we'll build a trellis, probably out of bamboo, to the south and grow deciduous vines, maybe grapes that will create shade in the summer but will die back and allow sun to access our solar floor mass in the winter.

Private workshop. On the west, we plan on creating an arch-shaped armature (probably just by running string between the two porch posts) and growing a deciduous plant or annual, perhaps beans, that will help shade the window as well as create privacy and a beautiful dappled light. Also, since greywater from both the inside and outside sinks will empty into a mulch basin just past the patio edge, we'll put plants here to use up the water and also add to the privacy of this side of the building.

Public courtyard. The area to the north of the building will eventually be transformed into a large courtyard, probably with a slate or brick floor, that will span between the planned shop and the cottage. For this project, we'll excavate more of the hill to the east (the place where our retaining wall fades into the ground at the left of this photo) and continue our stone retaining wall around to the south and east. We're going to build a little building into this wall to house our composting toilet, situating it close to the cottage's east roof overhang so that it'll only be a very short, dry walk away.

Roof room. Notice the gravel path that starts at the south (left in the photo) side of the living roof. This path leads to a circular patio on the other side of the roof. We plan to build some sort of little bridge from the stonewall onto the roof to access this patio. It's a wonderful place up there surrounded by lots of interesting plants with a great view of the surrounding mountains.

Garden. The area to the east of the building above the retaining wall will be a vegetable garden.

Children's sleeping porch. The future of this outdoor room is still uncertain. At present it's a place to store garden tools. Once the shop is done, we'll probably move the tools to that building and create the children's sleeping porch here that was part of our pattern language design.

THE INSIDE

Because of our integrated design, we'd been creating our building's interior since early in the construction process. If you look back through this book, you'll see it slowly taking shape. In fact, in one sense everything we've done has been in service to our building's interior. That's a bit frightening to admit because after all of that work, we have a 12 x 10-foot interior space to call home. Yet, time and again, I've heard visitors say that it doesn't feel small. In fact, it's a complete house that really contains a number of overlapping rooms defined not by interior walls, but by the careful way we crafted the space, always using the world outside to enliven, enlarge, and enhance the interior.

Indoor Rooms

The "study." This desk sits under the north window next to the couch. The wide windowsill can serve as a shelf for books, and the high window gives a glimpse of the mountains while maintaining privacy and limiting distractions.

The "living room." *Above:* The built-in sofa against the east wall is designed so that two people can sit and talk face to face, one person leaning against the straw bale wall, the other against a small partition at the other end of the couch. The windows are situated so that each person sitting on the couch can read by the light of one of them. The lintel above the windows creates a protruding lower ceiling, giving the couch the feeling of being in a space that's gently separated from the rest of the room, a bit enclosed and secure like a window seat. The area between the couch and the cob wall has hooks set into the cordwood and serves as an open closet. We'll probably eventually build in some shelves and a drawer or two here where guests can keep their clothes. *Left:* This is the backrest at the south end of the couch. We shaped it so that the view out the cob window wouldn't be obstructed.

The "dining room." By moving the desk a few feet from its perch in the study, it becomes a table that can seat four people, one on each side of the L-shaped couch and two on chairs. One chair comes from in front of the desk, the other from just a few feet away at the cob window.

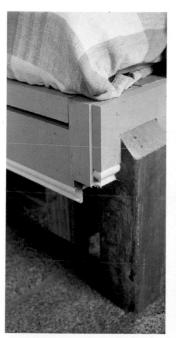  

The "bedroom." The couch easily pulls out into a queen-sized bed. The big east windows will be a gentle alarm clock, bathing sleepers with the morning sunrise.

The "kitchen." Tim designed and built these beautiful shelves. The cable supports are fun and save a lot of shelf space compared to under-the-shelf bracing. Notice how we've tied the new shelving into the built-in cob shelves. The sink was salvaged from a house remodel job. The counters are more of the salvage granite we've used throughout the building. The counter and sink framework is built with 2x4s, salvage plywood, and trim leftover from our house.

The "family room." *Left:* This photo doesn't completely capture it, but there's a lot of open space when the cottage is set up in study/living room mode. The wooden shelf and bottle designs high in the cob wall above the arched window somehow lend a more expansive feeling to the small space, almost like the effect of a large fireplace mantle in a big old drawing room. The open area serves as the main solar heat collection mass in the winter. In fair weather, the double doors can be opened wide to connect the interior with the patio. *Above:* The fact that both interior and patio floors are slate creates a feeling that they're the same room, greatly increasing the perceived size of the space.

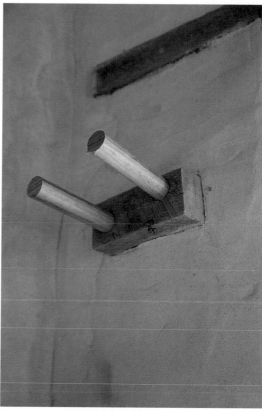

The "entry room." More coat hooks and a chair placed by the door create a little entry room, a place to stop and take off your coat, or sit and put on your shoes before venturing outside.

Design comes alive. It's a special feeling to experience something imagined come to life. If you review our design discussion in chapter 4, you'll see much of what we discussed has been realized, including many seemingly esoteric subtleties. Here, different kinds of glass (including bottles), deep window and door reveals, varied wall and floor materials, and a carefully considered color scheme provide a variety of kinds and patterns of light that create distinct places in this single tiny room.

SYSTEMS

The systems for our cottage are going to be very simple. The small size of our building, passive solar design, and complete insulation cocoon will really cut down on our need for an external heat source. We've planned for a small direct-vent propane heater to do that job. One reason we picked this particular site is that the water pipe from our spring reservoir to our house passes right by the cottage, so we simply have to cut into that line to supply our building with gravity-fed spring water. We'll use this water for both sinks and to create a nice outdoor bathing grotto, probably on the hill to the south looking out over the pond. Greywater from the sink will go to a planted mulch basin off the west slate patio. We plan on building a composting toilet set into an extended stone retaining wall on the east side. We've decided not to have electricity in this building for now. The light of an oil lamp bouncing off the plaster and around the thick window reveals is magical at night. If guests want to keep things cold, there's plenty of room for an ice cooler under the sink. In the winter, a cooler on the north side of the house would keep food cool without ice. Eventually, we plan to equip our cottage's kitchen with a tabletop, two-burner caterer's stove with built-in broiler that runs off propane.

Heating and cooking. Our small direct-vent propane heater will be installed here right next to the counter and the propane caterer's stove. The trimmed box on the wall is for the vent. A small propane tank will sit outside under a workshop shelf. Both the heater and caterer's stove will be within 5 feet of the tank. The propane pipe will come through the chase we set into our stem wall (visible at lower right in the photo).

Cooling. All of our windows are casements or awnings, which means they open wide. The small, open interior space and wide window and door openings create excellent cross-ventilation. This fact, along with the shade of our porch overhangs and correct passive solar siting to maximize roof shading, will keep the cottage's interior nice and cool in the summer.

Water. The water pipe from our reservoir to our house is buried under this grass only a few feet from the cottage. Water is piped from our springhead into the reservoir, which is sited high enough above the house to create good water pressure at the faucets. This is called a gravity-fed water system because gravity, not electricity, is the power source behind the water's movement. We'll tie into this line to send water to the cottage and to a private outdoor bathing area. If you've never taken a shower out in the sun, you don't know what you're missing!

Electricity. Even though we decided not to bring electricity to the cottage, we ran a chase through the stem wall in case we want electricity here later. A tiny photovoltaic system would be adequate for lighting and to run a little stereo or some other gizmo.

WHAT WE'VE ACCOMPLISHED

In modern residential construction, the "outside," if considered at all, is treated almost as an afterthought in a separate construction phase called "landscaping." I don't know how this strange amputation of the outside from the inside developed, but I do know it's a huge mistake. We, on the other hand, never really separated the two and as a result have been steadily working on the spaces both inside and outside throughout this project.

This integrated approach offered us many advantages. It allowed us to very efficiently heat and cool our interior by consciously interfacing with the sun and wind of the site. It guided us to access a clean source of water without pumps or electricity and to redirect the water from our drains for the use of plants rather than treating it as waste. It has given us ample sunlight and fresh air. It also created a building with both indoor and outdoor rooms connected with comfortable transitions. That means we'll never have to make the bizarre choice between indoors and outdoors; we'll enjoy both "places" simultaneously and move freely between them.

To put it more simply, though, this approach seemed the only way we could stay true to our imagination. You'll remember that we started this project with a process of careful imagining. We dreamed up a complete place, focusing on how we wanted it to feel. With that as our blueprint, we had no choice but to follow a building progression that worked simultaneously on indoor and outdoor spaces and the transitions between them. The result, amazingly, is that our little cottage comes very close to embodying the feeling that we imagined. In a down-to-earth, practical sense, we made our dream a reality. As far as I can tell, then, we've built the illusive "dream house" for which so many people seem to be searching.

Chapter 16

The Completed Cottage

To my mind, our building has been a success because it's moved from imagination through design, theory, and execution to come out the other end looking like imagination again. But what does that really mean? It's something that's hard to articulate. They say a picture is worth a thousand words, so perhaps the very big pictures on the following pages are worth 10,000 words each.

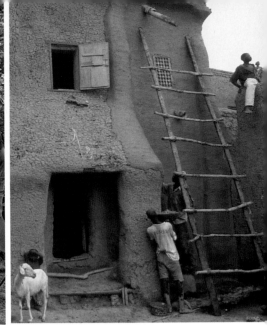

Epilogue
Your Green Building

Have you ever heard of "male answer syndrome"?

This is the dreaded psychological malady that, for example, will compel a guy with no clue as to how engines work to tell you what's causing that noise your car is making. In my experience this tragic affliction isn't confined to men, but I'd say we're the majority of its victims. In any case, we're really trying to make this book "male answer syndrome" free. That's why Tim and I are hundreds of pages into a book written to help you construct a green building of your own and all we've done is talk about ourselves. The fact is that we don't know you or anything about your situation, so we've been limited to showing you in depth the why, what, and how of a green building project that was right for us.

Okay, we've shown you our building, now what are you going to build?

I hope that all the information in this book has brought you much closer to being able to answer that question. But it just doesn't seem right to leave it at that. I want to hear about your situation, your dreams, your plans. Of course, I can't, but maybe at the risk of a "male answer syndrome" relapse, I can venture some general comments and even advice that I hope will help you in your own building projects, whatever they may be.

HOW MUCH WILL IT COST?

How much a building costs sounds like a simple thing to determine. You look in your wallet when you start and look in there again when you're finished and the difference is the cost, right? Actually, lots of other issues affect the true price of a building. I read articles all the time where people claim to have built a house for some tiny amount of money. Often, it's a sort-of-finished building chock-full of salvage materials and a huge time investment by the owners and lots of friends. The number quoted as the cost reflects only the price of store-bought materials, and it's presented in comparison to a finished, code-approved house built by a contractor.

To be kind, this is unrealistic. To be unkind, it's a lie. As we pointed out in the last chapter, salvage has hidden costs, like gas to drive around finding it and then bring it home, not to mention the time and money spent repairing it. More fundamentally,

Cost. The longer a well-constructed building lasts, the cheaper it becomes.

except in the cases of drug dealing, gambling casinos, and the stock market, money is essentially a measure of time spent. If, then, you want to compare the prices of two things, you have to factor in the time you spent on each. If you want to accurately compare the price of a contractor-built house with something you put labor into, then you have to set a value on your labor.

Even more important, we green builders see beyond the falsehood of a simple price tag. We know that the initial cost of a building is just the beginning and that spending more money in construction to create an energy-efficient building can end up saving huge amounts of money through the life of a building. Beyond that, of course, our decisions aren't driven simply by economics. We're dedicated to creating a building that's healthy for both its inhabitants and the environment. In a true accounting, the toll a building extracts from the environment should be a line item on its balance sheet.

In addition, as we've explained before, the longer a building lasts, the cheaper it is. And the longer you, the builder, live in your well-conceived green building, the cheaper it will become. In the end, all of these factors add up to a simple realization: Cost isn't a number, but a function of time.

As for estimates of costs you might incur in real dollars, they are meaningless without a lot of specific information. All I can say is that, in my experience, building always costs more than you think. The less experienced you are, the bigger the gap will be between your fantasized price and the eventual reality.

Tim's Take
Confessions of a Former Shack Dweller

Okay all you old geezers, step back. I'm talking to the idealistic youth now. I know that, for many of you, the concept of green or natural building conjures up an image of self-sufficiency. It represents the dream of taking charge of your own life by building an inexpensive, healthy home with your own hands without debt.

I'm no stranger to this goal; in fact, I've done it myself on several occasions. In the mid-70s while living in Vermont, I built a house with no cash outlay at all. It was made of snow—the ultimate in nontoxic and renewable building materials. I lined the floor with pine boughs that kept me up off the cold ground. It was big enough on the inside for me to sleep, read, and be sheltered from the wind and storms. I lived there for a number of months. After that, I lived in a small shack that I banged together from recycled lumber. It was about 8 x 10 feet with a 5 x 6-foot wing. Compared to the "igloo," this was the Ritz-Carlton. It didn't have a door because I didn't really see the need for one. The roof did a fine job of keeping me and my meager possessions dry.

In neither of these two places did I own the land where I lived. In fact, I'm not even sure that the people who did own it knew that I was there. I had neither running water nor electricity, and in both instances I had to hike in and out a fair distance and rarely (actually never) had visitors.

It isn't difficult to build a shelter out of a variety of different materials for little money. The difficulty for most people comes in matching this shelter to their lifestyle. Most of us want to feel secure that we can't be thrown out of our house for squatting. We also want to be able to drive to within a reasonable distance of our home. Well, with these two simple needs, we've already pulled ourselves abruptly out of funky shack makin' and into plain old deal-with-the-modern-world building. Regardless of your chosen building method, you still have to pay to buy land and build roads. Similarly, if you want electricity, plumbing, heat, energy-efficient glass windows, and the like, these costs are going to be very similar for a given design, whether your walls are built of cob, cordwood, straw, stick-framing, or gold.

Zach's shack. This is Zach. He built this little hut for almost nothing in a few weeks on land owned by his parents. Access is by a steep overgrown path through the woods. There's no water, electricity, heat, or even a door. He lived here for most of a year, including through a cold winter. It was his chosen lifestyle, not the particular design or materials of his building, that made this project a success.

From my experience as a professional builder over the last 25 years, I've found that people almost always share one trait: they want more than they can afford. Even if you think you're going to step out of the rat race and into shack living splendor, ask yourself: is your image of an inexpensive cottage based on imagination or actual research? Have you truly soul-searched whether your imagined shack matches your real lifestyle? Maybe you've chosen a building design using materials you're confident you can pay for, but do you honestly know if you can afford the time it will take to build it?

I can't answer these questions for you, but I can remind you to think practically and realistically about the process of building. So as a starting point, unless you're talking about building a very temporary abode, here's some advice for idealistic youth from a hardened former shack dweller:

1) Buy land. I know private property is evil, and you don't want to kowtow to "The Man," but do yourself a favor and sign on the dotted line. Building is just too much work (and social relations are just too uncertain) to trust a handshake, good will, or fate when it comes to the status of your building site.

2) Access is critical and life is short. The ability to move yourself, tools, and supplies to your site should be made as simple as circumstances allow. The 20-year-old you are may disagree, but the 50-year-old you will become will be thankful.

3) Find water. Easy access to water is paramount, as a perusal of the history of human building will attest. Finding a spring is rare. Digging a well is expensive and basically a crapshoot. Municipal water usually comes with a hefty "tap" fee and is getting more and more expensive by the day. Don't build until you have a clear understanding of where and how you're going to get water.

4) Realistically design heating and/or cooling systems. Though the design, siting, and materials used in your building can greatly reduce your dependence on these systems, most modern lifestyles in most climates require one or both of them. Be realistic. For example, if you think you'll always need just a woodstove, consider installing radiant floor tubing in your mass floor anyway. This step is inexpensive and cannot be retrofitted later without huge expense if you decide to upgrade your heating.

5) Plan for electricity. Even if you think you'll never use it, plan for it. I know from experience that there's a huge difference between a young, single woodsman philosopher, and an older, married guy with kids. If you don't want grid power, price a photovoltaic system and ask what you should install during construction to make a future retrofit easier. Consider hydro or wind. Whatever the source, just take the time to plan for it at the outset. I'm willing to bet that you, or someone living in the house you build, will be thanking me later.

Time. If you don't pick a project that fits your skill level, you'll probably never get it done.

HOW LONG WILL IT TAKE?

You know me well enough by now not to expect a simple answer to this question. Okay, I'll surprise you. Here it is: MUCH longer than you think. To exemplify, I'll make an embarrassing confession. When creating a budget for our cottage project, Tim and I claimed that we could basically finish the building in two months, meaning completing everything but the indoor and outdoor room definition covered in chapter 15. About eight months later we limped to the finish line. I was plastering in November, sometimes until 10:00 pm, hoping the strangely long fall would hold out so that the plaster wouldn't freeze. At this point, I hadn't even collected any firewood for the winter, which meant I was really behind on the basics of my survival.

So listen, friends: Here are two experienced builders—one with more than 25 years of experience and a contractor's license—taking a full four times longer to complete a building than estimated. In retrospect, I really don't understand how we came up with that ridiculous original estimate. It's simply a mystery to me; something I wouldn't believe if it wasn't documented. Luckily, I'm sure all of you complete beginners who might be reading this will never make such a stupid mistake. At least, I'm sure you're convinced you won't.

Please don't misunderstand me. I'm not trying to discourage you. I'm only trying to scare you straight.

HOW DO I GAIN EXPERIENCE?

Probably the main factor in both the cost of your building and how long it will take is the amount of experience you bring to the project. Even if you aren't building it yourself, the more you understand the intricacies of the process, the smoother your project will go and the better the results will be. What are some ways that you can gain experience?

Experience. There's simply no substitute for hands-on experience.

READING AND LISTENING

I guess it's obvious that I'm a firm believer in having a theoretical underpinning to what you do. I've met very experienced builders who didn't have basic theoretical concepts in their heads—things like the path of the sun through the sky or the fact that a thick concrete or stone wall has almost no resistance to heat movement. Because we modern builders don't have the advantage of generations of experience with the same materials in the same climate, I don't think that we can make the best building choices without the help of theoretical concepts learned from books, magazines, websites, and lectures.

As for what you should read or whom you should listen to, I'm going to avoid going into a protracted bibliography here. (You can find a bibliography in my first book, *The Good House Book*.) Instead I'll proffer some general guidelines.

First, use the Internet. I love Internet research because it's so democratic. You'll almost always find dissenting opinions on even the most basic topics, like whether to insulate under a mass floor or determining the correct plaster approach for a given situation. Though on the one hand this can be frustrating because you won't find definitive answers, I think it reflects the real world very accurately. In the end, it's going to be up to you to sift through all the information and make your own decisions. That's true whether you like it or not, and shutting yourself off to dissenting opinions by choosing the first guru who comes along won't change it.

Second, read a wide variety of books and magazines. Don't think that just because you're pretty sure you want to build with straw that you only need to get a book on straw bale construction. Buildings, no matter what they're made of or how they're constructed, are more similar than they are different. You'll find useful information in many sources no matter what you're going to build. Conventional books with information on framing, plumbing, and water detailing have a place right beside your books on straw bale and cob.

For the most basic library, I'd start with design. Of course my favorites are *The Timeless Way of Building* (New York: Oxford University Press, 1979) and *A Pattern Language* (New York: Oxford University Press, 1977), but others may be right for you. A book that goes into the specific intricacies of passive solar design in your climate would be a smart thing. Next, I'd probably get a basic book on stick-framing. I have one called *Graphic Guide to Frame Construction: Details for Builders and Designers* (Newtown, Ct.: Taunton Press, 2000), which is really nice. Besides the fact that you'll probably use some kind of stick-framing somewhere, books on the topic often have a lot of good information on flashing and other details that are conceptually the same across a wide variety of building approaches. I'd also get a pocket reference that has useful conversion tables, math formulas, and all those simple things that are so easy to forget, like the number of pints in a quart.

Next, I'd start collecting books on some of the different materials and techniques that interest me, like straw bale or cob. I haven't seen any that I didn't think were worthwhile, but they do vary quite a bit. Some are designed for the do-it-yourself eco-warrior trying to extricate him or herself from the modern world as much as possible. Others are more geared toward people looking for a sensible, energy-efficient, green option for a home that they intend someone else to build for them. Some books are heavy on construction details; others are heavier on advice. Match your needs to the appropriate books. On the other hand, books are an incredible value and they work better in groups. If you think a book might be of use, take a chance and get it. I referred to my library constantly while building our cottage and writing this book.

As for magazines, the advantage here is that they keep you up to date with specific topics. If you're thinking about going with photovoltaics or a hydro system, subscribe to a magazine like *Home Power*. Over time you'll pick up the basics by reading the beginner's articles, and you'll simultaneously be keeping up with the latest on who's making what gizmo for which purpose. If it's starting to become clear you'll be using some form of straw bale construction in your projects, get *The Last Straw* now so you'll be privy to all of the ongoing conversation, debate, and camaraderie that is the straw bale movement today. Innovations and adjustments to accepted assumptions are a constant in many areas of the building world, so it's good to keep up with the latest information.

OBSERVING

Perhaps the most overlooked avenue for gaining experience is simply studying existing buildings. Every building with which you come in contact is a 3-D glossary of building information. Observing structural characteristics, trying to determine what's causing that water damage, and studying siting choices and their consequences are just a few of the things that buildings will teach you much better than any book or person. You know enough now from the fundamentals presented in this book to study, critique, and ask probing questions about any building with which you come in contact. Once you get into the habit, it's really a fun game, and, like learning a language by living in a foreign country, you'll wake up one day and realize that you've absorbed an incredible amount about buildings and what makes them tick.

Observing. Every building is a puzzle to be unraveled. What's holding it up? Why is it cold, damp, or wonderfully cozy inside? Why exactly do you like or dislike it?

BUILDING

Of course, the best way to learn about building is to build, but how does one go about getting building experience? In this realm, a motto might be: Work for others before you work for yourself. If you find the right projects with the right people running them, there's nothing better than being paid to learn. You'll get to experience all the aspects of construction without shouldering much of the mental stress, organization, or decision-making of the process. You'll also learn things that someone like me can tell you, but that you won't really know until you try. Comments like "building is hard work" have no real meaning until you've woken up sore all over after a day of trench digging, rafter installing, cob mixing, or any number of other tasks that produce the same effect.

If you're looking around for projects to work on, definitely try to find something that matches your building goals as they stand now, projects that are using the materials, techniques, and general mindset that interest you. Such perfect matches are often hard to find, but don't despair—you can learn a huge amount working on a conventional framing crew, for example. You'll learn even more on a job where the same crew installs the foundation, walls, roof, and interior and exterior skins. Being involved with the construction of a conventional house from beginning to end will teach you an enormous amount of skills, many of which will relate directly to your project.

Finally, you'll also probably learn firsthand about a lot of the things that are wrong with modern building. There's nothing like watching the pile of plywood, lumber, insulation, and other "waste" pile up on a conventional construction job to convince you there has to be a better way. Sometimes in the grip of your own project, the memory of something done the wrong way can push you through a difficult moment and give you the perseverance to do it right.

Of course, it's a big commitment to take on a full-fledged construction job. For one thing, there's the pesky fact that you might have a job already. In that case, a common way for beginners to get experience with a lot of interesting, less-mainstream building approaches is through workshops. These can vary in length from afternoon or daylong straw bale raisings or earth plastering sessions to multi-week practicums to longer internships with experienced builders or organizations. Some are free; others can cost hundreds or thousands of dollars. You need to realize that a lot of what you'll be doing is working for free or paying to work on someone else's project. If you're not in the right mindset, that can be a stumbling block.

If you're considering spending a lot of time and/or money on a workshop, I suggest researching it thoroughly before committing. Call the presenter, ask some specific questions, and get a very clear idea about what's actually going to be built, how much instruction time is included, etc. I'm not in any way calling into question the integrity of workshops here. I just know people and the difficulties inherent in communication. Someone else's concept of a start-to-finish workshop covering all aspects of construction may not match your own. Some workshops are heavy on the politics, others have a strong New Age slant, while others just focus on building. Each of these will be perfect for some and torture for others. Just do some research to find the right workshop for your needs and personality.

WHAT AM I GETTING MYSELF INTO?

If you don't have a lot of experience building, even the detailed information in this book might not give you a feel for what's really involved. It may seem like the decisions we made along the way were clear, obvious, and all made at once long before the process of building began. The reality is that you have to get very good at making decisions in all sorts of situations and adjusting what you're going to do tomorrow based on what you've experienced and learned today. Of course, that's what getting good at anything is really about. If you decide to dive into the world of building, you'll quickly learn what I'm talking about. In the meantime, here are a few entries from the diary I kept during this project that might illustrate the point.

Complications. Once you put a building project into motion, it takes on a life of its own. You have to learn to adjust what you're going to do tomorrow based on what you've learned today.

Site Work:

Wed – Apr 2

Retaining walls. Really scrounging for the final cap rocks, crawling around in streams, scamming rocks from everywhere I can imagine to look. Very heavy and backbreaking due to distance I had to carry them to the truck and terrain/brambles I had to traverse.

Foundation:

Fri – Apr 4

Tim and I had extended discussion about stem walls: concrete block with perlite infill or poured vermiculite concrete.

Issues: Block with infill might be easier, but there's a thermal break involved and would need to cover with structural stucco. Also, since no mortar, would be difficult to get a level lay, though that isn't critical with these wall infills. Poured would be more work, but more insulating, easier to get really level, and a better deterrent to termites, won't necessarily need structural stucco and will look cooler.

Decision: Poured.

Other issues: Need to set posts at level of stem wall for termite barrier, but can't set them on stem wall because insulated concrete will be too weak structurally. Need to pour a small column on piers to level of stem walls.

Frame:

Wed – May 14

Installed barge rafters. Squared up roof and leveled trusses. Tim will bring power planer tomorrow because some truss members are badly bowed. Cut trusses to length. Installed subfascia on east. Discussed roof edge detail, but we were tired and didn't come to closure. Concern that we are using a lot of plastic lumber, which is expensive. Tim concerned about stem walls where trusses bear on columns in west wall. He came up with a cool wall truss to redirect loads to concrete corner piers. Decided to maximize overhangs on east and west: 4' 6" to subfascia. Finished site cleanup. Looked at water supply. Where I thought it would come off of main to our house is right where a footer will be for porch posts. Should stub out water under west small rock wall and mark well for future hookup.

Cob:

Tues – July 15

Wrestled with the wet mix from yesterday. It was a real bear. I added more sand and tried a bit of vermiculite. I added lots of straw. It ended up seeming like a really nice mix, but I'm not going to mix that way again. This clay is incredibly hard to break down. I'll try paddle mixer on drill next. Finished arched window buck including stops and bracing. Window will be left in as form. Lisa helped me place the window and we discussed sill possibilities. Window will be in center of wall with large granite sills to both sides.

Cordwood:

Mon – Sept. 15

More cordwood. Going very well. Used David's concrete mixer today and was able to keep myself in mud. It's still a lot of work, takes a lot of organization to do it alone, keeping a bunch of things going on different fronts. Vermiculite and perlite both work great as infill insulation, and sawdust is very good, but I don't think it fills gaps as completely. It doesn't blow as easily as the others, though. Installed both window bucks. Lisa pointed for me at the end of the day because I had gotten behind. Took a very long time to clean mixer, perhaps because I let it sit a long time at lunch. Didn't finish everything until 9:00. Remember to add a bit more lime to mortar because of coarse sand; it really seems to help.

Straw Bale:

Fri – Oct. 3

Tim came. We prepped straw wall and started installing bales. Made final decision on window buck placement and placed first three courses of bales and the buck. However, after Tim left, I realized we hadn't put the vapor barrier on the first course of bales. I dismantled bales and installed a felt barrier, but it didn't work because of furring strips. Decided we needed building wrap and started calling around to see if a friend has an extra piece. An entire roll would be too expensive to buy.

Plaster:

Mon – Oct. 20

Mixed a 6 sand/1 lime/1 clay/½ straw mix for cob wall but didn't like the way it felt going on. It would've been difficult to keep the organic contours of the wall with that mix, so I used it to start plastering the inside of the west wall. Before doing that, I made a small mix of 1 sand/3 lime/½ straw and tried it on the cob wall. It was much easier to work with. After I used the other mix on the inside of the west wall, it was almost 4:00. I made a new mix anyway and plastered the cob wall until almost 10:00.

Stick-Frame:

Thurs – Oct. 30

Based on the long-term forecast, I decided to let the lime soak one more day. I worked instead on prepping the west wall interior for plaster. I got into some time-consuming little chores. I decided to box out and insulate the water supply zone, which turned out to be a real pain. Then, I decided to make a sill for the window out of granite and slate. That turned out to be a real project, but it's beautiful. I reset the window hinge so that it would close with the new sill. I put in plaster stops and blocking for the sink. I found out how big the cellulose blower hose is and started prepping the top of wall for the cellulose installation.

WHAT MATERIALS AND TECHNIQUES ARE RIGHT FOR ME?

Perhaps the one thing I'm the most convinced of based on my building experience is that there is no magic material or construction technique. That's frustrating for busy modern people because our lifestyles are set up to favor the quick answer. As soon as we decide to do something, hundreds of other things are pulling on us for attention. In housing, that unfortunately sometimes leads to the tendency to fetishize a certain building material. We read something about a wonderful straw bale house or get a chance to visit a sweet little cob cottage, and that's it. We've found our dream house and all we have to do now is build it. I hope that this book has been a convincing argument that good building is more complex and more creative than that, but the habit of simple truths is hard to break.

In my opinion, this malady is compounded by the fact that we humans seem to have a tendency toward the evangelical, meaning that we tend to think that what's right for us is right for everyone. I don't think that idea ever works, but it's definitely a dud in building. In fact, it's the main critique of modern building that we presented at the beginning of this book: the generalizing of something very specific. Building is very climate-, site-, and person-specific. What works in one situation might be a disaster somewhere else.

Patience. What works for someone else may not work for you. The right materials and techniques for your situation will become obvious as you learn more and gain experience.

Facts. Discovering the "facts" is like going fishing. You cast your net and see what you catch today.
It's your responsibility, no one else's, to choose what to throw back and what to keep.

Building materials and techniques are simply tools. Just as you don't know to grab a hammer or screwdriver until you've seen the nail or screw, you can't decide what material or approach to use until you know exactly what need it's going to fulfill. Don't limit your options by deifying materials. The right materials and techniques for your particular situation will be obvious when you know enough about building in general and your project in particular.

WHAT ABOUT CODES?

I don't want to get into a big discussion about codes. Are they good or evil? Who cares? There they are, a fact of life that has to be dealt with. First of all, not every locale has building codes. Where I used to live in Texas, there were no building codes outside the city limits. That meant you were free to build an eco-paradise. It also meant that your neighbor was free to build a racetrack or unofficial toxic dump. Find out the code situation where you're going to build. Also, the building materials and techniques that are code approved vary widely by region. For example, as far as I can tell, one form or another of straw bale construction is gaining acceptance in a wide variety of locales around the United States. Cob, on the other hand, seems to be having more trouble in that regard.

Local inspectors often have a lot of latitude to decide whether something fulfills the "intent" of the code. They are often also allowed to give experimental permits that fall outside of the letter of the code. Where I live, a building has to be longer or wider than 12 feet in order to fall under the codes. If you're trying to get code approval for a building approach that isn't familiar to your local inspectors, start the process well in advance of any plans to begin construction. It could literally take years in some situations. On the other hand, it could conceivably be a breeze. The determining factors are going to be the attitude of the inspection department and your degree of preparation. The more documentation you have for your chosen materials and techniques, such as code approval in other jurisdictions and engineering and fire-rating data, the better your chances for a smooth permitting process.

Your best resource is other people in your area who have built before you. After hanging out around the green building water cooler for a while, you'll get a clear scoop on what you need to do, who you need to talk to, or who you need to avoid.

Codes. As flawed as they may be, on one level, building codes exist to protect us from each other and ourselves.

CAN MY HOUSE MAKE ME A BETTER PERSON?

Okay, we're all friends here, so I can get a bit personal as I sign off. Part of your interest in green building rises from your feelings of guilt. You know that we humans have screwed things up. I mean, can anyone seriously argue that a sea of asphalt, concrete, glass, smog, and shag carpeting is an improvement over a forest? What's more, though we like to blame governments and corporations, you and I also know that we're all complicit. We've created this mess together. That's depressing, and you're looking for relief. You want to do better.

Anyone serious about lessening their personal environmental impact has to eventually examine the buildings they use. In fact, the buildings that we live in and use daily may be the main measure of our impact on the world through the course of our lives. For that reason, creating a sturdy, energy-efficient, functional, fun, healthy building can be a transformational act. Such a building can instantly reduce your environmental footprint, empower you by lowering your monthly bills, and, if designed carefully, make your daily life easier and more enjoyable. In short, it can make you a better person.

At the same time, you have to be careful about throwing the baby out with the bathwater. You're a complex entity, and the intricate map of your needs simply isn't going to be reflected in anyone's summaries of green, natural, or alternative building. If you really want your building to work, you're going to have to build it for the real you, or at least a very possible you, not a fantasy.

Take me, for example. I believe without a doubt that we're in serious danger as a species. The ozone hole, global warming, melting ice caps…I mean come on! I'm constantly in awe of the deer, rabbits, and ants that I run across daily around my house. They live simply without all of this human edifice, and on some level I really believe that we lost everything when we abandoned their lifestyle.

As a result, I've gone to great lengths to change my familiar way of life. I'm constantly trying to create a more sustainable existence, searching for ways to have less of an impact on my poor, little planet. Yet, I am a long way from being a rabbit. I'm a child of the modern world whether I like it or not. I still respond on a visceral level to visiting big, filthy cities. I love the sound of an electric guitar and am fascinated with the art of movie making. I've found that these feelings and many more like them are real—just as much a part of me as anything else. I've learned from experience that if I completely ignore them, if I try to pretend I'm something other than I am, then I meet with failure.

When it came time to build a house for this strange conglomeration of influences that is me, I knew I had to create something that would help me constantly stretch toward self-sufficiency while at the same time allowing me to keep connected to my urban roots and my society at large. My process was much too complicated and personal to fit any building ideology exactly. I didn't find my situation discussed in any book or listed in a chart.

Ultimately, because I was honest with myself, I created a compromise that seems to have made everyone in my head happy. As a result, my environmental impact is way down, not only because my house is energy efficient but also because it was designed to let both the city and country mouse in me work and play at home, therefore vastly reducing my need to drive.

I firmly believe that such a look-yourself-in-the-mirror, soul-searching attitude is an integral part of good building design. In the end, though you can seek help from professionals, you're really the only expert on your personal, undoubtedly idiosyncratic, complex, and unique situation. Such is modern life. Whatever you come up with, it's not going to perfectly fit any ideology, and it isn't going to save the world. At best, it's going to serve you faithfully, help you live a happy healthy life, and reduce your impact on your environment. If you can pull that off, that's a lot.

Feeling. Like any meaningful relationship, the connection between human and home takes a huge amount of work and many years to mature. This is the house Lisa and I built. We're just starting to get to know it. Our garden soil needs a lot of work, our shade trees are tiny, and our list of projects is long. But we've got a solid beginning, and now that we're here, we've got the rest of our lives to nurture this spot. It's the beginning of a beautiful friendship.

METRICS CONVERSION CHART

To convert from U.S. units to metric, multiply by the number given in the middle column, and then round the resulting number up or down. Example: To convert 10.1 feet to meters, multiply by 0.3048; the answer is 3.078 meters, which can be rounded to 3.08. To convert from metric units to the U.S. system, divide rather than multiply.

	U.S. "INCH-POUND" SYSTEM	MULTIPLY BY	TO DETERMINE METRIC EQUIVALENT
LENGTH	Inch	25.4	Millimeter
	Foot	0.3048	Meter
	Yard	0.9144	Meter
	Mile	1.609344	Kilometer
AREA	Square inch	645.16	Square millimeter
	Square foot	0.09290304	Square meter
	Square yard	0.8361274	Square meter
	Square mile	2.589988	Square kilometer
	Acre	0.40469	Hectare
MASS	Ounce	0.02834952	Kilogram
	Pound	0.45359237	Kilogram
	Ton	0.9071847	Tonne
VOLUME	Fluid ounce	29.57353	Milliliter
	Gallon	3.785412	Liter
	Cubic inch	16.387064	Cubic millimeter
	Cubic foot	0.02831685	Cubic meter
	Cubic yard	0.7645549	Cubic meter

U.S. "INCH-POUND" SYSTEM	MULTIPLY BY	TO DETERMINE METRIC EQUIVALENT
TEMPERATURE		
Degrees Fahrenheit	Formula: Minus 32 times 5 divided by 9	Degrees Celsius
OTHER APPLICATIONS		
	Pressure	
Pounds per square inch (PSI)	6.896	Kilopascals
Feet head of water	2.988	Kilopascals
Feet head of water	0.3048	Meters head of water
	Energy and Heat	
British thermal units (BTU)	1055.06	Joules
R-value	0.176110	RSI
	Velocity	
Miles per hour (mph)	1.6093	Kilometers per hour (km/hr)

GLOSSARY

2 X. Standard width of structural lumber, which is actually 1½ inches wide.

Across the Grain. Parallel to the growth rings of a tree, i.e., from bark to bark.

Active Solar Design. Planning for the storage of solar energy collected in one place to be used in another; examples: photovoltaic electricity and hydronic floor heating.

Adobe. Air- or sun-dried blocks made from a mixture of clay, sand, water, and sometimes straw.

Aggregate. Sand and stone particles of different sizes that combine with a binder to create the structural strength of concrete, cob, mortars, and plasters.

Alis. Paint made using various combinations of water, wheat paste, colored clays, finely chopped straw, mica, and other additives; often used to cover earth plasters.

Along the Grain. Perpendicular to the growth rings of a tree, i.e., from the roots toward the sky.

Altitude Angle. The number of degrees that an obstacle, or the sun at a given time, is above horizontal, i.e., unobstructed ground level.

Applied Skin. Protective coating applied to a building surface; example: plaster.

Azimuth Angle. The number of degrees that an obstacle, or the sun at a given time, is east or west of south.

Bale Needle. Thin, long, strong piece of metal or wood used to thread string or wire through straw bales.

Barge Rafter/Truss. Rafter or truss assembly at the outer edge of a gable that completes the roof overhang.

Beam. Horizontal structural member.

Berm. To surround parts of a building with earth.

Blackwater. Water that contains potential toxins (such as synthetic chemicals or human feces) as it leaves a building through a drain.

Bottle Block. Glass unit installed in cordwood or cob walls made of bottles surrounded by reflective metal.

Box Beam. Assembled beam often made from two-by lumber and plywood to create added width or to achieve necessary strength without using large timbers.

Breathable Wall. Wall system designed to allow air exchange through its volume.

Buck. Structural window or doorframe.

Casein Paint. Water-resistant paint containing lime putty or clay and milk protein as a binder; often used over earth plasters.

Cellulose. The primary constituent of the cell walls of most plants; in building, the term usually refers to recycled newspaper insulation, though straw and wood are both also forms of cellulose.

Cement Plaster. Mix containing Portland cement, hydrated lime, and sand; often called "stucco."

Chinking Compound. Flexible material that fills gaps between logs in log wall construction; can also be used over mortar in cordwood walls to seal shrinkage gaps.

Clay. Soil component that is water absorbent becomes plastic and sticks to itself when wet and hardens when dried; originates from feldspathic rock, such as granite.

Clay-Slip Straw. Loose straw coated with a clay slurry (clay particles suspended in water); also called "straw clay," "light straw clay," and *leichtlehmbau.*

Cleat. 1. A piece of wood or metal used to strengthen or support the surface to which it's attached. 2. A device used to secure rope.

Cob. Mixture of clay, sand, straw, and water—the clay and some or all of the sand usually come from the site or locally harvested subsoils; sometimes called "monolithic adobe."

Cobber's Thumb. Tool used to weave straw between courses of cob to enhance structural strength.

Collar Tie. Horizontal beam in a triangular truss assembly.

Column. Vertical structural member.

Composite Block. Hollow cavity block made of crystallized wood chips bound with Portland cement; can replace conventional concrete block in many applications.

Composite Lumber. Extruded lumber made primarily from recycled wood and recycled plastic.

Compression. Squeezing force.

Condensation. Liquid water that results when air becomes saturated with water vapor.

Conduction. The transfer of heat from molecule to molecule through a material.

Control Joint. Break in a plaster coat that prevents cracks from spreading.

Convection. The transfer of heat by physically moving molecules from one place to another.

Convective Loop. A heating cycle often fueled by direct solar energy in which a liquid or gas confined within a closed system is heated in a collector and rises into a storage area, consequently allowing cooler liquid or gas to flow into the collector to be heated.

Corbel. Literally means "bracket;" in construction, "corbel" means to create a structural contour by offsetting progressive courses of a material.

Corbel Cob. Specially made cobs reinforced with extra straw used to create corbelled shapes.

Cordwood. Air-dried logs cut to length (and sometimes split) that are laid with mortar to build walls.

Cripples. Small columns in stick-framing, used between bottom plate and windowsill or header and top plate.

Dead Loads. Static, permanent forces on a building.

Dead Man. Object, such as a small log, buried in an adobe or cob wall to be used as a structural connection for window/door bucks or roof framing.

Dew Point. Temperature at which a sample of air at a given relative humidity will produce condensation.

Drainage Box. Outer edge of a living roof that holds materials in place but allows water to escape.

Drainage Plane. Seamless or overlapping membrane designed to redirect water away from vulnerable building materials.

Drip Edge. Shape or groove that breaks the flow of water, causing it to fall away from a building.

Earth Plaster. Clay-based mixes possibly containing sand, chopped straw, and a variety of other materials.

Earthbag Construction. A variant of rammed earth construction wherein durable bags are filled with earth, laid in courses, and tamped into place.

Earthship. Building system using tires as permanent forms for rammed earth, passive solar design, rain catchment, and other integrated systems to create low-impact, energy-efficient structures.

Eave. Projecting overhang created by roof rafters.

Embodied Energy. Amount of energy required to extract, process, transport, and install a given building element.

EPDM. Synthetic rubber.

Evaporative Cooling. Cooling strategy based on the fact that evaporating liquids take heat from the surrounding air.

Expansion Joint. Control joint.

Fascia. Trim board attached to rafter tails; also attached to sides of rafters on the gable ends of roofs.

Flashing. Sheet material used to cover building joints to prevent water entry.

Floor on Grade. Floor whose entire volume is supported directly by the ground.

Footer. Foundation.

Form. Structural enclosure used to shape a building material.

Foundation. That part of a building that transfers loads to the ground.

Foundation Drain. Assembly, usually including a perforated pipe, installed to direct water away from the foundation of a building.

Frame. Box holding a window or door that isn't designed to carry structural loads.

Freeze/Thaw Cycles. Water in contact with a building (under the foundation, in a material such as cob or concrete, in pipes, or nestled in cracks in plaster or a roofing material, for example) will expand and contract in response to fluctuations in temperature above and below 0°C (32°F).

Frost Heave. Lifting of building due to expansion of freezing water under the foundation.

Frost Line. Depth in the ground below which water will not freeze; distance from surface varies depending on climate.

Gable End. Sides of a building with a gable roof where the wall reaches all the way to the ridge.

Glazing. Glass used in doors and windows.

Grade. Elevation of the ground around a building.

Grade Stake. Stake set in the ground to mark a given elevation.

Gravel Trench. Trench dug below the frost line and filled with gravel to serve as a building foundation.

Greywater. Water that contains no potential toxins, (such as synthetic chemicals or human feces) as it leaves a building through a drain.

Hawk. Hand-held platform that holds plaster for application.

Hay. Dried, hollow stems of grass plants without seed removed.

Header. Lintel attached to the main structural framing system of a building.

Heat Island Effect. Phenomenon by which cities have higher air temperatures than surrounding rural lands, caused by the replacement of plants that transpire water (therefore lowering surrounding temperatures) with concrete and asphalt, which are thermal masses that collect solar heat (therefore raising surrounding air temperatures).

Humus. Layer of organic material on top of subsoil, also called topsoil.

Hydroelectricity. Electricity generated by falling water.

Hydronic Floor Heating. Heating system in which a heated liquid is passed through tubing embedded in or under flooring material; also called radiant floor heating.

Hygroscopic Wall. Wall system using materials that can take on and give off some amount of water vapor in response to humidity changes.

Infill. Nonstructural material filling volume in a wall.

Insulated Glass. Glass unit made up of at least two panes separated by a sealed space filled with air or other gasses.

Insulation. Material used to resist the movement of heat.

Integrated Skin. Protective coating integral to a building material; example: the surface of stone.

Jack. Stick-framing studs set under headers.

Jamb. The side member of a door or window frame.

Jig. A device for guiding a tool or holding a material in a specific position while being worked.

Joist. Floor beam.

Key. Plaster or mortar that wraps around a building element creating a mechanical connection.

King. Stick-framing studs set next to jacks and attached to headers.

Ladder Truss Framing. Framing system used to make wide cavities for loose infill insulation; so named because the framed "columns" look somewhat like ladders.

Lateral Load. Transient load approaching a building at an angle.

Lath. Wooden strips or metal mesh that provide a surface for plaster to grip.

Ledger. Horizontal member attached to a vertical surface to create a ledge on which other horizontal members can rest.

Level. Of equal elevation.

Lime Cycle. Limestone ($CaCO_3$) is burned to form quicklime (CaO), water is added to form lime putty ($Ca(OH_2)$), which is mixed with sand to form plaster, which is spread onto walls and slowly absorbs CO_2 to become limestone ($CaCO_3$) once again.

Lime Plaster. Mix containing lime putty, sand, and sometimes a fiber such as chopped straw.

Lime Wash. Watered-down lime putty sometimes with color added, used as a sealer for earth- and lime-plastered surfaces.

Lintel. Beam spanning a window or door opening.

Live Loads. Transient forces on a building.

Living Roof. Multilayered roof skin consisting of a waterproof membrane, insulation, drainage layer, growing medium, and plants.

Load-Bearing. Material installed to carry loads.

Loads. Forces on a building.

Mass-Enhanced R-Value. Potential of thermal mass wall and roof materials in very specific climatic situations to exhibit a higher effective insulation value than steady state R-value lab tests would indicate.

Modified Post-and-Beam. Framing system wherein post and beams are constructed (usually out of dimensional lumber and plywood-type materials rather than milled from single logs); this is done to create a wider wall profile to accommodate straw bales or other infill wall systems requiring added width.

Modified Stick-Frame. Approach to stick-framing that greatly reduces the amount of materials used by avoiding sheet materials such as plywood and drywall and by placing structural members only where needed to carry loads.

Monolithic Structure. Building approach that distributes loads throughout the entire volume of a building section.

Mortar. Any of a variety of mixes that bind stacked units in a structure; adobe can be laid with a mud mortar, cordwood can be laid with a cob or Portland cement-based mortar, etc.

Mortise and Tenon Joinery. Technique for connecting materials wherein one member has a projecting piece called a tenon that fits into a cavity called a mortise on a second member.

Mud. General term used for any building material that is installed wet and dries hard, such as mortar, concrete, or cob.

Paddle Mixer. Metal shaft with integrated paddles that attaches to an electric drill and can be used to help mix cob and plasters.

Passive Solar Design. The conscious placement of a building and associated materials so that the sun's direct energy is manipulated to affect the temperature inside the building.

Pattern. Configuration of physical elements that encourage a repeated series of events.

Pattern Language. An interconnected group of patterns that come together to create a place, such as a building.

Perlite. A volcanic glass that can be expanded through heating to produce a light, airy material used, among other things, as infill insulation.

Photovoltaics. The direct production of electrical current from solar radiant energy.

Pier. Water-resistant column built on top of a foundation and designed to lift vulnerable materials away from insects and water.

Plaster. Mixture of a fine aggregate, a binder, and water to create a seamless building skin applied wet that dries to a hard, protective coating.

Plaster Stop. Barrier that serves as the edge of a section of plaster.

Plate. Top or bottom horizontal wall member, usually in a stick-framed wall.

Plumb. Perfectly vertical.

Point Load. Load concentrated in a small area.

Pointing. The process of cleaning, filling gaps in, and compressing fresh, partially cured mortar.

Portland Cement. Mineral binder used in concrete and plaster mixes; made by burning limestone, clays, shales, or other ingredients containing alumina and silica.

Post. Column.

Post-and-Beam. General term for skeletal framing system using strong members that allow for wide spans between posts.

Purlin. Permanent horizontal bracing between rafters that also provides a surface for attaching the roof skin.

Quick Lime. Calcium carbonate ($CaCO^3$), often in the form of limestone, which has been burned to form calcium oxide (CaO).

Radiation. The transfer of heat through space by means of electromagnetic energy.

Rafter. Sloped structural roof member.

Rain Catchment. Collection of rainwater in cisterns for domestic or other use.

Rain Chain. Chain that replaces a gutter downspout in directing roof water away from a building.

Rainscreen. Siding approach wherein an air space is created between wall and siding materials.

Raised Floor. Framed floor platform lifted off the ground on piers or stem walls.

Rammed Earth. Earth mix packed between forms to build walls, sometimes requiring addition of water and/or Portland cement.

Reactivated Solar. Solar energy stored in a physical form, such as petroleum or wood, then burned to release the energy for use.

Rebar. Steel bar used to increase tensile strength of concrete.

Relative Humidity. Ratio of the amount of water vapor in a sample of air to the greatest amount of vapor that sample of air could hold at the same temperature.

Reveal. The area in a window or door opening between the buck or frame and the trim or wall surface.

Ridge Beam. Beam at top of roof to which rafters are attached.

Rigid Insulation. General term for a group of rigid sheet materials used as insulation. (All rigid insulation used in this book is extruded polystyrene.)

Rough Opening. Structurally reinforced hole created in the structural framing of a wall to accommodate a window or door.

R-Value. Measure of the resistance to heat flow of a given thickness of a material; the higher the number, the better the resistance.

Sand. Finely ground rock particles (.05 to 2 mm) that do not absorb water and are a component of most soils; sand is the correct size to serve as structural aggregate in cob and plaster.

Shake Test. Simple test for roughly determining the composition of a soil sample.

Shear. Force that causes two parts of a body to slide past each other in a parallel direction.

Shingles. Small units laid in overlapping courses to cover a roof; can be made of a variety of materials, including asphalt-impregnated felt, recycled plastic, slate, concrete, and clay.

Sill. Bottom member of a door or window frame.

Sill Plate. Water-resistant horizontal wall member attached to a stem wall.

Silt. Very finely ground rock particles (.002 to .05mm) that do not absorb water; silt is too small to be of value as structural aggregate in cob or plaster mixes.

Skeletal Structure. Building approach that distributes loads by placing strong structural members at strategic points throughout the volume of a building.

Skin. Interior and exterior surfaces of a building, including walls, roof, windows, doors, etc.

Slaking. Process by which water is added to quick lime (CaO) to produce lime putty ($Ca(OH)^2$) and, as a side effect, produces a large amount of heat.

Specific Heat. The amount of heat required to raise the temperature of one gram of a substance one degree Celsius; a material with a high specific heat is said to be a good "thermal mass."

Spirit Level. Tool that establishes how level or plumb a surface is by means of an air bubble suspended in liquid.

Spud. A flat-headed, sharpened tool used to debark logs and trim cob walls.

Stem Wall. Water-resistant wall built on top of a foundation and designed to lift vulnerable wall materials away from insects and water.

Stick-Frame. Skeletal framing system using thin columns spaced closely together.

Stop. A surface against which a hinged door or window closes.

Straw. Dried, hollow stems of grass plants with seed removed, usually leftover after cereal grain harvesting.

Structural Insulated Panel (SIP). A structural unit made up of an insulative core sandwiched between two thin rigid outer layers.

Stucco. Plaster containing Portland cement.

Stud. Thin column used in stick-framing.

Subsoil. Soil directly under the humus or topsoil.

Superadobe. A building technique pioneered by architect Nader Khalili in which long fabric tubes are pumped full of damp earth and coiled into domes.

Swale. Valley created as part of site work to slow water run-off for absorption by land and to redirect excess away from the building.

Tarpaper. Heavy paper impregnated with tar used as a drainage plane on walls and roofs.

Tension. Pulling force.

Termite Barrier. Obstruction that forces termites out into the open where their tunnels will be seen.

Thermal Bridge/Break. Component with considerably less resistance to heat movement than surrounding materials; example: wooden stud in an insulated stick-framed wall.

Thermal Mass. Material chosen for its ability to store quantities of heat.

Thermosiphon. The natural, convective movement of a gas or liquid due to differences in temperature.

Timber Frame. Skeletal framing system using wood posts and beams connected with wooden joinery.

Toe-Up. Area between finished floor and top of stem wall where vulnerable wall materials begin.

Top Plate. Thin beams at the top of stick-framed walls; can also be used in cordwood and possibly cob as a surface for attaching roof members and creating a more even distribution of roof loads.

Torsion. Twisting force.

Transit. Device consisting of a leveled scope on a tripod used to measure relative elevations.

Trim. Component of building skin used to seal joints.

Trombe Wall. Passive solar design strategy that uses a glass-covered interior mass wall set close to the building exterior and facing the winter sun—as the air in the space between wall and glass heats up, it rises and passes through holes in the top of the wall (thermosiphon), which causes cooler air to be pulled into the space through holes in the bottom of the wall, creating a heating cycle called a "convective loop."

Truss. Assembly of members, often arranged in triangles, that form a rigid framework to support a roof, bridge, or similar structure.

Uplift. Force caused by wind pulling up on protruding sections of a building, usually the roof.

Urbanite. Recycled concrete used to replace natural stone in stacked stone walls.

Vapor Barrier. Material placed in an attempt to stop the movement of water vapor into areas of a building where it could cause damage.

Vermiculite. A hydrous silicate mineral (mica) that can be expanded through heating to produce a light, airy material used, among other things, as infill insulation.

Volumetric Shrinkage Factor. Estimated percentage that a given species of wood will shrink in volume when kiln dried from a green (freshly felled) state.

Water Level. Device that uses the property of water to seek its own level as a means to measure relative elevations.

Wattle and Daub. Interwoven sticks covered with clay-rich plaster, often containing straw, used to infill space between post-and-beam structures.

Wind Power. Electricity created by wind spinning a turbine that in turn spins the rotor of a generator.

Wooden Tie Strip. Thin strips of wood placed on each side of a straw bale wall and tied together to connect the bales to each other and, in an infill bale wall, to the skeletal structure of the building.

ACKNOWLEDGMENTS

THE BUILDING

Lisa Mandle is a fabric and visual artist who has a good bit of building experience and also happens to be Clarke's wife. She helped design the building, especially during the initial pattern language sessions, and often lent a hand with construction. You'll see her pictured throughout this book, measuring sun angles; mapping site contours; grading foundation drainage; installing porch posts; mixing, laying, and sculpting cob; making and placing bottle blocks; putting in stone shelves; and insulating the roof. She was also responsible for several pivotal building elements, such as the bottle pattern and the sculptural design of the cob wall; the design and installation, along with Christopher Mellow, of the living roof growth medium and plantings; and the design and execution of all the painting on the building. In addition, she had the dubious task of putting up with this ridiculous project from start to finish. Obviously, there's no conceivable way we could have done it without her.

Christopher Mellow is a plant wizard who not only offered his great horticultural expertise in helping to design and install our building's living roof, but also supplied most of the plants by relocating a huge portion of his sedum collection to the roof garden!

Rob Pulleyn is a retired emperor who lent us his tractor on several occasions, donated a couple of salvaged windows, and also custom made the beautiful water basin that catches rainwater coming off our building's roof.

Paul Gurewitz is a Jewish carpenter who lent us various tools for a LONG time so that we could finish this project.

Josh Sinz is a cool guy who put in some volunteer time on the construction site until we scared him away.

Chuck Marsh is a permaculture/ecological-design teacher and consultant. He also knows a lot about natural building and gave us some good advice on our living roof and earth plaster mixes.

Shannon and **Natalie Callahan** are concrete paver decorators who can be convinced to mix cob on occasion.

David Parrish not only lent us his cement mixer but also delivered and picked it up! Our backs thank you!

D.T. Ramsey Lumber Co./ Big Pine Log Homes in Marshall, NC, is a family-owned mill close to our building site. They supplied us with our poplar logs for cordwood, moved a lot of wood around to get us just the right pine porch beams, and even milled our locust corner posts for us.

Wilma R. Penland at Reems Creek Valley Nursery in Weaverville, NC, graciously helped us design the right growing medium and plantings for our living roof.

Hank Strauss owns Mountain Marble and Granite in Asheville, NC. Most of the natural stone in our building was salvaged from Hank's cut-offs and remainders.

Fredrica (Fred) Lashley and Wolf Alterman own the Unturned Stone in Mars Hill, NC, a company that does expert dry-stacked stonework. They hooked us up with the opportunity to salvage much of the stone used in our building.

Marilyn Held and Steve Michaels gave us the sink out of their old kitchen. After more than a five-year hiatus resting in the barn, it's now ensconced in the guest cottage.

T.W. and Mary Wynns Gregory donated the wood for our cob door buck.

Ed Caskey, Betty Clark, Ann Snell, Eileen Mandle, and Jane Tuttle all got their hands (or feet) dirty in various ways helping out on the building.

THE BOOK

Special thanks to Carol Taylor, Publisher, President, and 5-Star General of Lark Books, for persevering with this large, complicated project.

Terry Krautwurst was a major force in shaping this book. He tirelessly took confused scribbles and turned them into actual sentences with punctuation, meaning, and all of that stuff. If we were stranded on a desert island and could have only one editor along, it would be Terry.

Kathy Sheldon took over for Terry when he had to move on to other projects. She somehow figured out what was going on and dragged this book's tired carcass to the finish line. Okay, we'd also want Kathy along on the desert island.

Kristi Pfeffer deserves infinite thanks for her sublime art direction and also for not stabbing us with her ominously sharpened jewelry.

Jackie Kerr is a freelance graphic designer who did much of the actual layout for the book, somehow getting all of those pictures close to the relevant text.

Olivier Rollin is a multi-talented artist who did the amazing color illustrations for this book.

Don Gurewitz is, among many other things, a wonderful photographer. Thanks, Don, for traveling the planet with your camera and giving us access to a wide variety of buildings from around the world. You can view more of his photos at www.dongurewitzphotography.com.

Mollie Curry is an experienced natural builder, writer, and photographer who contributed a number of photos of interesting buildings and also turned us on to the suburban straw chopper (i.e., mulching leaf-blower).

Janell Kapoor supplied photos she's taken of a number of buildings all over the globe. She is the founder of Kleiwerks (www.kleiwerks.com), "an international grass-roots natural building organization, teaching people how to build their own, appropriately designed, hybrid homes with affordable and indigenous materials." The photos of adobe-making in chapter 8 were taken during a Kleiwerks workshop.

David Eisenberg supplied a variety of photos illustrating many aspects of straw bale construction. He's the executive director of the Development Center for Appropriate Technology (www.dcat.net).

Rob Roy contributed a collection of photos of cordwood masonry projects. He's the author of a number of books on cordwood masonry construction and a variety of other topics. He's also the director of the Earthwood Building School (www.cordwoodmasonry.com), which "offers courses in cordwood masonry, earth-sheltered housing, and megalithic stonework in northern New York, and around the world."

Tom Wuelpern, of Rammed Earth Development (www.rammedearth.com), contributed a photograph of the beautiful rammed earth home he designed and built outside Tucson, Arizona.

Iris Photographics is a great photo shop in Asheville, NC, that developed all of our slides.

A general debt of gratitude to the Cob Cottage Company, in our view the group most responsible for the exciting cob renaissance in North America. Many cob terms and techniques in common use today have a genesis in their work.

Finally, a general scream of "Thanks!" to all the people not mentioned by name who as a part of the collective consciousness of construction have developed tools and techniques utilized in this book. Even if we don't know who you are, we are nonetheless deeply indebted to you.

TIM'S ACKNOWLEDGMENTS

It would have been impossible for me to undertake, much less complete, this work without the support of my wife Margaret—thank you, my dear, for keeping the home fires burning. A quaternity of men have been particularly influential in helping me to learn and grow in my professional life; I give thanks to Don McNair, Bob Yunaska, Stuart Savel, and Michael Landman for their friendship, encouragement, and kind critiques. The hard work of Terry Krautwurst was invaluable in shaping this book; thank you for having faith in us. A special draft of gratitude to my dear friend Clarke Snell, whose unwavering focus and dogged determination are what really "got it done." And, of course, none of us gets anywhere without the support, inspiration, and interference of unnamed and unnamable hordes. To all of you who I have loved, and to those who have driven me mad, my deepest appreciation.

CLARKE'S ACKNOWLEDGMENTS

Between building, photographing, researching, writing, and—in a final bizarre twist—editing, this project has been a marathon that has taken up most of my waking hours for the last two years. I want to thank everyone who has had to put up with me during that period. To anyone I've neglected, angered, or stared at blankly while making little whining sounds, please forgive me. I want to thank Tim Callahan for being a genius and Margaret Callahan for not hating me (as far as I know) for getting Tim involved in this quicksand called a book. Most of all, I want to apologize to my kidneys for all of that coffee I drank. I promise I'll make it up to you.

PHOTOGRAPHY CREDITS

Clarke Snell
All photographs not otherwise credited are by Clarke Snell.

Don Gurewitz
Pages 14 (bottom left); 15; 18 (top); 23; 26 (center); 31 (top left, bottom left); 32 (top right, middle right); 41 (bottom); 45; 46 (top right); 48; 57; 67 (bottom); 72 (top right, bottom left); 74; 75 (bottom); 85 (right); 89 (left); 100 (top right, bottom left); 101 (left); 111(bottom); 117; 209 (left); 217 (top); 218 (top left, bottom left); 222; 223 (left); 257 (right); 290 (right); 398 (top left, top right), 399 (top left), 480; 484 (top right); 486 (top left); 508 (right); 509 (top right); 528 (right); 580 (top right, bottom left); 581; 584; 591; 592; 593

Stewart O'Shields
Pages 2; 5 (top, bottom); 6; 9; 12 (left); 13 (top left); 14 (bottom right); 46 (bottom left); 72 (bottom right); 83 (bottom); 91 (top right); 100 (bottom right); 145; 256 (bottom right); 257 (left); 325; 440 (bottom right); 457 (top); 469 (right); 484 (bottom right); 503 (bottom left); 506 (top left); 532; 533; 534 (top right, bottom left); 544 (top left); 545 (bottom left); 547; 551 (top right); 553 (bottom right); 554; 555 (top, bottom right); 556 (top left, top right); 557 (top, bottom right); 558 (top right); 562; 563; 564; 565; 566; 567; 568; 569; 570; 571; 572; 573; 574; 575; 576; 577; 578; 579

OTHER INDIVIDUALS

Povy Kendal Atchison: 340 (top right); 341 (right); 352 (right)

Paul Bardagjy: 293; 346 (top left, bottom left); 538 (top left); 580 (bottom right); 586

Tim Callahan: 163 (top left)

Dan Chiras: 212; 213 (bottom)

Molly Curry: 210 (middle); 292 (top); 343 (bottom); 345; 348; 352

Laurie E. Dickson: 118 (bottom right); 137 (middle right); 143 (bottom); 224; 225; 473 (bottom); 513; 515

David Eisenberg: 143; 340 (top left, bottom right); 384; 385; 387; 388; 390; 391; 392; 394; 396 (top left); 409 (bottom)

Dency Kane: 77 (right)

Doug Keefer/Nelle Gregory: 343 (top)

Janell Kapoor: 14 (middle right); 20 (top); 91 (bottom); 101 (right); 139; 211; 218 (bottom right); 219; 285; 287 (bottom left, bottom right); 294 (top right, left); 296 (middle left); 338; 486 (middle left); 487 (top right)

Lisa Mandle: 10; 14 (top); 21; 99 (top left); 183 (middle)

Rob Roy: 296 (top right); 297 (right); 306; 335; 337; 475 (bottom right); 489 (bottom)

Simonton family: 341 (bottom)

Michel Spaan: 100 (top left); 108; 436 (top left, top right); 485 (top)

Alan Stankevitz: 305

Phillip Van Horn: 288 (left)

Tom Wuelpern: 288 (right)

OTHER SOURCES

The California Institute of Earth Art and Architecture: 32 (bottom right); 289 (top)

Durisol Building Systems, Inc.: 20 (bottom); 210 (right)

Earthship Biotecture: 34; 55; 213 (top)

MWB R-Pro: 221 (bottom); 427 (left)

Optigrün International AG: 489 (top)

Southwest Windpower: 70 (left)

Thatching.com: 508 (left)

U.S. Dept. of the Interior, Bureau of Reclamation, Lower Colorado Region: 64 (middle)

Wellington Polymer Technology, Inc.: 509 (top left)

ABOUT THE AUTHORS

Clarke Snell (left) has decades of experience in green building, sustainability, and low-impact living. Author of *The Good House Book* (Lark, 2004), he lives in the mountains of western North Carolina with his wife in a partially bermed, passive-solar house in a small intentional community they helped create.

Tim Callahan (right) is a practicing general contractor, with over 30 years' experience in a broad range of design and building projects. Tim is currently focusing on residential work of unique character for unique characters.

Clarke and Tim collaborate on a number of projects, including workshops, lectures, consulting, and building. For more information, see their website at www.thinkgreenbuilding.com.

INDEX

NOTES